Freedom, Civility, Commerce

Freedom, Civility, Commerce

Contemporary Media and the Public

Sukumar Muralidharan

Three Essays
COLLECTIVE

First Edition November 2018

ISBN 978-93-83968-23-7

Three Essays COLLECTIVE

B-957 Palam Vihar, GURGAON (Haryana) 122 017 India
Tel: 91-124 236 9023, +91 98681 26587, +91 98683 44843
info@threeessays.com Website: www.threeessays.com
Printed and bound at Chaman Offset Printers, New Delhi

To my mother

and the memory of my father

Contents

Acknowledgements

This book is in part about experiences and impressions gathered over two decades as a journalist and roughly seven years spent in press freedom campaigns, advocacy and training. I had opportunities to meet with a vast number of journalists and media practitioners in these times and to all of them, especially those courageous individuals in some of the conflict zones I travelled to, this book is a gesture of solidarity in shared struggles.

This work was set in train by a suggestion from Sanjay Kak who by pure chance happened to see an old article that circumstances led me in 2013 to recycle and share within a small social group. My intent in recycling a near-decade old article was limited, merely to capitalise on the possibilities offered by the social media and present some observations on a subject that seemed to have a renewed topicality. Sanjay was interested enough to get in touch and ask if there were some ideas in there that could be worked up into a book. I was then in the mood for taking up a challenge that went beyond my usual deadline driven existence and Sanjay was happy to support the effort with a grant from the Zindabad Trust. Since then, Sanjay has been regular with his inquiries and his counsel, once making the effort to go through an entire draft and offer detailed comments on every part of it.

Distractions along this long journey have been many and this book emerges in current form thanks to a number of friends who I have had the good fortune to call on for support and advice. I must especially thank a group of friends who I was able to sound out about the ideas that emerged as I went along: Pamela Philipose, Vibodh Parthasarathi, A.S. Panneerselvan, Siddharth Narrain, Geeta Seshu, Laxmi Murthy, Ammu Joseph, and Sajan Venniyoor, who went through parts of this work in the various forms it has taken over time.

I carried this book along in partially finished form to the Indian Institute of Advanced Study, Shimla, where I spent two years on a fellowship beginning April 2014. It was a frequent, but not unwelcome distraction from the research proposal that gained me the fellowship. I was helped along in that pursuit by the director Chetan Singh, always willing to support a diverse range of activities. In particular, a seminar he proposed I organise in October 2014, helped in bringing together a large number of journalists and media scholars. They will see some bits of our conversations from then and later in these pages.

A part of this material has been road-tested in other forums in rather different shapes and forms. My two principal forums since before this work began – and while it was in process – were the *Economic and Political Weekly* and the quarterly journal, *Social Scientist*. I thank the editors of these journals through the relevant periods, C. Rammanohar Reddy and Rajendra Prasad.

A few of the iterations of the ideas presented here were published in *Himal SouthAsian*, that remarkable magazine which recently relocated from Kathmandu to Colombo. For those opportunities, I thank Kanak Dixit and Aunohita Mojumdar.

For their patience and meticulous attention through the last mile, I thank Asad Zaidi and Nalini Taneja.

As this goes out of my hands into the public domain, I hope that it will be of some use to younger and aspiring media practitioners, including current and future student cohorts at the journalism school in O.P. Jindal Global University, Sonipat. I wish them a future when they match and excel the outstanding professional standards I often had the good fortune to witness from up close.

Shobhana and Mallika, the two pillars of my existence in recent years, helped me stay positive through the huge mood swings of seeing this work through. Vinod and Lakshmi, my two oldest and best friends, urged me on from the background, mostly without knowing it.

Finally, there are debts that can never be repaid to my parents, to whom this book is dedicated in deepest love and gratitude.

Introduction

Speech is a basic human faculty, normally granted untrammelled freedom at least in the formal sense. Problems begin to arise in the fine print. There is in the real world, no such unconditional investiture of rights in an individual, since he is a social being, obliged to live at peace and not entitled to encroach into another's autonomous domain. Yet a doctrine which isolates an individual within his own skin is a denial of the basic human characteristic of being a *zoon politikon* or social animal. Where should the lines be drawn and who is to play the arbiter in such matters? No person can be a judge in his own case and yet neither can he be made the hapless object of another's whims. Harmony emerges when two individuals are in perfect accord in their understanding of what can properly be said among themselves. In a larger social milieu, this becomes a far more complex compact to arrive at, especially when competitive politics is thrown into the mix. Identities often clash in the maelstrom of electoral politics and the outcome is not the conciliation of these differences, but their deepening. A broad political consensus may be feasible in purely theoretical terms, but often could break down in practice, as with one group's exercise of its free speech right being regarded by another as an affront to its identity.

In the years of optimism since World War II, modernity and liberalism came to be seen as the best solvents for all such particularities, with the potential to wrap everybody into its egalitarian spirit. But much of the world was introduced to modernity within the political grid of colonialism. And the years following independence from colonialism, especially since globalisation became the reigning ethos towards the end of the 20th century, have been – despite all claims of cosmopolitanism – a period of massive displacements and dislocations in space and time. There was a time when these were regarded rather benignly, as difficulties that would be easily overcome. What used to be regarded rather patronisingly as a "cultural lag" that the less fortunate peoples had to overcome became a still more indulgent construct. The more fortunate societies rushed in eagerly to adopt the doctrine of multiculturalism, of a collective generosity that would allow multiplicities of culture to not merely coexist but also flourish. Civility was built not upon the confinement of cultural specificities to private spaces, but on an easy tolerance towards their presence in the public arena. This tolerance was built on a presumption that certain values of mutual respect, of concern for the dignity of those of another culture, were deeply enough imbedded in the individual and social psyche.

But that was when times were good. The 21st century has brought a more contentious spirit in the encounter between cultures, internationally as well as within the nation state. Certain societies imposed a demand on citizens to make a public and ostentatious display of their loyalty in every civic engagement. Basic citizen entitlements were contingent on loud proclamations of fealty to the singular faith of the land. That faith could be one handed down through the ages and interpreted for the times by a power clique, or even a modernist constitutionalist ethos, hardened into dogma. Thus we have in France and other European nations, a sensibility which insists on every faith being fair game, where the willingness to publicly disdain or laugh at every cultural emblem that failed to measure upto a rigid template of modernity was essential part of the civic commitment. The particular vantage point of the gaze is immaterial, whether interior to the faith or exterior. Laughter is enjoined as the inescapable duty of citizenship.

There are of course socially recognised limits to laughter, where civility itself is transgressed and typically the process of the law would be triggered. But in the mix of cultures which modernity has wrought, these limits are a matter of perception. Areas of disagreement are enlarging rather than shrinking. Frequent recourse to lawless behaviour to enforce the limits of free speech – the politics of outrage – are a feature of contemporary reality, provoking in turn sharply polarised responses which remain in most part, inattentive to context and history.

Laughter in unequal societies is either a privilege or a rebellion against disempowerment. When exercised in the public space, it could be regarded in two completely opposed ways: as a marker of social power relations or a determination to disregard and subtly overturn these. There is a settled pattern of life that every member of the civic order is accustomed to, which has its own permissible codes of public behaviour. Laughter in one of its guises could be a way of reinforcing every iniquity of this order; and in still another variety, an expression of resistance to these. But humour is an occasional intruder in ordinary lives that are lived by established codes, the "habitus" that in the sociologist Pierre Bourdieu's terms, determines practice. The reproduction of everyday life is about individuals in conformity with assigned identities, which mark them out as "mainstream" or "marginal". And then there are those regarded as beyond the pale.

Speech is exercised through organised apparatuses that in a famous characterisation, have a significant influence over identity, over the formation of both social solidarities and particularities. "Print capitalism" was once regarded as the forge in which nationalist consciousness was shaped and it is a role that continues to be played by the very much more complex media industry today. In an older regime of technology, the homogenisation of distinct identities into the dominant nationalist mould may have been a relatively simple process. But in the newer regimes which operate in far more complex social milieus, media industries perform the role of not merely affirming the national character, but also continually reproducing the other, the minorities without whom the dominant identity would remain disturbingly fluid and undefined.

Loud proclamations of loyalty to a civic definition of nationalism usually do not amount to more than formal obeisance. Media portrayals of "in" and "out" groups reflect concurrent sensibilities of dominant majorities, which may not be politically empowered in the formal sense, but set the boundaries within which the competitive processes for gaining governmental authority are exercised. Most regimes of nationalist legitimacy rest on subtly or otherwise enforcing a number of identity based tests.

Assertions of a right to belong by those who are deemed to be outside the majoritarian consensus, are often regarded as a threat to civic order. Nobody contests the right to free speech in itself. He only contests the right of another person to exercise the right, especially when he is not deemed to be part of the "in" group. The fear of disorder today provides fertile soil in which the rioters' veto proves decisive. Offence has become an organised social industry and individuals would suffer in silence, allowing every manner of outrage, rather than risk stirring up its furies.

Free speech as a right is often narrowly read, as residing within the confines of the media industry in its widest definition, which includes the news media as well as the culture and entertainment sectors. It may at one time have been necessary to access a media platform in some manner to exercise the right to free speech, which has no meaning except as the right also to be heard. That platform access is now no longer an absolute necessity. Contemporary democratic societies enable the creation of various kinds of platforms from where the right to speak and be heard can be reasonably exercised.

Free speech is a subject that is deeply implicated within the complexities of politics, law, and the interface between the two. It is an interface where rights and wrongs are determined, though most questions that arise have a disturbingly unsettled character, even in democracies with loudly declared commitments to the rule of law.

Since the dawn of liberal democracy, free speech has been regarded as a worthy goal for society to collectively pursue and protect. Yet the benefits arising from the untrammelled exercise of the right are not obvious in cultures where self-interest is regarded as a special virtue, where it is an irresistible temptation to privilege the rights of oneself or one's immediate – not to mention more remote – community. To transport that perception to a wider social setting would effectively make democratic coexistence impossible, since it rules out respect for the "other" or makes it an exceptional matter of grace. That may partly explain why the history of free speech jurisprudence in India, most complex among democracies, is one of tortuous twists, of hopes awakened and then betrayed, of a trajectory always falling short of its ultimate goal of an unconditional investiture of rights.

As Gautam Bhatia points out in a recent volume on free speech under the Indian constitution, the law finally is not of great material importance, since "courts are not the primary battlegrounds of free speech in India". Most speech offences are cognisable under Indian law, allowing enforcement agencies to act without warrant. The object of suppression is normally met in the hiatus between executive action and judicial review. It is called the "chilling effect", when speech is either killed or paralysed by the forbidding prospect of arbitrary legal action. Process is punishment in the Indian judicial system, which makes the right to speak one's mind, even on matters of urgent public importance, something of a hazard or a luxury enjoyed only by a few. Most citizens would rather waive the right, when the alternative is running the gauntlet of a weakly institutionalised judicial process and risking a capricious outcome.[1]

The year 2016 brought its fair share of free speech controversies in India. A long discredited law on sedition was resuscitated to bring to trial student activists of Delhi's Jawaharlal Nehru University for questioning certain aspects of what would be considered the sacred topography of the Indian nation state. One of the accused was brutally belaboured by officers of the law – who discarded their civic personae to don the vestments of patriotism – when produced in court. A bail plea that he entered was only granted after a sermon from the bench that effectively prejudged guilt and demanded from him a more penitent standard of conduct while the special benediction of liberty was granted pending trial.

A film that tackled the growing contagion of drug addiction in a state of India was held up by a film certification board which under a newly appointed chair had begun to assume the role of moral arbiter. Since elections to the state were due within a year, the film was read as an attempt to influence its outcome by discrediting the party that held power. Dark hints were dropped about a partisan motive and a possible financial linkage with a political party with growing interests in the state. With the powerful Mumbai film industry rallying to the cause, this matter went swiftly through a judicial hearing, where the preposterous demands placed on the film maker were roughly dealt with.[2]

1 Bhatia (2016): 325.

2 The film in question was titled *Udta Punjab* and was released to fairly indifferent receipts at the box office. Reviews and assessments of its commercial value can be found at multiple sites on the internet.

Similarly quick outcomes are a luxury beyond most ordinary citizens. Working journalists and creative writers most often suffer the worst of a weakly institutionalised legal regime, where precedent seemingly has no value.

Where does the incentive lie for society in upholding the free speech right, rather than silencing those who may represent a minority viewpoint, or indulging the perverse delight of persecuting somebody who does not conform to a narrow definition of belonging? The years since 2014 have brought about a frequently voiced demand that all who seek to belong should be prepared to swear a common catechism of nationhood. It was proposed that only those willing to chant the glories of the nation as a mother merited the rights of citizenship, even if the faith a person is born into forbids any such declaration of filial attachment. That was the newest turn in the politics of speech in the service of the nation: not merely to outlaw certain of its emanations, but to actually impose a threshold to gain the fundamental rights of citizenship.

Free speech is recognised as a desirable end in the hoary tradition of liberalism going back to John Stuart Mill, because it is how society collectively seeks the truth and corrects itself from error. But what is the time horizon over which this corrective function should be given its run? In that interim period, is it permissible under free speech doctrine to indulge grossly offensive and harmful speech, such as the advocacy of racism or ethnic cleansing? Liberal optimism in the "passage of the ages" being a reliable corrective, is obviously of little use for those who may be on the wrong side of these malevolent public utterances in contingent circumstances.[3] There is a clear need for a wider rationale, which views speech as a form of self-fulfilment, an entitlement that every individual can claim. And this is also about the right every person has through speech, to shape the moral and ethical environment she lives in. Free speech could then be thought of as a necessary component of all forms of democratic self-government.

This does not yet exhaust the value it brings to society, since free speech is essential to cultural change, to shedding the detritus of ages as society moves towards change and more inclusive conceptions of social cohesion.

---

3 Bhatia (2016) addresses this question in its various complexities.

Beyond the self-fulfilment rationale, there is a more radical construct which views free speech as means by which a person authors her mode of engagement with the reality outside the individual self. That was the manner in which Enlightenment philosophy, as conceived by Immanuel Kant for instance, saw an individual ascending to the civic state. Yet for Kant and for various other thinkers in that lineage, background conditions were to an extent immaterial. To be a woman was disqualification, as also to be a wage slave who had to sell his faculties to earn a daily subsistence. Free speech was not a merited right in these instances, since the subjects were not deemed quite ready for the civic state.

How far then would free speech doctrine need to be attentive to background conditions, to inherited debilities that prevent a full and free articulation of particular opinions? How far should law and policy go in seeking to equalise these conditions of access to the sphere of public deliberation? The correction of inherited disabilities may involve the abridgment of existing liberties – the narrowly constructed freedoms in the Friedrich von Hayek sense – which potentially include the freedom to impose a viewpoint or a way of life. These social negotiations traverse several layers of complexity. Economic regulation, as with legislating minimum standards of wages and decent working conditions for media employees, would not be regarded as a violation of free speech rights. That point has been established in a continuum of cases in which the Indian Supreme Court has tacked in a fairly consistent direction, though only in terms of the doctrine of balancing between competing entitlement claims.

In recent times, this "balance of rights" rationale has been transformed into a wider context: as a stronger and positive affirmation of the liberty and autonomy of the news gathering and dissemination functions, and derivatively, of the social right to speak and be informed. Media industry structures, particularly within the neoliberal policy dispensation, are seen to lend excessive and undue importance to the advertiser and demote the voice of the public. A possible antidote could be the "public service journalism" construct, which could direct financial investments as a matter of policy, into news gathering and job security assurances that would enable media practitioners the freedom to actively pursue the public interest. But that solution founders on the age-old dilemma, that he who pays the piper has the right within liberal ideology, to call the tune.

More acute dilemmas arise when rules of access to the public sphere are the issue. This question could be rendered in terms of another, about modes of social control over the infrastructure of communication. A newspaper that enjoys the strongly entrenched patronage of corporate advertisers could sustain a higher volume of circulation and find greater traction for its editorial content. This could be to the exclusion of other, perhaps more representative and legitimate views on civic and political matters. In fact, since the positive reinforcement between readership volume and advertisement support is very strong, this is a circumstance that could lead to media monopolies and the extinction of pluralism in the marketplace for ideas.

Regulatory efforts in India were attentive to this reality, though they stumbled at the first legal challenge. In a celebrated case in 1962, the Supreme Court held that a policy restraining newspapers from leveraging advertisement access to establish a selling price advantage over the competition, was violative of the free speech guarantees. The free speech clause allowed for some restraints, but nothing could justify the limitation of the rights of one category of citizens, i.e., the large newspapers, to better protect the rights of others.

A similar rationale of privileging big media against competition from smaller players was part of the 1972 Supreme Court ruling in the Bennett Coleman matter, disallowing newsprint rationing in a situation of acute scarcity. Just over two decades later, when deciding on the norms by which the broadcast spectrum should be allocated, the Supreme Court resoundingly upheld a principle of public control. In terms of operational benefit thought, this very significant ruling has been of little consequence. The colonisation of the spectrum by big media has only accelerated after that very salutary ruling.

A notion that free speech in its untrammelled exercise could undo social cohesion lies at the root of most efforts at curbing the right. The infamous sedition law in turn draws its justification from the premise that the "state" as ultimate guarantor of social order, deserves gentle treatment in all forms of political speech. Anything that tends to undermine its legitimacy, or bring it into disrepute is a threat to the liberty of all, since the "state" ultimately is all that stands between order and the Hobbesian dystopia of a "war of all against all".

Sedition has been the most stubborn of the "speech crimes". It is a legal clause that has been recognised as dysfunctional in any democratic order, since its ultimate purpose has at all times been to exclude certain persons and collectivities – sometimes chosen arbitrarily but most often with deliberate purpose – from the public discourse. Yet for all the accumulated evidence that it is offensive to every notion of democratic rights, "sedition" refuses to be rubbed out of the statute book.

In the euphoria of newly won freedom, India's Constituent Assembly witnessed spirited demands for deleting the crime of sedition, the imposition of a colonial regime seeking to suppress dissent within a nation held by conquest. Inheritors of the mantle of governance opposed that demand, but gave in under pressure, to a limited degree.

Sedition was removed from constitutional grounds for restraints on free speech, but still remained on the penal code. The Constituent Assembly also resolved that articles of law inconsistent with fundamental rights provisions would be deleted. What followed was an elaborate fudging of principles, and despite subsequent remedial efforts, when vagueness has been dispelled and stronger affirmations made of the free speech right, the legacy in 2016 is of a partiality towards constructing free speech as a restricted right.

There is a philosophical posture, perfectly reasonable, that views the remedy for an abuse of free speech in encouraging more speech. It is a sound proposition, but presupposes a basic substratum of civility for carrying out a social dialogue. This is the great intangible in all such debates. "Civil society" has been a constant presence in the liberal democratic discourse on freedom and rights, from its very beginnings in the 18th century. But it is a notion that is unformed and rather vaguely formulated in most debates. In recent years, Edward Shils has spoken of civility as an essential component of national solidarity and, a little more questionably, Robert Putnam has pointed to the vanishing of this virtue as part of the crisis of modern times. Civility has been defined as respect for another's dignity. But social actors are now quick to construe an affront to their dignity in a manner that denies another the freedom to speak the unvarnished truth as seen from that perspective.[4] Here again is the tendency for homogenisation at work, which insists on particularities being abolished since there is an overarching "general interest" that demands it.

In the absence of this substratum of civility, uncertainty reigns over the limits of free speech. Random speech acts done without the slightest hint of malafide intent, could trigger threats of violence, providing room for state authorities to step in and impose order at their will. Free speech requires fearless listening. But as long as states revel in portraying themselves as fragile and societies remain uncivil arenas, the rewards from taking on that burden of fearlessness would just not seem worthwhile. Free speech would remain in the circumstances, the exclusive privilege of the powerful.

Speech is also strongly associated with assertions of identity. And the collision of identities could often end in bloodshed, as the *Charlie Hebdo* killings in Paris in January 2015 showed. This incident drew worldwide condemnation and something equivalent to a culture war between western values of scepticism and irreverence, and the supposed obscurantism that large numbers of another world religion were mired in.

It did not take long for the matter to segue into more overtly political issues, like immigration, assimilation and minority rights in a republic which putatively enshrines the universal values of equality and liberty. These principles are self-evident in terms of theory, but their interpretations in practical politics have been varied and often conflicting. And the French interpretation has been particularly problematic in the rigour with which it seeks to banish all displays of religiosity from the public space and condones the mocking of the belief systems of perceived "others". Equally difficult has been its appropriation of the privilege of laughter – at others and at oneself – by those who by historical circumstances, wield a higher degree of power than those they laugh at. The *Charlie Hebdo* affair showed that laughter does little to bridge social differences when it is a narrow privilege enjoyed by those of power.

Could the free speech right be problematised within the paradigm of positive and negative liberty associated with Isaiah Berlin? This is a

---

4 Garton Ash (2016) is an important work which addresses several among these issues with a wealth of empirical detail.

framework that does not work beyond a point, though a more credible effort could be made within the terms of the reconstruction that the political theorist C.B. MacPherson attempted.

The Indian experience has been that an unconditional investiture of the fundamental rights in the constitution was gradually rescinded as an increasing number of exceptions were introduced. The boundaries of free speech were then negotiated through the years, with reasons of state security becoming a ground for increasing restrictions. Because of a lack of clarity in phraseology and the inevitable hiatus between executive action and judicial review, the reality became one where powers of restricting free speech by state and civil society actors became virtually untrammelled. Judicial precedents in matters involving the basic rights were weakly established and often disregarded.

Quite apart from weak institutional processes, there are a number of tensions inherent in the dual construction of information: as a commodity and as a human right. The media functions by transacting two kinds of information. Media output is a product that is sold twice over. This unique feature means that lower subscriber prices might not serve the cause of consumer sovereignty, since that would imply higher leverage for the advertiser. The maintenance of a reasonable balance in the advertisement-editorial chemistry has been a matter of social concern. Policy has sought to ensure that the advertiser's preemptive claim to media space does not skew the competition in the marketplace for ideas. But these efforts have been unsuccessful and the larger failure has followed, of advertiser power gradually taking over editorial space.

Advertising has been among the most loosely monitored areas of global business. It also merited under most constructions of the fundamental rights, a lower level of protection than other forms of speech. Recent turns in judicial interpretation though have tended to bring advertising on par with editorial speech. This represents a collapsing of the distinction that was a strong and time-honoured convention in the media. The corrosive impact on editorial independence has been evident, as has the loss of media autonomy to the new global advertising giants.

Scholarship has in recent years unearthed the many mechanisms through which nationalist identities are consolidated. Benedict Anderson's contribution has been particularly noteworthy, with its affirmation of the importance of "print capitalism" as an underlying force. Reading deeper into his work, certain clues emerge towards understanding the troublesome persistence of the term "fourth estate" in later nationalist writing as a clichéd reference to the press in a democratic political order. This term tends to suggest that the press enjoyed a status almost akin to other recognised estates as a part of the established order of political governance. In reality, a plain reading of the evolution of liberal democracy would reveal that press freedom was never even remotely an assurance till very late in its career. Rather the press was always intimately connected with one or the other political interest group and when not on the right side of the dominant power structures, always subject to persistent censorship efforts.

It is only when "civil society" as a construct became embedded in the liberal democratic order, that press freedom gained a degree of latitude. By then, the need for coercion to compel the sustenance and reproduction of the liberal capitalist order had begun to abate. "Civil society" as a construct crosses over seamlessly into that of the "public sphere", which the media is instrumental in creating. This is a space that is sustained on the "mythology" of universal access for all citizens. Myth is the term of art that has been given to this process of fostering a public discourse that makes what is contingent seem eternal, that strips the history out of the social reality and makes it appear as part of the natural order.

Over the course of 2011, mass movements sprouted across various parts of the globe. Uncoordinated and for the most part lacking an identifiable leadership structure, these movements, all focused around the need for change of an undefined sort, soon gained the epithet of the "social media revolution". Yet the roots of the mass unrest remained obscure and the leaderless revolutions either meandered into a dead-end in quick time, or descended into a state of full-blown political chaos.

Robin Jeffrey has fused Benedict Anderson's idea of the nationalist imagination as moulded by print capitalism, with Ernest Renan's characterisation of the newspaper as a daily referendum on the nation. Since roughly the end of the "emergency" regime in 1977, in Jeffrey's narration, India's newspaper revolution has brought larger numbers into the political process, and served as a means of recruiting citizen loyalty to the nation. The purchase of a newspaper is "a vote in favour" of the nation, a gesture of belonging. Since that diagnosis was offered, the media scene in India has been transformed beyond recognition by the arrival of satellite television and the internet. This period has also been one of growing economic inequalities both in India and globally. In the character of the discourse that it promotes, the media reproduces and amplifies these inequalities. These disparities in voice have a linguistic and a technological dimension: one determined by the relative privileges enjoyed by those who use the English language, the other by entry barriers into the new universe of the social media.

In turn, the faceless corporations behind the new social media have begun to be the hidden persuaders that make consequential political decisions with far-reaching implications. This explicit political agenda was evident during the 2011 social media revolutions and the particular course they took, with the potential for anti-system dissent emerging in an organised shape in the capitals of global neoliberalism being quickly scotched, while chaos and anarchy were allowed to spread elsewhere.

The Indian nation was imagined by early ideologues in English print. The polyphony of regional discourses came into the scene at a later stage and in a distinctly hierarchical relationship that mirrored the social pecking order of caste and community. If there was a construction of nationalist identities incipient in the growth of print capitalism, so too was there a linguistic evolution that tended to identify the minorities as a distinct, even alien, component in the social matrix. Following independence when print capitalism – and later, broadcast and digital capitalism – set an autonomous course, the alternate discourses representing the voices of those characterised as minorities by "mainstream" consensus, began to be increasingly marginalised. The promise of the development state that was constituted with independence from colonialism, involved an implicit assurance that identities would be immaterial in the distribution of the fruits of modernity. But reality belied this promise, fuelling a fresh resurgence of narrower identities and an effort to submerge these in a hegemonic construct of nationalism.

India is unique in having a legislation protecting wages and working conditions of journalists as part of its legal framework on media freedom. The link has not always been obvious, since the media industry has in repeated onslaughts against the law, portrayed it as an active impediment to the constitutional right to free speech. These efforts have not quite brought rewards, though realities on the ground in terms of the practice of journalism have altered radically. With journalists' unions fragmenting and the newspaper industry organising to safeguard its interests, the prospects have turned adverse for decent work in the media profession. The consequence has been, among other things, an epidemic of corrupt practices in the news industry. The evolving jurisprudence on the protection of journalism as a profession has been of some help, but the collective response in civil society has failed to uphold the basic values of the profession, at a time when media technologies potentially make every citizen a participant in the news domain.

The chapters that follow seek to tackle this broad range of questions. The first of them considers how freedom of speech has been constructed as a fundamental human right that can contrary to promise, be abridged in particular situations. With all the philosophical inquiries into the question, it appears that the criteria for actually instituting restraints upon this freedom are loose and arbitrary. They do not lend themselves to generalisation, except paradoxically, in a context dependent manner. The need to sustain civic peace is always a concern, but enforced very disproportionately in practice, focused on cultural difference rather than the real value of speech. An overarching circumstance would be the established patterns of delegation of the right to speak within a particular social order. These are always subject to disruption which could be a positive circumstance if the outcome is a fresh equilibrium that expands the ambit of the right. In concrete situations though, the balance could also be restored through instruments of coercion that deny the right to large numbers.

The following three chapters look at a triad of terms that are increasingly part of the political discourse in a time of growing illiberalism: nation, state and civil society. Taken for granted as a locus of collective loyalty at one time, the nation has been theorised in recent literature as an artefact of the imagination, moulded in part by the collective worship orchestrated by the media. Human imagination is a fickle and shifting terrain, an uncomfortable place for a supposedly eternal form of human association such as the "nation" to be situated. As a remedy for the fallibility of this definition of the nation, there is the solidity of the state on offer, an active agency of collective intent that embodies the law.

The current reality is that the law is itself a muddled terrain, which the state expresses through arbitrary actions attacking the speech right, while waiving like sanctions against expressive acts that seem clearly to breach accepted bounds. That arbitrariness is believed to originate in part, in infirm contacts between the state and the entity referred to as "civil society", where the norms of harmonious coexistence are supposedly worked out in regular, quotidian fashion. Since the bipolar contest for world hegemony broke down in 1991 and the neoliberal era began, the construct of "civil society" has acquired greater prominence in public discussions.

New technologies of communication and information dissemination have sharpened this focus on "civil society", now seen as a domain immensely empowered by technological possibilities. Real life experiences show that the convergence of technology with civil society, could produce outcomes that defeat the objectives of democracy. The lazy assumption that technology necessarily contributes to positive social and political change has to be challenged and this is a matter that current thinking on the media has to accommodate.

Civility is premised upon respect for people of other beliefs and convictions. The collision of ideas could often be expressed in satire, perhaps even in mockery. Every individual is given the freedom to mock another, within mutually agreed definitions of civility. But like the archetypal "black swan" which crops up to disrupt all established modes of thought, these accepted definitions could break down without prior warning, with potentially lethal consequences, putting the entire edifice of civility under threat of catastrophic collapse in an action-reaction spiral.

The following two chapters look at unstated but immutable principles of access to the public sphere. The market is the principle on which the media universe functions, and advertising is the magic carpet that brings words that would otherwise remain unspoken to audiences, whether interested or otherwise. The market is supposedly an open sphere, where nobody will encounter the slightest barrier to entry. That is a long way removed from the reality, where the market is constituted by a tight nexus of business enterprises which work in something of a simulation of competition, but agree at a more profound level on the principles that are in their best mutual interests. The media market has two sides to it; the media industry purveys a product that is already sold to the advertiser before it reaches its audience. That has caused a convergence of two distinct information genres – advertising and editorial – whose separation was part of the compact that the media made with its audience and indeed is the basis on which it claims to be an institutional bearer of the social right to free speech.

Where does this leave the craft of journalism? Once viewed as a part of citizenship in evolving liberal democracies, journalism was later categorised as a distinct profession within an established structure of commerce. Despite this, the civic role of journalism as a commitment of democratic citizenship never fully receded, creating an incentive for society and state to render it a special and protected status. That special status is no longer a social or political priority, in part because of the collective defaults of journalism itself, but perhaps more so because of the inexorable logic of a system that forces information transactions into the narrow mould where commerce becomes its sole rationale.

Early technological optimism induced by the new media ecosystem, is proving misplaced since these resources are perhaps being coopted into the existing substratum of global power relations, to sharpen its worst abuses. Democratic control over the media will not magically dawn by any manner of internal logic of technology. It has to be achieved in constant political struggle.

A Patchy Freedom

Commerce, class and the value of speech

A notion of freedom that does not protect speech is quickly recognised as a patent absurdity. Yet there are few national systems of law that protect speech in an absolute sense. That is a paradox that liberal democratic theory is yet to resolve, or even find a pathway towards resolving.

Free speech as a codified right originates in the late-18th century republican revolutions in France and the United States of America. In successive constitutional formulations, the French revolutionaries first elevated and then demoted free speech, deeming it now a basic entitlement and the next moment, a threat to the republic's survival. In a situation of less political volatility, free speech as a principle received a significant impetus with the First Amendment in the U.S. in 1791. This seeming triumph was almost immediately neutralised by the enactment of a law to severely sanction the crime of "seditious libel". For several decades that followed, jurisprudence on the sin of "blasphemous libel" remained similarly inattentive to free speech guarantees. The republican revolutions were followed by years of imperial expansion and an effective division of the world into the enlightened few and the benighted many. Doctrines of liberty remained in this sense, patchy in their application.

Free speech suffered a fate very much like the putatively inalienable rights – life and liberty – which could be severely abridged if the claimants lacked certain virtues. Finer points of legal propriety remained unresolved as two 20th century conflagrations involving industrial scale savagery created a crisis of conscience that inheritors of western enlightenment traditions needed to assuage. The Universal Declaration of Human Rights (UDHR), adopted by the United Nations General Assembly in 1948, by far the most widely honoured international covenant, conferred upon humanity in both its enlightened and benighted quarters, the benediction of uniformly applicable rights and entitlements.

In the language of the UDHR, equality in the investiture of rights originated in the equal endowment that all human individuals had of "reason and conscience". This conceptual breakthrough effaced the easy and lazy ascription to certain categories of individuals – the working class in the imperial nations and perhaps all but a small westernised minority in the colonial territories – of lesser wisdom and moral judgment. Ironically, this happened at just the time that the early western faith in reason was beginning to erode, a scepticism expressed in Max Horkheimer's 1946 work, *The Eclipse of Reason.*

Any person asked if she had a sense of what was meant by reason, Horkheimer pointed out, would be hesitant to speak, if not embarrassed. And that was not simply because the answer seemed self-evident. Reason, in ordinary speech, referred to the adequacy or otherwise of procedures employed for "purposes more or less taken for granted and supposedly self-explanatory". Yet this subjective understanding was a world removed from the sense in which the term "reason" was embedded in western enlightenment traditions, where it was "a force not only in the individual mind but also in the objective world".[1]

A reconciliation of sorts was accomplished in the doctrine of pragmatism, which in essence held that "a theory is nothing but a scheme or a plan of action". Theory was tested for its truth by how successful or effective was the action it led to.[2] Success was key and once truth gained this identification, the measure of commerce came into play. Money was the measure. That was for Horkheimer the natural destination of liberalism, which created conformity and social bonding, through "the levelling principle of commerce and exchange which held a liberalistic (sic) society together". An industrialised culture would en-

1 Horkheimer (1946): 1-2.

2 Ibid: 28.

force the "principle of conformity", which would proclaim itself, emancipated from the cult of individual liberty, in the "rank of an ideal".[3] Lost in the process was any sensitivity to the larger mass of humanity that remained outside the liberal ambience, where different idioms of communication prevailed. Horkheimer ended on an exhortatory note, urging philosophy to cultivate greater sensitivity to diverse languages and their "muted testimonies" which carried layers of meaning, "embodying the thought forms and belief patterns rooted in the evolution of the people who speak it".[4]

These subtleties took the philosophical perception well beyond the limitations of liberalism, but were not quite within the gaze of the committees that drafted the UDHR, in a deadline-bound, consensus-oriented procedure. Yet the UDHR put forward a construct of free speech as an absolute investiture of rights, unbound by distinctions of status or national frontiers. There was little equivocation in the language of the UDHR, which held in its article 19 that "everyone has the right to freedom of opinion and expression". This included the "freedom to hold opinions without interference and to seek, receive and impart information and ideas through any media and regardless of frontiers."

In the real world, this radical investiture of rights stood not the faintest chance of being implemented. Possible grounds for abridgment were set out in the International Covenant on Civil and Political Rights (ICCPR), drafted under UN auspices in 1954, adopted and opened for signature in 1966 and effective as part of the "international bill of rights" since 1974. After restating the free speech right in its broadest form, the ICCPR set down a charter of responsibilities, presumably creating a threshold of civic duty every individual had to cross to gain free speech and related entitlements. All exceptions, the ICCPR cautioned, needed to be specified under law, not left undefined or defined so broadly as to allow every manner of arbitrary suppression of speech or so-called thought crimes.[5]

---

3 Ibid: 98-99.

4 Ibid: 118.

5 "The exercise of (these) rights... carries with it special duties and responsibilities. It may therefore be subject to certain restrictions, but these shall only be such as are provided by law and are necessary: (1) For respect of the rights or reputations of others; (2) For the protection of national security or of public order, or of public health or morals."

Provisos introduced by the ICCPR tacitly recognised several tensions in the UDHR formulation on free speech. While identifying the complexities, it yielded minimal ground to calls for a dilution of the right. One person's speech could not be an invasion of another's rights. A second proviso put national security and public order on a higher pedestal than the citizen's right to free speech and this has expectedly, become a zone of sharp contestation. Who defines the state of "national security" and when is "public order" disturbed sufficiently to warrant invocation of the doctrine of necessity?

The paradox of rights

A knotty paradox arises here. In the absence of "national security" and "public order", individual citizens would be deprived of not just speech, but all freedoms. Chaos and anarchy would prevail, a Hobbesian state of "war of all against all". An individual enters a social contract with fellow beings to live at peace with them, in part by delegating responsibility for life and liberty – most prized among all possessions – to an external agency. State sovereignty is an outcome of multiple such acts of delegation, of the ceding of the individual's vital stake in preserving himself, to a body that stands above and beyond individuality. Underlying the compact is the tacit recognition that the sovereign power would determine when its most severe provisions are invoked, involving in most cases, perceived threats to its own existence. The human rights dilemma is in some ways derivative, or closely connected, with the paradox of sovereignty that Giorgio Agamben among modern political theorists has drawn attention to.[6]

The state functions under the law but also determines when exceptions could be made. A speech act that undermines the authority of the state could be punished if seen to endanger the fundamental rights of all.[7] In lesser situations, acts by any one individual, imagined in one

6 Agamben (2005: 3) defines the "sovereign" as "he who decides on the state of exception", and (1998: 12), he points to the paradox of sovereignty: "The sovereign is both outside and inside the juridical order".

7 Garton Ash (2016: 7028) presents this imagined dialogue between state and citizen, which could as well have been written by that master of modern satirical drama, Harold Pinter: "S: You can't say that. C: Why not? S: We can't tell you. C: Why can't you tell me? S: It would endanger your security. C: Why? S: We can't tell you why it would endanger your

context as a legitimate exercise of rights could elsewhere be seen as an intrusion into another's rights. Article 4 of the ICCPR offers a codification: exceptions could be made in "times of public emergency" when a threat to the "life of the nation" is manifest and "officially proclaimed". Parties to the ICCPR could then take "measures derogating from their obligations", but these would have to be strictly proportional to situational needs and consistent with every other legal obligation, including equality of treatment irrespective of "race, colour, sex, language, religion or social origin". Specifically prohibited are derogations that abridge the right to life, or involve torture or enslavement.

As salutary as they sound, these strictures against discrimination on any ground need to be assessed against prevalent constructs of nationalism. The sense of belonging to a "nation" has always been an identity assertion, which makes for an easy transition from declaring a threat to the "life of a nation" and acting against those who do not share that identity construct. Public sanction for coercive action against an alien other – an enemy within – is often sought and obtained on these grounds.

Beyond well-intentioned statements of principle – general to the point of banality – practical experiences in legislating free speech exceptions have been slippery. At a fundamental level, it is impossible to legislate the state of exception which stands at the intersection between politics and law, since the "state of necessity" on which it is founded cannot have a juridical form. Contingent adjustments have been made, every one of them specific to a particular place and time. Principle here is very much in the grip of history. Invariably then, the safest recourse for political authority has in most cases been to slip into a regime of selective proscription. Principle counts for little when the sustenance of the State is at stake.

An early text arguing for free speech goes right back to the mid-seventeenth century and the turmoil of the civil war in England and Cromwell's dictatorship. John Milton's *Areopagitica* couches its argument in loyalty to the state. A free citizen requites his obligations to the sovereign by speaking the clear, unvarnished truth, enabling him to rule wisely by sparing him the false comforts of courtiers. It was

---

security because to tell you that would endanger your security. C: So I may not know what I may not know and I may not know why I may not know it? S: Next caller please."

not a cause that gained much traction at the time. In a state of intense struggle, none among the three combatants – monarchy, nobility and ecclesiastical order – felt inclined to grant the other the least latitude.

By the eighteenth century, the notion of the free and autonomous individual began to take root, shifting the focus of debate to the means by which the body politic could be constituted in a manner that embodied the individual's sovereignty within a collectivity. Utilitarianism was an early philosophical trend which economic theory has since made its guiding light, and though it gained a degree of respect in early years because of the passion which the rising British middle class brought to its espousal, its identification of society as an arithmetic aggregation of isolated individuals fails every test of authenticity. Social contract theory was a rival doctrine that better retained the Enlightenment spirit of inquiry, seeking to plot the pathways through which the mutual dependence of individuals within society could be consolidated in bonds of solidarity and mutual gain.

From a state of nature to the civic bond

Early thinkers posited the social contract as mankind's evolution out of the brutality of the state of nature, which in turn was seen as the historic datum – an actually existing situation – of endemic conflict that humanity naturally tended to fall into. Rousseau did away with this contrivance, postulating the state of nature rather, as merely a hypothetical reference point. The "social order" was for him, a "sacred right" and "the basis of all other rights", originating not in nature but "convention". It was essential before considering the process by which a people chose their government, to "examine that by which it has become a people". Between a hypothetical natural state and its civic being, the human species made the big transition from instinct to justice. A sense of morality – lacking in nature – became indispensable, and a "well-ordered" society would necessarily have to agree on a shared moral code for its sustenance.[8]

Every individual was sovereign in terms of rights and the collective was the basic unit of legislation. Facts were created in accordance

8 Rousseau (1762): 165-6, 173, 179. This notion of shared morality being necessary within the "basic structure" of a "well-ordered society" became an integral part of the political philosopher John Rawls's celebrated twentieth century theory of justice.

with the perfect constructs of rights, but this transition from the world of hypothetical rights to the realm of facts, was not seamless. If the "sovereign" – which embodied the general will – were to assume executive power, "right and fact would be so confounded that no one could tell what was law and what was not". In that situation, the "body politic, thus disfigured, would soon fall a prey to the violence it was instituted to prevent". Representative democracy was the solution fashioned to resolve the tensions of the transition from feudal autocracy to a popular democracy. Rousseau saw this as a deeply flawed and contradictory pursuit since sovereignty was inalienable and belonged to every individual. Sovereignty was impossible to delegate; it lay in the general will and did "not admit of representation". The moment a people allowed itself to be "represented" was when it lost its freedom. From then on, "it is no longer free: it no longer exists".[9]

Immanuel Kant dealt subtly with Rousseau's dissent, in part by distinguishing between the contract by which individuals organised themselves into a social state and all others. The difference lay in the constitutional principle by which individuals entered into the "civic state". A perfect constitutional order was the inevitable outcome of competition and conflict. Such an order would enshrine "the right of human beings [to live] under public coercive laws by which every man's [right] is determined and secured against the interference of every other man".[10]

Kant saw a superior purpose guiding man's actions, an intent concealed in individual human nature, but manifest in species characteristics. He saw the antagonism of men in society becoming, "in the end, the cause of a lawful order". The unlawful tendency would become the foundation of the law. Antagonism was "the unsociable sociability of man, i.e., the propensity of men to enter into a society, which propensity is, however, linked to a constant mutual resistance which threatens to dissolve this society". Virtue and vice were not innate properties of the individual, but outcomes of the social state. The species property of man to seek association was decisive and only in the social state would he be "capable of developing his natural faculties".

---

9 Ibid: 240, 242.

10 Kant (1793): 419.

Averse as Kant was to a state that would assume powers over the citizens of a nation, his perceptions of human nature involved a logical conundrum. How does harmony emerge by some miracle, from the collisions of infinitesimal individuals who share nothing except the instinct for acquisition and a tendency to allow their egos to take over their existence? In his *Critique of Practical Reason*, Kant provided his best effort to resolve this conundrum, proposing among his most crucial axioms, that the human will should "freely" submit itself to the law. In this sense of "free" submission lay the preservation of individual liberty. Every individual, under the reign of reason, would be enjoined to act as though the exercise of his will could "always at the same time hold good as a principle of universal legislation".[11] A state of enlightenment for Kant involved an escape from the tutelage of older authorities – typically of the ecclesiastical sort – and each individual acting with a sound and well-formed judgment of the principles of "universal legislation".

Civic state and market

It is roughly here that we could date the origins of the construct of the "marketplace of ideas" as the ultimate arena for valuing what gets to be spoken and heard.[12] The argument of the marketplace being unfailingly fair as arbiter, has retained a powerful influence within the liberal democratic approach to basic rights, including free speech, though its credibility as a guarantee of authenticity and democratic equality has been questioned.

Writing in the relatively more settled and equable conditions of the mid-19th century, John Stuart Mill was absolute in his commitment to free speech, though not quite so strongly compelled to exert himself over press freedom. Perhaps the press did not merit distinct consideration since like all liberal thinkers of his time, Mill assumed that with laws that met libertarian standards, all voices would be heard. The power to restrain the expression of any point of view, he held inher-

11 Kant (1788): 238.

12 At a much later date, a judge of the U.S. Supreme Court, Oliver Wendell Holmes, rephrased these arguments in the realm of ideas, making a case that the relentless collision between rival viewpoints would create conditions in which the best would prevail and gain general acceptance.

ently illegitimate, no matter if the voice being silenced was hopelessly isolated and demonstrably in error. The possibility of the majority being in error could not be ruled out, and even if indisputably in the right, the grasp over truth could only be sharpened in a collision with error. To prevent itself from lapsing into the "deep slumber of a decided opinion", society needed always to encourage those who would question established beliefs and express contrarian opinions.[13]

With all that, Mill concluded "in sober truth" that "the general tendency of things throughout the world is to render mediocrity the ascendant power among mankind". The "public" could be variously constructed: in the U.S., it was the whole white population and in Britain, "chiefly the middle class". Irrespective of these distinctions, the "public" was always a "mass", or in other words, "a collective mediocrity". The singular novelty Mill observed in his time was that the mass did not take its opinion from the authorities held in awe in earlier times – the church and the state – or from the ostensible leaders of society. Rather, "their thinking is done for them by men much like themselves, addressing them or speaking in their name, on the spur of the moment, through the newspapers".[14] The "marketplace of ideas" in terms of the most salutary outcome, was likely to impart greatest buoyancy to the best. In the real world of the mass production of ideas for the market, it was mediocrity that more likely triumphed. The Late-Victorian period is when press freedom became something of a discernible reality in Britain but the impact on freedom of thought and speech was ambiguous.

A hierarchy of rights

Aside from the triumph of mediocrity, this variant of the liberal doctrine also had the unhappy outcome of stratifying rights and entitlements in a manner that negated its fundamental premise of equality. Liberal thinkers of the twentieth century pointed out that the Kantian formulation of liberty involved a possible hierarchy in status, between the rational and the empirical individual. The rational person would find liberty as Rousseau said, in "obedience to a law that he prescribes to himself". The empirical individual would remain slave to irratio-

13 Mill (1859): 154- 179.

14 Ibid: 190-1.

nal passions whose public expression would be illegal when measured against the standards that he *should* willingly comply with, if he were in full possession of his rational faculties. This was the recognised paradox at the heart of the Enlightenment doctrine: the willing submission of the rational individual to the law is no submission because no law written in the spirit of reason could possibly deprive a person of freedom. Only the irrational would need to be coerced to submit to the laws of reason.

There was a common assumption underlying these doctrines, Isaiah Berlin pointed out in his much cited work *Two Concepts of Liberty*: "the rational ends of our 'true' natures must coincide, or be made to coincide, however violently our poor, ignorant, desire-ridden, passionate, empirical selves may cry out against this process". Freedom did not come with the sanction to be "irrational, or stupid, or wrong". It was no "tyranny, but liberation" to compel empirical individuals to abandon their follies, and adopt "right" patterns of conduct.[15]

It was an irony for Berlin that the enlightenment liberalism seemed to meld in this respect into the opposite authoritarian stream. Indeed, the theoretical tradition which saw liberation in man's release from all forms of tutelage, seemed to wander here into the rather strange ideological embrace of its opposite: the authoritarian, state-focused philosophy that Johann Fichte, one of many epigones in the Hegelian tradition of western thought, seemed best to express, with his belief that "compulsion is also a kind of education". In seeking a resolution to this dilemma, Berlin was led towards an exposition of liberty in two distinct manifestations: the positive and negative. Positive liberty in Berlin's estimation involved the right of unbridled action, but also carried a potential for excess, for the oppression of individuals in the name of a larger cause; for the arrogation by some of the right to decide the larger social good and compel others to acquiesce in the loss of their freedoms.

Berlin saw an inexorable transformation of positive liberty – in a manner consistent with liberal-democratic orthodoxy – into an oppressive doctrine. Since every individual's self-assertion could potentially impede another in his exercise of rights, liberal-democratic theory worked out a moderating principle. Every such affirmation of

15 Berlin (1958): 219.

individuality and rights was to be restrained by reason, which in turn was imbedded in law. Caprice and individual whim would cease being part of a citizen's public actions once he accepted the restraints consistent with universal principles of legislation. Those unwilling to follow the law as dictated by a universal rationality, would forfeit their right to the protection of the law and could be suitably sanctioned or deprived of their liberty.

In effect, this created two categories of individuals: those socialised into the higher rationality and the recalcitrants who needed to be coerced. Positive liberty as Berlin saw it, could be deeply damaging to the fabric of a society committed to diversities of opinion and belief. It had a salutary value to the extent it asserted an individual's right to be part of the political sovereign, or the state. The downside was that it could potentially sanction an intrusion into the freedom of fellow citizens. A greater hazard would arise in that a positive construct of liberty could empower a faction ensconced within the apparatus of the state – claiming the legitimacy of the majority – to impose any manner of arbitrary action upon others.

Far more manageable for Berlin was "negative liberty" which demarcated a zone of inalienable freedoms where individual sovereignty could not be breached, whether by another person or by any entity claiming sovereign power. From being the licence to act in a manner of his choosing, liberty would in this "negative" construction become a safeguard for an individual's most preciously guarded entitlements. Negative liberty though did not create any manner of legal entitlement against the presumptive powers of national states. So the best guarantee available for liberty was a commitment to pluralism, an attitude of tolerance towards difference, a forbearance towards all ideas without advancing any manner of a claim of "eternal validity" for any among them.[16]

Freedom and justice

A conception of justice, widely agreed and shared, was identified in a late-20th century revival of social contract doctrine, as an essential part of a "well-ordered society". Within liberal traditions, John Rawls sought an anchorage for a principle of equality which would be an effective foundation for a liberal order. A just order needed to satisfy two

16 Ibid: 191-242.

fundamental principles: first, that each person would have "an equal right to the most extensive basic liberty compatible with a similar liberty for others"; and second, that social and economic inequalities would be "arranged so that they are (a) reasonably expected to be to everyone's advantage, and (b) attached to positions and offices open to all".[17]

Rawls recognised that differences in status and wealth would tend to negate these principles, but argued that human endeavour could work through these difficulties to establish a fair social order. Key here was a sense of justice that every member of society could consent to. There were two relevant positions that "for the most part" each member of society held: "that of equal citizenship and that defined by his place in the distribution of income and wealth". Individuals entering into a relationship of cooperation would be guided by "publicly recognised rules and procedures" and within this "basic structure", the element of justice would be appraised "from the position of equal citizenship".[18]

How was a state of "equal citizenship" to be forged in a context of wide and growing inequality? Rawls' solution was premised upon what he called the "difference principle". The "higher expectations of those better situated are just", he argued, "if and only if they work as part of a scheme which improves the expectations of the least advantaged members of society".[19] Society would negotiate its principles of justice – involving equal liberties and "fair equality of opportunity" – from an "original position", which would "nullify the effects of specific contingencies which put men at odds and tempt them to exploit social and natural circumstances to their own advantage". Such a state is attained when it is assumed that all the parties "are situated behind a veil of ignorance": "They do not know how the various alternatives will affect their own particular case and they are obliged to evaluate principles solely on the basis of general considerations."[20]

17 Rawls (1971): 60.

18 Ibid: 96-7.

19 Ibid: p 78.

20 Ibid: 136-7.

What emerges when these principles are worked into the domain of free speech and the narrower construct of media freedom? The competition between media organisations to platform the contest of ideas is the perfect example of the marketplace that ostensibly allows the best to rise and gain public attention. But since the media functions in an environment of scarcity – of the essential material resources of the trade such as newsprint and broadcast spectrum, to name just two elements – open access to the media is not an assurance that can be held out to all. In the circumstances, those who hold the megaphone in society are obliged under the difference principle, to provide fair voice to all who may have a viewpoint to articulate.

Rawls has had his fair share of critics, several of them focusing on how viable this negotiation from an "original position" would be in a concrete historical conjuncture. C.B. Macpherson, a perceptive late-twentieth century critic of liberal doctrine, thought that Rawls's assumption on the inevitability of inequalities betrayed a vision limited to the horizons of a market economy. After a promising beginning, when Rawls posited equality as a desirable end, he moved seamlessly towards the premise that there are certain situations in which inequality is justified. In its basic structure, a just society would ensure that the situation of inequality has acceptance across the scale of income and wealth, since all of society would be seen as benefiting from the good fortune of those at the upper end. Macpherson simply asks if Rawls does not blind himself to the whole range of possibilities that society could explore, by ruling out a classless society. He remained limited in essence, to a "liberal-democratic capitalist welfare state".[21]

Rawls and Berlin concurred in ruling out poverty and inequality as substantive violations of liberty and justice. Poverty did impede the enjoyment of liberty, but this was different from being deprived of liberty itself. G.A. Cohen disagreed and in 1983, resurrected the Marxian case for "proletarian unfreedom", arguing that workers alienated from ownership over the means of production, are effectively deprived of their liberty. The premises of the capitalist model, that every individual worker had a pathway to prosperity, were worse than specious.[22] Yet even while strongly emphasising this, Cohen found "more free-

21 Macpherson (1971): 87-94.

22 Cohen (1983).

dom in the proletariat's situation than classical Marxism asserts", a consequence perhaps of his use of the British context as datum, as also his dependence on abstract logic rather than the empirical realities of global capitalism.[23]

Money and freedom

In a later lecture published as part of a posthumous collection, Cohen argued that the lack of money was a denial of freedom, that indeed those who argued otherwise were prey to the fallacy of regarding money as a "thing". Berlin and Rawls tended to see freedom and economic well-being as "distinct values" which needed to be reconciled as a matter of compassion or political prudence. This did not stand up to rigorous logical testing. If unfreedom was a state of being liable to "interference" by other people, a lack of money signified precisely that state.

The right wing argument opposed interference with the rights of property, but endorsed the "interference with access by the poor to that same private property". Even without going into the "comparative moralities of protecting and violating private property", it would be evident that there is an abridgment of freedom there. The right wing would argue that a person is rendered unfree only if he suffers interference in doing something that he has moral entitlement to. But such a case could not be made until the issue of the moral legitimacy of private property itself is resolved.[24]

These were themes anticipated in Macpherson's 1973 critique, which pointed out that Berlin's division of an indivisible human entitlement failed to account for constraints on individual conduct imposed by the grossly unequal distribution of "the means of life and the means of labour".[25] An individual lacking such means for no fault other than birth in the wrong lineage, would be obliged to transfer his powers to another, conferring on the latter an "extractive power" over his capacities. In this state of unfreedom the individual would be deprived of all choice and would lack all opportunity to develop his talents and personality.

---

23 Ibid: 11.

24 Cohen (2011): 187.

25 MacPherson (1973): 94.

Berlin had performed a useful function in calling attention to the harm inherent in positive liberty. And the one sense in which he was willing to uphold the concept – an individual's right to be part of the political sovereign – was consistent with his construct of negative liberty, in that by securing his voice within the actions of the political sovereign, the individual could guard against an intrusion by the state into his domain of autonomy. Macpherson was convinced that "positive liberty" needed to be understood more broadly than in its "debased" sense as the "imposition of a 'rational' freedom", as indeed a broader "absence of impediments to men's developmental powers".[26] Liberal doctrine failed consistently in getting a true measure of these impediments.

Beyond logical formalism, if the matter were to be viewed in historical context, the little detail Berlin missed out, was property. Even in the absence of an actively coercive state apparatus, which in libertarian theory was the principal source of iniquity, the alienation between vast sections of the people and the means to make their labour productive (and their voices heard), meant that liberty remained an illusory promise.

A liberal heterodoxy

As a possible resolution of this dilemma of liberal political theory, Macpherson posed two alternative conceptions: "counter-extractive" and "developmental" liberty. The former endowed an individual, even if he lacked the means to realise the productivity of his labour, with the power to resist the extraction (or the exploitation) of his faculties by another. The latter was a positive affirmation which went beyond the preservation of individual sovereignty and enabled the exercise of freedoms for developing an individual's unique personality.[27]

How did these principles fare when imported into the domain of free speech? It is a question of special relevance at a time when socialisation patterns are over-mediated, when an individual is unable to choose a mode of civic engagement without being barraged and hectored by media messages. Consider the U.S. media and its deceitful conduct in the months leading to the U.S. invasion of Iraq, on grounds

26 Ibid: 96.

27 Ibid: 95-119.

that were known to be false, concocted only to serve the lust for power of a narrow, morally bankrupt ruling clique.[28] Counter-extractive liberty could in the circumstances be interpreted as the right to be free of manipulated information and images that violate an individual's sovereign right to form an independent opinion, to insist that consent for corrupt and unethical actions cannot be won through sustained dissimulation and indoctrination, carried out with active but unstated media connivance.

Developmental liberty in the context of the free speech right would be the power to put forward a viewpoint and have it assessed on intrinsic worth, rather than disparaged or buried under. As a universally held right, free speech would be an entitlement that could not under any circumstance, be taken away. To voice a point of view within an empty room, where it does not rise beyond the level of soliloquy, is no exercise of free speech. Free speech also involves the right to be heard. Just as Berlin conceived of positive liberty – in one of its more acceptable variants – as the right to participate in the affairs of the political sovereign, "developmental liberty" would empower every citizen to be part of the organised apparatus of information dissemination in society.

It was recognised in liberal doctrine that there could not be in law, any prior restraint on the right to speak and be heard. But if it was to be retrieved from a welter of contradictory principles, liberalism also had to add the positive guarantee that nobody would be deprived of the right to be heard by reason of a lack of means. Nobody of supposedly superior status or faculties was entitled to take that right away: neither those of ample purses who owned the press; nor the self-regarding professional cadre of journalists.

Macpherson's effort at the retrieval of liberal democratic theory never quite achieved consummation in practical terms. The closest approximation it could be said, was the liberal democratic welfare state, which he was highly critical of in other respects. State guarantees that every citizen would have the franchise right, and access to essential needs of nutrition, health, education and recreation, could be read as an assurance of counter-extractive liberty. In the realm of information,

---

28 The trail of disinformation, beginning with the first stirrings of war lust within the George W. Bush cabal has been usefully traced by Mitchell (2008).

the practice of public service broadcasting, adopted as official policy in many among the liberal democracies, ensured the semblance of a place in the public arena for voices that remained unheard in earlier contexts.

Free speech absolutism and its critics

Over time, especially with the neoliberal triumph of the 1980s, these commitments, always infirm, began to be whittled down and the competitive ethos reaffirmed in undiluted form. In a later neoliberal phase, with its erosion of national frontiers through capital and information flows and the mixing of cultures, a fresh set of sensitivities, which could broadly be described as the politics of cultural offence, began to intrude into the debate over free speech. How far does the risk of offence to one element within a complex social milieu warrant restraints in the exercise of free speech? In a globalised context, that question would apply to instances where speech acts in particular corners of the map trigger adverse reactions in faraway locations.[29]

Answers have been mixed. Free speech absolutists have argued the case for retaining the broadest possible protections. Anthony Lewis's "biography of the U.S. First Amendment", traces the back and forth movement of free speech doctrine in law, from the first affirmation of the principle in 1791 to its abridgment in the law of "seditious libel" within a mere seven years, to the greater dents inflicted by the "Espionage Act" in the early twentieth century. There were then a host of rulings which upheld the security of the state as the preeminent principle, before which citizen rights had to yield.

This rather up-and-down career has led some to infer that the U.S. First Amendment was no real guarantee of freedom, only a protection against prior restraint on speech acts. Once in the public domain, all speech acts would be, despite the First Amendment, subject to legal sanction. Lewis nods towards this interpretation but then discounts it, making perhaps a little too much of the fact that the person who made it ultimately recanted. A quarter century after advancing that decid-

29 Garton Ash (2016) deals at length with the many complexities involved in the contemporary information age, where national frontiers no longer contain information exchanges, if ever they did and every global citizen seemingly inhabits the same seamless space of the worldwide web.

edly modest claim on behalf of the First Amendment, the person who had made it declared that even if "legal theory remained repressive", the press in reality "conducted itself as if the law scarcely existed". The press was not merely highly critical of politicians, it was almost "habitually scurrilous".[30]

The reality nonetheless was that speech acts – printed, pamphleted or spoken – attracted sanctions till well into the twentieth century. It was that late when the U.S. Supreme Court began to acquire first a dissident fringe and then a fairly voluble and consistent majority, who would stand up for an expansive interpretation of the First Amendment.[31] Lewis identifies 1931 as the turning point, when the Supreme Court struck down a state law that proscribed the display of a red flag "as a sign, symbol or emblem of opposition to organised government".[32] This shift in judicial standards has since been consolidated except for what seemed a retraction in a "hate speech" case in 1952, when the Supreme Court upheld a penalty – important only symbolically since it was derisory in magnitude – against a white supremacist calling for a determined pushback against "mongrelisation" and the "rapes, robberies, guns, knives and marijuana of the negro".

Lewis contends that the standard established in this case, *Beauharnais v Illinois*, will not survive the Supreme Court decision from a decade later, in a matter involving an advertisement in the *New York Times* alleging illegal means by Alabama state officials to target civil rights campaigners working for minority enfranchisement. In this matter, *Sullivan v New York Times*, the court quashed a half-a-million dollar fine imposed by an Alabama court, and held that "public officials and public figures cannot recover damages for libel unless they can prove that a false statement of fact (sic) was published knowingly or recklessly". This very expansive protection of free speech was later reiterated in a

---

30 Lewis (2007): 5.

31 Notable prosecutions which ended in convictions were those involving the Socialist Party leader Eugene Debs (Ibid: 27), the case of *Abrams v United States* in which four young radicals were found guilty under the Espionage Act for distributing pamphlets denouncing U.S. intervention in the newly established Soviet Union (Ibid: 28); *Whitney v California* which involved a communist organiser brought to trial for the propagation of what were called "syndicalist" views (Ibid: 157).

32 Ibid: 39.

case involving the libel of an individual, "as in *Hustler* magazine's attack on Jerry Falwell".[33]

In later years, in a case involving a Ku Klux Klan leader calling for the "return" of the "nigger" to Africa and the Jew to Israel, the Supreme Court unanimously held a lower court conviction unlawful since there was no proof that the speaker was inciting "imminent lawless action", instituting what has since been called the "Brandenburg test" after the defendant in the case. And in what seemed a step too far in free speech permissiveness, the U.S. Court of Appeals in 1977 held that local government ordinances to stop a neo-Nazi demonstration in the village of Skokie near Chicago, were unconstitutional. It did not seem of any material importance that the town in question had a substantial Jewish population including survivors of Nazi death camps, or that the leader of the Skokie march, ultimately cancelled, was credited with the view that "Hitler should have completed the job". The Supreme Court declined to hear the case, allowing the Appeals Court's decision to stand.[34]

Lewis generally lauds these rulings, but admits to a certain unease over some of the practical consequences. This reveals much about the blindness in his ardour for free speech. "In an age where words have inspired acts of mass murder and terrorism", he concedes, "it is not as easy for me as it once was to believe that the only remedy for evil counsels .. should be good ones". A potential resolution of this knotty dilemma presented itself in the legal provision which allowed suppression of speech, when "violence or violation of the law are intended by speakers and are likely to take place imminently". In tacit reference to the heightened mood of public insecurity since the beginning of the twenty-first century, Lewis suggests that "judges and the rest of us ... (would) be more on guard now for the rare act of expression ... that is genuinely dangerous". It remained an option to punish that manner of speech which "urges terrorist violence to an audience some of whose members are ready to act on that urging".[35]

---

33 Ibid: 159.

34 Ibid: 160. Also, Waldron (2012): 34.

35 Ibid: 166-7.

A test of intent

This establishes a threshold of "terrorist" intent for speech which could be punished using the test of imminent violence. Lewis is not quite able to explain why he imagines that the Nazi strut through Skokie to express regret at Hitler's unfinished job, did not meet this test. Well after the fact, he is prepared to give it a certain legitimacy, since there was no violence manifest either in Skokie, or in nearby Chicago city where the Nazi parade took place after the case was won. But the *ex post* test is not quite sufficient in safeguarding valued social objectives, however they may be defined.

Are these standards acceptable as general principles? To give effect to these standards, there would have to be some agency – judicial or executive – that determines where speech assumes dangerous forms, and is fit to be categorised as "terroristic". Lewis's ardour for an absolutist interpretation of the First Amendment, collapses quite abjectly into an apologia for the heightened paranoia that gripped the western world after the September 11 terrorist attacks on U.S. territory.

These were among the many serious flaws identified by the British philosopher Jeremy Waldron in a review of Lewis's book. There was to begin with, an obvious problem in Lewis's effort to apply the *Sullivan* standards to *Beauharnais*, when the differences were more than obvious. The "African-Americans labelled ... in *Beauharnais* were not public officials who had taken on the burden of office", only "ordinary citizens who may have thought they had a right to be protected from scattershot allegations of the most severe criminal misconduct".[36] Lewis's insistence that the likely harm from regulation would outstrip any possible good, Waldron said, was to beg the question. The object of all who advocated sanctions on hate speech was not to enter minds and control thought processes, but to prevent real social harm from hateful public utterances. "The issue", said Waldron, is "the harm done to individuals and groups through the disfiguring of our social environment by visible, public, and semi-permanent announcements to the effect that in the opinion of one group in the community, perhaps the majority, members of another group are not worthy of equal citizenship".[37] Some degree of caution was warranted in imposing a hate speech code which

36 Waldron (2012): 28-9.

37 Ibid: 32-3.

held the danger that "vigorous dissenters" from an officially sponsored consensus would as Lewis put it, "be hunted, humiliated, punished for their words and beliefs". That was not a hazard to be discounted, but to focus on this possibility alone, while ignoring "other ways in which waves of public hysteria (could) threaten freedom" was fairly useless.[38]

Civility and citizenship

Equal citizenship is key and Waldron here draws upon Rawls's application of the principle. A "well-ordered society" for Rawls was one where "anything and everything may be published, even when they tended to question the foundations of social organisation". Waldron is unsure though, if Rawls is willing to apply this advocacy of speaking the unspeakable about "the fundamentals of justice", as for instance, "attempts to advocate publicly for the exclusion or subordination of a given group, or their disenfranchisement, segregation, enslavement, concentration, deportation, or whatever".[39]

Rawls's dictum about tolerance of the intolerant is widely cited, though most often for opportunistic purposes. In all fairness, Rawls showed extreme scruple in his advocacy of the principle. Even the intolerant were to be given the whole range of their freedoms, except in situations in which "the tolerant sincerely and with reason believe that their own security and that of the institutions of liberty are in danger".[40] This is a heroic effort to retrieve a theory of justice and liberty from majoritarian abuse, though finally debilitated by terminological imprecision. Who is to judge when the liberties of the "tolerant" are threatened, and who to begin with, could claim membership in this privileged category?

Much of Rawls's empirical detail is derived from the clash of religious orthodoxies in the west during the late-medieval and early-modern periods. He reads into the "original position" an irresistible tilt towards upholding the principle of "equal liberty of conscience". Notions of majoritarian privilege would not pollute the discourse here because persons in the original position could not "take chances with their lib-

---

38 Ibid.

39 Ibid: 70-1.

40 Rawls, *Justice*: 220.

erty by permitting the dominant religious or moral doctrine to persecute or to suppress others if it wishes". In the original position, "there is no way of ascertaining the relative strength of various doctrines", and typically, the "veil of ignorance" would lead to "agreement on the principle of equal liberty".[41]

There is an obvious difficulty in applying the liberty principle to religious sects, which impose a duty that is "absolute" and "cannot acknowledge any principle at all for limiting their claims on one another".[42] Here liberty would allow "freely organised" associations with the choice of an "internal life and discipline", though absolutely conditional on all members having the "real choice of whether to continue their affiliation". The "right of sanctuary" would enjoy full state protection, "in the sense that apostasy is not recognised, much less penalised, as a legal offence".[43] Liberty of conscience could only be limited when there was "a reasonable expectation that not doing so (would) damage the public order which the government should maintain". This was in line with early expositions of social contract theory as in Rousseau and Locke, who urged that liberty could be limited on "the basis of what ... were clear and evident consequences for public order". "If Catholics and atheists were not to be tolerated it was because it seemed evident that such persons could not be relied upon to observe the bonds of civil society."[44]

That finally is decisive: the preservation of civility. Law rests on a substratum of civility where custom and mutual consent determine the rules of social engagement. Laws are intrusive in that they hold in reserve the threat of coercion, often viewed with suspicion as a potential weapon of aggression against freedom. But discussions of the free speech right, most often carried out on the terrain of the state and the law, belong at least in equal part, in the realm of civil society. Remedies for an abuse of freedom can be found in allowing more freedom. This perfectly sound proposition is premised upon certain foundations of civility that can support a higher volume and intensity of speech, however contentious. If the foundations are infirm, social dialogue could

41 Ibid: 207.

42 Ibid: 208.

43 Ibid: 212.

44 Ibid: 212, 216.

be engulfed in rancour, with possibly the threat of violence providing room for state authorities to step in and impose order at their will.

Free speech also requires fearless listening. And as long as states revel in their ostensible fragility and societies remain uncivil arenas, the potential rewards would not seem worthwhile for anybody to take on that burden of fearlessness. Civility has been theorised in political philosophy since the late middle ages, as with Hobbes, who saw "manners" as key in a society that was successful in taming its inherent tendencies to fly apart as a result of the mutually repellent egoism of individual members. He did not mean by the term the embellishments and fripperies that may at the time be in vogue, but "those qualities of mankind, that concern their living together in Peace, and Unity".[45] In later years, Montesquieu was also to raise civility to a highly prized virtue for social coexistence. Civility he saw as preferable to politeness or what would be called good manners: "Politeness flatters the vices of others, and civility keeps us from displaying our own".[46]

In the contemporary context of prickly sensitivities over free speech, Edward Shils has described civility as "respect for the dignity and desire for dignity of other persons", a characterisation that resonates strongly with Waldron's definition of the threshold of hate speech. Civility is seen here as the internal defence of a well-ordered society against the abuse of rights. It is an undoubted virtue, whose antecedents could be traced in certain other notions that have cropped up over the centuries in social and political theory. A ready example would be Adam Smith's exchanges with David Hume on the sentiment of sympathy that bound the human community together. Theorisations of this virtue though have not been systematically carried out. As Timothy Garton Ash points out, the term has a long provenance in English and French, but does not translate very well into other languages and cultural contexts.[47]

Civil society: history of an idea

In 1809, Hegel wrote in his diary that the daily newspaper habit had become a serviceable substitute for the ritual of the morning prayer.

45 Hobbes (1651): 160

46 Garton Ash (2016): 4495.

47 Ibid: 4502.

Hegel was as he wrote these lines, still at an early stage in his thinking on civil society and the state. For early enlightenment thinkers, "civil society" and the "political state" were interchangeable terms, representing mankind's liberation from the "state of nature". Hegel dismissed all this as muddled and misguided thinking, since nature and society were united in mystical synthesis in the "Idea". Separate, individual existences were united in "civil society", which represented the fusion of "particular subjectivities". Above all this, the "State" represented the universal objectivity. Kant conceived of private opinions being rendered public through practical reasoning, expressed through the franchise and the daily press among other means. Hegel found a mystical process through which the infinity of private viewpoints became a coherent whole in the public sphere.

In Hegel's system, the principles at which public opinion arrived would be in perfect consonance with liberty, justice and all the other modern political virtues. These were not ends that the human species had to bring to fulfilment, but a preordained state born in the ineffable wisdom of the "Idea" that governed the world.

For those inclined to wade through endless pages of obscure prose and futile reasoning, there is a passage in Hegel that provides a summary approaching a basic standard of comprehensibility. "Formal subjective freedom, implying that individuals as such should have and express their own judgment, opinion, and advice concerning affairs of state, makes its appearance in that aggregate, which is called public opinion", says the sage: "In it what is absolutely universal, substantive, and true is joined with its opposite, the independent, peculiar, and particular opinions of the many.... Public opinion contains therefore the eternal substantive principles of justice, the true content and result of the whole constitution, of legislation, and of the universal condition in general".[48]

Years later, Karl Marx, as one among a group of young radicals swept up in the turbulence of political transition and trying to reckon with Hegel's mystification of reality, asked in absolute stupefaction about the possible sense that the sage intended to convey. Man had a dual existence in Hegel's doctrine, Marx observed: he lived in the political community as a "communal being" and in "civil society", where

48 Hegel (1820): 252.

he was "active as a *private individual*". "The relationship of the political state to civil society", Marx concluded with some irony, was "just as spiritual as the relationship of heaven to earth". And after digging into a particularly obscure passage from the sage, he wrote with the triumph of having unravelled an immense mystery that it was only in going "*above* the *particular* elements, that the state constitutes itself as universality".[49]

The question has a bearing on free speech. Of all voices only a limited number would assume influence. Hegel elides that issue by transforming the whole process into a mystical synthesis. In his critique of Hegel, Marx had without quite calling the philosophical authority of the sage into question, wondered at his patently self-contradictory propositions. The material world, its institutions, its political structures were all various stages in the development of the Idea, its grand coming into being. And in dealing with legislative institutions and their power to determine the constitutional order, Hegel tied himself up in knots of amazing complexity, because of his aversion towards materiality and human agency as realities rather than manifestations of an unseen divine.[50]

Civil society as process

"Civil society" as a theoretical construct in Hegel's doctrine, was about submerging antagonisms in a higher, divinely ordained sense of concord. To the extent that the Hegelian perception has a bearing on contemporary understanding, "civil society" could be understood not as a "thing" but as a "process" – of transforming minute particularities in a complex and evolving society into a unified perception which feeds into state policy. Yet within the Hegelian system of thought, it is an infirm concept, indifferent to material realities, which calls upon some mystical process to bring all the diversities of society into a union or-

49 Marx (1844a): 220.

50 Here for instance, is how Marx (1844b: 117) deals with Hegel's denial of human agency in political processes: "The 'legislature is itself a part of the constitution' which 'lies absolutely outside the sphere directly determined by it'. But the constitution did not create itself. The laws which 'require fresh and extended determination' must surely have been somehow established. A legislature must exist or have existed *before* the constitution, or apart from the constitution".

dained by divinity, serving the higher purposes of the "State". Where civil society did not have the means to bring all individuals within the compact that would preserve unity and solidarity, Hegel was prepared to invest the "State" with that coercive power.

Many years later, as a young journalist seeking radical social change, Karl Marx confronted the reality of press censorship in the Rhineland province of Prussia. He had before him a number of propositions on how far press freedom would be consistent with the broader objects of the social order emerging from feudalism. Marx observed that there was no other sphere in which the "specific estate spirit" – the interests of the various orders of society – was "more clearly, decisively and fully expressed than in the debates on the press". This was especially so in the various rationales advanced for opposing press freedom. It was, Marx observed, "in opposition to a *general* freedom that the spirit of a definite sphere in society, the individual interest of a particular estate and its natural one-sidedness of character are expressed most bluntly and recklessly".[51] Freedom of the press, understood in its broadest sense as every individual's right of self-expression, was a general freedom. But every public figure showed his social class (or estate) interest, in the position he took on the issue, despite florid pretences of speaking for the generality of citizens. These were estates speaking through their individual representatives, expressing the collective intent to deny all others the freedom they claimed as an exclusive right.

There was thus a representative of the "princely estate" who urged the cause of censorship, which ostensibly was a "lesser evil than excesses on the part of the press"; and another who argued that despite press censorship, there was "neither in speech nor in writing" – both in Rhineland and the wider German federation – "any shackles to be seen on our true and nobler spiritual development". Disinclined to give this vapidity a pass, Marx added the ironic comment here that the "noble lustre of truth in our press is supposed to be a gift of the censorship".[52]

A similar tendency was manifest in another speaker's justifications of press censorship: "Man, individually and in the mass, is always one and the same. He is by his nature imperfect and immature and needs

51 Marx (1842): 138. These comments on the Prussian censorship were written by Marx between January 10 and February 15, 1842.

52 Ibid: 138, 139.

education as long as his development continues, and it ceases only with his death". Marx found this an especially droll argument, observing that "in order to combat freedom of the press, the thesis of the permanent immaturity of the human race has to be defended". And then followed a summation that foreshadowed some of the philosophical principles of Marx's *Theses on Feuerbach*, still a few years in the future: "What undergoes development is imperfect. Development ends only with death. Hence it would be truly consistent to kill man in order to free him from this state of imperfection. That at least is what the speaker concludes in order to kill freedom of the press. In his view, true education consists in keeping a person wrapped up in a cradle throughout his life, for as soon as he learns to walk, he learns also to fall, and only by falling does he learn to walk. But if we all remain in swaddling clothes, who is to wrap us in them? If we all remain in the cradle, who is to rock us? If we are all prisoners, who is to be the prison warder?".[53]

The moral impossibility of speech restraints

As he embarked on a lifelong mission of radical political transformation, free speech was among the first of the rights Marx focused on. On view then were a range of political postures, several verging on the absurd. Among the speeches Marx heard while watching the proceedings of the provincial assembly of Rhineland, was one by the representative of a princely estate, which held that "the fetters with which the press is shackled, prove that it is not destined for free activity".[54] The absurdity here was evident as was its inspiration in Germanic romanticism, which saw the law and the state as the point of arrival, a state of perfection that was the very apotheosis of human endeavour. Marx's ironic refutation, which became the basis for a much wider reflection in later years on the denial of basic liberties under capitalism, was that freedom is the natural state of man and no law could be written to negate that. "No man combats freedom", he wrote: "at most he combats the freedom of others".

Any fetter on a particular individual's freedom must then be at the instance of another. A social class similarly, would be restrained

53 Ibid: 153.

54 Ibid: 138.

in its freedoms only to serve the interests of another. Every manner of freedom had always existed, at times as a "special privilege" and at others, as "a universal right". In Enlightenment doctrine, the physical universe was often seen as the repository of "law", the domain from which society could draw the best options on how to organise itself. A "law of society" had in this sense, the same immutable and infallible status as one of the physical universe. Marx was convinced that legislation constraining human freedoms while invoking the authority of law, was absurd on the face of it. "Laws are in no way repressive measures against freedom, any more than the law of gravity is a repressive measure against motion", he wrote: "Laws are rather the positive, clear, universal norms in which freedom has acquired an impersonal, theoretical existence independent of the arbitrariness of the individual. A statute book is a people's bible of freedom. .. Therefore *press law* is a *legal recognition of the freedom of the press*".[55] A press law that constrained the operation of the institution it was supposed to govern was in other words, a contradiction in terms, an illegality on the very face of it.

Since the 1990s there has been in the social science academy, a new vogue for theorising in terms of "civil society" – which mirrors the belief derived in some measure from Hegel – that "civil society" is a process that the individual goes through in successive levels in his engagement with the state. These serve to harmonise diverse interests between individuals and convert potential sources of conflict into a superior harmony. Hegel got his perceptions upside down, banishing the real world to the ether and investing a transcendent being that existed only in his imagination, with ultimate and decisive powers over matters great and small. This inversion infects his entire system and colours his construction of civil society.

There is in the modern conception of "civil society" no predetermined destination these interactions are working towards, though there is a strong suggestion that civil society – at its most civil – is an essential part of a successful democracy. Since being dismissed as a dubious theoretical construct by Marx, "civil society" receded as an element of active theoretical engagement. The maturing of bourgeois society meant however, that it acquired a practical relevance impossible to ignore. For a later generation of Marxists and in particular for one of its most perceptive thinkers, Antonio Gramsci, "civil society"

55 Ibid: 162.

was a fact of life, part of the hegemonic apparatus of bourgeois society. In developing Marx's analysis of the first stages in capitalist evolution, Gramsci found that "civil society" was vital to the stability of the edifice, though not quite in the Hegelian manner. A social group had to establish its hegemony before winning power and this meant securing the consent of the governed as the democratic veneer over underlying economic relations of coercion.[56]

Bourgeois society deemed those without means as effective wage slaves, not sovereign individuals capable of exercising the rights and liberties of citizenship. This was a doctrine violently in conflict with the practical compulsions of bourgeois society. Working class people had to volunteer to serve in the armies that fought national wars and more importantly, be available to sell their labour-power for wages, to perpetuate capitalist accumulation. But any possible identity of interests between the bourgeoisie and the working class was contingent and tenuous, liable to regular and violent disruption.

When consent replaces coercion

A generation after Gramsci, the Marxist philosopher Jurgen Habermas rendered some degree of clarity to "civil society", in terms both of concept and historical fact, with his construct of the "public sphere". The context again was different and bourgeois society had changed vastly since Gramsci's times. For Habermas, the "public sphere" was no politics-free domain. Rather the "public sphere" took on political functions specific to that period of "the developmental history of civil society as a whole in which commodity exchange and social labour became largely emancipated from government directives". Coercion yields to consent in perpetuating the commodity exchange on which the bourgeois order rests: the recruitment of social labour in the reproduction of capitalist relations. It is a consensus arrived at in a complex fashion, never conforming to any predetermined or predictable template. It is in part determined by the manner in which social forces are represented in political institutions and by the bargains struck over economic and social policy.

"Civil society" here departs from its Hegelian roots, where it is the embodiment of a divine will acting through family and guilds to

56 Gramsci (1935): 235.

achieve a fusion with the will of the state. It becomes a "public sphere", where social groups contend and engage through organised apparatuses of information exchange and political bargaining. The final outcome of this engagement is in the happiest instance, the perfect liberal-constitutional order seen in a number of its variants on the European continent in the nineteenth and early twentieth centuries, where a gradual widening of the franchise fostered the illusion of an inclusive polity. And with the transition to the "welfare state" as organising principle, beginning with the Great Depression of the 1930s – and officially blessed as sensible policy following the Second World War – the nature of the public sphere, as Habermas viewed it, underwent subtle but significant transformations.

Universal access was the principle on which the public sphere "stood or fell", since a sphere that excluded specific groups on account of identity or class, was indeed, "not a public sphere at all". As a construct, the "public sphere" needed the necessary safeguard that "economic and social conditions" would not deny anybody admission, that specifically, all who desired could "earn the qualifications for private autonomy that made for the educated and property-owning person".[57]

At the level of theory, the "public sphere" as a construct normalised the rampant inequality that Marx had identified a century-and-a-half before. Beyond anodyne expressions of commitment to democracy as an eternal value, the rules of entry that the public sphere enshrined, stood in stark contradiction with the juridical promises of equality held out by the State.[58] The growth of an industrial press homogenised the idiom of the public discourse to some degree, and the simulation of an editorial function entirely divorced from ownership propped up the mythology of equal access. At a later stage, these fictions merged with the institution of concrete and specific welfare measures that made the social "inclusion" promised in the bourgeois order at least a faintly perceptible reality.[59]

Built on commercial foundations the mass press works on the basis of tacit and mostly unstated rules of entry, a bit like the most expensive restaurants. Yet the mythology of egalitarianism had to be

57 Habermas (1962): 85-6.

58 Ibid: 124.

59 Ibid: 168ff.

kept afloat, while ensuring in the real world that privilege and property remained securely protected: contrary objectives served in some manner, through stripping the political element out of the public sphere. Mass media, Habermas observed, "was based on the commercialisation of the participation in the public sphere on the part of broad strata designed predominantly to give the masses in general access to the public sphere". Or to put this in plainer terms, those invited into the public sphere had to pay their way, even if this involved reneging on a commitment of unfettered access. By imposing a commercial threshold for entry, the "expanded public sphere lost its political character .... In the case of the early penny press it could already be observed how it paid for the maximisation of its sales with the depoliticisation of its content..."[60]

"Culture" and "politics" are what mould the terms of the public discourse. And as bourgeois society evolved, the masses were rapidly transformed from agents who create culture and critically reflect on its many dimensions, to being passive consumers. The culture propagated by the mass media as Habermas said, is "a culture of integration": it integrates "information with critical debate and the journalistic format with the literary forms of the psychological novel into a combination of entertainment and 'advice' governed by the principle of 'human in-

---

60 Ibid: 169. "Penny press" is a reference to newspapers that began circulation in mid-19th century Britain, before advertising growth began affording a means of meeting printing and distribution costs. The first newspaper to achieve a circulation in excess of fifty thousand in Britain was the *Political Register*, edited by the agitationist William Cobbett, who suffered relentlessly from sedition charges and imprisonment, and opted for a period of voluntary exile in the United States to escape the persecution unleashed by British liberal democracy. Operating within the "penny press" logic, this paper began publishing in 1802 and was transformed into a weekly pamphlet in 1816 to evade duties imposed by the government of the day. It had explicit political objectives and refused to be confined to the neutral and sanitised process of disseminating "news". By 1817, with its relentless campaign for political reform, the *Political Register* had exceeded all existing publications in circulation and earned the disdainful sobriquet of "two-penny trash". It was a title that Cobbett eagerly adopted as a badge of honour. With the political reforms of 1832, Cobbett made the transition from persecuted agitationist to honoured member of an elected parliament. He died soon afterwards and the *Political Register* folded almost immediately, though its place in the history of free speech remains an honoured one. (Curran and Seaton, 1985: 16).

terest'". It is also "flexible enough to assimilate elements of advertising, indeed, to serve itself as a kind of super slogan that ... could have been invented for the purpose of public relations serving the cause of the status quo". This effectively becomes a "pseudo-public" sphere since the consumption of culture was carried out within the "private" confines of the family and the home, even if manufactured through a media process that had a "public" appearance.[61]

The reality that Hegel's dictum about the newspaper ritual gestured towards, was that moment in industrial society when people united in allegiance around common symbols of belonging, getting over their disenchantment at the waning power of god and king, by constructing an alternate theology of the "nation". It was a sense of belonging brought home to them every day by a printed broadsheet. That was a radically redefined sense of community, manufactured in quite the same way as a broadsheet. But over time, the promises of equality, of the right to participate and contribute to the public discourse, were diluted, since a social order built on privilege could not fulfil these. An early profession of editorial autonomy within the media-determined public sphere, created the illusion of an accessible world. But then it became necessary to market the "editorial section" which in turn became a function connected with advertising. Editorial autonomy had till then sustained the illusion, since the individuals creating the terms of discourse could credibly claim that "they constituted a public". But with the triumph of advertising, the press "became an institution of certain participants in the public sphere in their capacity as private individuals; that is, it became the gate through which privileged private interests invaded the public sphere".[62]

Roland Barthes provided deeper insights into the manner that a discourse inspired by narrow interest is recast as a widely shared credo. In his *Mythologies*, published in the 1950s, he considered the "remarkable phenomenon" that with all that had changed in France since 1789, "a certain regime of ownership, a certain order, a certain ideology remains at a deeper level". In terms of naming this regime, there were other strange conventions at work. The "bourgeoisie" could be named with little reserve as an "economic fact", but transiting to the realm

61 Habermas (1962): 175.

62 Ibid: 185.

of politics, the same class showed serious difficulty in "acknowledging itself". There were no "bourgeois" parties in any of the chambers of popular representation, nor indeed, in the wider political fray. The bourgeoisie was "defined as the social class *which does not want to be named*". Class descriptions in the capitalist order, as indeed the nature of the order itself, were "the locus of an unceasing haemorrhage". This incessant bleeding deprived these characterisations of their meaning: indeed, "meaning flows out of them until their very name becomes unnecessary". And politically, the haemorrhage was "effected through the idea of *nation*". It was once a "progressive idea, which served to get rid of the aristocracy", Barthes observed, but "today the bourgeoisie merges into the nation, even if it has, in order to do so, to exclude from it the elements which it decides are allogenous (the Communists)".[63]

Particular interests take the general form

The "nation" afforded the bourgeoisie with the means of synthesis to gather various other strata into its fold, notably the intermediate or "shapeless" classes. This was a project accomplished through ideological means, providing "through the press, the news and literature", the varnish of the "national" and by extension, the "natural" on all that was associated with bourgeois hegemony. "The bourgeoisie is constantly absorbing into its ideology a whole section of humanity which does not have its basic status and cannot live up to it except in imagination, that is, at the cost of an immobilisation and an impoverishment of consciousness".[64] Myth is the term of art that Barthes bestows upon this process of fostering a public discourse that makes the contingent seem eternal, that strips the history out of social reality and makes it appear as part of the natural order. Myth is in other words, "depoliticised speech", construed as an active process continually carried out through the media and other instruments of mass indoctrination. Politics is here constructed in its fullest meaning, "as describing the whole of human relations in their real, social structure, in their power of making the world". But with this degree of conceptual clarity achieved, Barthes

63 Barthes (1957): 164. Barthes' sense in using the term "allogenous" evidently refers to the determination by the bourgeois order that the communists were a relic of an older order that had survived when they should by all rights have become extinct.

64 Ibid: 167.

confessed an inability to carry out a serious study of the "social geography of myths": such an undertaking indeed, would remain difficult as long "an analytical sociology of the press" was lacking.[65]

The media does not hold up a mirror to reality, it creates that reality. For long years, media functioning was studied almost exclusively in terms of a "transmission" model, which underlined the autonomy of the institution and its ability to influence social perceptions through "indoctrination" processes. The audience in this model was anonymous and inert, passively absorbing the messages imparted by a mass media it had little influence over. Audience autonomy was limited to the consumer decision of selecting or "buying" a primary news source among the choices available. And in most cases, national States that managed the airwaves purporting to know what was best, could deny the element of choice by tightly controlling the media.

The passage of years altered the reality of the relationship between the media and its audience. Media came to be understood, not as the transmission of a message through "neutral" mechanical and electrical processes, but as the propagation of a system of meanings that audiences variously associated with. In this sense, the modern sociology of the media views it as an apparatus, or more so, a process, of creating shared meanings that an audience can identify with, that equips people with the vocabulary and the empirical knowledge to engage in a public conversation. The media is not just about answering a community's needs for information; it is as much about constituting that community. The media cannot be understood except as an institution organically linked to the evolution of modern social identities, whether acceptable (and respectable) "national" identities or more narrowly defined sectarian identities.

Discourse ethics as a solution

The new vogue for civil society mirrors the belief that individual citizens go through levels of mediation in their engagement with the State. These serve to harmonise diverse interests between individuals and to convert potential sources of conflict into a superior harmony. Kant's categorical imperative as a basis of moral action saw the intense com-

65 Ibid: 174.

petition between individuals in a market society as the foundation of progress. This potential for conflict was to be given full play since that was the only way that "reason" would triumph. For Habermas, this categorical imperative was the outcome not of a logical process within an individual mind, but of social discourse conducted in accordance with certain ethical norms. "Discourse ethics" was the term adopted for the "moral argumentation" that led to the normative justification of any course of action.

This argument stood and fell with two assumptions. A statement made on ethical grounds could have exactly the same claims to truth as one made from an empirical observation. A claim to ethical truth was not devoid of a concrete knowledge claim. Indeed, "normative claims to validity have cognitive meaning and can be treated like claims to truth". But to make this potentiality real, there was the need for a "real discourse". This was not a possibility in "a hypothetical process of argumentation occurring in the individual mind".[66]

Like with John Rawls's "original position", there was a notion of the "equalisation of power" in these later Habermas postulates. The "validity of norms" could be tested through a process of practical discourse. Any norm could be proposed for adoption in a "hypothetical" sense, but would have to bring in content from outside its frame of reference to fulfil the ethical requirement. Rival claims to ethical truth would have a meaning within the "horizon provided by the life-world of a specific social group". And discourse ethics was all about dealing with "real conflict in a concrete situation in which the actors consider it incumbent upon them to reach a consensual means of regulating some controversial matter".[67]

Because he traversed a wide terrain, it has been difficult to reconcile Habermas's later scholarship with earlier theoretical constructs. The fundamentals of "discourse ethics" which allow for an equalisation of power and a dialogue conducted between equals, do not square with the asymmetries that Habermas unravelled in his early work, where he seemed convinced that ethics and fairness in the public discourse would be impossible on account of structural constraints built into the bourgeois public sphere. It may well be the case that the concept of

66 Habermas (1983): 68.

67 Ibid: 103.

"discourse ethics" occludes the capitalist context of the social dialogue in its effort to achieve a state of equalisation of power.[68]

The conundrum is partly unravelled in the 1993 paper where Habermas addressed Rawls's theory of justice. It was a philosophical exchange curated by the *Journal of Philosophy* and introduced as an event of historic consequence.[69] Its value today lies partly in signposting Habermas's rather conditional embrace of the liberal political creed and his effort to convert this into a pragmatic doctrine that could yield just and egalitarian outcomes in reality. Many years later, Amartya Sen was to look back on the exchange and retrospectively say he was persuaded that the two approaches were not "in fact, radically different in terms of the respective strategies of reasoning".[70] That assessment may be accurate, though a plain reading would suggest that Habermas's main concern was to bring Rawls into a real-world context, where high abstractions were translated into practical propositions.

It was axiomatic for Rawls that contracting parties in the original position would agree on the principles of "justice as fairness". This would be the evident choice that individuals in their autonomy would arrive at, when autonomy was itself defined as a compound of two parts: a morally neutral component seeking "rational advantage" and a "morally substantive" part which involves every individual's acceptance of a fair system of cooperation in a well-ordered society. Curiously, the second value-laden commitment was rendered superfluous by the device of the "veil of ignorance" which made it a matter of rational calculation for every individual to take account of what was "in the equal interest of all". Because the veil of ignorance blocks off any foreknowledge of the positions they will occupy in the society that they are setting out to structure, said Habermas, "they find themselves constrained already by their self-interest to reflect on what is equally good for all".[71]

Kant's "categorical imperative" is replaced in Rawls's framework, "by an intersubjectively applied procedure which is embodied in par-

68 Townshend (2016).

69 Habermas (1995) and Rawls (1995).

70 Sen (2009): 43.

71 Habermas (1995): 111.

ticipation conditions, such as the equality of parties, and in situational features, such as the veil of ignorance".[72] This response to the reality of pluralism neutralised "the multiplicity of particular interpretive perspectives from the outset", but threw up unique problems as it proceeded. In the original position of limited fields of vision, participants would have to guard themselves against "unpleasant surprises" as the veil of ignorance was lifted through successive stages, from the writing of the constitution, to the legislative process and finally, the actual implementation of the law. As new information began to flow in, these would be harmonised with "basic principles already selected under informational constraint". This in turn would mean that the "theoretician himself would have to shoulder the burden of anticipating at least parts of the information of which he previously relieved the parties in the original position".[73]

Participants in the original position have this heavy burden to carry, with the ever-present possibility of a misstep taking them adrift of justice as fairness. Habermas proposes that this burden could be lightened by "operationalising the moral point of view in a different way", that is, by adopting a "more open procedure of an argumentative practice that proceeds under the demanding presuppositions of the 'public use of reason' and does not bracket the pluralism of convictions and worldviews from the outset".[74]

Value, power and voice

There have been few theoretical efforts to reconcile the later Habermas's reading of the public use of reason with his early propositions on the structural impediments that make a truly equitable social dialogue impossible. There is no explanation in short of Habermas's drift away from an "original position" in Marxism towards a fairly ardent embrace of the liberal credo. While that remains a mystery to be unravelled, the economist Amartya Sen has taken the notion of the "public use of reason" into a case for justice that departs substantively from Rawls. The pursuit of an absolute doctrine that transcends situational constraints and specificities is effectively abandoned, in favour of

72 Ibid: 116.

73 Ibid: 118.

74 Ibid: 119.

a procedural fairness, of "democracy by consultation" that brings on board all voices in situations of absolute equality of access to sources of information and the means of their dissemination. Sen is led to strongly underline the importance of media freedom in ensuring an outcome of fairness for all. This he says, is "one of the central issues to consider for the advancement of public reasoning in the world". In this respect, "the traditions established in Europe and America over the last three hundred years", he argues, "have indeed made a gigantic difference". "The lessons derived from these traditions have been transformational for the world as a whole, from India to Brazil, and from Japan to South Africa, and the need for a free and vigorous media is being rapidly learned across the globe".[75]

It is rather piquant that a tradition which began with a trenchant critique of the sociology of the press in a capitalist order, and found that it imposed very real and substantive limitations on freedom, should pass through imperceptible stages into a restoration of a liberal orthodoxy that has been unmindful of these real world constraints. In recent years, Manuel Castells has revived discussion of the public sphere and the creation of meaning within a networked context, where older hierarchies are preserved and communication occurs at the highest threshold of information transmission, the speed of light. The "construction of meaning" in the public sphere and its assimilation by various social actors "creates the conditions for the legitimate exercise of power". The basis of legitimacy of course is not fixed and absolute. In the manner of its exercise, power which is a representation of the "values and interests of citizens expressed by means of their debate in the public sphere" would be decisive in setting the norms of legitimate action.[76] The network society excludes large masses of citizens who cannot afford the material means of access. Even among those who manage to cross the entry threshold, the network picks and chooses, only amplifying the articulated values of certain among them in a manner that gains traction with the state.

Castells speaks of the network state as an artefact of the burgeoning growth of information processing industries. Yet it is worth asking how many of the putatively inherent markers of the network state

75 Sen (2009): 335.

76 Castells (2009): 12.

are really unique to the phase of the global economy he refers to. At least two of the features that Castells identifies as unique are present to varying degrees in earlier phases of industrialisation and global economic integration. In identifying "innovation as the source of productivity growth", Castells seems only to be echoing a point made back in the 1920s by Joseph Schumpeter. The "networking of production and management", again in Castells's view a crucial ingredient of the twenty-first century global economy, could likewise, be read as the essential breakthrough achieved with the advent of the Taylor-Ford system of industrial organisation in the 1920s. Exploring further, these features could be seen – even if they did not merit the characterisations that later came into vogue – from very early days of industrial society. This leaves open the question of how different in a substantive sense a readily recognisable twenty-first century feature – "computer-networked global financial markets" – is from periods of integration through techniques such as the telegraph and the railways. Is the difference one of degree or of kind?

Networks are a "fundamental pattern of life" and ample archaeological and historical research exists to demonstrate "the pervasiveness and relevance of networks as the backbone of societies", many thousands of years in the past.[77] There were nonetheless, spatiotemporal bounds specific to every phase of technological evolution. Since the industrial revolution, the nation-state was viewed almost axiomatically, as the locus within which this relationship was exercised and the "State" was regarded as the entity with the monopoly of legitimate violence, which also determined the permissible bounds within which information transactions could occur. In a network society, these power relationships were "global and local at the same time" leading to a transformation of the boundaries of societies as also of "the frame of reference of power relationships that transcend the national".[78] Society by definition would seem to have a boundary, but networks made possible "open-ended and multi-edged" societies. These would expand and contract over time in accordance with certain measures of "compatibility or competition" between the "interests and values pro-

77 Ibid: 21.

78 Ibid: 18.

grammed into each network" and those they encounter in their "expansionary moments".[79]

"Information society" as a term of art, does not quite mask the reality of the flow of commodities – raw material and industrial products – that undergirds it, both to create the infrastructure and architecture of the global network and to fulfil numerous other human needs. As material flows through the nodes and channels of the global division of labour, there is a countervailing flow of value denominated in money terms.[80] Within the global division of labour, the flow of value is mediated by the boundary conditions that supposedly sovereign nation-states could enforce. And in fact, the epoch of globalisation begins with most nations within the developing world downgrading currency parities in relation to developed country counterparts. Assuming wage rates that stay unchanged in domestic currency denominations, this means that the owner of a dollar – ultimately, the U.S. as sovereign power – would be able to recruit more labour in the developing countries than before.

Social structures, in Castells's words, "originate from the processes of the production and appropriation of value". But what in turn determines value? In Castells's terms, it is power that determines value and perhaps *vice versa* too. "There is no change here (in the network society) in relation to earlier social structures in history: value is what the dominant institutions of society decide it is".[81] But then the conclusions he draws are far from definitive. Despite being an "old question of industrial society" and indeed "the cornerstone of classical political economy", the question of what constitutes "value" has "no definite answer in the global network society": "Value is what is processed in every dominant network in every space according to the hierarchy programmed in the network by the actors acting upon the network.[82] Clearly, "value" as Castells conceives it, is a flow through both the material network of the division of labour and the nodes of the information network. It is a flow whose magnitudes he is not quite able to quantify, aside

79 Ibid: 19.

80 "Value" may or may not correspond with price. The so-called transformation of value into a price that is transacted in the market is determined by political bargaining that in turn, reflects relations of power.

81 Castells (2009): 27.

82 Ibid: 29.

from asserting its close association with the character of power relations in society. Value is a construct that has a long genealogy in the analysis of power relations, and in its contemporary form, it has been used from at least the mid-17th century. For Hobbes, the British political philosopher and propagandist writing during the civil war, value was something every individual possessed, measurable in terms of the "price" that would be given for the use of his "power". And "power" was in turn judged by his "present means, to obtain some future apparent good".[83] Some two generations later, John Locke constructed his theory of value on a somewhat different basis, as an expression of embodied human labour: "For 'tis Labour indeed that puts the difference of value on everything", and this was most evident in comparing an acre of land planted with a commercial crop with one that was lying in "common". It would at once be clear that by far "the greater part of the value" arises in such situations, from the "improvement" that labour makes.[84]

Elie Halevy concluded in his monumental study of the British liberal tradition, that Locke's "economic theory of value was, at the same time and indivisibly, a juridical theory of the right of property".[85] Among contemporary academic specialisations, property is a field of study in politics and law. It is among the unstated and unexplored background conditions in economics, where the concept of "capital" embodies property as a legal right, but is somehow rendered in the theory into a sanitised object that can be touched and felt and most importantly, measured. This rather shaky construction of "capital" has been called out for being logically dodgy and practically vacuous. When used as a concept in any manner of practical application, it requires to be embellished with a number of what were earlier considered intangible elements. Most of these attempts at retrieval of the concept emerged in response to the need to theorise about growth and development potentialities in the world's poorer countries. Once put down to their lack of that measurable entity called capital, poverty came at a later stage to be attributed to a multitude of deficiencies, among them capital in the human, social and civic dimensions. Yet all these elements within the portmanteau of capital were regarded as distinct. Within economics,

83 Hobbes (1651): 150-2.

84 Locke (1688): Article 40.

85 Elie Halevy (1928): 96.

all efforts at theorising on the manner they relate to each other and interact in reality have been futile.

The power to speak

For the sociologist Pierre Bourdieu, "capital" is an entity with many dimensions, all closely interrelated. It is "accumulated labour" in the embodied form which could be appropriated by social agents to augment their power. Easily discernible in its economic dimension, where it is "immediately and directly convertible into money" and "institutionalised in the form of property rights", capital also exists in cultural and social incarnations. These different modes are related in various ways, though not predictably so. The intersections between these different dimensions of "capital" fix an individual within the social matrix, though not in entirely determinant fashion, because this is only a "synchronic" definition, applicable at a particular moment in time.[86] An individual's practices could not, however, be defined exclusively in terms of the "position occupied in social space" at any given moment. Fuller comprehension would involve a reckoning with the "initial capital" and "present capital" of the individual, which would provide some notion of the "trajectory effect". Linking the past and present position of the individual in the social field would open up an understanding of the trajectory on which the individual was embarked, and also enable a deeper understanding of class affiliation, political loyalty and possible electoral behaviour, all within a definite time frame.[87]

This is a model taken from the physical universe, somewhat in the manner Hobbes centuries before made material acquisitiveness without limit an inherent trait of the human species, much like infinite motion was the property of all objects in the physical universe unless restrained by an external force. What mattered in the social universe was a sense of "one's place in the world", imbibed through multiple sources – the education system and the media, the former featuring prominently in Bourdieu's framework – and inscribed in people's minds. Logical conformity, a term borrowed from Emil Durkheim, was the objective, which meant that "categories of perception of the social world" would be "adjusted to the divisions of the established order" and would to all

86 Bourdieu (2011): 83-93.

87 Bourdieu (1984): 456.

minds steeped in the dominant discourse, "present every appearance of objective necessity".[88]

Social actors are secured within their respective "habitus", a term strongly associated with Bourdieu, which refers to the "internalised form of class condition and of the conditionings it entails".[89] In this form of conditioning, the "propensity to speak politically, even in the most rudimentary way ... is strictly proportionate to the sense of having the right to speak". Yet the sense of being a "person" also involves the belief in a "personal opinion" that deserves to be voiced. Certain strata, which Bourdieu refers to in the fashion of his time, as the *petit bourgeoisie*, are zealous in guarding this right to a personal opinion and resisting any form of delegation, especially in politics. The working class, Bourdieu sees as more realistic, in not falling prey to the "naïve belief in formal equality" and "seeing no choice... other than simple abdication, a resigned recognition of status-linked incompetence, or total delegation, an unreserved remission of self, a tacit confidence which chooses its speech in choosing its spokesmen".[90]

In bourgeois societies generally – though with particular vigour when densely networked – there is as Castells puts it, a "bipolar opposition" between the "abstract universalism of global networks" and the "strategies by which people try to affirm their identities". This becomes the source of new forms of social struggle.[91] "Generic labour" is the term that Castells uses to describe how the network economy homogenises the working population, drowning out diversities in the accumulation of capital. The term resonates with the concept of "abstract labour" – as distinct from "concrete labour" – that Marx used to work out his theory of value. Labour stripped of all particular features, including the individuality of the worker, is the tendency of capital in its pristine, undiluted form. That is the origin of the production of value and the reproduction of capitalist social relations. Over these abstractions, we have reality that manifests itself one layer over another. In its reproduction, capitalism in the real world has to constantly reckon with the manifestations of the political strength of labour as expressed

88 Ibid: 471-93.

89 Ibid: 105.

90 Ibid: 412-8.

91 Castells, *Communication Power*: 43.

in trade-union action and political mobilisation. This concreteness is constantly being undermined by the reproductive drive of capital, and an index of the potential degree of success the strategy would enjoy, would be the unconquered geographical frontiers and the size of what Engels called the "reserve army of labour". In constantly eliminating the concreteness of labour and reducing everything by abstraction to a common denominator, capitalism depends upon the "reserve army of labour" – the unemployed and the underemployed, whose constant presence as prospective workers who could displace an existing labour force, invariably acts as a deterrent to political assertion by the working class.

Nationalism provides the bonds to paper over these schisms between social classes and the grossly unequal disposition of rights within the bourgeois order. This is a form of "imagined community" that the media has a special role in cementing. Benedict Anderson's famous exposition of how bonds between people dispersed in space and not even aware of each other's existence are created in a regime of print capitalism is relevant here. The imagined linkages as Anderson put it, derived from "two obliquely related sources". The first was simply "calendrical coincidence": "the date at the top of the newspaper, the single most important emblem on it, provides the essential connection – the steady onward clocking of homogeneous, empty time. Within that time, 'the world' ambles sturdily ahead". A second source of imagined links lay in the "relationship between the newspaper, as a form of book, and the market. ... In a rather special sense, the book was the first modern-style mass-produced industrial commodity .. (and) the newspaper is merely an 'extreme form' of the book, a book sold on a colossal scale, but of ephemeral popularity". In its obsolescence within a day of its printing, the newspaper created an "extraordinary mass ceremony: the almost precisely simultaneous consumption ('imagining') of the newspaper-as-fiction".[92] In creating an information universe that a mass of people drew from, the newspaper also cemented the large-scale solidarity of a shared perception of the world.

In comparison with print capitalism, a network society shapes the imagination of community in subtly dissimilar fashion. As Anthony Giddens has remarked, modernity creates a "transformation of space and time". The sense of community arising from shared time is

92 Anderson (1983): 33-35.

delinked from shared space. "The separating of time and space and their formation into standardised, 'empty' dimensions cut through the connections between social activity and its 'embedding' in the particularities of contexts and presence". Social relations are "lifted out" of the "local contexts of interaction" and restructured "across indefinite spans of time-space".[93]

This constitution of a "community" of ideas through networked mediation impinges on the politics of the nation. New communities that identify themselves by that portmanteau term "civil society" are constituted while others disintegrate. And this process influences the imagination of the nation in profound ways. Even when a nation identifies itself by its democratic credentials, the constructions emerging from the network society influence that imagination and in turn have a bearing on how democracy is practised.

Networks of value and capital do not confine every individual to a determined slot and eliminate any possibility of human agency in the creation and articulation of meaning and culture. A useful distinction made between "programme" and "text" – applicable especially in the context of the electronic and visual media – emphasises the autonomy of the audience construction of meaning, which could often deviate from the intentionality of the producer. Such limited and finite deviations could accumulate into a phenomenon of significant social power as an alternative to hegemonic constructions of meaning. Possibilities here would be conjunctural, subject to several contingencies and as Bourdieu might suggest, subject to the geometry of power determined by the lines of force emanating from varieties of capital. There is an intent that the producers who disseminate news may have but it is far from certain that this will be carried out. Indeed, there is a struggle over meanings that occurs on a constant basis between the homogenising forces working "top-down" and the diversifying pressure working "bottom-up". Knowledge is never neutral as John Fiske reminds us: "it never exists in an empiricist, objective relationship to the real". "Knowledge is power, and the circulation of knowledge is part of the social distribution of power. The discursive power to construct

---

93 Giddens (1990): 17-21.

a commonsense reality that can be inserted into cultural and political life is central in the social relationship of power".[94]

The "truths" that emerge from the organised apparatuses of information dissemination in any society would depend upon mechanisms of control. But with the possible channels of information flow multiplying, there are likely to be diverse scraps of information – ways of seeing – that contend for influence at any time. This seeming competition of equals is overdetermined by other forms of the assertion of power, including through organised apparatuses of coercion of the State and the influence that rioters and others covered by that broad rubric of "non-State" actors, could bring to bear. Official covenants and laws promise a free and open domain for speech acts of all. Yet that promise of formal equality is in substantive manner skewed by property regimes and other forms of power. Full possibilities of speech acts are constrained by uncertainties in the nature of the public response they are likely to elicit. There are categories of citizens – formally equal before the law – who live with the certainty of retribution for stepping out of line; there are others who work with the assurance of impunity for any excess. Predictive frameworks are possible though they would be of limited utility. Descriptive exercises that uncover the conditions under which speech acts are made and the challenges they face in gaining acceptance within the chain of social value creation, may yet open up avenues along which future struggles need to be waged.

---

94 Fiske (1989): 149.

Nationalism
Citizens Great and Small

It may at one time have been considered a serious transgression to bring the "nation" – regarded in all but the most deviant imaginations as an entity integral to contemporary life – under any form of scrutiny. It would also have been thought equally outlandish to propose that the "nation" had anything to do with the media industry.

Beginning in the 1980s, for reasons as much about European ennui and the awakening of a questioning spirit in erstwhile colonies, the "nation" as political organisation and emotional anchor began to be put through a degree of critical examination. It was among the more audacious breakthroughs of this phase of inquiry, to banish the nation from the solidity of the real world, into the mists of the human imagination. Against the theological norm, that the "nation" had been handed down as a primordial bond that none could deny or disclaim, the scholarship of the 1980s posed an alternative that the "nation" was the distillate of a process of imagining the past in selective (and frequently contested) readings. As a construct of the imagination, the nation required continual renewal and reaffirmation in various rituals of citizen loyalty: from the morning newspaper to the evening sports broadcast and talk show, the periodic electoral contests, the singing of the national anthem or even the daily paeans of praise for the dictator.

For as long as the nation was an enterprise in progress, it remained a tug at the heart, a call to action, an emotional bond that escaped clear definition. "What is a nation?" was a question that even the most ardent nationalists evaded, while still insisting that it was an indispensable unit of political organisation. Making it an artefact of the human imagination was a big breakthrough in demolishing this theological claim. The human imagination is a site of great fecundity, where even the worship of an unseen divine could flourish. It is also a space where a sense of mutual belonging could be achieved between people separated by vast distances, knowing little of each other and unable for the most part, to talk to each other.

Benedict Anderson came up with his celebrated formulation on the nation as an "imagined community" in 1983. Particularly relevant was the distinction between linguistic affinity as a marker of national identity – inaccurate as a reading of history – and "print language" as the artefact around which a sense of mutual belonging, key to cementing nationhood, was constructed. The growth of mass media was the accompaniment and accessory to the consolidation of nationhood. Till not far back, it was assumed that a nation was constituted by people who could speak a mutually intelligible language. Yet, mutual intelligibility was not inherent in any unit of human organisation beyond, perhaps, the family. Both the idiom of discourse and the rules of public engagement had to be evolved and agreed upon, as the scale of human community ascended from the family to the clan, the tribe, and then the nation. In the mythology of established nations, that ascent acquired the character of teleology – of a prior and predestined goal that diverse elements in the past were seen to work towards. All earlier modes of human community in effect became incremental steps towards the singular object of achieving the finality of the nation.

Beyond the mythology, it was never easy finding that ladder which took the human community from elemental forms of association towards that supposed apotheosis of the nation. The least familiarity with history showed that this was no mystical progression but a pathway strewn with extreme conflict and coercion. Those who were brought into the nation against their will were characterised as misguided and misinformed, though amenable to correction through the didactic processes of the nation-state. Those who resisted their induction into a collective they shared no sense of identity with, were represented as plain enemies of civilisation.[1]

In his inquiry into the imagining of a nation and the creation of its idiom of public discourse, Anderson found neither primordiality nor spontaneity. The process rather, was something akin to manufacture. From a variety of mutually unintelligible modes of thought and speech – the vernacular idioms as they are called – nationalism created a unified language of communication and other bonds that were stable, durable and could be the foundation of a number of individual acts of commitment to the wider network, called "patriotism". As the primary mode of interaction between individuals, language was where this manufacture of unity and mutual solidarity really began.

Anderson observed that the spread of a standardised vernacular for use in daily social intercourse – even by communities otherwise isolated from each other – contributed to the growth of a very basic and preliminary ("proto") nationalist consciousness. With the burgeoning ambitions of a capitalist class intent on turning every opportunity into profit, the media in turn, spread into unexplored geographical nooks, inviting far-flung communities to partake of what was beginning to be defined as the spirit of the nation. Mass printing technologies allowed "for reaching larger constituencies, for validating each local community with its own linguistic identity and for providing the underpinning for a common effort… not compromised by tensions of class, community, locality or denomination".

---

1 This is needless to say, a finding of special relevance to all countries in South Asia which have taken the pathway of consolidating freshly minted nationalist identities by imposing linguistic homogeneity. That coercive attempt to impose a linguistic identity has invariably created a backlash against the idea of a unitary nation, shaking its foundations and in some instances, destroying it. The rioting that occurred in East Pakistan against the imposition of Urdu, is rightly regarded as the first stage in the dismantling of the country that was created with pretensions of being a Muslim homeland in South Asia. Turmoil and spiraling violence followed the introduction of the Sinhalese only policy in Sri Lanka. And of course, in India, there was the anti-Hindi agitation in the early-1960s, which almost brought the assiduous nation-building efforts of the Nehruvian leadership in India to a virtual naught soon after Nehru's death, before a precipitate retreat restored a semblance of stability.

National identities Anderson pointed out, could be constructed in a "modular" fashion, drawing on at least three earlier models. Between the "official nationalism" that relies on civil and military educational systems, the popular idiom sustained by elections, party rivalries and cultural celebrations, and the citizen-republican ideals of the French revolution, today's nationalist elites draw on a wide range of legitimisation strategies. And in all these, they rely on far more powerful modes of communication that multiply the power of "print capitalism". Radio and television and "multilingual broadcasting" embody the possibility of bringing "illiterates and populations with different mother-tongues" under the spell of the imagined community.[2]

"Ruling coalition" is a term in common use as a description of the fissuring and cementing of political alliances in competitive electoral politics. Anderson introduced "reading coalition" as an arresting analogue from the early days of nationalist consolidation. Print capitalism as the instrument of emotional integration presumed the agency of people who could utilise it, of people who possessed the required competence in the linguistic idiom involved. Till as late as the 1840s, almost half the population in Britain and France, "the most advanced states in Europe", were illiterate. In "backward Russia", illiteracy stood at 98 per cent, a level guaranteed to overwhelm and indeed defeat the idealism of the most committed reformer or nationalist moderniser. The "reading classes" in these contexts also meant people who were otherwise endowed with a degree of social power: "More concretely, they were, in addition to the old ruling classes of nobilities and landed gentries, courtiers and ecclesiastics, rising middle strata of plebeian lower officials, professionals, and commercial and industrial bourgeoisies".[3]

The fourth estate and the rise of the bourgeoisie

The growth of print as an element of the industrial structure was linked diversely with the diffusion of mechanised processes in other sectors of the economy. Of equal if not greater importance were the messages print conveyed, that cemented the sense of belonging, inviting larger numbers of people within a territorial expanse to partake of the new

---

2 Anderson (1983): 135.

3 Ibid: 75-6.

nationalist consolidation. The typical agency driving this process was "a coalition of lesser gentries, academics, professionals, and businessmen". It was not a coalition formed with deliberate design. But in their own ways, these disparate elements coalesced around the common endeavour and shared symbols of collective loyalty.[4]

Anderson drew attention towards the circumstances in which the press emerged in the role of a "fourth estate" in early nationalist projects. Reading a little deeper into his work, certain clues emerge towards understanding the persistence of the term in later nationalist writing as a clichéd form of reference to the role of a press in a democratic political order. "Fourth estate" is a term commonly attributed to Edmund Burke's reference to the opening of British parliamentary proceedings to the press in 1787. Politics till then was the preserve of the three recognised estates of the polity – the "lords spiritual and temporal and the commons" – and Burke was alluding with his coinage of a new term, to the potential transformation of the political discourse that the press could bring about.

Yet it was insufficient for the press to enter into parliamentary deliberations in a passive reportorial capacity. That reporting also had to be an element in a wider political discourse. The "fourth estate" in this sense was a fairly useless appellation, unless it was part of the active political project of one among the other three "estates", or of the excluded sections that none of the three recognised.

In later years, the "fourth estate" as a commonly used term was embroidered with several layers of mystique. In the loose and somewhat self-serving sense that the term soon acquired, the media is regarded as a fourth pillar of the system of governance, without which the other three – executive, legislature and judiciary – would prove dysfunctional. This feeds professional conceit and embellishes the mythology that the media industry reflects and represents society in all its complexities. It also does considerable violence to fact and historical authenticity. The "fourth estate" when it referred to the press and propaganda function, was understood in terms of a specific and rather close relationship with competing elements within the larger political milieu. It had no rights conferred by law, other than as an element within ongoing political contestation.

4 Ibid: 79.

In an important and enduringly useful work, Curran and Seaton deflate claims of a steady onward march of press freedom under a liberal democratic order. Newspaper sales were at all times, "inadequate to cover the costs of producing a paper" and it was hence the "growing income from advertising which provided the material base for the change of attitude from subservience to independence". It would be no exaggeration, indeed, "to say that the growth of advertising revenue was the most important single factor in enabling the press to emerge as the Fourth Estate of the realm".[5] The liberal understanding of press freedom has withstood an abundance of contrary facts. But the truth, as we learn from this work – written in the 1980s, but now into a seventh edition that brings the discussion up to speed for the internet age – is that this interpretation has been sustained all these years by focusing narrowly on the "mainstream commercial press, while ignoring or downplaying the development of alternative radical newspapers". Indeed, the story of press regulation through the nineteenth century was one of narrowing the scope of public discussion so that only the voices that were "safe" for the reproduction of a bourgeois order, gained a reasonable chance of being heard.

Newspaper multiplicity (such as it was) in the early years of the nineteenth century, was the outcome of an effort by the growing industrial proletariat and those who could speak for them, to make their voice heard against the deafening chorus of the bourgeoisie in their moment of triumph. A "stamp duty" on newspapers, levied on every printed page and published advertisement, was one among the means of control. In the early part of the nineteenth century, when Britain was engaged in the effort to push back against the tide of republican radicalism arising in France, the stamp duty on newspapers was doubled. But stamp duty evasion was rampant by the late 1820s, when burgeoning social unrest became a concern for the rising British industrial bourgeoisie. In fact, the circulation of unstamped newspapers published by various radical factions was soaring, probably even exceeding the reach of the conformist newspapers.

The response of the Whig government (whose descendants today occupy an obscure "liberal" corner in British politics) was significant and perhaps set the template for modern-day neo-liberalism. In 1836, it cut the stamp duty on newspapers, but armed itself with sweeping

5 Curran and Seaton (1985): 7-8.

powers of search and seizure, including the prosecution of any individual found in possession of an unstamped newspaper. The industrial system was at just about the same time, kicking in with the promise of advertising as an alternative revenue stream for newspapers, emboldening the *Times* of London – today the pride of the predatory Rupert Murdoch's stable – to announce that it would stop the practice of receiving advance notices from the government for publication, since that would be contrary to the journal's "pride and independence". Being in the good books of the government was immaterial, since the *Times* had a sufficiently large number of backers within the industrial and commercial bourgeoisie, to help it prosper.

By deliberate design rather than coincidence, a movement for the abolition of the duties on newspapers began in 1848, just when the tide of radical politics began to ebb in Britain. Though it pretended to be broadly inclusive, the campaign had a rather narrow class basis. Richard Cobden, thriving textile manufacturer and leading Whig politician put it with admirable clarity: "we comprise steady, sober middle-class reformers". It was a campaign carried out with amazing efficacy. In 1853, the duty on advertisement was withdrawn, followed in 1855 by the stamp duty and in 1861 by the tax on paper. In 1869, ten years after John Stuart Mill had published his classic tract of democratic liberalism, *On Liberty*, security regulations on the press were themselves abolished.[6] The British bourgeoisie was triumphant in the battle of ideas. From then on, mediocrity bearing the distinct bourgeois stamp – already a threatening prospect in Mill's time – would reign with little challenge in the press domain.

Imagining the Indian nation

In his 1994 study on "propaganda and the press in the Indian nationalist struggle", Milton Israel pointed out that "in significant measure, the ideal of an All-India nation state that emerged out of the Indian nationalist struggle was imagined in English print". This was not really a unique situation since in most colonies, the early nationalist stirrings were articulated in the language of the imperial power, in a borrowed vocabulary of rights. Pragmatic considerations also played a role, since English was the only language that "reached beyond regional borders

6 Ibid: 28-9.

– especially those that separated the north and the south". In terms of the orthographic techniques available, English again afforded vast advantages over other languages. And advertising support was extended with greater willingness for English language newspapers since these were assured of reaching an audience which disposed of higher incomes. In these formative years of the nationalist identity, the "collectivity of distinctive entities ... produced their own illusions, myths and utopias", and often "competed and accommodated". The particular nature of the relationship between these diverse claims of identity depended on "images of the nation in place or the nation in making", which were "propagated in print".[7]

In its early years, the Indian National Congress (INC), that unique platform of nationalist striving, conducted its deliberations entirely in English. And the first session of the INC in 1885 had a number of newspaper editors in attendance, though most of them would have counted themselves principally as social reformers and political activists: G. Subramania Iyer of *The Hindu* from Madras, G.G. Agarkar from the *Maharatta* of Pune, B.M. Malabari of the *Spectator* from Bombay, Narendranath Sen of the *Indian Mirror* from Calcutta, and a host of others.[8] Among them, Subramania Iyer was accorded the honour of moving a resolution demanding an official commission of inquiry into the working of the Indian administration.

Iyer was also engaged in journalism in the Tamil language at the time, having begun the *Swadesamitran* as a weekly in 1882. In 1899 he transformed the paper into a daily and took leave of all responsibilities in *The Hindu*. In a tumultuous period of world history between then and the end of World War I, *Swadesamitran* became as Natarajan put it in his widely-cited history of Indian journalism, an avidly devoured newspaper whose account of each of the events of the time set a certain standard in the promotion of an informed public discourse. The newspaper was no mere passive conveyor belt of news. Rather, says Natarajan, it "contributed to the development of the Tamil language". The newspaper was in this sense, an experiment in social engineering. "It was not easy in those days to conduct a daily newspaper in the Tamil language": "Thanks to the Pandits and the Pulavars, Tamil

7 Israel (1994): 21.

8 Natarajan, (1955): 118.

remained for long hide-bound and impervious to new thoughts and ideas which came from the west and knocked at the doors incessantly. (Iyer) experienced much difficulty in expressing modern events and ideas in a language which would easily be understood. He coined new phrases and liberally used but in parenthesis English words… in Tamil and they became quite familiar to the people".[9]

The record of developing an idiom for discussing affairs of an emerging nation in native Indian languages, was not uniformly successful. In particular regions, the mode of expression chosen in the local language stirred up deep insecurities among the colonial authorities. The Vernacular Press Act was introduced in 1878 to rein in what the British regarded as the intemperate course of journalism in the Bengali language, perhaps most menacingly embodied in the *Amrita Bazar Patrika*. In moving the bill through the Legislative Council, the Lieutenant Governor of Bengal Ashley Eden dismissed as "imaginary rather than real" the difficulty of applying a measure "to a portion of the press and exempting another". The reasons as he put it were simply that firstly, English language newspapers were "written by a class of writers for a class of readers whose education and interests would make them naturally intolerant of sedition". These were also "under a sense of responsibility and under a restraint of public opinion", which could not exist by their inherent nature, in "ordinary and native newspapers". There was in this sense, nothing amiss about exempting from the harsh new orders, all those newspapers "written in the language of the ruling power".[10]

Coverage of the Ilbert Bill controversy in the native press further deepened the suspicions of the colonial authorities. And the gulf between English and the native idioms widened during the public agitation over the Age of Consent bill. The *Amrita Bazar Patrika* in 1891 threw itself into this agitation with considerable fervour.[11] On the western flank of the *raj*, Bal Gangadhar Tilak parted ways with Agarkar, following profound differences on social and political matters, and assumed exclusive proprietorship of *Kesari* and the *Maharatta* in 1890. Among the first causes he committed himself to was the Age of Con-

9 Ibid: 126.

10 Ibid: 101-2.

11 Ibid: 129.

sent bill, when he made no secret of having drawn inspiration from the *Amrita Bazar Patrika* example.[12]

Nationalism could not remain the preserve of the genteel Anglophone for long. As larger numbers began entering the political sphere in the early years of the twentieth century, aspirations shifted up a notch from claiming equal rights of citizenship under the British crown for those of education and wealth, to securing a measure of autonomy and self-government. Journalism was transformed accordingly, and the new linguistic idioms crafted to deal with the changing universe of political ambitions resonate with what Benedict Anderson called the "revolutionary vernacularising thrust" of print capitalism. Indeed, just as print capitalism created "particular solidarities", it engendered new schisms and deepened older fault-lines.

Looking at the northern regions of the *raj*, Jyotirindra Das Gupta has observed that Hindustani and its derivatives, which then could be understood in terms of a Hindi-Urdu compound, were widely used, but distinctly lacking in the prestige of a high literary language. With the stigmatisation of English as the symbol of an oppressive foreign power, came an effort to emulate it in terms of the range and diversity of human experiences it could capture. This created the grounds for a profound divergence between the Muslim elite of the North Western Provinces and Oudh (NWP&O) – broadly corresponding to contemporary Uttar Pradesh – and the Hindu intellectuals in the eastern part of the same province. As the two drifted further apart, Gandhi intervened with an admonition that the "Hindu *pandits* of Prayag" and the "Urdu *maulvis* of Aligarh" were "exaggerating the mutual differences". A large part of what these two sectarian interest groups disdained as "mixed forms", Gandhi pointed out were, "in fact commonly employed throughout North India". A common language for all of India, he urged, "should build on popular usage and convention and not on literary injunction".[13]

Alok Rai's work on "Hindi nationalism" recognises the historic significance of the replacement of Persian with local vernaculars as the language of British colonial administration. Occurring in phases over the fourth decade of the 19th century, this was a crucial moment in the

12 Ibid: 135.

13 Das Gupta and Gumperz (1968): 157ff.

evolution of the modern variants of Tamil, Marathi and Bengali, which were adopted as official languages in British presidencies administered from Madras, Bombay and Calcutta.[14]

In the northern region of India, the directive on official language engendered much local variation. Hindustani, as the vernacular was called in much of this region, was in reality, a vast diversity of spoken dialects. The written idiom, typically associated with the official purposes of the *raj* and the incipient print industry, saw a supplanting of the Persian script with Nagari during the 1870s and 1880s in most parts of present-day Bihar and Madhya Pradesh. In the vastness of undivided Punjab, the Persian script showed a greater resilience, lasting into the early years of the 20th century as the official mode of written communication.

The decisive contests in the emergence of modern "Hindi nationalism" occurred in the NWP&O. The "McDonnell moment" was decisive here, when an imperial governor of the NWP&O, haunted by memories of the 1857 uprising – which rendered a shattering, near fatal blow to the British imperium – decreed that the official correspondence of the province would be conducted in "Hindustani" written in the Nagari script. This was a reward to the loyalist Hindu upper-caste element that had diligently waited upon him in quest of this demand. It was also a clear signal to the Muslim community that they were principally held responsible for the trauma inflicted on the *raj* in 1857 and would pay a high price for their rebellion.

The new nationalist element in the NWP&O was prepared to reject the Persian script because of its ostensible foreign origin and oppression of native idioms. It earned a receptive audience among the masters of the *raj* by constantly playing upon the supposed truth that the rebellious elements of 1857 enjoyed custodianship over Persian and would persist in their defiance if the idiom and script continued to be privileged much longer.

An alternative script to Nagari then existed, called Kaithi, which has now passed into history, little remembered by all save the more assiduous linguistic scholars. More widely used than the classical Nagari, Kaithi was deemed inappropriate to the communication needs of the new nationalist elite. Among the many reasons it did not qualify, Rai

14 Rai (2001): 27.

recounts, was its "association with Hindustani rather than with Sanskrit". Moreover, it was a part of the linguistic practices of both Hindus and Muslims and provided no basis for differentiation.[15]

Identity definitions are malleable. The Indian "national identity", in the early stages of its formation, elevated emotive ties of kinship and community and conferred on them the status of nationalist, or failing that, at least, proto-nationalist bonds that stood above and beyond personal and familial relationships. There is a deeply respected convention in Indian historiography that ascribes the divisive and bitter acrimony of early nationalism to a sinister British policy of "divide and rule". Yet a more reasonable reading would view the proliferation of identity claims that colonial India witnessed, as the response of a diverse social milieu to the dislocations of modernity. People who are sucked into force-draught modernisation would seek defence mechanisms. And calling upon ties of kinship and community would be the first protective reflex in a situation where no other anchorage is available.

Print technologies and the "normalising" tendency

Coupled with this were the technical imperatives of the new print technologies, which demanded standardisation and led quite naturally to what Rai calls a "normalising" perspective. "Standardising grammar… (and) … orthography … were 'natural' imperatives built into the new printing technologies".[16] Many of those who turned to classical Sanskrit sources for inspiration saw the proliferation of the print industry as an impediment to the discovery of the true cultural identity of India. The printing presses, they complained, were sowing confusion, allowing shallow pretenders to hold the field and impeding the recognition of Sanskrit's undeniable claim as the national language.

A similar worry over coarser idioms infiltrating the high literary discourse was evident in the Bengal region. Anindita Ghosh, in researching the development of print in colonial India, portrays a new vernacular idiom in the Bengali language, evolving under multiple social determinants. There was the need to refute the European criticism of Bengali as an inferior language and cultural form – a challenge that the "cultivated classes" took on, in part, by underlining how they were

15 Ibid: 52.

16 Ibid: 23-4.

different from the lower strata in linguistic and cultural practices. In general, the Islamic cultural presence was identified as the alien "other", a pervasive influence that needed to be contained and isolated.

This elite response, in turn, created a contending politics of culture within the Muslim community, which set about retrieving its own traditions from the rubble of history, refurbishing these to meet the demands of the new climate of colonial modernity. In 19th century Bengal, as indeed in various other milieus where colonialism was dominant, the vernacularising thrust of print capitalism did not create cultural uniformity. Rather, it sharply polarised the manner in which primordial identities were imagined. Cultural differentiation fed and reinforced the social stratification that was ever more deeply embedded as Bengal was absorbed by imperialism into the global chain of commodity transactions.

"By 1860s", says Ghosh, "a standard Bengali purged of its syncretic associations and modelled strictly on Sanskrit had established itself". Concerns over the lower sensibilities creeping into public spaces, aided by the new mass printing techniques, were perhaps best expressed by the pioneering novelist in the Bengali language, Bankim Chandra. The scourge, he said, could be directly attributed to the spread of "little education", which while "creating an enormous body of readers, had not produced a commensurate body of 'decent' literature". The peculiar condition in Bengal, Ghosh observes, "which had created not only readers, but also authors out of the category of the 'little educated' or *olposikshita*, had led to a common appreciation for the vulgar and obscene".[17]

Rival understandings of the original linguistic identity of the nation contributed to the growing estrangement between communities. "The Sanskritisation and 'Hinduisation' of the Bengali language", says Ghosh, "led to a parting of ways for its speakers". As upper caste Hindu strata came to closely associate themselves with a "*tatsama*-based vocabulary", "Muslims remained faithful to the Perso-Arabic dominated earlier version, even consciously inflecting it with a more 'Islamic' character".[18]

---

17 Ghosh (2006): 78, 91.

18 Ibid: 259; the term *tatsama* refers to Sanskrit loan words in vernacular Indian languages.

Meanwhile, on the western side

This excursus into history could be concluded with a brief consideration of parallel processes on the western seaboard of the *raj*, where the idiom of spoken and written Marathi developed a similar internal stratification under the challenge of colonial modernity. We read in the introduction to a recent anthology of the great social reformer and visionary, Jotirao Phule's writings, that he remains a relatively unrecognised figure in the history of Marathi literature. This, says G.P. Deshpande, editor of the volume, is "strange and sad", since "Phule's prose, his use of nineteenth-century colloquial speech, his system of argumentation, his ferocious polemics, (and) his poetry", all merit serious discussion, as too would "his assessment of various Bhakti poets which amounts to the beginning of Marathi socio-literary criticism". Those who do refer to these aspects of Phule's work, including his searing critique of the caste system titled *Gulamgiri* (or Slavery), only do so to point out that he never quite conformed to the requirements of the dominant literary canons of the time.[19]

Despite political careers that converged in time, there is no recorded evidence in the official historical canon, of any serious tension on matters of ideology or strategy between Jotirao Phule and the more orthodox and militant nationalist, Bal Gangadhar Tilak. They had rather different ideas about the retrieval of the supposedly primordial identities that gave substance to the Indian nation. It is also clear that despite strong reservations, Phule found himself more in tune with the sensibilities of the modernist reformer Mahadeo Govind Ranade, rather than the Hindu orthodoxy of Tilak.

Unsurprisingly, the Hindu nationalists, while constantly rejecting Ranade as dangerously misguided in his affinity for western values, focused their ire to an even greater degree on Phule. Tilak's close political associate, Vishnu Shastri Chiplunkar, recognised as a pioneer of the modern Marathi literary idiom, once referred to Phule in these disdainful terms: "In my estimation, a Rao Bahadur (a reference to Ranade) is an infinitely more creditable name than all Dayanandas and Jyotibas put together. If my tone is more respectful towards the Rao Bahadur than towards the great author of *Gulamgiri* that is due to the

19 Deshpande (2002): 16-7.

unspeakable difference between the first man of the age and the sorriest scribbler with just the clothing of humanity on him".[20]

Chiplunkar's vitriol and his intemperate criticism of Phule was purportedly grounded in aesthetic sensibility, but as Veena Naregal has pointed out, there was no mistaking his basic disregard of the "norms of liberal communicative reasoning". Writing in his journal, *Nibandhamala*, an early platform for the development of Marathi's high Brahminical idiom, Chiplunkar in 1877 excoriated Phule in terms that would today be regarded as verging on hate-speech: "Under the present conditions (it needs to be considered) how wise and really courageous it is for fools like Jyotiba to shamelessly bark away at Brahmins, and to vie for crumbs that may be thrown at them according to the convenience of those in power". And in tones of patronising and haughty superiority, he urged Phule to realise the futility of his polemics: "Mr Phule is thus notified – that if he is indeed concerned about the uplift of his caste-brothers, then it is little use for him to be composing books like the *Gulamgiri* to abuse those who are his superiors in every way. However unjust or wicked Brahmins may be, one fact is incontestable: that they retain possession of the keys to the storehouse of knowledge. And there simply are no avenues for the other *jatis* to have access to education/knowledge without their help".[21]

Later history writing tended to collapse Phule, Tilak, and other social and political activists of the period into one single current of what is identified, from the vantage point of today's nationalist orthodoxy, as a renaissance in the Marathi language region. This retrospective judgment sees the upsurge of nationalist thinking as widely based, enriched by the cultural strivings of diverse people. Indian nationalism in this portrayal, originated in internal harmony and concord, from multiple individuals all imbued with similar visions of the future. An

---

20 Quoted in Tucker (1972): 134-5. Dayananda here is a reference to the founder of the Arya Samaj and Phule is referred to first as Jyotiba and then as the "great author of *Gulamgiri*". Phule's *Gulamgiri* (Slavery) is needless to say, recognised today as a seminal tract in the awakening of the social rebellion against the new constructions being placed on tradition by the likes of Tilak. Jotirao Phule is how G.P. Deshpande (2002) chooses to spell his name for reasons specified. However, he will also be referred to in subsequent paragraphs as Jyotiba or whatever else the original source dictates.

21 Naregal (2001): 256, 258.

isolated event, such as the reception Phule organised in Pune (then Poona), after Tilak was released from prolonged incarceration on sedition charges, is picked up as evidence of an underlying harmony of perceptions.[22]

From another work of Veena Naregal, which relates evolving print media idioms with regimes of power under early colonialism, we learn that the creation of a native aesthetic in Marathi was an essential part of the new intelligentsia's assertion of hegemonic political claims. This sphere of "vernacular" knowledge did not, in its creation, involve a challenge to clearly recognised hierarchies of wisdom or power. The "English" sphere was acknowledged to have unique claims to superior status. There were indeed, few "evident signs of hostility" towards the language of colonial administration in the evolving vernacular sphere. Rather, "the consolidation of the vernacular sphere was strategically achieved through a virulent anti-lower caste discourse".[23]

Excluded sections raise the flag of rebellion

The picture that emerges here is of the co-constitution of the nation and its minorities. Print capitalism with its normalising tendency created a particular sensibility, which then ascended by elite agreement, to the status of a nationalist identity. As it imprinted the caste Hindu sensibility into the vernacular idiom, the awakening nationalism banished two categories of colonial subjects to the margins. There was first, the alienation of those identified with the Islamic faith. Till then relatively unpoliticised in terms of social identities, long used to living in comfortable syncretism with people nominally of another faith –

---

22 At the foundation day of Maharashtra state in 1960, Y.B. Chavan, the first chief minister of the state, hailed Phule as one of the architects of the Marathi renaissance, alongside Tilak and Ambedkar. Dhananjay V Keer, has written biographies of Phule and Tilak without ever going into the nature of their mutual relationship. In his biography of Phule, Keer (1964: 105) has allowed himself the following critical remarks about Tilak: "Chiplunkar's attack on the reformers retarded the growth of social cohesion and social revolution in Maharashtra. Not long afterwards, Tilak, on whose shoulders fell the mantle of the leadership of the Chiplunkar school of thought, ruthlessly moved his intellectual steam roller over the social reform movement in Maharashtra. … The followers of Jotirao (Jyotiba) kept themselves aloof from Poona politicians…"

23 Naregal (1999): 3446.

and partaking of the same social observances – the Muslim community reacted to the consolidation of the Hindu nation with an invention of its own traditions.[24]

A rebellion of the lower castes began along a different fault-line within colonial modernity, acquiring a variety of shapes and forms and peaking with the Communal Award of 1932, which recognised them as a separate political category. Gandhi's "epic fast", undertaken to prevent the "vivisection" of Hinduism, marks the point at which the "untouchables" are enfolded back into the "mainstream" nationalist domain. Yet, Gandhi's disdain for the muscular ideologies of nationalism espoused by many on the right-wing of the Congress – virtually indistinguishably from active proponents of Hindutva – made this a potentially benign embrace.[25] And far from being a unitary conception, the new idiom that was crafted recognised differences and separateness and accorded certain special privileges to the "untouchables".

The Muslim community presented an alternate claim to nationhood during the anti-colonial struggle. At some stage, though there could be long and inconclusive debate on precisely when, the assertion of another identity crossed a critical threshold and became a declaration of secession. Indian nationalist historiography identifies the moment of separation as the "Pakistan resolution" of the All India Muslim League in March 1940. An alternative perspective identifies successive moments of alienation leading to the final schism, going back to the first half-hearted transfers of power from the British *raj* to native

---

24 Ghosh (2006: 42-3, 50) in *Power of Print*, identifies certain developments in the 19th century that lay behind the "split" in the "large secular, syncretic Bengali language". Among these were, the "abandoning of Persian as the official language of administration in 1839 and the recasting of Bengali in a Sanskritistic mould under the influence of educated Hindus". This does not exhaust the causes that Ghosh lists, but Rao (2010), in a work on Tilak, has an entire chapter titled "Inventing the Enemy", which speaks of precisely this definition of a Hindu identity through differentiation with the Muslim "other". An early work in this respect is Cashman (1970).

25 Ambedkar (1945: chapter 3) writing on Gandhi's attitude towards the "untouchables", characterised it as one of "killing with kindness". But perhaps it was the kindness that seemed most in evidence then, with the intent to "kill" being far from any public perception of Gandhi's strategy.

elites.[26] The quite deliberate and calculated vivisection of the topography of the *raj*, was a partition that the Muslim leadership had decidedly little interest in, since it left several of their core areas of interest – centres resonant with the syncretist Islamic traditions unique to India – inside what became by reverse analogy, a "Hindu India". Within the territory that came to be known after partition as the Republic of India – as opposed to both the civilisational idea and the colonial definition – the Muslim community, which till then had proclaimed a contending claim to nation-ness, was reduced to a minority status within a putatively secular and democratic polity.

Citizenship in the Indian nation that emerged out of colonialism was conferred by the territorial circumstances of birth. There was no other criterion required under the Indian Constitution adopted in 1950. In terms of the actual enforcement of these laws, there were serious discrepancies between persons who chose to leave the country under the compulsion of the partition – who were effectively told that there was no way they could reclaim their Indian nationality – and those who left to explore other options, such as citizenship in the newly emerging Zionist State. In the former instance, opting out of Indian citizenship was irrevocable, not so in the latter.[27]

Aside from this seemingly minor difficulty at the fringes of the new nation-state, the constitutional guarantees of equality before the law, freedom of conscience, right to education (and all others), were applicable to all citizens. But in a concession to post-partition realities, and in particular, the raw wounds of the Muslim community, two clauses on minority rights were inscribed into the constitution. There was a mention of a minority being "distinct" in terms of religion, cul-

---

26 Jalal (1985) provides the most comprehensive and authentic statement of this thesis. The revisionist thesis on partition won an unlikely convert in a senior politician of the Hindu-nationalist Bharatiya Janata Party. Jaswant Singh (2009) authored a biography of Jinnah that earned him a prompt expulsion from his party. This was predictable, though Singh's greater object may well have been to contest the Congress party claim that it was always an unswerving advocate of Indian unity against the Muslim League's demand for a parting of ways.

27 See Zamindar (2007): 199ff.

ture, or language, but no reference to the benchmarks against which this "distinctness" was to be measured.[28]

In this conceptual vacuum, a variety of perceptions have flourished. But the hegemonic vision that the Indian State sought to represent, was that identities were immaterial. The State would serve as the focus of nationalist allegiance and in turn would treat all citizens equally, recognising no identity as having a bearing on citizen entitlements, except his or her existence as a locus of material needs and aspirations.[29] The model of "economic man", a construct which effaced all facets of cultural identity, was key to the implementation of economic planning by the Indian State – a process that would lift the general level of social well-being by uplifting the status of each citizen.

Two recognisable minority categories

History had led to two recognisable minority groups within the Indian nation. One was the residue of a national community that had chosen to secede, to partition the topography of India. The other was a group that had been persuaded to abandon its quest for separate nationhood, in return for the assurance of separate treatment. The promise India made as it embarked on its journey towards planned economic development, was that over time, these boundaries would be effaced and an enveloping Indian national identity established.

By the mid-1980s, these expectations were all but abandoned. Since they were never overtly articulated, it is difficult to find a moment of explicit disavowal. But increasingly, the political discourse through the 1980s began to be infused with a notion of "Indianness", as defined by certain cultural attributes, in turn derived from a pristine civilisational source or Hindutva, that existed in an identifiable form through millennia. This provoked an opposite reaction within certain segments, which determined that an insistence on separateness was the only available defence against the new hegemony of "cultural nationalism".

---

28 A 2007 report by a National Commission for Religious and Linguistic Minorities constituted by the Government of India, made the telling observation that the term "minority" occurs at numerous points in the Constitution of India, but is never precisely defined.

29 This is an argument rather well elaborated by Partha Chatterjee (1997).

On another front, the belief that the special treatment given the "untouchables" would over time become superfluous, was rapidly being belied. The political call for expanding the scope of affirmative action to include segments of the Indian population left out by the first enumeration of the disadvantaged – a list that subsequently became a "schedule" to the Indian Constitution – was growing.

In the 1980s, Hindutva political forces resumed mobilisation over a cause that had rather sporadically excited their attention earlier. The target was the Babri Masjid, a Muslim place of worship in the northern Indian city of Ayodhya, a rather modest structure which had in the Hindutva imagination, been built over the hallowed birthplace of a revered Hindu god-king. It was an enduring symbol of the humiliation that the Hindu nation had to efface from its collective memory.

The gates to the structure, long shut to all faiths after a surreptitious introduction of the idols of another faith in 1949, swung open in 1986 after a judicial order crafted quite patently under political guidance. The faithful were now permitted to enter the portals of the ancient structure to offer their veneration where the idols had been placed in an act of trespass. This was the third in a sequence of judicial events that had led to a state of near panic among people of the Muslim faith. In 1985, an injunction by the Calcutta High Court against the Quran on the grounds that it preached holy war, though quickly vacated, held the field long enough to stir up anxieties. This was followed by a Supreme Court order directing that an aged Muslim woman be granted maintenance by her husband after the annulment of their marriage.

The judgment in the Shah Bano case, as this matter was called after the petitioner, became a handy weapon for community leaders who were worried about an erosion of their authority. The Congress party's leadership which then held an unprecedented degree of power, soon caved in, abandoning fairness in an effort to placate the more reactionary elements by legislating a reversal to the judicial verdict. The Urdu language media expectedly took a strident line against the verdict, while the cause of a "uniform civil code" to supercede all faith-based personal laws, drew together an unlikely coalition of the political left, progressive Catholics and extremist organisations arguing the Hindutva cause.[30]

30 Mody (1987): 943-4.

The Masjid theme: a lesser nation

The most vigorous debate, featuring all shades of opinion, occurred in the English language press. Yet, there was a more than ample use of essentialising tropes in this discourse, such as a supposed crisis of the Islamic faith and the community's tendency to privilege extra-territorial loyalties at the cost of their civic duties toward national constitutions. As was later pointed out, most of the English language press, "shied away from acknowledging the crucial reality that the communal divide generated by the bill was undermining the unity of the masses, strengthening political conservatism, and perpetuating the policy of divide and rule." And among the most revealing media responses was the complete neglect of the issue, except for an isolated interview with Shah Bano, by the "most potent mass medium available – the government's television agency, Doordarshan".[31]

The final upshot of the bill was a majoritarian surge, fuelled to a considerable extent by the judicial order opening up the structure at Ayodhya to worship by the faithful. This mobilisation was fragmented in some measure by an August 1990 decision by a government elected nine months earlier, to implement the recommendations on affirmative action for those disadvantaged by origin in one of the "socially and educationally backward classes" or "other backward classes" (OBCs) within the caste hierarchy. These recommendations arose from a ten year old report of an officially mandated body, the "Mandal Commission", which inquired into the social debilities faced by these classes. The Indian parliament had a rare moment of unanimity in 1980 when it received the report and accepted it with little demur. But the Mandal recommendations were a political hot potato that few among the governments that followed were willing to grasp.

Prospective implementation of the Mandal recommendations in 1990 threatened disarray in the majoritarian ranks. The Bharatiya Janata Party (BJP), which had taken up the cause of Ayodhya with complete conviction after the ruling Congress fumbled with an issue it hoped to control, launched a nation-wide mobilisation under its president L.K. Advani, to restore unity within the ranks. The ritual procession or *yatra* he inaugurated from the western coastal town of Somnath to Ayodhya left a trail of bloodshed in the various towns it passed through and was

31 Ibid: 950.

only interdicted at the point of its entry into Bihar. Advani's arrest triggered the BJP's withdrawal of support to the uneasy coalition which had governed for close to a year with the support of left and right wing formations anxious to keep the Congress out of the portals of power.

Soon after these events, Advani offered a stocktaking in the English language press, confessing himself "pained" at the suggestion that he had contributed to the embitterment of communal relations and rejecting any suggestion of a correlation between his motorised odyssey and the violence that had recurred through the weeks since he started it. Unity, not division was the underlying message of the *yatra* and indeed, this was the sense in which it was seen by the many who took part. In a term that he had unique claim to authorship of, he denounced those who felt otherwise as "pseudo-secularists" who had made a career out of pandering to the minority community and were beginning to feel the insecurity of an assured vote-bank slipping out of their hands.

For Advani, the undue deference shown to minority sensitivities was a denial of the basic genius of the Indian nation, which was and would remain Hinduism. It was vital to embrace the Ayodhya movement as a platform of cultural consolidation, since the alien other had won significant political victories and been emboldened to press its claim for a niche within the nation that was above and beyond the law of the land.

The narration that Advani then unfolded is worth recalling in some detail. "It all began", he said, "with the Congress Government's capitulation on the Shah Bano issue and its readiness to undo a Supreme Court judgment in 1985". Though the judgment was fundamentally sound, the government capitulated. This victory emboldened "them" – a category that Advani never really identified in specific detail – to form the Babri Masjid Action Committee, to reverse the judicial order that allowed Hindu worshippers access to the structure at Ayodhya. Having "tasted blood" in reversing a Supreme Court judgment, overturning a lower court order seemed a rather trivial matter. Because of its nationalist resonances, it was a legitimate issue for political mobilisation to resist this stratagem and complete the transformation of the Babri Masjid into a temple honouring the revered God-king of Hindu mythology.[32]

32 Advani (1990).

Shortly after a New Delhi rally in April 1991 demanding the restoration of the hallowed site at Ayodhya, an editorial in the English daily, the *Indian Express*, (April 6, 1991) summed up the state of stirred up public emotion. There was a "groundswell of Hindu self-consciousness in the country" which, like it or not, every political calculation had to take note of. From that seeming observation of fact, the editorial quickly switched to an advisory role about the movement spearheaded by the Vishwa Hindu Parishad (VHP). It would not be appropriate for the new political assertion to narrowly focus on the object of a temple to supplant the Babri Masjid at Ayodhya. A broader purpose had to be pursued, nothing less than the restoration of the hero of the Ramayan epic to a deserved central position in the nationalist pantheon. For the BJP, which was fighting the battle at the political level the object would be to enlarge the platform, beyond the immediate objective the VHP had adopted. It was not just the strip of real estate in Ayodhya that was the issue, but the status of the epic hero Ram, "as a symbol of an Indian identity that predates the arrival of Islam in India and endures to this day".

As elucidated in this editorial, India's political agenda since independence had suffered the fatal flaw of bringing on board the Islamic cultural strain, which had a nationalist claim if at all, very much inferior to the ancient epics such as the Ramayan. This abuse of the Indian practice of secularism needed correction. Focusing narrowly on a temple and the removal of the offending alien presence of a mosque in Ayodhya, would likely lead to violence. By a broader focus on Ram, the matter could be taken forward peacefully, with the debate being pitched at the level of "the true content of secularism rather than a specific combative assertion on the location of a temple".

Jammu and Kashmir, India's sole Muslim majority state, broke out in insurgency late in 1989. A harsh crackdown followed, presided over in the initial phase by a state governor, Jagmohan, who was appointed to the post a second time within days of the trouble erupting. Jagmohan was removed after a few months on the job, after a particularly egregious incident in which a funeral procession was fired upon with grievous loss of life. Later in 1990, he published an account of long years of service in Kashmir, inclusive of his earlier tour of duty as governor. The key to a resolution of the problems of Kashmir, he suggested as he wound up an interminable and for the most part self-serving account of events, would be "a reformed, reawakened and rejuvenated Hinduism".[33]

In an article inspired by a reading of this book, Swapan Dasgupta ruled out the possibility of a "permanent Muslim rapprochement within the Indian republic" and suggested that there may be no alternative but the "demographic Indianisation" of the Kashmir valley.[34] And just around the same time, another widely read columnist Arun Shourie, was laying out the *modus operandi* for such a process: all the security personnel involved in the operations in Kashmir, he proposed, should be given title to buy land in Kashmir and presumably, to make the Valley their home.[35]

This variety of locution was by no means exceptional in that time when a new majoritarian assertion seemed to threaten every principle on which independent India had sought to build a constitutional order. In terms of the categories discussed earlier and Jeremy Waldron's warnings about free speech ending where the "dignity" of others was at stake, these are speech acts that step far beyond relevant red lines. To suggest that an entire class of people are undeserving of the freedoms that a constitutional order guarantees, is a breach of the code of civility that makes peaceful coexistence possible. The Ayodhya movement normalised these utterances in public spaces.

The Mandal theme: a seamless nation

Another variety of media discourse emerged once implementation of the Mandal recommendations became stated governmental intent. To take a sample of the English-language press, often referred to as the "national" press (indicating not so much an all-India presence as the continuing imagining of the nation in English), *The Times of India* (*TOI*) in an editorial headlined "Back to the past" (August 9, 1990) bemoaned that the decision on extending reservations in government employment to the OBCs threatened to undo "at one stroke" all that had been achieved over four decades of independence, in building a "modern, egalitarian order". While anxiously underlining that it was

33 Jagmohan (1991): 627.

34 Dasgupta (1991).

35 Shourie (1991).

not opposed to rendering OBCs a fair deal, the *TOI* pronounced that reservations would "enshrine casteism, undermine meritocracy and excellence and work against the creation of a pan-Indian identity". Rather than reservations, the disadvantaged sections could be helped to improve their "competitiveness" – that word much favoured by the upwardly mobile – through the provision of "abundant educational, health, nutritional and other social welfare benefits".

The Hindu the same day responded with greater restraint in an editorial titled "A populist move". Operating from the southern state of Tamil Nadu, where reservations of upto 68 percent are the norm, the newspaper had good reasons for caution. But its editorial tone was disapproving. The move was imprecisely grounded in social reality and politically unimaginative. It provided an incentive for every social group to develop "backwardness" into a "vested interest". Echoing the *TOI*'s editorial line in at least one respect, *The Hindu* argued that it may have been by far preferable if the government had undertaken "special development programmes targeting the OBCs", apart from launching "all out efforts to change the socio-economic structure which is heavily weighted against these communities".

This range of reactions must be considered moderate in comparison to the furious, frothing pronouncement that *The Indian Express* (*IE*) came up with. "Ruinous" was the *IE* editorial headline (August 9, 1990), under which it argued that reservations were a contingent political promise made exclusively to a defined section of India's population – "the Scheduled Castes and Scheduled Tribes". It was a promise that could not be extended to larger sections without serious risk of a "further deterioration of the state apparatus and heightened social tensions". The decision to extend reservations to castes which were "rich and dominant in several parts of the country" was "crassly opportunistic" since the new beneficiaries, aside from being undeserving, were also active oppressors of the lower orders.

Fomenting mass disturbances

Aggrieved elements who saw the expansion of reservations as a constriction of opportunities, were soon out on the streets. As the agitation began to spread, the *IE* pronounced it "clearly in defence of the national interest". In an evident breach of editorial responsibility, if not an open incitement to riot, it urged the students fomenting the disturbances to fulfil their "responsibility to spread and intensify them" (editorial, August 15, 1990). The *TOI* was editorially more circumspect (August 18, 1990), calling for a firm hand in controlling the violence, but still tilting strongly towards seeing the protests as a just cause. *The Hindu* similarly (August 14, 1990), reacted adversely to the spreading violence, but was prepared to lay the blame on the government for doing what was "manifestly populist and dramatic" rather than "approaching the question dispassionately and with circumspection".

From the first stirrings of unrest on the street in August 1990, official spokesmen sought at several junctures, to calm the student disturbances. But the message failed to win a receptive audience and there is a credible argument to be made that the media managed to amplify the discord by drowning out alternative viewpoints. Public dialogue on the matter became in other words, a conversation between the agitationists, each keen to outbid the other in anger. In the process, the media came perilously close to entrenching a perception of caste exclusivity, to upholding the notion of the "organised sector" of relatively better paid and secure jobs being the rightful preserve of the privileged. Indeed, the crowds in the streets were invested with a unique claim to speaking not merely for themselves, but on behalf of the entire nation.

The *IE*, late-August, denounced the official effort to mitigate the sense of grievance within the student community. Jobs in the Central Government, it argued, however minuscule their contribution to total employment, were by far the largest contributor to opportunities within the "organised sector". To try and shift the focus to the jobs scene in general was in other words, disingenuous, since the focus of the anti-Mandal agitation was the organised sector. In a later edition, the *IE* ran a story on how job reservations in the Indian Railways were perhaps responsible for its poor safety record.[36]

With the media unequivocally behind it, the anti-Mandal agitation was by this time conspicuously displaying its contempt for those of lesser privilege, who were seemingly condemned to unending toil in the unorganised sector. Students from Delhi's elite colleges were

36 Saraf (1990) quoted from various commissions of inquiry into railway accidents but the argument was weak, since one inquiry merely relied on the findings of preceding ones, embellishing it with some impressionistic accounts derived from staff that it managed to interview.

trooping to the *dhobi*-ghats on the Jamuna riverfront to exercise their laundry skills in full view of the national media; others chose strategic street corners to sit with shoe-shine kits, offering their services to any passer-by. This display of elitist contempt for the sole livelihood recourses of large numbers, proved the complete alienation of the "anti-Mandal" forces from the populist vein essential for sustaining a mass movement. The movement had evidently lost its moral compass and inevitably, the momentum of the agitation was beginning to die out within a month. This is when in circumstances that still remain obscure, a Delhi student, Rajeev Goswami, began a cycle of self-immolation attempts in full view of the media. Goswami survived that attempt, but the picture of him ablaze was featured prominently on the front pages of the *IE*, the *TOI* and a number of other newspapers. It became emblematic of the anti-Mandal agitation and soon enough, sparked off a series of copycat attempts, several of which proved fatal. The first fatality in Delhi, involving an associate of Goswami's, S.S. Chauhan, was featured prominently, again on front pages, by both the *TOI* and *IE*.

Breaching well accepted media codes

Media coverage here was in obvious breach of well-accepted journalistic codes, but few seemed inclined to pause and think when brazen excess seemed the rule. Between the middle of August, when the agitation was beginning to move into high gear, and the end of September, the Delhi edition of the *IE* devoted 1,915 column-centimetres (col-cm) of front-page space to news reports on the anti-Mandal disturbances. Within the same interval of time, 3,311 col-cm off the front-page were used exclusively for coverage of the agitation. The *TOI* was only marginally behind, devoting 1,554 col-cm on front page, and 3,229 col-cm off it, to the rampage on the streets. Only *The Hindu*, with its reputation for sobriety and moderation and with the relative unconcern of a newspaper headquartered in the distant south of the country, chose to devote to the agitation less than half the space that the other two major national dailies did individually.[37]

---

37 By way of a baseline for assessing these figures, the *TOI* and the *IE* on a typical day then, had about 350 column-centimetres of space on their front pages and about 420 column-centimetres on a typical interior page. *The Hindu* because of wider columns, had about 250 column-cen-

Both the *IE* and the *TOI* were lavish in their visual coverage too – in both cases, the total space allotted came very close to the print coverage. However, in the scale of priorities of *The Hindu*, the movement merited no more than a quarter of the visual space that the other two dailies devoted to it. In terms of editorial comment however, all three dailies were roughly comparable.

These figures would not mean much unless they could be assessed against a credible benchmark. A possible baseline would be media coverage of the confrontation then underway, along another of the fault-lines in the Indian polity, involving another of the "minority" groups created in the consolidation of Indian nationalism.

In September 1989, a spark of sectarian blood-letting was lit in the northern region of the country in the course of a nationwide mobilisation by the forces of "cultural nationalism", intent on reclaiming a hallowed site at Ayodhya. Beginning in small towns in the states of Rajasthan and Uttar Pradesh, the fire spread into Gujarat, Madhya Pradesh and Karnataka by mid-October. It then simmered and spread slowly across the Hindi-belt, until it broke out violently in Bihar. Bhagalpur in Bihar state was soon engulfed in a firestorm of violence against the Muslim community, comparable with the very worst witnessed in independent India: Ahmedabad, 1969; Jamshedpur, 1979; Moradabad, 1981, Bhiwandi, 1984, and Meerut, 1987.

What was the reaction of the media? To arrive at a scale of values, a comparable period of 47 days may be taken between October 1 and November 17, 1989. Moreover, the reasonable – though admittedly arbitrary – assumption may be made, that the impact of visual coverage is twice as great as that of print coverage. We then find that the *IE* devoted 12.81 times as much space to the anti-reservation agitation in 1990, as it did to the anti-Muslim riots of October-November 1989. The corresponding ratio for the *TOI* would work out to something like 9.81, while for *The Hindu*, it would be the rather more humane figure of 5.75.[38]

---

timetres on the front page and about 320 column-centimetres on the interior pages. A typical daily edition of these newspapers consisted in all of 16 pages, excluding the occasional supplements. Between 40 and 50 percent of total space would be on an average day, devoted to advertisements.

38 It has to be underlined here that *The Hindu*'s relatively modest ratio is not because it provided what might seem duly merited coverage to the

Adding further weights to these figures to reflect the number of lives lost, one would arrive at the perfectly perverse conclusion that a life lost in defending a few hundred thousand jobs against the claims of the disadvantaged, is in the estimation of the *IE*, worth 75 times more than one that is snuffed out in the cause of building a shrine to a god-king of Hindu mythology. Corresponding ratios would be in the region of 60 for the *TOI* and around 35 for *The Hindu*. Evidently, the principle of "one man, one value" considered in Ambedkar's famous locution as a fundamental principle in the practice of democracy, had acquired a rather misshapen form in the imagination of the Indian national press.

To the extent that "communities" are defined by difference, the media would reflect, sometimes subtly though more often rather crudely, the perceptions of "otherness" without which communal boundaries would remain uncomfortably fluid. But there are also sections of the media that claim to represent a "national" perspective, untainted by narrow pulls of community loyalty. Penetrating the subtleties of the "national" media discourse is often a challenge, since it succeeds in most cases, in disguising communal predilections in the pretence of a larger solidarity. This practice of the media embodies the conceit of a segment that views itself as the "national mainstream", which stands above and beyond the clamour of minority groups seeking to assert their sectarian claims.

Changing tone of the "mainstream" discourse

This so-called national mainstream though, does not represent an unchanging sensibility. As circumstances change, so too would its perceptions and priorities. The dynamics of these transformations emerge from comparing the media discourse between two distinct points in time: the period just dealt with, when the country was convulsed by the Mandal and Mandir agitations, and the communal carnage of Gujarat in 2002, a decade on.

If in the earlier period, the media in most parts of the country was guilty of not opposing Hindutva communal adventurism with suffi-

---

deaths of Muslims in the Ayodhya mobilisation, but merely because it had been relatively less inclined towards hyperbolic coverage of the anti-reservation agitation.

cient passion or principle, the media in the Hindi speaking region was actively engaged in the abetment of these forces. This is no subjective judgment. Rather, it was the firmly established view of the Press Council of India, which in 1991 went into news coverage and editorial comments in four major Hindi language dailies during an especially fraught moment in the Ayodhya agitation. The conclusions were unequivocal: the newspapers had "lost their balance" during the period. Following the repulsing of an effort by volunteers of the Hindu nationalist parties to storm the mosque at Ayodhya, these newspapers carried "wild rumours and exaggerated reports" about thousands being killed. One of the newspapers distributed five-thousand copies free of cost in the city of Ranchi, with contents so provocative that communal riots were soon fanned aflame.[39] The editor with one of the newspapers, *Dainik Jagaran*, quit his post when he found that there was an institutional compulsion that he was helpless to combat, in carrying "distorted, malicious, blood-soaked gutter material, which if published, would only result in creating further dissension between the two communities".[40]

There is a different pattern discernible in the coverage of the Gujarat pogrom. With the exception of the Gujarati press – where a clear tilt was evident towards blaming the victims, towards lurid exaggeration and incitement to violence – the rest of the press nationwide, both in English and the Indian languages (or *bhasha*), earned wide credit for their unflinching portrayal of the brutalities of Gujarat. Indeed, the pressure was severe enough for the Gujarat chief minister, Narendra Modi, to frequently put the blame on the media for what he on at least one occasion referred to as "secular riots".[41]

There had evidently been a significant cultural change in the media over the preceding twelve years, especially in the Hindi language press. The crucial factor here could well be the tremendous growth in the reach of the Hindi press since the days of Ayodhya. One estimate puts the total number of readers of Hindi dailies in 1990 at around 7.8 million. By the year 2001, it was over 21 million. In 2013, the two

---

39 *The Hindu* (1991). Also, Robin Jeffrey (2000): 158.

40 Kamleshwar (1991).

41 Varadarajan (2002): chapter 8. Also see Editors' Guild of India (2002). The references to "secular riots" are from the latter source. On the language media, see *Times of India* (2002).

leading newspapers in Hindi alone, were estimated to have a total readership of 40 million.[42] This quantitative explosion led to certain qualitative changes.

This brings up the Hegelian dictum once again, about the daily ritual of a newspaper being akin to a form of prayer, a mass ceremony which individuals in their social isolation pursue, to establish a social solidarity overwhelming the barriers of anonymity that otherwise surround every person in mass society.[43] The decade between Ayodhya and Gujarat was when the Indian middle class with its multiple identities, entered into an embrace with the cult of globalism. As the decade progressed, the English language media began to reflect, increasingly, the sensibility of the globalised/globalising middle class. It served in most part, a metropolitan audience at a time when India's metropolises were being transformed into something akin to a melting pot of cultures. The prime target audience for newspapers and the media in general (the age group between 25 and 40) – even when rooted in imagined primordial identities – worked with the self-belief of having detached itself from active political engagement and being at best, indifferent towards the politics of identity.

Like the English language media sought to forge the globalising identity, regional media began increasingly privileging the local. The advertising revenue to fuel readership growth came for the regional media from closely tailoring content to local demands. Location and purchasing power, rather than identity became the key parameters driving media strategies. The Indian media through the decades of glo-

42 These figures are obtained from the bi-annual surveys conducted by rival market research organisations: the National Readership Survey and the Indian Readership Survey. Though these surveys often produce contradictory figures, reflecting the rivalry between media groups, they are in the instances cited, in agreement on broad aggregates.

43 The analogy with mass prayer is advanced with due acknowledgment to Hegel, by Benedict Anderson (1983): 35: "The significance of this mass ceremony … is paradoxical. It is performed in silent privacy, in the lair of the skull. Yet each communicant is well aware that the ceremony he performs is being replicated simultaneously by thousands (or millions) of others of whose existence he is confident, yet of whose identity he has not the slightest notion. Furthermore, this ceremony is incessantly repeated at daily or half-daily intervals throughout the calendar. What more vivid figure for the secular, historically clocked, imagined community can be envisioned?"

balisation brought the "economic man" – stripped of the particularities of identity – closer to reality than the years of economic planning had. This was a consumer whose cultural universe could be easily moulded to fit snugly within the imperatives of the advertising industry: cricket, cinema, crime and celebrity worship.

The persistence of exclusion

At the same time, there were other forms of social exclusion, other kinds of particularities, that remained as unstated premises of media functioning even through this phase of transformation. It is not necessary to go any further than the news coverage and editorial comment that accompanied the presentation in 2006 of the Rajinder Sachar committee report on the status of India's Muslims, to grasp how the new processes of exclusion work. As in the Mandal-Mandir chapter, the media in its approach to this and other issues that came up concurrently, unwittingly opened before the public the entire panorama of how it creates and consolidates "minority" identities.

The Sachar report's presentation in Parliament on November 30, 2006, coincided with an outbreak of violence in Maharashtra over the vandalisation of an Ambedkar statue in Uttar Pradesh. The following day, *TOI* confined the Sachar report to the news digest section, occupying about 3 column-centimetres on the first page. Considerably more attention was devoted to the violence of the Dalit protests in Maharashtra, with the picture of a train that had been set afire between Mumbai and Pune getting marquee space on the front page. Top honours on the frontpage though, were reserved for the composition of the Indian cricket team for an upcoming overseas tour, with the recall of a former captain being featured as its salient feature.

The Sachar Committee earned significant space in the inner pages of the *TOI* that day, though the Dalit protests continued to enjoy far more. What the *TOI* chose to put front and centre in its coverage of Sachar was the government's uncertain resolve about introducing reservations in education and employment for the minorities. The institutionalised discrimination suffered by the Muslim minority was transformed in the *TOI* discourse into a concern over keeping India's enclaves of modernity secure from the ingress of the underprivileged.

On the Dalit protests in Maharashtra, perceptive media critics have pointed out that the consistent refrain of the mainstream press, in both English and the *bhasha*, was the ease with which the inherent violence of Dalit agitators could be provoked. There were references to the Khairlanji massacre of September 29, in which four members of a Dalit family, a mother and three persons/children, including a visually challenged youth, were killed. This was in a sense, an oblique acknowledgment that the atrocity in Khairlanji could have been a contributory factor in the upwelling of Dalit rage. But there was in evidence, no effort to make amends for a shocking record of media neglect of the crime. Indeed, the record of the media since the massacre was to underplay it, to see it not as an expression of the unrelenting social prejudice and persecution that Dalits suffer, but as a regrettable case of moral vigilantism carried to excess. Surekha Bhotmange, the mother who was killed, was with many a conniving nudge and wink, held responsible for having invited the terrible retribution by her licentious conduct. And it spoke eloquently of the blinkers the media had fashioned for itself from the social conditioning of its staff, that it took a Dalit-owned newspaper in Maharashtra to investigate and bring the crime to light after weeks of arduous effort.[44]

Evidently, *The Hindu* was subject to some serious questioning over the silence. Acknowledging that public anxiety was high, the Readers' Editor – an ombudsman that had just then been created to address audience concerns – wrote that the "charge of media indifference gets substantiated when the treatment of this incident is studied". "The attack", he continued, "took place on September 29. The first report appeared (in the English press) in a Nagpur daily on October 3, with a heading of '4 of family murdered.' The reason was said to be an 'illicit affair'. There was no mention that it was a Dalit family. A Mumbai paper gave a brief account of the happenings on October 7. A national TV channel picked up the story only on November 1".[45]

The media donned a rather different set of blinkers when dealing with the Sachar committee findings. Various alibis could be offered for the initial phase of neglect the report suffered, though none would stand serious scrutiny. It could be argued that the social and education-

---

44 See Jyoti Punwani (2006).

45 Narayanan K. (2006).

al handicaps of the Muslim community are not exactly a news flash. But then, neither was the choice of the Indian cricket team. Those familiar with the dynamics of competition in the newspaper business, might ascribe the relative disinterest in the Sachar committee to another factor. *IE* had in media jargon, "scooped" the main findings of the committee well over a month before its report was formally presented, considerably reducing the incentive that other newspapers might have had to feature it as a high-priority item. The *IE* coverage appeared in a compact series of articles on the front page, through the last week of October. The newspaper then chose to pronounce its final editorial verdict on the issue by urging the political leadership to acknowledge an undeniable verity: that economic growth was the only way out of social backwardness.[46] In effect, the *IE* succeeded in submerging the complexity of the Sachar committee's findings in a simplistic nostrum much favoured in the prevalent neo-liberal climate.

While the *IE* was constructing this narrative of discrimination on its news pages and paying obeisance to the virtues of globalisation editorially, a quite different picture of willing thraldom to superstition was being assembled in another quarter of the print media. Between October 24 and 29, the *TOI* carried no fewer than 6 articles – both news reports and comments, of which two were on the front-page and one on the editorial page – on the case of a young Muslim woman raped by her father-in-law and stigmatised by the Muslim clergy for her temerity in seeking to bring the criminal to justice.

On October 25, the *TOI* ran a story on the young woman on page one, right alongside another one on the confusion within the Muslim community about when precisely the Eid festivities were to be observed. This latter story led off with a description of the subjectivity underlying the precise date on which the most significant of Muslim religious observances is celebrated and the tension that this set up with modern notions of scientific precision.

The story on the rape victim seeking justice and the accompanying article on Eid enjoyed roughly the same priority in terms of space allocation and placement. But these stories were topped off by a large pho-

46 Chishti (2006) provided a series of six reports between October 23 and 29, outlining the main findings of the Sachar committee. These were preceded by an editorial in *The Indian Express*, dated October 23 titled "Not by fatwas".

tograph, occupying marquee space on the front page, which showed the touring Pakistani cricket team offering Eid prayers at Chandigarh, their port of call at the time during a tour of India. The picture was boldly captioned "Champions of the faith?" with a marked emphasis on the interrogatory tone.

With this mystifying juxtaposition of stories and visuals, the *TOI* managed within about a third of the space on its front page, to reinforce several stereotypes about the Muslim community, not least the common suppositions about their extra-territorial loyalties and their aversion to modernity.

Yet the *TOI* could not remain oblivious to the news emerging from another quarter on the findings of the Sachar report. On November 4, it ran an editorial giving its considered view on the main findings, beginning with deprecating reservations as a "blunt instrument" that failed to reach the core of the problem. Other forms of "positive discrimination" it urged could be thought of instead, including building "quality schools" and "providing healthcare" in "backward districts" that have high settlement densities of Muslims, Dalits or tribals. Government contracts could be preferentially allocated to these disadvantaged social groups, to "facilitate their participation in the modern economy". In turn, the *TOI* chose to place a special onus on the "Muslim leadership" to "encourage the community to take to modern education in larger numbers".

These are, of course, far from being newly minted prescriptions. Article 350A of the Indian Constitution mandates precisely such positive discrimination in favour of minority communities where State investments in education are concerned. Backward area development policies adopted by the central government, not to mention various states, have also sought to direct special attention towards economically stagnant regions, without giving it the touch of class or community-orientation. The *TOI* showed admirable percipience in waking up to the reality that backward areas are in most parts of the country, also predominantly populated by people who would fall within the broad rubric of "backward classes". But this realisation was not informed by any effort to understand why backward area development policies have also proved fairly ineffective in redressing disparities, indeed, why they have proven an even blunter instrument than reservations.

On November 8, the *TOI* carried an article on Islamic schools or *madrasas* on its editorial page. Titled "Beyond Terror", the article argued that the debate on these institutions had remained for too long confined to the issue of terrorism, which was in essence a superficiality. Because the Muslim community was under pressure in times of global concern over terrorism, it had responded – the *TOI* editorial continued – with a spirited defence of these institutions as uniquely equipped to impart a moral and spiritual sensibility. This attitude in turn simply evaded the reality that the *madrasas* have a tendency to "promote a narrow, insular mindset". And as long as security concerns remained the principal impulse behind the debate, there was little chance that matters of immense import to the "welfare of millions of children studying in *madrasas*" would be addressed.

Though not formally released, many of the key findings of the Sachar committee were in the public domain by the time of this article. On the issue of *madrasas*, the conclusions were fairly clear: fewer than 4 percent of Muslim children in the relevant age group attended these institutions; at an all-India level, their number was not the "millions" as the commentator in the *TOI* suggested, but just marginally over one million, of which three-quarters were in the primary stage.[47] Far from

47 Arshad Alam, a researcher and scholar who has studied education practices and their social implications within the Muslim community, has disputed the Sachar Committee findings on the number of children enrolled in *madrasas*. Far from being the rather modest figure of 4 percent of all Muslim children of schoolgoing age, he says, the figure is likely to be between 12 and 14 percent. Alam (2011) dissents with the Sachar Committee which he believes under-estimates the number of children of school-going age enrolled in *madrasas* and also fails to take note of the ideological influence exerted by these institutions on social life. The Sachar Committee, Alam argues, only takes into account the number of students enrolled in *madrasas* that are registered with state boards of education and follow their stipulated syllabi. There is another category of institutions which are autonomous of state boards and governed by so-called state-level *madrasa* boards. If these are taken into account, then the number of school-going children of the Muslim faith enrolled in these institutions would number between 12 and 14 percent of the total, according to Alam's rough calculation. The matter perhaps needs deeper inquiry, though this does not seriously dilute the argument being advanced here on the quality of media reporting on minority issues, since the figure of "millions" that was freely used in the *TOI* editorial needed justification in the face of a contrary finding by the Sachar Committee. That this justification was not provided, speaks of a tendency for the media to fall back on easy stereotypes and

being an institution of choice, *madrasas* were "often the last recourse of Muslims, especially (of) those who lack the economic resources to bear the costs of schooling, or (of) households located in areas where 'mainstream' educational institutions are inaccessible". And for all the odium heaped on them, *madrasas* had very often been found to "have indeed provided schooling to Muslim children where the State (had) failed them".[48]

A few inconvenient facts though, were not going to stand between the *TOI* and what seemed a compelling narrative of backwardness and ghettoisation by choice among India's Muslims. It was mid-November 2006 by the time the *TOI* returned on its news pages, to the theme of the Sachar committee. On November 17, it reported that the committee's recommendations had put the ruling coalition, the United Progressive Alliance, in a "fix". The following day, it published front-page, a report arguing that the committee's recommendation to increase the Muslim share in several sectors of employment would in effect "give rise to the demand for a community quota leading to a full-scale political confrontation". Having begun its coverage of the Sachar report by viewing it through the narrow frame of the reservations issue, the *TOI* undoubtedly saw no reason to change course when more details were available.

Quantitative growth that kills diversity

To look at the media today is to look at a complex, dynamic and evolving scenario, to consider a quantitative explosion that bridges older particularities of identity. Numerical growth would normally lead to a multiplicity of choices, but the high degree of congruence between the world-views of advertisers who drive media content, ensures that diversity suffers. This is a reality apparent in the explosion of the TV media, especially since India entered onto what was claimed to be a new economic growth trajectory around 2003. Despite the rapid increase in the number of news channels, every one among them seemed locked into an imitative mode of programming, consistently seeking out the lowest common denominator of audience taste.

---

not unduly bother to check out facts, when minority matters are under discussion.

48 Cabinet Secretariat (2006): 99.

In its approach to minority matters, the media may well have ironed out some of the rougher edges evident in the early-1990s. That was the time the Muslim minority was stigmatised as legatee to the various injuries and indignities inflicted in the past on India's original, primordial cultural identity. The lower castes were at the same time, portrayed as interlopers and intruders in the enclaves of modernity of the Indian State, whose noisy claims to assured representation would severely impair efficiency and effectiveness.

In later years, particularly since terrorism became a global obsession, the Muslim minority was portrayed as an impediment to the glittering promises of modernity that lay ahead for India as it sought a merited place in global councils. And "terrorism", portrayed as a virtual monopoly of fundamentalist Islam, was the weapon deployed by those anxious to thwart India's march towards global prestige and modernity. Media reporting that conformed to this template was assured of wide and uncritical diffusion, basic norms such as factual accuracy being easily dispensed with.

On September 19, 2008, the Special Cell of Delhi Police, with the electronic media providing real-time coverage, raided a fourth-floor flat in a tenement in Batla House, a crowded south-eastern suburb of the city, neighbouring the campus of the Jamia Millia Islamia university. The "encounter" resulted in the killing of two youths and the capture of another. Since the supposed intelligence report that led to the police raid had identified five known terrorists hiding out, the Delhi Police admitted with some regret, that two among their quarries had escaped the cordon thrown around the area. One police inspector suffered grievous injuries in the operation and later the same day, died in hospital.

Despite losing an officer, the Delhi police were exultant. As reported in the local press, Atiq, killed in the encounter, was a key link in the terrorism ring that had set off serial bombs in a number of cities, at enormous cost to human life. According to *The Hindu* (September 20: 1), he was the operative of a shadowy terrorist group called the "Indian Mujahideen" and had "played a major role in the Jaipur, Ahmedabad, Hyderabad (and) Delhi serial blasts", all of which had scarred the urban Indian landscape in the months prior.

In this sequence of four serial bomb attacks in as many months, the last was in Delhi on September 13. Two days afterwards, *TOI* ran an editorial which ominously declared: "We are at war. The string of blasts (in Delhi) .. which killed 30 people and injured 90 is the fourth attack by terrorists on a major Indian city in the span of four months". The people of India, the newspaper advised, should get used to the idea of surrendering some accustomed liberties. This would be a necessary, short-term sacrifice, since the enemy they confronted was an even greater threat to human freedom.

It could be asked if this editorial prescription from *TOI* would cover the freedom to ask questions and expect the state agencies – including the police and intelligence – to conduct themselves with a measure of accountability. Though no explicit suggestion was made to that effect, the conduct of the agencies suggested an intent to silence all awkward questions. And the ideological shroud under which inquiry was suppressed, was the construct of "Islamic terror" or *jihad*.

In the days before, the supposed terrorist ring in India was portrayed in the media variously and with disturbing inconsistencies. Prior to the emergence of the Indian Mujahedin, a central position within the narrative of the Islamic *jihad* was reserved for the Students' Islamic Movement of India (SIMI), a once obscure body of uncertain provenance, vaguely believed to be affiliated to the Jamaat-e-Islami-e-Hind, banned in 2001 and except for a brief interlude following the change of government at the Centre, an outlaw organisation ever since. When Safdar Nagori, the putative SIMI general secretary, was arrested in March 2008, a security analyst well-known for his feverishly speculative commentary, observed that "SIMI cadre have been involved in almost every Islamist terror strike since (2000), ranging from the Mumbai serial bombings of 2003 and 2006 to attacks in Uttar Pradesh, Karnataka, Andhra Pradesh, and Delhi."[49]

The individuals behind the *jihad* mission similarly, were variously identified, their disparate names having little in common other than an Islamic provenance. First there was Waliullah who was assigned the role of main inspiration of the "Indian Mujahedin"; and then there was Abu Bashar Qasmi, a 25-year old cleric, snatched from his home in Azamgarh district of Uttar Pradesh by the Gujarat police and identified to be the man behind the Ahmedabad bombings of July 2008.[50]

49 Swami (2008).

50 *The Hindu* (2008b).

In still another variant, there was Shahbaz Hussain, arrested in the dead of night from his home in Lucknow by the Rajasthan police and charged with prime responsibility for the Jaipur attacks of May 2008. Looming over the whole conspiracy was the spectre of Mohammad Altaf Subhan – later identified as Abdul Subhan Quereshi, and variously described by the alternative names, Taufeeq and Tauqeer, by which he was allegedly known in terrorist circles – a computer hardware specialist missing from his home in Mumbai's distant suburb of Mira Road, since 2006.[51]

With Shahbaz's firm implication in terrorism, an elaborate chain of linkages began to be drawn between the Jaipur and Ahmedabad blasts. Nagori, Shahbaz and Qasmi were all reportedly, members of a secretive cell that underwent explosives training in camps as far afield as Kerala and the jungles of Gujarat and Madhya Pradesh. Subhan *alias* Tauqeer, was the supposed technical brain behind the ingeniously designed bombs and the e-mail messages, replete with intense Islamic religious symbolism, sent out celebrating each terrorist strike in the heart of urban India.[52] When Delhi was gutted by three simultaneous bombings in September, Tauqeer was almost by reflex, identified by every investigating agency as the mastermind. Working its way through the chain that connected Tauqeer with Qasmi and Shahbaz, the Delhi police quickly identified the other links in the terrorism plot, all from Uttar Pradesh: Abdul Rajib, Mujib, Alamjed Afridi and Qayamuddin.[53]

"Tauqeer" was the chant on every journalist's lips when the Delhi Police began their operation in Batla House on September 19. When the dust had settled, the story took a dramatic twist: it was no longer Tauqeer, but Atif – one of two youths killed that day – who was the terrorist mastermind. Some among the media clung onto the name of Qasmi, since he had been arrested just days before. But there were inconsistencies and contradictions within the narrative that suggested a shocking failure to check facts. Any report, it seemed, that conformed to the template of *jihad* and had a sufficient number of names of Islamic provenance strewn about, would pass the editorial test.

---

51 *The Hindu* (2008a) and *Indian Express* (2008).

52 *The Hindu* (2008c and 2008d).

53 *The Hindu* (2008b).

The Hindu reported the Jamia Nagar encounter as top story on September 20 and quoted Delhi's chief of police in the following terms: "Mr. Dadhwal said the Batla House operation was carried out solely by the Special Cell and it had no connection with the presence of Abul Bashar Qasmi, main accused in the Ahmedabad blasts, in the Capital on Thursday". Another police officer was quoted as saying that Bashir, an alleged militant killed in the encounter, had no connection with Qasmi.

Right under this lead story though, a correspondent seemingly specialised in Islamic terrorism, pronounced a judgment that sharply contradicted the Delhi Police Commissioner's disclaimer on Qasmi's role: "Based on the phone records of the alleged Indian Mujahideen cadre held in Gujarat, the Intelligence Bureau concluded that (a wanted terrorist) Bashir was likely hidden out in safehouses… in the Jamia Nagar and Okhla areas of south-east Delhi.... However, these could be located only when Qasmi was brought to New Delhi and driven around the Jamia Nagar area on Thursday night."[54]

In just a matter of days, with the arrest of five in Mumbai on September 24, the Nagori-Qasmi-Shahbaz chain of culpability was history. The Mumbai Police now definitively identified 31-year old Sadiq Sheikh, a resident of the Cheetah Camp slum sprawl near the city's north-eastern suburb of Chembur, as the inspiration and the mentor for all the terrorist actions of the preceding months. Four others were arrested alongside, including a computer software expert, an alleged car thief, and two supposed specialists in bomb making. The final twist came a month later, when a senior policeman from Maharashtra's anti-terrorist squad brushed Tauqeer aside as a complete fiction, a creation indeed, of the media.[55]

Terrorism, media and civic life

Serial bombs that target vital nodes of a city's civic life, are intended to produce the effect on an average citizen's psyche as "shock and awe", the war doctrine implemented by the U.S. in Iraq in 2003. The purpose

54 *The Hindu* (2008e) for the quotes from the Delhi Police Commissioner, and right below, *The Hindu* (2008f) for the account of how Qasmi contributed towards identifying the location of the "terrorist" ring.

55 Punwani (2008).

is to create a real life montage of simultaneous destruction that would be enveloping in its scope and would defeat popular loyalty to a regime or a political dispensation. The wider lesson that this tableau of destruction seeks to impart is that the average citizen cannot count on duly constituted political authorities for protection, and would need to assume the individual right to self-defence. Applied across a wide social expanse, this would become the recipe for a descent into the law of the jungle, a "war of all against all".

That the people of India have defied this calculus despite repeated provocation, speaks of resilient faith in rule of law and the democratic order. An old maxim about the rule of law holds that it is a lesser iniquity that several guilty go unpunished than for one innocent person to pay for a crime. Inquiries into the terrorist attacks through the first decade of the millennium in India, have seen this iniquity writ large. The profiling of those of a certain faith as inherently prone to terrorist action while others function with blatant impunity, corrodes public faith in the rule of law and could potentially fuel a self-perpetuating cycle of vigilante action. In this respect, the hamhanded and cynically biased investigations into terrorist strikes are succeeding where the bombs have failed: in cementing the widespread belief among the country's largest religious minority, that the institutional discrimination they suffer is being ever more deeply imbedded. If a united and well-informed citizenry is the prime requirement for a successful defence of civil society and the State, the official investigations may well be creating conditions for the reverse outcome.

A similar official attitude has been manifest as the Maoist insurgency has gained momentum in recent years in areas of India where indigenous communities or Adivasis have a large presence. Internally much more differentiated than Muslims or Dalits – since they have been more remote from the forces of modernity which drive homogenisation – and yet to achieve real coherence in their political challenge to mainstream nationalism, Adivasi communities could rapidly be emerging in the hegemonic media narrative as a distinct category. Much of the new narrative involving Adivasis is likely to be constructed in response to episodes of violence that erupt in their main areas of settlement in the central forested plains of India. What idiom the media will invent for the Adivasi identity still remains to be determined.

The attitude towards Dalits and backward classes is at once patronising and anxious. The affectation of a benign superiority blends with a certain wariness about the threat these sections pose to the enclaves of modernity the media celebrates. This is as much a consequence of those who speak through the Indian media, as of who it speaks to. In 2006, a survey of the British media found that of the senior journalists with decisive influence over news priorities and editorial policy, a significant majority is drawn from a narrow, privately-schooled, Oxbridge-educated elite. Indeed, as British society becomes more diverse and the political system grapples with the challenge of inclusion, the media – if a comparison were to be made with similar data from the mid-1980s – has tended to become an enclave of class privilege. As reported in the *Guardian*, the dominance of the upper crust was strong enough to ensure that it is "difficult for those from other backgrounds to get a foothold".[56]

These findings from distant shores were published in 2006, at roughly the same time that a decision by the Indian government to set aside a fixed proportion of seats in the higher education system for classes of citizens disadvantaged by history, had ignited a debate on the quality of representation afforded by Indian democracy. Among the institutions that came in for examination, though rather briefly, was the media.

A survey prompted by the decision to expand the scope of reservations – labelled Mandal II – found that in a sample of 315 journalists in the national capital with the authority to determine media agendas, not one belonged to either a Scheduled Caste or Tribe.[57] No fewer than 49 per cent of the sample was drawn from the Brahminical strata. And if all caste Hindu groups were to be considered in addition to the so-called *dwija* or twice-born, their share in the total was no less 88 per cent.

Where Scheduled Castes and Tribes are concerned, the argument over affirmative action was settled as part of the nationalist compact which brought India its independence. That the media should be a zone of liberation from the participation of these classes, well into India's sixth decade as a sovereign, self-governing nation, should surely

56 Gibson (2006).

57 Varadarajan (2006).

be occasion for introspection by a social institution that has pretensions to objectivity and fairness.[58]

It is a far from settled point that one is where one comes from. An individual's social origins do not determine his outlook: indeed, that notion of determinacy would be completely antithetical to all conceptions of individual liberty. It could be a valid proposition though, that a psychology of conformity could operate within large aggregations of individuals. Particular individuals could well transcend the limitations imposed by the circumstances of their origin and their accumulation of lived experience. Personal commitments and convictions though, could well get submerged in large groups, in the overriding pressure to do what is accepted.

In 1990, when the Indian media faced its first significant challenge on the question of affirmative action for the backward classes, it responded by invoking the sacred trope of a seamless Indian national identity and denouncing the divisiveness of caste. Having identified the augmentation of "competitiveness" within the backward classes as a national priority, the media then lapsed into a phase of inattention. When liberalisation and globalisation kicked in as India's official economic policy in 1991, the media eagerly joined the chorus of acclaim. The withdrawal of the State from domains where its interventions were not essential, the media confidently forecast, would enable it to more effectively meet the basic needs of a wider mass of the population. In its turn, the easing of the onerous burden of taxes that the more affluent bore, would ignite the spark of entrepreneurship, since individual self-aggrandisement was the most powerful incentive for productive economic activity. As the size of the national product increased, the diminution in rates of taxation would more than pay for itself in buoy-

58 On the missing Dalit in the Indian newsroom, see also Jeffrey (2010): 200-215: "For now, Dalits are too vulnerable either to proclaim their 'Dalitness' to their newspapers when they do have jobs or to start newspapers of their own. The handful in journalism in the 1990s must try to 'pass' and to write the sorts of stories their superiors expect. Readers will continue to receive newspapers which are the outcome of Dalits' 'not being there', and which reinforce ideologically the material weaknesses from which Dalits suffer. Newspapers tell readers that Dalits are poor, naïve, ignorant; victims, and sometimes perpetrators, of violence; in short, people who almost never travel, eat, or get married." Also see the more recent article by TV news anchor Ravish Kumar (2015).

ant tax revenues, empowering the State with ample means to address its basic welfare commitments.

It took the resurrection of Mandal, this time in the shape of reservations for backward classes in institutions of higher education funded by the Central Government, to reawaken media interest in the gigantic defaults of social welfare policy through the 1990s. Initial editorial reactions to the notification of a wider scope of reservations for the OBCs in 2005 tended to be fairly uniform in their emphases. By providing preferential access to higher education, the government had effectively reversed priorities, said the media. Remedying inherited social disabilities was undoubtedly a national priority, but these needed to start with the basics of the learning process. Higher learning should be reserved as a domain where merit alone prevailed, where selection processes were entirely free of extraneous concerns. This national priority would not conflict with others, such as the redressal of the iniquities of history, if opportunities for all sections were to be equalised through a universal and non-discriminatory system of school education.

These recommendations carry a strong patronising flavour, with an inherent suggestion that the backward classes were yet to prove their worth for the professions, since they had not quite passed the threshold of qualifying through the primary education stage.

Media neutrality as a myth

Rather than risk further alienating public sentiments by incessantly hammering away at this theme, the media chose a line of retreat. In an early editorial, the *TOI* argued (May 31, 2006), that the available data base for public policy on affirmative action was seriously flawed. This made a "caste census" in India a "necessary evil". Later, the same newspaper (June 14, 2006) deprecated the fact that *ad hoc* decisions had for long held the field when "the need of the hour" was a "coherent justification" and a "clear roadmap for future policy on reservations". Since several of the classes that had reservation benefits through earlier generations had graduated out of backwardness, there was a case for a continuing process of review of beneficiaries. And the quantum of reservations itself needed to be revisited, since a "blind application of the maximum permitted reservation… speaks very poorly of government policy".

The *IE* though remained fundamentally unreconciled, arguing that reservations threatened to fatally erode India's potential to contribute to the global knowledge economy, where its competitive advantages were well established. Editorially (June 5, 2006), it poured scorn on the political opportunism of ambitious individuals that had ostensibly triggered off the furore. It warned that the "space for liberal policymaking (had) been won after a long political fight". In the course of this struggle, the more "intelligent leaders" of Indian politics, had realised that "quality and efficiency, in most fields, cannot simply be mandated by fiat". This hard fought gain, the *IE* bemoaned, was at risk of being squandered in the pursuit of political advantage by ambitious individuals.

The Economic Times belatedly awoke to the merits of an alternative to the reservations process that has for long been established practice in Delhi's Jawaharlal Nehru University (JNU). Editorially, it urged the Central Government to "universalise" the JNU admissions model, "which awards booster points for various kinds of backwardness..". "Scarcity accentuates social fissures", it warned, and any *a priori* segregation of seats for particular classes would deepen the sense of grievance among those who did not have the privilege to call themselves "backward".

Editorially, *The Hindu* (May 25) urged that three imperatives be borne in mind in implementing reservations. The commitment that discrimination in favour of the backward classes would not diminish opportunities for others needed to be operationalised. This meant that the central government had to "get serious about strengthening (the) physical and academic infrastructure" of the institutions it was directly responsible for. "Funds", the newspaper commented "should not be hard to come by, given the buoyancy in revenues". Second, the newspaper urged that in "the larger interests of the nation", certain institutions were "to be retained as islands of excellence, their entrance standards uncompromised even by socially desirable goals". And finally, the central government should steer clear of the political trap that several states had fallen into, of viewing affirmative action as merely the institution of quotas. A far more serious approach towards basic education was essential if the ultimate purposes of protective discrimination were to be met.

Editorially, the media tended in comparison with the first visitation of Mandal, to adopt a more restrained tone of commentary in relation to the second. But editorial comment is perhaps the lesser role the media plays in moments of deep social turmoil. By far the greater influence is exerted by the tone and content of news coverage. And in this respect, some of the biases that were blatantly in evidence during Mandal I did resurface, though they were expressed with noticeably greater restraint.

Politics of outrage: an Indian story

India has had several close encounters with the politics of laughter and outrage, those opposed but symmetric responses to words that challenge and images that stir. In 2012, a textbook designed by an official body, the National Council for Educational Research and Training (NCERT), was found to have a cartoon that allegedly made an object of ridicule of B.R. Ambedkar, revered by millions at the bottom tiers of an ascriptive and oppressive caste Hindu order, as a liberator who showed the way to a just order. This cartoon referred to Ambedkar's other role, which in his own perception, was the lesser one, as chair of India's constitution drafting committee soon after independence, and was featured in textbooks designed and printed under the supervision of an NCERT expert body.

The cartoon in question appeared in a textbook for class 11 and was sourced from the 1949 work of one of India's pioneers in media satire, K. Shankara Pillai, commonly referred to as Shankar. It referred to the early difficulties encountered in evolving a consensus on the Indian constitution and portrayed Ambedkar perched atop a snail, seeking hard to impart some pace to its slow and clumsy movement. Prime Minister Jawaharlal Nehru meanwhile stood to the side, with a whip in his hand seemingly administering a chastisement of the flesh to Ambedkar. A crowd of people stood and gazed in evident amusement at the situation while the cartoonist's caption read: "at a snail's pace".

India's parliament came to know of this cartoon in May 2012, triggering an immediate furore.[59] The cartoon trope of a whip that Nehru employed against Ambedkar was deemed an inexcusable reference to

---

59 Early academic reaction tended to see the furore as a big fuss over a trivial issue, See *The Hindu* (2012b).

oppressive caste tradition, an invocation of the casual brutality that brahmins and others at the top of the hierarchy inflicted upon those deemed of lesser birth. Parliamentarians from the Dalit strata, which Ambedkar had few qualms about identifying as the "untouchable", were particularly vociferous in demanding that the slight be remedied and appropriate apologies rendered.

An exegesis of the cartoon and its author's intent followed. It was found that Shankar made frequent metaphoric use of the whip in his work, with at least one other instance coming to light when Nehru was administering similar chastisement to quite another politician – this time of brahminical birth – in his impatience at the glacial pace of reform and change India had sunk into following independence. That alibi though was quickly and with some justification, dismissed as insufficient since cartooning tropes necessarily referred to larger contexts. By way of analogy, the whip in the hand of a western white man would be unremarkable if portrayed in any manner of a relationship with another of kindred race. But were a black man pictured as receiving the ministrations of the whip, the reference would be explicit to slave plantations and the regime of brutality black people were subject to. It was in other words, no extenuation for the cartoonist that he had portrayed Nehru applying the whiplash to the very brahminical chief minister of Bombay State at the time, Morarji Desai. There was still the distinct stench of casteism that remained undispelled, in the representation of Ambedkar as recipient of the lash.

Others pointed out that Ambedkar too held a whip in his hand which he was applying to the snail that he sat on. The snail evidently was a representation of the Indian Constituent Assembly which comprised largely, men of the upper castes. So the alleged indignity inflicted on Ambedkar was simultaneously being transferred to another collectivity of persons from the same upper caste cohort as Nehru. The insults were evened out, leaving no reason for any sense that Ambedkar was being singled out because of his origins in the "untouchable" strata of Hinduism.

Questions then turned to the crowd of people standing around and laughing at the spectacle of Nehruvian ire at the snail's pace of constitutional writing. Was this not evidence that Ambedkar was being subject to caste derision? Yet here again, a riposte of some credibility was quick to emerge. The sense of popular mirth was in terms of historical context, accurate and directed at the prolonged agonising in the Constituent Assembly over fine matters of detail, rather than at the person who was guiding its deliberations.

If text and context were subject to conflicting and often ambiguous interpretations, there were a number of misgivings over transporting the cartoon from its distant location in space and time into a contemporary milieu where caste prejudices still flourished. In the eyes of a school teacher steeped in caste-based prejudice, the cartoon would have a significance very different than intended by its author or by those who in their naivete had rendered it a pedagogical tool.

Yet this argument seemed to pre-empt the outcome – if any such singular result could be predicted – of a complex process of social engagement with a cartoon that could be and was read at multiple levels. Within the textbook, the cartoon was part of a wider background describing – in words – the complexities of constitution writing in a newly independent India. It was intended moreover, to provoke the reflections of a student body which brought diverse experiences to bear in its response to specific textual and visual stimuli. School environments tend to import and on occasion intensify prejudices from the wider social milieu.[60] A cartoon of very benign intent dropped into this toxic environment, it was argued with seeming good reason, could trigger unforeseen reverberations.

The assumption that an encounter between a cartoon from a different era and the bruising contemporary realities of caste oppression should necessarily end adversely, in a deepening of prejudice, was however, open to question. There were several who saw the possibility of a positive outcome. Prejudgement in the matter, especially in the imposition of a form of censorship on a satirical production that for its time, was a well-intended reflection on history in the making, seemed to verge perilously close to escapism, the determination to keep all cultural production of multiple and ambivalent meanings out of the public discourse for fear of pushing beyond the limits of a safe and sanitised social discourse.

---

60 The range of reactions is portrayed in *The Hindu* (2012c), which ends with an assertion that cartoons should not be spared rigorous interrogation merely on grounds of tolerance for humour.

Positions soon hardened and members of the panel that had designed the textbook quit their posts under pressure of the public inquisition. That same day, the office of one among them, in the city of Pune, was raided and ransacked by irate political activists. Under a government *diktat*, the offending work was purged from the textbook, ensuring that cartoons would remain suspect as a didactic device for long.[61]

A similar frisson of outrage over alleged caste insult followed a few months later, involving the social psychologist and current affairs commentator Ashis Nandy. As a determined critic of modernity and self-declared gadfly always in quest of orthodoxies to demolish, Nandy is a highly sought after participant in media events and celebrity salons. During one such salon, the Jaipur Literature Festival in January 2013, he was called upon during a marquee conversation with a well-known publisher, to comment on the upsurge of public outrage over official malfeasance and corruption in the months and years just past. His response was by all accounts, a monument to the art of mis-speaking in public. On that, there was little disagreement. But there was also a case made that his statement reflected malice and an unapologetic pandering to caste privilege, utterly demeaning to those struggling against formidable odds for a life of dignity.

Prefaced with an explicit acknowledgment that he was about to tread into the territory of the "vulgar", Nandy tackled the question he was pitched by ascribing most of the corruption witnessed in India to those of lesser caste status. He then threw in a note of irony. Contrary to the popular belief that corruption corroded the innards of democracy, he seemed to celebrate it as a form of sustenance of the republican order. Amid interruptions and some outrage, he continued after pinning all that was corrupt on those of lesser privilege to declare that "as long as this is the case, (the) Indian Republic will survive".[62]

It was evident that Nandy had stumbled in his quest for an idiom that would be clever, outrageous and sympathetic to the under-privileged at the same time. And the response from the ranks of Dalit activ-

61 *The Hindu* (2012a).

62 Anand (2013) provides a full account of the controversy, though from a standpoint particularly opposed to Nandy's case and conceding him no slack.

ists did not disappoint. Those with a foot in the political realm called for Nandy's prosecution under the law that criminalises insults in word or deed to those excluded under the caste hierarchy. Others did him the magnanimity of sparing him criminal prosecution, since that would be an absurd situation when impunity was the law for perpetrators of brutal physical atrocities, including mass killings, against Dalits. Nandy's locutions nevertheless became an exhibit in the continuing narrative assembled by Dalit activists over the abuse of free speech by those unaware of their caste privilege. The ironic moral inversion in his words, which transformed corruption from an unmitigated evil to the lifeblood of the republican political order, was missed out in the process. There are elements of truth undoubtedly in the demand that those who posture as public intellectuals need to be more attentive to the sensibilities of those unlike them. But the test of intent that is customarily used to determine when free speech steps beyond acceptable bounds cannot be dispensed with. Nor can the demand that free speech should be assessed only against the template of fearless listening, in which an ear for irony – even of the most unsubtle kind – is an irreplaceable component. Fearless listening and a willingness to grant the benefit of the doubt, are necessary parts of the compact of civility without which speech of any form would be impossible.

Social conflict and the limits of media objectivity

Its proximity with community identities makes media functioning in a situation of conflict especially crucial. Is the function of accurate reporting uppermost, even if it is disconnected from moral judgments? Or is an ethical posture inherent even in the most dispassionate account of any event or sequence of events? Does a well-considered effort at ascribing responsibility for a state of inequality, which does not hesitate to name winners and losers, aggravate an already inflamed situation? Or does it, by focusing attention on the sources of injustice, impel society at large to root out the viruses within its fold?

If any convincing answers have been devised to these questions, they are yet to be elucidated. Neither are they evident in the existing practice of the media. Publishing media content that is in conformity with a placid and uncontested paradigm of social evolution would be acceptable conduct, because it serves elite interests and safeguards their social preeminence. Anything that departs from this idiom would be behaviour warranting stricture and quite possibly, sanction.

Similar is the dilemma that arises when dealing with media functioning in a context of social conflict. Persistent states of inequality which the media does not pay serious attention to, often contribute to outbreaks of violence in which the victims of inequality themselves become prime targets. Should the media then report things as they are, putting the violence in context and seeking out its roots in the state of inequality that nurtured it? Or disguise these facts for fear of aggravating the immediate violence, obscuring the structural violence of persistent inequality?

This spawns a host of derivative questions which have no obvious answers, since they touch upon the very fundamentals of media functioning. After long years of smug acquiescence in the agenda of globalisation, realities caught up a decade into the twenty-first century, compelling the media to come up with persuasive answers. It was obviously unrealistic to expect an instant departure from the mainstream narrative and a media discourse more accommodative of differences of perception and reflective of the diversities of the social milieu. At just that time, new options for self-expression presented by evolving technologies emerged, potentially presenting the public with various strategies to steadily undermine and finally extinguish the power of the privately-owned, profit-motivated media, in determining broader social agendas.

A noted scholar on the Indian media recently wrote, following Ernest Renan, that if "nationalism is a daily referendum", then purchasing a newspaper constitutes a vote of affirmation.[63] Clearly, there are also inherent in this daily ritual, multiple layers of meaning of who constitute the nation and who are its "minorities". In the years since 1990, the Indian elite which continues to imagine the nation in English (though with the growth of the electronic media, no longer exclusively in print) has stepped more confidently out of its sequestration and become a player on a global stage. But it is yet to figure out a satisfactory answer to the troublesome question of how it is to deal with the "minorities" within the fold of the nation, which are represented and reproduced by the media in the image that the "mainstream" would like to cast them in.

63 Jeffrey (2000): 6.

The State
Exceptions and the uses of ambiguity

In June 2008, police in the city of Ahmedabad in Gujarat state, brought charges of sedition and criminal conspiracy against two journalists and the local edition of India's largest English language newspaper, the *Times of India* (*TOI*). The complaint named the resident editor and a reporter in the *TOI*'s Ahmedabad office, as the principal accused, aside from the publisher who held ultimate responsibility for all material appearing in print. This followed a series of reports that looked at the service record of the city's police commissioner, O.P. Mathur, and found disturbing evidence of abuses of power and liaisons with the underworld.

Inducted into the elite Indian Police Service (IPS) in 1975, Mathur had been subject of a number of administrative inquiries, most of which had failed to turn up any evidence of wrongdoing, partly because of the Indian bureaucracy's unique innocence of the notion of a conflict of interests. This in turn resulted in every administrative inquiry being entrusted to either the agency under scrutiny or its siblings in the clerical order of the Indian state. On top of this came the caste exclusivity of the IPS cadre and its determination to disallow the ignominy of criminal prosecution to any among its own.

The two journalists and the publisher of *TOI*'s Ahmedabad edition were granted bail pending full hearing of the case.[1] Police commis-

1 The stories published over four days on the front page of the *TOI*'s Ahmedabad edition, tell their story rather vividly in their headlines:

sioner Mathur meanwhile served out his term, retiring in March 2009 and securing a happy post-retirement billet as head of an Ahmedabad-based university dedicated to security training.[2]

In April 2012, the Gujarat High Court finally ruled on applications seeking that sedition charges be quashed, quoting from two key judgments of the Supreme Court from 1950 and 1962, seemingly lost till then in the thicket of contrary rulings that followed. From the *Romesh Thapar* judgment of 1950, the Gujarat High Court drew the lesson that "criticism of Government exciting disaffection or bad feelings towards it is not to be regarded as a ground justifying restrictions on the freedom of expression and of the press unless it is such as to undermine the security of or tend to overthrow the State". From *Kedar Nath Singh*, the court drew the principle that "a citizen has a right to say or write whatever he likes about the Government or its measures, by way of criticism or comment, so long as he does not incite people to violence against the Government established by law". It would be a deep violation of the constitutional right to free speech to invoke the sedition clause even without these conditions being satisfied, i.e., to say that the "use of words .. which merely create disaffection or feelings of enmity" against the Government is sufficient cause for prosecution.

The Gujarat High Court on this occasion also called up one of its own rulings on a related theme. It had held as "well-settled judicial precedent" that "words, deeds or writings" could be deemed seditious "only if they incite violence or disturb law and order or create public disorder or have the intention or tendency to do so". Summoning up all these long forgotten precedents, the Gujarat High Court ruled that "a

---

"How can Ahmedabad be safe in his hands", (May 28); "OPM Ahmedabad can do without" (May 29); "Crooked path to the crown" (May 30); and "Latif an ISI man and Mathur a Latif man" (May 31). OPM is a reference to Mathur and Latif to an underworld don who controlled the bootleg trade in the prohibition state of Gujarat. He was accused of complicity in a devastating serial bombing in the western city of Mumbai in 1993, arrested in 1995 and killed while allegedly trying to escape from custody in 1997. The International Federation of Journalists posted a media release on its website on June 4, 2008, reporting all details of the chargesheet filed against *TOI* by Mathur.

2 Mathur was the first Vice Chancellor of the Raksha Shakti University, set up by the Gujarat State Government in 2009. Details on the university and how it was conceived can be found at its website: http://www.rakshashaktiuniversity.edu.in/.

citizen has a right to say or write whatever he likes about the Government, or its measures, by way of criticism or comment, so long as he does not incite people to violence against the Government established by law" or contribute with intent to "creating public disorder". Promoting disaffection and disloyalty is not the same thing as "commenting in strong terms upon the measures or acts of the Government, or its agencies, so as to ameliorate the condition of the people or to secure the cancellation or alteration of those acts or measures by lawful means".

To question the prudence of an appointment at a high-level in the police hierarchy, to wonder if the Government has applied "due diligence" in arriving at its decisions, to identify certain individuals who may have vitiated the decision-making process, and to challenge a chief executive of the state government to disprove the reasonable inference that these factors collectively cast a shadow over his claims to being a champion of the struggle against terrorism, did not amount to the crime of sedition.[3]

Silence as servant of public safety

In deciding on the legality of restricting basic rights on grounds of a putative threat to "public safety", the Supreme Court in the case of *Romesh Thapar* found that "public safety" as a rationale for extraordinary exercises of power, could cover a number of eventualities, such as an outbreak of disease, or an epidemic of rash driving on the streets. Admittedly, these were not quite as serious a threat as an effort to overthrow political authority and the rule of law. But even while acknowledging that element of triviality in bringing these diverse situations within the same judicial logic, the Supreme Court felt compelled to caution against the assumption of extraordinary powers by the State. Once granted, this extraordinary power to intrude into the freedom of others could not be effectively contained. There was no "guarantee", the Supreme Court held, that "those authorised to exercise the powers under the Act will in using them discriminate between those who act prejudicially to the security of the State and those who do not". Once armed with extraordinary powers, the officers of the State could not be trusted to make adequate distinction between traffic offenders – where summary punishment may be warranted consistent with the magni-

3 Gujarat High Court (2012).

tude of the crime – and those who they see as inconveniences or impediments to the unfettered assertion of their authority.

TOI was able to secure a relatively quick release from its travails with sedition law. Four years to secure a full discharge of criminal charges under Indian penal law must be considered a state of bliss, when the accused have not had the misfortune of spending a day in the custody of the law. Quite conceivably, the intent of the Ahmedabad police in bringing charges of sedition against the biggest entity in the Indian media scene, was not to take the matter to prosecution – merely to silence the newspaper long enough for an officer with obvious political patronage to serve out his tenure in a prize posting. Media groups endowed with financial muscle and political clout should in any case, be expected to have an easier time negotiating the vagaries of the law. That luxury is not available to most media practitioners who work outside the patronage of big business groups.

Multiple instances exist, concurrent with the *TOI* case, when individual journalists working with small and independent media platforms have been slapped with equally severe charges and suffered considerably more.

In September 2011, a tribal youth actively involved in citizen journalism networks, Lingaram Kodopi, was arrested on charges of raising funds for Maoist insurgents in the central Indian state of Chhattisgarh. As a journalist from an indigenous community, Kodopi was a rarity in the state, with unique access to the lives of a very substantial part of the population which remained under-represented in most institutions. Kodopi had been active in bringing these most often unheard voices into the public discourse, filing reports for the mobile phone and internet-based citizen journalism service *CGNet Swara*. These in turn had been instrumental in bringing to light serious civilian casualties inflicted by a major anti-insurgency operation in Tarmedla in a southern Chhattisgarh district in March 2011. Though he had no direct role in that particular news report, Kodopi's arrest was widely seen as retribution and a signal to any others who may volunteer for citizen journalism. The authorities clearly had no use for any mode of information transaction that potentially expanded the public discourse beyond the manufactured consensus of Chhattisgarh's mainstream media.

Reports indicated that Kodopi had a history of victimisation at the hands of the state police force. He was arrested in August 2009 and held for forty days and only released early in October after his family filed a *habeas corpus* petition in the state high court. In July 2010, he was named by the Superintendent of Police in the southern district of Dantewada in Chhattisgarh, as the mastermind behind an attack on the residence of a local political leader, in which one person was killed. He was at the time, enrolled in a journalism institute in a suburb of Delhi, undergoing a year-long training programme.

Kodopi's aunt Soni Sori, a schoolteacher, also detained along with him, was reportedly severely tortured in prison. The charges against them included the transfer of a large sum of money from a big mining enterprise with major stakes in Chhattisgarh, to units of the Maoist underground. The corporate official arrested for being the primary source of the funds, was since released on bail, while Kodopi and Sori continued being held.[4]

The clear double standards that smaller publications suffer in relation to the larger and better organised media organisations, especially where they involve the Adivasi and the Dalit, have been evident in a number of other cases. On January 2, 2011, police in Wardha district in India's western state of Maharashtra, arrested Sudhir Dhawale, as he was on his way back from a convention on Adivasi and Dalit literature. Editor of a magazine of dissenting opinion titled *Vidrohi* (which translates literally as "rebel") and a freelance contributor to numerous other publications, Dhawale was booked under provisions of the law dealing with sedition and waging war against the State. According to police accounts, the basis for his arrest was the purported interrogation of a leader of the banned Communist Party of India (Maoist), taken into custody a few days before. Dhawale was held in custody for forty months, repeatedly denied bail, before finally being discharged on all counts in May 2014.[5]

Several abuses occurred under the rubric of the "global war on terror", with its axiomatic premise that Islamic extremism was the

---

4 The details are recorded in IFJ-SAMSN (2012): 25.

5 Details of the case are recounted in Dhawale's own words in an interview with the New York based Committee to Protect Journalists, see Dhawale (2014a), also Dhawale (2014b).

singular fount for the malevolent ideology that "civilisation" was in unrelenting struggle against. Investigative journalist K.K. Shahina was charged with criminal conspiracy to intimidate witnesses, after her story published December 2010 in the weekly magazine *Tehelka* appeared to cast doubt on the prosecution on terrorism charges of a prominent Islamic cleric and political figure. Shahina's story was based on interviews with key witnesses cited in the case made by police in the southern state of Karnataka against Abdul Nasar Madani, an Islamic cleric who heads the Peoples' Democratic Party, active mainly in the neighbouring state of Kerala. Madani had been arrested and charged by Karnataka police for conspiracy to detonate a series of low-intensity bombs in the state capital of Bengaluru, hub of India's information technology industry, in July 2008. Shahina's story cited several of the witnesses named by the Karnataka police as saying that their testimony had been misinterpreted or distorted in making out charges against Madani.

Investigative journalism that held up actions of the police to the light of public scrutiny was transformed in this manner, into a cause for criminal prosecution.[6] Facing the possibility of arrest since January 2011, Shahina was granted anticipatory bail by the Karnataka High Court in July 2011. Following summons issued after charges were formally laid against her in January 2013, Shahina appeared before a court in Somwarpet in Kodagu district of Karnataka, to renew her bail. The courtroom where the bail hearing was scheduled was besieged by activists of the right-wing political group, the Bajrang Dal, just as Shahina made her appearance. Shahina and a few friends who accompanied her to the hearing, were reportedly threatened by the activists, who also insisted that a cameraperson show them the visuals he had recorded, to ensure that they could not be identified in public.

Iftikhar Gilani, a Kashmiri journalist based in Delhi, was arrested in June 2002 and held for seven months on charges of espionage and violations of the Official Secrets Act. The basis of his arrest was the discovery in his possession of certain documents, relating to men and materiel of the Indian Army. This information was then in the public domain and freely available on various websites. India's Defence Ministry initially made a submission in the trial court hearing his case that the documents were indeed, classified information. It later changed

6 See IFJ-SAMSN (2012): 19 for full details.

this plea and filed an affidavit that stated the reverse. Gilani was discharged after seven months in detention. The probable reason for his arrest was a vendetta against a near relative, who was for long among the most prominent of the dissident political leaders in Kashmir, insistent that the issue of the state's accession to India was a far from settled matter.[7]

Channels available for self-expression have proliferated with the arrival of the internet. Access to the public space – where information is exchanged and opinions ventilated – has escaped older modes of control. Many among the new entrants into the public sphere believe they are at liberty to express themselves – indeed that they have secured a way around the constraints imposed by older patterns of media ownership. Within the larger context of the steady retreat of the Indian State from the constitutional promise of free speech, police and other agencies in India have responded to a rapidly changing scenario with a deliberate disregard of judicial precedent. Invocations of the law on sedition have become a favoured recourse in pursuing localised and personal vendettas. And in virtually all these instances, actions are taken with the knowledge that charges brought will never stand up to the rigour of the trial process, though they would serve the expedient function of silencing critical media commentary and quashing dissent.

A short history of crimes against the Indian state

Views expressed during India's Constituent Assembly (CA) debates on fundamental rights, clearly were reflective of the sense of deprivation suffered under the repressive colonial *raj*.[8] One of the demands made was for the right to bear arms, specifically denied under the *raj*, since some among the Adivasi communities found peaceful assembly as a right incomplete, unless it allowed weapons displayed as an emblem of identity. A speaker also argued for repealing the Arms Act – an inheritance of the *raj* which restricted the right to bear arms – since that would make the people more courageous and "manly". H.V. Kamath, a member of Subhas Bose's Forward Bloc who split over its decision to

7 In his book, Gilani (2005) provides a full account of the circumstances of his arrest, his mistreatment in prison, and the tenuousness of the case against him.

8 Parliament of India (1948).

withdraw from the CA, argued the case for both press freedom and the right to bear arms. Kamath was perhaps inspired in some measure by the first and second amendments to the U.S. constitution which have ever since been a contentious inheritance, especially in the mandate that judges of a "strict constructionist" persuasion claim from the latter, in blocking any sane effort at controlling violent gun crime.

Kamath was followed soon afterwards by Ananthasayanam Ayyangar, who refuted the case for explicit recognition of press freedom or the right to bear arms. The right to bear arms was especially troubling, since it could descend into lawlessness in exactly the Hobbesian sense. The use of force had no place in a democracy and even when called for, had to be "concentrated in the State". Unwittingly or otherwise, Ayyangar was echoing Max Weber's famous formulation of the state as the agency with a monopoly of "legitimate violence". Ayyangar drew Kamath's ire by suggesting that those of youthful and impetuous disposition did not need arms to impose their will on others. He was quick with the disavowal of any personal imputation and an intervention from the chair cooled frayed tempers. Ayyangar went on to dismiss the explicit guarantee of "freedom of thought", which certain members had insisted on, as a superfluity. Nobody could really interfere with another's thought processes; what was germane indeed, was only the right to free speech, which would make "press freedom" a needless embellishment.

Summing up, B.R. Ambedkar acknowledged that all Ayyangar's points could as well be his own. The press would have no specific charter of rights under Indian law, he said: its rights and entitlements, no different from any citizen's, would be enshrined in the fundamental rights section of the Indian Constitution and in particular, article 19, which was about freedom of expression, commerce, association and much else.

Convinced of the centrality of fundamental rights within the constitutional scheme, the CA discussed the relevant section over several days. As one of the speakers then put it, article 13 of the draft constitution (which later became article 19) was truly the "charter of our liberties" and "probably the most important article in the whole Draft Constitution". Several among the members felt the draft provisions did not reflect the range of aspirations of the Indian people. Indeed, there were suspicions that the bureaucracy – an inheritance of colonialism interested more in order than liberty – had introduced far too many restrictions on the fundamental rights as defined in a 1947 draft.[9] The overhanging trauma of the killings and mass human migrations that occurred with the partition of India was an obvious deterrent and it is a tribute to the CA members who made the pitch for a strong fundamental rights section, that this experience did not dilute their insistence on a broad charter of liberties, rather than one severely qualified by fear of disorder.

Granville Austin, an early scholar of the Indian constitutional process, has described this phase of debate as a triumph of "liberty" over "bureaucracy".[10] Two notable drafting changes reflected this pushback against bureaucratic privilege. "Sedition" was removed from the conditions under which the fundamental right to free speech could be restricted. It did not seem right in the aftermath of freedom, that the robust criticism of established authority – a duty Mahatma Gandhi had enjoined as a citizen's basic commitment – should be criminalised. A second important change was a test of "reasonableness" on every restriction of the fundamental rights. This introduced a test akin to that of "due process", where judicial review would be applicable as a fetter on the arbitrary exercise of power.[11] A balance was restored to appease the bureaucracy, with the "restrictions" clause incorporating a number of contingencies where free speech would not limit the application of existing laws. In the language of the constitution as originally adopted, these contingencies were: "libel, slander, defamation, contempt of Court or any matter which offends against decency or morality or

---

9 Ibid. Kengal Hanumanthaiah, (later to be Chief Minister of Mysore state and Union Railway Minister) put it on December 2, 1948 as follows: "For the last sixty and odd years during which the freedom movement was taking shape, we made innumerable speeches and sacrifices in order to win the fundamental rights that are incorporated in this article. But, the point of view of many members here as well as the opinion of some people outside is that these fundamental rights have been so much curtailed that their original flavour is lost".

10 Austin (1966): 74.

11 Ibid. Curiously, in what seems oversight, "reasonableness" was not set down for any restriction that might be introduced in the free speech right.

which undermines the security of, or tends to overthrow, the State".[12] Neither would the free speech right impede the enactment of any law that stipulated how precisely these red lines would be honoured.

Fear of disorder

The entire exercise was swathed in ambiguity, allowing both for the manner of generalisation that Austin provides and for its exact opposite. Paul Brass has argued that the republican constitution of independent India was born "more in fear and trepidation than in hope and inspiration". There were in Brass's reading, several factors that contributed to the unsettled national mood, notably partition and war in Kashmir, near-insurrectionary conditions in Hyderabad state, and memories of famine and acute food scarcity from the war years. The "fear of disorder" was a looming presence all through the CA debates, leading to a number of qualifications being inscribed into the fundamental rights clauses, especially in matters of free speech and association. The numerous emergency powers assumed by the Central Government were also, Brass argues, a direct outcome of this sense of "trepidation".[13]

Within this confused melange, the constitution voided all laws "inconsistent with or in derogation of the fundamental rights", though only "to the extent of such inconsistency". Given this mix of immiscible principles – colonial repression and republican sentiment – challenges were quick to emerge in the political and judicial domains. The sequence of judicial determinations that followed was not distinguished for consistency of principle.

Within weeks of the adoption of the republican constitution, a challenge emerged on the left of the political spectrum, from Romesh Thapar, editor of the Communist Party journal *Crossroads* which was banned from circulation in Madras under a state statute.[14] In deciding

12 Effectively, this clause set up an unresolved tension with the fundamental rights clause – article 13 of the Constitution as adopted on November 26, 1949 – which required that all laws in violation of the provisions of the Constitution as it stood then would stand repealed.

13 Brass (2000): 66.

14 The law in question was the Madras (Maintenance of Public Order) Act, 1949, since superseded.

the case of *Romesh Thapar versus the State of Madras*, the Supreme Court held that the restrictions on *Crossroads* were unsustainable even after factoring in all exceptions to the free speech right. It was beyond doubt that "freedom of speech and expression includes freedom of propagation of ideas, and that freedom is ensured by the freedom of circulation". The restrictions imposed on the journal on grounds of "public security" did not pass tests prescribed under law. Indeed, said the majority on the Supreme Court bench: "Our attention has not been drawn to any definition of the expression 'public safety', nor does it appear that the words have acquired any technical signification as words of art".[15]

The Supreme Court majority noted that the CA had with deliberate intent omitted the word "sedition" – freely applied in the call to ban the newspaper – from the final text of the Indian constitution. As the five-judge majority read it, this underlined that "criticism of Government exciting disaffection or bad feelings towards it is not to be regarded as a justifying ground for restricting the freedom of expression and of the press, unless it is such as to undermine the security of or tend to overthrow the State".

On the basis of article 13 of the Constitution which required the deletion of all laws falling short of the standards of protection specified in the fundamental rights chapter, the Supreme Court held unconstitutional the provision of Madras provincial law under which the ban on *Crossroads* was enforced.[16]

---

15 Supreme Court of India (1950a). With elaborate apologies for seeming to trivialise the argument, the bench asked if a rash of reckless driving that caused traffic accidents; or an epidemic outbreak of disease, which also endangered public safety, would warrant similar restraints on free speech.

16 Another principle was upheld in the ruling: of the Supreme Court as the final guarantor of the fundamental rights. Romesh Thapar had then taken his plea for judicial remedy not to the High Court of Madras state which would under normal principles of judicial procedure, have had original jurisdiction in the matter, but to the Supreme Court. And the Supreme Court found this to be reasonable in terms of procedure. Even if a lower court had concurrent jurisdiction, the Supreme Court could not, as "the protector and guarantor of fundamental rights ... refuse to entertain applications seeking protection against infringements of such rights". Arguments of inappropriate choice of forum, drawn mainly from U.S. jurisprudence by advocates appearing for the respondents,

Brij Bhushan v State of Delhi was a challenge from the right, decided by the same bench on the same day, by a majority of five against one dissent. At issue was an order by the administration in the state of Delhi requiring that *Organiser*, a weekly magazine of extreme chauvinist dispositions, subject itself to pre-censorship. In the deeply fraught aftermath of independence and partition, administration efforts to maintain order were deemed to be dented by the journal's espousal of a virulently partisan position. Some journal content was also thought to be offensive to the fledgling government in the neighbouring state of Pakistan, whose cooperation was considered necessary for redressing the injuries of partition. In rendering its judgment, the Supreme Court held in *Brij Bhushan* that there was no constitutional basis for prior censorship of newspaper content.[17]

The logic of these judgments was carried towards a *reductio ad absurdum* of sorts by the Patna High Court which held in the matter of *Bharati Press*, that with public order disallowed as ground for restraining speech, "if a person were to go on inciting to murder or other cognisable offences either through the press or by word of mouth, he would be free to do so with impunity and that such utterances would not fall within the restrictions authorised by article 19(2) of the Constitution". This was a conclusion that the judges arrived at with obvious reluctance and with a tacit signal towards the Supreme Court to fill in the missing details. As one of the judges party to the judgment put it: "I wish that my decision on the point … would sooner than ever come to be tested by the Supreme Court itself and the position reexamined in the light of the anomalous situation pointed out above".[18]

Reasonable restrictions

Quick to correct what it saw as a gross misconstrual of its decisions, the Supreme Court still clung to the "security of the State" as its rationale, seemingly disinclined to give the criterion of "public order"

the Supreme Court held, were not on point since the constitutional system there was quite different.

17 Supreme Court of India (1950b).

18 Press Commission (1954:1): 362. More will be said on the formation and mandate of the Press Commission later, since this was perhaps the first attempt in independent India to evolve a theory of the media in a democratic order.

any degree of prominence. Disapproving the flippancy of the challenge that had been thrown its way from Patna, the Supreme Court held that "speeches or expressions on the part of an individual which incite to or encourage commission of violent crimes such as murder cannot but be matters which would undermine the security of the State and come within the ambit of law sanctioned by Article 19(2) of the Constitution".[19]

Parliament and the government seemingly did not have the patience to await a clarification from the highest judicial bench. The *Thapar* and *Brij Bhushan* judgments, along with a few others that held affirmative action for those disadvantaged by custom and tradition contrary to the "equality clause", were the immediate trigger for the first amendments to the Constitution, introduced by Prime Minister Nehru in the Lok Sabha in May 1951. The amendment bill inserted the rather broad term "in the interests of", to propose that "reasonable restrictions" on free speech could be imposed for a variety of ends. Among these, "friendly relations with a foreign state" was introduced as a ground specifically to counteract the *Brij Bhushan* judgment and "public order" to neutralise *Romesh Thapar*. The first amendment also removed the explicit reference that a speech act should "undermine" or "tend to overthrow" the State, to attract legal sanction or prohibition.[20]

The first constitutional amendment was given retrospective validity, retrieving from the trash bin a number of laws deemed violative of fundamental rights by the *Romesh Thapar* and *Brij Bhushan* rulings.[21] Soon afterwards, Parliament passed the Press (Objectionable Material) Act of 1951 (hereafter, POMA) which allowed the seizure of printed material and provided for the forfeiture of assets of newspapers that fell foul of the law. In contrast to the general formulations employed in the first amendment bill, POMA laid down very specific conditions in which harsh punitive measures could be employed. It would for instance, apply to printed material that urged withholding of food and essential commodities and services to any section of the people, induced acts of insubordination or disloyalty by members of the armed

19 Ibid: 363.

20 Parliament of India (1951).

21 Press Commission (1954:1): 378.

forces, or contributed to any criminal act such as extortion or blackmail, murder or mob violence.[22]

The law had a curious genesis. Even prior to final agreement on the language of the constitution, the Government had appointed a committee to review and recommend changes to the entire range of laws applicable to the press. The committee submitted its report in May 1948 after reviewing a number of laws, some of them enabling extraordinary controls and restraints, such as the Indian Press (Emergency Powers) Act of 1931, the Official Secrets Act of 1923, the Indian States (Protection) Act of 1934, and a number of "public safety acts" at the provincial level. A complex mix of legislative measures was proposed, including outright repeal, amendment, and the incorporation of some of the provisions of these laws into ordinary civil and criminal law. Rather than sample this complex menu, Parliament in 1951 – soon after adopting the first amendment – enacted POMA, which echoed the Emergency Powers Act of 1931 in several unsettling respects.

The blow was softened to an extent, by providing for trials by juries drawn entirely from the press, for anybody indicted under the act. But this was regarded as a lame safeguard, since the law imposed sanctions unknown in other countries. It also imposed a double jeopardy on journalism, potentially holding practitioners liable under its clauses, aside from ordinary civil and criminal law. Some among India's senior editors then argued that the mere existence of the law was a stigma on the press.[23]

In 1950, with these constitutional debates underway, the Indian Federation of Working Journalists (IFWJ) was formed as the first nation-wide representative body of the profession. At the moment of its founding, the IFWJ presented a charter of demands that through public inquiry and reasoning, the newly independent nation identify the appropriate place for journalism within its civic space. This articulation converged for contingent reasons, with the views of other actors. To the government of the time, a body that would inquire into the role of the press in society seemed the best way to settle serious discord over the First Amendment to the constitution. Media owners saw the restraints on free speech as a threat to their liberties. Elements

22 Austin (1999): 49.

23 Press Commission (1954:1): 378-94.

within the ruling Congress party – notably Home Minister C. Rajagopalachari – also insisted that the legislation would only stifle freedom, when the press should be allowed space to work out its own regulatory modes through internal institutional mechanisms.

Society and the press

When a Press Commission to address this whole range of concerns was constituted in September 1952, with a distinguished jurist, V.G. Rajadhyaksha as chair and a membership comprising "a veritable galaxy of eminent persons", the IFWJ was effusive in welcoming it.[24] This was quite the opposite attitude as that of the Indian and Eastern Newspaper Society (IENS), an industry lobby set up during the war years and since renamed the Indian Newspaper Society (INS).

In the twenty months of data it had to study the application of POMA, the Press Commission recorded one hundred and thirty-four cases of publications being arraigned under its provisions. A vast majority – no fewer than eighty-six – were lodged under section 3(vi) of the act, which applied to the rather loosely defined term "scurrilous writing". Other cases had been lodged under the portmanteau section 3, which defined the entire range of purported "offences".

To the representation that POMA represented double jeopardy, the Press Commission demurred. "All that the (act) provides", it argued, "is that in the case of a first violation, newspapers can be called upon to furnish security and if there is a second violation the security is liable to be forfeited. As a consequence of this forfeiture the registration of the press and the declaration made by the publisher (would) stand cancelled with all the results flowing from such cancellation".[25]

The Press Commission was at pains to emphasise that a "large section" of the Indian press was "sober and responsible" and did not engage in "yellow journalism". This was especially so for the English language press, which was "by and large ... free from objectionable writings". However, there were elements in the press which sought to "flourish on blackmail, sensationalism and obscenity". And the Press Commission observations that follow are so rich in insights into early

---

24 Bhargava (2005): 36.

25 Press Commission (1954:1): 388.

insecurities of the Indian nation-building project, that they deserve quotation at some length:

> A section of the Tamil, Telugu and Malayalam Press which carries objectionable writings abounds in indecent or grossly obscene matter concerning Ministers and cinema stars. Recently there has been a tendency for some papers to create feelings of enmity and hatred between different classes of citizens. In the border States of West Bengal and Punjab the yellow Press tends to promote feelings of enmity and hatred between Bengalis and non-Bengalis, Hindus and Sikhs and Hindus and Muslims as also between neighbouring countries. A section of the Sikh Press both in Urdu and Punjabi seeks to incite violence in the name of the 10th Guru for the formation of a separate Punjabi State. A very small section of the Marathi Press was found to idolise (Gandhi's assassin Nathuram) Godse. There are a few periodicals in Marathi that indulge in obscenity. Recently there has been a tendency in the Gujarati and Marathi papers to resort to unjournalistic language in carrying on controversy for linguistic States. A section of the Gujarati Press in Saurashtra has tended to incite violence against some Ministers of the State Government. Perhaps the Urdu Press is the most culpable in this regard. There are comparatively more newspapers and periodicals published in Urdu than in any other regional language taking all the States of the Union together. A large section of the Urdu Press is controlled by communalists, Hindus as well as Muslims. It is not uncommon to find in those publications reproduction of inflammable (sic) writings from the Pakistan Press with the intention, on the one hand, to rouse Muslim feelings or, on the other, to charge the non-Muslims in India with callous indifference to the anti-Hindu spirit said to be prevalent in Pakistan.[26]

The mood was clearly shifting by the time the Press Commission completed its deliberations. Despite receiving a number of entreaties for repeal of the law, the Press Commission confessed its inability to convince those who mattered. It did conclude, though, that POMA's "continuance is not necessary or justified and ... it should not be allowed to remain on the statute even for a temporary period".[27] However, in what has been described as a "curious affair", POMA was amended several times before being repealed in 1957.[28] There is no known record of any serious challenge to its validity on constitutional grounds. There was reportedly one case heard in a High Court which upheld some of its more severe provisions. And in the ambience of indignation at what Prime Minister Nehru called some of the "wretch-

---

26 Ibid: 386.

27 Ibid: 447.

28 Austin (1999): 50.

ed rags" that had appeared on the publishing scene, a number of state governments enacted equally coercive laws that enabled them when required, to enforce compliance in the press.[29]

A problem area flagged by the Press Commission became in the next months, the flashpoint for another coercive effort at imposing a political *diktat* on the press. When bitter discord engulfed Punjab in 1957 over language policy, a number of orders were issued under the Punjab Special Powers (Press) Act. This was a special state law enacted in the aftermath of the first amendment, prohibiting the publication of content that could aggravate tensions between Punjabi and Hindi speakers. Orders issued under the act in 1957 empowered the government to prevent entry into the state, of publications even remotely seen to be carrying content that met that definition of aggravating linguistic differences.

In the case that came up soon afterwards, the Supreme Court held that a decisive change had been introduced by the first amendment, which replaced a vague phrase on national security with the broader definition, "in the interest of". Society was invested in free speech, but it had greater stakes in public order: "Although free propagation and interchange of views are ordinarily in social interest, circumstances may arise when social interest in public order is greater and the imposition of reasonable restrictions on the freedom of speech and expression and on the freedom of carrying on trade or business becomes imperative".

Relevant here were the circumstances in which the impugned law was passed , as too the "extent and urgency of the evil it sought to remedy". In its intent, the law was to be assessed against the background of the enormous power wielded by the "Press"[30] with its "modern facilities of quick circulation", which created the very real risk of abuse. Taking into account all these factors, the Supreme Court held that "restrictions imposed by the impugned Act must be held to be reasonable".[31]

29 Dhavan (1987): 122.

30 Every reference to the "Press" as an entity is capitalised in this judgment, almost as a matter of underlining its seeming power.

31 Supreme Court of India (1957). The serious sense of threat perception recognised in this judgment from the "power of the press" – which was then as now, subject to a twenty-four hour cycle of news gathering, verification and dissemination – offers a faint foretaste of the sense of

Sedition stays on the penal statute

In 1962, the Supreme Court pronounced in *Kedar Nath Singh versus the State of Bihar*, that an earlier ruling by the Allahabad High Court holding section 124A of the Indian Penal Code – on the purported offence of sedition – violative of the fundamental rights, was valid, though only up to a point. The constitutional utility of the clause was retrieved by a consideration of "the history of sedition". In any event, its application was to be limited "to acts involving intention or tendency to create disorder, or disturbance of law and order; or incitement to violence".[32]

Here we see a much looser standard in the application of this most draconian of clauses. In just over ten years, the Supreme Court moved from an insistence on demonstrable intent to undermine or overthrow the State – the vanishing point of all rights since these ultimately were only guaranteed by the sovereign authority of the State – to merely requiring a tendency to create disorder. By this time, "liberty" was in tumultuous retreat and the voices of order dominant. Naga tribes in the north-east of the country had meanwhile, raised secession as a political object worth pursuing, as had a party of regional cultural assertion in the Tamil speaking region, the Dravida Munnetra Kazhagam (DMK).

The border conflict with China in 1962 inflicted a deep wound on the nationalist psyche. And it did not help that the Punjabi *suba* and Dravida movements in the north and deep south were around the same time, beginning to cause spasms of extreme anxiety in the central leadership over a possible unravelling of the constitutional order.[33] The *Kedar Nath Singh* judgment of the Supreme Court has rightly been held to suffer the infirmity of overbreadth, in being insufficiently attentive to the potential for mischief inherent in the ambiguity of the situations it describes. It also allowed for a speech corrosive criterion of a "tendency" to create public disorder, without specifying a firm test to establish a direct causal link. In terms of jurisprudence, this implied

---

absolute panic that occasionally seems to grip the law and order authorities in matters involving the rapid spread of information over the internet today (not to mention the mobile telephone network).

32 Supreme Court of India (1962).

33 Austin (1999): 153-5.

a regressive movement in relation to certain other cases that had been decided with a firm insistence on establishing such a causal connection.[34]

The Sixteenth Amendment to the Constitution was moved on 18 January 1963, when the country was still under a state of "Emergency" following a brief but bitter border war with China. In his "statement on objects and reasons", Law Minister A.K. Sen described the purpose of the bill as giving effect to a recommendation by the National Integration Council, that article 19 be amended to empower the "Union" to do all that would be necessary for "preservation and maintenance .. (of its) .. integrity and sovereignty".[35] In the space of just over a decade, the "Union" stood transformed by legislation and judicial rulings, from a body that would enshrine the collective will and protect the fundamental rights of those who constituted India into a sovereign republic, into an organism that could potentially extinguish the sovereign rights of citizens in maintaining itself.

The years that followed were unhappy for the Indian nationalist spirit. In December 1963, civil disturbances broke out in Kashmir over the disappearance of a sacred relic from the Hazratbal shrine in Srinagar. Within days, violent reprisals began against the minority Hindu community in East Pakistan, provoking in turn, retaliatory attacks on Muslims in Calcutta and other parts of West Bengal.[36] Very soon, communal riots had engulfed a vast swathe of territory in India, representing the worst crisis of national reconciliation since the injuries of partition.

In May 1964 the death of a Prime Minister seen as parent as much as political leader, added to the drift in the national conscience. A further wound came from successive monsoon failures in 1965 and 1966 and agrarian catastrophes which raised the prospect of rampant infla-

---

34 These and a range of other issues related to the law on free speech in India are dealt with subtly and with considerable authority by Bhatia (2015).

35 Parliament of India (1963); Also, Austin (1999): 154.

36 The sequence of events is described in Ministry of Home Affairs (1965): 25. Interestingly, this was the first time since independence, that a specific section on the "communal situation" was introduced in this annual account of the activities of the Ministry, which constitutes a report to Parliament and the people.

tion and civil unrest. It was in this mood of heightened national anxiety that the Unlawful Activities (Prevention) Act (hereafter, UAPA) was passed into law in 1967, its purpose being to operationalise the philosophical shift that the Sixteenth Amendment had signalled.[37]

For the constitutional scholar and commentator A.G. Noorani, UAPA was a law "that spared the heretic only if he remained silent", one that eminently deserved to be struck down by the Supreme Court. For Granville Austin, it was "undemocratic" and "intellectually wrong-headed".[38] Far from being struck down, the UAPA was in the years that followed, embellished by no fewer than five amendments, each adding to the range of special powers held by the state. Amendments are invariably enacted in anger at specific terrorist outrages, as in December 2008 when the fifth amendment was passed just days after the November 26 attacks and three-day long terrorist siege in the city of Mumbai . UAPA in its evolving *avatar*, has sections which could put anybody in a conflict situation under serious risk of legal action. Section 13 says that anybody who actively takes part in or commits an "unlawful activity" as defined by the law, or "advocates, abets, advises or incites the commission" of such an act would be liable for up to seven years imprisonment. Section 22 lays out a similar broad demarcation of offences.

Growing room for arbitrary actions

In years that followed, the Union Government enacted laws that provided still greater room for arbitrary exercises of power. There was no clear purpose in adding to the array of repressive laws it could call

---

37 The Statement of Objects and Reasons of the UAPA reads as follows: "Pursuant to the acceptance by Government of a unanimous recommendation of the Committee on National Integration and Regionalism appointed by the National Integration Council, the Constitution (Sixteenth Amendment) Act, 1963, was enacted empowering Parliament to impose, by law, reasonable restrictions in the interests of the sovereignty and integrity of India, on the (i) freedom of speech and expression; (ii) right to assemble peaceably and without arms; and (iii) right to form associations or unions... The object of this Bill is to make powers available for dealing with activities directed against the integrity and sovereignty of India." See: Parliament of India (1967). Also, Parliamentary Research Service (2011).

38 Austin (1999): 53.

upon, since most of the powers assumed under the special security laws that came in a torrent following the 1980s, could as well have been read into the UAPA. But with an insurgent threat emerging in Punjab and later in Kashmir, the executive branch may have just decided to empower itself still further – to add an extra layer to the armour of impunity already built up.

In 1987, the Union Government, with an eye on troubles ongoing in Punjab, enacted the Terrorist and Disruptive Activities (Prevention) Act (or TADA), which lowered the standards of proof required for conviction of putative offenders in the broadly defined category of crimes called "terrorism" and allowed for the presumption of guilt in certain contingencies. TADA also recycled the language of the UAPA, in that anybody deemed to "advocate, abet, advise or incite or knowingly facilitate" a terrorist act would attract some of its most severe provisions.[39] Further, the law included within its definition of "disruptive activity", punishable by up to five years imprisonment, any act of speech "through any media", which "questions, disrupts or is intended to disrupt, whether directly or indirectly, the sovereignty and territorial integrity of India; or ... which is intended to bring about or supports any claim, whether directly or indirectly, for the cession of any part of India or the secession of any part of India from the Union".[40]

Aside from considerably lowering the standard of proof required for a terrorism conviction, TADA included a broad definition of "abetment", which seemingly did away with the need to prove any manner of intent. "Abetment" was defined as engagement in any form of "communication or association with any person or class of persons ... engaged in assisting in any manner terrorists or disruptionists". Also covered in this over-broad definition was the "passing on, or publication of, without any lawful authority, any information likely to assist the terrorists or disruptionists, and the passing on, or publication of, or distribution of, any document or matter obtained from terrorists or disruptionists".[41]

Though initially enacted with the limited validity of two years, TADA was renewed with almost mechanical regularity by Parliament

39 South Asia Terrorism Portal (2013): section 3(3).

40 Ibid: section 4(2).

41 Ibid:section 2(1)(a).

till 1995. The Supreme Court in 1994, ruled authoritatively that the act was in conformity with all requirements of constitutional governance and the protection of fundamental rights. But while doing so in *Kartar Singh versus the state of Punjab*, it concurred up to a point with the petitioners in holding the definition of "abetment" rather "vague and imprecise". It was imperative in this regard that provisions of ordinary criminal law requiring proof of criminal intent be read into that particular section of TADA, the Supreme Court ruled.[42]

There was no way of testing the efficacy of the Supreme Court's prescription for a kinder and gentler TADA, since the momentum for its repeal was by this time building up irresistibly. By 1994, the newly created National Human Rights Commission had begun speaking up against TADA as an aberrant presence within a political order based on rule of law. And unlike in earlier contexts, the political audience for this message seemed rather receptive at this time. This was partly occasioned by anxiety over the parliamentary general elections due in 1996 and the costs likely to be inflicted by the blatant misuse of the law against persons of the Muslim faith. TADA had in fact become a plaything of a ruthless and unaccountable police force, a means of imposing its will on those who even otherwise bore the brunt of social prejudice and discrimination. This was an inference considerably strengthened by the very poor rates of conviction obtained under the law. For instance, statistics available in 1995 indicated that Gujarat, a state with no recognisable symptoms of terrorism, accounted for the largest number of arrests under the law: well over eighteen thousand, in which convictions had been secured in fewer than one percent of cases. In states like Assam and Jammu and Kashmir, the number of arrests exceeded ten thousand, of which not one case had resulted in conviction.[43] In June 1995, TADA passed into history with both houses of Parliament allowing it to lapse, though not without compensating for this seeming relaxation in the vigil against terrorism, by incorporating certain of its provisions into the Indian Penal Code. In effect,

42 Supreme Court of India (1994).

43 For the context and the background to the growing public demand for TADA's repeal, see *Frontline* (1994): 4-9.

this created a permanent refuge within ordinary criminal law for special laws dealing with the exceptional situation of terrorism.[44]

The "terrorism" bug had by this time infected the political conscience. Quite apart from the turmoil in Kashmir and Punjab, a major contribution to this perversion of the democratic sensibility came from growing majoritarian political aggression, particularly with the assertion of *faux* nationalist pride known as the Ayodhya movement, which convulsed Indian politics for the second half of the 1980s, before arriving at a brutal consummation in December 1992. The accompanying pogroms implanted a deep psychosis among members of the Muslim faith, leading in turn to strategies of resistance that often strayed beyond bounds of legitimate political action.[45] This whole range of resistance strategies came to be tarred as "terrorism", a definition that failed to gain much traction because of plentiful evidence of a quiescent Indian State that had not just failed to take a stand against majoritarian aggression but had indeed encouraged it for partisan gain. The consistent effort to message the theme that India was a democracy beset by malign forces of terrorism and obliged to abridge due processes of law to win this life-and-death struggle, failed to win many adherents, except among right-wing Hindutva cabals.

Terror obsession overwhelms all

September 11, 2001 was the moment of salvation for this manner of securitarian fantasy. As news of the airborne terrorist assault on major landmarks of U.S. world supremacy inundated global airwaves, the Indian government's priorities mutated rapidly, from preparing for a summit meeting to discuss issues that had for long divided it from a truculent neighbour, into its exact opposite: an eagerness to sign up for any international effort that would dismantle Pakistan for its supposed patronage of international terrorism.

44 See for the legislative jostling and bargaining that preceded the lapse of TADA, *Frontline* (1995).

45 The history of the Ayodhya movement is scattered across a variety of scholarly and journalistic sources. A compendium of relevant documents, as also media reports and commentary, is available in Noorani (2003) and Noorani (2014).

Having suffered wounds on home territory it had never refrained from inflicting on others, the U.S. which still enjoyed recognition as the singular global power, issued an edict through the U.N., requiring all member nations of the world body to enact domestic legislation specifically targeting the scourge of "terrorism". India was among the first to step up with legislation that recycled much of the language of TADA and added greater firepower to the assault on civil liberties.[46] If TADA had a definition of "abetment" that was "vague and imprecise", the Prevention of Terrorism Act (POTA) of 2002 had none at all. Further, article 14 of the law placed the onus of revealing information deemed relevant to an investigation on all who may be suspected of possessing it. The section titled the "obligation to furnish information", was unambiguous in what it demanded: "an officer investigating any offence under the Act" would be entitled, after gaining prior approval from a superior of the rank of a police superintendent or above, to seek information in relation to any offence from any individual or entity, if he had reason to think that this would advance the investigation. Failure to provide the information sought or the deliberate furnishing of false information would attract a term of imprisonment up to three years.[47]

A campaign and advocacy body, the Peoples' Union for Civil Liberties, took the matter up in a writ petition arguing that this coercive law failed the test of legislative competence since the subject of "public order" under the Indian Constitution fell within the jurisdiction of state governments. The law moreover instituted an overbroad definition of the term "abetment", which enlarged the scope for abuse and arbitrary action. In compelling the disclosure of information, moreover, it eroded the independence of certain professions, such as lawyers and journalists and endowed the police with undue powers of coercion.

The Supreme Court held all these arguments invalid. Fundamental rights would be secure from the threat of overbroad interpretation of the crime of abetment, it held, since in the absence of an alternative, the definition laid out in basic criminal law would hold the field. With the need to prove criminal intent being already an integral element of

46 A notable dissent to this course of legislation was entered by J.S. Verma, former Chief Justice of India, then the chair of the National Human Rights Commission. See Verma (2001).

47 Parliament of India (2002).

basic law, there was no risk that the undefined crime of "abetment" under POTA would provide room for trampling on civil liberties.

On the compulsion to reveal information sought by a terrorism investigator, the court was particularly brusque, holding that it is the "settled position of law that a journalist or lawyer does not have a sacrosanct right to withhold information regarding crime under the guise of professional ethics".[48] This statement of the obvious elided the inconvenient fact that in empowering the police beyond anything that ordinary criminal law would conceive and writing in a vaguely worded provision on "aiding and abetting", POTA endowed security agencies with the power to construct a crime where the ordinary sensibility would not see one. Indeed, in addressing the question of how "abetment" should be understood, the court seemed disinclined to entertain these complexities, preferring to stay with formulaic reiterations of the rhetoric on terrorism that had gained global traction since September 2001.

Journalism is about reporting on and reflecting the ordinary human sensibility in all its variegated social milieus. A political order that allows all voices to be heard is a remote prospect, forever probably fated to remain within the realm of aspiration. But a political order where the law enables officers of the State the very broad liberty to define the offence of abetment, is one that will with virtual certainty, result in the suppression of inconvenient truths. Reporting a call to attack symbols of the State could be construed as the crime of abetment for instance, compelling self-censorship by journalists rather than honest observation and documentation. In 1951, while deciding *Romesh Thapar*, the Supreme Court held that even the most slender probability of a clause under criminal law being basis for an abridgement of constitutional liberties meant it had to be declared void. The clause invoked in imposing the ban on *Crossroads* was in this respect, contrary to the liberties that the citizens of republican India had just given themselves through the Constitution: "So long as the possibility of its (i.e., the clause's) being applied for purposes not sanctioned by the Constitution cannot be ruled out, it must be held to be wholly unconstitutional and void."[49]

---

48 Supreme Court of India (2003).

49 Supreme Court of India (1950a).

Shrinking space for dissent

From this ruling by the Supreme Court, it was a long journey towards the outlawing of dissent under TADA and POTA, both extraordinary laws soon deleted from the statute books, but only after the political sensibility they represented had been deeply imbedded within the executive apparatus of the Indian State. Considering the number of convictions secured under these statutes, their utility in meeting stated ends can be discounted. Their significance rather has lain in signalling to the police and other agencies engaged in the enforcement function, that in the hiatus between executive action and judicial review, they could assume virtually untrammelled powers in cracking down on dissent. A significant contribution came from the incoherence in the judicial apparatus, where precedents in matters involving the basic rights were weakly established and often disregarded, especially when arguments of the special circumstances involved in combating terrorism were placed on the table.

As a collective body, India's journalists face most severe threats in regions where conflict has become endemic, simply because "consent" has not emerged spontaneously, nor has the "State" been able to foster it in sufficient degree to rule without frequent displays of its coercive might. These regions could from the 1990s onwards, be identified as Kashmir, the north-eastern states, and the Maoist-insurgency areas in the forested central plains, which stretch across the states of Andhra Pradesh, Chhattisgarh, Orissa, Maharashtra and Jharkhand.[50] These threats were manifest in the May 2011 advisory sent out to all media organisations in the north-eastern state of Manipur, warning against the publication or broadcast of material "directly or indirectly in support of the unlawful/illegal activities of various organisations".[51] Multiple pressures led to several mass closures of the press in Manipur. One such closure came in January 2011, after the arrest of an editor in the

50 The challenges facing journalism in Kashmir over recent years of political unrest have been reported by a number of international press freedom bodies. Two instances from the recent past are IFJ-SAMSN 2010: 21-2; 2011: 19-20; 2012: 19-21; and 2013: 26-8. Also, CPJ (2016b). On the issues facing journalists in the Maoist insurgency areas, see IFJ-SAMSN, 2010: 19-20; SAMSN, 2011: 23-4; and 2012: 25. Also see CPJ (2016a). On issues in the north-eastern states and in particular, Manipur, see IFJ-SAMSN 2010: 19; 2011: 19-22; and 2013: 29-30.

51 IFJ-SAMSN (2012): 25.

state capital of Imphal, in what appeared to be a police "sting" operation.[52] Just a few months before, threats and counter-threats from rival underground factions had compelled Manipur's newspapers to shut down for three days in protest at the increasingly insecure environment for journalists.[53]

In November 2015, newspapers in the north-eastern state of Nagaland reported a statement by an outlawed militant group that it intended to selectively target lawmakers who stood in the way of its armed struggle. A week later, all of them received a letter from an officer of the rank of colonel in the Assam Rifles – a military regiment under India's Ministry of Home Affairs – warning that the newspaper reports could be "construed as providing support to an unlawful association". The militant organisation concerned, the letter pointed out, had been outlawed under the UAPA. Reporting its statements was by implication, also an unlawful activity which would attract penalties under the act.[54]

By way of background, the militant group – led by an ethnic Naga from Myanmar called S.S. Khaplang – had entered into a ceasefire with the Indian government in 1998 and begun peace talks. It had unilaterally abrogated the ceasefire in March 2015 and two months later, ambushed a patrol of the Assam Rifles – widely used in India's north-eastern states in both anti-insurgency and policing the border – inflicting heavy casualties. In reprisal, Indian Army units had carried out a cross-border raid, to disable and destroy Khaplang's militant camps operating out of Myanmarese territory.

Whatever its status under law, the Khaplang group obviously had a footprint in India's north-eastern states and retained sufficient firepower to be a security headache. It was also in a position to influence the course of civic life, disrupting its normal flow, often at will. The law willed that it should vanish from the landscape of India's north-eastern states, but reality determined otherwise. A question arose, which the peremptory *demarche* from the Assam Rifles colonel seemed wilfully

52 IFJ-SAMSN (2011): 21.

53 Aside from September 2013, mass closures of the Manipur press have occurred in January 2011, November 2008 and July and October 2010. Details available in the following statements issued by the IFJ-SAMSN (2010, 2011).

54 *The Hoot* (2015b).

to butt its head against: did a legal determination about the unlawful status of a militant group oblige the media to efface it entirely from the public discourse?

The judiciary had shown a similar wilfulness in imposing itself on a recalcitrant reality, even at risk of an outcome of patent absurdity. In May 2015, the High Court in Shillong, capital of the north-eastern Indian state of Meghalaya, criminalised all media reporting of the activities and statements of a particular militant group believed to be operating from the neighbouring territory of Bangladesh. The judgment bore immediate reference to a militant group committed to the sovereignty of territory inhabited by the Khasi tribe of Meghalaya. But it also included a broad prohibition on reporting on unnamed groups, referred to under the broad category of "any other organisation which may have the effect of disturbing the even tempo of public life in the state of Meghalaya having a long international border with Bangladesh".[55]

This rather severe judgment was the outcome of the judges taking *suo motu* cognisance of the disruption to public life from a forty-eight hour general strike or *bandh* called by the underground group. Using press clippings and other information sources assembled for it by the Registrar of the High Court, the bench presided over by the Chief Justice, invoked a ruling by the Kerala High Court in 1998, that an enforced general strike or *bandh* is on the face of it, an illegality and a violation of the fundamental rights of the common citizen. The Kerala High Court judgment was since upheld by the Supreme Court in a summary, one paragraph order, though without quite dispelling its many ambiguities. There was for instance, despite the endorsement by the Supreme Court, no clarity on how a *bandh* – understood as a coercive imposition on society at large by a few actors – differed from a *hartal* which was acknowledged as a legitimate and supposedly unforced exercise of the right to free speech and expression.

Judicial ruling outlaws reality

The foundations were not very sound. But the Shillong High Court went so far as to order that notice be issued to all shops and business establishments, and in particular to medical shops, hotels and taxi-op-

55 Meghalaya High Court (2015).

erators, for "staying away from their lawful avocation and for keeping their establishments closed despite repeated .... assurance(s) issued by the state government that they shall be provided adequate protection on their place of occupation/business". All state and central government offices similarly were required to file "affidavits regarding the position of attendance of staff" on the day of the bandh and in the event of any future such event. This indicated an intent by the court to institute some manner of punishment against those deemed delinquent in their discharge of assigned official duties.

Effectively, this was the judicial usurpation of individual autonomy. The militant group that called the *bandh* had been declared unlawful, but its actions were acknowledged to have implications for daily life. The court did not pause to consider whether there was a public interest involved in reporting its intent to call a general strike, which in turn would enable an informed decision by citizens on how they should deal with all contingencies likely to arise from it. Where was the line to be drawn between fulfilling a legitimate information need and playing an overtly partisan role? Should the media after receiving notice of a *bandh* have suppressed it, with the consequent risk that the public would be deprived of the opportunity to make an informed decision, that individuals could indeed come to harm from being seen in defiance of an armed militant group?

These are obviously questions that the established agencies of the state and in particular the security services, have little time or patience to negotiate. The consequence has been a host of arbitrary actions that endanger journalists and impede the right to information, with security agencies supplanting the public interest with their own narrow construction of self-interest.

In the eastern state of Orissa, where a Maoist insurgency took root in the early years of the century, Laxman Choudhary, a reporter for the daily *Sambad*, was arrested on September 21, 2009 on charges of "waging war against the state". This followed the discovery of a parcel of Maoist literature addressed to him, in the possession of a bus conductor in the hill district of Gajapati in the state. Media reports in Orissa indicated that Choudhary was a popular figure in his home district and had acquired a reputation for exposing police corruption. Orissa's Chief Minister was on record within a week of Choudhary's arrest, sharply criticising the effort to muzzle the press. Yet it was not until December, after almost four months in prison, that Choudhary was released on bail, ordered by the High Court of Orissa. Charges of sedition continued to hang over him till well after, constraining his functioning as a journalist and essentially requiring him to exercise extra diligence to not risk offending any among the police officials in his district.[56]

The neighbouring state of Chhattisgarh, enveloped in a Maoist insurgency since the late years of the 20th century, brought its own challenges for journalists, who are often threatened and restrained from reporting on major security operations. Under a draconian security law enacted in 2005, "unlawful activities" were defined broadly and flexibly, in a manner that suited every police constable's most fervent fantasy. Among these were "acts written, spoken or through visual representation", that interfered or had a "tendency to interfere" with the maintenance of public order; posed an obstacle to the maintenance of public order, or had a tendency to pose such obstacle; which interfered or "tended" to interfere with the administration of the law or "its established institutions and personnel", which encouraged or preached disobedience to "established law and its institutions".[57]

There was much else in the Chhattisgarh Special Public Safety Act that was seen as nebulous – perhaps kept so with deliberate intent – to enable just about any act by the agencies of the State under the broad rubric of the fight against left-wing extremism. And the culture of impunity for actions that are grossly transgressive of the constitutional rights was, since the enactment of the law, manifest in a number of actions. Around September 2009, the Union Government in partnership with police in the states most seriously affected by the Maoist insurgency began a security operation that rapidly escalated into a state of virtual lawlessness.[58] This created a palpable sense of siege among journalists in Chhattisgarh. In October 2009, two journalists working for widely circulated Hindi-language dailies were asked to reveal their

56 IFJ-SAMSN (2010: 20).

57 The full text of the Chhattisgarh Vishesh Jan Suraksha Adhiniyam (or Chhattisgarh Special Public Security Act) 2005, can be found at Chhattisgarh (2005). Specially relevant are the definitions of an "offence" which are in article 2(e) of the law.

58 The undeclared state of war in the Maoist insurgency regions was described in a front-page report in *The Hindu* (2010)

sources by police in the district of Dantewada in the southern part of the state, for a report suggesting that innocent villagers were killed in an anti-insurgency operation by security forces. In a separate case, a TV news reporter was asked to present himself to police in Kanker district, for broadcasting a Maoist claim of responsibility for the murder of a local political figure. A senior police officer in Chhattisgarh was also reported to have sanctioned aggressive measures, including firing at journalists who crossed into the state from neighbouring districts of Andhra Pradesh to report on operations then underway.[59]

Some very special sensitivities

Several ironies of the judicial position on free speech become evident when the lesser offence of defamation is brought into the equation. In June 2011, the Indian Institute of Planning and Management (IIPM) – an educational setup of sorts based in Delhi – filed suit against *The Caravan*, a monthly magazine of political and cultural commentary, for the sum of INR 500 million.[60] Headed by an individual named Arindam Chaudhuri, the IIPM is an establishment that conducts training programmes and a graduate course in business management. With an annual advertising budget estimated at the time of this incident at INR 300 million – probably the highest among all India's educational institutions – IIPM has a high-profile media presence and the exemption from scrutiny that the strategic use of advertising budgets can buy.

The Caravan had in its February 2011 issue, featured an article titled "Sweet Smell of Success: How Arindam Chaudhuri Made a Fortune Off the Aspirations — and Insecurities — of India's Middle Classes". The article was a substantive pre-publication excerpt from a book by U.S.-based journalist Siddhartha Deb, due for publication in July 2011. The IIPM lawsuit named the author, the publisher Penguin Books India and the India office of the internet search portal Google

---

59 IFJ-SAMSN (2010): 20. The wireless message from the police officer recommending that journalists be fired upon was intercepted and leaked to the local press. It found its way to Sanjay Kak's documentary film *Red Ant Dream* released in May 2013. Though the source of the leak remains unknown, the officer issuing the order has been identified with a fair measure of certainty.

60 The details of the lawsuit were explained in a note from *The Caravan* editors in its issue of July 2011 (*The Caravan*, 2011).

as respondents, other than *The Caravan*, accusing them of "grave harassment and injury".

The lawsuit was filed not in Delhi, where both IIPM and *The Caravan* are based, but in Silchar town in the north-eastern state of Assam, over two thousand kilometres away. IIPM was the second petitioner, the first being a Silchar businessman associated with the institute as a recruiter. At the first hearing of the case, the civil court in Silchar granted IIPM a preliminary injunction, enjoining *The Caravan* to remove the impugned article from its website. This decree was issued *ex parte*, without any pre-hearing notice to the magazine. In August that year, the Supreme Court ordered a stay on the defamation proceedings against *The Caravan*, though without lifting the injunction granted in the lower court. The article has since failed to turn up in search operations conducted through the Google portal. In July 2015, IIPM announced its decision to shut down after being inundated by a tidal wave of public criticism over questionable business methods and virtually worthless instruction. The court case filed by the IIPM's rather shady owner remained unsettled till at least a year-and-a-half later.

In February 2013, IIPM secured an injunction from a court in Gwalior in the state of Madhya Pradesh, blocking a vast number of websites and social media posts which questioned the quality of the instruction it imparted. Yet again, the order was issued *ex parte* and the Department of Telecommunications (DoT) in the Indian government with uncharacteristic alacrity, jumped to attention to order all internet service providers to comply.

This came as part of a phase of uncharacteristic hyper-activity for the DoT. Within the space of just forty-eight hours, this directive was followed with four other orders to internet service providers (ISPs). In all, the DoT's zeal to protect the Indian public from information that could potentially harm, meant that no fewer than 164 URLs or web addresses hosting specific content were blocked. All five orders were issued in unquestioning and unreserved compliance with *ex parte* orders emanating from courts. No reasons were given, though as things transpired, these were not very difficult to figure out.

Of the five orders, three were issued with clear intent to clamp down on protests in Kashmir after the execution of one-time militant

Mohammad Afzal Guru, sent to the gallows after a trial process widely seen to have fallen short of every norm of fairness.[61] Physical movement in all of Kashmir had been blocked by pre-emptive curfew imposed that morning. As news of the execution trickled out, local news channels and newspapers were told to suspend operations. And though the internet remained available through broadband, the more widely used modes of access in the valley – mobile telephones and wireless datacards – were disabled. The information lockdown persisted five days in the case of newspapers and an entire week for internet users. For local TV news channels, it continued for months afterwards. But through the pores in this blanket of censorship, the people of Kashmir were still managing to make their anger and bitterness heard. The DoT directive, calling specifically for the shutting down of a number of pages on the social networking site Facebook, was obviously about blocking even that channel of dissent.

For a region where rights to life and liberty have been in suspension, an information blockade may seem a lesser injustice, though it is part of the same apparatus of repression that targets any possibility of an occupied people conducting a social dialogue beyond the constraints of location and space. Yet for all that, there was nothing really unusual about the effort to tighten the information blockade on Kashmir, a region that has long been in a state of exception in the Indian political map, where even the pretence of guaranteed rights and entitlements does not apply. Indeed, a blockade on mobile telephone services had been imposed in the valley just a fortnight before the Guru execution, while the rest of India was celebrating the anniversary of its republican constitution. Communications between the people of Kashmir was shut down since that could potentially have enabled a mobilisation of dissent on an occasion observed in the rest of India as an affirmation of republican commitments.

A second category of website blocks ordered in the DoT's February round of sweeping censorship, applied against the mimicking or parodying of important public institutions, such as the Bombay High Court. Few dissenting voices were raised here. If anything, there may have been some reservations about the recourse to heavy-handed cen-

---

61 In regard to the execution of Afzal Guru and its illegality, see Muralidharan (2013); also editor's introduction and essays assembled in Roy (2013).

sorship, where the task of sifting between the authentic and the fake, might well have been left to the judgment of the internet user, worries that the DoT action may have cast the rare visitor to these sites as an infant in need of the guiding hand of a nanny state.

What really raised hackles and triggered a war of attrition on the internet was the third category of order issued by the DoT, blocking seventy-three specific addresses ranging over a total of fifty websites, all of which pertained to the IIPM. The formal order addressed to all ISPs, began with a peremptory, "it has been decided", much like an edict issued from a sovereign that is beyond challenge. After listing the sites to be censored, it entered an enjoinment of secrecy on all recipients of its communication, uncharacteristic for a sovereign acting with absolute authority. Letters of compliance to be filed by all those at the receiving end of the edict were not to mention the identity of the blocked URLs. If the intent of that caution was to conceal the identity of the guiding hand behind this extraordinary measure of information denial, it did not go far. The common element in the seventy-three web addresses that were blocked was soon discovered to be the IIPM.

Cryptic in content and opaque in its legal basis, the DoT order for the most part, applied to blogs and independent initiatives by consumer groups and civil society actors to promote a dialogue on issues of public concern: such as the quality of service offered by various civic and commercial institutions. The IIPM, unsurprisingly for an institution with a high media profile, had come in for some searching scrutiny and been found wanting. Several of the postings on these sites, drawing on first-hand experiences of the services offered (or lack of it), were trenchant in tone and content. The Gwalior court it emerged, had issued its order under provisions of the Indian Penal Code (IPC, section 499) dealing with the offence of defamation and the Information Technology Act (IT Act, section 69) which enabled government authorities to demand the blocking of certain sites by ISPs and intermediaries such as Google and Facebook. Evidence that the court had applied the tests of intent, accuracy and public interest that are the preliminaries mandated by law before sanctions are imposed for defamation, was conspicuously lacking. And what literally leapt out in the DoT edict was the very first URL on the list, which belonged to a public institution, the University Grants Commission (UGC). In a notice issued in July 2012, ostensibly in compliance with a directive from the Delhi High Court in ongoing litigation, the UGC had recorded its finding that the IIPM was not a university under applicable law. It was in other words, not empowered to grant degrees in business management or any other discipline of study.

In holding the UGC liable for defamation, the Gwalior court obviously omitted any serious engagement, either with the history of litigation involving the IIPM, or with the law. Section 499 of the IPC is explicit about certain exceptions where in circumstances to be judged by the courts, the offence of defamation would not apply. These include, the "imputation of truth which public good requires to be made or mentioned," the "public conduct of public servants" and the "conduct of any person touching any public question". Clearly, any assessment that the UGC may have made and communicated to the public about the academic credentials of the IIPM, fell potentially within the scope of these exceptions. That the Gwalior court overlooked these aspects of the law pointed towards an egregious omission.

In a subsequent hearing, the Gwalior court undoubtedly a little unsettled by the torrent of public outrage, reversed its earlier ruling. But the patently irrational order had held the field for a whole fortnight by then. It is a case study that vividly illustrates the syndrome that the legal scholar and senior Supreme Court counsel Rajeev Dhavan has highlighted: that "in most civil defamation cases, the real mischief takes place right at the beginning … when injunctions are freely granted to prevent the publication or dissemination of an existing or proposed publication".[62]

For IIPM's owner, courts were clearly meant to be used as instruments of censorship with the deeper purpose of creating a favourable business atmosphere. Education became a major advertising category, particularly for the print media, since liberalisation of policy in the 1990s allowing greater private sector participation. The ranking of educational institutions, a bandwagon that one print publication after another jumped onto with extreme alacrity, became in turn a major money-spinner for the media, through the collateral advertising revenue it brought in. IIPM rode this wave for a while, but fell off the crest when found to be providing dubious figures to embellish its achievements, particularly in the matter of job placements for students. A phase of

62 Dhavan (2010): 112.

extreme acrimony ensued, with IIPM filing suit against a number of publications on grounds of defamation.[63] There was extreme irony then, in IIPM securing just a few months afterwards, a significant ruling from a magistrate's court in Delhi upholding its own right to free speech, when its injunction against *The Caravan* still held. This was a fascinating case of role reversal. *The Sunday Indian*, a magazine published by Arindam Chaudhari as part of the seamless business empire that includes the IIPM, had in November and December 2012, following an official audit inquiry that laid bare gross irregularities in the allocation of coal mining concessions, run a number of stories about a mining and energy corporation, Jindal Steel and Power Ltd (JSPL), that seemed to have engaged in illegal business practices. One of the stories in this sequence held the company guilty of seeking to subvert media freedom through threats and financial inducements offered to a broadcasting company.

JSPL was quick to take the matter up in a defamation suit. In deciding the case, the Delhi magistrate held, contrary to fact but with a certain scruple in a matter of principle, that *The Sunday Indian* is a magazine with "a wide circulation and reader base". It held further, that a democratic polity could not afford to give too much leeway to defamation suits since this would potentially impede the public right to know. "The tone and tenor of the articles only convey general observations regarding a current topic of national interest. There is nothing contained in the said articles which is especially meant to damage the reputation of the complainant."

Getting away with hate speech

This narration about the speech acts that attract legal sanctions of various degrees of severity would not be complete without a consideration of some notable instances when prosecution has faltered despite being eminently justified. If the touchstone of possible violence and public disorder were used to judge when article 153A would be applicable, then a case that literally called out for prosecution involved Bal Thackeray, leader of the Shiv Sena, a major political party in the state of Maharashtra. In 1993, Thackeray used the party newspaper *Saamna* to exhort his cadre into a ten-day long rampage of death and destruction

63 *Mint* (2013) provides a detailed run-down of these judicial encounters.

in the city of Mumbai (then Bombay). There was little ambiguity here, nor was there any effort to disavow responsibility for the hundreds of deaths that followed, mostly of members of the Muslim faith.

Soon afterwards, a group of public-spirited individuals from the city filed a petition before a local court, demanding Thackeray's prosecution for actions that contributed directly to an orgy of violence. Mumbai city police opposed the petition on the grounds that the matter fell within the jurisdiction of the Press Council of India – an unwieldy and inept body crippled at birth, with no more than the power of censuring delinquent behaviour in the press.

The petition filed in the public interest was thrown out at that point. In 1998, Thackeray and his party were held directly responsible for the violence by the B.N. Srikrishna Commission of Inquiry, set up shortly after the riots. A further move for his prosecution was initiated, which enjoyed somewhat better fortune principally because it had the explicit backing of an estranged crony who then happened to be Home Minister in the state government. In July 2000, a judicial order was issued seeking Thackeray's arrest and prosecution. After a series of monitory riots by Shiv Sena cadre and much bluster about the imminent prospect of the city going up in flames, the state government finally secured Thackeray's submission to the law. But the case against him was held void soon afterwards, because it was barred by the statute of limitations.

Further illustration of the impunity enjoyed by those with political clout came during India's parliamentary general elections of 2009. Varun Gandhi, a candidate of the right-wing Hindutva party, the Bharatiya Janata Party from a constituency in Uttar Pradesh that has a substantial number of voters of the Sikh and Muslim faiths, was recorded urging voters of the Hindu faith that it was their religious obligation to vote for him. Any hand that was raised with intent to harm a Hindu, he warned, would be ruthlessly severed. And as if these were not in themselves enough, he ended with a particularly gross reference to those of the Muslim faith, in terms of their religious practice of circumcision. A similar pejorative, though not quite as crass, was also hurled at those of the Sikh faith.[64]

64 For details of this infamous campaign speech, see Varadarajan (2009).

Varun Gandhi spent twenty days in prison on charges of incitement to violence and other provisions of criminal law. This did not prevent him winning the seat by over 300,000 votes, among the largest victory margins in the country in that particular electoral round. Gandhi was acquitted in both the trials that followed, with one witness after another turning hostile and the prosecution showing a marked disinterest in securing a conviction. It was later revealed through a sting operation carried out by a web-based news portal and broadcast over a widely watched news channel on May 15, 2013, that the whole trial had been a charade orchestrated by local power-brokers cutting across party lines and partisan divides. With a smart political trade-off involving the barter and exchange of seats in elections held to the Uttar Pradesh state legislative assembly in 2012, Varun Gandhi had in effect secured himself against any possibility of prosecution. The hard work of fixing the witnesses was left to his ally who happened to belong to an opposing party, committed to securing a fair deal for those of the Muslim faith.[65]

A general inference seems warranted by this history of a slow erosion in the constitutional assurances of the free speech right and the special rewards reserved for its abuse by those with political clout: first off, that far from being institutionalised, this was a right that had to be continually negotiated. It was moreover, a right enjoyed only by those who were fortunate enough to be invited into the small tent where the negotiations took place. Negotiated freedoms were liable to be revoked at any time, without prior notice. In terms of the realities of journalism at the local level, this tense dynamic between the exercise of a basic right of citizenship and bureaucratic insecurity was seen daily to be at work, especially in regions of conflict and insurgency. Where the free speech right was abused to create an atmosphere of hatred leading to acts of lethal violence, the leeway granted was vast and the principal protagonists seemingly indemnified against any form of legal sanction because they had negotiated their freedom in that tent where only the privileged few had access.

The online speech community, particularly the growing tribe of social media users in India had a moment of triumph in March 2014, when the Supreme Court of India rendered judgment on a batch of writ petitions filed by activist groups and individuals, challenging the

65 *Hindustan Times* (2013).

constitutional validity of section 66A of India's Information Technology (IT) Act. The IT Act was passed in 2000, principally as a measure to facilitate the potential of e-commerce through India's burgeoning IT services industry. Sections 66A, 69A and a number of others were added on in 2008 in response to the growth of the social media.

A moment of triumph for online community

Section 66A was scarred at the moment of its birth by a certain looseness of language, almost inviting rampant abuse. Curiously, it was adopted in parliament along with other amendments after the merest formality of a debate. It may have been a knee-jerk reaction to the wave of public outrage generated by the 60-hour terrorist siege of the western Indian metropolis of Mumbai in November 2008. The two principal sections introduced by amendment – 66A and 69A – were different in that the former was couched in phraseology that was broad and ill-defined, while the latter clung closely to the grounds listed in the provision of the Indian constitution, article 19(2), that provides for certain "reasonable restrictions" on the right to free speech. This seemingly saved 69A in judicial review, though it was seen to be no less prone to frequent and arbitrary use.

Section 66A was added as a sub-clause to a legal provision that dealt with the offence of hacking. Though the offence of "hacking" was defined with a fair degree of precision, 66A added a huge burden of ambiguity, making it a punishable offence to post online any "information that is grossly offensive or has a menacing character". Alternately, anything posted in the knowledge that it was false, for the "purpose of causing annoyance, inconvenience, danger, obstruction, insult, injury, criminal intimidation, enmity, hatred or ill will", to "deceive or to mislead", would be liable to criminal prosecution. Section 69A was more precisely worded, augmenting the powers of intercepting or ordering the decryption of coded information, with the authority to block websites or order offensive information removed from online circulation.

Since its passage, section 66A had been the basis for the arrest of two college students who questioned the shutdown of the commercial metropolis of Mumbai for a politician's funeral, a university teacher who posted a caricature of the chief minister of the state of West Bengal and a cartoonist who depicted the Indian parliament building in what was deemed an offensive fashion. There were a number of other cases where arrests were effected and prosecution launched on matters of equal or greater triviality.

It was the arrest of the two college students from a town near Mumbai in November 2012 and the similar fate of a businessman in the southern city of Puducherry after he posted a comment about the son of the Finance Minister at the time, that led to a petition before the Supreme Court invoking the writ jurisdiction of the higher judiciary in defending the fundamental rights. As the petition was admitted for hearing, the Chief Justice of India wondered aloud in open court about how the clause had evaded judicial scrutiny for quite that long.

In defence of what seemed a lost cause, the government just hours before the petition came up in the Supreme Court, notified a number of procedural changes in the manner 66A was applied. It was for one thing, made mandatory for a police officer of a certain rank to sign off on every arrest made under the law. In every such instance, moreover, the matter was to be heard before a judicial official of an appropriate rank within a defined period of time.

Abuses continued though, as arguments proceeded in the matter, listed as *Shreya Singhal versus the Union of India*. When the Supreme Court rendered its verdict on the matter, it was almost like a conclusion foregone.[66] Section 66A was by virtue of its vague phraseology, its attempt to create offences that were not recognised within Indian penal law and evidence of its abuse, just awaiting judicial execution. Government counsel sought to retrieve it by reading provisions of existing criminal law into the intent of the section. This effort failed on account of its inherent illogic. The offence of defamation was clearly defined under Indian penal law and its maximum sentence, even where it was a cognisable offence, was considerably less than provided under 66A. Moreover, it had a specific clause requiring that an individual prove "damage to reputation" to ensure that it stuck. No such requirement was invested in section 66A which could be triggered when some undefined threshold of "annoyance" was crossed.

66 Much of the history of section 66A is recounted in the judgment rendered by the Supreme Court on March 24, 2015. See Supreme Court (2015).

Efforts to bring an element of consistency between the application of section 66A and legal provisions dealing with permitted restraints, as when "contempt of court" was involved, were similarly dealt with. Finally, the rationale used was simply that "a section which creates an offence and which is vague must be struck down as being arbitrary and unreasonable". "Sufficient definiteness (was) needed", India's Supreme Court held, "to define penal law". And this was clearly not the case with 66A, which tended to "arbitrarily, excessively and disproportionately invade the right of free speech and upset the balance between such rights and the reasonable restrictions that maybe imposed on such right". Reiterating a finding from an earlier case, the Supreme Court observed: "The law should not be used in a manner that has chilling effects on the freedom of speech and expression".

Importantly, the Supreme Court firmly rejected the notion – advanced in a number of assurances by government counsel – that a bad law could be used in a benign manner. Such assurances would have no value, it observed, in a situation where "governments may come and governments may go, but Section 66A goes on forever". Such a commitment to use the law with extreme circumspection "even if carried out, would not bind any successor government".

As final recourse, government counsel advanced a notion of "severability": that the clause could be retained to the extent that it was consistent with other parts of the constitution, including its fundamental rights guarantees. This was termed as a "vague" proposition since it did not specify any part of 66A that could be saved. Neither was it consistent with settled law in India on the fundamental rights. The upshot finally was simple: 66A did not "fall within any of the subject matters contained in Article 19(2)". Its possible application for purposes outside those subject matters was clear. And there could be no escape from the firm judicial inference that "no part of 66A is severable and the provision as a whole must be declared unconstitutional".

Petitioners also asked for a definitive pronouncement that held any ruling made under 66A to be discriminatory, in violation of article 14 or the equality provision of the Indian Constitution. It was not acceptable practice that internet users should be subject to a different regime of laws than other media users and consumers. The Supreme Court seemed disinclined to hear this plea: "The intelligible differentia is clear – the internet gives any individual a platform which requires very little or no payment through which to air his views". It was seemingly solely on the grounds of its wider accessibility that the court ruled in favour of a different framework of law for the internet. In view of this "intelligible differentia between speech on the internet and other mediums (sic) of communication", it observed, "separate offences can certainly be created (for the latter) by legislation".

With these preliminaries indicating its philosophical outlook, the Supreme Court proceeded to uphold 69A as a legitimate legal provision, consistent with the fundamental rights. In this, an altogether too brief a section of its judgment, the court seems to have put its faith almost entirely in the procedural rules prescribed. Yet it was a procedural anomaly that the petitioners had sought to highlight. Unlike in the criminal procedure code, which allows stakeholders in a newspaper threatened with forfeiture to appeal the decision at the level of the high court, 69A provides no such safeguard. Anybody seeking redress for a perceived wrong would for this reason have to invoke the writ jurisdiction of the higher judiciary. This entire range of problems was dismissed by the court as trivial. The procedure prescribed before an order to block a website or take down specific bits of information, it ruled, had sufficient internal checks to prevent abuse.

Yet as Apar Gupta, a lawyer who represented one of the litigants in the matter wrote, the safeguards that the court pinned great faith in, were never "evidenced in practice". There had not been a single instance of a hearing being afforded to the affected parties before blocking orders were issued. The rules themselves provided the privilege of "confidentiality to any complaints and actions taken by the government to block websites". Applications made under the right to information law that had sought disclosure of the rationale for specific blocking orders, had as a rule, "been unsuccessful or at best provided incomplete information".

The safeguards prescribed in the criminal procedure code were read in the Shreya Singhal judgment as specific to the print medium, with little utility in the online domain. This was in line with the court's reading that regulatory rules and regimes specific to the internet – and not to other media – would not offend against the principle of equality before the law. Gupta pointed out that in setting what could conceivably be a lower standard of protection for online speech, the court seemingly endorsed "the legislature's tendency to view the internet as an inherently dangerous medium, one that deserves greater regulation with decreased safeguards for civil rights". This, said Gupta, was "a cause for worry".[67]

Governments and legislatures were still working with memories of certain key recent incidents which spotlighted the potential for lasting social damage in the online media. In August 2012, there was a mass flight of people of north-eastern ethnicity from several of India's most prosperous metropolises after rumours were circulated over mobile phones and social media that they would be targeted for violent attacks. Activists then and at several junctures since, pointed out that the answer lay in better policing in the streets, and not over the internet, indeed, that a few well focused prosecutions in cases of wrongdoing could neutralise the damage potential of rumours spread with intent to do harm. That failed to win much sympathy from legislatures and governmental authorities mired in older habits of command and control. The transition from the old media domain of print and broadcast to the more dispersed and individualised modes of social media, occurs in a time of considerable legal ambiguity. With all the years of experience with operationalising constitutional guarantees of free speech and expression, the realm of practice remains shrouded in uncertainty. Section 66A was quickly dispatched to the ash-heap of history because it was a matter that was pressed with a sense of urgency by a large, energetic – and affluent – community of social media users in India. That exception aside, various curiosities could be identified in the history of constitutional debates over free speech in India, since most of the key questions about the full amplitude of the right have remained unsettled. Invariably, only those matters reach a stage of authoritative judicial determination where free speech is a convenient camouflage for the commercial calculations of the media industry.

67 Gupta (2015).

Civil Society
Media and the Politics of Anti-Politics

It has been called, variously, the defining idea of the 21st century and an antidote to all ills caused by the breakdown of the bipolar world order of the late-20th century. But it would take a brave person to seek a pathway through the haze of obscurity that surrounds the term "civil society".[1] Over the two decades of globalisation since the collapse of the Soviet bloc, "civil society" was seen on numerous occasions to assert itself through colour-coded revolutions that toppled well-entrenched regimes – most commonly after elections portrayed in dominant power circles as rigged or manipulated. The year 2011 was a proving ground, when civil society is believed to have exerted itself in pristine form to overturn numerous repressive regimes. Because these occurred in a region as volatile and strategically important as the Arab world, they were seen to be especially far-reaching in their impact.

Early optimism dissipated as developments in these countries departed rapidly from script. A popular revolt against decades of political stagnation in Tunisia was the trigger for similar uprisings in Libya, Egypt and most destructively, in Syria. Tunisia managed a transition to what seemed a stable democratic order within a reasonable period of time. The other nations on which the perfervid western imagination was scripting the scenario of an "Arab spring" or an irreversible march

1 This fuzzy element is flagged in the introduction to Kaviraj and Khilnani (2001).

towards democracy, soon collapsed in ruins. The democratic transition in Egypt was rolled back by the restoration of the old military authoritarianism. Libya, where the quirky forty-year reign of Muammar al-Gaddafi ended in a grisly public lynching, descended into chaos, with the forces of Islamic fundamentalism, which the west was ostensibly engaged in global war against, gaining a decisive edge within two years of western intervention. Syria sank into a brutal civil war which expectedly spilled over into Iraq, aggravating the severe sectarian animosities that had been festering through three rounds of elections since the U.S. invasion of 2003.[2]

Fantasies about a new dawn of democracy in a strategically complex region were rapidly dispelled. Seemingly, the west opted then for a situation of unending chaos.[3] Well before this squalid turn in what was touted as the unstoppable onward march of liberal democracy, *Time*

---

2 For an account of the geopolitical complexities unleashed by the "Arab spring" and its ominous implications for the region and beyond, see Muralidharan (2012). With the turbulence still ongoing at the time this is written, there is little by way of a retrospective assessment available at the time of this writing.

3 The rise of the Islamic State (IS) is one of the great mysteries of the chaos that began in the West Asian region and Arab world with the U.S. invasion of Iraq in 2003. A 2012 intelligence estimate by U.S. agencies, declassified mid-2015, seemed to have ample forewarning about the emergence of an extreme ideological regime in the trail of chaos created by the U.S. invasion of Iraq and the uprising in Syria that began in 2011. Al-Qaeda in Iraq (AQI), which was the precursor to the IS, is believed to have "regressed" in western Iraq between 2009 and 2010 and then picked up steam due to the insurgency in Syria. "The Salafist, the Muslim Brotherhood, and AQI are the major forces driving the insurgency in Syria", the intelligence report documented, before identifying its supporters as "the West, the Gulf countries and Turkey". Given the persistent military stalemate, there was strong possibility of the situation unravelling, when there would be "the possibility of a declared or undeclared Salafist principality in Eastern Syria", which was "exactly what the supporting powers to the opposition want, in order to isolate the Syrian regime". There would be complications in the "Iraqi situation" since such a Salafist takeover in Syria would create "the ideal atmosphere for AQI to return to its old pockets in Mosul and Ramadi". But that evidently, was a complication that the U.S. security and intelligence establishment was prepared to live with. A link to the severely redacted intelligence report, which reveals sufficient information to form certain definitive findings, is available in Milne (2015). Broadly similar findings were reported by the veteran British journalist Patrick Cockburn (2014).

magazine – that tireless champion of U.S. power – voted the "protester" as the "person of the year" for 2011. It was a distinction earned by virtue of the momentous changes protesters had brought about in a strategically important region after years of political stagnation.[4] The changes sought by the protesters might not always have been precise in their articulation, but on the conviction that business as usual would not be tolerated, they seemed absolutely certain.

These are extraordinary situations where civil society emerges in a forceful assertion against the structures of state power. There is also an ordinary reality, when civil society acts to enforce conformity in places where the formal machinery of the state does not reach. And this conformity is not about the written law, the civic law that all are putatively committed to honour, but about customary law. Civil society here emerges in its everyday incarnation, subsisting in comfortable harmony with the state, preserving order and contributing to the reproduction of daily life through processes of custom and consent.

Civil society as a concept in modern western political theory, Sudipta Kaviraj has remarked, is used in at least three different senses, all of which are "based on dichotomies or contrasts". It is a curiosity that civil society "appears to be an idea strangely incapable of standing freely on its own": it always needs a "distinctive support from a contrary term". These binaries have been variously expressed. In an early version of the term, the opposite number was the "state of nature". In a later understanding, it was about "political society" or more specifically the "state". Overlapping with these was the notion of the "community" against "civil society".[5]

If civil society is defined by what it is not, there should be ample doubt over its capacity to bear the heavy burdens thrust upon it. Is civil society something that can be touched or felt? Evidently not. It is a lived in experience or more accurately perhaps, a construct of the imagination, a region of shared values for every citizen. In that sense, it is very much an imagined community in the sense that the "nation" is now understood to be.

---

4 Anderson (2012).

5 Kaviraj (2001): especially 288-307.

Media as revolutionary accessory

The mass movements of 2011 were described in some quarters as the "social media revolution" and there seemed ample reason why that characterisation should stand. Media, especially the new networking techniques enabled by mobile phones and the internet, undoubtedly did facilitate the protests and multiply their impact. Group solidarities among protesters were formed through widely accessible and extremely flexible social networking sites on the internet, such as Facebook and Twitter. And the images of the demonstrations that arose were transmitted through the video sharing site YouTube.

To quote the *Time* cover story on the protesters and their impact on the events of 2011: "Calling the Arab uprisings Facebook and YouTube and Twitter revolutions is not, it turns out, just glib, wishful American overstatement. In the Middle East and North Africa, in Spain and Greece and New York, social media and smart phones did not replace face-to-face social bonds and confrontation but helped enable and turbocharge them ... And in police states with high Internet penetration ... a critical mass of cell-phone video recorders plus YouTube plus Facebook plus Twitter really did become an indigenous free press.... America's great 21st century contribution to fomenting freedom abroad was not imposing it militarily but enabling it technologically, as an epiphenomenon of globalisation".[6]

The civil uprising against the state came to India not as a demand for regime change, but as a statement of mass disgust at the corruption believed rampant at all levels of government. Its focus was the creation of a powerful new body that would oversee the integrity of the governance process: receiving public complaints, investigating suspected acts of malfeasance, and prosecuting wrongdoers. Even if regime change was not its stated objective, its ambition of instituting a process of oversight and accountability that would spare none in its reach, spoke of a similar ambition. There were two phases of intense activism in the movement, both in 2011 and involving indefinite hunger fasts by Kisan Baburao Hazare – commonly referred to as "Anna" or elder brother – then a seventy-four year old political activist from Ralegan Siddhi village in the western Indian state of Maharashtra.

Hazare chose prominent public spots in the national capital for both these fasts, undertaken under the unwavering gaze of the media,

6 Andersen (2012): 89.

with a steady stream of onlookers coming by to express support. Solidarity actions were organised in other parts of the country, always with a very attentive media presence. Social media technologies were a key tool of mobilisation. India Against Corruption (IAC) and a number of other non-governmental organisations (NGOs) that provided the logistical backbone for Hazare, set up websites rich with campaign material. Mobile phone "apps" were designed and distributed, that enabled the campaigners to stay engaged and committed.[7]

The Hazare movement differed from the protests that swept the Arab world, in enjoying an absolute monopoly over the attentions of what could be called the "mainstream media". It did not have to depend exclusively on alternate channels since it did not by any stretch, suffer the neglect of India's primary news platforms. In fact, the opposite was the case: Hazare was for the duration of both his hunger fasts, the dominant item on the agenda of the Indian news media. The protesters in the streets of Cairo and Tunis in contrast, had to depend on external media signals beamed in through satellite and the internet to be aware that the world was indeed taking notice.

Its enabling role cannot be questioned, but there are few who would accept a determinant role for technology in these movements. If technology is considered the means, then every mass upsurge in recent times, indeed in recorded history, has borne a distinct imprint. When the East European regimes were toppled, beginning in 1989 and ending with the collapse of the Soviet Union in 1991, people put it down to the new possibilities opened up by satellite communication. It may more plausibly, have been the consequence of a people catching up with more mundane realities, such as print technology, in societies where publishing the written word had for long remained a state monopoly.[8]

---

7 The range of media strategies used by the movement to mobilise numbers in support, was posted on the website of the campaign which till at least June 2012, could be accessed here: http://www.indiaagainstcorruption.org/index1.html. The website has since turned inoperative.

8 David Remnick spent many years in Moscow as correspondent just ahead of the Soviet breakdown and documented how the liberalisation of printing contributed to a vast spread of an alternative political consciousness, fuelling the social movements that led ultimately to the demise of a seventy year old socialist empire. See Remnick (1994).

In 1979, a tyranny was overthrown in Iran by a movement that organised itself around the revolutionary exhortations of an exiled religious cleric. It was technologically a less sophisticated time and the medium of disseminating the message was the cassette tape – cheap, portable and difficult to interdict, but capable of moving multitudes when played over the public address systems of mosques, then the hubs of community life. Yet this event, which had a deep impact on the geopolitics of the time and continues to this day to exert its influence, was not identified as the cassette tape revolution. It was set into motion by identifiable human strivings and once consummated, gained an identity by the religious ideology that claimed it as exclusive patrimony.[9]

Technological delusions

To identify epochal movements involving large masses by the technologies used would be equivalent to naming the 1848 uprisings in Europe – which overturned despotism and created the circumstances in which liberalism ran triumphant through much of that continent – after the railway and telegraph. And in the breathless ardour of its celebration of 2011, *Time* magazine did indeed reach for 1848 as the closest historical parallel.[10] Other facile inferences followed, including one on the supposed parallels between then and now in the use of newly minted technologies to articulate a powerful striving for political change.

---

9 This is a theme dealt with by Mohammadi and Mohammad (1994). A review by Tehranian (1995) provides the following summation of its message: "The revolution may be thus interpreted as a triumph of the oral tradition of the mosque, augmented by cassette tapes of messages from the religious leaders and duplicated by the xerox machines in government offices, against the mediated communication system of the national press and broadcasting. I would argue further that the demystifying power of television demythologised the monarchy in the same fashion that it is currently demythologising Islam and the clerical leadership. Exposure demystifies and absolute exposure demystifies absolutely! In their great enthusiasm to be constantly displayed on television, dictators thus risk a permanent legitimation crisis". This manner of determinism though is at best, a partial explanation since messages conveyed through various channels are "socially negotiated and mediated through primary (family and peer group) and secondary (work and voluntary associations) communications networks".

10 Andersen (2012): 66.

The main actors of 1848 referred to the mood then as the "springtime of the people". And the political ferment of the time inspired two young radicals, Karl Marx and Friedrich Engels, to write the text that looked ahead to a world embodying the most revolutionary visions of the time. The *Communist Manifesto* was not by any means representative of the majority or the mainstream of the visions of the world that coalesced to make the 1848 movements what they were. As Eric Hobsbawm has recorded it, the 1848 revolutions ran like a "brushfire across frontiers, countries and even oceans". They represented "potentially the first global revolution", which within a matter of weeks had overturned governments "in an area of Eürope which is today occupied by all or part of ten states". And yet, within six months, their "universal defeat was safely predictable".[11]

Movements of such scale and expanse, whether 1848 or 2011, spring from diverse motivations and dispersed individuals whose strivings coincide at a moment in time, but could then potentially diverge. It does not take great analytical skill to conclude that the narrative adopted with some alacrity by western commentators – that the social movements of 2011 are an epiphenomenon of globalisation, driven by the goal of securing the freedoms the U.S. has otherwise been enforcing through military force – has to prove itself against its polar opposite. There is on the face of things, equally compelling evidence to suggest that 2011 was the year of mass movements against the worst of globalisation.

Complex judgments are called for in deciding between these sharply polarised inferences, and such an inquiry would stumble at the very first conceptual challenge, of understanding and contextualising the phenomenon of globalisation. Till around the time that the Soviet Union passed into history, the term probably did not exist in any but the most obscure dictionary of the English language. A decade on, there were few debates of consequence on economic and social matters that did not profusely invoke the term. Since then, the term has itself not had quite the same frequency of usage, reflecting a certain ambivalence among its most breathless proponents towards its social and economic impacts.[12]

---

11 Hobsbawm (1962):22.

12 For a review of various perspectives on the issue, see Kiely (2005).

Polarised political terrains

In some measure, this ambiguity originates on the political terrain of the country at the centre of it all. Immediately after the inauguration of Barack Obama as U.S. president in January 2009, the angry white middle class rose in insurrection, putatively against the growing intrusion of the "government" into daily lives and the burgeoning deficit on the federal budget. An undertow of racial resentment at the election of an African-American to the presidency was apparent, as was unbridled animus at the entitlements of the small number of socialised welfare recipients.

Much of this rancour surfaced in a mass mobilisation against the Obama administration's first major legislative initiative: a comprehensive health care bill that sought – very cautiously and with due regard for the delicate sensibilities of both pharmaceuticals companies and the insurance industry – to provide the modest assurance that no U.S. citizen would be ruined for life by a medical emergency in the family. In little time, the veneer of political civility – such as it was after close to three decades of right-wing dominance in national politics – was ripped aside and the Tea Party movement, with the assiduous backing of a vast segment of the media industry, became the civil uprising that the political establishment simply had to deal with.[13]

The Tea Party uprising dominated the campaign for the mid-term elections of 2010 and succeeded in denting the solid majority that Obama's Democratic Party had in the U.S. Congress. It then evidently decided to press ahead, to throw rationality overboard and make conformity to a rigid template of conservatism the touchstone for anybody aspiring to the U.S. presidency.[14] But as the massed forces of civil society pushed rapidly to the right, a mobilisation on the other end of the spectrum began with the "Occupy" movements. Deviations from the pristine ideological foundations of the American way were not the issue here, but a more worldly reality, of masses of people left behind in stagnation and threatened with a plunge into poverty by the global rampage of finance that enriched a few. "We are the ninety-nine per-

13 There was no segment of the media that was quite as perfervid as Rupert Murdoch's Fox News in boosting the Tea Party movement. For one among several accounts of this phenomenon, see Butler (2011).

14 For an account of how this ideological civil war has taken possession of the Republican Party, see Taibbi (2012).

cent", said the Occupy protesters as they laid siege to Wall Street and other sites where the levers that controlled global capital flows were located.[15] This was a threat not merely of shifting the centre of gravity of the system, but of overturning it. And the authorities responded with force, clearing out protesters from several locations they had thronged to as the movement spread through the U.S. and the U.K.[16]

In parts of the globe where liberal democracy has been a remote and abstract entity, the social movements of 2011 took diverse forms. Early unity and coherence around the single message of change tended to fray once limited success was achieved, as movements fell apart in sectarian rivalries. Particularly in the Arab world, fierce divisions based on ancient constructs of identity were quick to emerge as these movements shifted focus from their original striving for a basic charter of democratic rights.

Were the protests of 2011 about people seeking the liberal freedoms of western political traditions? Or were they about regaining a lost way of life steeped in indigenous traditions, unsullied by western influence? Still again, were they about overthrowing the legacy of two decades of globalisation, which had enshrined a charter of rights for capital and provided working people with the semblance of the liberal freedoms, unmatched by the prosperity most of them saw at the upper end of the scale and were expected to draw a vicarious sense of achievement from? Were the 2011 movements, in short, about the breakdown of the social consent that was the foundation of two decades of growing global inequalities in wealth and income?

The proliferation of signals is a hazard of the information age that threatens to overwhelm the most diligent effort at comprehension. Sifting through the medley of voices requires an understanding of how the "primary" signals as they originated within these movements, were refracted through the media prism. Though this project tends often to be defeated by the phenomenon summed up in the McLuhanian aphorism that the medium is the message, it is one that needs to be un-

15 On the origin of the slogan, see Anderson (2012): 73.

16 See Roberts (2013) for an account of how the protests were dispersed. For a more optimistic view which believes that the protests will re-emerge with potentially transformative impact, see Ross (2013).

dertaken in the various arenas, including India, where media fuelled social movements have influenced recent historical events.

India: referendums predetermined

Robin Jeffrey has fused Benedict Anderson's insights into the conditioning of the nationalist imagination by print capitalism with Ernest Renan's characterisation of the newspaper as a daily referendum on the nation. Since roughly the end of the "emergency" regime in 1977, in his narration, India's newspaper revolution has brought larger numbers into the political process, and served as a means of recruiting citizen loyalty to the nation. The purchase of a newspaper is "a vote in favour" of the nation, a gesture of belonging.[17]

Since Jeffrey wrote, several new dimensions have been added to the Indian media landscape, notably a trend towards the concentration of ownership. Competition in its rawest form emerged in the English newspaper market in 1994 with the *Times of India* (*TOI*), then Mumbai's largest newspaper but a distant second in Delhi, aggressively making a play to raise its market share in the national capital by slashing prices sharply and handing out huge incentives to vendors. With the competition being forced to follow suit – since the alternative of keeping prices unchanged and offering a better mix of information did not seem viable strategy – the newspaper industry effectively downgraded readership and circulation.[18]

The internet made a quiet entry into India in 1996 and began a phase of rapid growth from the early years of the millennium. Satellite broadcasting, confined till the late-20th century to vapid entertainment

---

17 Jeffrey (2003: 9) explains some of the dynamics through which print capitalism fosters widely shared identities: "Capitalism in the late twentieth century liked large markets. Such a liking fostered the unity of the Indian state by making successful newspaper proprietors all-India actors and members of the 'national' elite. There were two elements to this process. First, such proprietors relished the status and prestige. But more important, newspapers that flourished had to operate with an all-India focus to secure the advertising that brought financial success. It was very difficult ... to maintain a newspaper on selling price alone. Thus pressures of both status and economics encouraged successful newspapers to project the fiction that all of India was at breakfast together each morning".

18 This is part of the case study offered in this volume in chapter vi.

programmes, transformed the news dissemination landscape from roughly about 2004. The 24-hour news channel has since been a major participant in the national dialogue.[19]

Though liberalisation became the reigning *mantra* in 1991, the first approval for a private news broadcaster operating from India was only granted in early-1998, for a venture launched under the deliberately misleading title of an "election channel". This was outcome of assiduous lobbying by Rupert Murdoch, once considered the man who could make and unmake national governments, and also by far the world's least favourite media baron through the 1990s and beyond.[20] Once granted Murdoch's Star TV, there was no credible basis to deny other broadcast companies – especially those owned by Indian nationals – the right to uplink to broadcast satellites from Indian soil. Those changes in policy were made in later years, though with extreme reluctance. The government had little problem allowing an international media moghul to breach its monopoly of the air-waves, but considered it quite another thing granting locals a similar privilege. Perhaps it is a measure of the growing confidence and clout of Indian capital in those years that the government could not hold out against the illogic of the policy for too long.

Despite the newly permissive policy dispensation, the number of broadcast channels that sought uplinking rights was initially rather modest. It took till 2004, when the Indian economy seemed firmly embarked upon an altogether new growth path, for the media industry to shed that seeming modesty of ambition. The figures say it all: in 2004 according to official data from the Ministry for Information and Broadcasting, there were a total of 130 channels registered in India. By 2013, the figure had increased six-fold, to 784. Half of these were registered for news broadcast and a large number of them (though this figure is not precisely known) were exclusive news and current affairs channels.

---

19 These aspects of the story are also dealt with later in this volume.

20 On Murdoch's early successes in transforming Indian media policy, see Guha Thakurta and Seabright (2011). An account of the early phase of confusion in India's broadcast policy can be found in Ninan (2000). Successive changes in India's broadcast policy can be followed from relevant links on the official website of the Indian Government's Ministry of Information and Broadcasting: http://www.mib.nic.in/.

Quantitative expansion may promote the quality of the public discourse, but the connections are not obvious. There are deeper realities at work here, in which the sources of media growth are deeply implicated. Reflecting the extra stimulus to growth in the Indian economy since 2003, total advertising spending is believed to have doubled by 2008. Clearly, this five-year interval was a window of opportunity the Indian media had never seen before. The 24-hour news channel acquired a pervasive presence across all regions and in the mix of channels broadcasting in languages that were understood, partly understood – and actively misunderstood – the English language broadcast assumed an influence disproportionate to actual viewership.

Understanding Media Demographics

The English-language audience simply had more purchasing power. So if advertisers tended to cluster around the English media, it was only because that was where the vanities, ambitions and anxieties of India's globalising middle class were represented. A disaggregation of India's growth process and a closer identification of its main beneficiaries would shed further light on the process.[21] Globalisation widened the gap between the upper and lower tiers and two decades into India's encounter with globalisation, it was an open question whether people at the lower end of the scale were better or worse off in absolute terms.

Media growth was a sub-plot within the broader story of disequalising growth and widening economic disparities. It was propelled by advertising expenditure which, as invariably happens, outpaced aggregate rates of economic growth, but mirrored underlying patterns of consumption growth.[22] The reason simply, is that advertising expenditure is targeted towards the top few strata in the scales of income and wealth. In its distribution between various media platforms, ad

---

21 For a survey of the state of inequality in the Indian economy, see Weisskopf (2011); and also Himanshu (2011).

22 For obvious reasons, advertising expenditure in the economy is a parameter that is much more difficult to track than most others. The leading Indian chamber of commerce, FICCI, has in recent times been tracking this parameter, though its methodology remains unexplained. According to information posted on the website of this organization (www.ficci-frames.com).

expenditure would be expected to reflect the widening gulf between consumer strata.

Purchasing power is not a measurable entity. It has to be assessed through proxy variables. Among the first of these would be language, since there is one group where linguistic ability overlaps with economic privilege. India's largest English language newspaper, the *TOI*, provided a useful public analysis of the demographics of newspaper readership when it was described in the context of a competitive battle against another major newspaper, as catering to a "middle-class" audience. Favourable judgments about its editorial and reporting tone were most welcome, the *TOI* sternly retorted, but the "middle-class" tag certainly was not.

As the *TOI* explained with an abundance of patience, its total readership of 7.4 million constituted just 0.60 percent of the total Indian population. In relation to the estimate by an international financial institution – that the Indian "middle class" was 420 million strong – the *TOI* readership numbered a mere 1.8 percent. It was logical to assume that the *TOI* audience knew English, "still the language of the elite in India". If the "incomes and spending power" of the *TOI* audience were taken into account, it would be clear that "they form the very peak of the pyramid". Though "small in numbers", the newspaper explained with unconcealed didactic relish, *TOI* readers "wield(ed) disproportionate economic and political clout", which made it a seriously unfair description to "collectively club them under an omnibus 'middle class'" description.[23]

It would be intuitively obvious that the audience for the English-language media is separated by a wide gulf from the constituencies served by regional language media. This gap in audience demographics is never easy to quantify because media economics is an area of great opacity. Fortunately, the 2004 decision by one of the country's biggest media houses – the Hindustan Times – to float a public issue of shares and then to hive off Hindi language titles in a separate company, provides a window through which a few insights could be gathered.

---

23 The online reference at Times News Network (2012) vanished soon after being posted on February 1, 2012. A comment on the piece was posted on a well-known blogsite of media commentary (Churumuri, 2012) which provided major extracts from it.

In its statement to shareholders for the financial year 2014-15, HT Media Ltd (HTML), which publishes all English-language titles of the group, reported earnings of Rs 15.75 billion (1,574.7 crore), of which Rs 11.64 billion (1,163.7 crore) came from advertisements. For the same year, Hindustan Media Ventures Ltd (HMVL) – which took over all the Hindi-language publications after being spun off as a subsidiary company of HTML in 2009 – reported total earnings of Rs 8.75 billion (875 crore), of which Rs 5.96 billion (596 crore) came from advertisements.

Readership figures for the *Hindustan Times* (principal publication of HTML) and *Hindustan*, (main revenue earner for HMVL), were available from the relevant rounds of the Indian Readership Survey. These were reported for the year 2014 as respectively, 4.515 million and 14.75 million.The simplest of calculations would show that HT Media earned Rs 2,578 as advertisement revenue for every reader it reached, while HMVL earned Rs 404.[24] The English-language audience in other words, was worth over six times more to the media company than its Hindi readers.

Unpacking "civil society"

This has obvious implications for the way the civil society dialogue is carried out through the media. Inequalities are nothing new in modernising societies and the core of the problem in India obviously lies in these four in every ten that remain beyond the reach of all media. But these sections of the Indian nation, which include many of those living in absolute poverty, remain unseen and unheard. Political leaders claim to speak for them, as do various civil society actors. But these assumptions of the moral right to speak for the voiceless gain little traction within the media, even when authentic in some measure.

---

24 The calculations are precise but do not represent the exact comparative picture since both HT Media and HMVL derive minor revenue streams from lesser publications. Adding on the estimated 310,000 readers of *Mint*, to the *Hindustan Times* readership would not substantively change the comparative picture. HT Media provides data in two formats, one of which includes the income of all subsidiaries. The figures used here refer to HT Media's standalone revenues, which reflect the earnings of its English titles alone.

Inequality as a reality has been reconciled through several devices with the republican promise of equality before the law. In the metropolitan centres of world capital, the concept and practice of the "welfare state" summed up the active political intent to neutralise the worst disparities of a capitalist society. Soon after World War II, i.e., at roughly the same time that the "welfare state" became the dominant mode of political organisation in metropolitan centres of the world economy, the newly independent post-colonial societies adopted the paradigm of the "developmental state". Regimes that came to power in the euphoria of liberation from colonialism promised fairness and equity, where no citizen would suffer discrimination on grounds of race, ethnicity, gender or religion.

Beginning in the early-1980s, the welfare state began to be dismantled in the west, with the counter-revolution initiated against economic common sense by Ronald Reagan in the U.S. and Margaret Thatcher in the U.K. The Latin American debt crisis which broke out as a direct outcome of the Reagan-Thatcher counter-revolution, sounded the death knell of the developmental state. By the closing years of the decade, the Soviet empire was tottering and seemingly all set for the fall. "Civil society" entered policy discussions from then on as an active variable. It soon afterwards became the basis for mobilising social movements in pursuit of specific policy outcomes. Older references to specific interest groups – such as trade unions, chambers of commerce and consumer organisations – were superseded by a new hold-all term.[25]

The information society has undoubtedly complicated the older narrative of the newspaper as a daily referendum on the nation, but perhaps not by very much. The media discourse is one among many ways in which particularities are evened out and a sense of "community" achieved. Linguistic segmentation – a feature of the Indian media landscape – is potentially an impediment to the harmonisation of various particularities. Though each linguistic zone could evolve a "civil society" viewpoint through the media discourse, there is yet no

25 "Social capital" became in a sense the method of promoting developmental objectives by fostering a sense of community among citizens in a sphere autonomous of the state. This was, as Harriss (2003) pointed out, a gigantic vacuity in policy, in seeking to take out of the equation the vital element of politics.

assurance that it could become an element in the "national" dialogue. As within the national context, the regional dialogue too tends to be skewed in favour of those with the purchasing power to be of interest to the advertiser. And as the English-language media has spoken the language of globalism, the regional media has, impelled by its own relentless commercial calculus, adopted the language of localism. As pointed out by Jeffrey, news content here tends to be tailored towards providing the right "context" for advertisements that have a strong local flavour.[26]

The pan-India dialogue, carried out for most part in English, draws in another slice of "civil society", and would for reasons of history and economics, have an influence over the policy agenda "disproportionate" – as the *TOI* very grandiosely put it – to the actual size of the audience reached. With regional media being sequestered in distinct linguistic spheres, the English language media is where the national elite speaks for and to itself. Segmentation and stratification in the media would seem logically to suggest not the harmony of particularities, but the dominance of one particular discourse masquerading as a "consensus" vision. The alternative would be sheer incoherence in the civil society dialogue.

Overcoming linguistic incoherence

The story of globalisation in India suggests that there is in the real world, a political dynamic which prevails over the logic of linguistic segmentation. Concord has been secured in matters of state policy, in part by recruiting regional elites into national politics through coalitional arrangements. By about 2003 moreover, the economic horizons seemed to be expanding rapidly enough to accommodate the burgeoning ambitions of all interest groups, from the regional to national elites.

Though fallen on bad times since the global economic downturn of 2008, the policy of "special economic zones" (SEZs) unfurled with much fanfare in 2001 and implemented in a fever of enthusiasm by various state governments since an enabling law was passed in 2005, would be an important case study of how important debates were conducted in privileged circles and reproduced in a feast of concord by regional and national media. State governments gained something akin

26 Jeffrey (2003).

to the power of eminent domain under the law: they could acquire large swathes of territory and notify them as SEZs to be developed by chosen corporate entities. From the point of view of the national elite, this was a way to expand "globalised India" to benighted regions of deficient infrastructure and unskilled people. From the perspective of the regional elite, it was a means for a few to find liberation from the drudgery of agriculture, escape the monotony of rural life and secure a niche in the modernising enclaves through which the glitter and affluence of globalism were diffusing.[27]

For as long as the economy was buoyant and the prospects bright, little in the media discourse suggested the possibility of a disturbance in the placid surface of consent. Protests that broke out over the mega-development projects conjured up in this time of burgeoning national ambition – including the SEZs and the many extractive industries sanctioned across the lands where India's indigenous communities lived – caused no more than a ripple in the larger "civil society" dialogue. And then came the cataclysmic events that let loose the rebellious spirits of the elite, amplified as always by the media.

The terrorist landing on the shores of Mumbai on November 26, 2008 and the bloodbath that followed as the affluent southern tip of the city was held under siege for sixty hours, were broadcast live and with competitive outrage by the news channels. Earlier terrorist atrocities had struck with sudden and lethal violence, but allowed for a reconstitution of civic solidarity in the immediate aftermath. Mumbai 26/11, as it is now remembered in the media discourse – because every terrorist atrocity has to seek a shorthand that rhymes with the 9/11 attacks in the U.S. – sapped civic confidence in the state. For sixty hours, it drowned out every other issue in the national conversation. And aside from a few conspicuous acts of bravery by police personnel and spe-

27 The SEZs policy was important enough at one point to have an entire research programme devoted to it, though its output has slowed in recent times. See http://www.indiasezpolitics.org/aboutus.php#a3 for details. For an analysis of the policy and the complexities of local political dynamics it unleashes, see Vijayabaskar (2010), who presents a classic case study on how regional elites gained enormous space within the discourse on globalisation by leveraging their political clout through coalitional arrangements. For the uncertain economic benefits of the SEZs policy, see Dutta (2009). For an account of how the land acquisition for SEZs was viewed in states where consent was not easily manufactured, see Balagopal (2007).

cial forces commandos, there seemed little in the response of the state agencies to restore public faith.[28]

Civil society votes down a government

Spasms of outrage followed at the "political class" which was accused of caring little about the challenges ordinary citizens faced in their daily lives. But if Mumbai 26/11 was expected to cast a long shadow over the general elections to Parliament that followed in 2009, the impact finally was minimal. By far the more dramatic elite referendum on the government came in 2011, with the Anna Hazare movement. Measured by the tone of media coverage, this was a referendum with a decisive outcome: "government" was held to be in flagrant default on all responsibilities and the sole remedy available was the civil society voice as articulated by Anna Hazare and his confidants, who had by now acquired the collective identity of "Team Anna".[29]

Significant changes had taken place in the landscape between Mumbai 26/11 and the moment when Anna Hazare managed to convert the Indian media into a virtual megaphone for his idiosyncratic view of politics and society. The September 2008 financial bubble-burst in the U.S. had swept over the global economy, hitting enterprises large and small. Media companies in India, which till late-2008 had few worries in prospect, were rudely awoken to the insecure foundations on which their fortunes rested. Many of the most prominent news channels which had been earning a fair profit till then sank deep into the red. For the newspaper industry, the hazards were great enough for some of the luminaries in the trade to line up hat in hand and plead for a special bailout package.[30]

An uptick in the economy in the year that followed was neutralised by raging inflation. Older certainties about the growth path the Indian economy had entered seemed suddenly shaky and fallible, and the confidence of the elite discourse began distinctly to fray, betraying acute symptoms of insecurity and anger. These found a natural focus in

---

28 See two analyses of the media coverage of Mumbai terrorist attacks in Muralidharan (2008 and 2009).

29 Muralidharan (2011a and 2011b) consider the Anna Hazare agitation with particular focus on the mode of media coverage involved.

30 This event is separately dealt with.

the rampant official malfeasance that came to light in the months since the 2009 general elections. There were few who paused to reflect on the irony that most reported acts of corruption arose from the transfer of resources from public to private hands. Corruption was in this sense, not an unwarranted intrusion into the economic growth story, but perhaps its inseparable accessory. But as long as the story-line remained strong about India being firmly on the trajectory towards global eminence, the sub-plot of rampant corruption went unremarked.

Legal luminary Anil Divan, who has done much to institute a credible regime of accountability in governance processes, made the case for a tough new law against corruption in a comment published by a leading national daily.[31] The basis for heightened public anxiety over corruption was in his perception, very clear: inflation had pared off the equivalent of Rs 230 billion (2,30,000 crore) in value from household expenditures over the year. This was of the same order of magnitude as the loss caused the public exchequer by the gross irregularities in the allocation of slots in the frequency spectrum for the second generation of telecom services (the "2G spectrum scam" in media shorthand). Reining in corruption in other words, would make ordinary lives more liveable – and less anxious – by a like magnitude.

In popular reckoning, there is a direct link between the distress caused by inflation and the money lost to illicit acts by those in authority. This connection becomes in the elite imagination, a causal link: all economic hardships are seen to originate in the cynical self-aggrandisement of people collectively named the "political class".

More patient examination would show that the estimate of consumption loss caused to the Indian people referred to a past period of time, while the putative losses from the sale of 2G telecom spectrum below true worth were spread over a period of time stretching into the future.[32] Secondly, the earnings from the sale of spectrum would not go into personal consumption, but a whole complex of expenditure commitments that the state undertakes. Finally, even if revenue fore-

---

31 Divan (2011).

32 Any loss to the public exchequer from the sale of spectrum below an assumed cost could well become a benefit to the "public" in a broader sense, from the cheaper telephone tariffs that this enables.

gone leads, through deficit financing, to a spike in inflation, the precise impact is rather difficult to estimate.

Yet, the analogy is interesting since it reveals much about the mood of public anger and anxiety that took hold in 2011. Transparency in governance was a hard-fought goal of public campaigns over a decade and more, an object that seemed within grasp when the right to information (RTI) became law in 2005. The multiplying scale of corruption since then was evidence that this was rather too optimistic an expectation. Economic policy was by this time, acquiring new dimensions which evaded the scrutiny of even the most vigilant and public-spirited citizen. The financial sector had become an ever widening domain involving strange and unrecognisable players and instruments that taxed the most robust commonsense. Its customary opacity was compounded several times over by the accelerated adoption of "global" practices.

The reign of virtue

Corruption was for Anna Hazare the central concern, constructed almost in a theological sense. And the means to fight the scourge was a powerful oversight body created by law. The draft law prepared by Anna Hazare's IAC movement went through several iterations between the four-day drama of April and the brinkmanship of September 2011. The IAC draft bill conceived of a Jan Lok Pal (JLP), as a powerful agency, in a language and idiom more akin to moral lecture than legal text. This was apparent in the profligate use of ill-defined terms such as "immaculate", "integrity", "eminent" and "evil". To be "impeccable" and to possess "integrity" or "eminence" in the manner that the JLP required, was seen to be beyond most citizens.

In the early years of what is today called the "European enlightenment", the political philosopher Montesquieu famously identified "virtue" – or respect for the law – as the widely shared spirit within a society that made democracy as a system of governance possible. Even if widely shared, virtue is a frail and delicate attribute, which needed to be securely enshrined. Virtue would surely perish if power were to be exercised arbitrarily and the law abused. Excessive power, vested in any individual or institution, was the surest road to the collapse of democracy, making the separation of powers an essential safeguard of virtue.

The Anna Hazare movement worked on a rather different premise. Virtue was seen not as a widely held attribute but the monopoly of a chosen few. The institutions of democracy had in Team Anna's view, failed to function for the people since legislature, judiciary and executive had arrived at a self-serving and sordid deal among themselves, making accountability the principal casualty. Team Anna held out the promise that once its anti-corruption bill became law, ordinary citizens' lives would be governed by higher virtues, embodied in a chosen few who would assume stewardship of the JLP. Reflecting its disdain of the legislature, executive and judiciary, the IAC conceived of the JLP as a body that could impose its will on all three in any matter involving the suspicion of financial wrongdoing.

By the loftiness of its mission, the JLP had to be a body born in immaculate conception and untouched by the politics ordinary mortals were mired in. The origin of the JLP seemingly lay in a construction of "virtue" beyond ordinary politics. It was this moral purpose that defined the central theme and determined the trajectory of the Anna Hazare campaign. Aside from "anti-corruption" which was a slogan even more vapid than "pro-motherhood", the spirit of the movement emerged in successive drafts of the bill that Team Anna and the IAC put before the public. And it was an enduring contribution of the media to this episode in the national political conversation that it chose to ignore all the tell-tale signals of authoritarian intent these drafts betrayed.

Beginning with an early draft – themed around "men of virtue" – which spoke of empowering Nobel laureates of Indian origin, Bharat Ratna and Magsaysay awardees and five-star ranking military officers to appoint the Lok Pal, the JLP bill went through several modifications. It is fair to say that every version, despite seeking precision in terminology and a better fit with constitutional processes, bore the imprint of the circumstances in which the bill was conceived. Since the "men of virtue" draft was rubbished, a subsequent iteration by the IAC, labelled version 2.1, changed the appointment criteria. Still manifest was a stubborn refusal to yield ground to representative institutions, or individuals chosen through direct elections. In a selection committee comprising eleven members or more, only one qualified by virtue of being an elected representative, and this was the Speaker of the Lok Sabha, who made the grade by holding an office presumably above partisan loyalties. Retained in the selection committee were all armed forces personnel of the five-star rank, of whom there have been three in the history of India, with the sole survivor at the time of the Hazare hubbub being well into his 90s. Also included were the two most senior among two categories of judicial figures: Supreme Court judges and high court chief justices.

In the next round of change, version 2.2 changed the composition of the selection committee considerably. The total number on the body was brought down to ten, and the patently absurd requirement to have a military officer of five-star rank was deleted. The Prime Minister and Leader of the Opposition in the Lok Sabha were allowed admission into the selection committee. But in the category of judicial representatives, the criterion of choice was changed from the most senior among Supreme Court judges and high court chief justices, to the youngest in both these categories. The deliberations that led to these formulations were supposedly open and transparent. But few reasons were advanced for this violent switch of loyalty between seniority and its opposite.

Saving the people from themselves

Fundamentally, every formulation of the JLP bill resonated with the attitude that nobody could be trusted, that a presumption of guilt was warranted in any matter involving a broadly defined notion of "corruption". Against the imperative of deepening participatory democratic processes, the IAC draft sought a rigid, hierarchical structure, armed with extraordinary powers.

Anna Hazare was seemingly propounding the very antithesis of the European enlightenment. There was no way to retrieve the interests of the common man – by definition devoid of virtue – other than through a body that stood above all other institutions of governance. The Anna Hazare movement promised messianic deliverance from the difficulties ordinary people faced negotiating governance processes. But the sea refused to part as Hazare's chosen people were led to the water's edge. The Anna Hazare bubble burst of December 2011 remains to be analysed. For reasons yet unclear, the media in December 2011 withdrew its active sponsorship of the Anna Hazare movement. The "people" as constructed by the media, followed in withdrawing consent for

Anna Hazare's project of putting all institutions of democracy under a watchdog body that would embody all his virtue and righteous rage.

When the full story of the Anna Hazare movement is written, the reasons behind the implosion of December 2011 will undoubtedly come in for detailed scrutiny. Like other movements possessed of messianic fervour – such as the anti-reservations movement in both the 1990 and 2004 visitations – Anna Hazare could ignite the rage of the social strata that dominate the media discourse. But conviction failed at some point, when it seemed that the entire system was potentially under threat. A key moment may have been November 2011, when the government of Prime Minister Manmohan Singh, flailing desperately to extricate itself from a logjam in parliament, notified a policy allowing foreign direct investment in the retail sector. The announcement made through an executive order, was a quite brazen affront to parliament which was then in session, though prone to noisy and obstreperous disruption. The withdrawal of the change in policy, when a chorus of condemnation arose, was abject.

In that short interval of time, there was another fusion of the regional and national elite discourses. It proved transient and could not offset the rage occasioned by the Union Cabinet's disregard of parliamentary propriety. The entry of big capital in the retail sector was seen as a benefit by both globalising and localising India. Farm lobbies in states of such consequence as Punjab and Maharashtra endorsed it with little reserve. And the *TOI* spoke for large sections of the national elite when it commented editorially that opening up the retail sector was the government's "first big-ticket reform initiative in a long time". It had the potential, "when implemented" to "transform India's chaotic and predominantly unorganised retail sector, while hugely benefiting agriculture as well as the inflation-hit consumer". With the assurance of all these riches ahead, the *TOI* regretted that political parties, "even outside the staunchly anti-reform Left brigade have ganged up to disrupt Parliament".[33]

The Anna Hazare bubble-burst of December 2011 occurred on the back of visible signals of distress from the elected government. After pushing it to the wall through two rounds of Hazare's mobilisation, the media seemingly awoke to the reality that a further elite referendum

33 *Times of India* (2011).

that voted down the government could have unforeseeable and deeply damaging consequences. And this happened at precisely a time when elite perceptions – at least in the matter of allowing foreign investment in retail trade – converged briefly with the government's intent. A face-saving formula was available to tone down the fervour. Though still far from convincing in its response, Parliament did – while Anna Hazare floundered in quest of an audience for his December roadshow – put up a halfway credible public spectacle of debating a tough new law to ensure the probity of all government agencies. Figuratively speaking, that pulled the rug out from under the IAC agitation. Corruption ceased being an issue in the months that followed, till it was stoked back to life as an issue in the 2014 election campaign, when a person regarded as the least plausible candidate for a national leadership role became by some mysterious alchemy, the messiah of a new phase of economic dynamism and growth for the nation.[34]

December 16, 2012

Late on the evening of December 16, 2012, a young woman of twenty-three – a physiotherapy student – left a multiplex theatre in Delhi with a male friend. She was in an area not very well served by public transport and had a long way to go. At a busy city intersection, she found a bus with an eager crew hustling passengers on board with the assurance of taking them to their destinations. It was not an uncommon practice in that area and the woman boarded with her male friend. Well over an hour later, she was dumped out of the bus, not far from the spot where she boarded, severely injured and barely conscious. Passers-by went their way, unwilling to get involved, but one among them seemingly alerted the neighbourhood police who reached the young woman to the nearest medical care centre. Within a day, the nature of her injuries as disclosed in discrete yet vivid briefings from the doctors treating her, revealed a horrific crime of sexual assault and brutalisation. The young woman of twenty-three lingered on another thirteen days. For those few days it seemed the entire country was riveted on willing to recovery a person whose name remained unknown to all but a handful. The end, when it came, was a moment of extreme

34 The media contribution to the 2014 general election victory of Narendra Modi, then the Chief Minister of Gujarat and at the time of this writing Prime Minister of India, is dealt with in a later chapter.

public grief, with one news channel typically, headlining it as the death of "India's daughter".

That fortnight came to be seen as a deeply transformative moment, but it did not seem out of place within months, to ask what had really changed.[35] As one inquiry into this particular incident found, media coverage of the crime of rape was usually "narrowly focused on instances of sexual violence against middle-class and upper-caste women and ... tended to exclude ... violence as poor and lower-caste segments of the Indian population might experience". The reporting on rape was pervaded by the powerful emotion of "shame", which deeply influenced "media coverage the crime receives". And with all the elaborate codes devised to deal with the issue, the "patriarchal bias against the raped woman (was) fully in place and evident in the treatment meted out to the victim by the police, the criminal justice system, and the media".[36]

December 16 also provoked a "furore across the globe", leading in one estimate, to no fewer than 1,515 articles in the U.S. media within a period of two months.[37] International media coverage, this researcher found, represented the incident as "a putative battle between two India's: the first, new and modern, and the second, old and backward". The victim was portrayed as a woman of ambition, on the pathway to advancement through her commitment to a modern education. And her assailants were reported to have simulated a consuming, righteous moral rage at her temerity in travelling far away from home with a man she was not bound in marital ties with.

In media representation, the brutal assailants of December 16 were "migrant workers who lived in a local slum". They had been drinking

---

35 In December 2015, three years after the event, a coalition of three women's organisations issued a statement which said effectively, that nothing had changed: "Yet, in the three years since December 2012, women continue to face violence in every space they occupy, including their own homes, in public places, on public transport and at workplaces. There have been many attacks on women and girls, some accompanied by huge media coverage, but most taking place away from the public glare. Violence is the weapon used to keep them 'in their place' on the basis of their identities, including caste, class race, religion and dis/ability". See Scroll (2015).

36 Rao (2014): 154, 163 and 165.

37 Roychowdhury (2013): 282.

heavily that evening and were out on a predatory roam on a bus they had temporary control over. Feeding the narrative was a statement from politician Raj Thackeray, based in the distant western metropolis of Mumbai, about migrants from the Hindi heartland state of Bihar being perpetrators of most crimes in frontiers of urban modernity. The Chief Minister of Delhi at the time, Sheila Dikshit, added her own spin by pinning the blame on the "huge migratory population". Prime Minister Manmohan Singh with a moderate effort to be statesman-like warned of "footloose migrants" who were menacing society because they just could not find a toehold within the developmental process.[38]

Factually, all these constructions were sloppy and inattentive to detail. But the media seem disinclined to question the overarching narrative of an India of aspiration struggling valiantly against primitive forces from the rural outback. The popular dialogue here was constructed around basic urges of vengeance and retribution, which only admitted a limited range of possibilities: "incarceration, public shaming, and the possibility of state-sanctioned death".[39]

The December 16 coverage offers many teachable moments about a media universe driven by elite perceptions and profit calculations. December 16 was a Sunday, when most celebrity TV anchors were on holiday. The dark deed happened too late to be featured in the day's news bulletins. What triggered a cascade of public outrage the following day, may have been a briefing by the Delhi Police in the morning, which spoke of the crime as among the most barbaric ever encountered. Students from Jawaharlal Nehru University (JNU), located within a stone's throw of the crime scene, had mobilised by that evening for a demonstration outside the local police station. This spilled over onto nearby roads, choking traffic through some of the capital city's busiest thoroughfares.

The social media was meanwhile buzzing with outrage, propelling the mainstream media discourse in directions where the traditional principles of news reporting may have been sacrificed in order to better mirror public outrage. The electronic and broadcast media leaves a light imprint, but the tone of the print coverage accurately reflects the trend of the time. Because of the hour at which the crime was commit-

38 Ibid: 286.

39 Ibid: 286.

ted, the first print reports appeared in the newspapers of December 18. The headlines left no room for any ambiguity about the horror of the crime: "City Shamed: Girl gangraped in bus in South Delhi at 9.30 pm"; "23 year old gangraped inside Delhi bus, thrown out". Strong expressions of outrage followed from politicians and other public figures through a variety of forums including Parliament, where a number of women members raised their voices in strongly condemning the event and demanding action.

Till this time, there was no real hint of a chasm emerging between the political establishment and the public. The *Hindustan Times* (*HT*) on December 19 blazoned the theme of unity across its front-page story on the event: "India against rape: Parliament, public unite over Delhi horror". *The Hindu* had "A Nation Outraged" as its lead story on a day that it ran an editorial titled "A time to be ashamed". There was as yet no name-calling, no serious intent to play the blame-game, certainly none of the "civil society versus political class" mood that came to dominate the following days.

The mood shift began for some reason the next day, when *HT* chose to run a front-page headline that read: "Dear VIP, instead of shedding tears for Delhi's rape victim on TV, shed your inflated security". This seemed at the time an isolated comment, but the mood was infectious. On December 21, *TOI* devoted all of page five to the theme of VIP privileges that ostensibly denied the common person the security he or she deserved. Anger on the street was by then boiling over. Starting with a few candle-light demonstrations and prayers for the December 16 victim, the public mood was pumped up when the news channels chose for reasons uniquely related to their competitive calculus, to rapidly escalate the outrage factor. From then on, the media rhetoric and the anger on the streets fed into each other, creating for the embattled government, yet another serious crisis of a no confidence vote by the entity called "civil society".

At some point, senior officials in the government felt compelled to issue warnings to the media to tone down the rhetoric and not let the manifestations of public outrage spill over the limits of systemic tolerance. On December 25, Subhash Chand Tomar, a police constable assigned to patrol one of the sites of most vociferous protest, died on duty. The authorities were quick to blame his death on an unprovoked assault by demonstrators, while the media went to great lengths to establish that Tomar had died of natural causes, possibly accentuated by the stress of dealing with a situation he had not been trained for. As governance structures in Delhi sought to contain the eruption of public rage, Chief Minister Dikshit apparently sought an escape route by flying the victim of the brutal rape to Singapore for what she said was emergency surgery. For a sceptical media, this seemed just a way of getting the evidence out of the way before a final admission of defeat.

The death of the young woman was formally announced within two days, her identity still mostly unknown. Reporting her passing, *HT*'s front page lead on December 30 called the nation to action: "Wake up India, She is dead". Its black-bordered front-page editorial declared that the flame she lit would "burn on". The *Indian Express* (*IE*) announced an "outpouring of grief across India". "Rest in peace, Nirbhaya", said *TOI*, using a name that it had bestowed upon the unknown girl of 23. *The Hindu* alongside its news-report headlined "A young woman dies, a nation mourns", ran an editorial exhortation that there should be "no turning back". "Ordinary citizens", it urged, should step into the "leaderless vacuum". "Would the Indian political system and class have been so indifferent to the problem of sexual violence", asked *The Hindu*, "if half or even one-third of all legislators were women?"

The Hindu's proposal to legislate an assured representation for women in all legislative institutions, was one among several policy recommendations that followed. With the surfeit of advice it enjoyed, it would seem that the government would have had no difficulty in making the necessary changes in policy and procedure. Indeed, the high-level advisory committee that the government appointed under a former Chief Justice of India, J.S. Verma, came out within just a month, with a report of exemplary detail and analytical depth, proposing all necessary changes in the law and the manner of its implementation, not hesitating even from venturing into the more difficult domain of social values.[40]

---

40 J.S. Verma *et al* (2013). Introducing its recommendations (Ibid: 411), the committee observed that "existing laws if faithfully and efficiently implemented by credible law enforcement agencies, (would be) sufficient to maintain law and order and to protect the safety and dignity of the people, particularly women, and to punish any offenders who commit any crime". Nonetheless, the committee went on, this did not mean that "necessary improvements in the law, keeping in mind modern times, should not be enacted at the earliest".

With all this available, the government chose early in the budget session of Parliament in 2013, to introduce legislative amendments that made sexual assault a far more strictly punished crime. Changes in criminal law added a number of provisions to sections 326 and 354 of the Indian Penal Code (IPC) which respectively dealt with aggravated assault and gender crime, though without specificity or stringency. None of these changes in the law could have been applied to the trial of the six (later reduced to five by the ostensible suicide of one among them in prison) accused of the December 16 atrocity. The law is very clear here. Article 20 of the Indian Constitution, part of the fundamental rights section, specifically lays down the stricture that no person can be "convicted of any offence except for violation of a law in force at the time of the commission of the act", and cannot be "subjected to a penalty greater than that which might have been inflicted under the law in force at the time".

This clause embodies the common sense that nobody should suffer from the retroactive definition of a crime, a basic principle of the rule of law. Nonetheless, no such scruple prevented the media in the aftermath of December 16 from frequently wondering out aloud if the gallows were not the appropriate destination for all the accused. Even in respect of the seventeen-year old juvenile offender, there was frequently expressed disgruntlement about the maximum term of three years allowed.

A petition was presented before the Supreme Court by political operative Subramanian Swamy, always looking out for a chance to grab the limelight, asking that the law be changed and applied retroactively to the juvenile offender of December 16. All through this, the media remained on the sidelines, applauding patently illicit endeavours. In the months that followed, the media and the political establishment seemed to be in tacit alliance in feeding the mood of public illiteracy about the basic principles of the rule of law. Soon after the conviction of the four who went on trial on charges of rape, aggravated assault and murder, the leader of the opposition in the Lok Sabha then, Sushma Swaraj, whose curriculum vitae includes a claim of having practised law in the Supreme Court, was quoted saying that "as per the new law, rape and murder entails death penalty". Parliament indeed, had made that point, that "all four should be hanged."

The opposition leader's legal illiteracy was clearly a lesser sin in comparison with Union Home Minister Shinde's. Speaking soon after the conviction of the four by a Delhi court, Shinde referred to the new legislation he had piloted through Parliament, which amended the law on sexual assault. "The new law has provision for hanging in rarest of rare cases," he said.

The plain fact was that the maximum penalty the four were liable for, laid down in article 376 of the IPC, did not even remotely provide for death. It was only by tagging on the charge of murder, which is a more severe charge than causing death, since it requires the proof of intent to kill, that the four criminals of December 16 could have been sent to the gallows. Making this manner of charge stick would have required a far different procedure than followed in the December 16 prosecution. In their editorials following the imposition of the death sentence on all four accused, the media did not seem bothered with these subtleties. *The Hindu* welcomed the expeditious procedure adopted before concluding, in line with its editorial policy of opposing the death penalty, that the "decision to hang all four adult accused to death marks a step back — since it will have the effect of substituting the need for greater social, legal and even political efforts to tackle the epidemic of crimes against women with the false comfort of retribution".[41] *IE* commented that the crime of December 16 did not need any manner of judicial determination to meet the criterion of being among the "rarest of the rare" where the death penalty was appropriate. This was in *IE*'s words, "not just because of the brutality of the assault, but also in the way it wrenched attention to itself". The death sentence awarded four of the accused was "clearly meant as exemplary punishment for an exceptional crime".[42]

Soon after the sentences were handed down, *TOI* reported on its front-page that contrary to all the reporting logged till then, the juvenile let off with what seemed undeserved leniency, was perhaps not guilty as charged in the media. Quoting the findings of the statutory body that sent the juvenile criminal to a three-year remand - the maximum permitted under the law - the *TOI* reported that the evidence against the juvenile did not indicate that he was any more brutal

41 *The Hindu* (2013a).

42 *Indian Express* (2013).

than all others involved in the crime. The Juvenile Justice Board in fact, sharply criticised the "media hype" over the young offender's role. Neither the victim nor her companion on that ill-starred evening, had even remotely indicated in their testimonies that the juvenile had been a greater offender than the others. By pointlessly echoing and amplifying the hearsay which held him guilty of the most barbaric conduct that evening, the media had in fact, "brutalised" the juvenile offender.[43]

Two years later, when the juvenile offender in the case had done his time under law and was due to walk free, the media seemed possessed by a strange amnesia. Neither the appalling state of the juvenile justice system which is known to create potential offenders rather than correct delinquents, nor the specifics of the December 16 gang rape seemed relevant, as the call went out for harsh amendments to the law to keep the offender in confinement for a longer period. Failing that, and there were a few media platforms that recognised that the retroactive application of criminal law would be impossible, there was a demand to provide for the trial of juveniles accused of certain categories of crime in accordance with the normally applicable law. A favoured recourse was to juxtapose two elements: news of the imminent release of the juvenile offender with the tearful images and words of the parents of the December 16 victim. Rights campaigners arguing the case for retaining the law unchanged and attending to rampant abuses in the administration of the juvenile justice system were put through the same emotional wringer and came through distinctly the worse off in that contest of images.[44]

The orchestrated public hysteria had its impact. Parliament which was then in session quickly drafted an amendment to the Juvenile Justice Act and had it passed through both houses with unaccustomed alacrity. The amendments provided for trial of juvenile offenders in accordance with the law applicable to adults when the crime involved rose to a certain "heinous" standard. On December 26, the day after the upper house of Parliament passed the bill, *TOI* carried an advertisement for itself whose tone was nothing short of triumphal. With a collage of six of its headlines over the years since the December 16 rape – all calling for the trial of juvenile offenders in major crimes with

43 *Times of India* (2013).

44 *Huffington Post* (2015).

the severest provisions – the *TOI* celebrated its ability to "lead change", a practice it rather gloatingly declared, it had been loyal to through its one hundred and seventy-seven year history.[45]

Internet as a public space, policed by the state

The anti-corruption upsurge and the December 16 protests, brought out a situation of schism between state and civil society, best described by Manuel Castells. These were situations in which the articulation of the interests of society collided with organised structures of power, as embodied in the state.[46] Needless to say, such collisions are more likely to arise when the means available to articulate particular points of view are widely dispersed, and not amenable to any form of centralised control. Print media was domesticated through the power of advertising, and broadcast, when it escaped the legally enforced monopoly of the state, was soon brought under the same discipline. The internet and social media posed a different order of problem, but the logic of domestication has been at work in this space too. That is a story which remains incompletely told because its subject is itself in a state of continuing change. But certain broad contours are already discernible.

In May 2011, while under house arrest in the U.K., Julian Assange, founder of Wikileaks, received a request for a meeting from Eric Schmidt, Executive Chairman of Google. Assange was preoccupied at the time by the global crackdown on Wikileaks, the desperate attempt to staunch the flow of highly classified diplomatic communications that laid bare the shadowy world of global power politics. But a meeting with the head of the world's most influential company who was ostensibly engaged in writing a book on the power of ideas, was an opportunity he could not turn down.

Schmidt's collaborator on the book project was Jared Cohen, head of a division within the company known as Google Ideas. He was another of the elements referred to by the generic term "in and outers", constantly in transit through the revolving doors between the corpo-

---

45 The media watch website *The Hoot* (2015) made note of this self-celebratory advertisement in the *TOI* on 27 December. Among the headlines that the *TOI* chose to recount was one that celebrated bad spelling: "Lower the juvenile age to 16, punish them severly".

46 Castells (2009): 13.

rate world, policy think-tanks and government. As Assange later narrated it, Cohen had "been poached in his early twenties" by Google. He was famed for having served the U.S. State Department under two bosses – Condoleezza Rice and Hillary Clinton – and for his facility to invent smart sounding catch-phrases such as "Public Diplomacy 2.0" for every enterprise of marginal novelty. In 2010, Schmidt and Cohen co-authored a paper for the solid establishment journal *Foreign Affairs*, titled with a newly coined catch-phrase "Digital Disruption". It was a celebration of the new frontiers of human freedom, potentially within reach on account of networking technologies Google was pioneering. From the "reading coalition" that Benedict Anderson theorised about as a key player in the early days of the nation, here was a prophecy of how "coalitions of the connected" would cement a true global solidarity of enlightenment and freedom that went beyond the nation.

Schmidt and Cohen spoke of the dualism of the possibilities inherent in networking. Its benign uses were evident in Moldova, they pointed out, where crowds were organised to storm the streets in 2009 after elections they felt were rigged to sustain a discredited old regime in power. More malevolent uses came from the Taliban Islamic militia in Afghanistan, which had cleverly learnt to manipulate a newly installed mobile telephone network to coordinate actions, threaten and extort. Mobile handsets were even pressed into service to detonate roadside bombs and kill U.S and allied troops.

Within this polarised context, Schmidt and Cohen looked forward to the consolidation of an "interconnected estate, a virtual space that (would be) constrained by different national laws, but not national boundaries". It would be a space in which there could be no equivalent of "the modern system of nation-states". What would prevail instead would be a distribution of power in which "governments, individuals, nongovernmental organisations and private companies (would) balance one another's interests". The transition was likely to be turbulent, though there could be little doubt that "free-market and democratic governments will be the best suited to manage and cope with this maelstrom".

The Google maestros saw a certain typology among the world's nation-states. In China, they saw a state that was aware of the power of the new techniques of connectivity and intent on harnessing it to sustain its own "political and economic power". In India as in China, there were worries about the unsettling of established power structures and also a determination to use the internet and social media for building economic growth. Then there was the vast majority of nations where connectivity was partial, almost a privilege enjoyed by a few. Governments in these societies were tending to see "more costs than benefits" from the spread of technology.

Within this spectrum of responses, only one firm prognosis could be advanced: that continuous innovation and "the increasing population of the interconnected estate" would bring up new and difficult challenges for "people and governments the world over". Governments that "ride the technological wave (would) clearly be best positioned to assert their influence and bring others into their orbits". And in this respect, democratic nations that had "built coalitions of their militaries (would) have the capacity to do the same with their connection technologies".[47] The new technologies of connectivity in other words could become a hand-maiden of the same interests that in earlier contexts were served by military means. The forging of western military might in to a focused instrument of policy was one among the models for how the new technologies of connectivity and communication were to be harnessed.

Schmidt and Cohen were stepping into a terrain where they were assured of official blessings. Just months before U.S. Secretary of State Hillary Clinton had formally declared "internet freedom" a foreign policy goal, useful in the realm of values and also to serve more material ends. She was speaking at the Newseum, a museum located in Washington DC, showcasing the best and worst of U.S. journalism over the years. In attendance were some of the leading lights of the free speech cause in the U.S. and legislators from both sides of the aisle, testifying as Clinton said, to a "commitment that crosses party lines and branches of government".

The message that the top U.S. diplomat delivered at the time was simple. Powerful new means had been found to advance freedom, but with an inherent potential also to "undermine human progress and political rights". Steel could be used "to build hospitals or machine guns, nuclear power, to either "energise" or "destroy" a city. Information technologies similarly could be "harnessed for good or for ill".

47 Schmidt and Cohen (2010): 75-85.

There was already a subtle suggestion that moral and ethical markers applied in older technological paradigms would be seamlessly transferred to connectivity technologies. The arbiters of morality would be the same but unlike steel – and more particularly nuclear power – the U.S. here would "stand for a single internet where all humanity has equal access to knowledge and ideas". It was a responsibility that was enjoined on the U.S. republic from the moment of its birth. The State Department had in line with its foundational creed of the "free exchange of ideas", begun work in "more than 40 countries to help individuals silenced by oppressive governments", while also "supporting the development of new tools that (would) enable citizens to exercise their rights of free expression by circumventing politically motivated censorship".

It was a deep effort with considerable material and ideological commitment. Groups around the world were being funded "to make sure that those tools get to the people who need them in local languages". Along with access to the tools, these groups were also being given the "training they need to access the internet safely". In service of these diplomatic objectives, the U.S. State Department had "assembled a talented and experienced team to lead .. statecraft efforts" in the new millennium. Having "travelled the world helping governments and groups leverage the benefits of connection technologies", this team would stand up for a "Civil Society 2.0 Initiative to help grassroots organisations enter the digital age".[48]

Assange had cause to be interested when Schmidt and Cohen put in their request for an interview. Wikileaks was just turning out thousands of U.S. diplomatic cables exposing the inner mechanics of a system driven by principles almost completely opposed to those piously expressed in public. Social and political convulsions were tearing apart the delicate state system in the Arab world, plunging global balance of power calculations into a mire of uncertainty. The potentialities of political mobilisation through social media were suddenly the topic on everybody's lips. Despite initial panic at the insurrectionary conditions engulfing Egypt and threatening its loyal servitor, President Hosni Mubarak, the U.S. foreign policy establishment managed to turn his long delayed and grudging decision to leave office, into a seeming triumph for its values. Having failed to stem the tide of outrage stirred

48 State Department (2010).

up in part through the social media, the U.S. decided to swim along. Suddenly, as Assange recalled, "everyone wanted to be at the intersection point between U.S. global power and social media, and Schmidt and Cohen had already staked out the territory".[49]

Assange was familiar with Jared Cohen's record in the State Department. He came to public prominence after parlaying a tour of Iran during his graduate student days into a book, *Children of Jihad*. On official request, he later prepared a report on Iran that Condoleeza Rice, U.S. Secretary of State during the ill-remembered second term of the ill-remembered President George Bush, seemingly found valuable in understanding a country where the U.S. had gone four decades without diplomatic representation. He was hired for the policy planning staff of the State Department, retaining that position through the change of administration in the U.S. in January 2009. In July that year, he earned international notoriety by requesting a delay of planned maintenance at the micro-blogging site Twitter, so protesters using the platform to mobilise against a disputed Iranian presidential election would not lose momentum.[50]

In 2009, Schmidt and Cohen met in bombed-out Baghdad and compared notes over how far they could turn reconstruction in war-ravaged Iraq into a business opportunity. That was evidently a very stimulating encounter, since Schmidt the following year approached Cohen with the proposition that Google would fund a "Think/Do Tank" that he could head. The career shift was announced in breathless terms in diplomatic circles. As one commentator noted, Cohen had as the "youngest ever member of the policy planning staff ... (shown) .. how to use technology for diplomacy". As part of Google Ideas, he would "see if some of the thorniest foreign policy issues (could) be tackled from the private sector".[51]

The appellation "Think/Do Tank" set Cohen apart from the professional ideas industry that had flourished within the ecosystem of

49 Assange (2014): 6.

50 Schmidt (2010); *Financial Times* (2011) also carried a report on this enterprise of Jared Cohen's.

51 These were the words used on the website of *Fast Company*, a magazine that styles itself seeking to inspire "a new breed of innovative and creative thought leaders who are actively inventing the future of business". See Fast Company (2009).

the Washington DC Beltway. He would not spend his days spinning idle thoughts but would seek concrete results on the ground. And his tools were to be the entire information infrastructure, where his company was among the most influential players. It was an ambition that stirred deep unease among older mandarins of the U.S. foreign policy establishment. Joseph Nye with two tours of duty in the State Department and the distinction of coining the influential – though rather inane – term "soft power", foresaw a conflict with U.S. foreign policy objectives, though he was not sufficiently bothered to make a public issue of it.[52]

Schmidt and Cohen fixed a meeting with Assange for June 2011. They arrived separately and without prior announcement, Schmidt brought along Lisa Shields, his companion at the time and also the Vice-President for Global Communications at the Council on Foreign Relations (CFR). This is a "think tank" wrapped up in Beltway politics that presumably does not "do", but finds effective agency for its ruminations in the State Department and Pentagon.

Cohen arrived accompanied by an unannounced visitor, Scott Malcomson, introduced as the book's editor. As longtime member of the CFR, Malcomson was on the inner track of the foreign policy establishment. Three months after their meeting, Assange observed, he would enter the U.S. mission to the U.N. as lead speechwriter for Ambassador Susan Rice. At the time Assange wrote his book, he was communications director at another think-tank of global scope, the International Crisis Group (ICG), which identified itself as an independent non-governmental organisation working "through field-based analysis and high-level advocacy to prevent and resolve deadly conflict".

Assange observed that the group he was engaging with was one part technology industry and "three parts U.S. foreign policy establishment". He thought nothing further of it as discussions progressed. His account of the day is prefaced by sharp observations on each of his interlocutors and shrewd assessments of their stakes in the game. The conversations were carried out over roughly three hours. Assange's visitors had overlooked certain basic requirements of accurately recording interviews, which required his Dictaphone being pressed into service. As agreed at the meeting, recordings were shared in raw au-

52 Cited in *Financial Times* (2011).

dio form and the written transcripts exchanged and corrected by both sides.

Then under attack from governments around the world – U.S. Vice President Joe Biden's term, "high-tech terrorist" being among the choicest epithets flung at him – Assange found the conversation rather stimulating. As an interview subject facing four individuals from a different world, he had to move out of his "comfort zone". The outcome was an interview that Assange at the time rated among the best he had ever given. In the course of the conversation, he suggested with exaggerated casualness that Google should leak U.S. government information requests, which Wikileaks would be glad to platform. Suddenly rattled at this departure from script, Schmidt refused, "citing the illegality of disclosing Patriot Act requests".[53]

The conversation between Wikileaks and Google was in part about technical issues involved in securing a decentralised information architecture where multiple users could enter and access data. Wikileaks was Assange's effort to structure such a system. "In a Fourth Estate context", he explained, "the people who acquire information are sources; the people who work on information and distribute it are journalists and publishers; and the people who may act on it includes everyone". That was the "high-level construct", or the abstract objective being pursued. Things finally came down to "how you practically engineer a system that solves that problem".

Information of great public importance was often denied an audience. This variety of censorship operated in the form of a pyramid. At the top was the threat of violence against anybody who brought information into the public domain. At the next level was legal action, effectively the delayed threat of coercive force, which could result in imprisonment or the seizure of assets. But the "most significant form of censorship" had historically, been economic in nature, "where it (was) simply not profitable to publish something" because of the absence of a market. Self-censorship was common practice since no individual or social group really wanted to move up the pyramid to the point they became targets of physical attack.[54]

53 Assange (2014):18.

54 Ibid: 69.

The only defensive bulwark Wikileaks could build, given its lack of financial resources and political connections, was anonymity. Again, with legal methods being unavailable, anonymity had to be secured through purely technical means. Assange explained that anonymity could be assured for all Wikileaks' contributors, in part through a system "distributed at its front with many domain names, and a fast ability to change those domain names". Custom software was employed to hide the location of its back-end servers. And the Tor network which enabled anonymous browsing of the internet was used to "tunnel through" from the back to the front-end.

These were technical descriptions that Assange's audience that June day in Britain were able to keep up with, but only with patient pedantic explanations from his side. As he readied his transcript for publication, Assange took care to explain these matters to his prospective audience, taking into account the befuddled response of his supposedly better informed interlocutors that day. That particular phase of the conversation was summarised by Schmidt for Cohen and Malcomson who joined late, in "non-technical terms", as building a system where if "obvious things" were done to block content, it would "simply show up in another way". This was done by replicating content and using multiple names.[55]

With an occasional comic interlude, such as a glass of water spilling on Schmidt's laptop, the discussion cut a pathway through a variety of themes. Schmidt explained the benchmarks used in vetting content posted on Youtube and other sites that Google owned. The forty-eight hours of video content posted on Youtube every minute, made prior review impossible. The company was happy in the circumstances to leave the trigger in the hands of the user. Any material flagged as inappropriate would be reviewed and if required, removed. But the bar was set very high. For one thing, factual inaccuracy was not sufficient criterion for deleting material. Google made sure that its policies were well specified and understood by all users.

Assange had a rather different benchmark. Every manner of information was welcome and all who had useful material to share would have a place aboard Wikileaks. Authenticity was a clear requirement. Spurious information could have consequences, including danger to

55 Ibid: 71-3, 79.

life and limb. The Wikileaks team was obliged to perform a check for veracity on all the information it received. There had been efforts to plant spurious material, including one by a Kenyan source seeking to influence an election by showing a sinister opposition intent to introduce Islamic law across Kenya. Such material would be posted on Wikileaks with the caveat that it was spurious, since forgeries too had an important public information function. Cohen was interested in knowing how a forgery would be identified, to which Assange conceded that the Kenyan document posed certain difficulties, which were ultimately resolved by checking all the signatures involved. But the job was not as a rule, "hard work".

Days after the interview, Cohen flew into Dublin for a Google Ideas event, the Summit Against Violent Extremism, which brought together Islamic radicals, Nazi skin-heads, criminal gang-members and a variety of other reprobates in the official narrative, on a platform to discuss pathways to reform and endorse certain strategies of yoking the new cyber-technologies to the cause.[56]

When Schmidt and Cohen finally published their book to a chorus of public acclaim and encomiums from distinguished western warlords such as Henry Kissinger and Tony Blair, their tone was for the most part upbeat. There were worries that "Civil Society 2.0" as promise could well be transformed into the dystopia of "Police State 2.0". Nations could "balkanise" the Internet – like China introduced a "Great Firewall", Iran could presumably create a "*halal* internet" – but a vigorous argument could be made for connectivity technologies to build local resistance to such stratagems.

Schmidt and Cohen cited multiple instances where connectivity had created the kind of civic mobilisation to threaten regimes the U.S. was hostile to or uncomfortable with. Their omissions though, told a rather distinct story. Where the mobilisation was of a nature that caused anxiety in the Washington Beltway and Wall Street, a rather different standard applied. Portugal in March 2011 saw a day of protest involving a gathering of 300,000 people restive at the prospect of mass unemployment following the introduction of an austerity package to to salvage the country's membership of the European currency zone. In May 2011, city squares in Spain and Greece were in a state of siege as

56 *Financial Times* (2011).

thousands assembled to resist similar measures. And in September the same year, an "Occupy Wall Street" camp came up in New York's Manhattan district, not far from the capital of global finance, the switchboard from where the most perverse redistribution of global income in history has been carried out.[57]

These movements were celebrated in some quarters as a new dawn for "deliberative democracy", which used the apparatuses of communication available in the new information technology as a powerful accessory.[58] In time, with the mainstream media proving either indifferent or actively hostile, and the formidable coercive powers of the neoliberal state being called into play, these protests faded out. Through the years that the neoliberal dogma has held sway – of leaner governments making for better governance – there has always been one area where a deliberate exception was made. As Alasdair Roberts points out, both in the U.S. and the U.K., where neoliberalism as modern day doctrine originated, police forces were considerably augmented since the first waves of resistance were overcome in the 1980s. Expenditure on policing at all levels in the U.S., "more than tripled, even after adjustment for inflation, between 1982 and 2009". Figures over a comparable period in the U.K. are not available, but Roberts does find that expenditure on policing increased by 33 percent after adjusting for inflation, between 1988 and 1998. By 2011, it was crystal clear that the British police had "never been better resourced ... (with) more officers than ever before". As police forces became better organised and equipped, a new doctrine of "public order policing" emerged. A "central theme within this doctrine was the control of territory for the purpose of preventing disruption". The police were in fact, at the "front line of a social revolution" in the days of neoliberalism.[59]

The dissolution of older forms of collective organisation such as unions, was a singular objective of neoliberalism from its very early days. This had consequences for mass protests even when circumstances were especially aggravated. Without the "internal structure and self-discipline" of collective organisation, the masses of people gathered in the streets lacked the capacity and "will to impose order on

---

57 Roberts (2013): locations 60, 903.

58 Ross (2011): 107-9.

59 Roberts (2013): locations 1083, 1114 and 1143.

itself". "Police forces compensated for this change by developing new techniques that imposed discipline on the crowd".[60]

As he recounted the June 2011 encounter with Google Ideas, Assange observed with one eye focused on Cohen's eager sponsorship of events like the Summit Against Violent Extremism, that the world he inhabited seemed one event after another: "endless soirees for the cross-fertilisation of influence between elites and their vassals, under the pious rubric of 'civil society'".[61] The State Department *wunderkind* turned Google revolutionary was supposedly seeking to secure the boundaries of "civil society" for the advocacy of "things like human rights, free speech, and accountable government". But he was playing by a book of rules evolved within the western hegemonic enterprise. This was an enterprise that had flourished by raising to almost cultic status the idea that "civil society" was a sphere where ideas could be formulated independent of dominant structures of state and market. However, as Assange observed rather pointedly, this manner of relatively free association had long since vanished, ever since "authentic actors like unions and churches ... folded under a sustained assault by free-market statism". Civil society had then been transformed into a "buyer's market for political factions and corporate interests looking to exert influence at arm's length".[62]

Assange's disdain for the Google Ideas enterprise was more than repaid. Wikileaks as the model of a platform where all forms of information would be welcomed and hosted, Schmidt and Cohen concluded in the book that emerged after their interview with Assange, was a "dangerous" one. There was always going to be somebody with bad judgment who would release information that would "get people killed". On the terrain of principle, the Wikileaks model left the "question of discretionary power" unsettled. Why was it Assange, specifically, who "got to decide what information (was) relevant to the public interest"? And what would be the consequence if the person making such decisions was "willing to accept indisputable harm to innocents as a consequence of his disclosures"?

---

60 Ibid: location 1199.

61 Assange (2014): 25.

62 Ibid.

There has of course, been no documented case of anybody coming to harm on account of the Wikileaks disclosures. And there really are no convincing grounds that Schmidt and Cohen advance for Google's superior claims to being arbiter of public discourse. Social turbulence at the iniquities of neoliberalism and their aggravation by the crooked practices of Wall Street financiers, may be a genuine cause for mass grievance, a powerful trigger for political mobilisation outside the structures of the state and market. Google valuations though, rest on Wall Street and the corporation's interests are not served one bit by any disturbance to the functioning of the giant financial siphon that sucks in global savings to slice and dice it up into instruments of beguiling – but illusory – value. The silences in Schmidt and Cohen's book speak louder than its many words.

There is much substance in Schmidt and Cohen's assertion that "even the juiciest disclosures require a subsequent media cycle in order to have impact". The insurgent impact of Wikileaks was enhanced by its collaboration with the *The Guardian* and *The New York Times*, but then quickly lost momentum when the organised forces of state and market mobilised to counter it. Schmidt and Cohen use this observation to argue the case against a platform of the Wikileaks kind, since a highly decentralised landscape of secret-spilling websites would make it difficult for media outlets to "keep track of these sites and their leaks, and to gauge their trustworthiness as sources". This, the Google duo concluded rather sniffily, meant that the "Assanges of the world (would) exist in future, but their support base (would) remain small". The kind of whistle blower who would be more "welcomed" would "follow the example of people like Alexei Navalny, a Russian blogger and anti-corruption activist, who enjoys much sympathy from many in the West".[63]

That effectively was where the limits of dissent were set by Google, a construct that stays safely within State Department mandated foreign policy objectives and avoids any risk of disorder in Wall Street. Media freedom and the liberties that connectivity brings are ultimately about how much latitude those who control these platforms will permit. There are many who strive to push the envelope, to expand the range of issues the media deals with. But the logic of a commercially driven media which cannot take the conversation out of its core constituen-

63 Schmidt and Cohen (2013): 39–45.

cy's comfort zone, neutralises all such efforts. Even with the dust unsettled, the question that lingered from the civil society uprisings of 2011 was about elite commitment to basic democratic norms. And that was a question which could with equal pertinence, be directed at the media too. Always quick to spring to the defence of an abstract principle of freedom, the media needs to explain whose freedom, really, it is talking about.

Personal autonomy as corporate choice

In May 2016, the technology news portal Gizmodo reported that Facebook, a social network that had in less than a decade built up a global constituency of billions and fostered visions about a world of unmediated encounters that conquered space, was using a human interface in prioritising stories. This revelation deflated the widespread belief that an impersonal mathematical algorithm based on user behaviour, was the unseen arbiter of Facebook's choice of "trending topics" and the "news feed" that it created for the special attention of each of its subscribers.

Spasms of anger were unleashed within the U.S., then in the last phases of an intensely competitive season of presidential primaries, ahead of general elections later that year.[64] Outrage was especially loud at the conservative end of the political spectrum, where the supposed "liberal bias" in mainstream media (also often referred to as "legacy media") was alleged to have been seamlessly transferred to new media.

Facebook was not legally obliged to give equal traction to all political opinions but like Google, the dominant entity in internet search, its public profile was based partly on the claim of being a clear and unclogged channel through which its global constituency could see, hear and read each other. Discretion and choice were in the hands of the user. Any person who could cross the access threshold for entering the global community of the internet, was a potential user with equal voice as any other. Opinions and information would be propelled to the top of the users' attention span by the widely held power of the mouse-click. The visibility of any fragment of information would be a function merely of the number of clicks it registered. In a situation of explosive growth in "smart" mobile phone usage, this effectively

64 *The Guardian* (2016).

promised a phase of deep democratisation. The Gizmodo revelation however, seemed to suggest an unseen hand and an unwanted tutelary influence shaping the public discourse.

Till not long before, conservative and liberal – in the very specific sense these terms are used in U.S. politics – seemed in beautiful concord over the potential for positive political change the social media embodied. June 2009 was one of several instances when this beautiful harmony was in evidence, when protests broke out in the streets of the Iranian capital of Tehran, soon after results were declared in a presidential election that gave hardline Islamist Mahmoud Ahmedinejad a second term. As the social media site Twitter came to be a venue of mass outrage against the ostensible overturning of the popular will, a sense of ecstasy engulfed the western media and its wider ecosystem of think-tanks. Iran had begun to be perceived after the invasion of Iraq in 2003 and its catastrophic aftermath, as a powerful impediment to the U.S. plan to reconfigure power relations in west Asia. Salvation seemed to lie in the microblogging and social networking site Twitter.

"The revolution will be Twittered", pronounced a pundit normally associated with the liberal side. Resilience was the singular feature of the social media site in the face of systematic state repression. Its wide availability as a platform accessible through mobile phones would make it a powerful means of change. The editorial page of the *Wall Street Journal*, a redoubt of the right-wing conservative, argued that Twitter would accomplish greater change in Iran than "years of sanctions, threats and Geneva-based haggling put together". A former aide of the George W. Bush administration announced a signature campaign to secure the Nobel peace award for Twitter. And that was the juncture at which Jared Cohen, then a junior official in the U.S. State Department, sent out a message to Twitter asking it to delay a planned maintenance shutdown to allow the Tehran protests an uninterrupted course.[65]

The Iranian government was unimpressed and protested the intrusion. But just as the internet as a medium embodied the potential for channelling dissent, it also afforded a means to neutralise political turmoil. There were numerous messages posted on Twitter about the sites where protests would assemble, but no clear evidence these actu-

65 Morozov (2011): 3-9.

ally triggered or influenced the course of the demonstrations. Finally, few of the Twitter combatants calling the forces of democracy to battle against the theocratic tyranny were actually based in Iran. Using the facility of anonymity (which translates into unaccountability), Twitter users in the U.S. and other western countries were inundating the site with inspirational messages, confident in the belief that they would not have a price to pay when the inevitable backlash came. But the internet was not merely a zone of free speech, it was also porous enough to allow surveillance of moments otherwise regarded as private, for implanting contrary signals that confused potential adversaries, and for swamping political motives of one stripe by its opposite.[66] Finally, the intent of the majority of internet users was only remotely political. Two weeks into the protests in Iran, audience attention shifted dramatically away from an allegedly stolen election, to the death of music superstar Michael Jackson.[67]

"Net utopians" as Morozov has called them, also omitted an inconvenient matter of detail. Profit seeking companies could look at both sides of the supposed political divide to serve their ends: both freedom as portrayed in the western neoliberal discourse, as well as its opposite. There could be situations in which authoritarianism promised fewer risks. Garton Ash points out how after the December 2010 uprising in Tunisia that heralded the "Arab Spring" – soon to meander into the depths of a harsh and dark winter – "the head of the country's Internet Agency revealed that, under the *ancient regime* of Zine el Abidine Ben Ali, several Western companies had used the agency as a testing ground for internet censorship technologies which they might then sell to other friendly dictators".[68]

Decades before the internet became an object of veneration, Marshall McLuhan spoke of the western tendency to confuse "rationalism with a single technology".[69] He referred to the alibi advanced by a corporate leader of the burgeoning broadcasting industry, absolving technological instruments of the sins committed by "those who wield them". This, he said, is the "voice of the current somnambulism". There

66 Ibid: 15-19

67 Ibid: 66.

68 Garton Ash (2016): location 7965.

69 McLuhan (1964): 16.

was simply nothing in the statement that bore scrutiny, said McLuhan, "for it ignores the nature of the medium, of any and all media, in the true Narcissus style of one hypnotised by the amputation and extension of his own being in a new technical form".[70]

"Net delusion" expresses itself in the belief that a technological extension can stand for superior values and represent a rationality that transcends the limits and deficits of human nature. That claim of perfect rationality was at work in a study carried out on a massive sample of Facebook users by a member of the company's data science unit and two researchers from Cornell University.[71] Results were published in the *Proceedings of the National Academy of Sciences* with the confident declaration that all applicable norms in use of personal data were honoured. The object was to study if "emotional states" could be transferred from one person to another via "contagion". The phenomenon had been studied in laboratory experiments and found operative in the transfer of "positive and negative moods and emotions to others".[72]

The methodology was explained in elaborate detail, including criteria to determine the "valence" of a mood, its positive or negative character. But the ethics of the process did not merit the same elaboration, merely the claim that "it was consistent with Facebook's Data Use Policy, to which all users agree prior to creating an account on Facebook, constituting informed consent for this research".[73] The results, gratifyingly for the researchers, showed that "emotional contagion" was real and existent. "For people who had positive content reduced in their News Feed, a larger percentage of words in people's status updates were negative and a smaller percentage were positive. When negativity was introduced, the opposite pattern occurred".[74]

---

70 Ibid: 11.

71 Kramer, Guillory and Hancock (2014): 8788-90.

72 Ibid: 8788. Here is how the matter is explained: "Posts were determined to be positive or negative if they contained at least one positive or negative word, as defined by Linguistic Inquiry and Word Count software (LIWC2007) word counting system, which correlates with self-reported and physiological measures of well-being, and has been used in prior research on emotional expression."

73 Ibid: 8789.

74 Ibid.

Personal as an outmoded idea

It is a commonplace observation that an unyielding barrage of negative news tends to depress, while a steady diet of positive "feel-good" information could elevate the recipient's mood. The more enduring contribution from the research may well have been unintended, though one that dawned late. It was only after a month of seeming somnolence that editors in the academy journal woke up to the ethical implications. In an "expression of concern and correction", the journal pointed out that applicable guidelines in experiments involving human subjects required "informed consent" and an "opt out" clause. These were "best practices in most instances" and though adherence to this "common rule" was the policy of the academy, Facebook as a private enterprise, "was under no obligation to conform". The academy had published findings from a large-scale experiment involving close to seven hundred thousand subjects on the basis of the "information provided by the authors". It was however, "a matter of concern that the collection of the data by Facebook may have involved practices that were not fully consistent with the principles of obtaining informed consent and allowing participants to opt out".[75]

Meanwhile, mainstream media commentary painted a troubling picture of a social networking platform that "in exchange for an admittedly magical level of connectivity", was taking over entire lives "as content". Privacy settings were available for everybody who signed up, as also an element of choice in the information Facebook would be authorised to make available to advertisers. Business enterprises in their thousands were interested in tapping into the database of buying intent that Facebook was assembling. The Facebook business model was built on selling that intent to any among a number of entities, and the corporate interest was typically hidden in the small print.[76] Facebook's preference for an opaque and unaccountable system was apparent in its response to the controversy over manipulation of users' news feeds.[77]

The disquiet occasioned by the discovery of a human hand in Facebook, presumes that there is an alternative that meets higher standards of rationality. What could this be? From its origins in the late-1990s to

75 National Academy of the Sciences (2014).

76 *The New York Times* (2016).

77 *The Guardian* (2016b).

its triumphant debut in the stockmarkets in 2004, Google is widely regarded to have established the highest standards in algorithmic search. When the internet moved from "a stance of exploration" (occasioned by the question "what can I find out there?") to one of "expectation" ("there is something out there I know I can find"), Google was at hand, ready to propel the search. As expressed by a former editor-in-chief of Yahoo – the company that established an earlier industry standard before being supplanted as the most popular gateway into the web – "the shift from exploration and discovery to .. intent-based search" was inconceivable at one time.[78] That precisely is the change that Google effected. Since its formation, this is a company that has revelled in its seeming innocence of the hardboiled calculus of markets and celebrated the spirit of playful tinkering as the mainspring of innovation. Its success in search was built on two major assets: the distributed computing system where it stored its indexes of literally billions of web pages, and the "page rank" system which worked on a logic roughly analogous to academic citation indexing.[79]

Both these were the creation of two Stanford University students in the 1990s, Sergey Brin and Laurence Page. Standard practice at the time, typified by Yahoo, was to monetise search results through big display ads. Brin and Page though, were convinced that this would detract from the credibility of the search and cast a shadow of doubt over the results it turned up. The authority they cited in this respect was none other than Ben Bagdikian, dean of critical journalism studies in the U.S.[80] An alternative method of monetisation was then emerg-

78 Battelle (2006): 61.

79 Ibid: 78. In a paper written while students at the computer sciences department in Stanford University, Google founders Sergey Brin and Laurence Page spoke of how they expected the objective measure of priority they arrived at through the "PageRank" algorithm to correspond well with "people's subjective idea of importance". See Brin and Page (1998).

80 Brin and Page (1998: 16) explained their reservations by recounting their experience with running a search around the term "cellular phones". Among the top results they got was "The Effect of Cellular Phone Use Upon Driver Attention", which explained "in great detail the distractions and risk associated with conversing on a cellphone while driving". This search result was yielded by the Google algorithm, but for Brin and Page, it was "clear that a search engine which was taking money for showing cellular phone ads would have difficulty justifying

ing, pioneered in the main by a firm called GoTo.com, which made an unsuccessful effort to join forces with Google in 2001. The basis of the GoTo revenue model was simple: advertisers would bid for certain keywords used in search. Their ads would be ranked in accordance with the financial bids backing them.

Google spurned the GoTo merger offer because it was not comfortable with ad placements that were paid for. Its own choice – in a commercial gambit that led to a patents dispute with GoTo.com, that was only resolved on the eve of the Google public issue in 2004 – was to tweak the placement rule, leaving rank ordering of ads to be established by the number of mouse clicks each gained.[81]

This seemed the best way to reconcile the profit imperative with early scruples Google's founders had about ad financed search. Soon after hitting on this winning formula, Google introduced its email service with the promise of affording every user storage space beyond imagination. Brin and Page were confident that this was a winning offer, an irresistible one. Instead, the company found itself mired in a major public relations fiasco. The unstated premise of the service was that every message passing through its channels would be parsed for content that could conceivably be of interest to advertisers. Ads with any possible relevance to the content of the message would then be placed alongside it.[82]

The company managed to wade through this crisis, banking on its image as the youthful new entrant that was doing things differently. Its model of matching ad placements to search terms functioned in a state of permanent and dynamic instability. It gave advertisers and website owners an incentive to milk the system for advantage, contriving ways of beating the Google algorithm by placing decoys that would draw web surfers to their sites. On Google's part, the overriding objective was to keep the results of what it called the "organic search" distinct from paid advertising. Its effort to always stay one step ahead caused

---

the page". Moreover, given the historic experience with other media, as illustrated vividly by Ben Bagdikian in his classic work *The Media Monopoly*, Brin and Page expected that "advertising funded search engines (would) be inherently biased towards the advertisers and away from the needs of the consumers".

81 Battelle (2006): 142.

82 Ibid: 194-6.

continuing changes in algorithm, none of which was really subject to any process of public accountability.

There was no escaping the fact that the algorithm was a new form of editorial gatekeeper, "pulling up what it deems important, based on someone else's understanding of what is important". This in turn spawned "a whole industry of search engine optimisation (SEO) consultants who game the system by reconfiguring a website's code, content, and keywords to move it up in the rankings". Companies were also known "to pay for links in order to push them up in the rankings".[83]

Despite the pretence of objectivity, Google felt compelled at some stage, to claim U.S. First Amendment protection for the search results it turned up. In 2012, it commissioned two lawyers to prepare a brief arguing that algorithmic search still involved the human element and an exercise of the free speech right. The selection and sorting of material, they argued, "is a mix of science and art: it uses sophisticated computerised algorithms", which in turn are infused by "engineers' judgments about what material users are most likely to find responsive to their queries".[84] First Amendment protection applied not merely to what was said, but also to what was not said. Neither Google nor any other search engine should face legal jeopardy for omitting material from search processes triggered by particular keywords.[85]

Interestingly, all these assertions about constitutional protections for search engines, were drawn from jurisprudence on the legacy media. In a case involving the *Miami Herald* in 1974 for instance, the Supreme Court of the U.S. (SCOTUS) had held a "responsible press" to be an "undoubtedly desirable goal", which however, was "not mandated by the Constitution and like many other virtues (could not) be legislated".[86] From this finding, Google made the extrapolation that the mere fact that its search was driven by an algorithm did not mean that it could be deprived of First Amendment protection. There were two underlying reasons: the algorithms were themselves written by human agents; and then, part of the rationale of the First Amendment was

83 Halpern (2011).

84 Volokh and Falk (2012): 3-4.

85 Ibid: 7.

86 Ibid: 9.

anchored in the utility of free speech to listeners and readers. An automated search driven by algorithm brought up the most useful results for a wide range of web users. This alone entitled a search engine to the protection of the First Amendment.[87]

On December 4, 2009, Google announced its conquest of a new frontier in its relentless pursuit of the perfect search: "personalised search for everyone". From that day onwards, Google declared, it would use fifty-seven signals – including user location and earlier search history – to customise search results. The capacious memory banks it had built up in its data centres spread worldwide, were obviously brimming over with profiles of the numerous users gathered into its fold. From then on, it would use these profiles to provide just the kind of search results the user was likely to be interested in.

Eli Pariser tried to check out the practical implications, getting two friends of roughly similar political inclinations, to search Google for the same term. The Deepwater Horizon disaster, when an oil-rig in the Gulf of Mexico had started leaking at a catastrophic rate into the waters, was fresh in public memory at the time. But Pariser's two friends, whose search histories, as logged in the Google data centre could not have been wildly different, nonetheless obtained hugely divergent results from searches involving identical terms.[88]

User had become content. Was the future of news "machine-powered" or "user-powered"?[89] As trust in the legacy media collapsed, the internet came to be perceived as the great new hope, which would enable every user to choose just the right mix of news feeds for his needs. And as the cost for Google of producing a fresh item of news fell closer and closer to zero, the reward from personalising news content to a very narrow reader profile which would offer the best target for advertising, rose proportionately. Far from creating an ecosystem in which all voices would emerge and be heard, the new web architecture is creating a silo for every user, a ghetto where the bliss of solitude and isolation is assured.

---

87 Ibid: 11.

88 Pariser (2011): 3.

89 Ibid: 51.

Knowledge acquisition, it has been argued, is equally a process of assimilation within an existing cognitive scheme, and changing the scheme to accommodate findings that fail to fit. The new architecture of the web allows for "confirmation bias" that deeply entrenches an existing perception, since that is the best way of selling a user profile to the advertiser. Fed a constant diet of news and information that fits a template fashioned in a distant data centre, the web user would find few "meaning threats" – or the "confusing, unsettling occurrences that fuel (the) desire to understand and acquire new ideas"[90].

Tim Berners-Lee, the acknowledged creator of the worldwide web, was in 2010, sufficiently disturbed by these prospects to sound the alarm: "The Web as we know it, is being threatened … Some of its most successful inhabitants have begun to chip away at its principles. Large social-networking sites are walling off information posted by their users from the rest of the Web ... Governments – totalitarian and democratic alike – are monitoring people's online habits, endangering important human rights. If we, the Web's users, allow these and other trends to proceed unchecked, the Web could be broken into fragmented islands".[91]

Social media and the collapse of civility

On November 9, a man with no qualifications was elected to the post that is customarily called the most powerful job in the world. Donald Trump came into the election with a background of shady business deals, tax cheating and an image of surpassing vulgarity acquired through his enthusiastic participation in reality TV shows. He embellished an already unsavoury image with a trail of bigoted, misogynist and racist remarks through the campaign. He failed to win the endorsement of any single newspaper of consequence in the U.S. though the TV networks were always willing to feature him since a clown is always a boost for viewership ratings. Finally, when the votes were counted, he had won fairly comfortably in the so-called "electoral college" while losing the national popular vote by a significant margin. It was an outcome that the mainstream media had failed to call, leading in those quarters to an expected round of breast-beating and contrition.

90 Ibid: 85-9.

91 Cited in Ibid: 217.

What accounts for this outcome that was accurately seen to involve baneful consequences for the entire globe? If the media role were considered, the older news outlets clearly had lost influence over the popular mood, to newer platforms such as Facebook and Twitter. A large part of the stories that are circulated through Google, Twitter and Facebook, originate in older media houses, but their impact has been diluted, since stories that follow older rules of fact-checking and accuracy, count for little in the new social media. Their influence is waning in comparison to the social media, where patently spurious information put in play by interested parties has greater chance of gaining traction.

An analysis of the last days of the election campaign showed that a flood of spurious stories was unleashed on social media platforms. These were in some measure traced to individuals aligned with the Trump campaign, who capitalised on the old verity attributed to Mark Twain that a lie could travel halfway around the world before the truth even gets its boots on. Perhaps the more powerful mode of propagating false news came from the newly confected process of "botnets" – a portmanteau term for the marriage in the digital world of the metronomic persistence of the robot, with the network's potential to promote the viral spread of information.

Social media was imagined as the ultimate answer to older dilemmas of the gap in perceptions between media producer and consumer, which had widened under the regime of globalisation. User generated content is potentially an antidote for the skewed priorities of the public sphere in a time of media commercialisation. But when content aggregators follow the same old rules of promoting news items, user generated content is likely to generate vast spirals of spurious information, promoted by all those invested in its propagation. Information that people want to see would gain traction, rather than news that has gone through an editorial process that minimally checks for authenticity.

Soon after the U.S. presidential election turned in its shock result, Joshua Benton, a researcher at the Nieman media laboratory, tried to make sense of its implications for the media, with a special focus on Facebook which had wondrously brought in billions onto its platform within a mere decade. For all its rapidly widening spread, Facebook had "also become a single point of failure for civic information". Democratic practice had never been perfect but the 2016 elections suggested that its biggest hazard lay in the "sewer of misinformation" that Facebook had become. Some of the spurious information was driven by ideology, but a large part of it came from "the economic incentive structure Facebook has created". This ensured that fake stuff would "spread like wildfire", when it connected with the "user's preconceived notions or sense of identity".

Benton looked at a sampling of material posted on Facebook by the mayor of his hometown in the south, a conservative part of the country where Trump enjoyed a substantial advantage. For all that, what was in evidence was appalling: accusations that Trump's opponent Hillary Clinton had called for civil war if she lost, that the Pope from the distant Vatican had endorsed Trump, that the investigator in to real and imagined illegalities committed by Clinton had mysteriously turned up dead. Facebook had become a platform for not merely sharing information, but for the "active dispersal" of brazen lies. And it was a no contest, simply because Facebook users would simply will themselves to believe what they wanted. The Pope's supposed endorsement of Trump's candidacy, for instance, was shared 868,000 times on Facebook, while the relevant item debunking this claim on the Snopes website, which styles itself as the "field guide" to fake news, had a mere 33,000.[92]

Aside from these contaminants in the public discourse that had a human origin, there was another category that came from automated sources. Analysis by the Oxford Internet Institute found a "deliberate and strategic" use of automated Twitter accounts through the election campaign. This seemed to be occurring "most clearly with pro-Trump campaigners and programmers who carefully adjusted the timing of content production". Periods of particularly intense activity occurred during the campaign debates which drew nation-wide TV audiences of several million, and then the last nine days of the campaign. The purpose was to flood the Twitter space with pro-Trump messaging and "strategically colonise" Clinton's hashtags.[93]

Tweets for this statistical exercise were selected using hashtags that best reflected the themes that had been widely articulated during the electoral campaign. The 19 million tweets harvested through the last

92 Benton (2016).

93 Oxford (2016).

nine days of the election campaign were categorised in accordance with the cause they advocated. Pro-Trump hashtags were typically associated with names like #LockHerUp, #CrookedHillary, #riggedelection and #DrainTheSwamp, aside from some that affirmatively messaged support for Trump. Pro-Clinton hashtags mostly signalled support for the candidate, with a minority that questioned Trump's record on taxes and his loose connection with the world of fact.

There is no firm basis to assess the geographical location from where the tweets originated, since most users did not tag their coordinates to their posts. Most of the traffic tended to fall off after sunset on the U.S. land mass. The evidence from analysing 19 million tweets was that pro-Trump messaging enjoyed over 55 per cent of the relevant Twitter space in the nine days prior to polling. Clinton's Twitter campaign lagged far behind at 19 per cent, and the rest fell into a large zone of neutrality.

The study used the threshold of fifty Twitter posts a day to identify automated accounts. It was not a perfect criterion, since natural beings with a high level of Twitter activity could have achieved this threshold. But with all necessary qualifications, the figure was judged a reasonable criterion. There were also self-identified Netbots that posted material, which did not pose any such problem of categorisation. The study also identified a further category of "highly automated accounts", which generated 450 tweets or more in any given twenty-four hour cycle.

Highly automated bots became particularly active at key points during the election race. At the first campaign debate, this category of Twitter posts were about 23 per cent of the relevant sample, increasing to 25 per cent during the second and peaking at 27 per cent at the third and final debate. Automated Twitter posts then tended to fall in importance within the relevant universe, before picking up in the week before polling day. Trump easily out-paced his adversary in favourable Twitter messaging through this entire cycle, by a factor of 4.4 at the first debate, 4.2 in the second, and 6.9 in the third. This figure fell away in the ten days before polling day, but the percentage of pro-Trump messaging emanating from hashtags with a declared loyalty to him or those with a declared loyalty to Clinton – which were evidently infiltrated by his campaign – rose from the region of 66 per cent, where it hovered through the debate cycle, to 81 percent.

The U.S. election of 2016 will be analysed by historians and data scientists for long years, as its perverse outcome ripples across the globe. An early message to take away from the whole cycle is that far from the rosy outcomes forecast by prophets of new global coalitions of the networked, globalisation may well be headed towards a harsh new dystopia.

Satire

The Power of Laughter and Laughter of Power

Satire is an effective solvent for dogma, until it gets mired in a theology of its own. That theology could often merge into background conditions and become an entrenched consensus on which codes of civility in social life are built. Wide social consent is often taken for granted, even when not explicitly sought or expressed. Promises of equal treatment under the law then become skewed to reflect unstated biases and predilections of the theology of civil society.

Most strongly entrenched dogmas though, do allow for some variance at the margins, where the strictures are vague enough to allow for a range of seemingly contrary behaviour. *Laicite* or secularism is a principle deeply internalised within the French civil compact, though not always with strictly specified codes. It takes particular incidents, often deeply traumatic, to trigger that process of explication of what otherwise would be assumed but unstated.

Many such unstated premises were laid bare in March 2016, when terrorism claimed thirty-two lives in Brussels, all of innocent civilians who bore no blame for the grievances – real or imagined – harboured by their killers. In November 2015, Paris had experienced a similar mindless rampage of terror. And January 2015 was perhaps the beginning of that cycle of lethal violence, when two gunmen forced their way into the offices of *Charlie Hebdo*, a satirical weekly in Paris, and with cool-headed precision and ample premeditation, murdered eight of its staff. Another nine were killed in related violence across the city, including six in a kosher supermarket catering mostly to a Jewish clientele. One of the attackers at the *Charlie* venue loudly proclaimed that Mohammad had been avenged as he left the scene of the crime. It was seemingly just retribution for cartoons caricaturing the prophet of Islam.

Honoured as a free speech martyr since, *Charlie Hebdo* suffered no lack of certitude in identifying who bore responsibility for the March 2016 visitation of terror in Brussels. Three wrongdoers were identified, one with a specific identity and two more generic. Tariq Ramadan, a well-known professor of religion, active in making the case for a new compact between Islam and the west was the only one identified by name. Then there was an unnamed baker who typically would take over a Paris *boulangerie* and remove all offerings violative of his personal dietary taboos, and an ordinary woman complying with the sartorial demands of her faith, such as the head scarf or face veil.[1]

France had done serious damage to its basic values by its casual attitude, by what passed for tolerance in the lazy discourse of everyday life, said *Charlie*. Ramadan did not carry Kalashnikov rifles into the lecture hall to make his case for Islam. He was open to being challenged and refuted on every substantive point. And if ham sandwiches were not available with the local baker who happened to be of the Muslim faith, it was easy to move on and shop elsewhere. That woman in the veil similarly, was unlikely to be carrying a bomb under her enveloping attire. Yet in condoning this pattern of behaviour, France was guilty of a deep betrayal of principle, an offence against agreed principles of civility. These breaches in the compact of civic coexistence, *Charlie* darkly suggested, lay behind the violence in Brussels.

Soon after the lethal January 2015 attack on the *Charlie* premises in Paris, several who were otherwise rather repelled by its tasteless cartoons underlined that a basic principle of peaceful coexistence was at stake. In exercising its right to free speech, *Charlie* was not demanding universal approbation. Those who did not like its cartoons could just move on. But for some reason, *Charlie* was unwilling to grant that degree of latitude in matters involving symbols of Islam in the public

---

1 The editorial (*Charlie Hebdo*, 2016) was published on March 30 in French with a simultaneous English translation.

space. Observing the use of the *hijab* as an item of everyday wear, or listening to an argument on reconciliation between Islam and the west, or suffering the dietary taboos of a Muslim baker, could well be minor sources of dissonance in the onward flow of time, which do not seriously ruffle the surface of civic coexistence.[2] But that clearly was not how *Charlie* viewed the matter. It was all very well to "shut up, look elsewhere and move past all the street-insults and rumpus", but that would be at the risk of suffocating the spirit of public inquiry. Citizens were stopped from asking perfectly reasonable questions, such as "how the hell did I end up having to wander the streets all day with a big veil on my head?"; and "how the hell did I end up having to say prayers five times a day?".

For *Charlie*, these restraints on the spirit of inquiry were just the same as another, which prevented a French or Belgian citizen from asking "how the hell" he ended up in a taxi headed for Brussels airport, "with three rucksacks packed with explosives". Terrorism lay in a logical continuum with the professor arguing the case for an enlightened understanding of Islam, the benign but bearded baker with the "prayer bruise" on his forehead, and the devoted mother of a family who refused to shed her face veil. Secularism as a principle was increasingly being "forced into retreat" by the silences of political correctness.

Even the most extreme liberalism allows some public scrutiny over personal choices. These would be limited in matters sartorial or dietary, since there is little possibility of harm to others here, except in certain bizarre and unlikely scenarios. It is also an observed fact that France's Muslim community were not given to conspicuous emblems of their faith until recent years, when for complex reasons not unrelated to the retreat of the welfare state and the denial of equality, there may have been a reassertion of identity. Far from an accommodative posture, the French republic responded with ever more dogmatic assertions of its doctrine of secularism or *laicite*. This was in the most charitable view, little else than an effort at scapegoating, at blaming the large immigrant communities from former colonies, for their failure to integrate into an inhospitable social milieu. In further rubbing in its

2 In other words, an individual's habitus – in the sense the term is used by Pierre Bourdieu, in reference to his or her pattern of behaviour that is part of the dynamic of social reproduction – could easily adapt to these elements.

insistence that the free speech right would not recognise the slightest cultural sensitivity of immigrant groups or seek to engage them in a spirit of civility, France seemed to prefer a retreat into dogmas of colonial conquest and racist domination, rather than an honest reckoning with its baneful legacies. The more strident voices within French feminism called for the boycott of clothing lines that brought the *hijab* to the market. Others likened a woman's personal choice of the *hijab* to African-American acquiescence in their own enslavement in the 19th century.

Meanwhile, a blatant selectivity was manifest in enforcing the free speech right. In March 2015, a protester wearing a shirt denouncing the Israeli occupation of Palestine was arrested and interrogated. Hate-speech law by one count, had been invoked at the time to charge at least a dozen civil society activists calling for a peaceful campaign against Israel, under the rapidly growing "Boycott, Disinvestment and Sanctions" (BDS) movement. In January 2016, a group of French activists and writers signed a public pledge of support to the BDS movement, defying the declared governmental intent to criminalise any such call. Alongside its partisanship for Israel, the French government has also been unrepentant about the chaos it has fomented in seeking regime changes across a wide swathe of the Arab world, from Libya to Syria. This goes with the pursuit of commercial advantage in arms deals with regimes that promote the most primitive forms of religious fundamentalism, such as Saudi Arabia.

Carnage at *Charlie Hebdo*

Few minds were changed in the furious debate that followed the January 2015 carnage in the *Charlie Hebdo* offices. Every participant clung with a tenacity bordering on despair, to well-rehearsed scripts on free speech and its legitimate boundaries. Heat from that global debate had barely subsided when a fresh round of contention broke out over a decision by the U.S. unit of PEN, a global literary association, to honour *Charlie* with a free speech award. Six well-known writers, designated to perform marquee roles at the awards event, pulled out in protest, to shrill admonitions from the novelist Salman Rushdie. "Six pussies .. looking for a bit of character", said the Booker winner of South Asian origin, who lived over a decade in the shadow of a death sentence imposed by Iran's theocratic authorities. Undeterred by Rushdie's abuse, a substantial group of literary eminences joined the protests, while others stepped up to take their place in the ceremonies.

It was not long before bigotry in a more transparent form invaded the free speech arena. A far right organisation appropriately characterised as a "hate group" by anti-racism campaigners, assembled an event in a small town in the U.S. state of Texas, with the sole object of caricaturing Islam's prophet. With Geert Wilders, a particularly rabid immigrant-baiting politician from the Netherlands in attendance, a prize was reserved for the most hateful portrayals. Two men, both reportedly locals with known criminal records, attempted to storm the event but were shot dead by heavily armed guards. Though duty bound to protect what he identified as an exercise of the free speech right, the local mayor said that his job had been complicated by an ill-advised and ill-timed event. Another round of acrimony followed. Zealots for free speech attacked the suggestion that the organisers of the hate fest should have exercised restraint and *Charlie*'s defenders sought, in some embarrassment, to draw the distinctions that others could not quite put their finger on.

To follow the debate that *Charlie* triggered, is to recognise the brittleness of all standards. Indeed, the effort to establish a firm benchmark for the exercise of the free speech right might be futile. Contextuality and cultural relativism are ingrained in the notion. And to seek an absolute standard independent of the disposition of power is to chase a chimera.

George Packer in the *New Yorker* was among the first to sound the trumpet of approaching apocalypse when news of the *Charlie* killings broke, seemingly dispensing with the verities every journalist is taught, of ascertaining, verifying and sourcing information. There was a strong temptation to ascribe the attack to the essence of an alien, enemy faith and undoubtedly much political reward from doing so. Packer left no room for any suggestion that the event could be viewed in larger complexities as he called the faithful to war in defence of liberty. The murders in Paris were not about "France's failure to assimilate two generations of Muslim immigrants from its former colonies". Nor were they about French, or for that matter, western military actions that had in a decade reduced much of the Arab world to a state of seething chaos. "Least of all", said Packer, were they to be rationalised or understood as "reactions to disrespect for religion on the part of irresponsible cartoonists". The Charlie Hebdo killings were in fact, "only the latest blows delivered by an ideology that has sought to achieve power through terror for decades".[3]

The theme of imminent civilisational catastrophe was played up with deliberate intent. Writing for *The Atlantic*, from within the premises of the European Parliament in Brussels, Jeffrey Goldberg saw a lethal hammer blow aimed at all the ideals of "peaceable integration, tolerance, free speech and openness" that the institution was built on. Europe had been slow to recognise the symptoms, despite ample warning. Atrocities from the enemies within had been accumulating, though all of them paled in comparison with the *Charlie* massacre, which was "the most direct attack on Western ideals by *jihadists*". "We in the West believe that blasphemy is a right and not a crime", intoned Goldberg, "satire and the right to blaspheme are directly responsible for modernity".[4]

Blasphemy was certainly not the flavour of the day on January 11, three days after the killings, when church bells at Notre Dame cathedral rang out a message of unswerving western resolve to meet all challenges to its values. As French President Francois Hollande, much of his cabinet and several of the city's notables appeared in a solemn memorial for the *Charlie* victims at a site steeped in the history of Catholicism, church bells all over the country rang out their affirmation of the supposed values the *Charlie* cartoonists had died for. Days later, Paris witnessed an assembly of global leaders unprecedented in size, with Israel's Prime Minister Benjamin Netanyahu carefully avoiding any hint of proximity with Palestinian Authority President Mahmood Abbas, as they marched hand in hand with most of the European political leadership and a smattering from Africa and the Arab world, to reaffirm their commitment to free speech as a core value. The absence of any notable figure from the U.S. was noted and derided as a failure of will and commitment.

Those moments of mawkish solemnity enclosed several curiosities. *Charlie* was cast as a clear and uncompromising practitioner of equal opportunity irreverence, exactly as intended by France's official policy

3 Packer (2015).

4 Goldberg (2015).

of *laïcité*. But then there was no dissonance involved in the commemoration of their atheistic irreverence in a cathedral of almost iconic significance within French Catholicism. Did the politicians moreover, each with distinguished track records of repression of dissent and free speech – including in the case of Netanyahu, overtly racist conduct straight out of the colonial playbook – really have a standing in advocating the virtues that *Charlie* supposedly championed?

Another face of intolerance

Paris that day resonated with the message of intolerance and lawlessness that was sent out from the capital of the United States soon after the September 11, 2001 terrorist attacks: there is no middle ground; you are either with us or against us.[5] Early pushback against this demand came from Richard Seymour, who called out the French government's overtly "securitarian" response, which involved the demand that critical thought be suspended in the struggle against a "civilisational threat". This clearly unreasonable demand had culminated in the peremptory demand "to defend *Charlie Hebdo* as a forceful exponent of 'Western values', or in some cases even as a brilliantly radical bastion of left-wing anti-clericalism". That forced a false and easily avoidable binary. Without conceding anything to the notion that journalists could be targeted for their work, it was possible to identify *Charlie* as "frankly a racist publication".[6]

Charlie had been targeted in a fire-bombing earlier, though without loss of life. This followed a bunch of cartoons published on Islam's prophet in 2011. Risking the odium of victim-blaming, the incumbent chief in *Time* magazine's Paris bureau commented at the time, that the cartoons were "stupid and totally unnecessary", not to mention "offen-

5 Mamdani (2004: 230) points out the moral symmetry between the perpetrators of terrorism and those sworn to combat it: "Few would fail to notice the growing common ground between the perpetrators of 9/11 and the official response to it called the 'war on terror'. Both sides deny the possibility of a middle-ground, calling for a war to the finish. Both rally forces in the name of justice but understand justice as revenge. If the perpetrators of 9/11 refuse to distinguish between official America and the American people, target and victim, 'the war on terror' has proceeded by dishing out collective punishment, with callous disregard for either 'collateral damage' or legitimate grievances".

6 Seymour (2015).

sive, shameful, and singularly humour-deficient". The violence *Charlie* had suffered "was outrageous, unacceptable, condemnable, and illegal". But there was no escape from the conclusion that logic and reason dictated: "apart from the 'illegal' bit, *Charlie*'s .. edition (was) all of the above".[7]

The reaction to the fire-bombing of the *Charlie* office was the predictable "torrent of unqualified condemnation from French politicians, many of whom called the burning of the notoriously impertinent paper as 'an attack on democracy'".[8] To the commentator in *Time*, the incident just seemed part of the "idiotic, divisive, and destructive efforts" at Muslim baiting by sections which for some reason felt compelled to demonstrate that the west would not be dictated to by an alien "other". This led to "futile and childish .. Islamophobic antics" and invited the "very violent responses from extremists their authors claim to proudly defy in the name of common good".

In September 2012, after a particularly puerile issue of the magazine, France shut down its diplomatic missions, cultural centres and schools in twenty countries. *Charlie* opened its offering that week with the illustration of "an Orthodox Jewish man pushing a Muslim man in a wheelchair". In the following pages, it went on to portray a series of "ungainly caricatures, presented … as advertisements for a film". These were an obvious reference to an amateur movie production titled *Innocence of Muslims*, uploaded on a video-sharing website a few months before, to spasms of outrage in various parts of the world. The cartoons were, an observer noted, "only tenuously connected with the front cover's spoof" and involved the prophet of Islam, "labelled as such .. naked and bending over, begging to be admired", and in another panel, "crouched on all fours, with genitals bared".[9]

Local police contacted *Charlie* after getting an inkling of the tasteless and offensive work in progress. Editorial director Stephane Charbonnier – one of those killed in the 2015 attack – sent the issue's front and back covers to the police and politely declined to pull out the offensive cartoons. "Satire", he said, was "his bread and butter". *Charlie* hit the stands on a Friday, the Muslim day of prayer. An emergency

7 Crumley (2011).

8 Ibid.

9 Greenhouse (2012).

protocol to deal with anticipated violence was implemented with alacrity, though with loud grumbles from official quarters about the inconvenience. French Prime Minister Jean-Marc Ayrault criticised the cartoons as an "excess" and Foreign Minister Laurent Fabius asked if it was "really sensible or intelligent to pour oil on the fire". Others from the political establishment and the press concurred. *Charlie*'s work was variously described as "irresponsible, inopportune, and imbecilic", indeed, as "silly provocations" that would only feed grievance at the cultural insensitivity of the west.[10]

Extreme insouciance was *Charlie*'s response. Public excoriation of Islam, its prophet's shaming and the demolition of its precepts would continue, said Charbonnier, till "Islam is just as banal as Catholicism". The mere existence of a taboo was the precise reason why the prophet should be portrayed – in demeaning manner – since religions had to be "freely analysed, criticised, even ridiculed". This had been the French tradition "since Voltaire". Other newspapers including the left-leaning *Libération* joined the chorus, proclaiming blasphemy as a duty enjoined on all citizens who bore loyalty to French republican values. "Banning anything that anyone calls blasphemous", was itself "a kind of violence".[11]

Accusations of racism refused to die. In November 2013, Charbonnier and a colleague chose to frontally take these on in a brief polemic in the mass circulation newspaper *Le Monde*, bumptiously stating their central argument in the headline: "No, *Charlie Hebdo* is no racist". The "incredible slander" that *Charlie* was a "racist sheet" had been circulated in "wider and wider" circles and had gone too far. It was "anti-racism and the passion of equality between all human beings" that was the basic creed of the paper. The "definitive proof" lay merely in reading the journal. Those who insisted on the canard of racism "simply revel in an abominable rumour". *Charlie* embodied the "critical spirit of a generation", which mocked authority but was consistent and committed in "defending the human person and the universal values associated with it". The editorial team laughed, criticised and dreamt, and it was divided "between supporters of the left, the far left, anarchy and ecology". And while the journal spent much of its cover

10 Ibid.

11 Ibid.

space attacking the "papists", it saw no reason to spare Islam, a "flag imposed on countless peoples of the world". Charbonnier and his colleague ended with an aggressive chest-thumping dare: "Let those who claim and will claim tomorrow that *Charlie* is racist at least have the courage to say it out loud, and under their name".[12]

Satire oversteps a red line

There was one person, a former *Charlie* staffer, whose gorge rose as he read these lines. Olivier Cyran responded in a fortnight with abundant irony: "Not racist? If you say so". It was difficult to understand the bravado of the *Charlie* dare said Cyran, since "many people (had) been saying 'out loud' and 'under their real name' what they (thought) about (the) magazine and the effluent flowing out of it". Cyran had worked with *Charlie* till 2001. He quit in protest at "dictatorial behaviour and corrupt promotion practices", just before 9/11 when two "suicide planes made their impact on (its) editorial line". Till that moment, it was hard holding the journal to the stricture of racism. "There had been some Francocentrism", said Cyran, "as well as the editorials of Philippe Val (which) were subject to a disturbing fixation" to depict the Arabic-Muslim world "as an ocean of barbarism threatening to submerge … the little island of high culture and democratic refinement that was, for him, Israel".

These obsessions were at that time, confined to a column on page three and "overflowed only rarely into the heart of the journal". The 9/11 catastrophe was followed in the smaller context of *Charlie* by another, when "Caroline Fourest arrived in (its) editorial team". And then began the "ideological reformatting" that would change the character of the journal and its readership: "Little by little, the wholesale denunciation of 'beards', veiled women and their imaginary accomplices became a central axis" of *Charlie*'s editorial functioning. The magazine became a forum for publishing supposed investigative reports, "which accepted the wildest rumours as fact, like the so-called infiltration of the League of Human Rights or European Social Forum by a horde of bloodthirsty Salafists".[13]

12 Charbonnier and Nicolino (2013).

13 Cyran (2014).

In 2006, Val and Fourest took the initiative in drafting a statement titled "Manifesto of the Twelve against the new Islamic Totalitarianism", later published prominently on *Charlie*'s front page. The opening lines were little less than a call to battle: "After having overcome fascism, Nazism, and Stalinism, the world now faces a new global totalitarian threat: Islamism". In the background was the furore over cartoon depictions of Islam's prophet in the Danish newspaper *Jyllands Posten*, just then subsiding. Signatories to the manifesto were definitive in their judgment about the mortal danger civilisation faced from an implacable adversary: "Islamism is a reactionary ideology that kills equality, freedom and secularism wherever it is present. Its victory can only lead to a world of injustice and domination: men over women, fundamentalists over others. On the contrary, we must ensure access to universal rights for the oppressed or those discriminated against".[14]

Signatories to the manifesto included, as Cyran put it, the "most corrupt figures of the intellectual jet-set, such as Bernard-Henri Lévy (and) Antoine Sfeir". Others who signed up were novelists Salman Rushdie and Taslima Nasreen, and two globally known campaigners against hardline Islam – Ayaan Hirsi Ali and Irshad Manji – of whom the former at least had a known history of crude fabrications to embellish an image as hapless victim of fundamentalist bigotry.[15]

Just as a new intolerance began to be manifest towards personal acts of faith and family fealty among the Islamic minority in the western world, cultural entrepreneurs pandering to the demonisation of Islam were granted indemnity against every manner of fraud. *Charlie* had made France "a nastier place to live in", said Cyran. Women were forbidden from working in child care on grounds that their head covering would "traumatise the kids". A student who sought to partly accommodate the exaggerated political scruple over religious emblems

14 The statement was released on March 1, 2006 and published at BBC, 2016.

15 Blumenthal, 2015. Hirsi Ali also is with her usual shaky grasp of history, known for calling for a Martin Luther to lead a reformation in the Muslim world, and championing a Nobel peace prize for the far from peaceable Prime Minister of Israel, Benjamin Netanyahu. See Hasan (2015).

and wore a modestly sized bandana to college was judged to be displaying her faith with undue aggression and banished beyond the gates.[16]

A reply to Cyran's furious polemic came soon afterwards from a *Charlie* staffer whose name, Zineb el-Rhazoui, identified her as a member of the religious group ostensibly victimised by racism. She was nonetheless proud to claim the honour of having authored many of Charlie's putatively racist or "Islamophobic" articles. There were, she claimed, two possible designs behind Cyran's omission of her name from all he had brought up in his excoriation of *Charlie*: he was either reluctant to let *Charlie*'s critics know that one among the authors of its supposedly "racist ravings" was Muslim by origin; or, he did not think her "worth naming" since she could not be "anything but the house Arab", whose function was to render racism respectable.

Faith as accessory of state power

Lurking behind this omission and in fact, loudly proclaimed in the larger tone of Cyran's article, Rhazoui alleged, was "the most sophisticated variety of racism", an unsubtle clientelism that viewed people of the Islamic faith and Arab origin as "congenitally sealed off from the ubiquitous ideas of atheism", their identities "solely structured by religion". Rhazoui was educated and began her journalism in Morocco, witnessing up close how *Charlie*'s alleged racism had been a convenient pretext for a tyrannical monarchy and its accomplices in the clerical order, to quash all dissent. She saw a reprise of the same pattern after Cyran's article appeared, with Moroccan authorities eagerly promoting it through a number of compliant websites, where investigative articles on the corruption of the regime and the clerical reign of unreason, would be unheard of. That was sufficient proof of Cyran's disingenuousness: "A piece like yours is worth its weight in gold to the royalist police agents, who sponsored a 'dossier' against *Charlie* published in a gutter newspaper in Casablanca". This symmetry for

16 The UN Development Programme's annual report on human development in 2004 (UNDP, 2004) chose the theme of cultural liberty. It found that the French practice of denying denominational holidays on major festivals of the minority faith fell foul of its aggressive protestations of secularism. Neither was its political decision to ban the head-scarf, alongside other symbols of personal faith in public spaces, a norm that was equitably enforced or underwritten by wide social consensus.

Rhazoui had been intentionally ignored by *Charlie*'s critics: just as her pieces on Islam "might occasionally please" the racist National Front in France, *Charlie*'s critics were making the Moroccan dictatorship of King Mohammad VI rather happy.

From a Moroccan king repressing his subjects, Rhazoui then made a rather clumsy pirouette towards Mohammad, the prophet of a faith which in particular situations, served the ends of state power. Rhazoui's invocation of the Moroccan instance was apt, though she could as well have referred to more egregious examples, like Saudi Arabia and the Gulf monarchies.[17] The argument though was rather fragile. Apart from the cohabitation of monarchical power and clerical authority, there was also the placid and comfortable relationship these tyrannies enjoyed with secular and liberal governments in the west.

Just four months after the Charlie Hebdo murders, President Hollande chose to be the first foreign leader to attend a summit meeting of the Gulf Cooperation Council (GCC), the congeries of petroleum fuelled tyrannies where dissent is either bought off or more often, repressed under an ostensible divine mandate. His motive may partly have been securing contracts for French arms companies from increasingly unstable and beleaguered kingdoms, an unimpeachably secular purpose served by pandering to religious bigotry enshrined in state power.[18]

Quite aside from the instrumental use of religion by tyrannical states, there are multiple contexts in which faith is the basis of community life, of a sense of mutual belonging. This is a reality that *Char-*

---

17 In May 2015, French President Francois Hollande travelled to the capital of Saudi Arabia to be part of the summit meeting of the Gulf Cooperation Council, a consortium of regressive medieval monarchies that Saudi Arabia has formed with U.S. patronage. He spoke of the desirability of abolishing the death penalty at just the time that the Saudi monarchy was rapidly escalating the number of executions it was carrying out. And there is no recorded evidence of him having protested over the Saudi regime's conviction of Raif Badawi, a political dissident and blogger to ten years of imprisonment, interrupted only by the sentence of one thousand lashes, for the crime of calling for social and political reform in the country. Badawi received the first instalment of fifty of his thousand lashes in January just after the *Charlie* murders, though this matter did not feature at all in the international discourse on free speech.

18 *Arab News* (2015).

lie Hebdo and its vociferous defenders chose to ignore. In situations where large numbers of people are uprooted from native contexts by political turmoil or material deprivation – or the lure of a livelihood from fulfilling the more menial tasks within the European welfare state project – faith as remembered and reconstructed could be a thread that sustains a sense of identity in an alienating milieu.

The faith she reduced to a single-dimension signalled multiple meanings, but Rhazoui was content just considering it as an accessory of state power. "You've got to understand us, because you see, centuries after his death Mohammed is still imposing his law", she argued: "He is, in a manner of speaking, the head of state of this Umma that deprives us of our freedom of thought, and which forbids me, for example, to inherit property equally with my brothers or to marry a man of my choosing". Secularism in its French variant afforded a release from a centuries old tyranny. The "official representatives of the Islamic denomination in Europe" could not, for that reason, be allowed to "fix the limits of our freedom of expression".[19]

A number of motifs emerged from these exchanges. Cyran's focus was on the Muslim community in France and their observances of faith in a smaller context, expressed in sartorial, culinary and various other choices. The French policy of *laïcité* sanctioned state oversight of these personal choices. Much like *Charlie* claimed to take on all faiths and denominations in an equal spirit of irreverence, *laïcité* worked on the presumption of symmetry. Just as the head-scarf was banned in a public space, so too was a conspicuous display of the crucifix or the Jewish skullcap. This seeming imposition on otherwise inviolable personal choices claimed its legitimacy from the promise of assimilation of diverse people into the egalitarian ethos of the French republic. Cyran's furious polemic against *Charlie* suggested that this promise was never fulfilled; Rhazoui's riposte conceded that this probably was the case, but only because of the persistence of the atavistic pull of Islam in Europe. That was not a very convincing case and called for another form of appeal to past glories for its sustenance. As *Charlie*'s editor Gerard Biard explained in 2012: "We're a French newspaper, engaged in the defence of French values .... *Laïcité* is not just some abstract idea. It is a moral value ... (and) one must recognise that *laïcité* is perhaps the

19 Rhazoui (2013).

prime moral value of our republic".[20] Without secularism, the promise of "liberty, equality and fraternity" would itself turn vacuous.

The sociologist Emmanuel Todd was one Frenchman left unmoved by the mass public ceremonies after the Charlie Hebdo killings. *Who is Charlie?* was his reply, published a few months afterwards and translated into English within a year of the incident. The march in Paris and the cathedral ceremonies designed as affirmation of the core values of the French republic, seemed to Todd little else than a "moment of collective hysteria" which presented a unique opportunity to penetrate the layers of "ideological and political power" in French society. Secularism was ostensibly at stake, but there had been a deviation from the "tradition of secular values" and the voices that claimed to speak for the Republic were far removed from the republican essence. Once this mystique was dispelled, the January 11 events shone a light on the curiosities of a society that could bring millions out on the street to "show their solidarity with a magazine identified with a caricature of Muhammad, one that specialised in stigmatising a minority religion, Islam, and designating it as France's number one problem".[21]

Far from the simple-minded belief that a secular sensibility was driving these perceptions, the reality was of two distinct sub-cultures created in the banishment of Catholicism from the French public sphere. There was one part of the republic that had abandoned the church in the mid-18th century and forced the pace of social change in the decades that followed. There was another, broadly distinguished by region, that retained its fealty to the Catholic faith till around 1960, but then "finally kicked free and lost its belief". This disappearance of religion from the public sphere created other kinds of ideological bonds. And Todd describes the force that "emerged from the final disintegration of the Church in its traditional bastions" as "zombie Catholicism".[22]

20 Sayare (2015a).

21 Todd (2016): 12.

22 Ibid: 24, 28.

Zombie faith overturns egalitarian values

Egalitarian values were lost in this resurrection of Catholicism from its interment. Hierarchy was restored in society and as the European integration project gained momentum, compounded by a punishing monetary regime that ended all possibility of meeting the employment needs of emerging youth strata. A sense of rootless anomie grew in which the quest for a fresh set of moorings was consummated in the sacralisation of the republic minus its egalitarian promises. Traditional hierarchical principles of the Catholic faith adapted well to the newly secularised faith of the republic.[23]

Secularism as official policy in France dates from a 1905 law on the separation of church and state, which revoked the concessions to ecclesiastical authority that Napoleon had granted under his 1801 concordat with the Vatican. Prior to this Napoleonic conciliation, the French republic had in the heady fervour of the revolution introduced a law in 1795 which disestablished the Catholic faith, turning over all church properties to the state. Napoleon's *modus vivendi* was perhaps driven by the strategic purpose of restoring order to a polity just emerging from a prolonged period of internal turbulence and bloodshed, about to inaugurate a series of military adventures to create a hospitable environment for burgeoning imperial ambitions. As the polity shifted left with the arrival of mass working class politics in the late-19th century, public endorsement for the isolation of ecclesiastical authority grew, achieving fruition in the 1905 law.

The 1905 law was in its implementation, always negotiated with the Vatican and tempered by judicial interpretation. Over time, its rigidities abated considerably. There was at the same time, a lazy delusional attitude towards the popular faith of minorities, particularly those from the former colonies. The French state purported a certain benign neglect towards the irreverence that periodically surfaced in the public discourse on matters involving the majority faith. This was a convenient camouflage for the homage paid, almost absent-mindedly towards the Catholic faith. The memorial service for *Charlie* at the Notre Dame cathedral with virtually every significant French politician in attendance, was perhaps best evidence of the new reconciliation between church and state. As Todd remarked, Marianne, emblem of

23 Ibid: 39.

French revolutionary values, simply "got used to cohabiting with the Virgin Mary".[24]

Todd is prepared to go further: the "secular homogeneity" that France likes to claim as essential part of its republican identity is "pure fiction". What is being demanded of Muslims, "was never obtained from Catholics, in spite of more than one hundred years of violent conflict, including the 200,000 dead in the Vendee war".[25] Disengaged from an authentic mooring in history, the doctrine of "radical secularism" often expressed in a "militant atheism", became another dogma. In a truly republican order, it was a doctrine that needed "to be kept outside state schools just as much as Catholicism, Protestantism, Judaism and Islam".[26]

Laïcité was in short, another kind of dogma imposed by a notionally democratic state apparatus. Though prohibited by its secular commitments from funding any religious order, the French state "owns and maintains 39,000 churches which became state property" with the passage of the 1905 law. There are a further 5,000 places of worship built since 1905 by the Catholic church and still owned by it. In contrast, of about 2,500 places of Muslim worship, most constructed after the mass arrival of immigrants from Africa and the Arab world since the 1960s, not one enjoys any form of support from the state.[27]

This schizoid construct of secularism originated in an undying belief that French colonialism had brought lesser people boons they could not otherwise have imagined. Many of the French colonial territories, despite being innocent of metropolitan systems of franchise and representation, were given the status of provinces within the nation.[28]

24 Ibid: 28.

25 Ibid: 187. The Vendee war between 1793 and 1796 was a particularly brutal part of the bloody afterlife of the French revolution, read then as a royalist uprising with the backing of the Catholic church. Historians have applied the term "genocide" to the means adopted by the revolutionaries to crush the uprising in the Vendee region of France. This remains a contentious point, though there have been few who have questioned the scale of the bloodshed involved.

26 Ibid: 175.

27 Sayare (2015b).

28 Bleich (2001).

Following decolonisation in the early-1960s and the first arrivals of immigrants in the metropolis, the ends of equal opportunity and assimilation were in part addressed by legislation that took effect in 1972 to prevent any form of discrimination on grounds of ethnicity, race or religion. While the U.S. and the United Kingdom sought to recognise different cultural identities and if appropriate, introduce policies for inclusive employment and educational practices, France chose the path of asserting the singularity of its culture and the unique opportunities it afforded to all, irrespective of identity.

France's anti-discrimination law provided no civil remedies. Parliament considered empowering "civil parties" to bring to trial cases of discrimination on behalf of individual claimants. A brief debate later, this clause was deleted, reflecting an old French superstition that any manner of intermediary loyalty between citizen and state would be corrosive of the republican values. As finally adopted, the law allowed a limited eligibility for civil groups that had been in existence for a minimum of five years, specifically to disentitle activist organisations that sprang up during the nation-wide turmoil of May 1968. Within this circumscribed range, civil parties could take up litigation only with the explicit consent of an aggrieved individual. Proceedings were to follow the criminal law, in which the agencies of the state would bear primary responsibility. Yet in the absence of a specific agency – separate from the local police – to follow up cases of discrimination, the law remained weak and poorly implemented.[29]

The real face of discrimination

Minority assimilation and incorporation into the republic remained patchy and sporadic. Elected legislatures till well into the twenty-first century, had virtually no membership from people of the Muslim faith or African extraction. In 2007, a reporter with the U.S.-based magazine *Time* spoke of a "bigoted chorus" and "growing racist chatter in the French mainstream". This included a TV commentator musing that the "black penis" may be responsible for famine in Africa and calling for the infusion of sexual discipline in the continent through mass sterilisation. A prominent Socialist Party politician meanwhile, bemoaned the loss of white pre-eminence in the sporting arena, as rep-

29 Liberman (2001).

resented by the nine black players in the starting line-up of the French football team. Another public figure, a philosopher and prolific author known to be an ardent Zionist apologist, complained that the French football team was "black-black-black … and the laughingstock of Europe". In 2005 interior minister Nicolas Sarkozy, already front-running contender for the presidential election due in two years, responded in outrage as riots broke out in some of the country's most deprived urban quarters, using a crudely racist epithet that fuelled a further spiral of violence.[30]

In 2012, a government advisory body reported a 23 percent rise in racist acts, with the vaunted 1972 law being by and large, ineffective. The official response was a further retreat into the delusional cocoon. In 2013, the French government outlawed the term "race" in all relevant articles of the penal code, or alternately, its replacement by the term "ethnic". Expectedly, this led to a torrent of acerbic comment, one of which purported to see a durable fix for all public health issues in abolishing the term "disease". Defenders of the terminological solution argued that "disease" had an objective basis in reality and existed in an identifiable form, while "race" was a political construct that only obscured the fundamental principle of equality before the law.[31]

This assertion was obviously in troubling conflict with reality. French census enumerations stopped gathering information in accordance with race and religion ever since colour-blindness became official policy. By 2004, there was reason to believe however, that the preceding decade had witnessed a dramatic change in the composition of the country's prison population. Persons of the Muslim faith, though only an estimated 10 percent of the population were then believed to constitute 60 percent of prison inmates in France. And the prison system, presumably because of the unique seductions of the French secular pretence, was yet to adapt to the requirements of handling this shift. There was for instance, an obdurate refusal to employ Muslim clerics to counsel the prison population, because "inadequate screening could unleash potential militants into the system". Prison inmates of the Muslim faith complained of being "ignored in a system devised for a Christian population". There was no regard for Islamic dietary

30 Crumley (2007). See also, Pulham (2015).

31 *The New York Times* (2013).

laws and no "religious services for Muslims, even though most Catholic inmates (could) attend Mass once a week".[32]

The depth of this unique and rather conceited construct of cultural integration in France – and the casual manner it was viewed – were underlined in 2008, when roughly 70 percent of the prison population in the country was estimated to be of the Muslim faith. Since official policy made an enumeration in accordance with faith impossible, a proxy indicator was used in the number of prisoners who declined pork as a part of their prison diet. Muslim inmates continued to be denied counselling by persons of their faith. As reported at the time: "The prison system has only 100 Muslim clerics for the country's 200 prisons, compared with about 480 Catholic, 250 Protestant and 50 Jewish chaplains". With no hint of irony, an official of the national prison system was quoted holding out a rather perverse reassurance: "It is true that we haven't attained full equality among religions in prisons yet ... It is a matter of time".[33]

Even if cultural assimilation was going off the rails the French government failed to read the signs and in a mood of reignited colonial hubris, began as a matter of declared national policy, to step beyond international law in seeking regime change in countries predominantly of the Muslim faith, such as Libya and Syria. Poseur and *faux* philosopher Bernard-Henri Levi, fresh from his monitory warnings against the menace of Islamism, was among the principal public champions of the reawakened French civilisational mission.

France's national policy to nurture religious extremism for foreign policy goals was unlikely for long, to leave the domestic political landscape untouched. One of the *Charlie Hebdo* murderers, as also an associate who ran rampage through a Jewish supermarket the same day, were found after the event, to have met while spending time in jail. They were initiated into militancy in the cause of avenging the slights inflicted on their faith, by an individual serving a sentence for an alleged plot to attack the U.S. embassy in 2001.[34] Since the two shooters in the *Charlie* incident and their accomplice who triggered the carnage in another part of the city were eliminated, very little has come to light

32 Smith (2004).

33 Moore (2008).

34 Alexander (2015).

on their antecedents or motivations. One among the two brothers who carried out the *Charlie Hebdo* attacks did travel to parts of the Arabian peninsula in 2011 as a volunteer – witting or unwitting – in the stated French government policy of regime change in Syria.[35]

Though banished from public attention in the self-righteous ambience that prevailed, these questions showed a certain persistence on the fringes. It was pointed out that amidst its moral agonies over the human suffering in Syria and Libya, France had been making casual, almost offhand admissions about its constant shipments of arms to some of the most extreme elements combating established governments in these countries.[36] Other reports suggested that the arms blackmarket in Brussels may have been the source of the lethal, military-grade assault weapons that the *Charlie Hebdo* murderers and their accomplices used.[37] Following the secret burial of the three gunmen, cornered in an industrial warehouse and eliminated by French police, these questions were surreptitiously interred in the dark and capacious vault of national security which seldom disgorges its secrets.

Faith as strategic tool

The rush to declare *Charlie Hebdo* a martyr for free speech was more about shifting attention from tough questions about French domestic policy and foreign adventurism, than mourning individuals who worked exclusively through words and images, but were naive at best or insensitive at worst. The PEN America award announced in April 2015 was a further step in the canonisation of the weekly. When pushback occurred with six writers – Booker Prize winners Michael Ondaatje and Peter Carey, Teju Cole, Francine Prose, Rachel Kushner and Taiye Selasi – declining designated roles in the awards ceremony, PEN America President Andrew Solomon and Executive Director Suzanne Nossel took to the media to explain the questionable choice. Satire, they conceded, was often "vulnerable to being construed as hate speech, especially at first blush". *Charlie*'s valour lay in "their dauntless

35 Some part of the mystery of Said and Cherif Kouachi, the Charlie Hebdo attackers, is presented in the French news agency AFP's report datelined Paris and published January 9, 2015.

36 Cartalucci (2015).

37 Woolf (2015).

fortitude patrolling the outer precincts of free speech". It was a "far-flung territory" and there was no question that much "bigotry (could) lurk there". But without "those who stake out the border provinces, we would all be forced to dwell in an ever-shrinking expressive terrain".

This in itself would seem a rather weak endorsement of Charlie's virtues. It makes no more than a case for rewarding poor taste, since not doing so might constrict the free speech zone where quality could flourish. Abusive behaviour gets a free pass because it creates sufficiently large interstices, where words of value could potentially be uttered. This defence of poor taste gathers pace as Solomon and Nossel plunge further on. PEN America would not endorse the "content or quality of the cartoons", but was happy going along with the judgment that they did not constitute hate speech. A survey by the French newspaper *Le Monde* had established that "of 523 Charlie Hebdo covers published from 2005 to 2015, only seven singled out Islam for ridicule (ten were cited as mocking multiple religions); many more mocked Christianity and the racism of the French right". The "leading French anti-racism organisation", SOS Racisme had, moreover, called *Charlie* "the greatest anti-racist weekly in this country".[38]

The figures revealed in the *Le Monde* survey, though devoid of subtlety and even an effort to arrive at a deeper qualitative judgment, were widely quoted in the *Charlie Hebdo* defence. They failed to account for gross asymmetries in the application of the law and the discriminatory norms in place in the darker crevices where the law failed to reach. Also left out of consideration were the different ways in which people related to their faiths. SOS Racisme which provided the resounding endorsement that all *Charlie*'s defenders came to rely on, is in turn, an organisation with an interesting doctrinal history. Formed in 1984 when the earlier orthodoxy of colour-blind integration was losing ground to an alternative which foregrounded difference and a multiculturalist perspective, SOS Racisme soon found its main doctrinal principles appropriated by the right-wing. "Difference" was the principle to be defended, but then the racist National Front was quick to argue that difference needed to be kept at bay, preferably outside the national frontiers of the French republic. By the early-1990s, anti-racism campaigners were beginning to awaken to the limitations of the multiculturalist plank. As a leading philosopher of the cause then ar-

38 Solomon and Nossel (2015).

gued, the "right to difference" could soon degenerate into a "difference of rights". SOS Racisme bought into this revisionist doctrine, switching its focus from the ostensible "community logic" of multiculturalism, to a reaffirmation of the traditional colour-blind model.[39] Perhaps in the process, real differences in society and the denial of rights on grounds of identity stood banished into the shadows of official neglect.

Denial of difference soon passed over imperceptibly into the elision of how identity was often basis for an abridgment of rights. Its impact was apparent in the days after the *Charlie Hebdo* murders. "*Je Suis Charlie*" or "I am Charlie" was a nation-wide chant, but there were some who could not partake of the chorus. When the government decreed a minute's silence in all schools in respect to the victims, there were a reported hundred incidents of resistance. The number was modest in relation to the millions who go to school in France. Yet the marginal expression of dissent was reported by *Le Monde* under a panic-stricken headline and France's Minister for Education reacted with an assurance that punishment of appropriate severity would be reserved for the offenders, with "police investigating the worst cases".[40] *Laïcité* as official policy would be reinforced with a special emphasis on the "transmission of republican values" and changes would be introduced in the recruitment standards for teachers, so that a candidate was assessed in accordance with the ability "to explain and spread the values of the Republic". All students and their parents would be obliged to sign a "*laïcité* charter" and a special annual day designated for the commemoration of these values.[41]

These statements of official intent were unambiguous about the principle of the equal application of the law. A clear double standard – devoid of any ambivalence – was however in evidence in the wave of arrests effected after the Charlie Hebdo murders, on grounds of "*apologie du terrorisme*". As a writer in the *London Review of Books* noted just eight days after the murders, there were roughly forty cases registered within that time under this legal provision, fraught with "harsh consequences" since the law was changed the previous year. "Freedom of expression" was under scrutiny as a consequence of these arrests

39 Bleich (2001).

40 Sayare (2015b).

41 Ibid.

and it would be "even harder than it was a week (before) to speak up against Israel's occupation of the West Bank, or another onslaught in Gaza, without being accused of anti-semitism".[42] One of the most widely publicised arrests was Dieudonne M'Bala M'Bala, popularly known as Dieudonne, a comedian and provocateur of uncertain political provenance – an anti-racism campaigner who later made common cause with the racist National Front – for a social media posting in which he responded to the "*Je Suis Charlie*" chorus with a proclamation that he felt a bit like Charlie Coulabaly, the gunman responsible for killing four customers at a kosher supermarket. Here was a man who had gone on an expedition into the outer precincts of free speech and fallen over that tipping point into hate.

Different standards

Considerably more problematic was the arrest of a youth who put in circulation an ironic reprise of a *Charlie* cartoon mocking the victims of a crackdown on protests in Cairo which killed some eight hundred activists of the Muslim Brotherhood. Demonstrators had gathered at various points in Cairo city following the Egyptian army coup that toppled the country's first freely elected president, Mohammad Morsi in July 2013. In five distinct phases involving extreme use of force, the Egyptian army and police cleared up these gatherings, crushing the mass protest against an illegal seizure of power by the country's long dominant military castes. After a year-long investigation Human Rights Watch (HRW) concluded that the "systematic and widespread killing of at least 1,150 demonstrators by Egyptian security forces in July and August 2013 probably amounts to crimes against humanity". There were five distinct incidents involving the use of disproportionate force by the Egyptian army, beginning on July 5 and ending with the action of August 14, when a protest at the Rab'a al-Adawiya square in Cairo was dispersed, killing "a minimum of 817 people and more likely at least 1,000".[43]

In July 2013, *Charlie* ran a cover cartoon that depicted a victim holding a bullet-riddled copy of the Quran as a shield and hurling a scatological imprecation at the holy scripture of the Muslims. "The

42 Harding (2015).

43 Human Rights Watch (2014).

Quran is shit", he said, as gunfire perforated his body: "it does not stop bullets". Though unclear then and later if this was by accident or design, the cartoon appeared on the first day of Ramzan, the Muslim month of abstinence and penance.

Dieudonne's website, soon after the Paris carnage, published a cartoon presenting an unnamed person of French or certainly western mien, holding up this particular issue of the magazine and hurling an identical imprecation against *Charlie* for failing to stop bullets. This should have been an unexceptionable exercise in satire under the principle of equal opportunity offence, or certainly allowable within the broadly permissive ambience of what could be called gallows humour. Yet the youth who posted this ironic comment was soon afterwards arrested on charges of defending terrorism.[44]

Against this background of uncertain moral categories, Joe Sacco and Garry Trudeau, both legendary exponents of the art of pictorial satire, spoke up explicitly against the *Charlie* brand of humour. Sacco's work was presented in a one-page strip soon after the Paris carnage, using all the tropes of cartooning that *Charlie* had made its own, but turning it on people not customarily targeted by the satirical magazine. "Lines on paper are a weapon and satire is meant to cut close to the bone", but the question really was: "whose bone?" And if Charlie's defenders were to take a break from "holding up the middle finger", and ask "why the world is the way it is", they might also figure out "what it is about Muslims in this time and place that makes them unable to laugh off a mere image".[45]

Early-April 2015, just ahead of the PEN award though without being aware of it, Trudeau chose a ceremony honouring his lifetime work, to sum up the moral dilemmas involved. "Traditionally", he said, "satire has comforted the afflicted while afflicting the comfortable". By its very nature "satire punches up, against authority of all kinds". To ridicule those at the bottom of the social heap "is almost never funny – it is just mean". In punching down and "attacking a powerless, disenfranchised minority with crude, vulgar drawings closer to graffiti than cartoons, *Charlie* wandered into the realm of hate speech, which in France is only illegal if it directly incites violence". That rather stringent criterion, Trudeau said, had been met, since "voila – the seven

44 Abunimah (2015).

45 Sacco (2015).

million copies that were published following the killings did exactly that, triggering violent protests across the Muslim world". And for all the pompous claims made on its behalf, the "French tradition of free speech is too full of contradictions to fully embrace".[46]

When PEN America announced its honour for Charlie, six dissenting members tried to remind free speech dogmatists about these subtleties. There was a "critical difference between staunchly supporting expression that violates the acceptable, and enthusiastically rewarding such expression", they said. The argument that *Charlie* worked on the principle of "equal opportunity offence" was, even if true, only very partial extenuation, since "in an unequal society, equal opportunity offence does not have equal effect".[47]

From *Charlie*'s perspective, the inescapable comparisons were made when Pamela Geller infamous hate-group American Freedom Defence Initiative (AFDI) – with its credentialed claims that President Barack Obama is the love-child of the late black power leader Malcolm X – launched an event celebrating the most vile and hateful portrayal of the prophet of Islam. Speakers at the PEN awards took these accusations on in some hauteur, asserting that even if Charlie's drawings were "often vulgar" the "ideas behind them (were) rather sophisticated". The distinctions with the AFDI arose from three aspects, among which anti-racism and secularism were key. Yet again, the endorsement of SOS Racisme – with all its burden of ambiguity – was trundled out to support the *Charlie* cause, and secularism underlined as a fundamental condition for "freedom of conscience".[48] Another commentator dismissed the comparison as misplaced since it fudged the "distinction between hate and critique". Even if *Charlie*'s methods were not "always admirable or appropriate", its approach was avowedly secular. Secularism was not "state atheism, but rather, an impartial, detached policy

46 Trudeau (2015).

47 The letter was initially attributed to the six writers mentioned earlier, who withdrew from specific roles in the awards ceremony. A number of other writers subsequently signed up with the protest. On April 30, 2015, the number of dissenting PEN members was estimated at 204. See Greenwald (2015).

48 Kachka (2015).

that permits the coexistence of multiple faith groups and cultures under an egalitarian structure".[49]

Colour blind? Not quite

Claiming the honorific of secularism would be a rather shaky defence without a deeper interrogation of its content. On available evidence, the doctrine that *Charlie*'s defence was premised upon was secular in name but in reality, akin almost to religious dogma in its willingness to elide social reality and airbrush out of consideration the links between rights and identity, even within a republican order that purported to be blind to the latter. Certain identities obviously acclimatised better within the environment of *laïcité*, but this was not a complexity that the custodians of the French republican order were willing to look at, even as they closed ranks within the hallowed precincts of Notre Dame cathedral in a symbolic defence of secularism.

One of the dissenting writers within PEN called for sobriety as tempers remained frayed. "Why is it so difficult for people to make fine distinctions?" asked Francine Prose. No right thinking person would have the faintest qualm about standing "fully behind *Charlie Hebdo*'s right to publish whatever they want without being censored, and of course without the use of violence to enforce their silence". Honouring the magazine was a different proposition, since that suggested widely shared admiration and respect, which were "responses quite difficult to summon for the work of *Charlie Hebdo*". Personal taste and commitment aside, the plain fact was that "provocation (was) simply not the same as heroism".

Evidently pushed to extreme aggravation, Booker winning novelist Salman Rushdie fired back. To protest a peer honour for people killed for working with words and lines, amounted to a "public judgment" that the victims were at fault. In itself, independent of all the words spoken, this placed the dissenters "in the enemy camp". And then in language that recalled the tyranny of the "with us or against us" rhetoric used to intimidate a sceptical world into acquiescence in the so-called "war on terrorism", Rushdie warned: "In politics you can't

49 Flanagan (2015).

both be for and against. Your act says you are against. And that makes you fellow travellers of the fanatics".[50]

Charlie Hebdo as controversy is firmly embedded within the clash of civilisations foretold by the ideologue of U.S. power Samuel Huntington, years before it acquired full-blown malevolence in 2001 as the "global war on terror". Without explicitly stated intent, the main players in the controversy were playing out roles that had seemingly been assigned to them in the larger drama, consolidating the existing mood of public endorsement for violence as the only remedy. The PEN Award it turned out was not without a theology of its own which made it a weapon, witting or otherwise, in the hands of one of the global combatants.

PEN Executive Director Suzanne Nossel, a key figure in the drama over free speech, belongs to that tribe of "in-and-outers" who frequently pass through the revolving doors between the U.S. State Department and the flourishing ecosystem of think tanks and universities, nourishing that cross-fertilisation of ideas and agendas between academia and the U.S. security and foreign policy establishments.[51] Nossel's brief biographical sketch on the PEN America website credits her with inventing the term "smart power" which Hilary Clinton, during her four years as U.S. Secretary of State, made the "defining feature of U.S. foreign policy".[52] The article in question, published in the solidly credentialed establishment journal *Foreign Affairs* in 2004, described Nossel as an "executive at a media company in New York", and between 1999 and 2001, "Deputy to the Ambassador for U.N. Management and Reforms at the U.S. mission to the United Nations".[53]

Nossel served the State Department once again in a relatively junior spot, as "deputy assistant secretary" for international organisations after the Democrats regained control of the White House in 2009. This was when the U.S., seeking under President Barack Obama a kinder and gentler image than the preceding administration, with-

50 Flood (2015).

51 The term is used in Perry Anderson's very interesting work on the ruling ideology of the U.S. (Anderson, 2015).

52 The brief biography is available on the PEN website (PEN, 2015).

53 Nossel (2004).

drew its boycott of the Human Rights Council (HRC), formed in 2006 under a mandate of the U.N. General Assembly.

In 2011, Nossel explained the policy reversal as part of an effort to make the HRC "more legitimate and more credible". The U.S. was aware of all the body's "limitations and flaws" and hoped to correct these. First among the flaws of the body was a "persistent, one-sided, unbalanced, and almost obsessive focus on Israel". Still another was the dubious membership roster, with the HRC having "within its ranks member states whose own human rights records do not always reflect the kind of respect for human rights that (the U.S.) would like to see".[54]

Free speech standards as "smart power"

Nossel's paper on "Smart Power" clearly foreshadowed these themes. It called for reinstating the philosophy of "liberal internationalism" as a way of repairing the U.S. image, damaged by the aggressive militarism of the "global war on terror" and in particular, the 2003 invasion of Iraq. As a principle of U.S. global hegemony, "smart power" was an emanation of liberal internationalism, and could be defined as "assertive leadership — diplomatic, economic, and not least, military". The reference point for her, as in much latter-day liberal fantasies about the eternal character of U.S. power, was the immediate aftermath of World War II, when the U.S. found itself the "only industrialised country left intact by the war" and faced "challenges ranging from containing Soviet ambitions to rebuilding war-ravaged Europe". Far from seeking to go it alone, the U.S. "crafted an interdependent network of allies and institutions that included the U.N. and NATO". It stood at the centre of this order, but "shared the task of maintaining it". The long period of conservative pre-eminence in foreign policy had "tainted liberal internationalist ideals". It was time for the progressive wing in the U.S. to "take back the fight" since "entrusting the liberal internationalist agenda to the multilateral system (was) neither viable nor sound".

Though extremely critical of the "aggressive projection of unilateral military power" during the long conservative reign in the U.S., Nossel was herself prone to ample use of military metaphors. "Progressive policymakers", she urged, should "learn from the example of the U.S. military", and its recognition since long that the advantage in power comes not from size or destructive capability, "but from farsighted

54 State Department (2011).

strategy, sophisticated intelligence, professionalism and precise weaponry". U.S. foreign policy had failed to follow the excellent example of the military. In renewing the doctrine of liberal internationalism, there was need for explicit recognition of the mutual reinforcement possible between "military power and humanitarian endeavours". Being smart in the exercise of power meant "enlisting others on behalf of U.S. goals, through alliances, international institutions, careful diplomacy and the power of ideals".

These locutions from a "free speech" champion who saw the principle as an extension of U.S. power, different only marginally from the military firepower it had unleashed in diverse parts of the globe, should have been sufficient warning. Greater admissions though, were to follow. In rebuilding alliances and reforming the U.N., Nossel argued, a priority should be to break down the "long-standing, destructive anachronism ... (of) anti-Western developing-world blocs". A prime instance that she was able to cite of such an anachronism, was the Group of 77 and the Nonaligned Movement (NAM), both of which were "Cold War relics" that retained "outsized importance at the U.N., leading to such travesties as Libya's leadership of the human rights committee, Cuba's domination of budget debates, and constant scapegoating of Israel".[55]

Much like French secularism frowned upon intermediary loyalties between the citizen and the state, "smart power" required all nations to bend the knee to U.S. tutelage and forget allegiances that might dilute their servitude to liberal internationalist ideals. Nossel wrote at a time when the G-77 and NAM were well past their best days. Beyond symbolic affirmations of solidarity at their occasional gatherings – whether under the U.N. canopy or elsewhere – these bodies had little ability collectively or individually, to stand up against the demands of the U.S. and its allies. It took a particularly obsessive conviction to view the G77 and NAM as encumbrances to the exercise of U.S. power, whether smart or unsmart.

Nossel's tender concern for Israel was never concealed in her work as a practitioner and theorist of U.S. foreign policy. The attentions perhaps were repaid before, but definitely so after she assumed charge at PEN America. Soon after the ceremony honouring *Charlie Hebdo*, it

---

55 Nossel (2004): 131, 135-6, 138 and 141.

emerged that the Israeli Embassy in the U.S. was among the sponsors of the PEN America events, including a splashy series of celebrity literary events.[56] Within a galaxy where governmental bodies were generally scarce, Israel stood out for the ardour of its government's support of the cause of free speech, especially as embodied in PEN America.

The pencil and the bomb

The pencil became a powerful metaphor of freedom soon after the *Charlie Hebdo* murders. For a writer in *Vanity Fair* in January 2015, it was "a symbol of solidarity with the five cartoonists .. targeted for the paper's perceived insults to the prophet Mohammed". And when President Barack Obama delivered his State of the Union address on January 20, days after the *Charlie Hebdo* killings, members of the U.S. Congress held up yellow pencils to show their commitment to the cause of free speech.[57] In distant Australia, the Murdoch-owned tabloid *Herald Sun* had the most extravagant flight of fancy, depicting masked, hooded and gun-toting terrorists of an obvious Islamic stripe, gazing befuddled at the sky as a shower of pencils descended on them. It was an almost child-like fantasy of the western world triumphing against lethal arms through the sheer force of ideas. As an extended commentary on the website of the Stop War Coalition put it, "reality could not be more at odds with this ludicrous narrative". Ever since 2001, the U.S. had with varying degrees of support from other western nations, "rained violence and destruction on the Arab and Muslim world with a ferocity that has few parallels in the history of modern warfare". This was not a battle fought with pencils or ideas. Rather, it was the force of lethal munitions delivered with intent to kill, maim and destroy, "that left Iraq, Gaza and Afghanistan shattered and hundreds of thousands of human beings dead".[58]

---

56 An event scheduled for May 8, titled "A Literary Quest" identified a number of sponsors of which the only two governmental bodies were the Embassies of Israel and France. Information extracted from PEN (2015b). A second series of events, titled "World Voices Festival of International Literature, was scheduled between May 4 and 10 and identified the Embassy of Israel as a "patron". The Government of Australia was the only other governmental body that had a similar standing within these events (PEN, 2015c).

57 Sancton (2015) and Berenson (2015).

58 Oakley (2015).

The pencil as a metaphor – particularly as a destructive shower unleashed from the sky – made eminent sense within the framework of "smart power", where military force was held in reserve as final arbiter, to be deployed if the U.S. did not prevail through moral strength and an appeal to values. Free speech as PEN America chose to celebrate it, was another weapon of war, deployed with intent to dehumanise an enemy people and their culture, to prepare and inure public opinion for an unending war of destruction which would buttress the western claim to civilisational superiority through a destructive technological prowess that would "shock and awe".

"Free speech" was purportedly the purpose and intent of the cartoon-caricatures of the prophet of Islam that a Danish newspaper published in 2006. But the community of Islam saw it as grossly provocative, a licentious manifestation of western civilisation – or the lack of it – which had transformed free speech into the sanction to offend.[59] Further aggravation followed along this particular fault-line, with the release of a trashy amateur film production titled "The Innocence of Muslims" in 2012, which purported to re-enact a number of key episodes from the life of Islam's prophet, portraying him as a person of serious character flaws and uncertain paternity. Rumbles of anger were heard on the street in countries predominantly of the Muslim faith. And one of the direct consequences was possibly a lethal attack on a U.S. diplomatic compound in the Libyan city of Benghazi, where the west had just a few months before, consummated what it self-regardingly viewed as a democratic revolution against an unlamented Arab dictatorship.

With continuing self-regard, the internet giant Google Inc., which owns the web-based video-sharing site Youtube, refused to pull down the offending footage. A petition moved on grounds of a severe im-

59 It is important to recall this particularly bitter cultural encounter, because of the divided responses that emerged from the west. The press in Denmark published the cartoons and forwarded the material to colleagues in other countries with the explicit request that they be carried as a gesture of solidarity. France was divided, Britain totally opposed to the provocative action and the U.S. simply brushed off that whole episode as a needless diversion from more important issues. When the violence began over the provocation, all countries seemingly joined hands, though elements within the U.S. and British press did remind their Danish counterparts that the symbolic act of affirmation they sought was really quite pointless.

pairment of rights and life-threatening dangers by an actor who played a role in the film with no knowledge of the producer's provocative intent, brought no relief. It was only on appeal at a higher level of the U.S. federal justice hierarchy that the plaint was granted, on grounds that the aspiring actor held a partial copyright over her performance, which was violated by the producer of the video when he altered the title and intent of the film, and interpolated as part of her spoken part, words she had never uttered.[60] The first amendment to the U.S. Constitution guaranteed freedom of speech, but no protection for copyright violations, ruled the U.S. Court of Appeals for the Ninth Circuit.

On further appeal, the Ninth Circuit court held *en banc* i.e., with all its judges hearing the case, that the injunction against Google would not stand. It referred to the Copyright Office ruling that for copyright registration purposes, "a motion picture is a single integrated work". The aggrieved actor's contribution "was limited to her acting performance" and the office could not "register her performance apart from the motion picture". Granting copyright to every person who contributed to a film would be "a logistical and financial nightmare", and in performing a role assigned to her, the actor granted the director "an implied licence to incorporate her performance into the film". Though there was no denying the possibility of the actor's personal safety being endangered by the content of the film, the court could not grant her the desired relief since her copyright claim was not admissible. The protection of personal safety was not the intent of copyright legislation. If anything, the remedies sought by the actor lay within the domain of privacy laws rather than copyright. But that was a point on which the court preferred not to offer any "substantive view". If her ultimate objective was to have "her connection to the film forgotten and stripped from YouTube", the court was unable to grant her that

60 The character played by the plaintiff is shown asking "Is your Mohammad a child molester?" in the course of the film in which her services were recruited on the grounds that it was an action film set in the Arabian desert. Google took the plea that the demand for an injunction amounted to a prior restriction on free speech that violated the First Amendment to the U.S. Constitution. The right to an injunction was granted, with one dissent, on grounds that the First Amendment did not protect copyright violations. U.S. Court of Appeals (2014).

since the "right to be forgotten" though affirmed by the Court of Justice for the European Union, was "not recognised in the United States".[61]

Google wins one loses another

Interestingly, the issue of hate speech was never raised in any of the hearings connected with the trashy production. When the controversy first exploded and the U.S. consulate in Benghazi was attacked, U.S. President Barack Obama made an explicit suggestion that Google should contemplate the removal of the offending item from its inventory. The internet giant rebuffed that request with the claim that the film, though against the religion of Islam, was not against the Muslim people. It had blocked the film in countries like India and Indonesia, where it had country-specific websites and a violation of local laws was involved. Its policy for controversial content would take into account not just local laws but also community tastes and standards. As recorded by the company's top official for public affairs in its 2007 policy statement: "we have a bias in favour of people's right to free expression in everything we do. ... But we also recognise that freedom of expression can't be — and shouldn't be — without some limits. The difficulty is in deciding where those boundaries are drawn. For a company like Google with services in more than 100 countries — all with different national laws and cultural norms — it's a challenge we face many times every day".[62]

---

61 U.S. Court of Appeal (2015) for the Ninth Circuit, California, No 12-57302, D.C. No. 2:12-cv-08315-MWF-VBK; filed May 18, 2015.

62 *The New York Times* (2012). Garton Ash (2016: chapter 2) deals with this range of issues and points out how protests against the Danish cartoons in certain western societies, which included the incitement to violence, drew criminal indictments and convictions. One part of the Brandenburg test – the intent to cause violence – had been met. But had the two other criteria, likelihood and imminence? Clearly there was a judgment call there. This creates the further complication inherent in the Brandenburg precedent which accords hate speech a degree of protection, to assess when the threshold to "dangerous speech" is crossed. And a five-part test is available for making this assessment, attributed to Susan Benesch. Key here are judgments about how explicitly the speech act makes a call to violence, the identity of the speaker, i.e., does he or she have sufficient influence that others should take any exhortation to violence seriously. The character of the audience also matters, particularly its susceptibility to a call to violence. There are then two which require even more subtle acts of judgment, such as

In June 2009, Max Blumenthal, a young U.S. national well connected with the New York liberal intelligentsia, was in Jerusalem working on a book and a film about Israel's prolonged crisis of identity and territory. It was a night before U.S. President Barack Obama's scheduled public speech in Cairo, when he was widely expected to propose a new covenant in the relationship between the Arab world and the U.S. Blumenthal was asked by a friend who edited a progressive Jewish American blog, to gather a range of popular reactions on the Israeli street to the upcoming speech. The outcome was a brief recording that exposed the vicious racist undertow in the Zionist project. There had for long been a number of subtle indications of this virus lurking deep in the Zionist soul, but Blumenthal was able to capture a veritable orgy of drink and drug-fuelled racist animus, directed at Obama and at the Arab population that Israel had displaced to secure its place on the map.

Within twelve hours, as Blumenthal later narrated the story, "the video was ricocheting across cyberspace, generating half a million hits and counting". A young journalist for the liberal Israeli newspaper *Ha'aretz* commented that the video had been linked to a hundred political blogs and was "circling the internet at a critical velocity on a mission to humiliate the Jewish people". Others upbraided Blumenthal for his immaturity in both filming the youth, many of them holding dual U.S. nationality, in a moment of inebriation and incoherence. The video circulating through Youtube, others argued, was a case for sticking with trusted old media sources, since such material would never have made it past the gatekeepers they employed. Within twelve hours, after receiving a half-million hits on Youtube, the censors at Google stepped in to take the video down. Another video-sharing site, Vimeo did likewise. The formal explanation was that the video contained "explicit content".[63]

Though the original recording has since vanished, related material – though not half as vivid – continues to circulate under the title "Feeling the hate in Tel Aviv". In its contrast with "The Innocence of

---

the historic context and the means of propagation of the speech act. The last-named, Garton Ash points out, has been transformed in recent times. What good is the test of "imminence" he asks, "when everything online is, so to speak, immanent?"

63 Blumenthal (2013): 242.

Muslims", this case study offers interesting insights into the standards used in judging material that could be shared on the various platforms that Google owns. "Innocence" led to an actual outbreak of violence and also embodied the potential for physical injury to one of the actors who was induced to take a role in it on false pretexts. "Feeling the Hate" left no room for any doubts about its authenticity. Yet it held out the very real possibility of causing damage to the image of Israel, a vital U.S. strategic ally. Despite the triviality of the material involved in the former case, Google carried its fight through multiple levels of petitioning and judicial appeal, insisting that it had the right to keep a spurious video, created with explicit malafide intent, in public circulation. In the other, it set its censors to work with extreme alacrity, within a mere twelve hours. There has since been no appeal against this decision, though Blumenthal has posted a seven-minute sequel which refers to the preceding video.

In 2015, Google was estimated to have a share of close to 75 per cent in the internet search business. It has in this sense, decisive influence over what can and cannot be seen over the web. In 2008, a group of Greek nationals – in jest more than malice – posted material on Youtube which declared that the founder of the modern Turkish republic, Kamal Ataturk, was gay. The Turkish government retaliated by blocking Youtube access through its territory. Google sent a legal team to argue its case and agreed as part of a compromise to block material that was in clear violation of Turkish law. The Turkish government was happy with that deal but then raised the stakes, demanding that global access to the offensive material be blocked. Google refused and Turkey soon reinstated the ban on Youtube.

As one commentator observed, it was an incident that highlighted how Google had emerged as "the most powerful and protean of .. Internet gatekeepers". The giant corporation's legal team got to "decide what controversial material does and doesn't appear on the local search engines that Google maintains in many countries in the world, as well as on Google.com". As a result, this small group arguably had "more influence over the contours of online expression than anyone else on the planet".[64] Indeed, as Carne Ross, a British diplomat who quit after the convolutions of the truth he was compelled to perform in preparation for the Iraq war put it, the internet giants such as Google and Facebook

64 Rosen (2008).

today have the power to constitute the world and determine patterns of socialisation for millions. The algorithms these firms deploy, with supposedly benign intent, to optimise web browsing experiences, wrap users into a cocoon of their design. These are, as Ross points out, "intrinsically political decisions of considerable consequence".[65]

Expanding market share is the object and that clearly would mean that disposition of purchasing power between the various strata that access the internet would be of relevance. Some could pay for amusement and would always have the easy option of hiring entertaining clowns from the wide choices available. Others would perhaps have to worry about who or what they laugh at. The acceptable limits of satire would emerge from this unequal contest.

Laughter and power

In the mid-17th century in an England convulsed by strife between an older monarchical order and the parliamentary sentiment of the rising bourgeoisie, the political theorist and propagandist Hobbes reflected on the forces that could potentially contribute to restoring a semblance of order. His method, as the political philosopher C.B. MacPherson reminds us in an extended introduction to a 1968 edition of Hobbes's classic *Leviathan*, was deeply inspired by his contemporary Galileo, who set about unravelling the mysteries of the physical universe by first resolving it into distinct component parts and then composing them into a unified field where their mutual inter-relations would be clearly manifest. The resolutive part was where the basic propositions of human behaviour were enunciated. Then followed the compositive part which combined elementary propositions about human behaviour into society-wide generalities.

Among Hobbes' first priorities was to lay bare the origins or the "voluntary motion" commonly called passions, in the inner world of man. And he found a variety of such emotions that required vivid description in his taxonomy of the human passions: appetite, desire, hunger, thirst, aversion, love, hate, contempt, delight and numerous others. Soon after dealing with vain-glory and dejection, he turns to "laughter" and finds that it is a peculiar kind of "grimace" that originates in a sense of "sudden glory", caused in turn by "some sudden

65 Ross (2011): 98-100.

act of their own, that pleaseth them; or by the apprehension of some deformed thing in another, by comparison whereof they suddenly applaud themselves". Much of laughter occasioned by "the defects of others", was a sign of "pusillanimity". Great minds would not sink that low, since they would "help and free others from scorn" and "compare themselves onely (sic) with the most able".[66]

Laughter assumes various forms. Every milieu functions on social codes that determine when laughter is apposite and when not. The childlike proclivity to laugh out loud at the unclad emperor is actively repressed through socialisation processes, because authority has to be revered. Likewise, there are situations that by agreement and consent within the relevant milieu, as part of the social compact that keeps it afloat, should trigger a degree of expressive mirth. To deviate from expected patterns of behaviour would be to earn displeasure and be held unworthy of the benedictions supposedly being showered on all within the liberal environment of modern "civil society".

In writing his classic 1952 work *Black Skin, White Masks,* Frantz Fanon brought to bear his clinical observations as a psychoanalyst, on the varieties of repression that typically afflicted the colonised mind. Situations could often arise in which the benign laughter of the colonised subject would be called for, to assuage the anxieties of the coloniser. It was important for the colonised man to make that gesture of laughing it off, often enough for the coloniser to feel secure that his civilising mission was not in danger of being rudely rebuffed.

There are occasions when laughter becomes impossible. As with the black man who finds himself in a milieu where reactions to his presence are diverse and unpredictable, ranging from amusement to indulgence to outright terror. He seeks to laugh off each of these, but is unable to any more when a white child screams in a frenzy of irrational terror. That is the behaviour expected of him but he is unable to meet social expectations.[67] A particular form of acculturation imposed by colonialism convinces the black man that he is the child of the European enlightenment. But with a lately dawned sense of responsibil-

66 Hobbes (1651): 20-25 for MacPherson's introductory remarks on methodology; 118ff and especially p 125 for the treatment of the passions.

67 Fanon (1952): 84.

ity for his protégé, the colonialist is intent on ceasing older habits of thought, which identified the black man with the state of savagery. The black man is granted the ability to acclimatise himself within the culture of enlightenment, and savagery is portrayed as the state of a third people, racially akin to the black man but geographically placed elsewhere. There is always the cultural production that seeks to reinforce the image of the enlightened European by portraying the other in his state of nature, savage and uncivilised. For an individual who has been socialised into the belief that Europe is his parent culture, this poses the dilemma of how to respond.

Fanon finds the tensions especially acute in his native Antilles region. The black schoolboy here is reared on stories of "the Gauls" as his ancestors and in watching a cultural production involving the white conquest of dark and hostile lands, "identifies himself with the explorer, the bringer of civilisation, the white man who carries truth to savages". Watching a Tarzan film in the Antilles for instance, the "young Negro" would identify himself "de facto with Tarzan against the Negroes". In a European theatre that would be difficult since the audience he is watching the film with would "automatically" identify him "with the savages on the screen". A documentary film on Africa would produce similarly disparate reactions when shown in France and in a colony. The "bushmen and Zulu", Fanon is prepared to say, would "arouse even more laughter among the young Antilleans". The "reactional exaggeration" here, betrays a hint of recognition. But in France, a "Negro who sees this documentary is virtually petrified". He has no option of "flight"; he is "at once Antillean, Bushman, and Zulu".[68]

The tumult over *Charlie Hebdo*, Paul Michael Johnson observed in a reflection that followed, occurred at the four-hundred year anniversary of Cervantes's *Don Quixote*, a landmark in European literature and perhaps its first "comical novel". The varieties of laughter in the novel – described despite its comic overtones as a work of "hideous cruelty" – are many, though there are two that are of special interest.

In one of these, the faithful but intellectually feeble Sancho Panza is appointed governor of a small town in Spain. The duke and duchess who wield power in the region are looking for entertainment and spectacular failure by individuals they would normally disdain,

---

68 Ibid: 114, 118.

is one source of idle amusement. That perverse urge of indulging in the "laughter of superiority" remains unfulfilled for the ducal couple because Sancho is accepting of his lack of privilege and fashions his assertion of power accordingly. Far from being awed by his charge, he acquires by mysterious providence, the wisdom and sagacity to be a fair and competent governor, sensitive to popular sentiment.

Soon after leaving this post, Sancho meets up with a "morisco", a person of the Muslim faith compelled to leave his homeland by the Spanish inquisition. Cervantes carefully ensures that his description here does not run any risk of turbulence with the censors, yet portrays this meeting as a reunion "between old friends, marked by wistful nostalgia and longing for a time before the expulsion had created a morisco diaspora and sundered entire communities". After much friendly conversation and a convivial meal washed down with quantities of wine, "Sancho is overtaken by a fit of good-natured laughter that … lasts over an hour".

These two situations, among many in Cervantes's novel where the reader is invited to share in the laughter, involve polar opposites in the politics of humour. One invites participation in the "power of laughter", the other seeks the vicarious pleasure of observing "the laughter of those with power". Laughter is in its motivations, "both coopted by and constitutive of power". Representations of the prophet of another's faith in a posture of ridicule might elicit laughter, but only because it caused offence. In the smug satisfaction of the western sensibility, it was possible to look at the "indignation, pain, distress—and, yes, outrage" of the Muslim community, as just so much inconsequential froth. That variety of "malicious pleasure" was "less satire than schadenfreude".[69]

Johnson concludes that the "pre-modern superiority theory of laughter offers purchase for understanding the contemporary moment as well". It is no coincidence that the communities that seem all too prepared to take offence are the same that have suffered long histories of "colonial violence, religious persecution, and racial discrimination" and its members demonised by "popular, anti-immigrant movements of the sort that have gripped various parts of Europe". In other words, the "racial and socioeconomic privilege of the dominant majority is often coterminous with the privilege of laughing". It is an unseen priv-

69 Johnson (2015).

ilege that flourishes behind the smokescreen of formal equality. Those of lesser status have been cast for all their recent histories as inert masses to be moulded into a shape that would fit them for life within the enlightened west. And now with the end of multiculturalism all but official, they are being abandoned as unlikely ever to make the cut because of innate social and psychological handicaps. Their inability to share in the laughter of superiority only strengthens that motif of mutual cultural recoil.

The ghost of Albert Camus

As Edward Said points out, the notion of an Islamic population that is culturally and temperamentally averse to secular modernity is an ideological device that has been in the making since at least the 1970s.[70] That decade was decisive because it brought the threatening prospect of stagflation and the possible end to the long years of post-war western prosperity. Blame was easily assigned to petroleum-soaked gulf dynasties revelling in the power that their unearned riches brought. Regimes that seemed amenable to western demands in turn, suffered a contagion of political insecurity after the Islamic revolution in Iran swept aside a loyal client. The Saudi dynasty was threatened by an insurrection that took Islam's holiest shrines captive, necessitating a desperate plea for western military intervention to regain the hallowed sites. And right at the end of the decade came the Soviet invasion of Afghanistan, and the possibility of another variety of radicalism sweeping in from the eastern extremities of the contiguous Islamic territories.

It was a maelstrom of strategic confusion in which neither the secular nationalist nor the pan-Islamist seemed quite worthy of western trust. And the response unsurprisingly, was opportunistic, though consistently corrosive of any form of republicanism that could challenge the massive stakes the west had in the natural resources of the Islamic world. The underlying premise was simply that the Islamic world was incapable in its infantile state of mind, of negotiating the values of rationality that made possible a productive engagement within the global community of nations.

Nationalist consolidation in much of Europe, Said observes elsewhere, led to the commonly held view of the Orient as a "geographical

70 Said (1991).

space to be cultivated, harvested and guarded".[71] The oriental person was not to be trusted with agency, but could conceivably be subject to the tutelage of the colonist. Illustrations abound from the western literary canon. But Albert Camus offers a unique perspective here both because of the place of honour he occupies in French literary history, and for his own identity as a Frenchman of Algerian origins at a time when the colonial encounter was ending in violent mutual recoil.

The title of Camus's first novel, *The Stranger*, is strongly suggestive of how he viewed himself within the Algerian milieu of the 1930s. "Meursault" its main protagonist, takes his identity from a name that Camus often used in his early journalism. With the virtual cult status it acquired, the novel's plot is fairly familiar. It involves Meursault's conviction for the murder of an Arab and ends with him calmly awaiting his execution. Conor Cruise O'Brien who in a 1970 literary exegeses of Camus's work, set a standard that has not been surpassed or even remotely challenged, found it a rather implausible scenario for colonial Algeria, that a white Frenchman should face execution for the murder of an Arab who had drawn a knife on him. Yet that stretch beyond the realms of plausibility, was an essential device for Camus to make a larger point about his protagonist's unique moral qualities.

These emerge in Meursault's absolute indifference to all the verities of the ordinary bourgeois life, subtly presented from the very beginning of the novel, when he observes deadpan that his mother had died, though he was not sure when. The owner of the funeral home where the body is kept is mildly scandalised at his lack of emotion and disinterest in one final glimpse of his mother. Meursault's mind in the first person narrative that Camus employs is elsewhere, on thoughts of how he could have spent his time in the countryside rather agreeably, were it not for the filial chores he was compelled to perform.

Later that day, Meursault meets Marie, a woman he has earlier had a brief familiarity with. Through a pleasant enough meeting, Marie flinches ever so slightly at Meursault's impassive mien on the day he should have been mourning. They spend the night together but Marie has left when Meursault wakes the next day, leaving him to muse in solitude on passersby on the streets outside.

71 Said (1995): 219.

The next day he meets an unsavoury character, a local tough and pimp whose invitation for lunch he is glad to accept. He listens in confidence to the pimp's plan to deal with a woman who has been giving him a hard time. He drafts a letter on behalf of his newly won confidant and identifies the woman who is troubling him, from her name, as a Moor. Meursault meets Marie again that evening and as they go to bed, is vaguely bothered with her queries about his true feelings. Is he in love or not? Distinctly uncomfortable at the question, he says that he probably is not. They hear violence from a nearby room where Meursault's confidant, the pimp, is thrashing his truculent lady friend about. Marie is outraged and wants to intervene and if necessary, call the police. Meursault demurs, saying that he does not like the police.

The next day as he walks the street in the company of his friend of rather unsavoury character, he is stalked by a group of Arabs. One among them is identified as the brother of the woman who was roughed up the previous day. Revenge was clearly the intent and Meursault and his associate had a gun in their possession for self defence. Events then onwards moved in a quick and uncontrollable cascade, ending with Meursault drawing the gun as a knife was drawn on him, and shooting dead his assailant. He then fires "four more shots into the inert body, on which they left no visible trace". Yet he recognises "each successive shot ... (as) ... another loud, fateful rap on the door of (his) undoing".[72]

Prior to his trial, Meursault's defence attorney pleads with him not to reveal his record of indifference to all the accepted mores of the world he lived in. But there is no way these details can be concealed from the magistrate. Prosecution underlines Meursault's unfeeling attitude towards his mother and his very casual response to her death. Defence pleads "extenuating circumstances", but to little avail. Meursault is sentenced to death and in his last moments spurns the prison chaplain's offer of consolation in the faith.

It is an arresting story with vast areas of ambiguity about the hero's motivations, which Camus sought after a fashion, to explain many years later in a preface to the English language translation of *The Stranger*. Meursault was condemned to death because he refused to "play the game". He was a "stranger to the society" he lived in, drifting "in the margin, in the suburb of private, solitary, sensual life". Forgive-

---

72 Quoted in Cruise O'Brien (1970): 18.

ness was at hand and he could have earned a reprieve from a simple lie, which he resolutely refused to utter. Lying is a common recourse for those seeking to simplify everyday life. But Meursault "says what is true (and) refuses to disguise his feelings". Society is immediately "threatened" but Meursault is a man who, "without any heroics, accepts death for the sake of truth".[73]

O'Brien finds in these locutions a curious elision of the many lies that Meursault actually utters through the novel. He drafts a letter as part of a plan to entice an Arab girl to the violent deserts his shady friend has reserved for her, stands mute witness to her brutalisation and later lies to the police to get his friend off the hook. His inattention to the verities of Algerian bourgeois life also comes with a curious indifference to the humanity of the Arab. The woman who is brutalised by his French friend makes not the slightest dent on his conscience and as he shoots a brother who seeks to avenge her humiliation, he sees him as a blank, shapeless being. He is nameless, as is the woman whose thrashing Meursault connives in. When this Arab is killed in a hail of bullets, the "reader does not quite feel that Meursault has killed a man".[74]

Meursault though, will not lie to save himself from the trouble he got into on account of earlier lies. There can be no reason other than his own insistence on being true to his feelings. That construct of personal integrity for Camus is a compound of three parts, one of which is himself. "Three characters went into the composition of *The Stranger*", he has said: "two men(one of them me) and a woman".[75] Meursault in that sense, faithfully mirrors the colonial encounter that Camus witnessed up close in Algeria and presumably partook of. It was an encounter in which the two sides did not view each other as fully human. The Arabs who were embarked upon their mission of avenging a dishonoured woman were in Meursault's gaze, "staring at us silently in the way they have – as if we were blocks of stone or dead trees".[76] And Meursault's sense of personal probity, his vow to bear true witness to his authentic

73 Ibid: 20.

74 Ibid: 25.

75 Ibid: 22.

76 Ibid: 23.

inner voice, does not baulk at a sequence of gross falsehoods when the target is an Arab.

A very productive phase followed in Camus's literary life after *L'Etranger*. He wrote a deeply allegorical novel, *The Plague*, about the menacing imminence of fascism, engaged in the French resistance and emerged from World War II a recognised hero of French culture. Troubles, earlier subdued, had begun erupting with increasing regularity in the relationship between France and the colonies. Camus recognised the precarious nature of the colonial relationship, especially the hollowness of the pretence that Algeria and other colonies were equal participants and beneficiaries of French republican values. He made note of every episode of resistance, violence and bloodshed and seemed aware that the bonds with Algeria had been frayed by repeated acts of bad faith by metropolitan France. A new compact had to be found and that imperative was being deliberately trampled underfoot by the expedient militarism of the French response to resistance movements in the colonies.

Camus observed all this with a dispassionate sense of fairness, but still tilted strongly towards seeing one form of violence, deployed in the cause of the French republic, as justified. Other kinds of eruptions were deeply reprehensible in a moral sense, since they came from an innate tendency toward violence that certain political creeds possessed. Camus was especially reproachful of the communist ideology as enshrined in the Soviet Union at that time, though his gaze was perhaps directed equally at the Algerian anti-colonial resistance which had erupted in violent armed struggle by the mid-1950s.

In 1945, Camus wrote of justice – in the abstract – as the only basis on which the relationship of the French metropolis with its colonies could be constituted. "It is the infinite force of justice, and it alone", he wrote, "which must help us to win back Algeria and its inhabitants".[77] Camus did not return to the subject of Algeria till nine years later, when the war of liberation that would drag on till after his death, had broken out. In 1956, when the twin crises of the Anglo-French invasion of the Suez and the Soviet invasion of Hungary occurred, Camus fell back on an older understanding of violence being justified in one form and not in another. "The defects of the West are numberless and

77 Ibid: 65.

its crimes and faults real", he wrote: "But in the last analysis, let us not forget that we are the only people who hold that power of improvement and emancipation which resided in the genius of freedom".[78] Just over a year later, after receiving the Nobel Prize in Sweden, he seemingly felt sufficiently unburdened to state his basic credo with a certain rawness that had earlier been hidden in his very rich literary French: "I have always condemned terror. I must also condemn a terrorism which operates blindly, in the streets of Algiers for example, and which one day may strike my mother or my family. I believe in justice but I will defend my mother before justice".[79]

So that is where the loudly proclaimed values of the French revolution finally ended, in the trenches where filial ties and kinship superseded all else. Post-colonial France was willing to address, purely in a verbal sense, its guilt for the atrocities inflicted on subjects in an earlier era. But if necessary, they would as the *Charlie Hebdo* case showed, continue the cruelties in the intangible domain since these were consistent with the republican values as handed down from the revolution, through a number of colonial conquests, and the assumption of a superior civilisational role over the people of the benighted regions of the world.

A state of civility is often a state of suppressed conflict. To use Pierre Bourdieu's term, inequalities of status, wealth and power are often internalised within the habitus that each element within society lives, and organises his world around. Edward Shils, the theorist of civility as a constituent element in the social life of a nation, identifies an essential element of civic coexistence in a "macrosocial" map that every member carries in his or her mind. This is a cognitive mapping of the social universe, that helps to define "what that society is" and to fix "its boundaries and its internal properties".[80] Members bring their perceptions of status and position in the stratification of society and its distribution of power to the rhythm of their engagements with the civic world beyond individuality. They may not always be comfortable with that manner of identification as part of a stratified order, but would nonetheless retain their fealty since it "is evidence to them of

78 Ibid: 73.

79 Ibid: 75.

80 Shils (1972): 27-8.

that membership, even if it is an aspect of membership which they do not like".[81]

Humour is part of an accustomed routine for members of society, a habitus, though with diverse purposes that could be in deep conflict, depending upon where it comes from. Humour, satire and laughter could deepen an already unequal engagement within the civic order, or talk about the possibility of overturning it. Humour could be practised with intent to deepen a "sociocultural reality" that is otherwise deeply internalised in the ordinary reproduction of life. Alternately, it could act to subvert the more oppressive features of that reality.[82]

Laughter could be shared or directed against members within society who happen not to be in a very fortunate place. Typically in the latter case, the laughter of superiority has a clear cognitive message, of reinforcing hierarchies, or affirming that prevailing systems of stratification are naturally ordained and deserve to persist. Resistance begins with the laughter of those at the bottom of the hierarchy against their own acquiescence. That is a force of change. This could be followed in quick order, with the laughter of those who find ridiculous the pretensions of those who rule as a purported matter of right. This manner of laughter brings with it not merely resistance, but subversion. It carries the potential for liberation.

It takes long and arduous effort though, to gain liberty from the prison-house of nationalist ideology, when it has donned the vestments of universal law.

---

81 Ibid: 28-9.

82 This discussion owes much to Apte (1985).

The Market

Free speech and the commercial imperative

Media freedom is a specific category within a more broadly invested right. A self-serving myth holds the field in most commentary on the modern media, where it is portrayed as institutional bearer of the social right to free speech. This is a claim difficult to reconcile with the reality of the media as largely a privately owned industry oriented around profit. Speech that is free, but not heard may as well not exist and this leads with a certain logical inevitability, to the conclusion that as a broadly invested right that even those without access to media space or time enjoy, "free speech" is a fiction.

A perfectly piquant conclusion follows: free speech is a right that extends only as far as it serves profit.[1] For countries with weakly instituted cultures of liberal democracy, the intrusive and often paranoiac attention of the state security apparatus has been recognised at all times, as a serious threat to citizen liberties. The critique of corporate control as an equal if not greater threat remains undeveloped, because "free enterprise" manages to project itself as the only guise that true liberty can take. In this conceptual vacuum, a grand fusion has occurred between the authoritarian state and corporatised business interests, which poses multiple threats to citizenship and civil liberties.

---

1 Garton Ash (2016: 1052) reminds us of A.J. Liebling's famous aphorism, which has since acquired cult status, that press freedom exists only for those who own one.

To resolve the uneasy tension between information in its two *avatars* – as commerce and as a basic human entitlement – reliance is placed not so much on curbing the pursuit of profit, as on ensuring the sustenance of media diversity. Commerce need not be antithetical to the right to information, provided there are few barriers to gaining access to sources and a sufficient plurality from which the public can draw. A liberal democracy allows for few institutional restraints or regulations on the functioning of the media, leaving the marketplace of ideas as arbiter. In matters that vitally involve the public interest, where a risk exists of social disorder or offence to good taste, decisions are left to the prudence and social responsibility of the media.

Yet there are circumstances in which seemingly settled questions emerge with a fresh vigour. In 2003, the Standing Committee on Information Technology of the Indian Parliament urged the government to prescribe a "ratio for coverage of news contents and advertisements in newspapers". This was necessary since, the committee observed, there was "a tendency ... in the leading newspapers to provide more and more space for advertisements at the cost of news items".

The government for its part responded with a plea of inability, given judicial precedent. Regulatory devices of the nature proposed had indeed been under consideration for long, said the Ministry of Information and Broadcasting. But these matters had not proceeded far "owing to legal and constitutional complexities".[2]

Among India's preliminary exercises in enunciating a theory on the media in society, was the Press Commission appointed in 1952. It was an exercise launched in the rosy flush of India's independence, when individuals and groups active in the struggle against colonialism laid claim to substantive assurances, but found every definition of freedom seriously contested. For owners of the press, freedom meant a quite literal interpretation of *laissez faire* when they would be answerable only to the market, the profit calculus and their own sense of responsibility towards a newly independent nation. For journalists and their unions, freedom meant liberation from the tyranny of their owners' rather skewed understanding of what constituted news and the public interest.

2 Parliament of India (2003): 39-42.

A "statement of facts" that the Press Commission (hereafter called the First Press Commission or FPC)[3] required from newspaper organisations as a first step in its deliberations, remained unavailable for most part because publishers did not feel obliged to comply with the call to submit such a statement. FPC then decided to scale back the information sought just to ensure better compliance by news organisations. When even this concession did not dent the obduracy of the newspaper houses, the FPC – more in sorrow than anger – determined that it would not pursue coercive legal strategies, though it "had the legal powers to launch prosecutions against the proprietors of newspapers and periodicals for their failure to submit the factual information called for".[4]

Transparency is supposedly a premise of press functioning but even with that, the FPC did have to confront a thorny dilemma about the best mode of recording evidence. There was a strong inclination to conduct proceedings in a full spirit of openness, since the public had a stake in being fully abreast of "the progress of the inquiry and the nature of the evidence tendered to it". There was also the risk that closed-door or *in camera* hearings would "encourage some witnesses to make irresponsible statements". Yet, "many working journalists", the commission observed, "were reluctant to enter into a frank discussion of their difficulties in an open session for fear of being punished by their employers". There was also the reverse hazard that those with nothing to lose would "play to the gallery" in an open session, seeking to earn their brief moment of fame. The final decision was to keep testimony confidential for the duration of the commission's inquiry, but put out periodic reviews of the "progress made" and the "names of the witnesses examined".[5]

Principal among the obstacles the FPC encountered in assembling a narrative on the Indian media, was the absence of reliable statistics. And despite a year spent exploring every available source, the picture the commission constructed – even of a basic parameter such as the

---

3 The body appointed in 1952 was the first of two such bodies, though it had no way of anticipating its successor. The prefix "first" is added merely for clarity of reference.

4 Press Commission (1954): 6.

5 Ibid: 9-10.

number of active dailies and periodicals – was patchy. It noted none-theless, that there seemed every sign of a new vigour in the newspaper business post-independence, with a number of new ventures starting up in erstwhile princely states "where freedom of the press did not, in the past, come anywhere near to that in the rest of the country". There had also been a general increase in circulation across the country. Yet, with all that, the FPC observed, the "development of journalism (had not been) adequate in terms of the total population". A survey conducted at FPC instance had found that India's newspapers were "concerned with the town dwellers ... produced by them and ... read mainly by them."

Without undue fuss, the FPC moved swiftly to the core economic issue: the relative proportion between circulation and advertisement revenue, a crucial parameter in determining how far the press remained an institution serving the public interest. "The great advantages possessed by the metropolitan press has (sic) tended to draw away from the districts the talent that might have gone into the development of a local press", it said: "We do not consider concentration of the press in metropolitan cities a desirable feature, however inevitable it was in the early stages".[6]

Economics was key and FPC inquiries revealed that in comparison to the British industry – admittedly not the best datum – newspapers in India spent relatively less on services and editing. This conceivably was because of the higher relative price that Indian newspapers had to pay for newsprint. Earnings from newspaper sales displayed wide disparities between English and the various Indian languages. There were two seeming exceptions: the Gujarati language press, because it functioned in an area of high "industrial and commercial prosperity" had an average ad revenue in excess of other regional newspapers; and the Malayalam language press, because it had "outpaced the industrial and commercial progress of the region", had an average ad revenue considerably lower than counterparts in other states.[7] There was an inherent impediment in the situation to newspaper industry profitability. The "rapid spread of education" could lead to multiplying reader demand while ad revenue to support an increase in production volumes would

6 Ibid:19, 20 and 18.

7 Ibid: 57.

not emerge at quite the same pace, because of a lag of "commercial and industrial activity".[8]

These aside, the commission identified a number of shady practices in the industry, two of which compelled special attention: collusive deals with vendors, and package deals enabling a newspaper group to obtain advertisements in all its publications on the strength of one leading title.[9] With all these factored in, newspapers of established lineage had advantages that were seriously detrimental to competition. "Papers of long standing which have been able to build up large and stable volume of advertisement revenue are in a very advantageous position as compared to others who have just entered the field." One substantive advantage was the power to drive out competition through price warfare. FPC inquiries had shown that newspaper audience size was critically dependent on price: illustratively, two Tamil newspapers, *Swadesamitran* and *Dinamani*, which had in concert raised their price by a quarter to meet rising costs, witnessed sharp declines in circulation over the following three months, compelling them to reverse their collusive arrangement. But one took nine months to regain earlier circulation, while the other never recovered.[10]

Similar factors were at work in other industries, though their persistence in the press was worrying, said the FPC. "Newspapers serve as media for the free exchange of information and of ideas", it observed: "The proper functioning of democracy requires that every individual should have equal opportunity ... to put forward his opinions. We consider it therefore essential that measures should be adopted to reduce the differences due to economic advantages or other causes, and to enable newcomers to start with a fair chance of success. After examining various schemes that have been put forward for this purpose, we feel that to fix a minimum price at which papers of a particular size can be sold would be the most effective measure to bring about this end".[11]

---

8 Ibid: 59.

9 Ibid: 61, 62.

10 Ibid: 61.

11 Ibid: 73.

Price fetters to promote free speech

The price-page schedule was the instrument for the preservation of diversity, a regulatory process that by contemporary standards would distinctly smack of absurdity. In 1956, India's Parliament – not yet dazzled by the mystique of the market – passed into law an order which regulated newspaper price in proportion with number of printed pages, and specified a definite sharing of space between editorial material and advertisements. Using powers conferred by this law, the government in 1960 issued the Daily Newspapers (Price and Page) Order, an intrusive set of rules that sought to micro-manage various parameters of a newspaper's functioning.[12]

In 1961, in the case of *Sakal Newspapers versus the Union of India*, the Supreme Court of India held the Price-Page Schedule violative of article 19 of the Indian Constitution, which protects the rights to both free expression and commerce. Handing down its ruling in the case, India's highest court found that the order took away the freedom of the newspaper to charge whatever price it chose, constricted its ability to disseminate news and opinions, and cut into its commercial fortunes by limiting advertising space.

It was a curious and contrary case. The Supreme Court heard an argument advanced on behalf of the Indian Government, that the effect of the law would be "to promote further the right of newspapers in general to exercise the freedom of speech and expression", rather than the opposite. The space allocated to advertisements varied between 46 and 59 percent of total printed area and these brought in "substantial revenue" which enabled newspapers to be sold "below the cost of production". The consequence was that "newspapers of long standing" which had "large and stable advertisement revenue" would be in an "advantageous position" to "squeeze out" newcomers and "destroy the freedom of expression of others".[13]

The true purpose of the impugned legislation was "the prevention of unfair competition which (had) resulted in (the denial) to others (of) a right to propagation of ideas by publishing newspapers". The price-page schedule in that sense, did not "infringe the right or freedom of expression of a newspaper", but on the contrary, only "promote(d) and

12 Parliament of India (2003): 39-42.

13 Supreme Court of India (1961): 847-8.

encourage(d) healthy journalism".[14] Far from being an imposition on the newspaper industry, the Government submitted, the price-page schedule was introduced in part as a response to the insistent pressure of the "Indian Language Newspapers Association".

India's highest judicial body felt compelled to disregard all these arguments for a variety of reasons. Free speech as a right, it ruled, applied to all citizens of the country "not merely to the matter he (sic) is entitled to circulate, but also to the volume of circulation". By fixing a minimum price for "the number of pages (a newspaper) is entitled to publish", the Government aimed not to ensure "a reasonable price to the buyers" but to "cut down the volume of circulation of some newspapers by making the price so unattractively high for a class of its readers as (would be) likely to deter it from purchasing such newspapers".

Data on the price sensitivity of newspaper circulation were available to the Supreme Court from the FPC report, from which the judicial body drew exactly the opposite inferences, sketching a doomsday scenario for any newspaper entrapped in the coils of the "price-page schedule". "If the area for advertisements is curtailed the price of the newspaper will be forced up. If that happens, the circulation will inevitably go down".[15] The matter, in the judgment of the Court, could be considered in another manner: the higher the circulation of a newspaper, the larger would be its advertisement revenue. "So if a newspaper with a high circulation were to raise its price, its circulation would go down and this in turn would bring down also the advertisement revenue. That would force the newspaper either to close down or to raise its price. Raising the price further would affect the circulation still more and thus a vicious cycle would set in, which would ultimately end in the closure of the newspaper".[16]

The court admitted that commerce as a right could be curtailed in difficult circumstances, but not at the cost of free speech. And in a formulation that betrayed an uneasy awareness of the tension in the liberal doctrine between the two notions of liberty – the positive and the negative – the Indian Supreme Court held that nothing in the Constitution allowed the State to abridge the freedom of expression "on

14 Ibid: 850.

15 Ibid: 860-1.

16 Ibid: 862.

the ground of conferring benefits upon the public in general or upon a section of the public". The "reasonable restrictions" on free speech permitted under article 19 only covered a limited range of contingencies: the sovereignty and integrity of India, the security of the State, public order, decency or morality, friendly relations with other States, or the incitement to commit an offence. No reasonable restrictions on one person's freedom could be countenanced, in order to better safeguard another's.

In other words, freedom of the press was a fine principle for those who owned one, particularly if it happened to enjoy a dominant position in the market. For those less fortunate, free speech was a dispensable luxury, to be exercised at best, in the limited circles he or she moved in.

The fight for the commerce of free speech

Precisely on account of these ambivalences, the price-page schedule as an instrument of regulation retained a certain appeal for years afterwards.[17] A Committee on Small Newspapers in 1965 upheld it as a legitimate device for protecting the right to free speech. The Fact Finding Committee on Newspaper Economics in 1975 (FFC) though, did not seriously consider it as an option, perhaps since its inquiries were conducted in a juncture of acute newsprint shortage. It was a situation that newspapers individually and in combination had responded in a variety of ways to. Among the respectable and recorded means that the inquiry found, were the curtailment of number of pages offered, an increase in selling price or ad rate, and an alteration of the ratio of ad to news pages.

There were other practices uncovered in testimony recorded in the FFC, including bullying advertisers to pay special rates for an assurance of being featured at a time and place of their choice within the folds of the newspaper. It may not be unreasonable to assume that several among the coping strategies perhaps escaped the attention of the FFC, given the environment of information scarcity it functioned within. There was no way of accounting for the number of journalists laid off to meet financial exigencies, or for the kind of collusive arrangements

---

17 The following narration is sourced from Parliament of India (2003): 39-42.

with power-hitters in the political and business realms that many years later earned the title of "paid news".[18] The practice may have acquired conspicuous new proportions with the dawn of the millennium, when the Indian media rode the crest of a short-lived economic boom and expanded far beyond dimensions that underlying realities could support. But it did not spring into existence unheralded and may indeed, have had a long germination period.[19]

In a context of newsprint scarcity, the response of particular newspapers varied according to the competitive situation they were in and the calculations of their commercial departments. The FFC found that since about 1973, newsprint was the most critical element in cost escalation in the industry and that this was "substantially compensated" by a "reduction in consumption, ... (an) increase in sales revenue and in some cases by (an) increase in advertisement revenue".[20] The newspaper industry in short, had a variety of coping mechanisms at its disposal and would not, as the Supreme Court assumed in its *Sakal* judgment, be driven to ruin by any manner of external shock, whether emanating from the market or the policy domain. With this firm finding behind it, the FFC went on to suggest active regulations including legal stipulations requiring a degree of transparency in the functioning of the news industry. An intrusion of monopoly elements was to be curbed, though the potential problem areas were to be identified with extreme care. A small language group such as Konkani, for instance, may have a monopoly newspaper simply because the market could not support a second one. The FFC found that market behaviour, as in the phenomenon of "price leadership", was often an indicator of monopoly power and it was "patent" that "price increases (were) initiated only

18 Ministry of Information and Broadcasting (1975). For the information scarcity on the newspaper industry, see Introduction and p. 42; the strategies adopted to deal with newsprint shortage are in chapter 8; the bullying of advertisers is in chapter 9, especially pp. 137ff.

19 Press Council of India (2010). The Press Council of India commissioned an inquiry into the extent and magnitude of the practice soon after the 2009 general elections to India's parliament. The report of the sub-committee that carried out the mandate was suppressed, and a highly sanitised version adopted by the Council in July 2010. Following active public advocacy and petitions under the right to information law, the Council posted the entire report of the sub-committee on its website in October 2010.

20 Ministry of Information and Broadcasting (1975): 118.

by a small number of leading papers". Other papers just followed the example of the price leader.

Monopoly power was manifest in the collusive arrangements between newspaper concerns and distribution agencies, as also in the various inducements and subtle coercive pressures applied on advertisers. A first step towards eliminating dangers to the public interest from information monopolies was to separate the ownership of the news industry from others. This, the FFC approvingly noted, was a "legal measure" under active consideration by the government of the time. Once such a change was effected, "one of the major impediments to the study of the economics of the newspaper industry (would) disappear". A further step would be to implement the Press Commission recommendation that "every paper should be constituted as a separate unit so that its profits and losses (were) definitely ascertainable and both the proprietor and the employees know where they stand". A segregation of costs and revenues in accordance with purpose and source would be another essential part of the move towards transparency. Newspapers, the FFC recommended, "should keep their accounts on a uniform pattern and in a form which will be useful for analysis".[21]

These were the issues among a range of others, revisited by the Press Commission appointed in 1978 and reconstituted following a regime change at the Centre in 1980. Though the notion was implicit in earlier inquiries into the press, this body (referred to hereafter with the prefix "second" and abbreviated as SPC) in its 1982 report seemed for the first time to formulate a theory of the press as a "public utility". In line with this philosophical posture, the SPC recommended the application of existing monopoly laws to the newspaper industry, with the threshold for recognising a monopoly being one-fourth of the "effective market". The body empowered under the anti-monopoly act was to be invested with the power to launch investigations "if allegations of monopolistic practices by a newspaper undertaking come to its notice".[22]

The diffusion of ownership was another priority area for the SPC, as was transparency in accounting and a clear line of demarcation be-

21 Ibid: 200-4.

22 Press Commission (1989): 144. See also, chapter 10 titled "The Press as a Public Utility".

tween costs and revenues by purpose and source. The SPC registered its disagreement with the Supreme Court ruling in the *Sakal* case, observing that the mandatory linkage between selling price and pages printed was no abridgment of article 19 freedoms. On the contrary, the objective being "promotion of competition and prevention of monopoly, the law (would) advance freedom of speech and expression".[23]

Four of the eleven members of the SPC, including two of four working journalists, dissented with this finding. Given the temper of the times though, it was no surprise that the inquiry should have come up with this frontal challenge to the liberal orthodoxy on press freedom. Heading the commission was a former judge of the Supreme Court who had in a 1972 case involving press freedom, authored a famous dissent when the majority on the bench clung very closely to liberal orthodoxy. At issue then was a government notification, issued in a situation of acute scarcity, limiting newsprint supply in accordance with the reported consumption of newspaper companies. A 1972 order established quotas for every major publishing house on the basis of newsprint consumption over a defined interval of time. Newspapers that published in excess of ten pages were required to bring down daily offerings to that number. They were not permitted to reduce circulation to maintain page numbers at existing or increased levels. To provide a full day's complement of news, publishers needed to rationalise space allocated between editorial and advertisement matter. They could also explore the other option of curtailing news coverage to accommodate advertisements at then prevalent levels.

In October 1972, the Supreme Court decided that these norms imposed on newspapers violated the Constitution, in that they imposed restrictions well beyond permissible on the right to free speech. The judgment in the case of *Bennett Coleman and Company Ltd versus the Union of India* is of historic significance, since it lays out a whole range of principles on press freedom. In addressing the issue though, the Court seemed to oscillate wildly and indecisively, between a notion of free speech as a privilege that is enjoyed by the few, and a broader conception in which the unreserved exercise of a broadly held right by a few, could engender situations of denial and conflict.

23 Ibid: 159.

Among the first issues the Court confronted was *locus standi.* Did the petitioners, some of India's largest print media groups, have a legitimate right to challenge the stipulation on newsprint allocation? Speaking for the majority on the bench, Justice A.N. Ray observed that the "individual rights of freedom of speech and expression of editors, directors and shareholders, are all expressed through their newspapers".[24] But then a few pages on, the majority opinion effectively widened the ambit of the right: "It is indisputable that by freedom of the press is meant the right of *all citizens* to speak, publish and express their views. The freedom of the press embodies the right of the people to read. The freedom of the press is *not antithetical to the right of the people to speak and express*".[25]

Considered in every possible manner, the majority opinion held, the restriction on newsprint use by a newspaper meant a serious abridgment of the right to free speech. If the volume of news disseminated was reduced, that in itself was a loss to the public. And if the space devoted to advertisements were to be curtailed, the newspaper would suffer serious financial losses, "weaken" and perhaps "crumble".[26]

The rest of the judgment clung very closely to the liberal orthodoxy on the right to free speech: that governmental regulation is an evil more invidious than the prospect of private monopolies. Called upon to address the latter issue, the Supreme Court held by majority, without unduly bothering itself with facts – or seeking to engage with the findings of the FFC and the SPC – that "the press is not exposed to any mischief of monopolistic combination". And even if otherwise, newsprint allocation could not be a feasible "measure to combat monopolies". In equally treating "newspapers which are not equal" in terms of their "needs and requirements", the newsprint allocation policy fell foul of article 14 of the Indian Constitution, which upheld the principle of equality before the law.[27]

---

24 Supreme Court of India (1972): 759.

25 Ibid: 760, emphases added here and in further citations.

26 Ibid: 761.

27 Ibid.

A significant dissent

Of special significance here is the lone dissenting judgment from a bench of five, by Justice Mathew. The perspective here is reversed – rather than casually rule it out, the judge explicitly concedes the possibility of a conflict between the public interest and the profit motivations of the press. Using a "theory of the freedom of speech" that essentially views it in terms of twin entitlements – to speak and be informed – Justice Mathew observed that "the distribution of newsprint for maintenance of (newspaper) circulation at its highest possible level … (would)… only advance and enrich that freedom".[28] As a constitutional principle, "freedom of the press" was "no higher than the freedom of speech of a citizen".[29] What was essential in the circumstances was "an affirmative theory underlying freedom of expression", and due attention to the "various conditions essential to maintaining a workable system".[30] The purpose here would be to bring "all ideas into the market (to) make the freedom of speech a live one having its roots in reality". Necessary as a first step was a recognition "that *the right of expression is somewhat thin if it can be exercised only on the sufferance of the managers of the leading newspapers*".

Freedom of expression in other words, also involved the right of access to media space. And this requirement would be met only through "new opportunities for expression or greater opportunities to small and medium dailies", which would enable them "to reach a position of equality with the big ones". This was as important, "as the right to express ideas without fear of governmental restraint".[31] What was required was a free speech right which recognised "that restraining the hand of the government is quite useless ... *if a restraint on access is effectively secured by private groups*".

Posed in this manner, the newsprint allocation issue was easily dealt with, without undue strain on the "equality before law" principle. The "crucial question" was how the equality clause should be interpreted. Was it "merely a ban on the creation of inequalities by the State"?

---

28 Ibid: 764.

29 Ibid: 803.

30 Ibid: 805.

31 Ibid: 814.

Or, a command "to eliminate inequalities existing"? The answer was very clear: the State was obliged to adopt a "standard which takes into account the differing economic and social conditions of its citizens, whenever these differences stand in the way of equal access to the exercise of their basic rights". Free speech had an essentially "individual aspect". If a publishing group secures the right for itself, then launches more products and claims newsprint allocations accordingly, it would curtail the right of free speech for other individuals and entities. In a scarcity situation, the regulation of access to basic resources was essential to safeguarding fundamental rights.[32]

"Access" was one of the crucial questions raised in this minority judgment: access of the public to the media environment and of the media organisation to the essential resources of its trade. Though the latter was seemingly the sole issue before the bench, the dissenting judge tied this up with the larger one of the public function of a newspaper and its socially enjoined duty to reflect the variety and diversity of the milieu it operated within.

Interestingly, public access to the media space is under U.S. constitutional law, explicitly denied. This flows from the peculiar wording of the first amendment to the U.S. Constitution, which forbids any legislative curbs on the freedom of speech *and* the press. Scholars have since argued endlessly over the intent behind the specific mention of the "press" as a protected entity. Is this a redundancy, considering as in India, that the wider right of the public includes the narrower one of press freedom? While the scholars argue, the prevalent judicial orthodoxy – which accords with the "strict constructionist" doctrine – is that the authors of the U.S. Constitution must have had the intent of protecting the press as a specific entity. And since allowing the public access would be an intrusion into this freedom, no such right could be granted. It was an anomalous state, perhaps arising from a poor job of draftsmanship, since it created a situation where the press was immune to any demand from the public that a particular viewpoint should be accommodated, while the broadcast media was obliged under the "Fairness Doctrine", to ensure that different opinions gained a voice and that any issue should be reported from diverse perceptions.[33]

---

32 Ibid: 424.

33 Jaffe: 1972.

The "fairness doctrine" was an obligation imposed on broadcasters in 1949 since they were beneficiaries of a publicly granted right to use a scarce resource, i.e., the electromagnetic spectrum, for a commercial purpose. The argument for repealing the fairness doctrine was heard with increasing insistence through the 1970s and '80s, partly on the grounds that broadcast media should not be burdened by rules of public access that print media was unconstrained by. There were voices which argued the unpopular cause, guaranteed to gain little traction through all forms of media, that the way forward was to bring print under the same obligations as broadcast.[34] In 1987, the U.S. Federal Communications Council (FCC) voted unanimously to repeal the fairness doctrine, which never had the force of law and was no more than a norm that broadcast licence holders were encouraged to follow. The FCC chairman – newly appointed to his post by the doctrinaire right-wing U.S. President Ronald Reagan – announced the decision as one that eliminated the supposed discrimination between different media: "We seek to extend to the electronic press the same First Amendment guarantees that the print media have enjoyed since our country's inception".[35]

The right of access to media space and time

An individual citizen's access to the media, as a right, was in the Indian context the subject of a 1992 Supreme Court ruling in a case arising from a consumer advocacy group's scrutiny of the functioning of the Life Insurance Corporation (LIC). This critique of the insurance company, then owned entirely by the Union Government, was circulated widely among insurance policy-holders, entirely through the energy and resources of its author, Manubhai Shah and the activist group he headed. In a bid to dispel public reservations about its functioning, LIC commissioned one of its senior officials to write a rejoinder, which was published in a major newspaper headquartered in the city of Madras (now Chennai). Shah's response was also published by the same newspaper.

When LIC chose to reprint its paper in a journal published for circulation among policy holders, agents and employees, Shah demanded

34 Jacklin et al (1982).

35 *The New York Times* (1987).

the right to present his case through the same forum. This demand was turned down on the grounds that the forum was a house-journal of the LIC, where public access was not an untrammelled right. The Supreme Court in 1992 ordered LIC to publish Shah's article based upon two public interest considerations. The publication in question merited the status of a public forum in that it was available to the general public through subscriptions. And second, even if the status of the publication as a house-journal were to be conceded, LIC as a corporation owned by the government, fell within the definition of an agency of "the state" and had no authority to deny any citizen the right to free expression.[36]

LIC was a soft target – a government-owned corporation for which publishing was a peripheral activity. And in specifying two grounds and failing to clarify which among them was decisive, the Supreme Court bequeathed an ambivalent legacy. Clearly, if the criterion of wide circulation is decisive, then the same principle should apply even to elements of the privately owned media. But if the fact of the LIC being an agency of the State is the key consideration, then newspapers and the media in general would be exempt from complying with similar rules of public access. Though the matter has been the subject matter of a desultory public debate over the years, the right of public access to media space and time remains a neglected issue. The orthodoxy on the matter is laid down by the Press Council of India as a set of voluntary guidelines on the right of reply.[37] Matters are not greatly helped of course, by the lack of statutory enforcement authority at any level of the policy apparatus.

As an aside, the Supreme Court also chastised the government TV channel in the course of the 1992 ruling, for refusing to air a national award winning documentary titled *Bhopal: Beyond Genocide*, directed by Tapan Bose. It was a time when the government enjoyed an absolute monopoly over broadcasting and took the plea that it had its own standards and was not obliged to air every film found worthy by a national awards jury. The court ruled that the awards jury would inevitably have reflected the social and public value of a piece of art in arriving at

---

36 Supreme Court of India (1992).

37 The norms specified by the Press Council of India can be found on its website, through an appropriate process of search: http://presscouncil.nic.in.

its determination. As a monopoly broadcaster, the government channel could not refuse to air this film without seriously infringing the right to free speech.

Whose freedom: the advertiser or the public?

If this entire sequence of rulings were to be revisited in the light of India's subsequent media experience, a feature that emerges quite starkly is that the relationship between circulation and advertisement revenue is not quite as neat as the Supreme Court believed. Advertisement revenue is dependent not merely on gross circulation but, more crucially, on audience demographics. When the *The Times of India* (*TOI*) proudly proclaimed that it had crossed the magical threshold of a million in circulation in 1996, it did not, in the breathless ardour of this achievement, inform readers how its printing presses were sustaining this output when every additional copy was being sold at a price rapidly plunging below production cost. The answer simply was that the *TOI* had assembled an adequate war chest from its conquest of the advertising market, to be able to ramp up its financially draining output and reach the demographic segments of the most intense interest to advertisers.

The scenario was the exact converse of what the Supreme Court had sketched in the *Sakal* case – not of a newspaper being forced to raise prices because it was deprived of advertisement space, but of a newspaper able to slash prices and drive out competition after securing pre-eminence in the ad bazaar. Advertisers unlock the doors to circulation and vice versa. The newspaper that delivers the high purchasing power demographic segments to the advertiser has the potential to earn profits beyond the reach of others, even with relatively more modest circulation.

Print media criteria are transported to the broadcast domain with a little effort, since the underlying principles have a certain universality. Newsprint in the 1970s was regarded as a scarce commodity, much as the spectrum was in the early years of satellite broadcasting. Newsprint has since become abundant, much like frequency slots for broadcast channels. Advertisement revenue, once regarded as a limited resource, has since grown enormously, though the competition between newspaper groups for cornering increasing shares of this expanded cake, has greatly intensified. And even if the proliferating broadcast channels of the years since 1991 when the skies opened up for satellite television – and particularly since the Indian economy hit a purple patch of growth in 2004 – have not been very transparent in their financial accounting, the mere fact that they exist, is proof that the aggregate of advertisement spending in the Indian economy has been percolating, albeit in varying degrees, to all of them.

The principal restraint then to using the electromagnetic spectrum as a public resource, lay not so much in scarcity, as in the privileges the government had arrogated to itself. In terms of doctrine, the matter was settled in a 1995 ruling by the Supreme Court in a rather trivial matter involving the rights to broadcast a cricket match. Among the principles laid down was the public ownership of the spectrum, which the government enjoyed no inherent monopoly right over. In the words of Justice P.B. Sawant who wrote one of two concurring judgments: "the airwaves or frequencies are a public property. Their use has to be controlled and regulated by a public authority in the interests of the public and to prevent the invasion of their rights".[38] In other words, the uppermost concern in the deployment of the airwaves would be the preservation of the right to free speech and the related right to information. The challenge of regulation was to harmonise the two different aspects of the "right to freedom of speech and expression", which were the "the right to educate, to inform and to entertain" and the "right to be educated, informed and entertained". In the context of the broadcast industry, one was "right of the telecaster" and the other, "that of the viewers".[39]

This in turn, required a regulatory approach that departed from an absolutist notion of media freedom. "Broadcasting freedom", in the words of Justice B.P. Jeevan Reddy - author of the other opinion in the case - "involves and includes the right of the viewers and listeners who retain their interest in free speech". With public interest being dominant rather than private profit, "restraints on freedom of broadcasters are justifiable on the very ground of free speech", simply because "free-

38 Supreme Court of India (1995): para 124(i).

39 Ibid: para 78.

dom of expression includes the right to receive information and ideas as well as freedom to impart them".[40]

The airwaves judgment in short, urged the adoption of a new paradigm that transcended the dichotomy between government control and free enterprise. On one side, it asserted in Justice Sawant's words, the need to "rescue the electronic media from the government monopoly and bureaucratic control and to have an independent authority to manage and control it". When the electronic media was controlled "by one central agency or (a) few private agencies of the rich", there was a need for another body, "representing all sections of society".[41] The nature of this body was for the legislative authorities to determine. The central point simply, was that "private broadcasting, even if allowed, should not be left to market forces, in the interest of ensuring that a wide variety of voices enjoy access".[42]

With these being the central principles, the Supreme Court directed – in Justice Sawant's words – that "the Central Government shall take immediate steps to establish an independent autonomous public authority representative of all sections and interests in the society to control and regulate the use of the airwaves".[43] Justice Reddy laid down the principles on which this body should function: "it is the duty of the State to see that airwaves are so utilised as to advance the free speech right of the citizens which is served by ensuring plurality and diversity of views, opinions and ideas". Conceding monopoly control in any form would be "detrimental to the free speech rights of the body of citizens inasmuch as only the privileged few - powerful economic, commercial and political interests - would come to dominate the media".[44]

Despite the clarity of this ruling, official policy continued on its course of muddling through. Decisions seemed to oscillate between defensive responses to predatory moves by media corporations, particularly those of foreign origin, and pragmatic gestures of acquiescence in the larger designs of these corporations.

40 Ibid: para 181.

41 Ibid: para 107, 85.

42 Ibid: para 205.

43 Ibid: para 81.

44 Ibid: para 205.

Towards the end of 1996, News Television India Ltd., a corporate entity owned by the global media czar Rupert Murdoch, announced its readiness to start "direct to home" (or DTH) telecasts in India. This was followed by a print advertising campaign promising viewers a new deal that would secure their independence from the ever-unreliable local cable operator. By April 1997, this campaign had peaked and the Murdoch enterprise seemed all set to manoeuvre its way past areas of silence in policy, to begin an entirely new category of service. After months of silence construed as acquiescence, the government in July 1997, issued a formal notification prohibiting the transmission or reception on Indian soil of any broadcast signal above the 4800 megahertz frequency range, effectively ending any immediate prospect of DTH.[45]

If this was a defensive policy response, the official attitude towards uplinking from Indian territory for broadcast through satellite, bore all the scars of submission to an agenda set beyond the reach of regulatory efforts. The story begins in May 1991 when the Hong Kong based STAR TV network began beaming programmes into India, where audience interest had already been stoked by the satellite broadcast network CNN's coverage of the Gulf War some months before. The first of many committees to examine possible policy and regulatory responses, constituted almost immediately afterwards, submitted its recommendations by October 1991.[46]

Certain conditions were taken for granted in all early examinations of broadcasting reform. Though thinking on autonomy for the sector had evolved over the years, there was little acceptance yet that the government would have to yield its monopoly over the airwaves. The most that would be conceded was a modest degree of public access to broadcast platforms that would remain under exclusive government control.

The number of broadcast channels beaming into India was by now proliferating. Yet the government remained unwavering in its refusal to allow any Indian entity to establish a satellite uplink for broadcast diffusion over the country. This compelled a number of Indian broadcasters to physically transport their programmes on magnetic media

45 Ninan (1998): 18-9.

46 Ibid.

to other countries – notably Singapore – from where an uplink was established.

An inherent illogic in broadcast regulation

This was a situation rife with ironies. Singapore till the second decade of the new millennium – despite all the changes in attitudes – continued guarding its airwaves with a zeal bordering on fanaticism, allowing incoming broadcasts only with a time delay, so that diligent censors continually monitoring the signals could screen out any material deemed objectionable.[47] But despite all its authoritarian attitudes, the government of Singapore had little reservation early in the C&S television boom, in allowing signal uplinks from its territory. In contrast, the Indian government disallowed any broadcast uplink, but admitted that it was powerless to monitor or regulate incoming television programmes. To draw attention to this contrast is not to endorse the Singaporean policy of censorship, or to advocate a police regime that would monitor all broadcasts for conformity with an official line. It is only to underline the inherent illogic of the Indian government's position, which remained a persistent feature for long years into the Cable and Satellite Broadcasting (C&S) television boom.

By late-1996, a minor concession was granted with domestic broadcasters allowed uplink to satellites owned by India's Department of Space, for the limited purpose of gathering "news feeds" from remote locations. Though successive committees had recommended that uplink rights be granted Indian-owned entities, the government dithered endlessly.[48] By early-1998, the Murdoch-owned STAR TV contracted with an Indian production company to provide the feed for a 24-hour news channel. STAR TV officials, many of whom had prior to joining the Murdoch enterprise, been working for the Ministry of Information and Broadcasting (MIB) in positions of decisive authority, were then under investigation in matters involving possible conflicts of interest and even corruption. Prime Minister I.K. Gujral however, found little amiss in throwing open his official residence for the inauguration of STAR's 24-hour news channel. Uplink rights were granted, ostensibly

47 For an account of censorship in Singapore, see Aaron Rao (2014).

48 This complex regulatory history is summarised in two articles in the fortnightly magazine *Frontline* (1996 and 1997).

for a trial period of six weeks, so that the news channel could provide coverage of elections due to take place in that time.[49] And once the uplink right was granted to a foreign-owned broadcaster, there was no credible basis on which Indian entities could be denied.

Under the Supreme Court's air-waves judgment of 1996, the government was enjoined to transform a zealously guarded monopoly into a benign, democratic and inclusive public trust. Aside from the advisory bodies that were periodically commissioned to come up with creative solutions, the first concrete effort at legislation was the Akash Bharati bill, introduced in Parliament after much deliberation, only to lapse with the dissolution of the Sixth Lok Sabha in 1979. It is germane in this context to note that the Lok Sabha that passed into history that year was one elected in 1977 on a wave of rage at the suspension of democratic rights during the internal emergency declared in June 1975, when press censorship in its most explicit form was introduced and the government monopoly of the airwaves was transformed into a *mala fide* effort at promoting the personality cult of an incumbent Prime Minister.[50]

Akash Bharati's successor was the Prasar Bharati bill, enacted but not notified when the National Front government elected in 1989 – comprising numerous fragments from the political formation that had dominated the Sixth Lok Sabha – passed into history. It took till 1997, with another avatar of the National Front in power – now called the

---

49 This sequence of events is covered in concurrent issues of the weekly newsmagazine, *India Today*, especially in the special page titled "Teletalk", devoted to visual media issues.

50 A White Paper released in August 1977, after a regime change occurred at the Centre, provides essential details of the "misuse of the mass media" during the internal emergency (See Government of India, 1977). Censorship was imposed under the Defence of India Rules with the declaration of the Emergency on June 25, 1975. But then, conscious that the new procedures would not take immediate effect, the Government cut off electric supply to most Delhi newspapers that evening, resulting in them being unable to come out with reports on the "cataclysmic events" the following day (p. 8). A few months later, addressing a conference of the state-controlled broadcasters, Prime Minister Indira Gandhi reportedly "ridiculed all questions being raised about (its) credibility". Her words as reported in the White Paper (p. 8) were: "Quite honestly, I do not understand what it (credibility) means. Who has credibility? The newspapers, who had day in and day out printed falsehood?"

United Front - for Prasar Bharati to be notified and become the law of the land.

The government that followed the 1998 general election to the Lok Sabha, allowed the ordinance notifying Prasar Bharati to lapse and a few months afterwards, disbanded the board of trustees appointed to supervise the functioning of the public broadcaster. In all these respects, the Bharatiya Janata Party (BJP) – which had emerged as the haven of the Hindu nationalist element from the chaos of the Sixth Lok Sabha's disintegration – signalled its partiality towards strict control rather than freedom upheld by the Supreme Court. The entire episode underlined certain realities about the political tutelage that broadcasting reform has constantly laboured under. Where governments unsure of their tenure are in power, led by political formations convinced of their imminent mortality, there was always a possibility that the oppressive official hold over the airwaves would be relaxed. This narrow window of political opportunity would invariably be shut tight when governments assumed power led by parties that believed, for whatever reason, in their historical destiny as rulers.

The Congress Party's persistent record of default on the Prasar Bharati Act, the United Front's restoration of the agenda of broadcasting reform and the BJP's unceremonious termination of the experiment, underline the very strong warning issued by Justice Reddy in the airwaves case: "Government control in effect means the control of the political party or parties in power for the time being. Such control is bound to colour and in some cases, may even distort the news, views and opinions expressed through the media".

A monopoly over the airwaves was part of the initial conditions in India, in contrast with how the media evolved elsewhere. To take only the U.S., where broadcasting began as private enterprise and rapidly drew in a large assortment of players who were swiftly assembled into rigorously capitalistic monopolies by the laws of the market, it might appear that an oligopoly of private broadcasters – however small in number – would be far preferable to a government monopoly. Interestingly though, in the doctrine of fundamental rights laid down by India's Supreme Court, the fact of monopoly ownership over broadcast platforms, in itself, was not read as a curb on the twin rights of information and free speech. It was only in the denial of public access to broadcast media, that such an abridgment of the fundamental rights could be deemed to occur.[51]

After much dithering and default, when political partisanship seemed easily to have overwhelmed the public interest, the union government in August 2006 posted on the website of the MIB – in an uncharacteristic spirit of openness and candour – the first draft of a renewed legislative effort at media regulation. The Broadcast Services Regulation Bill (BSRB), was how the proposed legislation was titled and it sought among other things, to provide legal backing for the principle of the public ownership over the airwaves. Apart from this object, another stated purpose was to give legislative backing to the numerous regulatory orders on satellite broadcasting issued since the mid-1990s.[52]

Viewed in this context, it was easy spotting the many deficiencies of the BSRB as first conceived, particularly when measured against the stated purpose of making the airwaves judgment operational. Drafted in 2006, when the government monopoly had been irreversibly

---

51 The precise formulation in Justice Sawant's judgment is as follows: "A mere creation of the monopoly-agency to telecast does not *per se* violate Article 19(1)(a) as long as the access is not denied to the media either absolutely or by imposition of terms which are unreasonable. Article 19(1)(a) proscribes monopoly in ideas and as long as this is not done, the mere fact that the access to the media is through the Government controlled agency, is not per se violative of Article 19(1)(a)". (Supreme Court of India, 1995: para 61).

52 The text of the Broadcast Services (Regulation) Bill was for long a mystery, with one commentator going to the extent of observing as late as July 28, 2006, that despite all the talk, the Bill was not officially "in the public domain". This commentator, who happened to be chairperson of the Public Service Broadcasting Trust, had by his own account "requested a copy" of the bill from the MIB, and been told that he could not "legitimately" be given one. "This means", he wryly concluded, "that all those in possession of a copy of the Bill and those writing about it are in violation of the Official Secrets Act". (See Mehrotra, 2006). The full draft of the bill was finally posted on the MIB website on August 11, 2006, with the stated purpose of inviting public comments on an issue of general importance. Like much else that deals with media regulation, this particular initiative has passed into history, leaving very few traces. The full draft of the bill, as of May 2014, is available at the website of the Parliamentary Research Service, a non-governmental organisation that sought to provide policy advice to legislators in matters of urgent public importance. The full text is available from typing the title of the act into the search box at the website of the PRS: www.prsindia.org.

eroded, the BSRB should reasonably have taken into account the experience of corporate control over the airwaves, factoring this into its regulatory philosophy. At first glance, the BSRB did indeed pay due obeisance to preserving diversity of choice on the airwaves, though on closer examination, this turned out to be worse than mere tokenism. As a correlate, the clause vesting the government with the power to curb media monopolies was numerically imprecise and devoid of any modality of intervention to secure the public interest.[53]

The BSRB conceived of a transfer by official *diktat*, of all "proceedings pending" before the existing frequency spectrum oversight body – the Telecom Regulatory Authority of India (or, TRAI) – to a body under the MIB, which it proposed to name the Broadcast Regulatory Authority of India (or BRAI). Between June and August 2006 – with the BSRB being debated in public – TRAI sought for the first time to go beyond its assigned job of mediating between telecom companies, and adjudicating matters of frequency spectrum allocation and determining fair tariffs for C&S TV subscriptions.[54]

The new mission that TRAI embraced was within the mandate conferred in 2004, ostensibly to hasten the convergence between broadcasting, communications and information technology.[55] Yet it was never secret that the MIB was unhappy with this seeming encroachment into its domain and the emergence of the TRAI as regulator of C&S subscription rates. This caused a further sense of alarm within the MIB at a rival body winning populist acclaim in pursuit of a public cause. In the light of the subsequent oblivion the BSRB suffered, it is a credible proposition that it was no more than a temporary expedient in a long-running bureaucratic turf war.

Like many other legislative initiatives in the media sector, the BSRB displayed the conceit of governments that believed they could appropriate the mantle of speaking for the public. And where instrumentali-

---

53 Article 10 of the BSRB merely reserved for the Central Government "the authority to prescribe such eligibility conditions and restrictions with regard to accumulation of interest in the print and broadcast segments of the media as may be considered necessary from time to time, to prevent monopolies across different segments of the media as well as within the broadcast segment, to ensure diversity of news and views".

54 *Hindu Businessline* (2006).

55 Press Trust of India (2004).

ty was concerned, the BSRB displayed very little creativity, falling back instead on the discredited old device of reserving for the government the arbitrary – and in the final instance, overbearing – powers of police enforcement inherited from colonial law. Appearing only fleetingly in the public discourse, the BSRB was another legislative effort in media regulation that was defeated by a deficit of the policy imagination, not to mention the assiduous efforts of powerful lobbies.

As if to reaffirm that the power to mould public opinion was seriously skewed, the media industry was permitted by circumstances, to have its say on the BSRB well before the public was brought into the discussion. Public perception on a major legislative initiative was moulded by the industry that had the greatest stake in diluting the scope of the law. It was a situation abounding in curiosities, though there was little novelty in the media being, uniquely among business sectors, the arbiter of public opinion in matters involving its commercial interests.

Media groups have their say

Towards the end of July 2006, a leading newspaper with a significant presence in Mumbai, carried a sequence of articles warning that the proposed broadcast legislation was a significant threat to all the free speech guarantees of the Indian constitution. All three articles were published under the caption "Media Muzzled" and their basic purport was that the BSRB embodied a familiar pattern of official paranoia and unreason. "Every few years", began the first of the articles, "a nervous government decides that the media has gone overboard and must be subject to regulation. Democracy and free speech do not mean spreading canard about public authority, endangering national security and allowing for obscenity, runs the argument (sic)". The leaked draft of the BSRB had led to considerable "disquiet" over what looked like "another attempt ... to muzzle the media".[56]

Rather self-servingly, the media chose to highlight those draft BSRB provisions that endowed the official government machinery with punitive powers. *The Times of India* observed in its report, that the draft "expanded on the already existing draconian provisions", before going on to describe, with little attention to nuance or detail, the

56 *Hindustan Times* (2006).

powers of search and seizure the BSRB invested the government with. It concluded with an account of the penalties the media would be liable to if it were to incur official displeasure.[57]

A Mumbai newspaper, a recent debutant then seemingly representing the new era of cross-linked media partnerships, also had its say. Under a vivid and exhortatory headline, the newspaper – in which both India's leading satellite broadcaster and the company that owns the country's largest circulated newspaper had equity investments – urged that the BSRB be "killed", effortlessly conflating the rights of the media into those enjoyed by the public.[58]

Media rights are not a separate category

With all the fuss it engendered, the BSRB fell far short in ambition, of the bill mooted in 1997 as a framework of rules for private broadcasters. Drafted during a brief interlude of openness within the MIB, the 1997 bill provided for "inter-category restrictions on licences (for broadcasting) as well as on the number of licences within a category". It restricted the "ownership and control of a broadcasting company by newspaper proprietors up to 20 percent and vice versa" and specifically prohibited religious bodies, political organisations, foreign nationals and entities, and advertising agencies from holding broadcasting licences in India. Further, it limited a single person or entity to licences in any two (or less) of the following activities: terrestrial radio, terrestrial television, satellite television or radio, direct-to-home broadcasting, and local C&S delivery.[59]

57 *The Times of India* (2006).

58 *Daily News and Analysis* (2006). This newspaper was launched in the Mumbai market in 2004 and its principal financial backers were the Zee Telefilms group, which operates a number of entertainment and news channels and is by far India's largest satellite broadcaster, and the Dainik Jagaran group, publishers of the newspaper that was reckoned by concurrent rounds of the National Readership Survey, to have a readership of 21 million.

59 The full text of the draft is available in Price and Verhulst, 1998: 191-222. Also included in the volume (223-33) is a concept note circulated by the Ministry of Information and Broadcasting, explaining its overall approach to regulatory issues.

In the legislative vacuum that followed the lapsing of the 1997 draft, big media players altered facts on the ground, to make the job of regulation all but impossible. Powerful print media groups moved into the broadcast sector, and others that had begun as C&S broadcast companies, integrated horizontally into the newspaper industry. C&S companies in turn, ventured into the domain of retail distribution of television signals and established their dominance in the most lucrative markets. The ease with which the media industry mobilised forces to scupper the BSRB, altogether more lenient in intent than the preceding bill, highlighted how the conquest of new frontiers in a regime of liberalism, had greatly enhanced its power to mould public opinion.

Early in December 2006, the MIB announced detailed policy guidelines on community radio services (CRS), as long-delayed correction to the December 2002 policy which reserved community radio for "well established education institutions". Even so, the amended policy required CRS applicants to meet a number of stringent conditions. In the case of aspirants other than publicly funded and managed educational institutions, CRS sanction was subject to clearance from two ministries, Home Affairs and Defence, not to mention the allocation of a radio frequency by still another. Programmes were enjoined to serve a "specific well-defined local community" and have relevance to the "educational, developmental, social and cultural needs" of this narrowly defined human collectivity. Broadcasts related to "news and current affairs" or in some way "political in nature" were specifically proscribed. Sponsored programmes would not be permitted except where the sponsor was an arm of the government. Advertisements and public announcements that yielded revenue would be permitted to the limit of five minutes in an hour's broadcast. All earnings would necessarily have to be used in meeting operational and capital costs. A surplus, if available, could, with the explicit written permission of the MIB, be transferred into the primary activity of the organisation running the service.[60]

This regime of policy may be instructively compared with that prevalent in the realm of private radio broadcasting. In July 2005, policy guidelines were announced and bids invited for the second round of allocation of FM radio broadcast circles. Tendering principles made the entry-fee offered by each bidder the key factor guiding allocations

60 Ministry of Information and Broadcasting (2006).

of frequency bands. A share of annual revenue would be paid by the operator as fee for the use of the broadcast spectrum. Advertisements would be the principal revenue source, but there would be no limit imposed on the quantum of advertising that each broadcaster could carry.[61]

In terms of frequencies granted for FM radio, the government seemed inclined to view the airwaves as a resource to be auctioned to the highest corporate bidder. Following successive rounds of bidding, the vast majority of licences were granted to companies or entities already strongly established in other media sectors.[62] Entertainment Networks (India) Ltd., a company owned by Bennett Coleman, won 25 FM radio broadcast circles, to add to the seven it was running under its brand name, Radio Mirchi. South Asia FM Ltd., a company controlled by the Chennai-based satellite broadcaster, Sun TV, won no fewer than 23 FM circles in the northern part of the country. This was quite apart from the 18 it won in the south through its affiliate company, Kal Radio Ltd. Sun TV it needs to be added, had in early-2006, bought up the Tamil daily, *Dinakaran*, then ranked third in readership in Tamil Nadu state. With aggressive price-cutting, it had soon catapulted the newspaper to an undisputed second position and quite possibly the first in the readership stakes, though this remained contentious and was not resolved on account of the flakiness of available data.[63]

Sun TV began in the realm of cable and satellite (C&S) broadcasting and rapidly expanded its influence into print and radio. Bennett Coleman, initially headquartered in Mumbai and later in Delhi, of-

---

61 Ministry of Information and Broadcasting (2005a).

62 Details of broadcast circles awarded after this round of FM spectrum auctions were posted on the website of the Ministry and extracted at Ministry of Information and Broadcasting (2005b).

63 It may not be out of place to mention here that Sun TV is a business group controlled by the family of a one-time Union Minister for Communications and Information Technology, appointed to the post in 2004 as a first-term Member of Parliament from Tamil Nadu. Aside from the intrusion of the monopoly element into the media, the appointment of this person to a position of authority despite his lack of experience and family ties to the communications business, raised serious questions about conflicts of interest, which surprisingly, attracted little public comment or discussion. For a rare discussion in a public forum on the multiplicity of issues involved in Sun TV's expansion, see Ramanujan (2006).

fered a case study of a business group of considerably older vintage, diversifying out of print into TV, radio, internet advertising and a variety of other media ventures, with little oversight or scrutiny from official bodies tasked with protecting the public interest.[64]

These two routes to media consolidation, though different, would be regarded with equal concern under any reasonable regime of safeguards over the right to information. But with policy being inattentive, these were by no means the only pathways available for well-endowed business houses seeking to capture the information space.

It took only a cursory glance at the second round of licences allocated for FM radio, to see that any notion of cross-media ownership restrictions had effectively been shredded and the pathway opened up for growing media monopolies. Illustratively: *Rajasthan Patrika*, a significant player in the newspaper space in Rajasthan state, was awarded four FM circles, while *Malayala Manorama* and *Mathrubhumi*, the two largest newspaper groups in Kerala, were awarded four each in their home state, and the Mid-day group of Mumbai was given six circles, all of them in highly lucrative metropolitan cities. HT Media and Entertainment, a company controlled by the Hindustan Times group – with its significant print media presence in Delhi and Mumbai – was awarded radio licences in both these cities, with the two metropolitan centres of Kolkata and Bangalore also thrown in as a bonus.

Beyond this story of media consolidation, a significant new presence was entering the scene. Adlabs Films Ltd., flush with an infusion of funds after its takeover by the Reliance-ADAG group – one of the country's biggest industrial conglomerates – won no fewer than 45 circles in the second round of FM radio allocations.[65]

Growing corporate control over the airwaves

These quite unconcealed concessions to corporate control over the airwaves should be viewed in the context of global norms on cross-media

64 An account of *The Times of India*'s growth, consolidation and diversification, is available in a later chapter.

65 On the acquisition of Adlabs by the Reliance-ADAG group, see Ninan (2006). Details of FM broadcast circles awarded at the point were drawn from Ministry of Information and Broadcasting (2005b).

ownership restrictions. These norms indeed, were repeatedly affirmed in India by legislative drafts that curiously, seldom made it to the stage of enactment. Though the realities of convergence with information technology often allowed big media corporations to effect a flanking operation around them, cross-media ownership restrictions remain a valuable part of the statute in several countries. And although the media monopolies have nonetheless often found their way around these, the public effort at ensuring plurality of sources persisted, unlike in India, where it is yet to begin.[66] In 2002, a move by the Federal Communications Commission (FCC) in the U.S. to undo some of the restraints on cross-media ownership, was met with a vigorous public signature campaign that effectively forced the regulatory body to retreat.[67]

For reasons that have more to do with the evasion of tough decisions than with inherent difficulties, the rules evolved for radio were immensely more stringent than those applicable to TV. This was in part because the stakes in TV broadcasting were high and the power of the medium so great, that multinational media enterprises and big domestic corporations were always an aggressive presence influencing policy decisions.

It is easy against this background to figure why policy on radio continued to remain restrictive: the poor cousin within the broad-

---

66 The classic work here is Bagdikian (2004), first published in 1983. Detailed rules on the cross-media ownership restrictions in force in the U.S. can be found on the website of the Federal Communications Commission. Illustratively, the rules in force as of 2017, prohibit "common ownership of a full-service broadcast station (television or radio) and a daily newspaper if the station's service area completely encompasses the newspaper's city of publication". The FCC's 2002 effort to relax these rules, was met with an organised show of public dissent that compelled it to put the proposed changes on hold. It could be argued that none of the FM broadcast licences given out in India in this round of FM auctions is a "full-service broadcast station", since they are all explicitly forbidden from engaging in news and current affairs. But with understanding of media economics having progressed much further since the U.S. norms were written, it should be evident that dominance over the advertisement market, particularly in concentrated pockets of high-purchasing power demographic groups, is really the material issue.

67 Associated Press (2006). This story, issued just when the FCC was beginning a series of public hearings, usefully describes the level of mobilisation of consumer advocacy groups on the issue of cross-media ownership.

casting family simply had no powerful lobbies arguing its case.[68] A record of inconsistent standards was especially evident in the record on community broadcasting. The concept note prepared by the MIB in 1996, by way of a preface to legislative proposals, mentioned community broadcasting as an "extremely useful" device in "providing voices to the local community in managing their affairs and participating in (the) overall developmental process". It proposed moreover, to award broadcasting licences in restricted areas – "on the basis of either a restricted bid or no bid at all" – to local organisations "to facilitate better education and communication".[69]

In the years since these words were written, big business control over the airwaves was further consolidated and public access to the airwaves banished from the policy discourse. It was only several months after the spectrum auction for FM radio that the Union Cabinet finally approved a policy that would open up opportunities in community radio to entities other than privileged universities and institutions of learning. And with all the changes grudgingly allowed since, the policy on CRS remained restrictive in terms of eligibility, content and permitted revenue sources. In October 2013, the campaign group Common Cause filed a public interest petition before the Supreme Court demanding that the illogical ban on news content on CRS be ended. In admitting the petition, the Supreme Court wondered aloud about the possible reasons for this proscription.[70] Despite a few hearings since then, the petition remained to be dealt with till January 2017.

These multiple forms of control over CRS stood in striking contrast to the total absence of any regulation over TV broadcasts. Regulatory efforts in C&S TV in fact, were for long focused on the cable operator rather than the broadcaster. The onus of ensuring that broadcasts conformed with the "programme code" and the "advertisement code" rested entirely with the cable operator. This curiosity of Indian

68 Pavarala (2003) asks a pertinent question that still remains unanswered: "why does this government find Rupert Murdoch more trustworthy than a poor, unlettered Dalit woman who wants to use a media channel to communicate?" The piece referred to is the introduction to a collection of papers on broadcasting in India with a focus on community radio.

69 Price and Verhulst (1998): 233.

70 Common Cause (2013).

broadcast law was inscribed into the Cable Television Network Rules of 1994 and has held the field since, despite a number of desultory efforts to legislate a comprehensive regulatory framework for the media, each defeated by the combined power of the industry. The "programme code" in turn, was a bunch of fairly vacuous strictures that in practice was reduced to nullity.[71]

Inquiries on media ownership reach nowhere

Where regulatory efforts threatened to have a substantive impact on media monopolies and thus on the overall ambience of the right to information and free speech, these were swiftly abandoned for reasons that should not challenge an average intelligence. In July 2009, the Hyderabad based Administrative Staff College of India (ASCI), on a mandate from the MIB, completed a study on media ownership and arrived at findings that any informed observer would have thought perfectly reasonable. Concentration of ownership was identified as a possible impediment to a full diversity of opinion emerging in the public discourse. And for a country of India's diversity, disallowing any voice in the public sphere was an effective denial of democracy. This manner of denial was to be judged in terms specific to the linguistic competence of India's very plural population. To put it in very simplistic terms, a highly diverse media in the English language (even if it were a reality) would be of no consequence to an Indian citizen whose linguistic competence was Tamil, since his civic participation would be determined by the discourse in his native language. For a highly segmented media – which differed from ordinary consumer items in its intimate link to the information universe that India's population lives under – it was very important, when assessing monopoly power, to focus on the "relevant market". The English or the Hindi media may matter to the

71 Among other things, the programme code explicitly forbids the broadcasting of material that contains the "criticism of friendly countries" or "criticises, maligns or slanders any individual in person or certain groups, segments of social, public and moral life of the country". Material that "denigrates children", or projects an "ironical and snobbish attitude in the portrayal of certain ethnic, linguistic and regional groups" is also forbidden. And in a revelation that would surely be of interest to the numerous channels that begin the day with astrological predictions – and the sports channels that preface the telecast of important cricket matches with the wisdom of tarot-card readers – anything that propagates "superstition and blind belief" is also proscribed.

citizen in the Telugu or Malayalam language region, but only indirectly in determining the wider hegemonic discourse that the regional identity subsists within.

The ASCI report debunked the argument that sheer numbers were sufficient assurance of diversity. It was not just "availability" that was germane, but also "relevance". Alternate media such as the internet, did not quite mean that geography was rendered irrelevant. Aside from the small number of internet users – at the time of the survey this was estimated at just 12 million, almost entirely urban-based – there was the additional factor that people who access the new media for information invariably "rely on sites that are generally controlled by traditional media providers". Far from undermining the rationale for ownership regulations, "the permeation of the traditional media players into the new media markets such as the internet, reinforces their value".[72]

The ASCI report identified three segments of the media market that merited distinct attention: carrier, content and distribution channel. Safeguards were required against two kinds of ownership concentration, it suggested. Cross media ownership was a situation of enterprises in print acquiring broadcasting and new media assets, or the other way around. And vertical integration was another outcome to be avoided, as with content generating groups seeking dominant positions in carrier and distribution channel activities, or the other way around. On the face of things, there was evidence of concentration in the Hindi and English print media in India. There were, the ASCI report noted, 105 daily newspapers in the Hindi language in the national capital Delhi, but five among them had a combined market share of close to 50 per cent. And though there were 201 daily newspapers in the English language nationally, just three – *TOI*, *HT* and *The Hindu* – controlled among themselves, close to half the market. Add on the Hyderabad-based *Deccan Chronicle*, whose debt-financed expansion was exposed as rather fragile only after the ASCI report was written, and the share of four enterprises in the English daily newspaper market was estimated at 55 per cent.

Curiously though, using its preferred methodology of applying the Herfindahl-Hirschmann Index (HHI) to assess concentration, the

72 Administrative Staff College of India (2009). The study is no longer available on the official MIB website. The above citations are at pages 43 and 46.

ASCI report found that the English and Hindi daily newspaper markets were not seriously exposed to the threat of ownership concentration or monopoly.[73] Perhaps if it had applied another measure – the share of the top three dailies in total advertising spend in the English and Hindi newspaper segments – it might have arrived at another conclusion. Within the parameters of its chosen methodology though, ASCI found in three other "relevant markets" – the Telugu, Tamil and Malayalam regions where media penetration was relatively high – that ownership concentration was an ever-growing reality.[74] There was no justification in its estimation, for persisting on the path of policy default. The regulatory vacuum in which the entire media had functioned through the years of growth and diversification since 1991, was no longer a tenable state of affairs. This was a finding underlined by ASCI's analysis of the media regulatory regimes in six other national jurisdictions: the U.S., Canada, Australian, the U.K., South Africa and Malaysia.

The final recommendations from the ASCI study were clear enough. Cross media regulations, it urged, must be put in place after "detailed market analysis of well-defined relevant markets". These must "include broadcasting, print and the new media". Market surveys would need to be conducted at regular intervals that could illustratively, be three or four years, "and the ownership restrictions/rules may then be changed accordingly". In addition, "disclosure norms that make cross media affiliations and ownership clear to the viewer need to be publicised".[75]

For all its methodological rigour and the clarity of its findings, the ASCI report suffered a strange fate. The MIB mothballed it, putting it beyond the pale of public discussion. Close to three years later, the Standing Committee of Parliament attached to the MIB observed that the Eleventh Five-Year Plan document had "made an observation … that while policy .. imposes an obligation to observe cross-media ownership rules, … these rules have not been formalised so far". The result

73 HHI is the sum of the squares of the market shares of all players in percentage terms. It would be readily seen that the HHI could vary from a theoretical minimum of zero – when there are an infinite number of players in a market, each with infinitesimally small shares – to a maximum of 10,000, when there is one player with a hundred percent share.

74 Administrative Staff College of India (2009): 137.

75 Ibid: 139-40.

was that "print and electronic media integration (was) taking place", creating "behemoths (that were) acquiring a mind-share disproportionate to what is permissible in a competitive market environment". The committee took note of the ASCI report and the MIB's response that as a "first step" towards putting in place a sensible policy, the ASCI report had been uploaded on its website. Public reactions would be sought and "views so received would be shared with TRAI for a relook on the entire issue" and to "work out a set of rules and safeguards".[76]

There was of course, no explanation from the MIB for the long delay in placing a report on a matter of considerable importance in the public domain. Neither is it known how long precisely the document remained on the MIB website. A fortnight after the parliamentary committee's report was tabled in the house, the MIB secretary wrote yet another communication to TRAI, to initiate a further series of consultations on the issue of media ownership. "Many players are looking for expanding their business interests in various segments of print and broadcasting sectors", read the letter: "In this scenario, issue of media ownership and the need for cross media restrictions assumes significance". TRAI responded in February 2013 with yet another consultation paper, indefinitely extending the agonising pretence of seeking clarity in a domain where the government seemingly had no intention to act. What were recommended as concrete policy options in the ASCI report, became in TRAI's paper a series of open-ended questions on which "stakeholders" – as the term of art would have it – were invited to comment.[77]

Events that followed hewed very closely to the template set in earlier such junctures when public participation was invited in determining the optimal media regulation strategies. Media industry entities and their lobbies mobilised in force, deluging TRAI in verbiage that had one basic purpose: to establish the futility of any manner of regulation. Working journalists managed to put together a solitary submission through the Delhi Union of Journalists, commending the TRAI initiative and suggesting that the magnitude of the problem remained

76 Parliament of India (2013).

77 The consultation paper and all the responses sent in to it, were posted on the TRAI website (Telecom Regulatory Authority of India, 2013). The discussion that follows is sourced to this link without specific attribution to the response filed by each of the parties to the consultation.

to be accurately assessed. The market share of the major media entities was of course germane, but so too was the disproportionately large share they obtained of the aggregate advertising expenditure in the economy. From the ranks of what could be called "civil society", a Delhi-based organisation called the Citizens' Forum for Civil Liberties, submitted a cursory eight-page response, which showed a serious lack of engagement with the issues raised.

From the world of academia, the Centre for Communication Governance (CCG) at Delhi's National Law University, sent in a modestly sized submission which argued among other things, that cross media ownership restrictions may well reduce the dominance of particular voices in the public sphere, but would not in themselves ensure diversity of opinions. That would indeed, require specific incentives to elicit and disseminate the perspectives of excluded sections such as women and those disadvantaged by traditions of caste and inheritance. The CCG warned against investing any agency of the state – even an autonomous regulator – with the power to disallow the entry of particular entities into the media space. Such a power if granted would "create a substantial risk of abuse" and would be "detrimental to media freedom". There was perhaps merit in having a limited number of disqualifications in place, though this power should in reality only be invoked after "a prescribed series of warnings and other escalating action, along with a right to respond and be heard".

Two individuals, Vibodh Parthasarathi and Alam Srinivas – collaborators on a study of the digital media in India – sent in a five-page response to the TRAI consultation paper, arguing that equity holding was a necessary though far from sufficient index of ownership concentration. Financial transactions carried out through holding companies and various kinds of loans – including at a personal level – were known to be equally important means of ownership concentration. In the case of a diversified media company Network 18, a personal loan advanced to its promoter had been a means through which the industrial conglomerate Reliance had acquired decisive control.

Where media companies were not listed in the stock exchanges, private equity investors often obtained decisive power over management decisions even with a minority stake. A case in point was a deal between the multi-edition publishing house in Hindi, the Jagran group and the D.E. Shaw investment firm. An accurate measure of ownership and control required in this regard, not merely transparency in the equity structure of media firms, but also the full disclosure of all relevant agreements and contracts.

Yet these interventions paled in comparison with the arsenal assembled by media industry groups to dismantle the case for regulation. BCCL questioned TRAI's intrusion into the policy space on print media, where it had absolutely no jurisdiction. Disregarding the finer points made in the debate, that numerical proliferation does not necessarily entail diversity, the BCCL went on to assert that India's "plethora" of newspapers was sufficient to ensure "plurality of views".

ENIL, a part of the Times group tasked with managing radio broadcasting assets, put on record its "fundamental" belief that the "growth of media in a democracy as vibrant and heterogeneous as India is possible only if the industry is allowed to grow to its full potential; governed only by market forces and not restricted by suffocating regulations". And as if the group's interests were not adequately represented, Times Internet stepped into the fray with the stern admonition that "(i)nstead of trying to harm the Media Industry which requires to be present in all different forms of Media in order to be competitive and indeed survive, TRAI must be sensitive to efforts to protect the Media Industry against existing wrong practices like wage-boards for newspaper employees, which allows government the power to decide the salaries of journalists and non-journalists". This was obviously not within the zone of direct interest for an internet enterprise, being more relevant to a print company, but that was not to prove a deterrent to the Times group parading its entire laundry list of grievances against the regulatory prospect.

To complete the awesome parade of its corporate power, the Times TV Network came up with a positive celebration of cross media holdings: "An economically well placed media entity should be permitted to invest in Print, Television and Radio segments and vice versa. Restricting companies from making investments in other media segments will affect their growth and hinder expansion of business, which are vital for the media industry to progress. It would also deprive companies of opportunities to extend their expertise and goodwill to other media segments which would otherwise bring in enhanced quality, optimum utilisation of resources and most importantly will be able to cater to growing consumer demand for better information and entertainment services".

STAR India Pvt Ltd., the Murdoch controlled distribution platform which has since beginning India's first twenty-four hour news channel withdrawn from the arena to focus on entertainment – and more importantly, distribution – scoffed at the entire purpose of the consultation. In a response in which the operative portions ran to 120 pages, followed by nine appendices spread over 205 pages, Star argued that the "existing media ownership regime itself has outlived its relevance and is ripe for dissolution". An especially irksome example it cited was the 20 per cent direct shareholding restriction on a foreign player in the DTH sector, which imposed an ownership restraint on Murdoch's Sky Television. "Media companies", said Star, "continue to be stymied by rules passed more than a decade ago – a time that bears no resemblance to the modern one in which they operate". The media ownership reviews carried out by TRAI and other empowered bodies, had proceeded in "fits and starts", which in turn had "left the companies and its customers in an infinite loop with no apparent escape valve". "Media Plurality as a concept", it urged "should be restricted to an analysis of the news and current affairs segment alone". And in this context, there was a "clear need for creating a level playing field between Indian and foreign players". The restrictions on foreign players entering the "news and current affairs space" had no "legitimate basis" and could be dispensed with once a "protective framework which addresses national security and integrity concerns" was instituted.

Among other industry players, Bharti-Airtel, a telecom and internet service provider that had ventured into digital TV, clung to its narrow sectoral interest by making a case for restraints on vertical integration between content and carrier. Network 18, which had just passed into the control of India's largest industrial conglomerate, Reliance Industries Ltd., responded briefly and perfunctorily, avoiding a response to many questions but in the crucial operative parts, purporting to see no useful purpose in cross media ownership restrictions. Among organised commercial lobbies, the Indian Newspaper Society submitted a voluminous response to TRAI, in part echoing the point made by the BCCL, of an authority stepping beyond its jurisdiction in mooting rules for the print media. It also repeated the boilerplate statistics about sheer numbers of media outlets which putatively made any effort at preventing the entrenchment of monopoly an utterly pointless exercise.

It was yet another instance of the media industry succeeding in hijacking the agenda setting function, appropriating a role more suited to the public understood in the widest sense. In August 2014, TRAI finally came up with its own exploration of media ownership issues. There was an element of surprise in the recommendations it put forward. At issue, it said, were two among the constitutional rights: property and free speech. Property had been demoted in the reigning constitutional orthodoxy from being a fundamental right to merely a "legal right", but remained an entitlement protected with greater zeal than life itself. And free speech was of course a right of very wide amplitude that had in much public discussion been reduced to merely a matter of the media. Recognising that these were difficult knots to cut through, TRAI placed all its thoughts on the table and then chose to leave the task of unravelling the multiple complexities involved, to a future body, perhaps a commission "headed by a retired Supreme Court judge".[78]

TRAI stepped boldly beyond the limits of political feasibility in suggesting a course of action that would cut through the media industry's protective layers of self-serving propaganda. The media industry itself responded with studied indifference. A sampling of the English language print media where the policy dialogue is customarily carried on with the greatest vigour, uncovered a curious indifference, with most newspapers relegating the TRAI recommendations to an insignificant spot on an inner page, often avoiding a serious engagement with its most consequential recommendations.

In arriving at its recommendations, TRAI purported to be solely guided by its understanding of public interest, as too the reasonable premise that pluralism is a desirable end. Pluralism as an end was defeated by concentration of ownership, but when media entities were either protected by accounting confidentiality or enabled to conceal the controlling hand behind a complex mesh of interlocked equity holdings, concentration was a difficult parameter to judge. Market power likewise was difficult to estimate when linguistic segmentation was the rule.

---

78 Telecom Regulatory Authority of India (2014).

Partly by borrowing concepts from ASCI's 2009 report, TRAI managed to negotiate these complexities with fair success. Ownership was to be assessed by requiring media entities to follow a regime of transparency and there was likely to be little amiss in imposing more stringent disclosure norms on these firms, on grounds of public interest. The more difficult notion of "control" was to be quantified using equity ownership as a proxy variable. Where interlocking ownership occurred, the multiplicative rule was recommended, i.e., for an entity that owns a certain percentage of the equity of another, which in turn owns a known share in yet another, the degree of control could be assessed by multiplying the first shareholding percentage by the second. Equity holding of twenty percent or above, would under the TRAI recommendations, connote the degree of "control" at which corrective measures would be triggered. Similarly, any entity with the power to appoint more than half the membership of the board of directors of a media enterprise, or holding fifty percent or more of the voting rights, would be deemed to have a controlling interest. TRAI also brought loans into the reckoning, recognising that these had been used as a means of acquiring decisive influence over media agendas. Any entity which advanced a loan equal to or above fifty-one percent of the total book value of a media unit's assets, would be regarded as controlling its operations.

In its methodology for assessing market power, TRAI further developed ASCI's suggestion that the HHI be the relevant measure. Market share was to be assessed segment-wise, i.e., in accordance with the language of broadcast and the relevant region, and measured using circulation for the print media and viewership for TV news channels. The English language media, both print and broadcast, would be assumed to have a pan-Indian audience. TRAI suggested an HHI of 1,800 as a threshold figure, above which certain recommended correctives would be triggered. Any single entity with a contribution of 1,000 or more to the HHI in any market of interest (such as for example, the print media in the Tamil language) would not be allowed then to have a like contribution to another (as for example, TV news in the same language). The entity would then be required to dilute its control below the threshold level of 20 percent in one of the two markets of concern.

TRAI did not account for concentration of ownership across language markets, as with an entity controlling dominant shares in both the Tamil and English print media in a particular geographical region. In principle, the same procedure could be applied there too, of a threshold level of the HHI at which action to dilute control would be triggered. Data availability was a likely hindrance since circulation and viewership information would only be available after a certain time lag. Business units could argue that in a constantly changing market scenario, it would be unfair to subject them to legal sanctions on the basis of data pertaining to the past and having no reference to current and future realities.

TRAI recognised moreover, that any effort to legislate its recommendations would almost certainly run into a constitutional challenge. Particularly troublesome would be the proposal to prohibit certain kinds of entities, such as political parties and religious bodies, from entering the news broadcast domain. Legislation of this nature could presumably have been passed in 1997 when the United Front coalition that held power at the central level, brought in a draft bill on broadcast regulation. But facts had since been created on the ground to defeat any such effort: occupation being one-half of the law and the number of religious bodies and political parties with interests in broadcasting through thinly disguised front organisations, having multiplied since then, almost by the month.

Unsurprisingly, TRAI left these rather knotty legal issues to a future commission. Perhaps it did not quite reckon with the fact that the existing jurisprudence on the issue was not favourable, with the Supreme Court having held in two decisive judgments – *Sakal* and *Bennett Coleman* – that media freedom cannot be curbed on the grounds other than those strictly specified in the constitution. TRAI's study came at a time when the public mood over a runaway media was in a state of considerable aggravation, though it also should perhaps have reckoned with a consistent history of indifference by the government and obstruction by the media industry.

Interestingly, in regard to another regulatory initiative from the authorities, which involved possible limitations on time apportioned for advertising within the broadcast hour, the response of the industry was divided, indicating a play by the bigger actors to secure a competitive advantage that potentially could reduce the space available for smaller players.

In 2006, a move by the Central Government to limit the advertisement time television channels could carry was abandoned within a month of its announcement, without any kind of public debate.[79] While the proposal may have seemed absurd on the face of things, it has a long and hoary vintage as a regulatory device with a vital bearing on the fundamental rights. Indeed, this limitation could be regarded as almost an exact analogy of the regulatory device that the first and second press commissions urged to stop the growth of print media monopolies. As Justice Mathew found in his dissenting judgment in the Bennett Coleman case, this seeming intrusion into the rights of the larger media companies was often a necessary evil in the larger cause of safeguarding the rights to information and free speech.

Revisiting the ratio of advertisement to subscription revenue

In March 2012, TRAI put out a consultation paper proposing that India should follow other major media markets – such as Australia, the U.K and with some qualifications, the U.S. – in seeking to safeguard quality of broadcast services by limiting the advertising time allowed through the day and especially in the peak viewing hours. Though a theoretical ceiling of 20 per cent of total broadcast time was in place, this was widely flouted, because of slack monitoring and in part by the fudge of taking the entire broadcast day as the basis for calculation. This enabled channels to allocate a relatively greater part of their prime-time slots, when premium ad rates were applicable, and bring down the average through a sparse allocations in slack viewing hours. Studies carried out on a sample of five news channels showed that despite this artifice, they were on average carrying ads through close to 35 per cent of total broadcast time.[80]

TRAI's intrusion into a putative area of autonomy elicited a storm of protest from the broadcast industry. The accustomed barrage followed, questioning TRAI's assumption of authority in a jurisdiction where it had no clear mandate, and repudiating any relevance that global best practices may have in the Indian scenario. TRAI went right ahead and in May 2012, notified an amendment to the Cable Televi-

79 *The Hindu* (2006)

80 Telecom Regulatory Authority of India (2012a).

sion Network regulations, imposing a 12 minute ceiling on advertisements in every clock hour of broadcast time, i.e., this was a ceiling to be honoured through the day, including primetime broadcasts.[81] Broadcasters protested vehemently to begin with, claiming that their finances would be irreparably damaged. A phase of litigation followed and TRAI backed off from some of the tougher norms: such as requiring ad placements during live sporting events only during natural breaks in the action; avoiding part-screen ads which distracted viewer focus from programmes of interest; and maintaining a minimum time gap between successive breaks. But in the face of quite palpable public disenchantment at the relentless barrage of distracting commercials and declining programming standards, the broadcast industry agreed to comply on condition of being granted a reasonable transition period.[82] The News Broadcasters' Association of India (NBAI) and the principal lobby of the entertainment channels, the Indian Broadcasting Foundation (IBF), duly advised their members of the need to honour the new ad cap regulations.[83]

Despite the seemingly conciliatory attitude, TRAI was inclined to play hardball, filing suit in August 2013 against a number of broadcasters for failure to comply with the ad cap. In extreme panic, NBAI filed a suit with the Telecommunications Disputes Settlement and Appellate Authority (TDSAT), where initial appeals against TRAI decisions must be heard. It secured a directive that coercive measures against the broadcasters would be held in abeyance till the matter was determined

---

81 Telecom Regulatory Authority of India (2012b).

82 Mint (2013).

83 A measure of the TV channels's realisation that audiences were seriously irritated at the relentless barrage of ads was the prompter that several among them introduced about the length of the ad break before the programme of interest resumed. But as the widely read columnist Santosh Desai (2014) pointed out, even this concession to viewer sentiment came with a layer of deceit: "Last week, while watching an opinion poll on a news channel and waiting for the ad break to get over, I noticed that the helpful prompter that tells us how much time to go before the main programme resumes was lying to me. It counted down from 2 minutes and after 30 seconds, went back to showing that there were still two minutes to go. In other words, it misled viewers outright about waiting for two minutes when in fact they had to wait for two-and-a-half in order to keep them from switching channels".

in all aspects.[84] These rulings though became immaterial and infructuous in December, when the Supreme Court held that TDSAT did not have appellate jurisdiction over policy regulations introduced by TRAI. Broadcasters were advised to approach the Delhi High Court for any further hearing of their grievances against the ad cap and other regulations. Early signals from this quarter though, were not encouraging. In February 2014, the Delhi High Court observed while hearing a petition against the ad cap by a Hyderabad-based channel, that the regulatory device in question seemed "reasonable" in terms of its public interest implications.[85]

The broadcast industry was divided for reasons easy to figure. Despite layers of opacity, the revenue model of the industry was increasingly being exposed as audience unfriendly, all too willing to not just accommodate, but actively pander to the advertiser. Viewer subscriptions were a large share – roughly 67.5 per cent – of total industry revenue.[86] But the bulk of this money was retained by cable operators performing the last-mile function of delivering the signal to subscriber premises. Estimates of the total subscription value that the cable operators cornered, varied between 80 per cent[87] and 91 per cent[88] – either way, the share they kept for themselves sheltering behind the virtual impossibility of an audit of their widely dispersed operations, was regarded as inimical to quality and diversity in television content.

There were some among the broadcasters who could take the risk of compliance with the ad cap, given the transition to a digitally addressable system which assured both a more reliable audience measure and a fair revenue share. In preparation for the October 2013 austerity of twelve minutes ad time in the programme hour, broadcasters began raising ad rates starting August. This was done with a sense of uncertainty, but for the general entertainment channels (GECs) in the

84 Press Trust of India (2013a).

85 A year after it was notified, the many twists and turns in the introduction of a ceiling on advertising time were recounted in a research report titled "The Ad Cap Ghost" published on a web portal exclusively dedicated to media industry news (Television Post, 2014).

86 Open Society Foundations (2012): 105ff.

87 Ibid: 108.

88 Mehta (2008): 173.

Hindi language, it was a realistic option, since they reached the largest audience cohort with the purchasing power to ensure enduring advertiser interest. By January 2014, the Hindi GECs had trimmed their ad inventories to between 13 and 14.2 per cent during the prime time broadcast hours, and between 9.7 and 13.7 percent during the entire day.

Other broadcasting genres were not quite so comfortable with the new rules. Hindi news channels for instance, were maintaining ad inventories of close to 20 per cent of broadcasting time till January 2014, if anything, increasing their prime time ad placements to cash in on public interest in general elections to five state assemblies in the Hindi belt in December 2013. Sustaining revenues in the event of compliance with the ad cap norms, would have entailed a hike in rates by between 48 and 76 percent for the more successful among the Hindi news channels. Evidently, this was a commercial risk that few among them were willing to hazard. English news channels were similarly in breach of the 12 per cent ad ceiling, though not by the extravagant margins of their Hindi counterparts. Compliance would have entailed a hike of between 23 and 56 per cent in ad rates to keep revenues unchanged. There was a perception that the three big players in the English news market – Times Now, CNN-IBN and NDTV – could in concert effect such a rate hike without damaging each other's revenue prospects. But for a long while, especially with national general elections imminent in April-May 2014, none among them was quite willing to cast the first stone.[89]

In this environment of hesitancy and uncertainty, there was an earlier act of commercial bravado that passed without serious comment. And it was an incident that highlighted some of the dubious processes that influence ad allocation decisions, TV ratings and the larger impact on news content. On 20 March 2013, Times Now, the English language news channel broadcasting from Mumbai, raised advertising rates by 30 percent across all time-slots and 50 percent for its primetime show, the Newshour with Arnab Goswami, which airs at 9 p.m. through weekdays.[90] It was a move that bespoke a high degree of confidence, seemingly signalling that Times Now as a news channel

89 *Television Post* (2014):13.

90 *Indian Television* (2013a).

thought itself exempt from the iron law of the marketplace, that in times of faltering sales and uncertain prospects, a rate increase would – far from propping up the bottom-line – further erode profits.

Times Now's bold manoeuvre spoke of its confidence that advertisers would stay the course despite the higher costs. As the company chief executive put it: "Times Now has had a high base of loyal viewers through its focus on hard-hitting and incisive news analysis. We continue to reign supreme in the English news genre for the fifth consecutive year and look forward to setting higher benchmarks for ourselves and for the industry. With our ever-increasing viewership share, we are positive that Times Now will always be the primary choice for the advertisers."[91]

A news hour promotes the communion of nation, market and unreason

Shorn of the corporate-speak, this was a statement that imparted a high degree of clarity to the character of the media as a beast. Most business enterprises would be fearful about raising prices in a time of plunging sales and rising uncertainty. But then most industries only make their sales at one point, after the production process has run its course. The media in contrast, is sold twice over: to the advertiser prior to publication and to the consumer following that. The latter transaction channels news and entertainment to the consumer and the former brings an audience to the advertiser. The relative importance a news organisation places on the revenue streams of advertising and subscription, would reflect its judgment of the balance between two sets of values, reflected in two distinct questions. How much would the news consumer pay for the information he is provided? How much would the advertiser pay to get his message to the audience the news organisation reaches?

For news broadcasts which do not charge for content, the consumer pays nothing except the delivery fee. News content is in short, paid for entirely by the advertiser. Thus, to parse the Times Now chief executive's statement and render it more comprehensible: advertisers would not baulk at higher rates, because the channel assures them value for money. It would deliver to the advertiser the audience loyal-

91 Ibid.

ty of the particularly prized strata where purchasing power would be relatively unaffected by recession. The channel would in turn, use the higher revenues earned from advertising, to raise standards in news broadcasting, wrapping its audience of high net-worth individuals ever more tightly into its orbit.

The decision to hike ad rates at a most unpropitious time could not have been taken without a thorough analysis of the audience situation. And there was probably some basis for the Times Now management's belief that the purchasing power of the audience cohort it had succeeded in creating, would more than justify the higher rates an advertiser had to pay. And that, going by the larger rate increase imposed for primetime broadcasts, would seem to be especially the case during the Newshour with Arnab Goswami, when audiences tune in to watch an hour of noisy acrimony between an assortment of individuals arranged in a grid around a central frame, where the anchorperson conducts proceedings with noisy and querulous lack of decorum.

Aside from the material reality of purchasing power, the Times Now audience cohort was also seemingly, a spiritual community uniquely responsive to its message, especially at primetime. And this spiritual solidarity was reaffirmed with particular solemnity at that moment of communion when Arnab Goswami took to the airwaves. The 24-hour news channel has had a pervasive presence across the Indian media landscape since about 2004, unsurprisingly from about the time that the Indian economy was declared to have moved to a new growth path. If overall economic growth has since then been in the range of 9 percent annually, the media industry grew at 15 percent: for the obvious reason that advertising spending caters to the strata of higher wealth and income, which normally do better in phases of bubble-powered buoyancy. In this scrum of channels and programmes all competing in the race to the bottom, the "Newshour with Arnab Goswami" had done something different, to earn a special benediction from the corporate advertiser. The plain lack of civility, the rampant irrationality and acrimony that was the news anchor's patented style, in other words, was the idiom of public discourse that the advertiser saw as most appropriate. The approach that Goswami made his own was clear: leave no room for ascertaining facts since that basic requisite of ethical journalism could not possibly, stand in the way of the triple confection of bullying, bluster and outrage that he was obliged to serve up before his primetime audience. Guests on his talk show were customarily given the choice of taking the facts as he served them up, or suffering the coarsest insult.[92]

The hazards to a sane public discourse in the Goswami style of journalism were aptly described by one of the guests on his show early in 2015, as the "plunder of reason". This followed a characteristically insult-laden, innuendo-filled primetime talk-show in which Goswami dealt with the denial of travel rights to an activist engaged with the defence of tribal habitats in central India. The reason given for this quite arbitrary action was the governmental prerogative in defending developmental imperatives, which meant that large energy projects in tribal habitats were a matter of national interest. To oppose these was by that token, an "anti-national activity" and anybody seeking to travel abroad to campaign for halting financial sustenance for large energy projects in tribal habitats could legitimately be stopped. As the political activist Kavita Krishnan put it after a bruising verbal battle with Goswami in which she yielded no ground: "Reason must be turned on its head – and anyone who dared voice a reasonable argument, must be shouted down, heckled, turned into a verbal punching bag. If you, as anchor, shout 'anti-national' or its variants enough times and enact derision and mockery with enough authority, anyone daring to argue with you is already always going to look and sound 'guilty'. And if your guests surprise you by putting up a fight and giving punches as good as they get, you can declare them guilty of 'bad behaviour'".[93]

Again in March 2015, Goswami pumped up the outrage over the scheduled telecast of a documentary on the gang-rape and evisceration of a young woman in Delhi in December 2012 that led to her death. Promos for *India's Daughter*, produced and directed by a British filmmaker, began appearing on social media sites of news broadcaster NDTV 24x7 on March 1. These spoke of an interview with one of the accused, Mukesh Singh, since convicted and sentenced to death, which testified to his moral certitude and complete lack of remorse. Times-Now, living up to its reputation for being a caricature of serious news analysis and debate, went quickly on air with elaborately simulated indignation. And with Goswami oscillating wildly between contemptu-

92 A comprehensive account of Goswami's journalistic style can be found at Bhatia (2012).

93 Krishnan (2015).

ous aggression and unctuous deference to authority, the stage was set for a bonfire of free speech.

Early in 2016, when sedition charges were brought against a group of student activists in Delhi's Jawaharlal Nehru University (JNU), Goswami invited spokespersons of the ruling party to his show and with deliberate, if sly intent, encouraged them to play doctored video footage purporting to show the student activists shouting slogans calling for the dismemberment of India.[94] Some of the accused students were set upon by a rogue group of lawyers when produced in court following their arrest and when the faux patriots had exhausted their rage on the seditious activists, they turned their fury on journalists assembled at the venue. Times Now blanked the incident out of its coverage and conspicuously stayed away from a demonstration by journalists protesting this outrageous assault. Neutral non-partisan observers were repelled by this conduct and called for an organised boycott of the channel and its obstreperous anchor-person.[95]

In July 2016, as civil unrest raged in the Kashmir valley, Goswami was seen to have breached even his own outrageously loose standards by calling for the prosecution of journalists who failed to faithfully echo the official line that all the trouble was manufactured in Pakistan. A professional rival from a competing channel denounced this effrontery and declared herself deeply ashamed at belonging to the same industry. And in a thoughtful commentary, independent researcher Simantini Krishnan, placed him in context as uniquely representative of a widely prevalent elite pathology. Against the liberal democratic consensus which looked at the consent of the governed as an essential element of a stable political order, the Indian elite she argued, had internalised a "technocratic ethos". This put attributes such as neutrality, value-freedom and the purported claim to scientific rationality at the foundation of the governance process, "hence negating the very grounds for socio-political conflict". Dissent and conflict, if at all they arose, were simply to be ignored or ruthlessly stamped out. "Goswami's editorial positions (were) without exception strategically aligned with the technocratic perspective on every issue", argued Krishnan: "In

94 Varadarajan (2016).

95 Guha (2016).

the few instances where technocratic posturing is untenable, Goswami chooses silence or a diversion to other issues".[96]

Television, as indeed all broadcast media prior to the advent of large-scale archives that could be accessed through the internet, was unique in leaving no imprint except in the visual and aural memory. It offered a manner of congregational prayer where the liturgy was administered by the presiding priest, different in kind from a situation in which a written body of scripture was the basis of communion. Prior to the printed word, the scripture was the exclusive property of a small and incestuous clerical tribe that held all others in thrall because they had the word. In the print era, all who could read became possessors of the word.

The boom in the broadcast media empowered a new clergy to claim a monopoly of the spoken word, with the potential to reach across the barrier of literacy. English broadcasts though were limited in their reach, since the language in India remains a very narrowly based privilege. But simply because much of the purchasing power resided with the English language elite, advertisers had a tendency to cluster around these broadcast channels. The Times Now move to raise ad rates in a time of recession revealed a certain self-assurance that its message had a resonance with the high net-worth individual that the advertiser would continue to retain an interest in, despite the higher costs incurred. And in harvesting (potentially) a higher inflow of advertising money, Times Now offered the reciprocal benefit that it would strengthen its message and provide still greater value for corporations struggling to keep afloat in a recessionary environment. These were worrying pointers to the direction in which the elite discourse in India was drifting, or rather being goaded under the tutelage of an obsessively profit-driven media. The main features of the emerging discourse were already clear: intolerance of complexity, impatience with the institutional processes devised to ensure at least an appearance of a free and open society, and a willingness to impose authoritarian solutions conjured up by those of putatively superior wisdom.

The print media, despite all its traditions in India, began losing its rich plurality, as the pressure mounted for conformity with the demands of advertisers and the affluent. The broadcast media because of

96 Krishnan, Simantini (2016).

its specific features, was more prone to surrender its autonomy when faced with advertiser interests.[97] The public character of the airwaves as a resource, was in short, completely subverted by a sustained campaign of disinformation that essentially denied the public its right to know. Circumstances called out, through the media boom of the early years of the century, for a credible regulatory authority, committed to the public interest, to revisit the issue of advertisement and subscription revenue. But that never happened. And even the late spurt of interest by TRAI in 2012 and afterwards, was always destined to flounder.

The shape of Indian democracy has to an extent been determined by the strata that have entered the terrain of active political contestation in increasing numbers since the turn of the century. Its future will be moulded by the new voices that will resound in the political battlegrounds over the third and following decades of the millennium. In its present shape, the Indian media is equipped neither to give voice to these aspirations, nor to render the polyphony of emerging social classes into something approaching coherence. With little left by way of a positive contribution to the public discourse, the Indian media as an institution, could well be rapidly receding in terms of social relevance. That does not mean, of course, that its prospects for earning a profit are much the worse.

Internet traffic: commodity or public utility?

Early in February 2016, the Telecommunications Regulatory Authority of India (TRAI) formally ordered an end to any kind of "discriminatory pricing" of data services over the internet. Stated in bare essentials, this order would not challenge an ordinary grasp of principle,

97 The weekly newsmagazine *India Today*, part of a business group that includes two news channels – Aaj Tak in Hindi and Headlines Today in English – in 2013 ran a cover story that was rather evocatively titled "Tamasha News". The subtitle read: "Sensational, Shocking, Pervasive, Trivial". But in a one-line summation of the purport of its story, the newsmagazine refrained from exercising its judgment on the merits of the phenomenon, perhaps because it could not be seen in public to be engaged in an act of self-condemnation. "Intense competition has compelled news channels to feed the voyeuristic appetite of today's viewers", it said, "for better or worse".

since discrimination is a prohibited practice in any lawful order. From another perspective though, it would seem curious for the opposite reason, since differential pricing of network services is usually a price that beneficiaries have to bear, either as social obligation or as a means of ensuring comprehensive connectivity and network integrity.

Internet governance, long the subject of global debates, moved up a notch in public attention early in 2014, when service providers in the U.S. began talking about a "two speed internet", with one channel reserved for carriage of high-priced content. Internet was then classified as an "information service" and a Federal Appeals Court held that though the FCC had the authority to enact anti-discrimination rules, it was prohibited from doing so for an "information service" under the relevant law.[98] A four-month long public consultation followed when the FCC committed itself to take on board all relevant opinions on the matter.[99]

In February 2015, the FCC reclassified the internet as a telecommunications service while issuing a ruling summed up in three explicit prohibitions: "no blocking, no throttling and no paid prioritisation". Legitimate content could be transacted through the internet without impediment from the service provider, who would in turn not differentiate between traffic on the basis of content or origin. Service providers could not favour one type of content over another, either in charge levied for each unit of information, or for the speed of transportation.[100]

Protests followed about a violation of the free speech right as embedded in the First Amendment to the U.S. Constitution.[101] A particularly interesting critique came from the former head of one of FCC's bureaus, who held the rationale of the ruling inapplicable in internet governance. Under Title II of the U.S. Communications Act of 1934, telephone services were classified as a "common carrier" obliged to follow rules a broadcast station was exempt from. This distinction be-

98 Much of this detail is available in the ruling by the U.S. Court of Appeal (2016).

99 *PC World* (2014).

100 FCC (2015).

101 *Wired* (2015). The matter was since heard in appeal by a US Court of Appeal (2016), which upheld the FCC ruling on net neutrality.

tween "systems that disseminate information to the masses" and those that "provide private point-to-point communications between individuals" was well established in U.S. law. While the latter was subject to the access and transparency norms prescribed under the "common carrier" clause, the other could claim First Amendment rights, which included the "ability to exercise gatekeeper control". Broadcasters, newspapers and cable operators had "gatekeeper control over their audiences", and it was a point of law upheld by the Supreme Court, "that these media have a constitutional right to discriminate against the speech of others".[102]

This is a provocative proposition but accurate in its reading of judicial orthodoxy on the First Amendment. Sloppy legal drafting may have been responsible, or possibly there was a specific intent in the wording of this clause, which forbids any law that curtails the freedom of speech and of the press.

"Common carrier" obligations, though inapplicable to the media's commercial operations, are integral to its ethical posture and its claim to a protected place in society. The American Press Institute puts it in its code of conduct in particularly sharp fashion: "The news media are common carriers of public discussions, and this responsibility forms a basis for special privileges that news and information providers receive from democratic societies".[103] These contrary postures on basic identity create a potential for conflict between ethics and commerce which runs very deep in the media industry.

India's debate over net neutrality began with plans by two telecom companies to offer free services. One of these was explicitly premised on websites paying the cost, i.e., it was just about transferring the cost burden from one end of the chain to another. The other worked on the premise that advertising revenue would cover the cost of rendering the special favour of free access.[104] Ironically, the latter plan was dressed up as a special dispensation for those without means, where advertiser interest was likely minimal.

---

102 Campbell (2015).

103 API (nd).

104 *Hindustan Times* (2015).

Public petitions led TRAI to decree a temporary halt on these plans, following which a broader and more measured process of deliberation was instituted. A consultation paper was issued late in 2015, inviting comments on the proposal to create two strata within the internet.[105] In ruling on the matter, the regulatory body took on board submissions on both the positive and negative consequences of differential pricing. The positives were relatively easy to identify.[106] Free service would make "overall internet access more affordable ... (and) allow people with no access to gain entry to least a part of it". But then, it would result in the "classification of customers based on the content they want to access". Price differentiation would end the internet as "a neutral end-to-end carrier of information", investing service providers with gate-keeping powers. This would "restrict consumer choice" and work against "free speech and media pluralism".

Because of the "unique architecture of the internet as a global communication network", TRAI was disinclined to accept the plea that differential pricing was a "recognised" practice "across utilities". In traditional markets, including public utility services, there were "for the most part, distinct producers and consumers". But on the internet, users were also consumers. Allowing a service provider which was "at one edge of the internet to charge differentially for data that it does not alone process, could compromise the entire architecture". It would also result in the hazard of "allowing service providers to define the nature of access (which) would be equivalent of letting (them) shape the users' internet experience".

Citizen sovereignty is one definition of democracy, the principle that every individual should have the freedom to determine terms of engagement with the civic order. In a neoliberal order, the citizen seeking optimal civic engagement is supplanted by the alternate construct of a consumer seeking maximum utility. Every consumer's utility can be measured on a common ordinal scale and is determined in part by price. Citizen meets vendor in the marketplace of ideas. A social optimum emerges from this meeting of producer and consumer in a milieu of free competition and unhindered choice.

105 TRAI (2015).

106 TRAI (2016).

There is a complexity in the information domain that arises from the differentiated character of the commodity being transacted. In addition to price, there are factors, mostly intangible, such as relevance and quality of information. Advertising moreover, is a factor that exerts tremendous influence while pretending to be in the background, irrelevant to the quality of the media discourse. That is a myth that deserves to be confronted in its deepest lair and dealt with.

Advertising

Transparency as a virtue admired at a distance

As an industry that trades in information as a commodity, the media caters to a defined audience and broadly transacts in two categories: news and advertisements. The two are different in that claims of factuality and veracity are imbedded in one; while for the other, "truth value" is not an essential attribute. If at all, "truth" is an end to be served only on a collateral basis, since the primary objective of the information transaction is to induce a commercial decision.

Advertising has been among the most loosely monitored areas of global business. Yet it is of sufficient consequence in an average life to have gained the title of "the hidden persuader", the unseen accessory of corporate power which works its influence subtly on the mind of the consumer. Vance Packard, the U.S. journalist and social commentator who coined that phrase in a classic 1957 book, soon found himself demonised by the ad industry, which dismissed his work as an effort born in deliberate malice, to destroy the choices advertising opened up before the average consumer.[1]

Early pronouncements from relevant judicial forums seemed to classify advertising as "commercial speech" which would not warrant a

---

1 Crispin Miller (2007: 22), who recapitulates this sequence of events in a re-issue of the book. A typical rejoinder from the ad industry read as follows: "Paranoids like Vance Packard, author of *The Hidden Persuaders*, have made fortunes peddling the fiction that advertising is some arcane force that causes you to act against your will. It is hogwash".

strong measure of protection since it came lower in the scale of values. But subsequent rulings, not to mention the brute realities of a commercially organised media, effaced these subtleties. Advertising was soon a powerful driver of media content.

In his foreword to a golden jubilee edition of Packard's book, Mark Crispin Miller noted with a degree of understandable hyperbole: "The history of America since the Civil War is, in large part, a history of conquest by commercial advertising... the history of an ever-rising flood of corporate propaganda – and also of our various responses to it, as We the People have obscurely struggled to reverse it, or resist it, or to live our lives in spite of it, or have simply let it carry us away".[2]

U.S. jurisprudence zealously guards the right to free speech and has evolved among the most libertarian doctrines in protecting advertising speech. Early rulings held that constitutional protections would apply only to the informational content of advertising speech and only collaterally to the commercial motive. The most relevant statement of the grounds on which advertising speech could be controlled were laid down in a matter involving an advertisement placed by Central Hudson, an electricity utility, promoting energy consumption as an unrestrained lifestyle choice. In a context of fuel shortage in 1973, the electricity regulator held that utility advertising was contrary to public interest, since the energy company did not have sufficient supplies to meet a possible spurt in demand. Even with the easing of the fuel crisis in 1976, the regulator insisted that the advertising ban should stay in place, since promotional advertising was different from informational advertising which advised on appropriate patterns of energy use.

An appeals court held that the governmental interest in energy conservation trumped the advertiser's freedom to promote electricity use. This was reversed by the Supreme Court of the U.S. (SCOTUS) which set out a four-part test to determine how far advertising would be covered by constitutional provisions on free speech. First Amendment protection would be extended to commercial speech if it concerns "lawful activity and was not "misleading". Curbs could be imposed to advance a "substantial" governmental interest, but should be no more "extensive than is necessary to serve that interest".[3] The ban

2 Ibid.

3 SCOTUS (1980).

on electric utility advertising, the court held, cleared all steps except the last. The regulator had failed to demonstrate that its interest would not be served by less sweeping restraints. The prohibition decreed, moreover, risked unreasonably restricting advertisements that served a public information function.

One of Packard's major concerns was the manner that from about the 1956 presidential election in the U.S., democratic choice was manipulated by carefully constructed advertising images. Packard was unimpressed by this manner of advertising, premised upon the "depth approach" which mined deep into the human psyche to exploit its deepest vulnerabilities. In the years that followed, the power of the media to determine electoral outcomes rapidly increased, often with organised corporate power driving choices through advertising.

The Federal Election Campaign Act of 1971 sought to regulate the intrusion of money power into the election process, demanding disclosure of all campaign contributions and in 1974, limiting these. This left a window open for unregulated or "soft money" flowing into advertising that promoted a candidate or knocked down a rival. The abuses of this loophole became sufficiently corrosive of electoral integrity, for the U.S. Congress in 2002 to introduce amendments banning the use of the ample treasuries of U.S. corporations in election advertising, within a defined interval prior to the polling date.

Advertising gains parity

This narrow restriction, clearly defined in place and time, was in a January 2010 SCOTUS decision, held to fall foul of constitutional provisions on free speech. Of the nine-member bench, five signed up for what came to be the opinion of the court that "political speech cannot be limited based on a speaker's wealth". This indeed, as recorded by Anthony Kennedy for the majority in a deeply divided court, was a "necessary consequence of the premise that the First Amendment generally prohibits the suppression of political speech based on the speaker's identity". The limitation on corporate-speak through paid advertisements in close proximity to elections, had in a less enlightened past, been upheld on the grounds that "corporate funds may have little or no correlation to the public's support for the corporation's political ideas". But this was, in terms of the First Amendment assurance, "irrelevant", since "all speakers, including individuals and the media, use money amassed from the economic marketplace to fund their speech". The "anti-distortion" rationale – that money power should not overwhelm democratic choice – had often been advanced to justify restraints on corporate advertising at a time and place close to an election. This reasoning, the majority on the court held, could potentially lead to the dangerous conclusion that laws could be imposed that "ban political speech of *media corporations*".[4]

The SCOTUS majority stepped into contentious ground here, also unwittingly betraying serious confusion over any supposed right the corporate media may claim on behalf of the public. "Media corporations", as Kennedy wrote for the majority, were exempt from the "ban on corporate expenditures". Yet media corporations "accumulate wealth with the help of the corporate form, the largest media corporations have immense aggregations of wealth, and the views expressed by media corporations often have little or no correlation to the public's support for those views ... Thus under the Government's reasoning, wealthy media corporations could have their voices diminished to put them on par with other media entities". There was, said Kennedy, "no precedent for permitting this under the First Amendment".[5]

In a concurring opinion, Chief Justice John Roberts played a variation on the theme of imminent danger to the news media. The chief justice chose a broad reading of the prohibition on advertising in the near vicinity of electoral contests, as a suppression of corporate free speech. And after inflating the nature and magnitude of the restrictions, Roberts warned ominously of grave consequences: "The Government ... asks us to embrace a theory of the First Amendment that *would allow censorship not only of television and radio broadcasts, but of pamphlets, posters, the Internet, and virtually any other medium that corporations and unions might find useful in expressing their views on matters of public concern*. Its theory, if accepted, would empower the Government to *prohibit newspapers from running editorials or opinion pieces supporting or opposing candidates for office, so long as the*

4 SCOTUS (2010): Opinion of Justice Anthony Kennedy: 35. (Here and in all following citations of the judgments emerging from this litigation, internal quotation marks are omitted, capitalisation is as in original, and emphases unless otherwise mentioned, are added.)

5 Ibid: 35-6.

newspapers were owned by corporations—as the major ones are. First Amendment rights could be confined to individuals, subverting the vibrant public discourse that is at the foundation of our democracy". The problem as Roberts read it, was that the prohibition on corporate speak potentially recognised no frontiers and could seamlessly and insidiously, extend to the news media.[6]

Justice Antonin Scalia, who joined the majority of five in pronouncing the opinion of the court, separately explored how a corporate entity would fit into a constitutional assurance of the free speech right to individuals and their associations. Press freedom Scalia argued, was "widely understood to protect the publishing activities of individual editors and printers". These individuals often acted through newspapers, which were very much like corporations in that they "had their own names, outlived the individuals who had founded them, could be bought and sold, were sometimes owned by more than one person, and were operated for profit." A principle that applied unequivocally to the media corporation could not be held inapplicable for another corporate entity that had the same legal form.[7]

Writing a dissenting opinion that three other judges signed, Justice John Paul Stevens described the "conceit" that corporations merited the same rights as "natural persons" as "not only inaccurate but also inadequate to justify" the majority decision. Within the context of democratic elections, there existed a significant distinction between corporations and individuals. Though a part of contemporary reality, corporations are not actually members of society as conventionally understood.[8] These distinctions had been recognised and honoured in a number of cases decided by SCOTUS over the years, and in shedding this weight of precedent on the grounds that it was an "invidious novelty", the court was rejecting "a century of history". In a ninety-page ruling where the word "nonsense" appears twice, Stevens denounced the opinion of the court as a threat to "the integrity of elected institutions across the Nation."[9] And in arriving at its findings, the SCOTUS majority had consistently overstated the nature of the restrictions –

6 Ibid: judgment of Chief Justice John Roberts: 1 and 11.

7 Ibid: judgment of Justice Antonin Scalia: 6.

8 Ibid: judgment by Justice J.P. Stevens: 2.

9 Ibid: 5-6.

"time, place and manner" specific – to make them sound like a complete suppression of corporate free speech.

Within this strongly-worded dissent, Stevens critiqued the heavy reliance the court placed on the example of media corporations. It was "not at all clear" that the law as it existed would permit any manner of restriction here. "The press plays a unique role not only in the text, history, and structure of the First Amendment but also in facilitating public discourse", said Stevens. These had been recognised by SCOTUS in a ruling which underlined the difference: "media corporations differ significantly from other corporations in that their resources are devoted to the collection of information and its dissemination to the public." Yet with all this, Stevens was prepared to concede that the majority in the Citizens United case had raised "interesting and difficult questions about Congress' authority to regulate electioneering by the press, and about how to define what constitutes the press." Though not devoid of merit, the court was not required to address these questions.[10]

Among others, the importation of the news media into the argument over corporate free speech, a dodgy manoeuvre that the dissenting judges failed to frontally and substantively defeat, obliterated certain basic distinctions: between news, editorial, and advertisement. Part of the rationale for the news media being accorded a greater measure of constitutional protection than other corporations – which are indistinguishable in most systems of law – is its claim to disseminating information that bears the attribute of factual veracity. Editorials likewise, are both a contribution to the public discourse and a reflection of its temper. Advertising, especially in a matter of public and political consequence such as elections, represents a more narrow interest – of corporate directors operating often without the sanction of shareholders – to achieve a desired outcome. In this departure from the current of public opinion, political advertising by corporations could be restrained in the near vicinity of the polling date, to promote the free and fair exercise of the franchise. By failing to challenge the spurious rationale of the majority judgment, which saw the restraints on political advertising as precursor to a muzzling of the news media, the minority of dissenting judges rendered unwitting homage to the reality of corporations increasingly dictating political terms of engagement.

10 Ibid: 84-5.

The power of lucre

In the real world, it is not principle that determines media conduct, but the sheer power of lucre. Illustrations of this principle abound but none perhaps speaks louder than the wilful suppression of news about the potentially fatal consequences of tobacco use.[11] In 1953, the American Medical Association, following the discovery of the link between tobacco use and cancer, imposed a ban on tobacco advertisements in its journals. That year, a study of the *New York Times* index revealed 248 entries under "cancer", "tobacco" and "smoking". Only 8 percent of these mentioned anything about a linkage between the three and three-quarters of them dealt with tobacco industry denials of any linkage. The following year, of 302 entries in the *New York Times* index, only 20 percent dealt with the medical evidence while 32 percent were about industry denials.

From a print media survey as late as the 1980s, the American Cancer Society found fewer stories about cancer causes than flu, polio and tuberculosis. In 1978, both *Time* and *Newsweek* in the fervour of their competition, ran stories on cancer within a week of each other. In a six-page cover story, *Newsweek* let it drop with extreme discretion on page three, that tobacco is the "least disputed carcinogen". The following week, *Time* had a two-column story in which it mentioned very casually that "smoking and drinking alcohol have been linked to cancer". *Time* a few weeks later, carried an essay which stated its libertarian position that smokers should mobilise to push back legislation against tobacco. Stripped of scientific and medical evidence, the issue was posed quite plainly as upholding freedom of choice.

In the neo-liberal age, which could be dated to the demise of the Soviet Union in 1991, pressures on journalism from corporate advertising became explicit. In 1997, Fox News fired Steve Wilson and Jane Akre, two investigative journalists reporting from the U.S. state of Florida, after they declined a cash settlement to withdraw a story on serial violations of law by the biotechnology giant Monsanto. This was after the manager of the station where the two reporters worked, was summarily dismissed and replaced by an executive from Rupert Murdoch's News Corporation, which then and till this time, owns Fox News and all affiliates. The two journalists were told that Fox had paid

11 The following narrative is derived from Bagdikian (2004): 250-6.

three billion dollars for the stations, which invested them with the right to determine what the news is: "The news is what we say it is". The story was then rewritten about eighty times, without quite meeting the standard set by the new management.[12]

In litigation that followed, Wilson and Akre won in 2000, with a jury awarding them compensation under whistle-blower law. In 2003, this limited victory was reversed, with the broadcast station successfully arguing that the FCC policy on news distortion was not a "law, rule or regulation" and was as such, exempt from whistle-blower protection. In 2007, the FCC itself turned down Wilson and Akre's final challenge. The issue it held, related to an "editorial dispute ... rather than a deliberate effort ... to distort news".[13]

Since early days of neo-liberalism, when journalism began to be troubled by the growing intimacy of the cohabitation of the media with advertising, the new media has emerged to overturn several premises of the older revenue calculus. The response of traditional media has been to seek closer integration with the ad world, accelerating a trend towards devaluing journalism. In 1997, media analyst Russ Baker took note of the "worsening chemistry" between advertisement and editorial: "Corporations and their ad agencies have clearly turned up the heat on editors and publishers ... and some magazines are capitulating, unwilling to risk even a single ad.[14]

Advertiser motivations were clear. Products made for highly refined tastes, with virtues embellished through advertising, would be diminished when placed in an "editorial context" that referred to an underside where poverty and deprivation were rampant. An easily available illustration:"Colgate-Palmolive ... won't allow ads in a 'media context' containing 'offensive' sexual content or material it deems 'anti-social or in bad taste' - which it leaves undefined in its policy statement sent to magazines. (T)he company (has said) that it 'charges its advertising agencies and their media buying services with the responsibility of pre-screening any questionable media content or context'."

12 Andersen (2000): 12.

13 For a summary of the litigative process, see citation of the Goldman Environmental Prize, which was awarded to Steve Wilson and Jane Akre in 2001. Goldman (2001).

14 Baker (1997).

In January 1996, Chrysler Corporation, at the time fifth largest advertiser in the U.S., sent out a letter to all major media outlets – peremptory in tone – demanding that a responsible person from the editorial side sign and return it without delay as a gesture of compliance. The letter explained that "to avoid potential conflicts", the corporation was to be "alerted in advance of any and all editorial content that encompasses sexual, political, social issues or any editorial that might be construed as provocative or offensive". Every media outlet that carried Chrysler advertising would need to file with the company's ad agency, a "written summary outlining major themes/articles appearing in upcoming issues". These summaries were to be filed sufficiently prior to printing deadlines, "in order to give Chrysler ample time to review and reschedule if desired".

The American Society of Newspaper Editors responded immediately with a call for resistance. Renowned graphic designer Milton Glaser, responsible for several features of modern newspaper layout, made his dissent clear. It was always a prerogative of the advertiser to choose the right "editorial environment" in which to display his material: "but preemptive withdrawal is a new and repellent development. Censorship of this kind that acts to curtail the exchange of unpopular ideas is unacceptable for all those who care about human freedom and a healthy democratic society". When Chrysler responded with an elaborate affectation of surprise since it was in its own perception, only making a rather poorly kept secret public, Glaser noted with some asperity: "after the triumph of capitalism, American business is embracing the politburo practice (sic) of censoring ideas it deems unacceptable".[15]

Neoliberalism brought a subtle change in style from the celebrated Mobil editorials that Ben Bagdikian, the dean of critical journalism studies in the U.S., drew attention to in the first edition of his landmark book. The giant oil corporation's editorialising took the shape of philosophical reflections on contemporary political events that would typically occupy a whole page in the country's main newspapers. This was in the 1960s and 70s, when Mobil was a corporation easily portrayed to the average U.S. citizen as an embodiment of national might and prestige. Mobil could take on the entire media and win, even on its own strength and well before it merged with another descendant of the oil monopoly that John D. Rockefeller created in the early 20th century to

15 Andersen (2000): 8-9.

become Exxon Mobil Corporation, a synonym for environmental depredation and political repression in all countries where it has extractive interests. In placing its full-page editorial-ads in most U.S. newspapers that mattered, Mobil worked with the absolute conviction that its social prestige could be leveraged into a significant degree of influence over public opinion.[16] These attempts to mould the public mind were also premised on tacit knowledge of the persuasive power of the full page ads, of its cash value being sufficient deterrent against an editorial policy contrary to the corporate worldview.

In the 1990s, corporations in the U.S. began to step far beyond unstated pacts, demanding explicit commitments of compliance with their larger agendas. And simply because the media was not keen on risking its image in a major public dissection of its profit calculus, these changes in the ad-edit relationship escaped serious contemporary critique. In her 2000 book, *No Logo*, Naomi Klein reviewed the rapid convergence between media content and advertising, a feature of the tumultuous decade that had passed. The trends were bleak, but by no means all doom and gloom. "Advertisers don't always get their way", she observed: "Controversial stories make it to print and to air, even ones critical of major advertisers. At its most daring, the news media could provide workable models for the protection of the public interest even under heavy corporate pressure, though these battles are often won behind closed doors. On the other hand, at their worst, these same media show how deeply distorting the effects of branding can be on our public discourse – particularly since journalism, like every other part of our culture, is under constantly increasing pressure to merge with the brands".[17]

India: a partial freedom now absolute

In a media environment where commerce is the predominant motive, brute realities ensure that advertising will force its way through a half-open door, to claim full free speech entitlements. The legal position in India is that advertising is not covered by free speech guarantees: a determination made as far back as 1959 by the Supreme Court in the

16 Bagdikian (2004): 168ff. For the influence exerted by the tobacco lobby, pp. 250ff.

17 Klein (2001): 39-40.

matter of *Hamdard Dawakhana*, involving a challenge to a law enabling the prohibition of certain varieties of advertising (in this instance, one that promised magic cures and encouraged self-medication).

Summing up its findings, the Supreme Court bench held that when speech (or printed matter), "takes the form of a commercial advertisement which has an element of trade or commerce it no longer falls within the concept of freedom of speech". This was for the simple reason that "the object is not propagation of ideas - social, political or economic or furtherance of literature or human thought". As in the case under consideration, the matter could be about "the commendation of the efficacy, value and importance in treatment of particular diseases by certain drugs and medicines". In such cases, "advertisement is a part of business..... and (has) no relationship with what may be called the essential concept of the freedom of speech".[18]

It is worthwhile assessing this finding of the Supreme Court which presumably, is the definitive statement on the issue of advertising as free speech, against the declaration by the Vice-Chairman of Bennett Coleman and Company Ltd (BCCL) India's largest media group – with interests in print, television, radio and much else – that he sees himself as a player in the advertising industry, rather than news.[19] Clearly, this is a group that has put itself beyond the pale of the constitutional protection for free speech available under article 19 of the Indian Constitution.

A particularly egregious example of advertising taking over the journalistic function in the Indian context is related to media coverage of the experience with the genetically modified Bt cotton in certain parts of the Vidarbha region of Maharashtra state.[20] In October 2008, the *Times of India* (*TOI*) ran a half-page story on the massive benefits that Bt cotton had brought to farmers in certain villages of Vidarbha. There were no suicides any more among distressed farmers: Bt Cotton had changed all that. Close to three years later, in August 2011, the *TOI* carried a story identical in every respect, down to the punctuation marks. The only difference was that in a discrete corner of the page, the

18 Supreme Court of India (1959).

19 Auletta (2012): 55. The exact quote reads as follows: "We are not in the newspaper business, we are in the advertising business".

20 Sainath (2012).

supposed news report was identified as a "customer connect initiative", or paid advertisement. "There are no suicides" in the villages of Bhambraja and Antargaon of Vidarbha any more, the ad masquerading as a news report proclaimed. "The switchover from the conventional cotton to Bollgard or Bt Cotton here has led to a social and economic transformation in the villages in the past three-four years."

The *TOI* would have known if it had checked facts, that there had been fourteen suicides in the two villages, for the most part since Bt cotton entered into cultivation practices. This indeed was the testimony rendered by the villagers to a visiting delegation from the Parliamentary Standing Committee on Agriculture just five months before, in March 2011. *The Hindu* had verified nine cases of farmer suicides, perhaps occasioned by the failure of the Bt cotton crop, between 2003 and 2009. Five more it estimated, came in the months since then, corroborated by field level inquiries by activist groups.

The *TOI* was not merely being inattentive or sloppy with fact-checking. Over the week that followed its advertisement disguised as a story in August 2011, the *TOI* carried no fewer than five half-page advertisements by Mahyco-Monsanto Biotech Ltd., a joint venture between a Maharashtra based seed company and the global biotechnology giant Monsanto, proclaiming the benefits of Bt cotton. To be sure, the *TOI* was not the only beneficiary of this intensive ad blitz. Parliament was then in session and Monsanto and its Indian joint venture were anxious to see legislation enabling a comprehensive new framework for genetically modified organisms in agriculture. In the event, the legislation was not tabled because Parliament was preoccupied with other matters. The relevant point is simply that the largest and most successful newspaper group in the country showed little hesitation in shedding ordinary journalistic scruple to lend the corporate advertiser a helping hand, taking the public discourse on a matter involving the social impact of an emerging new technology, seriously off track.

The emergence of the ad industry behemoths

Advertising has always been the lifeblood of the news media. And yet, in the decades since capitalism declared itself triumphant over all opposition – and emerged in its newest *avatar* as neo-liberalism – there has been an unsubtle change in the equations between news media and the ad industry. Concentration of capital and ownership has been a feature of both, though there is an appearance of enormous diversification of sources and choice for the media consumer. Even where they have not been integrated into the same chain of capital and ownership, the news media and the ad industry have achieved a mutual harmony of interests, most often with the former willingly complying with the most unreasonable demands placed on it.

It may be the best of times or the worst of times. The health of the corporate balance sheet may vary but not the profit obsession. And irrespective of the temper of the times, reliable old pursuits such as mergers and acquisitions can be counted on as entertainment sport. At the end of July 2013, two giant conglomerates in the advertising business – one headquartered in Paris and the other in New York – announced a merger that would swamp cross-Atlantic linguistic and cultural dissonances in the sheer power of lucre. Groupe Publicis of Paris and Omnicom of New York were both creations of the furious wave of consolidation that began in the advertising world – indeed, in the entire global business scenario – in the 1980s. By the dawn of the new millennium, equilibrium of sorts had been achieved, with half the world's advertising agencies being under one or the other of four giant transnational umbrellas: WPP of the U.K., Groupe Publicis of France and Omnicom and Interpublic, both of the U.S.[21] Apart from the clout that came with the most prestigious corporate brands being their clients, the "big four" also consolidated their power over the media through strategic acquisitions across a spectrum of related businesses: notably market research and audience measurement. The media industry, which is quick to react to any possible threat to its autonomy – real and imagined – had surprisingly little to say about the implications of growing concentration in advertising, a business which holds the ultimate key to its own commercial viability.

The proposed merger on equal terms of Omnicom and Publicis paid equal homage to both the names it inherited. And in a studied attempt at neutrality, the new entity determined that its global headquarters would be in the Netherlands, cutting itself free of older geographic moorings. By combining their business accounts, Publicis and Omnicom sought to bring within their grasp a dominant share of advertising expenditure in the U.S. and a more than ample share across

21 Andersen and Grey, editors (2008): 64.

the globe.[22] But Publicis-Omnicom stirred up size envies just when competitive equations seemed settling into a stable four-way oligopoly (with a few small but significant players making up the peripheral cast). It was seen as the possible precursor to further rounds of furious consolidation in the ad industry. And entities that had been relatively quiet and stayed outside the main theatres of action – such as the Japanese conglomerate Dentsu – were seen as likely leaders in future rounds of business agglomeration.

The newly minted ad industry behemoth was expected to have a tough job of persuasion on its hands, since giant corporations that spent lavishly on self-promotion – CocaCola and Pepsico, Apple and Samsung, so-called "power brands" built up in equal parts through puffery and the denigration of rivals – were unlikely to be comfortable when their ample budgets for advertising being poured into a corporation that while pandering to their vanity would also be rendering similar services to their main competitors.

Conflicts of interests tnough, were the least of the anticipated problems, since the ad industry had long since airbrushed those possibilities out. Through their massive consolidation spree, agencies managed to appease client anxieties by erecting "firewalls" that completely segregated competing accounts. The Publicis-Omnicom merger was estimated to be valued at US$ 35 billion in combined share market value. On combined revenue of US$ 22.7 billion, arrived at by aggregating two separate accounts, the total "synergy" anticipated from the merger – or the savings achieved through pooling resources that would otherwise be deployed in repetitive tasks – was about US$ 500 million, i.e., just over 2 per cent.

A question cropped up in minds schooled in the grand tradition of *laissez faire* economics: was it really worthwhile having this manner of corporate agglomeration for a measly 2 percent gain in profit margin, when the preservation of competition and consumer choice was ostensibly the singular justification of free enterprise systems? In the practical realm at least, this question was rendered superfluous since corporate concentration in all domains of industry and business became the pace-setter of capitalist development in the years since the 1980s.

---

22 The *Guardian* (2013).

At a time of rising livelihood anxiety, the authors of the new cross-Atlantic alliance were keen to dispel any impression that "synergies" would be sought through job cuts. The merger's main objective, they explained, was to meet the challenge posed by the mass migration of advertising to the digital world. Traditional media were bleeding from the technical creativity of new media natives such as Google and Facebook. And the ad agency's function of brokering the best deal between the advertiser and the media platform that reached the audience of interest, was being severely challenged by user profiling algorithms that the main players in social media were continually developing to achieve near-perfect audience targeting. The large-scale and aggregative methods of audience measurement and identification used by old media really seemed no match for the precision that Google and Facebook could achieve, merely through logging every mouse click.

There were sceptics at the very outset, one of them being Martin Sorrell, the chief executive of WPP, which notionally lost its status as the world's biggest ad conglomerate when Publicis and Omnicom announced their intended merger. The merger he said, while on his first visit to India in September 2013, "does not make any sense at all". The two companies, Publicis and Omnicom, were "going in opposite directions" prior to the merger announcement and continued doing so since. In "structural" terms, the entity emerging out of the merger would prove extremely "clunky", with its proposal to have two chief executives and rotating chairpersons. Deciding every issue through a jointly constituted "committee" would prove unwieldy. The advantages of large scale applied in the business of media buying and he personally was not worried, since in the three or four years that the Publicis Omnicom venture would take to get things sorted out, WPP would have forged far ahead.[23]

Sorrell evidently knew what he was talking about. In less than a year of seeking to negotiate the pre-nuptial agreement, the alliance was called off following irreconcilable differences over who should hold the reins in the new entity.[24] Colliding corporate cultures made the merger an ill-advised alliance. For the rival WPP ad consortium, it was an occasion for celebration. As Sorrell put it, the deal was born in dubi-

---

23 *Economic Times* (2013).

24 BBC (2014).

ous circumstances, in compulsions of the "ego" and an "emotional desire to knock WPP off its perch".[25] There was little question moreover, that the more difficult global economic environment, when ad agency fortunes were under pressure on multiple fronts, had made agreement on the terms of merger elusive.

Through two decades of "globalisation" – a policy commitment that could be dated with some precision to 1991 – India also saw the transformation of media platforms into brands. It is a process that has been analysed from two ends of the spectrum: the corporations that drive the transformation of content and the journalistic practices that are the recipients of often unwelcome attentions. Once seen as a passive intermediary that would be content with a small sliver out of the ad monies that corporations pour into the media, the advertising industry under neo-liberalism acquired agenda-setting functions that could potentially make or break media fortunes. There was a longish time when the going was good and the collusive arrangement between the larger media houses and the ad giants held up without serious strain. It seemingly mattered not that the ad giants were also beginning to dominate the market research function, from where the numbers on the size and demographic composition of various media audiences were expected to emerge. The conflict of interests was obvious, since the ad agencies were main users of the data generated by members of their extended families.

A pact of silence

Truth-telling is the function the media ostensibly performs for the wider social constituency. But there are larger and lesser truths and some that are qualified, integrally connected to particular ways of seeing. Since recasting itself as an industry organised purely in accordance with the profit principle, the media has shown a certain discomfort with the "fourth estate" role that historical circumstances cast it in. It also developed a marked aversion to speak the truth about itself.

A rare breach in the pact of silence occurred in March 2013, though the truths uttered were by no means esoteric or abstruse. The occasion was an annual conclave on the media hosted in Delhi by the Federation of Indian Chambers of Commerce and Industry (FICCI)

---

25 *Wall Street Journal* (2014).

– where the most influential members in the business community assemble to make their collective voice heard. And it was by then, common knowledge that the media industry in India like elsewhere, was facing a serious crisis of viability. Uday Shankar, chief executive of the Rupert Murdoch owned Star TV network in India, chose to look at a different part of the canvas. India's media industry, he said in words that deserve to be carefully parsed, faced a massive deficit of reliable data. For a business leader, finding a pathway out of troubles involved a degree of reliance on data. And Uday Shankar in this respect, faced a deeply disturbing scenario: "Numbers are supposed to be the foundations of rational business decisions but how can we make decisions when professionals in the business of numbers can't get their numbers straight? … As a TV executive, I am surprised sometimes how I am even able to function. I do not know enough about my viewers – in fact I don't even know how many of them are there. There are 140 million cable and satellite homes but the measured universe is 62 million households. The country's premier media agencies can't even seem to agree on a fact as basic as the size of the advertising market".[26]

These utterances carry layers of meaning and also offer a rather rueful retrospect on two decades when the media seemed intent on expansion beyond inherent economic limits. The industry had additional reason for worry in that the dip in its fortunes had been accompanied by an upturn in government attentions and fresh intent to remedy its unregulated, virtually anarchic state. These unwelcome attentions could have been easily repulsed if the media industry had been true to its ethos of self-regulation in times of plenty. But in the roaring 1990s and the still more boisterous decade that followed, there seemed no need to attend to this task with any urgency. Assembling a reliable data-base was considered superfluous, since the moment promised infinitely expanding frontiers of growth.

Through the years of boom, the revenue model of the industry was seen – despite layers of opacity – to be shifting towards an increasingly audience unfriendly mould, all too willing to not just accommodate, but actively pander to the advertiser. Viewer subscriptions had a large share – roughly 67.5 per cent – of total revenue of the C&S television

---

26 *Indian Television* (2013d).

industry.[27] But the bulk of this money was retained by cable operators performing the last-mile function of delivering the signal to subscriber premises. Estimates of the total subscription value cornered by cable operators varied from 80 per cent[28] to 91 per cent[29]. Either way, the share they claimed, sheltering behind the virtual impossibility of an audit, was regarded as inimical to quality and diversity in television content.

A transition to "digitally addressable systems" (DAS), which would enable greater clarity in assessing viewership data, was the recommended remedy. This rather self-evident cure was kept at bay literally from the time it was first proposed, by the cable operators' lobby, which numbered in tens of thousands and had considerable heft in local politics. At the end of its tether by 2011, the Union Cabinet made DAS the statutory norm, though one to be enforced in stages.[30] All subscribers in the country's four largest metropolitan cities would be required to switch over by the end of June 2012. An ensuing phase of frenetic lobbying by the cable operators ensured that the deadline was extended to end-October.[31] Public indulgence for the cable operators was also beginning to wane by then. In April 2013, a second phase of digitisation began, covering another thirty-six cities.[32]

Recessionary trends

Digitisation fell well short of the saviour's role it was cast in. Broadcasters were not organised to start harvesting subscriptions. And the extra revenue that began trickling in could not quite remedy the ill-effects of the anaemic rate of growth in advertising spending. Predictably, the government came up with its stock prescription of infusing another dose of foreign direct investment (FDI) into the stricken industry. Its proposals on the media were one element in a broader policy initiative to snap the economy out of a spell of gloom and retrieve the Indian

27 Open Society Foundations (2012): 105ff.

28 Ibid: 108.

29 Mehta (2008): 173.

30 Reuters (2011).

31 Press Trust of India (2012).

32 Indian Television (2013c).

rupee from the swoon it had descended into. At the end of June 2013, the Department of Industrial Policy and Promotion (DIPP) in India's Union Government circulated proposals for raising the FDI ceiling applicable in various sectors, specifically limiting permissible foreign equity in print and other news media, to 49 per cent of paid up capital, up from the prevalent ceiling of 25 per cent.[33]

The proposal entered the public policy dialogue with little discord, strange in itself considering the agonising and exaggerated nationalist posturing that preceded the lifting in 2002 of the prohibition on foreign equity in the print media. Though voices of dissent were muffled, unanimity within the industry proved rather difficult to achieve. The Ministry of Information and Broadcasting (MIB) played coy about committing itself one way or the other since the industry ostensibly was divided. On a reference from the MIB, the broadcast spectrum regulator, the Telecommunications Regulatory Authority of India (TRAI) endorsed the Finance Ministry proposal to raise FDI ceiling in the equity of TV news channels and private radio broadcasters to a relatively liberal 49 per cent.[34] The Union Home Ministry expressed concerns over the security implications since foreign interests could presumably leverage media ownership into an undue influence over domestic politics.[35]

Mid-July 2013, when the Government announced significant measures of liberalisation in FDI policy, the media was left out of the mix. Since with all else remaining the same, national security was the residual basis on which the limits to foreign involvement in various economic sectors was determined, the implication here was quite clearly, that the media industry posed greater security dilemmas than telecom services, mining, insurance and defence equipment, all sectors where the raising of FDI limits was announced with little discord.[36]

This would undoubtedly have flattered the mythology of the media as a distinct entity – where the mind, the imagination and the civic sensibility are involved – where rules applicable in other business

---

33 *Mint* (2013c).

34 *Mint* (2013d).

35 Press Trust of India (2013b).

36 Press Trust of India (2013c).

sectors could not possibly be applied. It proved an image the media industry could not quite live up to. Within days, it was lining up abjectly, asking that all puffed up notions of its importance be discarded. Its hallowed status was simply misplaced, since it was just another business desperately in need of money. Within the broadcast industry, there was just a little indecision: networks with entrenched positions in the English broadcast segment – small in numbers but vastly better off in advertising support than more widely watched Indian-language counterparts – were supportive of the move.[37] But regional networks were unconvinced. And if the newspaper industry seemed initially undecided, its main lobby, the Indian Newspaper Society (INS) had within days – with only two regional newspaper groups from Kerala being in dissent – endorsed the proposal to raise the FDI ceiling to 49 per cent.[38]

Travelling back, for a longer perspective, to the early years of the century, the media was after a phase of fairly rapid growth, then gearing up for another. It was also a time when the industry took what would turn out to be its last stand on the ramparts of nationalism. In January 2001, the Standing Committee of Parliament on Information Technology began hearings on the longstanding policy of proscribing foreign direct investment (FDI) in the print media.[39] Beginning in January 2001, the committee held thirteen sittings at which it heard senior editors and journalists, media professionals and jurists.

A key decision on foreign equity

From around December 2001, with deliberations entering their final phase, the committee began to witness an insistent campaign, associated in particular with newspaper magnate and Bharatiya Janata Party (BJP) MP Narendra Mohan, to permit FDI in the print media to a limit of 26 per cent, subject to management and editorial control being securely in Indian hands. Mohan, who was chairman of the Jagran Prakashan group - one of the most successful media enterprises in the Hindi belt - succeeded to the extent that, when the committee met in February, it had two competing drafts before it. While one draft report

37 *The Hindu* (2013).

38 *Indian Express* (2013).

39 *Frontline* (2002).

reflected Mohan's position, the other firmly upheld the 1955 Union Cabinet resolution reserving the print media exclusively for Indian ownership.

With veteran left parliamentarian Somnath Chatterjee heading the committee, the revisionist position failed to gain great traction. A few procedural manoeuvres by Mohan at a committee meeting in February 2002, proved futile, with the left parties and the Congress firmly backing the 1955 position. The findings of the parliamentary committee though, made little difference to the subsequent course of policy, partly since the ranks of the Indian media industry were by then deeply divided. The Jagran group had for long had allies in the campaign for relaxing FDI norms in the *Indian Express* (*IE*), *India Today* (*IT*) and *Ananda Bazar Patrika* (*ABP*) groups. But this campaign, underway since the early part of the 1990s and deploying the seemingly persuasive argument that the media industry had no reason to hold out against the tide of liberalisation, did not make much headway since it was met by an even more formidable lobby espousing the high nationalist stand: an informal coalition of the country's three most influential English language publishers, the *Times of India* (*TOI*), the *Hindustan Times* (*HT*) and *The Hindu*.

The formidable clout of the big three was buttressed by many of the regional papers, particularly in the southern states, where they were well organised, innovative and financially powerful. To the argument that the print media had no worthwhile reason to resist or stand aside from the wave of liberalisation, this lobby responded with a seemingly powerful counter: the newspaper was a unique cultural product that had a deep influence on the public mood and the political agenda, even more so than the electronic media. To demand that the sector be opened up to foreign investment was to invite alien and potentially corrosive influences into the political process. Maintaining editorial control in Indian hands would be unworkable with the asymmetries of power that would emerge from the entry of a large foreign investor.[40]

By the early-2000s, the alignment of forces within the media industry had begun to shift. The principal switch in the balance was

---

40 For an example see the article by N. Ram (1994), a substantial shareholder in *The Hindu* of Chennai, a former editor-in-chief of all the group's publications, who later assumed the chairmanship of the company board of directors.

effected by *HT*, which had come through distinctly the loser in its home territory in Delhi, from an intense price war against *TOI*.[41] By early-2002, without explicitly acknowledging it, *HT* shifted discreetly to the pro-FDI corner. In June that year, the BJP-led government, reassured that it had sufficient backing to risk angering a powerful section within the newspaper industry, opened up the print media to FDI, to the limit of 26 percent of total equity. Editorial control was to remain in Indian hands and at least three-quarters of all senior positions with influence over news agendas were to necessarily be occupied by Indian nationals.[42]

The newspaper industry was split in its response. The apex industry lobby, the Indian Newspaper Society (INS) reacted with some asperity: the decision, it said, would lead to the death of the small and medium newspapers. Individual news industry groups, such as *Business Standard*, *IE* and *IT*, cheered it as an overdue measure to bring much needed capital and state-of-the-art practices to the country.[43]

HT's apostasy on FDI was complete by 2005, when it came out with an Initial Public Offering (IPO) of shares. Early conviction having evaporated in the heat of competition with *TOI*, foreign entities including Citigroup and the Henderson group, were invited to pick up sizeable chunks of the IPO. Other news industry groups to allow significant equity dilution through foreign investments, were Jagran Prakashan, Midday Multimedia and *Business Standard*. In the satellite TV sector, Asianet Communications, the market leader in Malayalam language broadcasting, attracted a significant equity investment from a Mauritius based enterprise.

Takeover of the ad space

While the newspaper industry was engaged in this series of skirmishes over FDI, a major operational manoeuvre was executed on its flanks, leading in effect to its complete encirclement by foreign interests. Being narrowly focused on the issue of ownership in the industry, the newspaper lobby failed to recognise the signals from a policy move

41 These events which shaped much of the future course of the newspaper industry, are dealt with in greater detail in a following chapter.

42 *Frontline* (2002a).

43 *Frontline* (2002b).

initiated in 2001 with little public debate or discussion, when the doors were opened up for 100 percent foreign investment in the equity of ad agencies and market research firms. At a time when over 65 percent of total newspaper industry revenue came from advertising – and ad placement decisions depended crucially on the results that market research firms turned in – these policy decisions of consequence for media passed without serious opposition, indeed without even a cursory examination in regard to longer-term implications for the print media.

In 2002, N. Bhaskara Rao, a market research professional and media analyst, wrote that the debate on foreign ownership in the media was superfluous, if not entirely futile. The entire public discussion had "quite overlooked the fact that increasingly, the pace and path of the media are being determined by advertising, and is influenced by market research and media planning strategies in which corporate (sic), Indian and foreign, have invested heavily".[44]

While the media and newspaper barons carried out their phony wars over FDI in their narrow turfs, the territory all around was rapidly being colonised by corporate interests, both Indian and foreign. The implications for the Indian media scenario are best illustrated in the career of the advertising conglomerate WPP, which was threatened briefly with losing its global rankings but restored to that position following the collapse of the Omnicom-Publicis deal.[45] WPP started operations in 1985 as Wire and Plastic Products in a business sector rather remote from advertising, manufacturing supermarket shopping trolleys in the U.K. It was a modest operation begun on the side by Martin Sorrell, then a senior executive in Saatchi and Saatchi, the U.K. ad agency that enjoyed a purple patch of growth through the 1980s by parlaying a public relations contract acquired from the British Conservative Party – the dominant political force through the decade – into expanding global influence.

In 1987, WPP created a major flutter in the business world with a takeover of the U.S.-based ad giant, J. Walter Thomson (JWT). Within two years, it had taken over another storied global player, Ogilvy and Mather (O&M). A string of other acquisitions followed.[46] Though

44 Bhaskara Rao (2002): 105.

45 *Mint* (2013e).

46 For the story of WPP's rise, see Sinclair (2012): 35-9.

it was yet to gain absolute control over operations in India because of limitations on foreign equity in the ad industry, WPP had already begun to exert substantial influence through the 1990s over associate companies of JWT and O&M in India, including the Indian Market Research Bureau (IMRB) which was promoted in 1970 by JWT affiliate Hindustan Thomson Associates (HTA).

In 1993, WPP formed the Kantar group within a complex web of holdings across the world, as its market research arm.[47] AC Nielsen, a firm named after the man who brought to market a technique of assessing audience tastes and aptitudes for informing advertising decisions on radio, was by this time acknowledged global leader in audience measurement. In 1996, AC Nielsen passed into the control of a finance conglomerate based in the Netherlands, VNU. In 1998, Kantar teamed up with AC Nielsen, to set up Television Audience Measurement (TAM), with the promise that it would offer a unique combination of skills, invaluable for the rapidly growing Indian broadcasting industry. The main competitor for this system of television audience measurement was INTAM, set up then by a rival market research firm, ORG-Marg.

In 2000, ORG-Marg was itself acquired by the VNU conglomerate.[48] TAM and INTAM then merged to offer a single, unified measure for advertisers to bet on various channels.[49] To complete this story of opaque and obfuscatory commercial manoeuvres that kept potential conflicts of interests beyond public scrutiny, in 2006, Nielsen was itself acquired by a conglomerate of private equity companies including Blackstone, KKR, and the Carlyle Group for an estimated value of $ 10 billion.[50]

Globalisation brought tumultuous change to the world of newspaper readership surveys. The National Readership Survey (NRS), promoted by a council of the same name, in which three distinct interest groups – the INS, the Advertising Agencies Association of India

47 The basic details are available from a variety of sources, including the Wikipedia entry on the Kantar group.

48 *Indian Express* (2000). For basic details on the IMRB's absorption into the WPP group, *Mint* (2013f).

49 Mehta (2008): 178-82.

50 New York Supreme Court (2012): 13.

(AAAI) and the Audit Bureau of Circulation (ABC) – were represented, remained the industry standard through much of the 1990s.[51] The NRS was a fairly indifferent process, which often failed to deliver – as between 1990 and 1995, there were no surveys conducted. It then became a little more serious about its biennial commitment, and carried out nation-wide surveys in 1997 and 1999.[52] The new sincerity was awakened in part by the emergence of a rival in 1995, when a newly constituted coalition of advertising and media companies floated the Media Research Users' Council (MRUC) and launched an alternate process which it called the Indian Readership Survey (IRS).[53] Directly challenging the indolence of the NRS, the IRS promised quarterly surveys, synchronised presumably with the reporting cycle for corporate enterprises.[54]

Advertising spending was increasing rapidly by this time, with liberalisation being the established motif of economic policy. The placid newspaper scenario witnessed a new competitive dynamic, focused entirely on capturing advertising spending. It was very important to secure bragging rights over readership surveys, since the reward for a podium finish in the survey was a significant share in advertising monies. Both the NRS and IRS were soon sunk in a competitive swamp where reason was diminished and volubility prevailed.

Dodgy figures

Early in the year 2000, *M&A*, a monthly magazine catering to the advertising professional, sought a comparison of most current results

---

51 Information on these two bodies could be found at their respective websites: http://www.auditbureau.org/about.htm and http://www.aaa-india.org/.

52 For two articles on the NRS process that are reasonably objective and analytical, rather than crassly partisan and celebratory of real and imagined achievements of the media platform involved, see *Frontline*, 1999 and 2002d.

53 Details and some of the background can be found at the MRUC website: http://www.mruc.net/index.php?option=com_frontpage&Itemid=1.

54 For some of the competitive dynamics between the two surveys, see *Mint* (2009a, b and c).

from the NRS and IRS.[55] The comparison yielded several interesting nuggets about competitive dynamics within the newspaper industry, one of the most piquant being the relative positions of the two leading Hindi language dailies. "Perhaps the most interesting views ought to come from the two players that are in sharp contention for the title of India's most-read Hindi daily", said *M&A*: "While NRS shows Uttar Pradesh's *Dainik Jagran* the leader, way and away, IRS almost reverses the figures (strikingly wide lead-gap and all), with Madhya Pradesh's *Dainik Bhaskar* in the clear lead". While the NRS reported just over 9 million readers for *Dainik Jagran* and a little under 4 million for *Dainik Bhaskar*, the IRS had virtually the same figures, but in reverse precedence.

The survey results further were not proving to be of great consequence in ad budget allocations. To quote *M&A* again: "media planning *per se* has lost some of its importance to negotiations and discounts. Publications with far less market share than the leaders offer huge cuts in ad rates to swing a campaign in their favour. Satellite channels are notorious for discounting of this sort".[56]

As competition intensified, major players saw little amiss in calling into question the whole exercise of audience measurement when it failed to serve their ends. Recriminations reached a noisy crescendo in December 2003, when *TOI* began a high-voltage campaign on its front-page, sharply attacking *HT* for allegedly seeking to suppress NRS findings which supposedly put it far ahead in the Delhi market.[57]

NRS shut shop soon after that public relations debacle, leaving IRS as the sole player in the field. Questions of methodology continued to swirl around the IRS in subsequent years. In 2006, it was compelled to substantially revise its initial readership estimates after a number

---

55 It must be kept in mind here, that the IRS and NRS results was privileged information, then as now, paid for by client organisations that decided on allocations of roughly ₹ 80 billion (₹ 8,000 crore) between different media platforms.

56 *M&A* has since stopped publication. The relevant articles can be found in the first quarterly issue of 2000.

57 On December 13, 2003, the *Times of India* (Delhi edition) had a front-page story asking "Now what's holding up the NRS?", along with an editorial page piece by a member of its staff, which rather disdainfully proclaimed: "The Losers Take It All: Facts Delayed is Truth Denied".

of publications that had signed on, threatened to withdraw patronage because they were allegedly given a raw deal.

In terms of the global dynamics, this meant that the WPP conglomerate, which dominated the NRS, ceased having a role in newspaper ad allocations. That role passed exclusively to the control of the Omnicom group, whose Indian subsidiary, Hansa Research had bid for and earned the IRS contract in the late-1990s with the patronage of a rival consortium of newspapers working outside the formal framework of the INS. In 2008, the NRS made a feeble effort at resumption, under the technical supervision of IMRB, part of the WPP consortium.

Authenticity in readership surveys was one among a host of problems in the print sector. Financial disclosure norms and transparency, it could be argued, were others of pressing urgency. Meanwhile, the TV news industry blundered into a credibility crisis of its own. Despite the growth in numbers of TV news channels, audiences by 2013 were convinced that they suffered a serious deficiency of choice. To confirm suspicions that the broadcast industry was no more than an elaborate charade, a shallow pretence of speaking truth to power, tapped telephone conversations between an industry lobbyist and a number of influential media professionals surfaced in November 2010, which showed how the media in fact, fed off the thriving nexus between big business and politics.

Privacy issues were undoubtedly involved in the leak of the tapped conversations, known since as the Niira Radia tapes after the industry lobbyist who was their main protagonist. Yet these clandestine recordings, leaked without any attribution but unquestioned in terms of authenticity, revealed much of public interest. The context in which they emerged was the heightened sense of public outrage over irregularities in the allocation of the radio-frequency spectrum for second-generation telecom services (dubbed the “2G scam” in India’s media shorthand).[58] Since India’s biggest industrial groups had vast stakes in spectrum allocation, many among them were players in determining the cabinet appointment to the Telecom Ministry after general elections to Parliament were concluded in May 2009. The Radia tapes revealed

58 This matter will be dealt with in a later chapter. An article that sought to address the range of issues involved in the telephone conversations that came to light and the deliberate effort by the media to suppress the information, is Muralidharan (2010).

the stratagems that went into determining this, among many other, ministerial choices.

As global winds in the advertising business gusted through the economy, the territory around the Indian media turned into an arena of intense corporate consolidation. In 2002, WPP like all other advertising conglomerates, moved its media buying activity into a separate clutch of companies. This was partly on account of the large number of media platforms that had come into existence through the 1990s boom, which made it difficult for individual ad agencies – focused on the rather self-regardingly named "creative" function – to decide on optimal ad placements. WPP's three ad agencies in India – JWT, O&M and Contract – agreed through this arrangement, to delegate the function of buying media space and time to the newly created firm, WPP Media Communications, which through this one move, became sole arbiter over roughly 30 percent of total ad monies spent in the Indian economy.

This pattern of consolidation was mimicked by all other ad agencies. By 2005, the media buying arms of the four global ad giants were believed to control no less than 80 per cent of the Indian market.[59]

Cooking the books on TV ratings

Despite losing influence in newspaper ad allocations with NRS shutting shop in 2006, WPP remained a powerful player by virtue of its control over television ratings. Signs of disgruntlement at its arbitrary methods and monopoly status were always evident. In December 2008, the Standing Committee on Information Technology in the Indian Parliament called for an end to the monopoly enjoyed by TAM, seemingly irked in particular, by the low ratings that TAM always turned in for the state-owned broadcaster.[60] Soon afterwards, Prasar Bharati, the supposed public service broadcaster, began negotiations with another market research company to start a rival television ratings system.[61]

That initiative did not get very far, but the mood of the broadcast industry was transformed with the economic downturn that in Sep-

59 Sinclair (2012): 125.

60 Press Trust of India (2008).

61 Rediff (2008).

tember 2008, stole up on its celebrations of good times. In December 2008, one of the newspapers that uncharacteristically chose to turn the gaze inwards and run an occasional story on the media industry, was reporting that "the most lucrative advertising has fallen by the wayside and huge discounting has started happening in print and on television as media houses try to mop up any ad revenues they can".[62]

An unforeseen consequence cropped up from commercial strategies the media industry adopted through the boom-years. It was not uncommon for media companies – following the lead of the biggest among them – to swap advertising for equity. The favour of equity acquired without cost would be requited through free ad space, which would help build brands and boost stockmarket valuations. As long as stock values continued rising, this would work to the mutual benefit of both: a win-win game riding on a buoyant stockmarket, assisted on its way by hyped up media coverage.

When the stockmarket crashed following the global economic meltdown of 2008, the media companies were left with massively diminished portfolios, though without being spared the obligation to meet free ad space commitments. The industry's quandary was put it in stark terms by another of those rare reports: many media companies were "stuck with no-cash ad deals stemming from their equity deals with companies even as the value of those investments... plunged". Several among the media companies cancelled or indefinitely postponed new launches and expansion plans.[63]

Another consequence of the meltdown was an unsettling of the easy concord between market research firms and India's main broadcast enterprises. In August 2012, a leading news channel, NDTV Ltd, filed suit for $ 1.4 billion against TAM in the Supreme Court of New York for allegedly falsifying records in exchange for a monetary consideration. NDTV, a news broadcaster in Hindi and English, claimed that TAM had caused it losses to the tune of $ 800 million by deliberately understating its viewership numbers. And this was done as part of a collusive arrangement with rival channels to earn an illicit fee.

---

62 *Mint* (2008). The issue of advertising treaties between media companies and other enterprises which became a common industry practice through the years of the stockmarket boom will be dealt with in greater detail in a following chapter.

63 Ibid.

TAM's joint owners – AC Nielsen and Kantar – the NDTV petition alleged, had sold off a chunk of shares to a consortium of private equity firms based in New York. These investments had begun turning sour after the September 2008 meltdown, putting an added onus on TAM to come up with earnings that would repay them at least in part. TAM had for this reason, failed to invest in the necessary expansion of its survey methodology. It had also resorted to a number of shady practices, such as revealing the identity of households within its sample, allowing several among NDTV's competitors to infiltrate the primary process – a household's choice of channel at different times of day – on which the ratings are based.[64]

NDTV did not have great success. Within a few weeks of its suit being filed, the Supreme Court of New York asked for substantial modifications and a submission anew. It also asked the defendants to move their petition for dismissal of the suit at an appropriate time, so that NDTV would have adequate opportunity to respond. In March 2013, a lower court in New York held that NDTV's lawsuit should be dismissed on grounds of inappropriate forum, since its grievances were best addressed in an Indian court.[65] A subsequent defamation suit brought against WPP's chief, Martin Sorrell, also stood dismissed.[66] And all this was despite it being common knowledge that the ratings system had been "cooked for years".[67]

By this time though, there was a generalised air of rebellion with numerous other broadcasters, all for their own reasons, ending participation in the TAM ratings system.[68] Each had its own motive and

---

64 Supreme Court of New York (2012).

65 *Indian Television* (2012 and 2013b).

66 *Indian Television* (2013b).

67 A report in *The Hindu* within days of NDTV filing suit in New York, pointed out on the basis of a series of interviews with media industry insiders, that the "alleged manipulation of television ratings has been an open secret among broadcasters long before NDTV opened a Pandora's box with last week's billion dollar lawsuit against TAM India". However, it pointed out, with "most channels being beneficiaries of the flawed system at some time or the other, vested interests have ensured that the elephant in the room remained overlooked". See *The Hindu* (2013a).

68 *The Hindu* (2013b)..

the meltdown of the TAM system seemed to have been precipitated by multiple causes. The Sony Network which held broadcast rights for the Indian Premier League (IPL), felt hard done by in the dismal viewership figures recorded for the hugely hyped cricket tournament in its 2013 season. That the entire tournament was conducted under the constant buzz of corporate corruption and match-fixing, which turned off a number of otherwise devoted viewers, was not considered germane. The news broadcasters' cabal, including NDTV, was turned off by the expansion of TAM's ridiculously small sample to take in some part of the rural audience. Unsurprisingly, with this very modest expansion of the sample, the state-owned broadcaster Doordarshan's viewership showed a substantial increase, puncturing the conceit of the corporate channels.[69]

With advertisers and ad agencies digging in and affirming their commitment to the TAM process, the stage seemed set for a deadlock in the media business.[70] A compromise formula of sorts was reached a month later with TAM agreeing that it would release absolute numbers of viewers of each channel, rather than percentages, which often tended to be misleading.[71]

Print industry in freefall and a political rescue act

Print industry fortunes meanwhile, were in freefall with the global economic meltdown of September 2008. In March 2009, the editor of the *Indian Express*, Shekhar Gupta, addressed a memorandum to all colleagues, saying that profitability had vanished in the entire media industry over the preceding six months and that indeed, there seemed "no end" to the crisis. It was a call to severe austerities of the flesh and the soul by one who was renowned for being among the most avid celebrants of the cult of material success. After all the ritualistic homage to the sales team of the newspaper, which had defied the downbeat market to record two months of record sales in October 2008 and February 2009, Gupta called for "sacrifices", which he assured the flock,

69 Some of these complexities were discussed in Ninan (2013).

70 *Mint* (2013g).

71 *Mint* (2013h).

would be borne most intensely at the higher editorial and managerial tiers.[72]

Despite Gupta's dark forebodings, the weeks that followed seemed to bring an elevation in the mood. Early in April 2009, he was telling a media news website that the crisis was only akin to a "tsunami" when his newspaper was programmed to "survive a nuclear war".[73] It was another matter that the stimulus for the recovery in industry fortunes came after a fairly undignified procession by some among the Indian media's more notable figures to the doorsteps of the MIB.[74] The special pleading was of course, grossly at variance with the robust free enterprise doctrine that these media enterprises advocated as firmly held editorial philosophy.

A week after Gupta and other notables of the print media industry made their pathway to the doorsteps of the government, the MIB announced an increase in the rate paid on government advertising by about 24 per cent. The Minister also managed, despite fiscal stringency, to persuade his cabinet colleague in Finance, to eliminate the customs duty on newsprint. Since parliamentary general elections, though not formally notified then, were widely expected within two months, the timing of the Minister's announcement seemed a transparent concession to the power of the print media.

It was a far from edifying sight for an industry that has always taken pride in its independence, to present itself as a supplicant at the doorstep of the government, while being a loud opponent of the coddling state in matters involving other business enterprises. A degree of unease was expressed by *The Hindu*, which chose not to join the delegation to the doorstep of the MIB and refrained in its editorial space from joining the chorus for special favours. N. Ram, a major shareholder in the business and then editor-in-chief, explained that import duty elimination on newsprint was a demand that *The Hindu* as a corporate enterprise supported. The sequence of events though, probably

72 Content Sutra (2009a).

73 Content Sutra (2009b).

74 The three print industry personalities who petitioned the I&B Minister for a "bailout" were Shekhar Gupta, Shobhana Bhartiya of the *Hindustan Times* and T.N. Ninan of *Business Standard*. The visit was reported and its purpose debated on a number of blogs and websites, including Content Sutra (2009a).

reflected an unstated tradeoff: "...that is the reality. When the elections come, they (the government) are wary of the media, they want to be nice to the media".[75]

Aside from these specific measures, the surge in advertising expenses during the national general elections of 2009 contributed in some measure to a short-term stimulus for the media industry. And then, a government that had earned an unexpectedly sweeping mandate, introduced strong budgetary measures to boost the flagging momentum of the economy. Things started looking more upbeat but by the latter half of 2011 the stimuli began to fade. A report commissioned by FICCI from the global accounting firm KPMG Ltd, found that this was in part because the "long-promised digital ecosystem began to impact various (media) segments".[76]

That judgment though, was questionable. The digital impact on conventional media remains the great unknown, allowing its deployment as an argument in both good times and bad. It was for long believed to have kicked in around the turn of the century, but if accurate as an assessment, seemed not to have prevented a phase of buoyancy in the traditional media following about 2003. The "digital impact" is a hypothesis that can be advanced in support of just about any proposition, and the opposite. Illustratively, the corresponding report from FICCI in 2007, when the times were distinctly better and the outlook rather rosy, had an epigraph from Bill Gates, icon of the modern information age, celebrating that a prediction he made at the beginning of the decade, that this would be a period "when the digital approach would be taken for granted", was being fulfilled even faster than expected.[77]

While recording the continuing severity of the downturn in 2012, FICCI also tacitly conceded that it had been essentially, unforeseen: "the economic slowdown hit the industry hard – especially advertising revenue. Advertising budgets were cut and plans had to be modified. Most companies had to revise previously robust projections to reflect a new macro-economic reality".[78] That rather infirm grasp of reality was

---

75 Content Sutra (2009c).

76 FICCI (2012): Foreword.

77 FICCI (2007).

78 FICCI (2013): Foreword.

again not really new, having been manifest in good times and bad. In its 2007 report for instance, FICCI had forecast five years of uninterrupted growth:

> Through this year's report we have undertaken to tell the story of the Entertainment & Media (E&M) industry's tremendous growth over the last year as well as its expected growth in the future. The E&M industry is expected to outgrow the Indian economy in every year from now till 2011. An impressive cumulative annual growth rate (CAGR) of 18 percent is forecast for the industry over this five year period. This growth rate is in part due to several positive measures taken by the Government. It has also been boosted by technological advancements, entry of large corporate players into all segments of the industry, an increase in disposable income amongst Indian consumers and several other factors.[79]

Despite frequently miscued interpretations, the FICCI report, released at an annual gathering of the media and entertainment industry, remains one of the few sources to tap for information that even remotely points towards the economic aggregates of the industry. Till 2009, FICCI had been contracting with PriceWaterhouseCoopers (later rebranded as PwC) to produce this annual report. As long as it was in charge, PwC used to preface its report with a subtle disavowal of faith in the authenticity of the information provided. Much of the industry, the report pointed out, did not have an "organised body" and hence "a centralised tracking agency that could ... provide .. accurate figures" was missing. This challenge "was exacerbated by the fact that most companies in the industry do not have their financial information in the public domain". The only comprehensive report on the state of the Indian media in short, was prepared on the basis of information sources that were vast and varied, by no means in agreement on their methods and objectives. Its accuracy was hence not something that even its authors could vouch for.[80] Beyond that plea of helplessness in dealing with an industry with a quite pronounced aversion to transparency, there was an explicit disclaimer of legal liability for any of the inferences or judgments arrived at in the report.[81]

---

79 FICCI (2007): Preface.

80 Ibid.

81 Ibid: inside front cover. The disclaimer reads as follows: "While due care has been taken to ensure the accuracy of the information contained in the report, no warranty, express or implied, is being made, or will be made, by FICCI or PricewaterhouseCoopers Pvt. Ltd., In-

With all the caveats, the annual FICCI reports remain the only aggregate estimates available of the size of the Indian media industry. On a sober reading, the picture that emerged from three successive editions of this annual report was of misfortunes yet to bottom out. A single indicator summed up the situation for an industry whose lifeblood is advertising: gross advertising expenditure in the Indian economy was estimated to have grown 17 percent in 2010 and a rather more modest 13 percent in 2011. In 2012, the growth rate had shrunk still further, to a mere 9 percent. The years since have brought little to lift the gloom. In September 2013, an account of the state of the Indian media summed it up in rather rueful terms: "Not the internet, but a slowing economic growth (sic), the falling rupee, a regulation capping advertising time on television channels, and years of indiscriminate expansion (and profligate spending), seem to have caught up with the Indian media". Newspapers had cut their daily page offerings, TV channels had cut back on programming; "several publications and channels (were) on the block".[82]

Dubious stock deals

Bagdikian has identified the growth of joint stock ownership and corporate control in the U.S. as a key moment when quality and traditional values of journalism were inundated by profit lust. Despite changes underway since the turn of the century, major print media groups in India, remain under family ownership, though they all began actively contemplating limited public offerings of shares after the misfortunes that followed 2008.

Corporatisation in the Indian context followed a different trajectory. Print media groups in many instances, ploughed profits into other corporate enterprises. In the case of the *TOI*, investments took many innovative guises, among them the arrangement known as "pri-

---

dia (PwC), as regards the accuracy and adequacy of the information contained in the report. No responsibility is being accepted, or will be accepted, by FICCI or PwC, for any consequences, including loss of profits, that may arise as a result of errors or omissions in this report. This report is only intended to be a general guide and professional advice should be sought before taking any action on any matter".

82 For an account of how the slowdown persisted into the following year, see *Mint* (2013j).

vate treaties", which involves an exchange of free advertising space for equity in particular companies.[83] Several other media enterprises followed suit, though without quite putting this strategy front and centre in their corporate identity. For instance, NDTV in 2010 announced that it was discontinuing participation in private treaties, without really clarifying when it had entered this enterprise.

An issue of public concern was flagged by M. Damodaran, chairman of the stockmarket regulator, the Securities and Exchange Board of India (SEBI) just as he prepared to leave his post in 2008. He chose to focus on the stock portfolios of business news anchors and experts appearing in analytical programmes on TV channels, but the monitory warning on the lack of transparency could just as well apply to the print media. The matter was serious and had a bearing on the trust that several million potential investors placed in the markets. "There are people who make statements that are very clear indications of talking up or talking down stocks", said Damodaran: "And what do we have by way of investor protection?"[84] Several news channels came up soon afterwards with assurances that they had policies to ensure appropriate levels of disclosure by their business news anchors, to protect against any possible conflict of interests.[85] The issue soon dropped out of public focus and there was no real occasion to test this claim against the actual conduct of the channels in times of market turbulence.

In August 2010, the stockmarket regulator, the Securities and Exchange Board of India (SEBI) came out with a directive, evolved in consultation with the Press Council of India, that all media enterprises with investments in other corporate entities should make full disclosure alongside any report involving these entities. The directive was for the most part, ignored by the Indian media in its news coverage. There has since been no indication of compliance at all.

---

83 *Mint* (2013k) for instance reported a 49 per cent equity investment by the company that owns the TOI in an underclothing manufacturer. It did not reveal the source of the information, but checked with the TOI management, which confirmed that the investment had been made but provided few further details. Inquiries with the underclothing firm elicited no response other than a refusal to engage with "market speculation".

84 *Sans Serif* (2008).

85 *Mint* (2008a).

Taking the best available current figures for the Indian print media, advertising accounted for about Rs 13,940 crore of total industry revenue of Rs 20,900 crore in 2011. Ad revenue dependence was thus just over 66 percent for the industry as a whole. In comparison, the *TOI* group earned close to 84 percent of total revenue from advertisements. Viewed another way the *TOI* group alone accounted for close to 29 percent of the total advertisement monies flowing into the print media. If the three top English language publishers were taken into account, their share in total ad expenditure would run to over 44 percent.[86]

The TV sector earns a relatively modest 35 percent of its revenues from advertising, though a vast share of subscription revenues goes towards carriage rather than content. And in defiance of the global commonsense that carriage and content should be kept distinct of each other in terms at least of ownership interests, India has had a number of TV broadcasters investing heavily in satellite transmission: Zee Entertainment Networks, Sun and Hathway, to name only three. But all these would appear to be bit players, when viewed against the entry of India's largest industrial conglomerate, the Reliance group, into the sector.

Early in 2012, Mukesh Ambani's Reliance group took a substantial stake in the broadcast and online news enterprise, Network 18. Through a subsidiary firm, Network 18 had ownership over a number of TV broadcast channels, including the English-language CNN-IBN, the Hindi-language IBN 7 and the Marathi-language IBN-Lokmat. It also had control of the business focused channels CNBC-TV 18 in English and CNBC Awaaz in Hindi. The quiet takeover was effected through a personal loan of Rs 40 billion extended to Network 18 promoter Raghav Bahl, by Reliance. Its object was ostensibly, for cutting some of the company's debt and funding a merger with Eenadu Television (ETV), a major multi-lingual broadcaster based in the southern Indian city of Hyderabad. In the following months, Reliance head Mukesh Ambani concluded a deal with his brother Anil Ambani's ADAG Group, to utilise the extensive fibre optic network owned by

86 Aggregate figures on advertising spending in the economy are from FICCI reports. The *TOI* figures are from the annual reports of the company (Bennett Coleman and Company Ltd or BCCL) that owns the title.

the latter's Reliance Infocomm Ltd, to transmit news and entertainment programmes.[87]

Network 18 was promoted in 1996 as a private limited company with interests in finance. It was taken public and listed on the Indian stock markets in 2006. Early in 2007, it acquired a distinct identity as a highly diversified media conglomerate after an issue of shares at Rs 312 on face value of Rs 5. The deal with Reliance followed the global financial meltdown and a reportedly explicit decision – which flowed through the corporate veins to reach every part of the enterprise – that Network 18 would from then on, be an unabashed votary of a pro-business message and right-wing politics.[88]

In August 2013, no fewer than 350 employees of the TV18 group were handed letters of termination. The layoffs affected well over a quarter of the total employee strength of the media group. The purported objective, though this can only be surmised in the absence of any formal statement from the company, was of cutting personnel costs to deal with a profit crunch. Yet as several observers then pointed out, this was a plea that did not stand scrutiny, since TV18 – and the larger business group Network 18 that it was part of – was known to operate through a large and complex management hierarchy, where a major share of the human resources budget was allocated. Nobody within this unproductive hierarchy of managers was at the remotest risk of retrenchment. Cost cutting was achieved almost entirely by scaling back news gathering activities.

Senior managers within Network 18 remained unavailable for comment and employees targeted in the layoffs were reluctant to speak out for fear of losing the modest compensation promised. The mass layoffs were believed to originate in a number of bad business decisions, involving a subsidiary company Reliance Jio which was the chosen instrument of the business conglomerate's plans for implementing its ambitions in telecom. In June 2013, Reliance Jio, for reasons that have not been quite seriously inquired into, put plans to launch "fourth-generation" (or 4G) telecom services on hold. The premium

87 *Governance Now* (2013).

88 The takeover and its implications for personnel management policies and editorial line, was the subject of detailed reporting and analysis by Bhatia (2013).

placed on Network 18 media content diminished rapidly after this decision. The decision to integrate the Network 18 newsrooms came soon afterwards and then followed the mass dismissals.

Soon after parliamentary general elections were concluded in May 2014, a new regime headed by Prime Minister Narendra Modi, whose campaign had enjoyed the complete and unequivocal endorsement of Reliance and a number of other corporate behemoths, took the reins of power. That day, the chairman and founder of Network 18 revealed at a routine prescheduled meeting of the company board, that he was leaving his post since Reliance intended to assume complete management control. In the days that followed, other top editorial staff followed the founder in a procession out of the company.[89] Reliance control was now absolute.

Concentration in the Indian media industry is an ever growing reality and the contribution made here by policy default cannot be ignored. But behind this evident failure is a larger collapse of the imagination and a craven submission by the policy establishment to the power of the media and the wider corporate sector it is embedded within.

In unprecedented degree, the period between 2009 and 2014 was rocky and turbulent for both the Indian polity and the media, not to mention their interface. From the terrorist siege of Mumbai to the mass upsurge against corruption and the protests against the December 16 gang-rape, the media repeatedly showed its newly won ability to orchestrate an elite insurrection that could send out an ominously clear signal of no-confidence in the elected government. Within the quinquennial electoral cycle, these sporadic uprisings came together in what seemed a decisive vote in the 2014 elections. But more than that vaguely defined entity called "civil society" it seemed that the corporate sector – exerting its power through newly consolidated media power – was the real winner of the 2014 election.

The 2014 general election was good news for the media because of the promised stimulus to advertising expenditure. As the campaign started moving up a notch in February, advertising expenditure in the economy was estimated to receive a possible boost of 11.6 per cent over the year, against 10 percent in 2013 and an anaemic 5.1 per cent

89 *Mint* (2014a).

in 2012. The most significant gains were expected to accrue to the print media, principally daily newspapers.[90]

In February, when the main political players were just beginning to gear up, the BJP alone was believed to have set aside a sum of INR 4 billion (Rs 400 crore) for political advertising through the campaign season.[91] As the party's campaign unfolded, it became abundantly clear that the initial estimate had been way too conservative. By the time the last ballot was cast, the BJP was estimated to have spent, conservatively, about INR 50 billion (5000 crore) on advertising, creating an aura of omnipresence around prime ministerial candidate Narendra Modi. Factoring in charter costs of the jaunty aircraft that Modi rode to his frenetic series of rallies across the country, the cost of the campaign was estimated to end up in the range of INR 100 billion (10,000 crore), which at the prevalent exchange rates, would be significantly higher than the money believed to have been spent in the re-election of US President Barack Obama in 2012.[92]

Modi's case for leading the country was posed as a presidential style referendum. And the reward he obtained, in the shape of a 31 percent national vote share for the BJP, may seem rather meagre returns for the money invested. It was as analysts pointed out after the results were in, the smallest vote share won by any single party with an absolute majority in parliament.

Much of the electoral battle in India is fought in the minds of the electorate and involves unsubtle play on the mix of fear and hope that individuals within a fractured social milieu bring to their political choices. A share of less than a third in the popular vote could bring disproportionate rewards if the opposition to the party that gains early front-running advantage could be divided. The decibels unleashed by the Modi campaign were not just about rallying the faithful to the BJP's saffron flag, but also convincing the large mass of the unconverted, that opposition was futile – indeed that they had more reason for fear from opposing the inevitable than from acquiescing in it.

Early anticipations that the 2014 elections would involve unprecedented use of social media were borne out, though with a ca-

90 *Mint* (2014b).

91 *The Hindu* (2014a).

92 Varadarajan (2014b).

veat. In the predominant manner of its use, social media conformed to an older template of propaganda in being insistent, single-themed and relentlessly one-way. Specific features of the social media, such as interactivity and the potential richness of its user-generated content, were nowhere in evidence.[93] Aside from this use of the social media as a battering ram, with armies of hired personnel taking on every hint of scepticism about the chosen man's destiny to rule with withering contempt and polemic, there was very little by way of an honest engagement with the public. The only television interviews Modi granted were with worshipping acolytes or BJP partisans like Madhu Kishwar and Rajat Sharma, till the very last fortnight of the campaign, when he had Times Now news channel's noisy and bumptious anchor Arnab Goswami interviewing him in a rare mood of docile submission.

Modi's record of achievement as Chief Minister of Gujarat was blazoned as a model that he could magically transpose to every corner of the country, bringing electricity, roads, ample water supply and prosperity. It was a different matter though, that the better informed commentary found the Gujarat experience in economic growth to be little different under Modi than under several of his predecessors, and in fact to have been seriously challenged in terms of social welfare benefits. On most assessments of overall progress in growth and human development, Gujarat ranked in the middle-range among India's states. Yet through Modi's "maximum campaign", this undistinguished record came to represent a model that the rest of the country could profitably emulate.[94]

---

93 *India Today* (2014), reports how a "National Digital Operations Centre" in the BJP's Delhi headquarters handled regular updates of Modi's schedule on Facebook and continually worked on creating a "Twitter buzz". Mallet (2014) reports how the campaign used technology to "reach out to people who don't have access to technology", deploying "hundreds of young volunteers – alumni of US universities or the Indian Institutes of Technology who took sabbaticals or resigned from companies such as JP Morgan, Deutsche Bank or their own companies" to reach out to an estimated 100,000 volunteers in the field, to "organise the campaign". Chaturvedi (2016) provided after a period of time, a first-hand account – indeed a true confession – from a member of the BJP's social media team which laid bare the aggressive tactics adopted to shame opponents and embellish Modi's unique claims to national leadership.

94 For an early articulation of this theme, utterly naive and deluded by the statistical fallacy that parameters measured as ratios could exceed the

Is there an unresolved mystery in the manner the media played along with Modi's marketing strategy? Perhaps not. Early indications were available that media, when not acquiescent, would be subtly coerced to fall in line.

In October 2013, the Kasturi family that owns *The Hindu*, India's third largest English language newspaper, abruptly removed a professional editor appointed just 20 months before. The board of the proprietary company was deadlocked over the proposal and it took the casting vote of newly appointed chairman N Ram, who had ironically initiated the move towards professional editorial control in 2011, to carry the resolution removing Siddharth Varadarajan from his position.[95] Responding to public queries afterwards, the board identified one of the factors driving the reversal of course in an ostensible "bias" in editorial policy against Modi in particular and the BJP in general that Varadarajan had introduced, including a supposed ban on front-page coverage of the candidate.[96] It later emerged that far from the supposed ban, Varadarajan had in fact issued a memorandum to all staff, detailing the principles to be followed in determining the placement of stories involving the Modi campaign. These principles were assessed as sound and indeed a model for how a newspaper of record should conduct itself through an intense election campaign.[97]

In November 2013, *Open*, a magazine that had been publishing for five years under the ownership of the RPG group, a diversified business conglomerate, announced the removal of its political editor, Hartosh Singh Bal. No specific reason was given though it emerged afterwards, that the editor of the magazine, Manu Joseph, had long been under pressure to sign off on the order of dismissal. After reportedly taking

ceiling of 100 percent, see Panagariya (2012). Effectively, the Gujarat model is celebrated by unsubtly debunking the developmental experience of Kerala on grounds that the improvement in literacy rate it registered in six decades since Independence only amounted to 47 percentage points, while even a poor performer like Bihar registered 50. It seems to pass the comprehension of the writer, a Columbia University economist, that an improvement that matched Bihar, would have put Kerala's literacy rate at 101 percent.

95 This sequence of events was covered in the daily press. See for instance *Mint* (2013i).

96 *The Hoot* (2013).

97 *Outlook* (2013).

his resistance to the limit of feasibility, he finally gave in only to ensure a more cooperative relationship with the ownership. It did not take great insight to gather that the main reason for the removal of a senior journalist was his strong editorial posture against Modi's claims to the prime ministership. Joseph himself quit his editorial position when a person regarded as a close confidant of the BJP leadership was appointed Bal's successor in January 2014. Around the same time, the Sun TV channel based in the southern metropolis of Chennai removed senior news anchor Veerapandian from his prime time spot, allegedly after receiving a letter from the local head of the BJP warning of his party's intent to withdraw from further participation in the channel's programmes.[98]

These were merely the more conspicuous triumphs the BJP secured in the effort to radically alter the public perception of its chosen standard bearer. The mission was partly accomplished through authentic conversions of faith on the part of senior media personnel, but the greater role was played by the unique alchemy that developed in the years of neo-liberal hegemony, between the media on one hand and the advertising and public relations industries on the other. The overarching reality here is the brute power of corporate India, which seemingly decided about halfway through the tenure of the government elected in 2009, that a switch in leadership was overdue.[99]

Projecting brand Modi

In February 2014, media reports suggested that the BJP, already riding high among punters on the election results, was in the final stages of identifying the agency that would handle its massive advertising budget. Such a decision in the past involved just one choice. But structural changes in the ad industry had made this a two-stage process, since it was almost universal practice for the ad agency function to be organised in two partly overlapping halves: the "creative" side where content is determined and the "media" side where ad placements are decided.

98 For these events, see Raman (2015) and Janmohamad (2014).

99 Varadarajan (2014a) deals with how the business lobbies lined up behind Modi's candidacy for the top political role, well before the campaign started.

Among the agencies believed to be on the BJP shortlist for the creative function was McCann Erickson. And the front-runner among the media buyers was Lodestar.[100] At first sight, it seemed like a great idea for clients seeking the best service to divide up functions between distinct enterprises. The only problem was that McCann belonged to the global advertising conglomerate Interpublic, headquartered in the US, and Lodestar was a media buying agency owned within the same chain of multinational capital.

The multinational conglomerate's credentials to handle the advertising account of a party that by its own lights, was the true and unsullied face of Indian nationalism, did not go unchallenged. The most likely competitor for the creative function was reported to be Contract Advertising, with Group M rumoured to be bidding strongly to acquire the media buying contract. Again, the story of a competitive free enterprise system working to ensure value outcomes bumped up against the rather inconvenient fact that both Contract and Group M belong to the WPP group, headquartered in London.

When the Congress party began casting its eyes around for a TV channel on which its young prince Rahul Gandhi should first be featured, it looked at the audience ratings available and picked out Times Now.[101] It went by audience measurement statistics available from TAM Ltd, a joint venture of AC Nielsen and Kantar. Nothing exceptionable there, except that Kantar is part of the WPP group, and Nielsen an enterprise owned by a number of private equity investors just then in rather bad public odour. As the broadcast enterprise NDTV pointed out in its lawsuit before the Supreme Court of New York in 2012, Nielsen had been playing fast and loose with television audience statistics in return for various kinds of financial rewards.

As election preparations began to get underway, the media got busy with sponsorship of opinion polls. Among the most active agencies in the early days was C-Voter, which had no manner of declared relationship with the global advertising and PR giants and laid out an elaborate menu of options for the principal political contestants. With Modi as declared leader, it found in an opinion poll in May 2013 – a

100 This and the points that follow are dealt with in *The Hindu* (2014a) and Rodrigues (2014).

101 *Hindustan Times* (2014).

year prior to the expected date when general elections were to conclude – the BJP could hope to win as many as 220 seats along with its coalition partners, comfortably beating the Congress-led alliance. Without Modi as declared leader, the BJP alliance, the poll found in an exercise commissioned by the diversified media conglomerate India Today, would end up trailing its principal rivals by a significant margin in terms of seats won. Under this scenario indeed, the Congress and its friends were projected to win 209 seats.[102]

C-Voter remained an active player on the scene in the months that followed. In July 2013, around the time that Modi secured his party's approval as head of a crucial internal oversight body, C-Voter turned in a forecast that put both the BJP and the Congress alliances in the doldrums: neither was projected to win a sufficient number to put them in sight of a parliamentary majority. The vacuum left by this deadlock between the two principal combatants, remained unfilled in this projection. In subsequent exercises done for the same media clients and others, C-Voter turned in results that showed the BJP inching steadily ahead of its main rival, while still giving the motley grouping categorised as "others" a determinant voice in the emergent parliamentary arithmetic of 2014.

In February 2014, or just when the real preparations for the elections were beginning, C-Voter was caught out in a sting operation, promising tailor-made results for any media client. Despite ethical dilemmas, the sting carried out by the NewsExpress TV channel had sufficient credibility to raise serious questions about the political agendas that C-Voter sought to serve.[103] It led to the India Today group, possibly among several other media entities, abruptly departing the league of C-Voter patrons, though without an explanation of how much they knew of the agency's modes of operation.

Though relatively more quiescent – at least in relation to the frenetic pace set by C-Voter – two agencies that are integrally connected to the global network of advertising and PR agencies, were beginning to pitch in with their own predictions on the election outcome. Nielsen stepped up in May 2013, forecasting under the conditions that existed

102 *Economic Times* (2014b) provides a summary of all the early opinion poll findings.

103 *The Hindu* (2014b).

then – without testing for various leadership contingencies involving Modi and his rivals – that the BJP and friends would beat the Congress alliance by a clear margin, but still fall seriously short of a parliamentary majority. Nielsen shifted its estimates noticeably towards the BJP, though by relatively small magnitudes, in the following two survey rounds done for the same client in January and February 2014.

Hansa Research, which is part of the US-based Omnicom group and thus Nielsen's rival among global ad-PR conglomerates, had its own forecasts underway, again for at least two different media clients. In a July 2013 forecast made for *The Week*, a news magazine published from the southern state of Kerala, Hansa Research forecast a three way break-up of seats, with the BJP being marginally ahead of the Congress though well short of a majority. It foresaw a large residual portion where regional parties and the undefined "others" would be determinant players. In a poll for the broadcaster NDTV in March 2014, Hansa shifted the numerical advantage distinctly towards the BJP and its allies, putting it roughly 40 seats short of a majority, but giving a mélange of regional and unaligned parties a large say in the future parliament. The following month though, Hansa's poll uncovered a slender majority for the BJP and its allies, though one rendered more potent by the diminution of the Congress tally to just over a hundred.

Nielsen was meanwhile, providing a variety of other election related services of a far less disinterested character. Media reports in February indicated that it had been engaged by the Congress party in a major exercise to assess public perceptions of a number of prospective candidates. The ruling party seemingly had two candidates in mind for every seat and required an expert research-based input on how good a chance each stood, a task it chose to entrust to Nielsen. In what seemed a deliberate policy of ambiguity, the Congress general secretary directing the entire operation and a Nielsen spokesperson chose not to confirm the tie-up, but to talk around it.

Around the same time, the men who would propel the BJP ad campaign announced themselves, though with an abundance of discretion.[104] Companies seemed unwilling to put themselves on the line, choosing instead to be known by their leadership tiers. Thus, it was not Madison Media, India's largest surviving independent ad agency that

104 Rodrigues (2014).

was named in media reporting as the entity directing the Modi image makeover, but its head Sam Balsara. Similarly, it was not McCann Erickson of the worldwide Interpublic conglomerate that was mentioned, but its head for India, Prasoon Joshi. Likewise, Piyush Pandey of the WPP-owned PR outfit Ogilvy & Mather was pulled in as a contributor to the smart selling proposition.

Media manipulation

Aside from the competition in forecasting the outcome, an Indian election campaign is also a busy time for media reporting of all the action. And this is where a new trend emerged in the 2014 campaign season: "pre-packaged" coverage, where the political parties delivered an entire finished product to any interested television channel. Reporters and other staff would have no reason to stir out of their offices or studios, since they could, if inclined, scatter their own comments or editorial observations through the body of the pre-packaged material obtained from the political parties.

This new practice was reported by the *Economic Times*, based in Delhi, early in February 2014.[105] The reporter concerned contacted all major news channels, but mostly failed to gain any kind of engaged response, including from Times Now, a channel owned within the same group. The only response came from the Hindi news channel India TV, well-known for its very colourful content – where ghosts and supernatural beings feature as prominently as mere mortals – which explained that the concern behind the new practice was just the plain logistics of deploying reporters and technical staff in multiple venues to cover several ongoing events. Security constraints could limit the number of news crews permitted to the venue of a political meeting, explained Rajat Sharma, editor-in-chief and chairman of India TV. The common sense option of creating a video news pool, from which all channels could draw, had not taken off because of a lack of cooperative spirit in an intensely competitive world. And the policy of making full disclosure of material that political parties directly fed into news channels had not gained traction. That was a more remote ethical issue, as the India TV chief explained, one which news channels had not had the time or inclination to think through.

105 *Economic Times* (2014a).

Here was an ironic retrospect on the phony war that the newspaper industry was torn by in the early years of the century. The battle pitched those who took a stand on what seemed high nationalist principle, demanding that "alien" interests be kept out of this one vital sector where the national political discourse was carried out, against those who argued that foreign investment would bring in much needed capital and expertise into an industry where these were sorely needed. It seemed to matter very little then, that the TV news genre, which was clearly assuming the agenda-setting functions that the print media seemed anxious to surrender, had been invaded by foreign capital, perhaps irreversibly. While the newspaper industry was engaged in these skirmishes over foreign investment, a major operational manoeuvre was executed on its flanks, leading in effect to its complete encirclement by foreign interests. Being narrowly focused on the issue of ownership, the newspaper lobby failed to recognise the signals from a policy move initiated in 2001 with little public debate or discussion, when the doors were opened up for fully foreign-owned ad agencies and market research firms.

The consequences were mitigated in part, because India drew a lucky number in the global casino in 2003. That is when the tide of speculative capital unleashed from the capital of the global economy, began washing up on the country's shores. Ever since 1991, India had been readying for just that moment when it would win out against lesser rivals in the global beauty contest for attracting the largest capital inflows. And when that moment arrived rather belatedly, judgments were disoriented and unhinged.

Within five years, the sheen had begun to come off what was touted as India's growth miracle, puncturing the blustery self-confidence of a newly empowered middle class. Elite circles then began resounding with the call for policy clarity. Only some manner of authoritarian direction, it seemed, could weed out all distracting claims from the great unwashed in a vast and clamorous democracy, restoring the country to the pathway towards growth and great power status.

In the circumstances, among a host of political actors who could potentially have been contenders for the leadership of a diverse democracy, the choice fell upon one who least reflected its pluralities and complexities. Far from being a disqualifying factor, Modi's record of intolerant speech and actions as a thrice elected Chief Minister of Gujarat, became a testimonial for his unique claim to the position.

Modi's anointment as a potential Prime Minister began within the chambers of commerce he had courted with special ardour. The annual "Vibrant Gujarat" conclaves organised by a global heavyweight in the PR business became the occasion for much fictitious capital being committed to investment in the state, creating the miasmic illusion that Modi could work the wonder of injecting new life into a stagnant economy. When the chambers of commerce show the way, it is only natural that the media should follow. Institutional memories within the media stood in the way. Several among the professionals who led the media had rather graphic memories of the horrors of Gujarat in 2002. And it just did not seem right to bury these in the newly minted corporate lust for decisive political leadership.

Demographic realities, though, could not be denied. The 2014 general elections brought into the arena an entire generation born after the Ayodhya atrocity of 1992, who were no more than pre-adolescents at the time of the 2002 pogrom in Gujarat. Whatever the strata they were born into, impatience was their hallmark. And the please-all style of the fumbling Congress-led coalition government just did not seem up to the task of meeting the burgeoning aspirations of the new demographic strata. From September 2011, when Modi sent out a tweet pronouncing that "God is great" to mark his supposed exoneration by the Supreme Court in a petition calling for prosecution of those responsible for the 2002 pogrom, the media found a way of putting its scruples behind and celebrating the arrival of the promised one. Every move he made since then was assured of saturation coverage in the country's noisy media space, where agreement on news priorities was otherwise rare.

Before Modi's anointment, every vacant space in the news agenda on a slow day was filled with feverish speculation, driven by aggressive anchor persons, about when the BJP would make that decisive leap and name him as its designated prime ministerial candidate. Far from framing an agenda for the public discourse, the media seemed intent on forcing its agenda on the party and the public. In normal circumstances, a state chief minister's boast that he would attract greater attention on the national observance of Independence Day than the Prime Minister's customary address from Delhi's Red Fort, would have been dismissed as an upstart's delusion. Modi in August 2013 succeeded in securing a free pass for this effrontery. To add to this privilege, he also obtained live coverage for a speech delivered from a remote corner of Gujarat that was all attack and empty promise, challenging the propriety of independence day addresses that by convention underlined the messages of hope and expectation.

Modi's victory when finally it was announced with ineluctable force on 16 May 2014, was read variously. Within weeks of taking office though, he had signalled how much store he set by social media as a communications tool for his administration.[106] His early directive to senior administrators and bureaucrats that they should utilise social media to meet specific objectives, but confine themselves to the Hindi language, had the unintended consequence of generating a frisson of linguistic tensions. A later meeting with a top executive from Facebook on a business visit to India, earned wide media coverage. The Prime Minister's account of the meeting, in which he spoke of his enthusiasm in using social media as an accessory of his development ambitions, earned many thousand readers within seconds of being posted.[107]

Whose freedom?

In January 2012, Naresh Chandra, who then headed the newly minted body called the National Security Advisory Board – and in a long career as a civil servant, had transited through numerous sensitive positions – delivered a lecture instituted in honour of the founder of India's top overseas intelligence agency. The occasion determined the audience, which was closely attuned to the discourse of "national security" and needed no guidance through its basic premises. The prerogative of intruding into private conversations in the cause of national security was after a fashion, taken for granted within this audience.

Naresh Chandra worried that conventional modes of intelligence gathering and enforcement were proving inadequate for the brave new world of new networking technologies. "A revolution in communication and the tremendous expansion of the internet has created a new situation", he said: "The utility of monitoring telephonic conversation or intercepting messages on wireless is hardly sufficient any more".

106 Reuters (2014).

107 NDTV (2014).

Aside from print and TV, "the social media has now a reach which runs into millions with extremely fast communication capable of creating a surge of public opinion and movement faster than any government agency can monitor, let alone control". Referring to the protests against the sin of corruption in India and the tidal wave of street demonstrations that had seized the Arab world, Chandra observed that through the year 2011, "highly centralised governments" had been "taken by surprise (by) movements springing on to the streets in unexpectedly large numbers united with a common intent". Yet, while flagging this "new destabilising phenomenon", Naresh Chandra had words of comfort too. The "impact of such events" he concluded, would "fortunately" be "less in democracies where the media is free and open".[108]

Since then it became the commonsense among the country's top police and security officials that the new media was part of the factors they had to account for in strategic plans. In an address to the country's top police officials in 2013, Prime Minister Manmohan Singh alerted them to the need to be vigilant on this count, though without going so far as to demand an abridgment of the free speech right.[109]

Freedom is partly about knowing the limits to which an individual or institution can press what are seen as the "rightful demands" of a particular constituency. Conflict is inherent in any regime of freedom, but an individual or social group that persistently pursues what it sees as "rightful demands", even at the risk of intruding into the autonomous domain of another, would risk endemic strife. Media freedom is about the pursuit of several objectives, not all of which are in harmony: profit, the public right to information and the fostering of dialogue. Over time, this freedom has been defined in terms of the unrestrained right to seek profits and the discretion to seek out target communities, while shutting out all others.

Common carrier principle: a reaffirmation

In the actual workings of the media as an industry – and especially the manner in which revenues are structured, the key difference between advertising and editorial functions has perhaps been obliterated. It needs to be restated that free speech protections apply only to the news

108 Chandra (2012).

109 *Hindustan Times* (2013).

and editorial content of the media. In being the means through which news and editorial material can be conveyed to an audience at an affordable price, advertising would count more as carrier than content. The growing encroachment of advertising considerations into choice of content, falls foul of the first principle of good media management, which involves the separation of carriage and content. The "common carrier" principle as earlier seen, is the foundation on which the media's claims to a special status are built. But the intrusion of advertising vitiates this status and also becomes an active agent of blocking certain voices. The media in its neoliberal avatar has in short, become an active agency of suppressing the free speech right. Early hopes that the internet would bring liberation from the constrictions imposed by older media remain unfulfilled. Search algorithms and social media sites, increasingly the dominant modes of negotiating the Worldwide Web, are a means of bundling a user's information needs with his perceived purchasing abilities and interests, using individual profiles secreted in data centres by the internet giants. Far from achieving any manner of separation of content and carriage, the internet promises its ever firmer integration into one seamless whole, where the worth of information is judged solely by its cash value to the advertiser.

Journalism
Paid Speech in Sold Media

In February 2014, the Supreme Court of India ruled on a number of petitions brought by the newspaper industry, finessing a three year long enterprise. This outcome did little to requite the investments made in retaining the country's most expensive legal luminaries in arguing the industry case.[1]

First in the media owners' wish list was a definitive judicial ruling that a 1955 Act that afforded a measure of protection to the wages and working conditions of their employees, violated constitutional provisions on equality, free speech and the freedom of commerce. As part of a mandate conferred by the act, the Government had in 2007, appointed two statutory boards to propose fair wages and working conditions for journalists and other industry employees. In line with two reports submitted by the boards in 2010, the Government had in November 2011 through the Ministry of Labour, notified statutory scales of wages for newspaper industry employees. Only those who were well protected in other ways - either by way of seniority or in terms of vested interests in the profits of media organisations - were exempt from the sweep of the wage boards' attentions.

In addition to a final resolution of the constitutional question, the newspaper industry also sought a lesser relief. The most recent of the

1 Supreme Court of India (2014).

statutory wage fixation processes, it urged, should be set aside as stemming from an unsound law and based upon improper procedure.

The relevant enactment, the Working Journalists' and Other Newspaper Employees'(Conditions of Service and Miscellaneous Provisions) Act (hereafter, WJA), was passed in 1955 and then amended significantly in 1973. Aside from the constitutional challenge the petitioners also advanced an argument that the passage of years had rendered the law redundant. Further allegations were made about a conflict of interest, the denial of a fair hearing, and an unseemly anxiety to appease one side to the bargain. What should have been a tripartite bargain involving employers, workers and the government had in the industry's perception, effectively become a collusive process between government representatives and journalists' trade unions, united in a cause that would seriously damage the industry's financial prospects.

The newspaper lobby's suspicions on procedure arose in part from the Labour Ministry which administers the wage boards, having nominated its principal official – of the rank of secretary – to be a member of the wage boards soon after his retirement. He filled a place under the quota reserved for persons putatively "independent" of all parties engaged in the tripartite process. This was consistent with a long record of civil servants seeking evergreen pastures by appointing themselves to secure post-retirement billets. Yet an issue that merits serious engagement in terms of administrative ethics has become so much a standard practice that the Supreme Court hesitated to take a firm stand. It relied instead upon a judgment from 1973, which held that a lack of independence in official conduct had to be established with material evidence, not just inferred on the basis of the concerned individual's past service.[2]

Moving on, the Supreme Court called out as sharp effrontery, the plea of the newspaper industry that it had been denied a fair hearing. The factual record showed that the wage boards had early in their life, sent out inquiries to a large sample of newspapers enterprises, inviting opinions on procedure. Relevant financial information was sought in an obvious effort to avoid a pitfall that had brought earlier wage board processes to grief: the alleged failure to consider the newspaper industry's capacity to pay. As noted in the Supreme Court judgment,

2 Ibid: para 33.

"a detailed questionnaire was in fact issued .. (and) this questionnaire was commented upon ..(and).. corrected". Newspaper enterprises that responded "also received replies".

When challenged with these facts on record, the newspaper industry "attempted to make a feeble argument that the said questionnaire was issued by the secretariat and not by the wage boards". This was an alibi verging on the frivolous, "fit to be rejected".[3] The Supreme Court noted "several attempts ... made by the wage boards to get the relevant information from the employers". Many among the petitioners though, "had not given financial data" and also "abstained from ... proceedings". Records showed that the questionnaire seeking financial information over a nine year period had been sent to an exhaustive number of establishments, listed in the directory of the apex industry body, the Indian Newspaper Society (INS). There was then "regular follow up with the employers .. and (a) series of letters .. issued to collect financial information". Responses remained patchy and sporadic and in July 2010, the wage boards issued a "summons" to "around one hundred and forty stakeholders" giving them one final chance "to submit the information within fifteen days". In all, as the Supreme Court observed, no fewer than five extensions of deadline were granted for all stakeholders to submit any information that in their judgment would have been relevant.[4]

The newspaper industry had at various times in the past, earned rich dividends through the expedient of denying information for a public purpose. In 1958, the Supreme Court struck down the award of the first wage board for journalists, on grounds that it disregarded the industry's capacity to pay. It declined at the same time, to entertain the larger demand that the WJA, enacted just three years before, be declared a constitutional violation. The mood of the bench in 2014 was very different. The limited responses received from the newspaper industry were in the opinion of the court, adequately representative and afforded a sound basis for the wage boards to arrive at fair determinations.[5] There was also little substance in the industry's plea that it had not been given sufficient time to deliberate on the findings of the

3 Ibid: para 44.

4 Ibid.

5 Ibid: para 46.

wage boards.[6] No case existed to allow the petitioners "to take advantage of their own wrong and impugn the recommendations of the wage boards as not being based on their data when they eluded to submit the said data in the first place".

For the rest, the Supreme Court in 2014 reaffirmed a number of its findings from close to six decades before, when it was first called upon to decide on the constitutionality of a law protecting journalists' rights. Obviously, not very much had changed in its understanding of the substantive foundations of free speech and other fundamental rights. Neither unfortunately, had the obduracy of the newspaper industry to resist a fair bargain with its staff.

The first wage board constituted under the WJA came up with an award mid-1957, applicable only to journalists since the amendment to bring other employment categories under legal protection did not happen till 1973. It was a contentious process, with employer representatives on at least two vital points voting against the chairman and the journalists' representatives: the classification of newspaper groups on the basis of gross revenue; and the fixation of entire wage scales rather than just minimum rates.

Once the wage award was notified the more serious mobilisation began. In a petition filed before the Supreme Court – a case cited as *Express Newspapers and Others versus the Union of India* – the industry argued that the WJA was an irksome intrusion into press freedom and bad in law, since it created "a class of workers whose benefits and rights are given a preferential enforceability". In this respect, it offended against Article 14 of the Constitution, which guaranteed equality before the law.

Working journalists constituted less than a fifth of the "total staff employed by various newspaper establishments", said the petitioners. Improving the conditions of service of just this category of workers would be a fraught and hazardous imposition. It would trigger similar demands from "other employees who ... were bound to be restive and likely to raise industrial disputes for betterment of their conditions of service". The snowballing demands would "impose an additional financial burden on the newspaper establishments and ... substantially affect their capacity to pay".

6 Ibid: para 50.

An "abstract" guarantee of the "freedom of expression", the industry argued, would be "meaningless", if it were not accompanied by the assurance that "all the means necessary for the practical application of the freedom" would be protected. Viewed in its entirety, the WJA "authorised the fixation of salary of working journalists at a level which disables the running of the press". This manner of a restriction on free speech – and the newspaper lobby was absolutely convinced it was one – was not permitted under the first amendment to the Constitution and was hence contrary to law.

The WJA was also attacked in the petition as an unreasonable restraint on the freedom to conduct a trade, again falling foul of Article 19(1)(g) of the Constitution which guaranteed the right to practise a profession and carry out any occupation, trade or business.

Why journalism?

The status of journalism was a key issue the court was called on to decide. Did the special dispensation for journalists imply in some way a status that was "more equal" than others? And did this constitute a violation of the principle of equality before the law?

Indian jurisprudence tends to view the equal treatment of unequals as an injustice. In the language it was originally written in, the Indian Constitution enshrined equality before the law as a fundamental right without sufficient allowance for this principle, leaving an affirmative action programme introduced for the benefit of the disadvantaged in the ritual caste hierarchy, in a zone of judicial vulnerability. In this and several other cases brought soon after the Constitution was enacted, the judiciary stuck closely to the letter of the law and rudely overturned the commitments of the political leadership. Pushback from the political realm soon began. The first amendment to the Constitution, moved in 1950, introduced several changes in the language of Article 14 (equality before the law), not to mention Article 19 which covered free speech and other fundamental rights.

Amendments in the equality clause created room for special legislation to improve the lot of "socially and educationally backward classes". Certain identified "classes" within the general mass of the population, could be rendered legislative protections in the larger public interest. The jurisprudence of affirmative action is among the most fascinating threads in the evolution of India's constitutional philosophy. Early interpretations held that affirmative action would enjoy sanction as an exception to the equality guarantee. In later rulings, the Indian Supreme Court held affirmative action a stronger affirmation of the equality clause, rather than exception.[7] For a nation liberated from colonialism, and seeking to institute a republican order, equality clearly did not mean the equal treatment of unequals.

It was never anybody's case that the special legislation introduced for newspaper industry workers had anything to do with affirmative action. But India's Parliament, through the first decade of its existence, was very attentive to the needs of journalists. And it found a rationale for identifying journalism, among a host of professions, as one meriting legislative protection.

What made journalism different? As the public debate evolved – within Parliament and outside – a number of possible reasons came up, though none was fully elaborated. For this reason, the special legislation introduced in defence of journalism remains half-baked – or to put a more positive construction on the matter – a work in progress.

With these constitutional debates incipient, the Indian Federation of Working Journalists (IFWJ) was formed in 1950 as the first nation-wide representative body of the profession. M. Chalapati Rau, editor of the *National Herald*, a newspaper founded in the 1930s by Jawaharlal Nehru and based in Lucknow, was IFWJ's first president. At the time of its founding, the IFWJ was associated with the freedom movement and Nehru's ascent to office as Prime Minister of independent India, a time of struggle for establishing principles of equality and justice and optimism over the broadly defined cause of nation building. As a journalist, Chalapati Rau was seen to reflect Nehru's political attitudes and priorities, then considered the most refined expression of the new nationalist consensus.[8]

---

7 These are issues dealt with in Galanter (1984), a key work in understanding the many interpretations that the equality clause can assume.

8 In his account of the Indian press since independence, Bhargava (2005: 160) offers the following account of the relationship between Nehru and Chalapati Rau: "It was said that Chalapati Rau shared with Nehru the flair for writing flawless English prose. International affairs were his forte. Nehru as the founder of the *Herald* watched Chalapati Rau run the *Herald* from close quarters. When he was in Lucknow Nehru would drop in at the *Herald* office at night to be with Chalapati Rau

IFWJ demanded an empowered body that would inquire into the status of the press in newly independent India and this was seen to be of assistance to Nehru's government in cutting through a number of dilemmas, including dissent over the advisability of the first amendment to the Constitution. A body that remained rather quiescent through this phase of the public dialogue, partly because of its anomalous provenance, was the All India Newspaper Editors' Conference (AINEC), inspired in its creation by Kasturi Srinivasan of *The Hindu*, who also had substantial ownership in the newspaper. The AINEC was in this sense, not the greatest exemplar of editorial autonomy. Indeed, the authority of the editor was on the wane during the war years, as newsprint scarcities and the associated ration system opened up new avenues of profit, making investments in quality news coverage a side-issue for most newspaper owners.[9] The AINEC drew its putative strength from the stature the editor enjoyed in the newsroom, but as "the financial conditions of the newspapers improved – during the war years and after mostly through the non-journalistic activities of the establishment – the editor became more or less a business executive, and the editors conference developed into a shadow of the Newspaper Society".[10]

An extended and deeply polarised public dialogue followed the submission of the Press Commission report in July 1954. In legislative forums and the community of journalists, the tone tended to be supportive, while newspaper lobbies – mainly because the smaller players among them were not heard – pitched in with contrary opinions. Among its many recommendations, the Press Commission advised special legislative protection for working journalists, and a fair competitive environment for small and medium newspapers against the predatory tendencies of the large.

---

as he brought out the main edition. Once Nehru picked up from the PTI ticker a news item of several persons being killed in a mine accident and thought it deserved to be front page. When Chalapati Rau demurred, Nehru asked how many deaths there should be for a news item to make the front page? Integrity was another hallmark of Chalapati Rau's journalistic career".

9 Bhargava (2005): 28.

10 Ibid.

As this public dialogue progressed, India's Parliament in March 1955, took up a bill to extend to journalists the Industrial Disputes Act, passed in 1948 with the stated intent of protecting industrial workers from whimsical and vindictive management actions. Political support was overwhelming and when the bill was introduced in the lower house of India's Parliament – the Lok Sabha – in March 1955, members extended their sitting to ensure its passage. Hiren Mukherjee, then at the start of a distinguished parliamentary career, put the case for the legislation thus: "some of the greatest figures in (India's) recent history have taken to the avocation of journalism, but in those days, as even today to a very marked extent, deprivation was the portion of those who took to journalism".

A robust denunciation of the ownership of newspapers followed. "The press has become a segment of big money, and that is why the right to start newspapers and rape (sic) the public mind is almost a fundamental right, which we cannot contest, of people who have been described by one of our leading journalists today as the Thugs and Pindaris of the press". "It is against these Thugs and Pindaris of the press", Mukherjee said, "that the working journalist wants some sort of protection".

Other notable speakers in favour of the bill were R. Venkatraman (later a Union Finance Minister and President of the Indian republic), N.C. Chatterjee (elected on a Hindu Mahasabha ticket, but then in the process of shifting towards an independent posture with an emphasis on civil liberties) and M.S. Gurupadaswamy (who served as Minister for Chemicals and Fertilisers in the Union Cabinet of 1989-90). For Venkatraman, the bill was nothing less than the "*magna carta*" of working journalists. For Chatterjee, it was long overdue legal protection for a professional community that had been victimised for merely being true to its conscience. And in Gurupadaswamy's estimation, the legislation had come not a moment too soon, since newspaper establishments he knew, had already begun squeezing out seeming recalcitrants in anticipation of the day that journalists would gain a measure of legislative protection.[11]

The political mood was influenced very deeply by context and history, particularly by memories – then still fresh – of India's freedom

11 Parliament of India (1955): 1633-65.

struggle in its climactic phase, which coincided broadly with World War II. The relative ambivalence of the owners towards the freedom movement – sympathetic but unwilling to sacrifice core business interests – and the unequivocal support rendered by the community of journalists and press workers, seemed clearly to mark out one category as allies and the other as adversaries.[12] Journalists then seemed

---

12 Special wartime rationing procedures made newsprint a rare commodity, invariably reserved for the more compliant newspapers. Concurrently, a "press advisory system" was instituted, complete with oversight bodies at the national and provincial levels, which determined what the limits of fair reporting and comment were. Critical historians have with great credibility, referred to this as a system of pre-censorship of news content in which the newspaper owners were willing accomplices. Others are inclined to give the newspaper owners the benefit of the doubt, since the wartime powers that the imperial government had assumed provided for summary seizure of assets – and few of the Indian newspaper groups could really afford to run that risk (Bhargava, 2005: 26).

India's newspaper owners were well aware by then of the limits of safe reporting and of where they should allow nationalist commitment to subside when undeniable business imperatives cropped up. Israel (1994: 46) has recorded that a certain kind of conservatism, "both personal and institutional" characterised the relationship between the imperial government and the emerging Indian press. Illustratively, when "Gandhi asked the editor of *The Hindu* to publish a proscribed book in 1919, he was told that they had made too large an investment in their presses to risk confiscation and ruin. As an alternative, an unregistered cyclostyled news sheet was produced denouncing the Rowlatt Acts – serving both *The Hindu*'s nationalist principles and its business interests". Many of the press owners and prominent journalists who became involved in the freedom movement, like the editor of *The Hindu*, were in the description of a prominent historian of modern India, "vicarious nationalists", who were quite content to allow others to bear the burdens.

Journalists suffered no such qualms and were quite unequivocally behind the struggle for freedom. Bhargava (2005: 31) points out that the *National Herald*, the official newspaper of the Congress Party was a particular target of the imperial administration, which found much in it that went against the canons of permissible reporting. The financial misfortunes that were inflicted on the newspaper as a consequence of imperial displeasure, brought it to the very verge of closure. But in a gesture of commitment, the workers of the newspaper – both journalists and others – volunteered to forego their salaries for several months in succession.

It also needs to be added here, that long after the Congress party transformed itself from a national liberation movement into India's pre-

credibly to have a claim to be spokespersons for the general public, irrespective of social strata or class, while newspaper owners were seen to represent a narrow sectarian interest.

A more positive affirmation of journalists' rights came with the passage of WJA later in 1955. Again, Parliament united across all partisan divides in approving the bill.[13] The WJA was introduced in the Lok Sabha by Information Minister B.V. Keskar, with the following remarks:

> In some ways, the Bill itself is not a major Bill. It is a small Bill. .. But, it is important.. that we are trying to apply it to an industry which up to this time was not able to get all these benefits, a piece of legislation, which, for the better working of our Press, for the better security of our journalists and therefore for a better, I would say, freedom of the press in this country ....[14]

This was one of the few occasions when journalists' job security was spoken of as an ingredient of the policy mix safeguarding press freedom. The basic provisions of the WJA, as explained by the Minister, involved protection of journalists against arbitrary dismissal or mass retrenchment, regulation of the hours of work and the creation of a gratuity fund which would be a safeguard against long-term financial insecurity.

Perhaps the most important provision of the WJA was its creation of a statutory wage fixing machinery. In response to a number of queries, the Minister clarified that the power of the statutory board would go beyond determining a minimum wage. This represented an important change from the way the law was initially conceived by the Press Commission. As the Minister put it:

---

sumptive party of governance, the workers of the *National Herald* went through a much longer period of similar adversity, though not this time by choice. Though a ruling party that had no serious issue with raising funds, the Congress in the 1980s clearly had little inclination to put any resources into the newspaper business.

13 The Act was originally titled Working Journalists (Conditions of Service) and Miscellaneous Provisions Act, 1955. As it now exists, it is titled the Working Journalists and Other Newspaper Employees (Conditions of Service) and Miscellaneous Provisions Act, 1955. Several of these key amendments were made in 1974.

14 Lok Sabha debates.

> The important change that was made ... was regarding wages. The original proposal was for a minimum wage board... We had the benefit of discussing this question again with the representatives of the working journalists and we came to a happy agreement. In the light of that agreement, we have changed this particular clause and instead of having a minimum wage board, there will be a wage board which will fix the rates of wages for journalists.[15]

The background to the judicial review of the constitutionality of the WJA, was the assessment of the Press Commission, which laid out the basis for the special treatment of journalism in the following terms:

> It is essential to realise in this connection that the work of a journalist demands a high degree of general education and some kind of specialised training. Newspapers are a vital instrument for the education of the masses and it is their business to protect the rights of the people, to reflect and guide public opinion and to criticise the wrong done by any individual or organization, however high-placed. They thus form an essential adjunct to democracy. The profession must, therefore, be manned by men (sic) of high intellectual and moral qualities. The journalists are in a sense creative artists and the public, rightly or wrongly, expect from them a general omniscience and a capacity to express opinion on any topic that may arise under the sun.[16]

Echoing some of these assessments, counsel for the respondents in the litigation before the Supreme Court, took the argument that the "work of a journalist is peculiar and demands a high degree of general education and some kind of specialised training". On this and numerous other criteria, working journalists "are a class by themselves". The equality clause in the Indian Constitution did not prohibit the identification of specific classes of people who deserved (or might need) special legislative attention. The classification of journalists as such a category was based on "intelligible *differentiae* which distinguish them from other employees of the newspaper establishments and ... other industries".

It was, moreover, established law that employers had no right to argue that legislation seeking economic and physical security for workers fell foul of the equal rights clause. There was in all these respects, no inherent discrimination in identifying journalists "for the purpose of ameliorating their conditions of service".[17]

---

15 Ibid.

16 Press Commission (1954): 198.

17 Supreme Court of India (1958): Headnotes.

Beyond this affirmation of the uniqueness of journalists and their claims to recognition as a special "class", there was an apparent hedging of bets. The WJA, the respondents argued, could be viewed as one among many "social welfare measures". The WJA in this rendition was a legislative protection being extended to journalists in the first instance for purely contingent reasons. It could potentially, just as well be extended to other occupational groupings when required. Even the most ambitious social welfare initiative needed to "make a beginning somewhere" and could not possibly be "all embracing" at the moment of its conception.[18]

The court acknowledged that this argument had some weight. To take up all industries together would be impossible and doing so "one by one" was merely a matter of expedient procedure. Within the newspaper industry, it would be "equally expedient to take a class of employees who stand in a separate category by themselves". This did not mean that any special category of preference was being created, or that a class of workers was being acknowledged as "more equal". Rather, the objective of the "amelioration of the conditions of those workmen" did not imply lesser consideration for any other category; only that all occupation groups would be given their turn in proper sequence.

These were convincing arguments and the court determined that restricting the right to free speech was not the intent of the Act and neither would it be the likely outcome. Simply put: "neither the intention nor the effect and operation of the impugned Act is to take away or abridge the right of freedom of speech and expression enjoyed by the petitioners".

A stronger case, the court held, could be made against the WJA on grounds of an impediment to the right to commerce, another constitutional guarantee derived from Article 19, though infirmly established within the hierarchy of rights, if some such construct is feasible. The only possible circumstances that could redeem the WJA were the "reasonable restrictions" granted on the right to commerce, where the test of "reasonableness" in turn came from "intelligent care and deliberation". On the face of things, there was nothing in the wage board process that offended against these requirements. Where industry existed, disputes were not merely possible, but likely. And in every such in-

18 Ibid.

stance, it would be a necessary remedy that a neutral body, with equal representation from all contending parties, should sit in judgment on possible solutions.

Procedural flaws in the wage bargaining process

Having disposed of all constitutional questions, the court took on the issue of procedural soundness: was the Wage Board a legislative body operating on a mandate conferred by Parliament or was it a judicial body? If the former, it could ordain appropriate scales of pay for working journalists. If the latter, it would be obliged to follow something akin to due process and hear all sides.

Against this benchmark, the Wage Board suffered the serious procedural infirmity that few newspaper owners were prepared to cooperate with its deliberations. Responses to the questionnaire it sent out, asking for information on newspaper industry finances, were patchy and incomplete. As recorded in the Supreme Court judgment: "Out of 5,465 newspapers (and) journals to whom the questionnaire was sent only 381 answered the same; and out of 502 dailies only 138 answered it".

Following the Wage Board award, newspaper managements proved rather willing to make a presentation of their financial parameters, in a patently selective and self-serving fashion, before the Supreme Court. On balance, the Supreme Court found insufficient attention paid to the industry's compulsions and points of view. Far from being a body delegated with legislative power, the Wage Board was an administrative agency constituted by Parliament to aid the legislative process, and was as such, obliged to follow certain procedures appropriate to judicial functioning. It would need to "elicit all relevant information and invite answers to the questionnaire or representations from the parties concerned, hear evidence and arrive at their determination after conforming to the principles of natural justice".

The Wage Board enjoyed a "wide discretion" to determine its "own rules of procedure". But this did not mean that it was "entitled to follow any arbitrary rules of procedure". The Wage Board was a "responsible" body entrusted with "the task of gathering data and materials (sic) relevant for the determination of the issues" before it.[19]

---

19 Ibid.

In effect, the Wage Board was asked to gather information it had no authority to access, since the newspaper companies, with few exceptions, were privately owned companies that had no obligation under law to reveal their financial parameters. As created by law, the Wage Board was not just about minimum wages but about fixing an entire scale of pay for journalists, and this was a mission that involved a deep dive into newspaper economics, both as it existed and was likely to evolve. To credibly fix journalists' pay scales, the Wage Board needed to project ahead and take account of newspaper finances over the time-horizon relevant to its award. Lacking information on newspaper finances, the Wage Board was unable to project ahead from an unknown present to a still more indeterminate future.

The Supreme Court found in this context, that the procedure of the Wage Board was about reconciling competing demands in a spirit of "give and take". For every demand from the journalists' side, the Wage Board sought to determine how far the newspaper owners were prepared to yield, and then sought a means of bridging rival perceptions – typically by splitting differences. There was no evidence the Wage Board had taken into account the capacity of the industry to bear the financial commitments it was imposing, since the classification of newspaper companies by aggregate revenue failed to account for numerous complexities which made revenue a very poor indicator of financial soundness. There was nothing in the WJA itself which went against constitutional guarantees, but the Wage Board award, the Supreme Court ruled, had been vitiated by unsound process and was in this regard, *ultra vires* of the WJA.[20]

An immediate consequence of the Supreme Court ruling was a narrowing of the discourse. In introducing the WJA, the Information Minister had spoken of a fair deal for journalism as a necessary part of the foundations undergirding press freedom. Far from developing on this theme, the Supreme Court characterised the WJA process as one among many methods of protecting the free speech right, and journalism as one among many professions. Journalism as a location for social welfare legislation, was a convenient place to begin, though not because of any intrinsic social value.

---

20 Ibid.

The press as "public utility"

This represented a significant dilution of the Press Commission doctrine that the newspaper was a "public utility", which by definition, was essential to the sustenance of the civic community. Viewing things from this perspective, the Press Commission could make a case for "some measure of restraint and regulation" on the "exercise of ownership rights" over the newspaper, which was much more than a business proposition to be milked for profit. Surveying the newspaper scene as it was then, the Commission found that against the benchmark it had set, the actual conduct of the industry fell very badly short.

The newspaper industry was of course in complete disagreement and *The Hindu*, which took a relatively sober attitude to the entire debate, put the case with detached eloquence: "We must in all respect, contest the Commission's unsupported conclusion that the conduct of newspapers is no longer a mission... It is true that journalism is no longer a camp-follower in a subject nation's crusade for freedom. It has grown and developed, however inadequately... It is slowly becoming professionalised, even while on the economic side it is fitting itself, as it must if it is to survive, into the general industrial infrastructure. It has no need to be ashamed of the progress from amateurish and often inadequate idealism to responsible professionalism".[21]

Viewed from the perspective of the newspaper owners, the changes underway were part of the organic process of evolution from public cause to industry. Politics in India, still heady with memories of the freedom struggle, remained unconvinced that this transition was either necessary or inevitable. And journalism faced a dilemma, or as G.S. Bhargava, a close and astute observer of the scenario observed, a "double irony or tragedy": "the idealism of the previous period had dried up and the press had become an industry but with the old practice of working journalists being expected to live on idealism, even if the newspapers were growing to be an industry".[22]

These ambiguities in interpreting the law contributed to an erosion of the quality imperative. Through the early years of India's independence, journalists worked with a certain self-belief, claiming their

21 Responses to Press Commission recommendations, Lok Sabha secretariat.

22 Bhargava (2005): 37-8.

entitlements on grounds of a credible, socially recognised role as representatives of the public interest. This was a claim that underwrote the claim that journalists deserved a fair deal from the newspaper industry ownership. Policy in its subsequent course, especially as determined through successive judicial rulings, has tended both to narrow the amplitude of the free speech right and make newspaper owners the privileged repository of that entitlement, and also spare the ownership of media organisations any obligation of financial disclosure.

Ownership interests were already unfettered by the early-1990s, when economic policy directions themselves underwent a radical transformation. In this sense, the Supreme Court's 2014 judgment on the constitutionality of the wage board process, marked an important breakthrough in disallowing obduracy and financial opaqueness as alibis. It may well have come too late in the day for an effective job of retrieval of the fundamentals of journalism. The journalists' trade union movement by then was showing all signs of having lost the means to leverage important findings of principle into optimal public advantage.

Beginning 1991, when India entered into a policy of economic liberalisation and integration with the global economy, the dynamics of the journalism function began altering. Technological changes, typified by the explosion of cable and satellite (C&S) television and the internet, were the most visible face of this new dynamic. But traditional sectors defied predictions, freely bandied about in the early years of the boom, about their imminent demise. Newspaper circulation and readership continued to increase, though with significant differences from earlier phases of growth.

Beginning in the aftermath of the U.S.-led war against Iraq in 1991 – when a cable news network that was till then the butt of jokes became the storied purveyor of global news around an unrelenting twenty-four hour cycle – satellite broadcasts began to breach the zealously guarded government monopoly over the airwaves. As private television channels began to open the breach wider and the government remained paralysed by indecision, there were forecasts made of the imminent demise of print as a medium, since advertising was expected to migrate in droves to the more widely diffused medium of television. Such did not in fact, come to pass and the story of how the print media in India responded to the challenges of the new policy and technological regime is a story of two kinds of responses: globalisation on one side and hyper-localisation on another.[23]

Globally, the new information environment, still at an early stage of development out of the old, attracted considerable scholarly attention towards reimagining the basics of journalism. The advance of satellite broadcasting stations such as the Cable News Network (CNN) was bringing "uncut reports of world events, from the Gulf War to peace keeping in the former Yugoslavia" into subscriber homes. The reporter at the scene of the event was "reduced to a mere purveyor of facts", leaving less room for exercising the traditional function of "critical journalism". "Getting closer" to the action meant "seeing less" and there were anxieties within journalism that the "combination of information management, instant news, empty analysis, and the best of intentions" threatened its future as a critical pursuit.[24] The questions that were raised by the new intersections of politics and technology were manifold. Was journalism on its way to redundancy, with the "advance of the direct registration of news" where the older functions of establishing the appropriate background and context were increasingly

---

23 Kumar (2011: 67-9) considers the dynamic between the local and the national: "In the newspaper industry it is common knowledge that local news sells. Mostly because local news has the specificity of event, place and people with which readers easily identify. However, despite the widely acknowledged value of the local news, the coverage of local news has been declining in many parts of the world. One of the main reasons is the high cost involved in news gathering, but in Indian journalism an additional factor was that the local news events and local politics did not carry the same prestige as national or state level news". Obviously, the compulsions of revenue and profit proved the best solvent for this snobbish refusal to give local news its due place. "Despite being national and regional in their operations newspapers such as *Amar Ujala* and *Dainik Jagaran* competed with local city and town newspapers to provide news content that was closer to the readers concerns, reinforcing the salience of local news... the journalists of *Amar Ujala* and *Dainik Jagran* explained that hyperlocalisation was their contribution in the reshaping of news. For example, the chief of bureau of *Dainik Jagran* in the early 1990s in Dehradun said, 'We tried to cover everything that we could as we had to fill the pages allocated to the Uttarakhand region'. He explained that the logic was simple – if there were people at an event, there had to be readers for the news about the event in the newspaper next day. To ensure that people bought the paper the next day one of the strategies adopted by the newspapers was publishing the names of most of the people who were there at the event"..

24 Bardoel (1996): 284.

being carried out by the news consumer? Or were things going to work out the other way, with individuals losing their way "on the information highway and (feeling) a greater need for journalistic direction"?[25]

There were various answers devised to these questions. In India, investments in the media industry continued to be driven by a conjunction of rising advertising spending, vanity and aspiration. With the economy increasingly driven by private consumption and the doors opening up for major consumer goods multinationals, the world of corporate advertising – once rather patronisingly tolerated or looked down upon – became a domain of bitter contestation between media organisations. Securing the best share in corporate advertising budgets, rather than audience or readership, became the touchstone of authenticity for media organisations. At the same time, there was a certain eagerness among business groups, both old and new, to leverage financial strength into a media presence, to burnish their claims to a voice in politics and policy.

By the late-1980s, segments of the regional elite and the media that they spoke through, were firmly on the national political scene. In 1993, the editor of *Punjab Kesari* was celebrating his arrival on the national stage, when even the Prime Minister would seek an audience with him. In his own estimation, he had won this status by fluke. Indira Gandhi had during her "emergency" regime between 1975 and 1977, imposed severe constraints on the paper's usual style of news coverage. As a special favour from the overseers of the media during that phase of suspended democracy, the *Punjab Kesari* owners asked for the freedom to publish fluff – or the "magazine" variety in the proprietor's words – on the front and back pages, which were natural focuses of reader interest. The formula was miraculously successful, bringing *Punjab Kesari*, a paper that had been scoffed at and disparaged, to the front ranks of the Hindi press. Post-Emergency, when the paper sought to go back to its older style, it was assailed by resistance from the readership, who had got used to the "magazine" style and would not brook any reversion.[26]

Big industrial families, such as the Ambanis of Reliance, the Singhanias of the JK group and Thapars of Ballarpur, had meanwhile en-

25 Ibid: 285.

26 The story is narrated in Jeffrey (2000): 95.

tered either with new newspaper launches or with older titles rebranded after being bought over. Some older print media enterprises sought despite a distinct lack of clarity in the regulatory environment, to enter the satellite broadcast space. It was a heady time and policies of liberalisation and integration with the global economy which had acquired a seemingly irreversible course in 1991, contributed in no small way to an unbound spirit of adventure and optimism. As a later and rather rueful account put it, "everything seemed possible" then. "The stock market soared, advertising flourished, media ambitions flowered, and costs went up and up". Established newspapers increased their offerings of "pages and sections", despite a plunging rupee which made newsprint imports costlier. For journalists, the times had never before been so good, with salaries doubling and tripling "as publications fought off staff raids by richer TV companies". A new category of "stock analysts" gained an entrenched and privileged place within the media. Where once "five figure salaries were rare, people ... began to talk of six-figure pay packets". More staff were hired by the new publications than ever before and with business journalism enjoying a new vogue, the number of specialists in that domain tripled over the decade.[27]

The good times did not last. By the end of the 1990s, most new entrants in the newspaper business were sunk in deep remorse. Industrial groups that sought media leverage to enhance their business prospects found the gamble not paying off. In one conspicuous instance – the Singhanias – the editorial freedom granted a newly launched newspaper in fact turned counter-productive, impeding the acquisition of much needed permissions for industrial expansion. Several of the media ventures launched in this rosy flush of optimism, soon began retrenching staff. Suddenly, the unending vistas of opportunity that seemed to be opening up for journalists began to contract. The bottom was beginning to fall out of what seemed an unprecedented sellers' market for the professional journalist.[28]

That is when the changes in employment terms that became widespread in the 1990s, but were ignored because of the illusions of plenty, began to cast a shadow over the prospects for journalism. The progressive transformation of tenured appointments to short-term contracts

27 *Business Standard* (1998).

28 Ibid.

and the wilful surrender of the protections afforded by the WJA were seen as risk-free ventures as long as the mirage of limitless opportunities persisted. The costs and hazards became apparent in the downturn that followed. By then perhaps, the process was too far gone to be reversed. Indeed the following years witnessed the steady erosion of professional rights beginning with the evisceration of the wage board process.

Globally, this was a deeply transformative time for journalism, invariably to the detriment of its independence and integrity. In a symposium carried in 1998, the *Columbia Journalism Review*, provided a description of some of these changes. A "grid system", as one contributor put it, had been designed for the evaluation of journalism, which required editors to "estimate the time it should take to produce a story". Benchmarks were specified: "A reporter was expected, for example, to produce as many as forty stories a week if each piece were based upon a press release and one or two cooperative sources – and about fifteen stories a week if each were based on meetings or police activities". Weekly measurements would be done of journalistic output in term of the "length of stories". Needless to say, goal achievement would be rewarded while the supposed slackers would be handed various disincentives. "Assembly line journalism" was the appropriate description and the new culture of the trade rightly likened without any aspersions on the many honest men and women with no option but to work in such establishments, to a "sweatshop".[29]

Another contributor to the symposium spoke of a "new era" in journalism, described in the words of a *New York Times* veteran as "a massively increased sensitivity to all things financial". The new ethos was causing a potentially "fatal erosion of the ancient bond between journalists and the public". Unlike in an earlier juncture, the news product that was increasingly landing "on newsstands, doorsteps, and television screens" was seen to be scarred by "a heightened, unseemly lust at many companies for ever greater profits". Editors were being compelled to subject their better judgments to that ambition, "surrendering part of their birthright to marketers and advertising directors,

29 Underwood (1998): 42.

and making news judgments based on criteria that would have (... only a few years before ...) been anathema".[30]

The new journalistic ethos was the outcome of more complex factors than merely unchained profit lust in media companies. There were suggestions in the symposium of a new dynamic in the relationship between the media and the "public". As a sequel to the illusion of the "managerial revolution" of the 1930s, when major family-owned companies passed into joint-stock ownership and managerial control, there was through the 1980s and '90s, a broadening of the base of corporate ownership, created in the main through a large-scale sell-off of public assets created through the years since the Second World War. Profit rather than public interest was becoming the benchmark around which all social activity would be evaluated. More U.S. nationals than ever before had acquired a stake in public companies of all kinds, and this gave them a sense of entitlement, seemingly, to shut out the bad news about these corporations that renegade journalists might want to convey. The "vastly expanded interests" of the investors in the stock-market demanded that the media should be tender in its treatment of the profit imperative.[31]

In India, the 1990s were a time of booming stock-market investments, when esoteric crafts such as share price analysis became a valued part of the journalistic skill-set. There was a growing mood of impatience with journalism that looked for nuance, and advised caution and a sense of scepticism towards predictions of an unending stock price boom that would enrich all. This public mood that favoured fanciful speculation rather than robust critical reporting, was in no small part fostered by the media industry, which saw it as an accessory of its profit objectives.

Media fortunes picked up after briefly flagging in the late-1990s. This was part of a purple patch of growth the Indian economy hit from about 2003, when for reasons that are yet to be fully understood, foreign investment started flooding into the country, both in their "direct" form to fuel the expansion of specific corporate enterprises in the booming automobiles and telecommunications sectors, as well as into

30 Hickey (1998): 29-30.

31 Ibid.

the share-markets to boost overall valuations and create the euphoria of the "wealth effect" for investors.[32]

As of December 2016, the Ministry of Information and Broadcasting had a list of 899 privately owned satellite TV channels that had been formally registered. Of these 303 had been registered formally as "news" broadcasters, in the sense that at least some part of their programme content would be devoted to news and current affairs. A significant number which still remains to be reliably established, was of channels exclusively devoted to news broadcasts around the twenty-four hour cycle. From among this number, over 250 had been registered for news broadcasts in the fiscal year 2004-05 and since (i.e., after April 1, 2004).[33]

Typical of the kind of print media enterprise that came up in this time of unfettered optimism, was *Daily News and Analysis* (*DNA*), launched in 2005 in Mumbai, perhaps India's most challenging newspaper market. *DNA* involved a collaboration between an old world print enterprise, the Dainik Bhaskar group headquartered in Bhopal and dominant in the Hindi readership segment, and Zee, a new satellite broadcast enterprise – smart enough to see the shape of things in the early-1990s and register a solid profile in the Hindi entertainment segment, which it steadily developed into a presence in news, films and sports.[34]

---

32 "Wealth effect" refers to a situation when the appreciation of assets prices creates a stimulus for consumer spending, even when income flows remain moderate.

33 The figures are from the Annual Report of the Ministry of Information and Broadcasting. More detailed figures involving earlier years, can be found at the website of the ministry: mib.nic.in.

34 The career graph of *DNA* is available in a number of sources accessible through internet search. An assessment of the newspaper's plans three years into its life, is available at *Mint* (2008c). This account from February 2008 speaks of the bold course the newspaper proposed to take, since the global financial meltdown was the proverbial "black swan" that nobody quite saw on the horizon. The founder of Zee, Subhash Chandra, merits intense study in his own right, particularly since he is one new media entrepreneur who actually succeeded in buying himself enormous political influence, winning a seat to the Rajya Sabha, the upper house of Indian Parliament in 2016. The electoral process was soon beset by allegations of corruption and vote-buying, leading to an unprecedented intervention by the criminal justice system into the privileged sphere of the elected legislature. These narratives would

By far the more dramatic growth was in television, with the phenomenon of news broadcasting around the clock, non-existent till then, becoming something of a commonplace. A number of journalists made their debut as natives of the new domain, but were obviously unable to find their way through the minefields of political and business reporting without appropriate guidance. A sense of continuity and institutional memory had to be established and there was no other way for news channels about to launch, than to trawl through the print media. Loyalists of print resisted the bait, others made that shift to the bold new idiom of communication. The terms of employment that these mass migrants from print encountered, were well short of the quality standards prescribed under the WJA, but generous pay packages tended to sweeten that pill.

Early in 2008, with the industry just a few months away from caving in, a media report that turned a celebratory gaze inwards, spoke of TV channel heads earning annual salaries in eight digits in rupee terms. "War for talent is getting fiercer by the day in the broadcast sector", it reported: a number of broadcast companies had scheduled their launches for the year ahead in "genres such as general entertainment and news" and this had pushed "the rush to hire experienced hands ... (to) ... a feverish pitch". The head of an executive search firm described the journalism job market in terms that suggested unending years of plenty: "Hiring is in full swing and cash-rich TV start-ups, mostly those backed by deep-pocket investors, are willingly doling out staggering sums for good professionals". Professionals at the junior tiers, with four or five years in the business, were assured of pay hikes of 30 per cent and more if they changed jobs, against a slightly lower incentive offered in the year gone by. Within particular organisations, salary hikes – theoretically based on performance, though it must be added that few were aware of concrete criteria of assessment – ran at between 25 and 40 per cent.[35]

---

take this particular narration along a different course, as too would the indictment of two top journalists from Zee in an extortion charge and their subsequent career in promoting an unrelenting chauvinist line in their news broadcasts, invariably in breach of accepted ethical conventions in journalism.

35 *Mint* (2008b).

September 2008 was the moment reality caught up with these fantasies. Perhaps the Indian media was so deeply immersed in its celebration of the good times, that it never really got a full measure of the ramifications of the global financial crash of 2008. Not for the first time but perhaps more sharply than ever before, the media industry had to face serious questions about sustainability. And the expansion of job opportunities for journalism, which had never looked under threat, though several other of the basic tenets of the profession were, could no longer to be taken for granted.

As the advertising pie shrank, survival strategies became more aggressive.[36] In an environment of economic deregulation, all possible restrictions on unfair competition in the media industry were already dismantled and most social controls ruled out of court. One of the key ingredients of the public image of journalists through the early years of India's independence – that they had the pulse of the public and were professionally committed to giving a voice to all of society – began to be unsustainable in a context of the strong assertion of ownership rights over the press. In the late-1990s, the *Times of India* (*TOI*), then galloping ahead of the competition and gaining profitability through an unabashed embrace of the new idiom of newspaper management – revenue driven, advertisement oriented and increasingly disdainful of older editorial verities – provided an invaluable case study of how far it could push news priorities to serve ownership interests. Unsurprisingly, the devaluation of the journalism function was an essential ingredient of this recipe for newspaper success. The slowdown that began in 2013 may have pushed its competitors to the wall, but the *TOI* was not by any means untouched.

The career of the *TOI* since the early-1990s at least, has been a saga of how the race to the bottom is the most profitable enterprise for a media institution. When newspapers were mired in old habits of thought, clinging to the belief that they served a public purpose, the *TOI* boldly proclaimed its exclusive devotion to the commercial calculus. It tided over a storm of derision, striking out along a determined strategy of squeezing out the last rupee of advertising revenue available in the market. And it succeeded not merely in maximising advertising revenue, but even in sharply boosting circulation and profitability.

36 An account of the serious damage caused to media profitability by the falling off of advertising spending is available at *Mint* (2013j).

Catastrophic success: a case study of the *Times of India*

Since India's whole-hearted embrace of the ethos of liberalisation, the *TOI* has been something of a role model not for its journalistic content, but for its ruthless business strategies. When the relevance of the medium to its traditional constituencies was itself being called into question, the *TOI* not merely remained relevant, but also created new constituencies along with the lifestyle paradigms it propagated. As a case study, the *TOI* is important for understanding the media as a social and political institution in the new world order. This is particularly true in the Indian context where Bennett Coleman and Company (BCCL), the company that owns the newspaper, was replicating what had been done by large media conglomerates elsewhere – the subordination of journalism to the whims of advertisers.

An entry against the newspaper in the internet based public encyclopaedia, Wikipedia, records that in 1907, *TOI* launched the first price war in the Indian media industry, cutting its price from 4 annas (or one-fourth of a rupee under the currency denominations then prevalent) to 1 anna.[37] An authoritative history of the Indian newspaper industry and its role in the struggle for freedom from colonialism, puts a rather different spin on the event. The *TOI*, it records was richer than the competition in the Bombay market and shared the power of its British patrons. But it was always under challenge from the nationalist minded *Bombay Chronicle*, particularly when the sympathies of the English-reading public in the city started shifting in that direction. Thus "when the *Chronicle* set its price at one anna, the *Times* felt compelled to reduce its single issue price to one anna in order to preserve its share of the market".[38]

However the game was played in Bombay in the early years of the 20th century, the 1990s witnessed radically different rules of engagement. Among the first of the consequential decisions made to signal the growing influence of BCCL Vice Chairman Samir Jain, was the closure of popular but indifferently profitable magazine titles owned by the company. *The Illustrated Weekly of India* – once synonymous with magazine reading culture in India – was shut in 1993. So too were

---

37 See the chronology available at the following web address: http://en.wikipedia.org/wiki/The_Times_Group.

38 Israel (1994): 23.

two very popular Hindi language titles – *Dharmayug* and *Dinman* – both of which occupied highly valued spaces within the Hindi literary universe, though without ever being big money-spinners. A profile of Samir Jain published in 2012, which honours him as the principal architect of the newspaper industry's evolution through the 1990s and 2000s, puts these decisions down not to narrowly commercial calculations, but to a deeper motivation to intimidate prospective competition.

It was the time when industrial groups with little legacy of direct involvement in the media were signalling their intent to enter that space. In particular, BCCL was focused on Reliance Industries, a vast business conglomerate, then planning an aggressive move into the news media space. By killing *The Illustrated Weekly* which was then one of the most prestigious titles within the BCCL, Samir Jain hoped to "unsettle his rivals". A prospective competitor would step back to take in the full implications and wonder whether Samir Jain had "something up his sleeve". Failing to find a reason in both commerce and corporate prestige, he would wait, just a bit hesitant before launching "an attack". In the case of Reliance, the group "stopped in their tracks" and then "retreated".[39]

It soon emerged that the *TOI* group had the larger ambition of establishing market dominance by leveraging the power of its daily publications, where profitability was a more assured prospect. Removing the clutter of publications was one way of concentrating forces in the group's principal weapons for waging all-out warfare. The Delhi market, dominated till then by the rather colourless and unimaginative *Hindustan Times* (hereafter, *HT*), was earmarked as the first battlefield. Owned by the Birla family – perhaps India's most powerful and influential industrial group at the time – *HT* was of considerably lesser vintage than the *TOI*. It had been parented by a factional leader of the Hindu Mahasabha using the finances of the Birla family, and since beginning operations in the 1930s, been under secure and settled ownership. Though Delhi had become a market of interest for three other major English newspaper groups – the *TOI*, *The Hindu*, and the *Indian Express* – *HT*'s dominance seemed assured and safe, until the rules were radically rewritten.

39 Subramanian (2012).

In March 1994, *TOI* sharply cut the selling price of its single issue from Rs 2.40 to Rs 1.50 on all days of the week except Friday. To guard against a catastrophic drain of revenues, the Friday price was raised to Rs 6, but soon enough cut to Rs 2.90. By early-May, the results as assessed by the *TOI* sales management team, were distinctly promising. Circulation in Delhi city, they estimated, had increased by about 20,000 on a sustained daily basis. Perhaps a quarter of this increase had been achieved at the expense of *HT*.

An unexpected hitch arose from another quarter. Newspaper vendors, an organised and powerful lobby in Delhi, were worried about a possible loss of income since their fees were computed as a fixed percentage of the newspaper's cover price. To assuage these worries, *TOI* agreed *ad hoc*, to increase the vendors' fee from 25 percent of the cover price, to the equivalent of almost 40 percent. It was unclear if an assurance was also conveyed that the old pricing scheme would be restored and all ad hoc and contingent measures eliminated. Newspaper vendors seemed to be under the impression that the revised price schedule of the *TOI* would be applicable for no more than three months. The *TOI* management had other ideas and three months into the new deal, vendor organisations, claiming a breach of commercial agreement, began a boycott of the newspaper. It was conjectured on the basis of fairly reliable bazaar gossip, that the *HT* management had actively stepped into the fray by then, leveraging its relationship of goodwill with the fraternity of news vendors to ensure that the *TOI*'s predatory forays were checkmated.

What followed were weeks on end, when the street corners where newspapers were bundled and packed for daily distribution, resembled battle zones. Newspaper vendors, with *HT* officials and employees seconded as their advisors and strategists, managed to disrupt every effort to have the *TOI* distributed. An injunction obtained from the Delhi High Court served little purpose against the raw muscle power deployed on the streets. Editorial columns in both *TOI* and *HT* became the medium through which the battle of ideas, such as they were, was fought. This was a world in a total disconnect with rude ground realities of brawling vendors and conniving managements, its vocabulary dominated by lofty notions of consumer sovereignty, of dealers coddled with an assured take from each copy distributed, and the noble instinct of sacrifice that had led *TOI* to slash prices and take a catastrophic loss of revenue in the readers' interests.

Peace was finally established between Delhi's principal combatants, but with a newspaper scenario transformed beyond recognition. Apart from *HT*, two other newspapers, the *Indian Express* and *Pioneer*, felt compelled to match the *TOI*'s offering by way of cover price. Among the majors, only *The Hindu* retained its older selling price, content in the realisation that its core commercial interests lay in the distant south of the country. With all newspapers published in Delhi facing a massive drain of circulation revenue, the race began in earnest for the conquest of the city's English reading demographic segments that would be of maximum interest to the advertisers.

The golden goose of advertising

Needless to say, the *TOI* emerged the winner in that pursuit of advertising gold. It could not have been otherwise, since the *TOI* by 1994 had long since internalised the most significant rule of competition in the market for advertisements. Simply put, the advertiser was king and the readership a distant abstraction that did not have any immediacy to the newspaper, except as a burden to be borne. A chronicle of the Indian media industry records that the history of the press in the country can be written in terms of a significant point of inflection. The print industry, for long mired in romantic recollections of its contribution to the Indian freedom struggle and deluded in the belief that it had a role in underwriting the quality of the public discourse, was shaken out of its reverie by Samir Jain who entered his family business as a decisive player around the mid-1980s.[40]

A breathless account of the *TOI*'s innovations in the newspaper industry informs us that Samir Jain's achievement was to use "simple marketing principles and good business sense to transform a down-

40 Kohli (2003: 22) records the advent of Samir Jain in two section heads in her chapter on the print industry. "Then came the business.." says the sub-head on page 22, registering the momentous impact of Samir Jain's entry with the following section, which bears the heading: "That Samir Jain changed". A bitter business rival of the TOI group is quoted grudgingly conceding that the entry of this individual was among "the biggest milestones in the newspaper business in India".

in-the-dumps publishing company into a profit machine".[41] It is a testament to its essential simplicity that the same strategy, when deployed in Hyderabad in 2000, encountered a rather better prepared opposition. Both *The Hindu* and the *Deccan Chronicle* with longer established bonds in the city, pre-emptively slashed prices to retain and even increase their market shares.[42]

Evidently, price competition was rather quickly exhausted as a strategy of expanding market share. The focus then shifted to the demographic character of the audience. Paradoxically, the segments of the newspaper reading public that set much store by price are of relatively less importance to the advertiser. People with high purchasing power and high individual net worth tend to be insensitive to price variables in newspaper buying decisions, since even a difference of a few hundred rupees a month is from their points of view, immaterial. The *TOI* marketing strategy then devolved upon a simple principle: to bring the universe of the high purchasing power demographic into the gaze of every reader. It was the decade of globalisation, when the cult of the celebrity acquired unparalleled proportions and a celebration of the good life of the few became a source of vicarious delight for the many. The *TOI* was instrumental in the creation of this ethos, since that was the editorial ambience best suited to the advertiser.

Initial conditions were strongly in its favour. The *TOI* had always been strongly entrenched in Mumbai (formerly Bombay) city, the commercial metropolis that was home to most of the country's prin-

---

41 Ibid: 25-6.

42 *Hindu Business Line* (2000) provides an assessment of how *TOI*'s strategy of a price war in Hyderabad was checkmated by rival papers with deeper roots in the city. The report comes from a news enterprise which was itself a combatant, but is objective for most part. An assessment by a media monitoring enterprise in July 2001, just under a year since the *TOI* launched its Hyderabad edition, provided the following summation: "*TOI* launched its edition here late last year. ... Most of *TOI*'s key moves in a new market, were by then, very well known... *TOI* was pre-empted much ahead of their launch. *Deccan Chronicle* was given a complete makeover... (And) even *The Hindu* wore war paint in anticipation. Almost a year and three Resident Editors later, *TOI* in Hyderabad seems poised for a long haul. It has barely 5 percent of the city's English readership universe...." This account of the Hyderabad newspaper market and various other print media battlegrounds is from Exchange4Media (2001).

cipal advertisement agencies. Till the 1990s shifted the locus of urban wealth towards newer centres less weighed down by legacy, Mumbai was the city that by far, disposed of the greatest purchasing power. Enjoying a near monopoly in this market for decades, the *TOI* by 1994 was estimated to have an advertisement ratio, measured as the proportion of total printed area devoted to ads, of 55 percent. In comparison, the *HT* in Delhi and *The Hindu* in Chennai enjoyed much more modest ratios in the lower 40s. This was the initial advantage that endowed the *TOI* with the confidence that it could launch a price war and stay the course better than the competition.[43]

The gains of the price war would have proved ephemeral though, if the *TOI* had not recognised that celebrity narcissism was the wave of the future. And for those who were not fortunate enough to share in the ethos of these charmed circles, the opportunity to gawk from a distance was an acceptable substitute. Either way, the celebration of the good life was just what the advertiser wanted.

The *TOI*'s distinction was in being way ahead of the curve in adapting editorial content to advertiser needs. Beginning in the mid-1990s, the *TOI* began a shift of content towards fashion, lifestyle and entertainment that had its loyal readership thoroughly flummoxed, used as it was to an intensely political discourse, intimately engaged with public causes. But even as many among the older audience cancelled their subscriptions in dismay, the newspaper succeeded in attracting new readers from unexplored demographic segments, like youth and high purchasing power strata. The results were dramatic.

On December 22, 2003, readers of *TOI* began their day with a veritable display of triumphalism by their daily habit. Blazoned on the front page that day was a message of thanks to the newspaper reading public of Delhi, which had ostensibly made *TOI* the city's premier newspaper. And as important as aggregate figures was the composition of the audience. "Over three-fourths" of its readers, proclaimed the newspaper, were in "the highest socio-economic category"; "almost a fourth" were "executives, businessmen, (and) self-employed professionals"; and the

43 These figures were drawn from conversations with newspaper staff engaged in advertising, principally in *The Hindu*, during the price wars in the Delhi market in the 1990s.

newspaper had established itself as the "clear choice" of the youth, with about 40 percent of its readers being below 24.[44]

The basis for the celebrations was the National Readership Survey (NRS) for 2003, which had put *TOI* ahead of *HT* in Delhi for the first time ever. In a pre-emptive manoeuvre, *HT* put out a story through its own columns the same day, arguing that the NRS findings were deceptive. "Circulation", rather than "readership", was the more reliable index of a newspaper's spread and influence, it argued. And circulation figures as gathered by the mandated body, the Audit Bureau of Circulation, still accorded *HT* a significant lead over all competitors in the Delhi market.

TOI hit back with another front-page salvo the following day. "At the top", it proclaimed in bold print, "there's room for only one". And with an abundance of pedantic zeal, it sought to explain what the essential differences were, between circulation and readership, and why its claims to leadership in Delhi were absolutely watertight.[45]

The celebrations continued for another day. The edition of the *TOI* on Christmas eve moved the venue of the festivities from page one to two. It featured two photographs, of the Dalai Lama and Hindi movie star Amitabh Bachchan, posing with editions of the newspaper, and a chorus of acclaim from well-heeled businessmen and executives, about the pioneering new path *TOI* had embarked upon. For those who were still a little squeamish at the cocktail of froth and celebrity vacuous-

44 *The Times of India*, New Delhi, December 22, 2003, p. 1.

45 "The ABC of NRS", *The Times of India*, December 23, 2003, p. 1. In explaining the issues involved, the *TOI* could not resist a gratuitous sneer at *HT*, which had apparently just a few months prior, debunked the rival, Indian Readership Survey and upheld the NRS as the exemplar of rigour and accuracy. The IRS in 2002 had put the *TOI* in the top spot in the Delhi market, while the NRS had stuck with the established order of precedence. Though this discrepancy may have been on account of differences in sample sizes and techniques, there have been other instances when the two rival surveys, which are backed by competing consortia of media organisations, advertisement agencies and market research firms, have reported starkly different results. This has led to some suspicion that the exercise of measuring a newspaper's reach and the demographic constituencies it serves, is not entirely an objective process. With the disposition of large volumes of advertisement money riding on these results, they could be permeable to influence from the organisations that sponsor them.

ness served up by the daily supplement issued with the newspaper, the *Delhi Times*, there was a celebratory article on that phenomenon of the publishing world. The *Delhi Times*, wrote a breathless reporter, was "where an infotainment (sic) revolution is shaped and reshaped every day". "In a day and age when the newspaper has outgrown its pristine format to assume a millennial avatar, *Delhi Times* – by being in sync with the pulse of its audience – is constantly in dialogue with its readers".[46]

The financial performance of the Indian media has always been difficult to monitor, since most entities are either private limited companies, entitled to accounting confidentiality, or unlisted public companies whose parameters remain the preserve of a select few. A website specialising in media related matters does a significant public service in collating the figures for India's major media players on a fairly regular basis. And the results that it uncovered were little short of astounding. In 2001 for instance, BCCL was the "second most profitable unlisted company in India", recording a net profit of Rs 2,059 million, which was well over twice the figure registered the previous year. In comparison, other media companies turned in distinctly anaemic performances. Kasturi and Sons Ltd, publishers of *The Hindu,* declared a net profit of Rs 222.5 million and the *Indian Express* group reported Rs 23.6 million. But the weakest performance, expectedly, came from the newspaper that had suffered the misfortune of encountering *TOI* at its most aggressive. *HT*'s net profits in 2001 were down by over 96 percent at Rs 5.8 million, and the company seemed rapidly to be plunging into the red.[47]

The misery was by no means over for *HT*. Figures available for 2003 from the same source report that BCCL's net profit for the year stood at Rs 1,664 million, while Kasturi and Sons earned Rs 315.5 million. *HT* again was languishing at the bottom of the heap. Though not quite as dismal as two years before, at Rs 18.4 million, its net profit seemed derisory in relation to the standard established by its main competitor.[48]

46 *The Times of India* (2003a).

47 *The Hoot* (2007a).

48 *The Hoot* (2007b).

Matters improved in the following years. In August 2005, the *HT*, which had been among the most obdurate naysayers in the matter of foreign direct investment in the print media, came out with an Initial Public Offering (IPO) of shares. Early convictions having evaporated in the heat of competition with *TOI*, foreign entities including Citigroup and the Henderson group, picked up sizeable chunks of the IPO. In an analysis of the attractiveness of the offering, *The Hindu Business Line*, a financial daily published by Kasturi and Sons, reported that the *HT* bottomline had improved for a variety of reasons. It had managed "to come through a difficult period with a substantial expansion in circulation for the New Delhi edition". Circulation had stabilised at the "one million plus level", contributing to "greater clout with advertisers". Advertisement rates had been raised in May 2005. And in March of the same year, the *HT* and the *TOI* had agreed on a concerted rise in cover price of about 30 percent. The "price-cuts that hurt profitability", the analyst concluded, were "a story of the past".[49]

With the declaration of the truce, the two media giants evidently accepted an uneasy coexistence. In terms of content and target audience, they now looked like clones of the same cell. But the media landscape in which the peace was established, was a very different place. Delhi once had a choice of close to ten daily newspapers published locally in the English language. The number of serious options declined badly in the wake of the price war. Several of the newspapers that used to offer competing menus and priorities to the public right up to the early-1990s, contributing in their own ways to the richness of the public discourse, were now hollowed out financially, compelled to reach ever deeper to appease politicians and advertisers, merely to bring out a day's edition.

BCCL itself ended its decade-and-a-half of rapid commercial growth with a much leaner portfolio of publications. Its daily newspapers, the *TOI* and the *Economic Times*, were far and away, the leaders of their respective market segments. But several other prestigious mastheads, once regarded as serious participants in the public discourse in the Hindi cultural area, had passed into history. Increasing profits and financial clout were achieved in short by a palpable loss of media diversity. That the ends of consumer sovereignty were not served by the price war in the newspaper market or by the aggressive advertise-

49 *Hindu Business Line* (2005).

ment-oriented strategy of the *TOI* group, is a conclusion that for many, seemed indubitable.

The emasculation of the editorial function

This transformation of the newspaper in the advertisement and circulation aspects, also meant initiating radical changes in the editorial function, which had to adapt to the new imperatives of providing a "feel good" ambience for advertisers to display their wares. Earlier editorial priorities, which bore a relationship to the world the majority of people actually lived in, had to yield before the demands of fostering the mania for entertainment and celebrity lifestyles. The task should have been by all indications, especially difficult in the *TOI*, which had a strongly entrenched journalistic culture and a team of writers and commentators that with some justification, took pride in running the most respected editorial page in the Indian media.

Samir Jain's disdain for these traditions was never a secret. Soon after assuming the office of Vice Chairman in BCCL, he is known to have begun a sequence of duels with the editor of the *TOI*, Girilal Jain (no relation) over the utility of maintaining an intensely political discourse on the editorial pages of the newspaper. The Vice Chairman's view was that the editorial page output served no purpose other than drawing the attention of the political and bureaucratic class, who needed no education in any case and contributed little to the financial fortunes of the newspaper. Girilal Jain, a man of strongly held views and ample professional confidence, was indulgent towards the man who he knew would at some stage inherit undiluted proprietary authority. But as far as the editorial processes of the *TOI* were concerned, he kept Samir Jain at arm's length.[50]

The chemistry between management and editorial deteriorated rapidly and soon after the *TOI* completed an ostentatious celebration of its 150-year jubilee in 1988, Girilal Jain was eased into retirement. From then on, Samir Jain's writ ran unchallenged. He finally stamped his authority on the editorial department in 1994, nominating a director of the company to serve as editor of the *TOI* during a three-week absence of the regular incumbent. At the same time, the editor's un-

---

50 An exhaustive account of changes initiated by Samir Jain in editorial and news gathering processes is available in Subramanian (2012).

derstudy, who should have assumed charge, was asked to attend to the management functions normally discharged by the director.

The message was clear: editorial was no different in its importance to the newspaper than any of the management functions. The sole concern was the bottomline and the *TOI* would only host journalists prepared to abandon all conceit about making a difference to the public discourse. In the years that followed, the designation of the "editor", an integral part of a newspaper, was itself chopped and changed. It underwent various transformations that were devoid of sense or logic, before the BCCL management finally settled on having editors for each market, defined in a territorial sense.

Media group runs into a sticky wicket

Early in 1997, the Enforcement Directorate, an agency of the Indian government that is mandated to pursue and prosecute offences under the country's Foreign Exchange Regulation Act (FERA) opened investigations into a number of possible violations by BCCL chairman Ashok Jain.[51] The case involved opening bank accounts overseas without authorisation, money laundering and other offences.

On March 30, 1997, Prime Minister H.D. Deve Gowda was told early in the afternoon that the Congress Party, vital to sustaining his parliamentary majority, had withdrawn its support. The decision conveyed in a letter to the President of India by Sitaram Kesri, president of the Congress, left most observers deeply puzzled, including other members of the senior leadership of Kesri's own party. Deve Gowda duly resigned after failing to win a vote in Parliament and a successor was nominated from within his party, who the Congress then undertook to support.

On May 1 that year, three journalists from *Frontline*, the fortnightly magazine published from Chennai, met Deve Gowda at his residence in New Delhi for his first extended interview since leaving office. The general impression was that he had lost favour with the Congress because of the spate of investigations launched during his tenure into cases of political corruption involving the party. When the issue was posed in this manner, his response was simple: while in office

51 FERA has since been repealed and replaced by a more lenient statute that seeks to control specifically the crime of money laundering.

his intent had always been to let the law take its course. Out of office, his greatest source of satisfaction was the belief that nobody could accuse him of ever having intervened in the due process of law, even where the appeasement of political confederates would have brought rich dividends. A question was then posed about Enforcement Directorate investigations into possible violations by "various individuals", which were reportedly being blocked by the political leadership. This had impelled a number of civic-minded individuals to demand in a public interest petition in the Supreme Court, that the investigation be given free rein, provoking an irate response from Deve Gowda – during his prime ministership – that this was little else than "political interest litigation".[52]

Out of office, Deve Gowda was less given to that rhetorical flourish, even less so to the defence of privilege. "Public interest litigation is the right of every citizen of this country", he said: "If he or she feels that some injustice is (happening), he or she can go seek redress through the courts". The lapse of two decades since then has presumably freed all those present from mutual assurances of confidentiality rendered once the tape recorders were switched off. Referring to the question that had been posed about "various individuals" managing to sabotage the course of investigations, Deve Gowda brought up the specific case of the FERA offences involving Ashok Jain, and he was categorical that the singular reason why Kesri had withdrawn support, was Deve Gowda's refusal to pull in and quash the investigations into the alleged offences by the newspaper baron.[53]

---

52 The full interview was published in *Frontline* (1997). This writer was one of the three journalists interviewing the former Prime Minister.

53 Obviously because of the sensitivities in a case involving one of India's leading media magnates, this case went largely under-reported. Ashok Jain himself went on record on a few occasions to deny all allegations of wrongdoing. He also was rather bitter about the lone newspaper that seemed then to have space to devote to the case, *The Statesman*. But he was candid about admitting his close relationship with Sitaram Kesri in the interview that was published in July 1997, three months after Deve Gowda's ouster (*Outlook*, 1997): "He (Kesri) is an old friend of the family. My parents were very helpful to him early in his political career. Subsequently, he rose on the political ladder completely on his own. My father died about 20 years back and Kesri has been a treasurer of the Congress party under three-four prime ministers. I can't remember having played any role in helping him rise in politics in the last 20 years. It was entirely on his own. He is not indebted to us in any manner

By March 1998, Deve Gowda's successor had also been unseated and a government of a completely different political stripe installed in office. Yet the Enforcement Directorate was not deflected off course. The *TOI* meanwhile, had begun a regular front-page column titled "Human Rights Watch", borrowing the name of an international advocacy body for the decidedly more mundane purpose of suppressing an investigation into an individual's business transactions. There were horrifying stories of harassment and torture, of the selective victimisation of particular communities, and testaments of support for the victims of investigative excesses, from businessmen and legal luminaries. These reports began appearing from the time that the Enforcement Directorate raided BCCL offices in Mumbai, Calcutta and Delhi in January 1998.[54]

In May 1998, the *TOI* management summarily dismissed H.K. Dua from the post of "Editorial Advisor" he had held for a year. His appointment to this rather vaguely designated post – it was not clear from the formal title whether his function was to advise the management or the journalists – was integrally related to the *TOI*'s effort to reduce the editor to a cipher. To meet the statutory requirement that an identified individual should be ascribed with responsibility for news items featured in everyday's edition, Dua's name was featured in the print-line of the *TOI* where the printer, publisher and editor are identified. It was perhaps a case of responsibility without power, which Dua may have been incapable of sustaining beyond a point.

---

for that. On the other hand, in the last 20 years, I can't recollect a single instance where Kesri has helped us". Veteran politician from the Socialist camp, George Fernandes, who was then in opposition and perhaps able on that account to speak with relative freedom, observed in an interview (Rediff, 1998), that "the Deve Gowda government fell for no reasons other than Sitaram Kesri's 40-year-old relationship with Ashok Jain of *The Times of India*. Kesri, in fact, was on the board of directors of one of the group companies as far back as 1967. Deve Gowda refused to oblige the Kesri-Jain combine on several issues… Deve Gowda had to fall. It was that simple".

54 Few concurrent reports on this campaign by the TOI group are available. Sudha Mahalingam, a correspondent with *Frontline*, closely followed the Enforcement Directorate investigations and unearthed valuable facts that have now become part of the public record. See Mahalingam (1998a and b).

In March 1998, Dua's name was removed from the printline of the newspaper and substituted with that of Pradeep Guha, an executive director of BCCL. Cut to the quick, Dua penned a letter to the BCCL chairman on March 22, accusing him of acting in an "unfair, illegal, arbitrary, administratively improper and *malafide*" manner. Ashok Jain, he said, had called from a hospital where he was undergoing treatment for a heart condition, to ask Dua "to lobby with political leaders to seek their help in the FERA cases he (had) been facing for some time". Dua refused on the grounds that the lobbying function was no part of his responsibility as editorial advisor. A few days later, he recorded, "Ashok Jain asked me to write articles in his favour to create a helpful climate before the Supreme Court (took) up his cases". Dua, in his own narration of these events, responded with some asperity, pointing out that as "editor", he was committed to the defence of the public interest, which was clearly not involved in the defence of Ashok Jain in a case involving financial malfeasance.[55]

TOI takes on the Press Council

After being rubbed out of the printline of the *TOI* in March 1998, Dua was formally served his dismissal two months later. The indignity inflicted on him roused several other professionals to action. Veteran journalist Kuldip Nayar, then a member of the upper house of the Indian Parliament raised the issue as one meriting action from a constitutional standpoint in defence of free speech. Social scientist Rajni Kothari, a highly respected public intellectual, condemned the event as "an attempt to humiliate the entire editorial fraternity". "The blame for this cannot be laid entirely at the door of the management", he said: "Journalists are also to blame, especially those who put together the 'Human Rights Watch' columns in the newspaper".[56]

With public indignation building up, the Press Council of India (PCI) in August 1998 issued an unprecedented stricture against the *TOI*, accusing it of "carrying on a campaign against the Enforcement Directorate with the manifest intention of pressurising and deflecting it from performing its lawful duties". The Indian Newspaper Society (INS), a powerful lobby representing the print media industry, re-

55 A reliable recounting of these events is Mahalingam (1998c).

56 Ibid.

sponded within a week with "a strong objection" to the PCI's action. With little concern for propriety, the INS president went on to question the credentials of the PCI chairman P.B. Sawant, a former Judge of the Supreme Court of India, whose rulings from the highest judicial bench were widely respected for their integrity. Sawant's remarks, said the INS, indicated an "ignorance of the ground realities of the industry as well as (an) absence of understanding of the climate in which India has created a free and independent media".[57]

This controversy soon exploded in public vituperation. The INS took exception to observations by Justice Sawant that private ownership of the print media potentially embodied a public interest hazard, which made other forms of control, including cooperative ownership, worthwhile options. The PCI in turn, responded by dismissing the allegations of "hostility" and "bias" levelled against its chairman. These "unfortunate, unwarranted and completely unjustified" accusations, it protested, were deeply offensive to "the Constitution of the land" which allowed for a variety of ownership forms over public institutions. The PCI made implicit reference to the dissent expressed within INS councils over engaging a distinguished public functionary in an unseemly verbal brawl, characterising the attack on its chairman as a violation of the "constitution of the INS", which betrayed "an outright partisan attitude".[58]

The controversy threatened to burgeon out of control, but with Ashok Jain's death in February 1999 while under treatment for a serious heart ailment in the U.S. city of Cleveland, Ohio, the belligerents called a truce. If anything, the equations between the editorial and business functions of a newspaper were left further embittered by these inconclusive engagements. And in the years to come, the *TOI* was to establish a new orthodoxy in the diverse manners in which the constitutional right to free speech, and the right to access media time and space were understood.

Pay your way to information as commodity

News in both the print and electronic variants is a commodity always sold at a price below its cost. But unfortunately, the news industry

57 Bhattacharjea (1998).

58 Mahalingam (1998d).

in India evolved along a trajectory that made it almost worthless. In March 2003, *TOI* announced an initiative that was professedly part of its effort to stay current with journalistic practices in rapidly changing times, finding a rather lofty idiom for an enterprise as crass as charging a fee for favourable editorial coverage. The "Medianet" initiative as it was called, was in the words of the *TOI* management, part of its urge "to drive the market, to constantly break new ground". The function of a newspaper, as the explanatory note put it, was "to act as an information provider". That definition had "remained unchanged over time" though the character of information had changed, as too had the means of information gathering. The network of correspondents maintained by the newspaper and all its subscriptions to news agencies, were simply failing to match the voracious appetite for information manifest among the larger public.

The deficiency of traditional news-gathering techniques was apparent especially in new areas of audience interest – such as "lifestyle, fashion, entertainment, events, product launches, social personalities and city happenings". Public relations agencies had a much more sensitive feel of the social pulse in these areas, and journalism had recognised this reality. Once considered rather suspect as sources of news, PR agencies had come in from the cold and were enjoying a new respectability as legitimate stakeholders in the domain of public information. Yet no feasible method of regulating the flow of news from this source had been devised and "Medianet" was the *TOI* management's offering towards that effort.

Subtlety aside, there were coded references there to the pervasive journalistic practice of accepting and even actively soliciting, monetary and other forms of gratification for news and editorial coverage of material benefit to particular individuals or entities. Through Medianet, the *TOI* was, in deference to established rules of market competition, curbing this corruption of the trade by institutionalising it. Objectivity and integrity of editorial content would no longer be at risk from the susceptibility of individual journalists to material inducements, since the news organisation itself would bear the onus of vitiating news content in pursuit of monetary aggrandisement.

After making "infotainment" a staple of the media industry, the *TOI* was now fostering a new hybrid entity called "advertorial", which would allow sponsored stories in its news columns. All this would be done, the *TOI* management rather implausibly said, "without breaching the boundary wall between advertising and content".[59] To make this vital distinction between "paid for" content and the rest of the news, the reader needed supposedly, only to look to the bottom of the item in question. A discrete legend printed there would alert him to the fact that a particular item was being featured under a Medianet sponsorship.

A year later, a rival media organisation in Mumbai that had been tracking the Medianet initiative, reported that the identifying legend had entirely vanished after a few months. In short, there was no way the reader could differentiate between an advertorial and an authentic news or editorial item. It was also reported that *Mumbai Times*, the city supplement issued with the local edition of the *TOI*, had been charging for front-page photographs at 1,254 rupees a square centimetre. An art gallery owner in the city, while declining to give precise figures, went so far as to admit that he had instructed his PR agency to set aside a budget for coverage in the *TOI*. And the fast food chain McDonald's saw little amiss in conceding that the coverage of the launch of its home delivery service, which featured a topflight female model, had been paid for. The Medianet rate card that had come to light then, revealed specific rates for coverage in a purported interview on page one of *Mumbai Times*, and other tariffs for being featured on pages two and three.[60]

A commentator from Mumbai said shortly afterwards, more in sorrow than anger, that for "millions of Indians (who had) grown up with the *TOI*, its growing crisis of credibility is like watching an old friend become mentally unbalanced from an addiction to greed and power.[61] Pradyuman Maheshwari, a journalist who ran a blog in his leisure time, often featuring trenchant satire on the bizarre new journalistic trajectories the *TOI* was exploring, had to close down his enterprise under the threat of legal action. A journalist with the *Maharashtra Herald* in Pune, Maheshwari received his first legal notice for reporting on his blog that a deal had been concluded between *TOI* and

59 The entire concept note of Medianet, in the words of its main proponent is available at *The Times of India* (2003a).

60 Asher (2004).

61 Raja (2004).

Reuters for launching a TV channel. The story was perhaps two years ahead of time and was soon picked up by other newspapers, testament to its essential veracity and quality in a journalistic sense. But Maheshwari was soon served a legal notice, and lacking the resources for a prolonged battle, compelled to take the story down and apologise. As a media analyst reported, "even the apology upset the (*TOI*), and they told (Maheshwari) to take it down so there wasn't a backlash against the paper".

When the public-spirited journalist carried 19 postings in the following weeks, including some that were bitterly critical of the Medianet initiative, he received a much longer legal notice. Among other things, Maheshwari was accused of being "constantly engaged in criminal conspiracy" against the *TOI* and causing the organisation "grave harm and loss of reputation". Now thoroughly intimidated, Maheshwari shut down his blog.[62]

Medianet was soon business as usual as the wave of adverse notice subsided and the bottom line of the company gained greater lustre. Profit finally proved the most effective solvent for all the ethics and principles that journalists, some clinging on quixotically to the values they learnt in an earlier day, chose to practice.

Just a little later, the *TOI* embarked on a new venture called "private treaties" under which it would swap advertising space for equity in particular companies. This assistance in "brand building" and "corporate image development", rendered *gratis*, would be more than repaid when the companies emerged with a public floatation of shares and sought listing on the stock exchanges. Through the boom years in India's stockmarkets, shares in most companies were known to appreciate wildly from the day they were listed, and the reward for unpaid advertising would come from capital gains. Once the practice was shown to pay off, other media houses joined in. There was little public questioning of the conflict of interest issues involved in "private treaties". With fortunes being made and lost on India's stock exchanges and investor decisions being critically dependent on information, i.e., media, there were calls in later years, to put the practice of "private treaties" under the scanner from an ethical point of view.

---

62 A thorough account of the episode is available in Niles (2005).

After effectively shutting down public scrutiny, BCCL decided to go a step ahead in the value chain. It had through "Medianet" allowed PR agencies to intrude into the news space and undoubtedly found a few years later that it had sufficient commercial clout to take over at least some part of the PR space. In February 2008, BCCL announced its participation in the launch of a new PR agency, in association with an established PR and advertising agency, Adfactors PR Pvt Ltd. Equity ownership would be distributed in a one-third to two-third ratio, with Adfactors – the PR industry native – holding the majority stake. The memorandum of association signed between the partners, explained the company's objectives as carrying on "the business of consultancy in India and abroad in the field of public relations and ... to manage and build up public image and reputation of firms, bodies corporate, autonomous corporations and multinational conglomerates, international governments, state and Central governments and other institutions and of any other person, Indian or foreign".[63]

This news report, carried in a publication that competed with some of the BCCL's own titles, took care to make full disclosure of potential conflicts of interest. It also invited a number of reactions from other industry participants. A luminary in the PR industry was quoted saying that "a media house owning a PR agency may not have short-term impact", though in the long term it would invariably "erode credibility of the media house". Others who were more concerned with the struggle for survival, simply argued that the hidden dynamics of the media industry needed to be brought out into the open and perhaps even embraced since it had become a survival imperative. "It's one of the worst-kept secrets of the media industry", said one: "Some people do it openly, some behind closed doors".[64]

With the 2008 recession soon beginning to bite deep and declared advertising spending falling, the news industry began pressing ahead in accordance with the inherent logic of the scenario. It was no state secret that individual journalists were often susceptible to material inducements to twist their coverage one way or the other. This form of individualised corruption was now institutionalised. It was soon official, though still unstated, that the media in India had been selling

---

63 *Mint* (2008d).

64 Ibid.

space for favourable news coverage, much in the manner of advertisements – though without acknowledgment.

The "cash for coverage" abuse was noted during the extended campaign for the general elections to India's Parliament, between March and May 2009. Further instances of cash payments being used to secure favourable media coverage for particular candidates and parties, were recorded during the general elections to three state legislative assemblies in October 2009.[65]

Individual journalists of some stature began speaking out against the abuse soon after the parliamentary elections were over. Their advocacy soon induced the PCI to commence a formal inquiry into the abuse. Within the media itself, aside from very occasional breaches, the wall of silence remained impregnable. That arrangement of convenience seemed to come asunder the day a major global conclave of the newspaper industry began in Hyderabad in December 2009. What lay behind this breach in the compact of silence was undoubtedly a question worth investigating. It was rumoured for instance, that *The Hindu* and an allied clique of newspapers had fallen out with a rival lobby over the use to which the real estate premises owned by the INS in a prime location in Mumbai was to be put. From the point of view of the public though, it was adequate that somebody in the major league of Indian newspapers had chosen to break the silence.

Cash for coverage

The headline news was that the Chief Minister of the Indian state of Maharashtra, for considerations yet unknown, managed to get identical stories about his achievements (both real and imagined, though mostly the latter) featured in a number of Marathi language newspapers, under different author bylines. Several newspapers also carried extensive supplements within their main editions, blazoning his glories, again without the slightest suggestion that this was advertising content. Bylines of well-established journalists were often tagged to these stories to lend them a veneer of credibility.[66]

---

65 Sainath (2009) brought some of this discussion into the mainstream media discourse.

66 See Sainath (2014).

The obvious inference – that all this content was paid for – put the Chief Minister in breach of the strict ceilings decreed by the Election Commission of India on advertising spending by a candidate in state assembly elections. Apart from that, it offered a telling comment on the new revenue model that the news industry had adopted to shore up its sagging commercial fortunes. The loser in the process, was the practice of journalism as an activity pursued in the public interest.

Newspaper revenue calculations played a role in transforming the character of journalism. For obvious reasons, the principal beneficiary of the boost to ad spending that came with neoliberalism, was the English language media. This is where the high purchasing power demographic strata were most likely to go for news – and advertisers valued the favours that the English language audience could render them. News and editorial content that seriously undermined the "feel good" ambience the advertiser sought to foster, was actively discouraged. For the global media, the years following the early 1990s were a time of celebrity obsession, when audiences were being invited to partake in the vicarious delights of the lifestyles of the rich and famous. The Indian media, led by the biggest player, was quick to follow suit.

The media in India's regional languages (or *bhasha*) did not have quite the same allure for the advertiser. As Robin Jeffrey has pointed out, till the early 1990s, it was rare that an advertising agency would have more than one person looking after translations of ad copy into the Indian languages. The work was normally contracted out and would often produce bizarre copy.[67] That began to change in the years of the neoliberal policy dispensation, but not significantly enough to sustain the ambitions of the regional language media. The way around this conundrum came in the aggressive pursuit of an agenda of localisation of content. Localisation in itself was not a phenomenon specific to the *bhasha* press. As Jeffrey puts it: "Newspapers localise because advertisers see a commodity that is worth buying: rural and small-town spending power".[68] The *bhasha* press was most aggressive in pursuing this agenda because it had little other recourse than reaching out to this audience in the continuum from metropolitan India to rural India that the English media had little inclination for.

67 Jeffrey (2000): 73. Illustratively, the ad slogan "we've now let the cat out of the bag" was once translated as "*Ab hamne thaili se billi nikaal di*".

68 Ibid: 75.

Localisation with a credible news gathering function would have been a high-cost operation and few media houses were really prepared to plough in needed investment. News gathering became a subsidiary activity of the main function of harvesting advertising and promoting the sale of the newspaper. Payment for news was by volume, though the greater incentive was reserved for the efficient harvesting of ads. Neutral or objective coverage of any local entity with some influence and power was likely to seriously impair the stringer's ability to tap local sources of advertising. The mix of stories filed by the typical stringer was fed into the local editorial bureau, and then channelled up the value chain. If it served a compelling profit purpose or met a contingent political interest at any of these stages, it had a good chance of being carried. Otherwise the story was most likely killed. Sevanti Ninan has pointed out that by 2005 or so, the alarming consequences of the hyper-localised news product had begun to seriously erode public confidence, prompting a rapid reversal of course.[69] That may have been a hopeful prognosis, likely killed by the onset of the recession in 2008.

Censorship by the media industry

Soon after general elections to the Indian Parliament were concluded in May 2009, eyes cast back in retrospection began observing a suspicious pattern in some of the media reporting. In June, the Delhi Union of Journalists (DUJ), in a communication with the Press Council of India (PCI), drew attention to widespread concerns over "money power having played havoc with the media coverage of the elections". The phenomenon of news that was paid for, the union said, was "unethical, unfair and an infringement of the right of journalists to report freely". Journalists who refused to comply with the management directive to tilt in the direction of those who held the purse, the DUJ claimed, had been victimised.

Similar observations followed a round of elections to state legislative assemblies later that year. Concerns were escalating since the abuse of "paid news" represented a gross violation of the media's tacit compact with its audience, and also a way for candidates to evade ev-

69 Ninan (2007):113-80.

ery campaign funding restriction in force.[70] In July 2009, the PCI appointed a sub-committee to inquire into the practice and recommend remedies. This was an important victory for journalism as a cause, but as it approached the final stages of its inquiries, the sub-committee encountered a deadlock within the full quorum. Newspaper industry representatives organised their substantial clout within the PCI to stymie any possibility of consensus. A single copy of the report with its carefully assembled evidence was then placed in the library of the PCI, safely beyond the gaze of the general public, while newspaper industry representatives proceeded to strip it of all substantive findings. What finally emerged as the official PCI report was a bland and anodyne thirteen pages which reduced the sub-committee's draft to a sixth of its original size. It was censorship in most brazen form, but of little substantive benefit to the thought police since the main findings of the sub-committee had already been widely disseminated and discussed over the alternative media.[71]

Growing wage and job insecurity within journalism was among the factors the PCI sub-committee identified behind the "paid news" abuse. The inquiry also recommended that punitive powers under election law be deployed against political figures found to be engaged in the practice. On the other side, it proposed that the search and sanction powers available under the income tax law be utilised against media houses that received undue and unaccounted financial favour for doctored news content.

In May 2013, a Standing Committee of Parliament completed its own inquiries into corruption in the news industry and took note of multiple submissions that attributed rampant abuses to the decline of journalistic independence.[72] Insecurity induced by short-term contracts which had almost entirely replaced tenure appointments in the industry, put journalists in a position of vulnerability, unable to resist demands from commercial and advertising departments. Compounding this were disparities within the journalistic cadre between those

70 Sainath (2009) and *Mint* (2009d).

71 Both the official report and the sub-committee report are available as of December 2016 at the website of the PCI by inserting "paid news" in the search box.

72 Parliament of India (2013).

at the top with proximity to the ownership structures and those condemned to toil away as news industry drones.

Since the defiance of wage board norms became the rule rather than exception, long established proportionalities within the news and editorial hierarchies, that would preserve a healthy and collegial working environment, had tended to vanish. Again, because of the opacity of newspaper industry accounts, it was difficult to get an estimate of the true magnitude of the disparities in pay and compensation within the ranks. Illustratively, an analysis of the BCCL annual report for 2013-14 showed that among the directors and employees earning the highest compensation packages, five were members of the proprietary family. These five between them received over 55 per cent of the amount involved in compensation packages above the statutory threshold for listing in the annual report. Among the seventy-six employees listed as drawing compensation packages requiring mention in the annual report, only nine were journalists. The highest paid journalist, who held the designation "editorial director", ranked eleventh in total value of remuneration. He was outranked by the three directors, a chief executive officer, an executive director, a chief operating officer, two directors of the advertising and circulation departments, and others with similar management responsibilities. Below him among the journalists – and at a considerable distance – were a number who were in charge of the financial daily of the group, the *Economic Times*, and a handful who discharged various functions in the business news channel.

The BCCL annual report for 2010-11, among the few such documents accessible by the public, showed that the company incurred salary and wage costs of ₹ 551 crore in 2010-11, on "operating revenue" of almost ₹ 4,500 crore and "other income" of about ₹300 crore. Manpower costs in other words, amounted to just over 11 percent of total revenue for the company. A breakdown of the "manpower cost" component revealed that ₹ 102 crore out of the total, i.e., close to 20 percent, was absorbed in remunerations to just 40 employees. This list of 40 included only four whose function was remotely connected to journalism.

Here is a corporate pecking order sharply at variance with WJA priorities, which offers one possible explanation for the obduracy with which the BCCL and other newspaper organisations have opposed a fair deal for journalists. In substantive terms though, their claims that the pay scales mandated by the wage board were a certain pathway to financial ruin, have been repeated too often to be of any credence.

Journalists' unions: certain inconvenient truths

Even in its glory days in the 1950s, the journalists' trade union movement tended to favour a certain proximity to those in authority as expedient strategy to secure its ends. Chalapati Rau's very intimate and mutually respectful relationship with Nehru brought contingent advantages, but he left the scene at a time that the Nehruvian consensus over "nation-building" was falling apart, with consequences over a wide domain, including journalism. By now entering dynastic control, the IFWJ failed to respond in a manner that preserved essential professional interests, continuing to depend upon favours rendered as reward for loyalty to dominant political forces.

At a certain point, the bargain proved unsustainable. In 1972, sections of the journalists' movement broke away in dissent at the politically compliant character of the mainstream trade union. The National Union of Journalists (India) – abbreviated as NUJ(I) – was constituted in 1972 at an inaugural session addressed by M.C. Chagla, an eminent jurist who had been a judge on the Bombay High Court and served subsequently in the Union Cabinet, before bowing out of active politics in 1967. He made no major statement as he left the political realm, but was widely seen to be out of step with the political culture that emerged after India's fourth general elections in 1967. Keeping Chagla company on the dais at the inauguration of the NUJ(I) was Frank Moraes, editor then of the *Indian Express* and among the most acerbic critics of the Indira Gandhi administration then in power.[73]

The IFWJ had meanwhile proven itself willing to take principled stands on issues, though not quite to push these through to definitive conclusions. In 1955, as recorded by the Press Commission, it argued as a matter of principle for the repeal of the Press (Objectionable Material) Act – passed into law in 1951 – but conceded that its substantive impact on journalism had been negligible. In 1966, it went along with the government's proposal to set up a regulatory body designated as a "council" and pressed for recognition as the sole representative of working journalists, to the exclusion of bodies such as the Newspaper

73 This information is taken from the website of the NUJ(I).

Editors' Conference. Despite being a fervent advocate of such a regulatory body, it contributed little towards evolving credible procedural modalities for the newly created PCI. The IFWJ remained opposed in principle as the Indira Gandhi government lurched into one of its worst crises and responded by clamping a draconian "emergency" regime in 1975. But its nominees served on the "accreditation committee" constituted by the Ministry of Information and Broadcasting, alongside the official designated as the Chief Censor, in the first and only formal effort at this manner of thought control in independent India. In transparently vindictive actions, the accreditation committee terminated the official credentials of fifty-five journalists through the "emergency" period.

On June 29, 1975, the Minister for Information and Broadcasting V.C. Shukla began holding regular meetings with his top officials to review the working of the media.[74] At a meeting on 5 July, participants noted that an official press release giving an account of a meeting between the Prime Minister and the IFWJ leadership had given an "unfortunate" narration of certain remarks by the Prime Minister. Subsequently, when the Minister unveiled his plan to merge all domestically owned news agencies into one, the IFWJ went along eagerly with the proposal on the grounds that it would contribute to greater efficiency and better working conditions.

With the lifting of the internal emergency in 1977, the IFWJ joined the NUJ(I) and other professional bodies in demanding accountability for all the attacks the media had suffered in that period. The system of IFWJ affiliates built up through the country was by now creaking and the failure to institute democratic procedures within, led to an erosion of the ties of solidarity. Contingent agreements were patched together when wage board negotiations were due and this sustained the collective unity of the journalistic profession, till the inauguration of the neoliberal phase of the economy in the 1990s, which heralded the accelerated migration towards contractual employment rather than secure tenures. In 1992, the IFWJ split once again, with several among its

---

74 The government that followed the "emergency" regime instituted a formal inquiry and issued a "White Paper on Misuse of Mass Media During the Internal Emergency" (Government of India, 1977). This and many of the following details are drawn from this white paper.

top leadership rebelling against the seeming monopoly on leadership established by its long-standing president.

The new body – the Indian Journalists' Union (IJU) – then claimed to have won over most of the IFWJ's regional affiliates. Successive wage awards – Palekar in 1980, Bachawat in 1989 and Manisana Singh in 2000 – had meanwhile been concluded, though with increasingly indifferent records of implementation by the newspaper industry. The growing dysfunction of unions was a major factor in the collapse of collective power within journalism. Technological changes were ushered in at a time when the economic policy regime was being rapidly transformed from a relatively cloistered, state-led model, to the rough-and-tumble of a competitive marketplace. Despite the favourable 2014 verdict from the Supreme Court on the Majithia wage board award, apprehensions were strong that the newspaper industry would continue to stonewall. The prolonged war of attrition waged by the industry, it was feared, spelt the end of the WJA as a protective measure for the news gathering function.

In 2012, the IJU itself split when a putative agreement under which the President and General Secretary of the body, who had both been in office since its foundation, fell apart.[75] The propaganda offensive from the newspaper lobbies meanwhile gathered momentum. Newspaper columns which had been strangely mute for the most part in addressing the malaise of paid news, proved a congenial forum for ventilating imagined grievances over a fair deal for journalists and other staff. June 2011 was a particularly frenetic time on this battlefield, when the newspaper lobby mobilised forces to take its case against the wage award to the Supreme Court. Within a few days of each other, *HT* carried a story attributed to unnamed "experts" that the wage board process was "outdated". It turned out that the only expert opinion it really needed to summon to the cause was the collective wisdom of INS, the newspaper industry lobby. Paragraphs attributed to "expert" opinion alternated with citations from the petition the INS had filed before the

75 These details of the journalists' trade union movement have not been formally recorded at any single place. The narration is drawn from the author's involvement in the movement, especially between the years 2007 and 2013.

Prime Minister, asking that the wage board recommendations be consigned to the trashcan of history.[76]

The chief executive of the publishing company known after its best known title, the newsmagazine *India Today*, also converted his editorial spaces into a forum for rubbishing the wage board. But the most zealous and committed campaign by far was run by the TOI, which in the space of a fortnight, carried four articles sharply attacking the wage award. It began with an article titled "Muzzling the Media" – an old staple to push back against accountability – and then went on with dark warnings that newspapers would be forced to shut down in droves, and that the future of the press was at stake. It then announced in seeming triumph, that the wage award had been challenged in the Supreme Court. In the midst of all this activity in the editorial space, the two principal group publications, *TOI* and the *Economic Times* allocated valuable advertising space – on terms that are not quite clear – to the INS declaration that the wage board process was a sinister ploy by the government to buy the "loyalty of journalists".[77]

Following the Supreme Court ruling on the validity of the wage board process, *TOI* ran an editorial denouncing it as a "grievous body blow" that would "financially weaken even the few strong companies that are left in an industry that worldwide is under crushing pressure". The judgment also was an evasion of a "larger issue", which was that "a government appointed wage board that fixes compensation for the private sector is completely anachronistic".[78] A few weeks later, it offered the hospitality of its editorial page to the editor of Kolkata-based *The Statesman* – a once great newspaper driven to terminal decline by whimsical management decisions – to hammer the same theme. The Supreme Court judgment, wrote Ravindra Kumar in his capacity as the incumbent INS president, "threatens to drive many of us to closure

76 *Hindustan Times* (2011).

77 Khanvilkar (2011) gives a fairly complete account of this phase of the campaign, while also noting the irony of the newspaper lobby's silence on issues such as paid news, private treaties, media concentration and predatory pricing, among a host of dubious practices.

78 *The Times of India* (2014a)

and it may do so after it has taken a severe toll on the industrial peace we have so carefully nurtured".[79]

Towards the end of 2016, the barely suppressed symptoms of the print media crisis broke out in another rash. Certain leading concerns in the newspaper world began sending out ominous warnings to their employees, about an imminent and brutal shake-out. The trigger for the crunch situation was supposedly the strange – and ultimately futile – decision by the Government on November 8 to scrap 86 per cent of currency value in circulation, and demand that all who held notes in the denominations that had suddenly ceased being legal tender, line up in endless queues to establish that their modest accumulations of wealth were not acquired in shady, criminal deals.[80]

An immediate consequence of the big currency scrap was a drastic economic contraction, as accustomed cycles of production and exchange were rudely disrupted. In its commentary on the matter, the media remained non-committal – perhaps even clueless – about the true intent and implications of the demonetisation. Some news platforms sought to get to the bottom of the matter and report at least in some detail, about how people normally outside the focus of media attention were faring in the context of their social and economic entitlements suddenly vanishing. The larger picture though, remained unclear.

Within the smaller context of media economics, demonetisation had severely aggravated what was feared to be a long-term slowdown in advertising spending. The shrinkage of ad spending was estimated to aggregate roughly ₹ 30 billion (3000 crore). It was expected to disproportionately impact the print media, since TV genres such as sport usually involved advance ad bookings, which would survive the slow-

---

79 *The Times of India* (2014b).

80 The demonetisation was announced at roughly 8 p.m. on the evening of November 8, 2016 and allowed a mere four hours for all who held the stigmatised currency notes to pass them on in some transaction. There has been a substantial volume of media commentary that has sprung up subsequently, mostly suggesting that the move was ill-conceived. Another category has proposed that demonetisation was sound policy, though poorly executed. There are several shades of difference in between, but few commentaries, except in the partisan press that has emerged around Narendra Modi's prime ministership, to suggest that the move has been anything but a disaster.

down. Ad bookings in the print media in contrast were made week to week and could easily be cancelled or rescheduled.[81]

Late December 2016, the chief executive of Hindustan Times Media Ltd (HTML), which publishes the second most widely circulated English newspaper and a Hindi daily that ranks among the top five, sent out a mail to all staff, warning that the large-scale currency demonetisation had made a bad situation considerably worse. Certain sacrifices had to be made, he said, which would impact all departments and across the hierarchy.

There was a sense of foreboding but seemingly no specific warning of the magnitude of the shock. On January 5, 2017, HTML employees received emails from the chief executive, announcing the immediate closure of four editions and seven bureaus. Anxious calls made to relevant persons in the management hierarchy, went unattended. Four days later, employees numbering in the hundreds realised that they were out of their jobs. The plans had been underway since at least October but were perhaps advanced in their implementation because of the demonetisation crisis.[82]

On February 2, Kolkata's *Ananda Bazar Patrika* (*ABP*) group which publishes the most widely circulated English newspaper in the eastern region – besides being the dominant player in every segment of Bengali language print – announced similar plans of shuttering several bureaus and editions. Again, there had been some indications since the senior member of the family that owns the enterprise stepped aside to be replaced by a younger brother mid-2016. But nothing seemed to prepare the affected workers for the shock and the suddenness with which the blow finally came.[83]

Alongside the brutal strike on jobs, there seemed to have been a gag order on the affected staff. A month after the mass layoffs in HTML, a media observer was commenting that it was still unclear how many jobs precisely were affected. Neither was much known about the terms of severance offered to laid off staff, who were estimated to number several hundreds in both the HTML and ABP groups. However, even if

81 *Television Post* (2017).

82 *Samrat* (2017) has an extended description of these events.

83 *Newslaundry* (2017a) gives an account of how this decision was announced and received by the staff.

the newspapers from these two groups made a virtue of silence, a rival publishing house proved eager to step up in their vociferous defence, though without revealing the most minimal detail about itself. On January 19, *TOI* ran an editorial page article bemoaning the rising tide of red ink in newspaper balance sheets. "Facts beyond its control" had begun biting deep into the industry's financial fortunes, said the *TOI* in an article that was at least thrice the usual length of its leader pieces and carried no specific attribution.

Yet again, *TOI* showed no inclination to reveal its own financial parameters, while smearing the wage board process with a broad brush. It did pick up some scattered bits of information, curiously, from the recent financial performance of its rival newspaper, *The Hindu*, and the news agency the Press Trust of India which the newspaper industry collectively owns, but keeps on a starvation diet. Both these establishments the *TOI* pleaded, were undergoing severe financial stress as a consequence of the "latest wage board recommendations". The consequence of the wage board was that "blue collar staff including peons, clerks and drivers in certain scales (were being paid) more than three times what they earn in any other industry". In concert with other adverse factors – "rock-bottom" rates for government advertising, the weak Indian rupee which pushed up costs of imported newsprint and demonetisation which had squeezed "spends across almost all categories of advertisers" – the newspaper industry faced "an existential threat".[84]

Journalists' unions were quick to respond to the sharp effrontery. One union veteran from Mumbai, M.J. Pandey, dug up the BCCL's own affidavits filed before industrial regulatory authorities, which showed that it had in the three centres where it had significant printing operations in the state of Maharashtra, a mere 263 employees on wage board mandated scales. This in turn broke up as 34 working journalists, 86 administrative staff and 143 factory staff.[85] With duly thorough intent at concealment, the affidavit omitted to mention how many employees BCCL has retained on contracts of various sorts. From a variety of sources though, the Mumbai unions managed to put together an estimate that the BCCL as a group had a total employee strength of at least

84 *The Times of India* (2017).

85 *Samrat* (2017): 15.

5,000. Adding on all the group enterprises, the total payroll strength was perhaps 11,000. For the company to argue that wage board awards were a financial burden was in this context, to inflict serious violence upon factual veracity.

HTML and ABP were only the latest, though they will not be the last, in a long line of eruptions that broke the surface calm and laid bare a long festering crisis. Since the short-lived boom ended in 2008, the higher profile newspaper groups have been quietly cutting staff, while seeking political guarantees by severely curbing critical coverage. Regional papers and news channels presented an even bleaker picture, with several of them employing journalists at less than the minimum wage for unskilled work. Journalists were also expected to "act as advertising and subscription agents" and meet "targets for revenue generation". Professionals bearing the weighty designation of "resident editors" in such news organisations were "responsible as much for editorial functions as for bringing in the money".[86]

Expectedly, the *TOI* neither revealed any details of its own financials, nor looked into the deeper causes of the newspaper industry crisis. It had no reason to highlight how managements had been asleep at the wheel for years, pursuing profit at the cost of the integrity of the industry's basic function of gathering news and presenting it in a credible fashion. Meanwhile, the boom and bust cycle of the global economy was playing havoc, each upswing managing successfully to divert attention from the need to return to the essentials, allowing managements to tie the fortunes of the industry increasingly upon advertisements, rather than expanding readership through quality news reporting.

The argument that the wage board award was proving a financial burden was thoroughly belied by the ease with which HTML and ABP managed – overnight and at the stroke of a pen – to dismiss a substantial number of their employees. These facts were evidently of little consequence in the post-truth environment that the Indian media had created in the age of globalisation. The effort to delegitimise the wage board process represented a continuation of the trend towards abusing editorial prerogative to argue a one-sided case for newspaper industry

86 Parashar and Krishnan V. (2017): 40. This article is rich with detail on the antecedents of the late-2016 media meltdown and provides a wide range of case studies from different parts of the country.

owners. The case that the *TOI* in particular made for being attentive to reader interest by keeping prices low, went against boasts propagated through its own news pages, about the affluence of its readers and their high purchasing power. It also glossed over the role it has played over the years in launching a corrosive "price war", which forced competition to follow suit and drove many other titles to the wall and destroyed pluralism and diversity in the press.

Even if devoid of immediate practical consequence or profit, the crisis in the media industry seemed to compel a review of some of the strategic choices it had made over two decades. It was asked, for instance, if the industry did the right thing by itself and its customers from about the mid-1990s, by tying its commercial success to advertising rather than audience loyalty. In the process, the journalism function was devalued and its essential tenets and processes forgotten, because advertising – always the greater contributor to revenue – needed not just to be accommodated, but actively pampered. The opacity that has been a matter of principle with the Indian news media as in the persistence with which it has resisted a fair wage bargain and decent working conditions, has been self-defeating strategy, corroding public trust and credibility. Regaining these would mean accepting certain norms of transparency that would involve a *gestalt* shift in the industry culture. That would be a transformative moment for an industry that has never felt the need to honour the transparency norms that it has sought to foist upon others.

In an age of data overload, the role of the traditional mediators of information flow is weakening. But their place is being taken not by more democratic and widely dispersed modes of access to the information world. Rather the shape of the future could be robotic forms of information aggregation and dissemination that serve little else than the compulsion of corporate profit. There has of course, never been a golden age of journalism, though there have been times when certain of its fundamental values were discussed and efforts made to honour them. Perhaps there never was a time when reaffirming these forgotten values has been more urgent. Perhaps there never was a time when the task has been more difficult.

Epilogue

This book goes to press to the very noisy accompaniment of skeletons rattling out in embarrassing numbers from the dark cupboards of the Indian media industry. It took a "sting operation", an ethically questionable procedure, to bring this particular bunch of the industry's shady secrets to light. Cobrapost, a native of the digital media universe, promoted by an individual long invested in sting journalism, has always stretched the envelope and with dogged persistence, ventured into contested ethical territory. Its ultimate reward perhaps comes from the growing recognition that its transgressions, though troubling, are orders of magnitude less than the dodgy practices they lay bare.

The May 2018 revelations from Cobrapost portrayed in vivid and disturbing detail, how some of India's biggest media corporations were eager to take up the advocacy of a political agenda for assured financial rewards.[1] Launched in 2017, Cobrapost's "Operation 136" took its title from the global rank India was awarded on the annual press freedom index compiled by Paris-based Reporters Sans Frontieres (RSF).

If that was a deeply mortifying moment, more bad news followed. In April 2018, RSF downgraded India another two places, on grounds that merit some attention. The hyper-nationalistic cohorts closely

1 The Cobrapost reporting, mostly consisting of covert recordings of conversations by reporter Pushp Sharma with a number of senior media executives and proprietors, can be found on video-sharing site Youtube, by keying in Operation 136 in the search box.

gathered into Indian Prime Minister Narendra Modi's orbit, the RSF argued, had assumed the authority to determine the forms of media practice that could be tolerated, and those that must be ruthlessly put down. Often enough, unquestioning faith in the political leadership was the touchstone. "Hindu nationalists", the RSF said, had been "trying to purge all manifestations of 'anti-national' thought from the national debate". These officially encouraged exercises in thought control ensured that "self-censorship (was) growing in the mainstream media and journalists (were) increasingly the targets of online smear campaigns by the most radical nationalists, who vilify them and even threaten physical reprisals".[2]

Operation 136 laid bare how the media industry was an eager participant in its own enslavement to the new hyper-nationalism, which came bundled with commercial incentives for anybody who signed up for it. Responding to the blandishments of an undercover operative from Cobrapost, top media executives expressed their eagerness to push the political agenda commonly referred to as Hindutva, since it could amply pay its way. It mattered not that the agenda was deeply destructive of basic civility, indeed a threat to the security and the basic constitutional rights of minorities and other vulnerable social groups. All that mattered was the commercial imperative. Freedom comes with the unstated obligation to abide by the basic codes of civility, but commerce often trumps that value.

Legitimate questions could be raised about the RSF's perceptions based index of press freedom, as too its beauty pageant style of awarding ranks. Yet, in entirely rejecting the RSF findings, India's officially accredited guardian of press freedom and ethics, the Press Council of India (PCI), chose to overlook even its more substantive points. PCI Chairman C.K. Prasad, a retired judge of India's Supreme Court, said in fact that "undue importance" was given to the rankings, since there was little "clarity on the inputs that weighed in the ranking of a country".[3]

---

2 Extracted June 2018, from the RSF website: https://rsf.org/en/india

3 See the story issued with dateline May 6, 2018, Delhi, by the Press Trust of India, and carried on the website of *The Hindu* under the title "PCI rejects World Press rankings citing 'lack of clarity'"; extracted June 10, 2018 at: http://www.thehindu.com/news/national/pci-rejects-world-press-freedom-index-citing-lack-of-clarity/article23791829.ece.

Operation 136 laid bare how the media industry was an eager participant in its own enslavement, merely because the new hyper-nationalism could pay its way as a political agenda and bring it assured commercial advantages. It mattered not that the agenda was deeply destructive of basic civility, indeed a threat to the security and the basic constitutional rights of minorities and other vulnerable social groups. All that mattered was the commercial imperative. Freedom comes with the unstated obligation to abide by the basic codes of civility, but commerce often trumps that value.

Media executives who engaged the Cobrapost provocateur rather than showing him the door, ended up revealing the most inglorious tricks of their trade. Most of them found nothing amiss in the proposal to begin an advertising campaign that would in its first stage, exploit mass sentiments of piety by deploying words and images from the legends of Krishna, a figure from the Hindu pantheon who unlike Ram or Ganapati, had been sparingly used in political mobilisation. From these first invocations of Krishna and his battlefield sermon of duty and commitment, the Bhagavad Gita, the campaign would escalate to a second stage, where its tools would be the mockery of Prime Minister Modi's political rivals. The third stage would seek active polarisation, to excite a sense of animus towards the "anti-national" social groups and promote Prime Minister Modi's sole claims to represent an India on the pathway to fulfilling its burgeoning ambitions.[4]

Some among the media houses that engaged with the Cobrapost operative seemed to realise their folly as the date of the launch approached. On the eve of the scheduled release of the videos, leading Hindi media group Dainik Bhaskar, also heavily invested in mining and energy, secured an *ex parte* injunction from the Delhi High Court. Like most such rulings rendered *ex parte*, this seemed curiously unmindful of fair procedure. Subsequent efforts by Cobrapost to vacate

4 The basic details of the Cobrapost findings were carried in a story published by the news website *The Wire*, dateline My 31, 2018. See Siddharth Varadarajan, "Forget the Cobra That Stings, We Need to Worry About the Media That Poisons"; extracted June 10, 2018 at: https://thewire.in/media/forget-the-cobra-that-stings-we-need-to-worry-about-the-media-that-poisons.

the injunction had not made much progress at the time these lines are written.[5]

Dainik Bhaskar earned itself a reprieve from embarrassing disclosures, but not the other media houses that had laid out the welcome mat for the undercover journalist. For reasons to do with media dynamics in the internet age, the platforms that picked up the story and ran it with what seemed the appropriate degree of prominence, were natives of the digital domain. Traditional media chose to either blank it out, or provide it the most cursory coverage, suffused with caustic references to the unorthodox methods employed and its author's previous encounters with the law, which had left him with a few bruises.[6] The prelude to the Cobrapost revelations and its aftermath illustrate how the media industry has stood for transparency only as a virtue enjoined on others, and how it shapes a public discourse that spares it the burden of accountability.

Cobrapost unfolds a fascinating story in several parts. Among the highlights is Vineet Jain, Managing Director and part of the proprietary family of India's largest media group, Bennett Coleman and Co Ltd (BCCL), nonchalantly throwing out a variety of routes by which the sum of ₹ 5 billion (500 crore) promised by Cobrapost's undercover reporter could be transferred to its coffers, without inviting the suspicion of income-tax authorities. Kallie Purie, who occupies a like position in the India Today media group, is eager to accept the offer of a lavish advertising campaign focused around Krishna and the Bhagavad Gita, but careful to add a caveat, that all possible political ramifications of the campaign would be liable to editorial critique in her media outlets. A senior advertising executive from her organisation is depicted another moment, in whole-hearted endorsement of the po-

5 See the news agency story from the Press Trust of India, datelined Delhi, May 20, published under the headling: "HC refrains from vacating stay on Cobrapost documentary"; extracted June 10, at: http://www.ptinews.com/news/9764243_HC-refrains-from-vacating-stay-on-Cobrapost-documentary.

6 Pushp Sharma, the principal author of Operation 136, had in 2016 run a story purporting to show a degree of institutional bias against persoons of the Muslim faith in recruitment policies of the Indian government's Ministry of Health. The report, ostensibly based on discoveries made using the right to information law, was sharply denounced as fake by the Ministry, which filed a police complaint and secured Sharma's arrest.

litical themes of the campaign and in a seeming excess of enthusiasm, tying up a ₹ 2.75 billion (275 crore) advertisement commitment from the Cobrapost provocateur.[7]

The chief executive of HT Media, which owns the second largest newspaper brand in English and one of the top five in Hindi, responds to the Cobrapost proposals with what seems impeccable reason. The price tag he attaches to his services though, is distinctly more modest. "If you are giving me a couple of crore rupees to talk positive about you", he explains, "automatically my editorial is under pressure not to go deep negative". There is an escape clause that he is careful to add: the editorial departments "cannot ignore the news", which is perhaps a coded reference to the compulsions of competitive news coverage.[8] Any news outlet could suppress particular news items in return for a monetary reward, but would be at risk of exposure if the competition were to delve deep into that area.

The large and highly diversified conglomerate Zee Media, with interests in television news and entertainment, print and satellite broadcasting makes an inevitable appearance, as a charter member of the new nationalist media brigade.[9] Zee brings much baggage into the fray, including the arrest of two senior news executives in 2012 on charges of extortion.[10] After their quality time spent in prison, that duo has risen higher in the Zee hierarchy, perhaps beyond the reach of the Cobrapost operative. Those who do appear from the chain of editorial management though, provide ample evidence of a flourishing culture of cash for coverage. The Zee executives are candid in their offers to

---

7 Ibid.

8 Arefa Johari, "'Automatically my editorial is under pressure': What the Cobrapost sting reveals about Indian media", *Scroll*, May 26, 2018; extracted June 10, 2018 at: https://scroll.in/article/880377/automatically-my-editorial-is-under-pressure-what-the-cobrapost-sting-reveals-about-indian-media.

9 "Cobrapost Sting: From Promoting Yogi to Running Down Akalis, Zee's Journalism Laid Bare", *The Wire*, May 31, 2018; extracted June 10,2018 at: https://thewire.in/media/cobrapost-zee-paid-news-black-money.

10 "Two Zee editors arrested for 'Rs 100-crore extortion bid'", *The Times of India*, dateline November 28, 2012; extracted June 10, 2018 at: https://timesofindia.indiatimes.com/india/Two-Zee-editors-arrested-for-Rs-100-crore-extortion-bid/articleshow/17391903.cms.

the Cobrapost operative and seem finally to agree on a deal worth ₹ 250 million (25 crore) of which half would be received in unaccounted cash. Along the way, the Zee executives also explain that they have a ready template to accommodate similar demands, the "advertiser-funded programme". Yogi Adityanath, the Chief Minister of India's largest state Uttar Pradesh, they reveal, has been a regular user of this facility, often getting his ads pushed as news.

Only two among the media houses the Cobrapost operative approached, the Bengali language dailies *Bartaman* and *Dainik Sambad* are shown firmly rebuffing his overtures. Others may have been fortunate in not having been visited by the operative during his wanderings through the back offices of India's media houses. But as eloquent as the words spoken by senior media executives to the undercover reporter, was the silence of the mainstream media that followed. One among the major English language dailies, the *Indian Express* chose to do a factual story which appeared in its major editions two days after the revelations were posted online. Carefully written with ample opportunity afforded to the victims of the sting to place their responses on record, this report followed all the expected norms and stopped short of pronouncing an opinion.[11]

Pratap Bhanu Mehta, a columnist for the newspaper who enjoys a certain autonomy on account of his academic eminence, found no reason for similar restraint. Cobrapost, he raged, had laid bare, "the thorough contempt Indian media has for the Indian citizen". Citizens were treated as "infantilised fools", willing to suspend disbelief given the "thinnest veneer, the smallest gesture" or pretence of covering the news. Readers did not pay for the news and were hence of little consequence to the media owners, which acknowledged some measure of accountability to only "those who allocate capital or use political power".[12]

---

11 Krishn Kaushik, "Cobrapost: Sting claims media houses open to 'paid Hindutva content', firms call it misleading", *Indian Express*, Delhi, May 27, 2018, p. 9; extracted June 10, 2018 at: http://indianexpress.com/article/india/cobrapost-sting-media-houses-open-to-paid-hindutva-content-firms-call-it-misleading-times-group-india-today-ht-paytm-5192702/.

12 Pratap Bhanu Mehta, "Where Anything Goes", *Indian Express*, Delhi, May 29, 2018, p. 14; extracted June 10, 2018 at: http://indianexpress.com/article/opinion/columns/cobrapost-sting-operation-me-

The Times of India ran a story rich in invective, denouncing the Cobrapost recordings as a case of doctored content and falsification, since no media organisation "named in it agreed to any illegal or immoral activity and no contracts were signed".[13] There were caustic references to the unorthodox methods in the sting and its author's previous encounters with the law.[14] Finally, there was the rather implausible claim that the BCCL executives in meeting with the Cobrapost operative, were "in the process of carrying out a reverse sting with a plan to make (him) commit a mistake or even sign legal contracts so as to expose the people and organisations behind him".

The Hindu took the trouble to explain through its Readers' Editor, that its decision to avoid the Cobrapost revelations was consistent with all applicable editorial norms. Unethical practices were no way to improve ethical standards. A large measure of scepticism was warranted about the authenticity of the information uncovered by sting journalism. *The Hindu* was no part of the Cobrapost revelations and it had never at any time been accused of accepting cash for coverage. It did not authorise any concealed means of news gathering and all its staff were expected to identify themselves in carrying out their responsibilities.[15]

Yet all this remained, except to those steeped in the culture of the media organisations named in the Cobrapost tapes, deeply unconvincing. A foreign correspondent wrote a few days afterwards about a "potential scandal" that struck at a "key pillar of Indian democracy"

---

dia-houses-corruption-black-money-5194752/#.WwzTvpxnv-c.twitter.

13 "Cobrapost's sting on media groups based on doctored content and falsification", *The Times of India,* May 27, 2018; extracted June 10, 2018 at: https://timesofindia.indiatimes.com/india/cobraposts-sting-on-media-groups-based-on-doctored-content-and-falsification/articleshow/64335830.cms.

14 Press Trust of India, "AYUSH ministry case: Journalist Pushp Sharma arrested", dateline May 14, 2016; featured at the India Today website and extracted June 10, 2018 at: https://www.indiatoday.in/india/story/ayush-ministry-case-journalist-pushp-sharma-arrested-323521-2016-05-14.

15 A.S. Panneerselvan, "Lying to Get the Truth", *The Hindu*, May 28, 2018, p. 9; extracted June 10, 2018 at: http://www.thehindu.com/opinion/Readers-Editor/lying-to-get-the-truth/article24007726.ece.

and yet was "barely being reported in the Indian media".[16] And even if the methods used by Cobrapost warranted a degree of "healthy scepticism", the questions raised were deeply troubling, particularly when India was just "a year away from a general election".

Another to find the alibis advanced by the Indian media deeply unconvincing was the editor of *The Wire*, a newly launched news portal that was among the few that gave Cobrapost a high degree of prominence. The scruples shown in avoiding the outcome of sting journalism, he wrote, did not square with the eagerness certain Indian media platforms had shown in embracing the Wikileaks and Edward Snowden revelations. Indeed, in their evasion of the issues raised in the Cobrapost revelations, the mainstream media may have been guilty of overlooking the single ground rule of responsible journalism: that of "compelling, overriding public interest".[17]

Evidently when weighed against their own commercial well-being, the mainstream media tends to lose focus on the public interest. The contrast in the responses of the traditional news media and the emerging digital platforms, points to several interesting possibilities. The energy shown by the online news portals in uncovering the Cobrapost revelations in their various facets may suggest a likely divergence in news agendas in the years ahead. There is a definite promise there of alternative news sources emerging to overturn the stifling monopoly of traditional media outlets, though there is equal likelihood of the opposite: that online portals could become a disinformation source even more menacing than anything known so far.

For every one emerging news portal that shows a certain commitment to the public interest and follows every rule in the book about fair coverage and fact-checking, there are many more that have emerged with the explicit mandate of propagating a shrill, partisan voice. Prime Minister Modi's arrival in the highest political office in India has nurtured and sustained a flourishing ecosystem of propaganda websites that work with determined ferocity to drown out and delegitimise all dissent. There is no doubt that "fake news" is a real problem, but the

16 Justin Rowlatt, "The Story Barely Reported by Indian Media", BBC World, May 28; extracted June 10, 2018 at: https://www.bbc.com/news/world-asia-india-44280188.

17 Siddharth Varadarajan, as in footnote 4.

regulatory response in India – as also potentially even in that home of free speech protection, the U.S. – could pick on the wrong targets, in a clearly tendentious manner.

In April this year, the Press Information Bureau of the Indian Government announced fresh guidelines on the accreditation of journalists, ostensibly to check the menace of "fake news".[18] Media accreditation is granted journalists after a specified number of years in the profession. If anything, this waiting period is at least partial assurance that professionals granted access to official corridors in the national capital, would be immune to the temptations of fake news. The April notification put journalists on notice of a "three strikes and out" policy. An accredited media person found to have propagated false news would be on notice after a first offence, and issued a formal warning after a second. A third transgression would be trigger for the termination of his privileges.

The notice was withdrawn, following strong protests from the media community. Yet, a day had not passed before the Prime Minister's Office announced the formation of a committee to frame regulatory rules for news portals and media websites. Five among the ten members of the committee were to be the secretaries of various ministries: civil servants who begin their careers administering a district and then serve various functional ministries in the states and the Indian Union. Others were to be the representatives of the PCI, and various associations of the news broadcast and entertainment industries.[19] Missing entirely were natives of the digital domain.

In December 2015, the Ministry of Information and Broadcasting in India, working through a fully controlled corporate body, invited technical and financial bids from qualified vendors to set up and maintain a "social media communications hub", ostensibly to ensure that citizens were able to access a regular and reliable flow of information

---

18 "Journalists found writing fake news will lose accreditation", dateline: New Delhi, April 3, 2018, *The Hindustan Times*; extracted June 10, 2018 at: https://www.hindustantimes.com/india-news/ministry-of-information-and-broadcasting-drafts-regulations-on-fake-news/story-43MaY6UjKaNJpxZZoctwTP.html.

19 "I&B Ministry forms committee to regulate online media", *Indian Express*, dateline: New Delhi, April 5, 2018; extracted June 10, 2018 at: http://indianexpress.com/article/india/ib-ministry-forms-committee-to-regulate-online-media-smriti-irani-5125324/.

about the Government's most important programmes. That was the stated purpose, though there was a plainly stated propagandist intent in the brief given to prospective vendors, to enhance the "reach of content on internet and social media sites" and find ways of "making the uploaded content viral". There was also a surveillance intent though relatively unstated in relation to the propagandist, which was to monitor, "individual social media users and accounts", "social media sentiments", and "overall trends on various social media platforms".[20]

Little more has come to light about that particular venture into the brave new world by the Ministry. In January 2018 though, the Ministry returned to the fray, this time with a seeming renewal of energy. In line with plans announced then, it floated another request for proposals in April 2018, inviting a fresh round of applications for creating the social media communications hub. The "scope of work" specified here involves harvesting all relevant information posted both on news portals and social media platforms, to assess the overall drift of public opinion, as also its more granular features. The hub, as the tender specifies, "should also support easy management of conversational logs with each individual with capabilities to merge it across channels to help facilitate creating a 360-degree view of the people who are creating buzz across various topics". The proposal will also allow room for "influencers" of opinion who could initiate these conversations in all of the country's many districts. The purposes could be manifold, though the request for proposals does mention the cultivation of "nationalistic" feelings to be among the more important of these.[21]

Prime Minister Modi's impact on the social and communal fabric over his four years in power, cannot be understood without reference to the tactical use his ardent flock has made of the internet and

---

20 Broadcast Engineering Consultants India Ltd., Request for Proposals dated 03-12-2015; extracted June 10, 2018 at: http://mib.nic.in/sites/default/files/RFPsocilamedia2MIB4dec15.pdf. The quoted sections are at pages 26 and 27.

21 Broadcast Engineering Consultants India Ltd., Request for Proposals dated April 25, 2018; extracted June 10, 2018 at: http://www.becil.com/uploads/tender/TendernoticeBECIL01pdf-04836224e38fdb-96422221c4e057f6c5.pdf. The quoted sections are from pages 28, 30 and 33. For an interesting comment on this move, see Apar Gupta, "A Plan to Control Minds", *Deccan Herald*, Bangalore, June 10, 2018, p. 8; extracted: https://www.deccanherald.com/national/sunday-spotlight/plan-control-minds-674182.html.

new media. The 2014 electoral contest made history with its use of high-technology in projecting Modi's claim to the top political job. And Modi's enthusiasm for the new media was evident in a meeting early in his tenure with Facebook's Chief Operating Officer, Sheryl Sandberg. According to an entry in Modi's personal website, Sandberg congratulated him at this meeting, on his "exceptional use of Facebook to connect with voters".[22] Soon afterwards, Modi reportedly instructed colleagues in the party and the government, to use social media to get the word out, but to stay clear of direct interactions with news media.[23]

The internet is being cast here not as a domain of vast possibilities, of the potential deepening of democracy through the richness of user generated content, but as a new mode of propaganda: not pluralistic and interactive, but relentlessly one-way and single-themed. This explains a great part of the media strategy that the Prime Minister has adopted, of disdaining any form of direct interaction with the media, leaving that to chosen functionaries who could set a suitable tone of truculence on the airwaves, and otherwise fielding a vast army of internet operatives to colonise that space. It also explains why larger sections of the mainstream media see no way out of the crisis of profitability they are facing, than mimicking the loud, obstreperous and intolerant tone that the regime seeks to foster through the social media. There are undoubtedly great potentialities inherent in the new media for enriching the flow of information. But these are rapidly being undermined by a determined political operation, which in fact is turning it to quite the opposite purpose.

Statistics may often have no more than transient utility in the rapidly changing scenario of the modern media, but they could be used provisionally to gauge which way the winds are blowing. In 2011, as Robin Jeffrey and Assa Doron set about researching their book *Cellphone Nation*, India had 100 million newspaper copies coming to market every day, and an estimated 600 million cellphones in use all over

---

22 "Prime Minister Modi meets Facebook COO Sheryl Sandberg", July 3, 2014; extracted June 10, 2018 at: https://www.narendramodi.in/asm/prime-minister-narendra-modi-meets-facebook-coo-sheryl-sandberg-6344.

23 Index on Censorship, "India's Modi bypasses mainstream media and takes to Twitter", August 27, 2014; extracted June 10, 2018 at: https://www.indexoncensorship.org/2014/08/india-modi-mainstream-media-press/.

the country.[24] These figures were regarded as portending momentous change, though the future relevance of the newspaper as a medium still seemed assured. By 2017, the figures had not changed very much in respect of newspaper numbers, though there were growing doubts over how much of it was substantive and how much mere artifice to keep advertisers interested. Cellphone users – or at least the number of active SIM cards, which is its closest proxy – had topped one billion by then.[25]

In September 2016 a new entity came into India's universe of information transactions, with a splashy celebrity launch in the western metropolis of Mumbai. Its entry into the telecom and internet space was itself an end-run around all regulatory norms, a manoeuvre carried out while regulatory agencies winked or looked elsewhere. In 2010, a little known entity, Infotel Broadband Services Ltd. (ISBL), was awarded a number of licences for data services incorporating "fourth generation" or 4G specifications and technology. Since licences came bundled up with spectrum, this award earned for the novitiate in the field, the right to colonise a wide swathe of the electromagnetic spectrum across the country. A few days later, Reliance Industries Ltd – India's largest business conglomerate with interests in energy, infrastructure, petrochemicals and various stated and unstated stakes in media houses – announced that it had acquired a 95 per cent stake in ISBL.

Soon afterwards, Reliance announced the launch of a high-speed data service under the brand name Jio. Capitalising on the concept of a universal service licence announced in 2013, it expanded the service to include voice calls.

In 2014, the official watchdog over public finances, the Comptroller and Auditor-General of India (CAG), sent a draft report to the Department of Telecommunications (DoT), urging cancellation of the licence issued IBSL. The CAG found after an audit of the process, that the "DoT failed to recognise the tell-tale sign of rigging of the auction right from (the) beginning". Rather implausibly, a small and obscure

24 Robin Jeffrey and Assa Doron, *Cell Phone Nation*, Hachette India, Delhi, Amazon Kindle edition, loc 4783.

25 *Ericsson Mobility Report*, November 2017, p. 4. The exact number estimated for the end of the third quarter of the year, i.e., September 2017, was 1.185 billion.

company was awarded an all-India licence on the basis of a licence fee bid that was over 5,000 times its net worth.[26]

In January 2016, an advocacy group, the Centre for Public Interest Litigation, filed a petition in the Supreme Court demanding revocation of the 4G services licence granted Jio.[27] In April that year, the Supreme Court dismissed the petition on grounds that it would not intervene in policy matters unless there was evidence of "blatant" malafide.[28]

With all impediments removed, the Jio 4G service launched in September 2016 with a variety of freebies on offer. Other telecom and internet service providers were rattled though their feeble protests to the regulatory authority went unheeded. Already vulnerable to mounting debt servicing obligations, India's telecom operators suddenly had a new threat to worry about.

In its June 2017 edition, the Ericsson Mobility Report which has become something of a standard reference source for trends in the telecom and internet domains, observed that total global "traffic in mobile networks increased by 70 percent" between the end of the first quarter of 2016 and the corresponding point of time the following year. "Part of this increase", it said, "was due to one Indian operator's introductory LTE offer that included free data traffic".[29] Mobile subscriptions

---

26 See the Press Trust of India (PTI) report datelined Delhi, June 30, 2014, published in the *Times of India* the same day under the headline "Auction rigged, cancel broadband spectrum held by Reliance Jio, CAG report says"; extracted like all other links in this section December 2017 at: https://timesofindia.indiatimes.com/business/india-business/Auction-rigged-cancel-broadband-spectrum-held-by-Reliance-Jio-CAG-report-says/articleshow/37488064.cms.

27 "All you need to know about the PIL against 4G licences to Reliance Jio", *The Hindustan Times*, dateline Delhi, January 12, 2016; extracted: http://www.hindustantimes.com/business/all-you-need-to-know-about-the-pil-against-4g-licences-to-reliance-jio/story-lgsvpvf8O-20j7ctvcztXKK.html.

28 "Supreme Court dismisses PIL against Reliance Jio's 4G rollout plan", *The Economic Times*, dateline April 9, 2016; extracted: https://economictimes.indiatimes.com/articleshow/51739233.cms?utm_source=contentofinterest&utm_medium=text&utm_campaign=cppst.

29 The term LTE refers to "long-term evolution" which is another term for 4G data services that follow a template believed to ensure optimal technological options for users and technology providers going forward. The quote is from *Ericsson Mobility Report*, June 2017, p. 2.

had registered a 4 per cent growth over the year. In terms of the net additions during the relevant quarter of 2017, India had the largest number at 43 million, with China second at 24 million. "The strong subscription growth in India", the report concluded, "was mainly due to an attractive LTE 'welcome offer' by one operator, with free voice and data".[30]

Globally, smartphones accounted for 80 per cent of the total number of new mobile connections in the quarter, a figure expected to increase rapidly. Data traffic over mobile networks in 2017 grew 70 per cent globally, with video signals accounting for over 50 per cent of total traffic. Even if not part of the report, it is a safe inference – without entering into the moral dimension – that pornography was a large part of video traffic over the mobile network.

Jio's entry in India had contributed to a dramatic growth in data traffic. Though the report uses a broader geographic category (India, Nepal and Bhutan), the vast part of the increase in data traffic in this region between 2016 to 2017 – 0.3 exabytes per month to 1.0 – could be attributed to India. Data usage per smartphone within this geographic region increased from 1.5 to 4.1 gigabytes per month over the year.[31]

Aside from the disruptive effect that Jio's arrival had on other telecom and internet service providers, it signalled a possible era of consolidation, when older and honoured lines of demarcation between media content and carriage for instance, would be discarded in favour of the relentless concentration of market power. The principle of separation was never very scrupulously observed, but with its stated and unstated investments in India's crisis-ridden media sector, there emerged a very real threat of evisceration from Reliance's entry into the mobile data domain.

India's trajectory is a few steps behind the global trend in some respects, though the magnitude of the transition, because of the sheer size of the country, has attracted global attention. The Reuters Institute for the Study of Journalism (RISJ) has since 2011 been carrying out an annual survey of the digital media with substantial samples drawn from a large number of countries. India is yet to figure in this annual

30 Ibid, p. 4.

31 Ibid, pp. 11, 12, 35. The term megabyte refers to one million bytes and exabyte refers to one billion or 10^9 megabytes.

survey, partly because the institute has not found an in-country partner. But the global trends it highlights are clearly applicable in India and the evidence comes both anecdotally and from assembling information from a diversity of sources.

In its survey published October 2017, the RISJ used a sample of 70,000 from 36 different markets across five continents, with internet penetration ranging from 50 to 98 per cent of the population. Though there were variations in these markets with their own distinct demographics, the directions of change discerned across them allowed for certain robust generalisations.

There was firstly, an increasing dependence on the smart phone for accessing news and information. "Distributed discovery" was becoming more important, with particular news sources being less likely to be remembered than the platform on which they were discovered. Beyond these platforms, the growth of "private" messaging apps such as whatsapp in news discovery was growing. And with this multitude of sources and choices, the vital attribute of "trust" was eroding. As the RISJ study concluded "confidence in both social media and news (was) low".[32]

The ambience was just right for power, rather than a shared belief in a universe of facts, to become arbiter of what gets to be seen, heard and read. And in a world of growing resentments and anxieties, facts became what you chose to make them, which fed the erosion of trust in established institutions and encouraged a spirit of vigilantism and summary justice in dealing with economic and social insecurities.

In India, social media in powerful alliance with the smartphone was creating what was accurately described as "a whirlpool of misinformation", which continued to spread "unwelcome ripples".[33] "Fake news" propagated in aid of a political cause, with intent to influence voter intentions and election outcomes, was a familiar phenomenon, which manifested itself in a mutant though still familiar avatar in the age of the internet. Neither was there any novelty in fake news spread

---

32 Reuters Institute for the Study of Journalism, *Digital News Report 2017*, October, Oxford, UK. See especially the executive summary.

33 Al Jazeera, "The growing tide of fake news in India", December 11, 2017; extracted at: http://www.aljazeera.com/news/2017/12/growing-tide-fake-news-india-171210122732217.html.

through the new media becoming the trigger for social violence. There was plenty there, of course, to explode the optimistic forecasts that access to techniques of connectivity would lead inexorably to greater enlightenment and harmony.

Connectivity may not have been the cause, but it was certainly a powerful instrumentality for the expression of deep-seated social pathologies. A particular gruesome incident occurred in the eastern state of Jharkhand in May 2017, when seven people without any obvious criminal intent, were lynched on suspicions of running a child trafficking racket. Four of the victims were cattle-traders who happened to be passing through the district at the time, belonging to a religious faith stigmatised for long in India for its ostensible disregard for the cow, sacralised as an object of veneration by certain elements within the majority faith. Rumours of the child trafficking ring that had circulated over Whatsapp for at least a month, may have fused with a heightened sense of vigilantism against people of the faith, to provoke the hideous act of violence.[34]

Photographs and video shot of the image on mobile phone were widely circulated through Whatsapp and other social media soon afterwards, feeding a certain ghoulish energy. There was nothing to suggest that the baleful mood had abated since then, though few seemed prepared for the horrendous crime of December 6 in Rajsamand district of Rajasthan. It was a day marking a quarter century since the demolition of a mosque at Ayodhya in a fury of vengeful mediaevalism. For elements of the extreme form of nationalism called Hindutva, it was a day commemorating their bravery, or *shaurya*. And it was the day chosen by a young man of middling means, born at the lower end of the caste hierarchy, to pick up a random migrant worker whose only crime was that he belonged to the Muslim faith, hack him savagely and after failing to decapitate him, set him alight. Shot on mobile phone by the man's 14-year old nephew, the crime was soon circulating in vivid and gruesome detail on social media, gaining a nationwide audience.

In an unhinged rant delivered to the camera after completing his heinous act, the murderer spoke of his determination to avenge the

34 "Two Arrests, Protests Follow After WhatsApp Rumours Lead to Lynching of Seven in Jharkhand", *The Wire*, May 22, 2017; extracted at: https://thewire.in/138667/whatsapp-message-turns-tribals-violent-leaves-seven-dead/.

insults that his faith had suffered. He spoke of the so-called "love jihad" – a fantasy concocted by fevered minds about men of the Muslim faith using their wiles to entrap and marry women of other faiths – as an established reality. Counterfeit notes that enemy nations had distributed through India, he raged, had fuelled terrorist acts, and funded films mocking the Hindu faith and distorting its proud history. A sinister Islamic conspiracy was afoot to ruin a whole generation of Hindu youth by getting them hooked on drugs, while mafia dons who ran the chain of criminal enterprises enjoyed safe haven in Pakistan. Despite waiting a quarter century since the courageous demolition of a mosque at Ayodhya, he blustered, Hindus had been denied their right to build a temple to their revered god-king Ram at the spot.

A team of human rights activists who visited the scene of the gruesome murder a few days later put together a story of a social milieu that had nurtured the crime, but felt curiously detached from the horror of it. The team found lawyers outside the house of the killer, volunteering to provide him and his nephew free legal aid. One among the lawyers, who had come from the state capital of Jaipur, brought a cheque of fifty thousand rupees to hand over to the family. Social media had meanwhile exploded with posts in support of the killer. The video of the murder had been shared by users using a variety of identities, such as "Jai Hindutva" and "Swachh Bharat", the latter being the slogan of a nation-wide campaign of public hygiene launched by the Prime Minister. Songs valorising the deed as a heroic act had been composed and morphed images circulated depicting the murderer in a posture of religious piety and contemplation. Within days, an effort at funds mobilisation had helped gather a reported ₹ 300,000 for his wife. The psychopathic killer of Rajsamand had drawn inspiration from the insistent campaign of hate propagated through social media. His deed had in turn, fuelled that campaign and notched it up one degree in the intensity of its hatred.[35]

Social media has shown the potential to get people killed in the real world, after the murderers commit themselves to an alternative

---

35 Harsh Mander, John Dayal and Kavita Srivastava, "Rajasthan hate murder: The other tragedy in Afrazul's killing is a famine of compassion, outrage", *Scroll*, December 18, 2017; extracted at: https://scroll.in/article/861826/rajasthan-hate-murder-the-other-tragedy-in-afrazul-khans-murder-is-a-famine-of-compassion-outrage.

universe of facts simply because they want to.[36] Social media and the legacy outlets – print and TV – have a mutual relationship that is not yet clearly understood. But it is a likely hypothesis that excess on one side could be dampened by sobriety and responsibility on the other. In junctures of inflamed sensitivities and a heightened vulnerability to violence, legacy media could conceivably play a role to lessen probabilities of a contagion effect. Yet a close audit of media content following the Rajsamand murder, showed that "the gut wrenching news .. was largely ignored on prime time". Instead, the channels seemed obsessed by a barb that had been directed at Prime Minister Modi by a political opponent in the heat of the campaigning then underway for the state legislative assembly in his home state, Gujarat. By twisting the sense of the term used into what seemed a deliberate caste insult, the channels were with obvious intent, seeking to deliver a partisan advantage to the Prime Minister.

These strangely skewed priorities were not confined to the news channels; a comparison of the Delhi editions of various newspapers underlined that it was shared in print too. "It is no longer surprising", the study concluded, "to see sections of mainstream media gloss over news that could put the establishment in the dock for its ineptness if not subtle encouragement to elements who are out to destroy the social fabric".[37]

In an environment of collapsing civility, the enforcement of censorship through formal and informal means intensified. A yoga guru turned spiritual entrepreneur, who built a fortune on claims to produc-

---

36 As these lines are written, a horrific incident of two youths being lynched in the district of Karbi Anglong in the north-eastern Indian state of Assam, is being reported. As with many similar incidents in the recent past, rumour of a child abduction and organ harvesting racket originated on Facebook and was amplified and propagated through Whatsapp, till a violent mob just happened to pick up two random individuals who looked different, since they were travelling through the district. See: "16 Arrested in Assam Lynching Case", *The Hindu*, June 11, 2018, p. 1.

37 This valuable analysis was written by Arjun Siddharth for the fact-checking website AltNews, which had emerged in a short span of time by December 2017, as a significant effort at establishing authenticity in the news disseminated over social media. See: "A man was hacked to death. What did news channels discuss on prime time?", December 8, 2017; extracted: https://www.altnews.in/man-hacked-death-news-channels-discuss-prime-time/.

ing consumer goods suffused with indigenous ingredients and knowledge, secured a court injunction on a book detailing the story of his rise to fame and fortune. The book apparently had a rather sleazy story to narrate about the founding and expansion of the business empire, of assiduously cultivated political contacts, mysterious disappearances of business associates and labour exploitation on a truly scandalous scale. A district court in Delhi very quickly granted the injunction which was yet to be lifted several months afterwards.[38]

A businessman with investments in the media secured a seat in the upper house of the Indian Parliament and was since nominated to a select committee on defence. He was at the same time pursuing a host of contracts in the defence sector for his companies. An article raising questions about a possible conflict of interests involved was taken down after an injunction issued by a court in the businessman's hometown of Bangalore (Bengaluru).[39]

Films involving the depiction of fictitious characters from history, since adopted as mascots of modern day community identity, drew fire and threats of physical liquidation of its creator and actors. Others that used popular and common names that happened to be drawn from the vast Hindu pantheon of gods, were compelled to alter their title and denied any form of sanction for participation in publicly sponsored film festivals.[40]

---

38 The story of the injunction obtained by yoga guru Baba Ramdev, who founded the business empire known by the brand name Patanjali, can be found in a variety of sources. The book in question, by Priyanka Pathak-Narain, was titled *Godman to Tycoon: The Untold Story of Baba Ramdev* and published by the Delhi based publisher, Juggernaut.

39 The incident, involving the businessman Rajeev Chandrasekhar and the news website *The Wire*, was reported by a rival news website, *Scroll* on March 7, 2017 under the headline "In highly unusual move, Bengaluru court orders The Wire to remove articles on Rajeev Chandrasekhar", extracted December 2017 at: https://scroll.in/article/831159/in-highly-unusual-move-bengaluru-court-orders-the-wire-to-remove-articles-on-rajeev-chandrasekhar.

40 The film *Padmavati* was a high budget production from the Mumbai film industry that built upon a mediaeval fantasy of love between an invading Muslim general and a woman in the Rajput court that he went to war with. It is widely believed that the character of the woman was an invention of Malik Muhammad Jayasi, an Awadhi sufi poet, at least two centuries after the purported incidents and was an allegory for unattainable beauty. The film *Sexy Durga* drew fire for what was called

Meanwhile, the most extreme form of censorship of those who spoke inconvenient truths, was on frequent display. In September 2017, Gauri Lankesh a journalist and human rights activist was shot dead on the doorstep of her home in Bengaluru. Her two assassins were waiting for her as she arrived home and sped away on motorcycles after their heinous crime. The method was eerily similar to that employed in three earlier instances involving the murder of public figures involved in campaigns against superstition and religious obscurantism. Narendra Dabholkar was murdered in the western Maharashtra city of Pune in August 2013, Govind Pansare in the southern Maharashtra town of Kolhapur in February 2015 and M.M. Kalburgi in the northern Karnataka town of Dharwar in August 2015.

After all the rosy prognoses of the new disruptions creating opportunities and fresh forms of social bonding, a former executive from Facebook came up with the astounding *mea culpa.* Speaking to a university crowd in the Stanford Business School in the U.S. in November 2017, Chamath Palihapitiya who held senior management responsibility for user growth in the social media giant, expressed deep remorse over his role in developing a means by which society was being ripped apart. "The short-term, dopamine-driven feedback loops that we have created", he said, "are destroying how society works. No civil discourse, no cooperation – misinformation, mistruth."[41]

These remarks echoed those by a former CEO of the social media giant, who had a role in how Facebook evolved from a curiosity in Harvard University to a global phenomenon. In remarks made in November again, Sean Parker spoke of Facebook as a site made to exploit human vulnerability. It created a "social-validation feedback loop" that encouraged a retreat into a cocoon where the gratification afforded by a "like" clicked by a user of similar sensibilities was sufficient to mitigate all real and imagined vulnerabilities in the individual's psyche.

---

a salacious epithet conjoined to a name of divine provenance. It was forced to alter its title to *S Durga* before being cleared for commercial release. However, despite being chosen for the International Film Festival of India after a rigorous peer review by film professionals, the directorate of the event declined to allow its screening.

41 "Former Facebook executive: social media is ripping society apart", *The Guardian*, December 12, 2017; extracted: https://www.theguardian.com/technology/2017/dec/11/facebook-former-executive-ripping-society-apart.

In September 2017, Facebook revealed that it had sold space to hundreds of entities based in Russia to run ads that precisely targeted users whose profile indicated a susceptibility to propaganda with a xenophobic and racist tinge. Siva Vaidhyanathan, a professor of media studies at the University of Virginia, wrote following this revelation, that the jury was still out on how far this social media campaign had influenced the outcome of the 2016 election. It was clear as daylight though, that Facebook had "contributed to, and profited from, the erosion of democratic norms in the United States and elsewhere".[42]

Given the rich possibilities of commerce, the sustenance of civility was proving a dispensable luxury in the corporate driven ambience of globalisation. Freedom itself was being carved up in ghettos of the mind, with a sense of hyper-sensitivity towards criticism evident from those who feared the loss of entrenched privilege, together with an intolerance for difference, a proclivity to dismiss all that was at variance with the ghettoised mind as inauthentic and fake. This new spirit of animus was perfectly epitomised by the man who held the position traditionally granted the honorific of "leader of the free world".

In less than a year since assuming office, U.S. President Donald Trump was estimated to have uttered at least one patent and gross lie on at least 90 days. Using another standard – of a "falsehood" when the speaker utters an untruth without awareness or intent – the *New York Times* estimated that he had spoken falsely on every one of his first forty days in office. The number since remained to be tallied, but there was a strong case to be made that occasions when Trump has failed to utter an untruth have been days when he has been absent from the public eye, or holidaying at one of his luxury resorts. All politicians, the authors of this research conceded, do utter falsehoods with intent on several occasions. Yet, there was simply no precedent for what Trump was doing: "No other president — of either party — has behaved as Trump is behaving. He is trying to create an atmosphere in which reality is irrelevant".[43]

---

42 "Facebook wins, Democracy loses", *The New York Times*, September 8, 2017; extracted: https://www.nytimes.com/2017/09/08/opinion/facebook-wins-democracy-loses.html?_r=0.

43 David A. Leonhardt and Stuart A. Thomson, "Trump's Lies", *The New York Times*, December 14, 2017; extracted: https://www.nytimes.com/interactive/2017/06/23/opinion/trumps-lies.html.

Never known to admit error, Trump has also normalised the practice of blaming the messenger for unfavourable news. The term "fake news" that he learnt to deploy against every critic who spoke the inconvenient truth, was since picked up by despots and dictators all over the world to push back against any notion of public accountability.[44] In the land of "first amendment fundamentalism" – where free speech is considered an absolute value that enjoys higher protections than elsewhere in the world – Trump has on various occasions suggested the cancellation of broadcasting licences for TV channels that pursue a persistent line of criticism. That is sure signal that traditional notions of freedom of speech are in grave jeopardy.

A possible defence of freedom could emerge from the new effort to rebuild and consolidate the collective strength of journalism as a profession. The first challenge is to check the alarming attrition in the profession caused by the crisis in the media and its unending wave of personnel layoffs.[45] That struggle in itself faces formidable odds and merely recovering the ground that has been lost will take years of arduous struggle. Failure moreover, is foretold if journalism continues along the pathways of the past and fails to establish a live and vibrant link to the public interest construed in the widest possible sense. An alternative may lie in new media platforms that place the restoration of public trust, rather than profit, as their foremost objective.[46]

---

44 "'Fake News,' Trump's Obsession, Is Now a Cudgel for Strongmen", *The New York Times*, December 12, 2017; extracted: https://www.nytimes.com/2017/12/12/world/europe/trump-fake-news-dictators.html.

45 "The media today: A unionisation wave across the industry", *Columbia Journalism Review*, November 20, 2017, extracted: https://www.cjr.org/the_media_today/union-los-angeles-times-vox.php.

46 There have been several such experiments in recent times, notably in continental Europe. For a recent example from Switzerland, see Christine Schmidt, "After crowdfunding success, Swiss magazine *Republik* charts a course to 'reclaim journalism as a profession'", Nieman Lab, Harvard, May 22, 2018; extracted June 10, 2018 at: http://www.niemanlab.org/2018/05/after-crowdfunding-success-swiss-magazine-republik-charts-a-course-to-reclaim-journalism-as-a-profession/.

Bibliography

Abunimah, Ali (2015): "France begins jailing people for ironic comments", *Electronic Intifada*, extracted December 2016 at: http://electronicintifada.net/blogs/ali-abunimah/france-begins-jailing-people-ironic-comments.

Administrative Staff College of India (2009): *Study on Cross Media Ownership in India*, Draft Report, 2009, placed on the website of the Ministry of Information and Broadcasting, www.mib.nic.in, in June 2012 and extracted then.

Advani, L.K. (1990): "*Interview*", *The Times of India*, November 20, 1990, p. 9.

AFP (2015): "Who is Cherif Kouachi, Suspected in Charlie Hebdo Attack?"; extracted December 2016 at: http://www.ndtv.com/world-news/who-is-cherif-kouachi-suspected-in-charlie-hebdo-attack-724655.

Agamben, Giorgio (1998): *Homo Sacer: Sovereign Power and Bare Life*, Stanford University Press, Stanford.

—— (2005): *State of Exception*, University of Chicago Press.

Alam, Arshad (2011): "Exempted Futures", posted online on August 11, 2001 and extracted in February 2012 at: http://www.outlookindia.com/article.aspx?278014.

Alexander, Harriet (2015): "What is Going Wrong in France's Prisons", *The Daily Telegraph*, January 17, 2015; extracted December 2016 at: http://www.telegraph.co.uk/news/worldnews/europe/france/11352268/What-is-going-wrong-in-Frances-prisons.html.

Ambedkar, B.R. (1945): *What Congress and Gandhi Have Done to the Untouchables*, in Writings and Speeches, Volume 9, Education Department, Government of Maharashtra, Bombay, 1991.

Anand, S. (2013): "The Nandy Bully", *Outlook*, February 11, 2013; extracted November 2016 at: http://www.outlookindia.com/magazine/story/the-nandy-bully/283765.

Andersen, Kurt (2012): "The Protester", *Time*, December 26, 2011- January 2, 2012, pp. 53-89 (U.S. edition).

Andersen, Robin (2000): "Introduction", in Robin Andersen and Lance Strate, *Critical Studies in Media Commercialism*, Oxford.

Andersen, Robin and Jonathan Grey (2008): (editors) *Battleground: The Media*, Greenwood Press, London.

Anderson, Benedict (1983): Imagined Communities, Reflections on the Origins of Nationalism, Verso, London, 1983.

Anderson, Perry (2015): *Americana*, Three Essays Collective, Delhi.

API (n.d.): "The Elements of Journalism", American Press Institute; extracted December 2016 at: https://www.americanpressinstitute.org/journalism-essentials/what-is-journalism/elements-journalism/

Apte, Mahadev L. (1985): *Humour and Laughter: An Anthropological Approach*, Cornell University Press.

Arab News (2015): "First GCC-France Summit Makes History", dated May 12, 2015; extracted December 2016 at: http://www.arabnews.com/columns/news/745666.

Asher, Hemal (2004): "Is this journalism?", *Midday*, May 11.

Assange, Julian (2014): *When Google Met Wikileaks*, Navayana, Delhi.

Associated Press (2006): "Media ownership issues return to spotlight", Dateline: Washington DC, October 3; extracted December 2016 at: http://www.reclaimthemedia.org/legislation_and_regulation/media_ownership_issues_return_to_spotlight.html

Auletta, Ken (2012): "Citizens Jain", *The New Yorker*, October 8, pp. 53-61.

Austin, Granville (1966): *The Indian Constitution: Cornerstone of a Nation*, Oxford, Delhi, 1982.

—— (1999): *Working a Democratic Constitution: A History of the Indian Experience*, Oxford, Delhi.

Bagdikian, Ben (2004): *The New Media Monopoly*, Beacon Books, (sixth edition).

Baker, Russ (1997): "The Squeeze", *Columbia Journalism Review*, September-October, pp. 1-7.

Balagopal, K. (2007): "Land Unrest in Andhra Pradesh: Impact of Grants to Industries", *Economic and Political Weekly*, September 29.

Bardoel, Jo (1996): "Beyond Journalism: A Profession Between Information Society and Civil Society", *European Journal of Communication*, 11(3), pp. 283-302.

Barthes, Roland (1957): *Mythologies* (English translation, 1972), Random House, London.

Battelle, John (2006): *The Search, How Google and its Rivals Rewrote the Rules of Business and Transformed Our Culture*, Nicholas Brealey, London.

BBC (2006): "Full text: Writers' statement on cartoons", published 1 March 2006 and extracted December 2016 at: http://news.bbc.co.uk/2/hi/europe/4764730.stm.

BBC (2014): "Publicis-Omnicom $35bn merger deal called off", May 8; extracted in December 2016 at: http://www.bbc.com/news/business-27336870.

Benton, Joshua (2016): "The forces that drove this election's media failure are likely to get worse", Nieman Lab, posted November 9, 2016 and extracted December 2016 at: http://www.niemanlab.org/2016/11/the-forces-that-drove-this-elections-media-failure-are-likely-to-get-worse/.

Berenson, Tessa (2015): "Lawmakers will hold up pencils at SOTU to honour Charlie Hebdo", *Time*, posted January 20, 2015 and extracted December 2016 at: http://time.com/3675310/state-union-charlie-hebdo-pencils/.

Berlin, Isaiah (1958): "Two Concepts of Liberty", in *The Proper Study of Mankind, An Anthology of Essays,* Pimlico, London, 1998.

Bhargava, G.S. (2005): *The Press in India, An Overview*, National Book Trust, Delhi.

Bhaskara Rao, N. (2002): "Foreign Participation in Media", *Economic and Political Weekly*, Volume 37, No. 2, January 12.

Bhatia, Gautam (2016): *Offend, Shock, or Disturb: Free Speech under the Indian Constitution*, Oxford, Delhi.

Bhatia, Rahul (2012): "Fast and Furious: The Turbulent Reign of Arnab Goswami", The *Caravan*, December 2012, available on the website and extracted in December 2016 at: http://www.caravanmagazine.in/reportage/fast-and-furious.

—— (2013): "The Network Effect", *The Caravan*, December, accessed December 2016 at: http://www.caravanmagazine.in/reportage/network-effect.

Bhattacharjea, Ajit (1998): "Pressures on a profession", *Frontline*, September 11, 1998, pp. 114-5; available online at: http://www.frontline.in/navigation/?-type=static&page=archive.

Bleich, Erik (2001): "The French Model: Color Blind Integration", in John David Skrentny, *Color Lines: Affirmative Action, Immigration and Civil Rights Options for America*, University of Chicago Press, Chicago and London, pp. 270-96.

Blumenthal, Max (2013): *Goliath, Life and Loathing in Greater Israel,* Nation Books, New York (Amazon Kindle Edition).

—— (2015): "Exposing Anti-Islam Author Ayaan Hirsi Ali's Latest Deception", posted on March 26 and extracted December 2016 at: http://www.alternet.org/media/anti-islam-author-ayaan-hirsi-alis-latest-deception.

Bourdieu, Pierre (1984): *Distinction: A Social Critique of the Judgment of Taste,* Routledge, London.

—— (2011): "The Forms of Capital", in *Cultural Theory: An Anthology*, Chicago.

Brass, Paul (2000): "The Strong State and the Fear of Disorder", in Francine Frankel, Zoya Hasan, Rajeev Bhargava and Balveer Arora (editors), *Transforming India, Social and Political Dynamics of Democracy*, Oxford University Press, Delhi.

Brenner, Daniel L. and William L. Rivers (1982): *Free but Regulated, Conflicting Traditions in Media Law*, Iowa State University Press.

Brin, Sergey and Laurence Page (1998): "The Anatomy of a Large-Scale Hypertextual Web Search Engine", *Proceedings of the Seventh International Conference on the Worldwide Web;* extracted December 2016 through google search.

Business Standard (1998): "Bankruptcy in media, Newspapers and television channels battle for survival in the action-packed story that the press does not report", Weekend edition, May 2, p. 1.

Butler, Mathew (2011): "Fox News' First 15 Years of 'Balanced' Journalism", *The Guardian* (U.K.), October 7, 2011; extracted in December 2016 at: http://www.guardian.co.uk/commentisfree/cifamerica/2011/oct/07/fox-news-15-years.

Cabinet Secretariat (2006): Government of India, Cabinet Secretariat, Prime Minister's High Level Committee, *Social, Economic and Educational Status of the Muslim Community in India*, November 2006.

Campbell, Fred (2015): "FCC's Open Internet Order Won't Stand Up to the First Amendment", Forbes, published May 21; extracted December 2016 at: http://www.forbes.com/sites/realspin/2015/05/21/fccs-open-internet-order-wont-stand-up-to-the-first-amendment/#5db320d2ad59

Caravan, The (2011): "IIPM's Rs 500-Million Lawsuit Against The Caravan", July 2011; extracted December 2016 at: http://www.caravanmagazine.in/perspectives/iipms-rs500-million-lawsuit-against-caravan-republished.

Cartalucci, Tony (2015): "A Timeline: Where did Paris Shooters Get Their Weapons?", Centre for Global Research, published January 8, and extracted December 2016 at: http://www.globalresearch.ca/a-timeline-where-did-the-paris-shooters-get-their-weapons/5423445.

Cashman, Richard (1970): "The Political Recruitment of God Ganapati", *Indian Economic and Social History Review*, Volume VII, Number 3, pp. 347-73.

Castells, Manuel (2009): *Communication Power*, Oxford.

Chandra, Naresh (2012): "India's Security Challenges in the next decade – The Role of Intelligence", R.N. Kao Memorial Lecture, January 21, 2012; extracted December 2016 at: http://soodvikram.blogspot.com/2012/01/rn-kao-memorial-lecture-by-shri-naresh.html.

Charbonnier, Stephane and Fabrice Nicolino (2013): "Non,'Charlie Hebdo' n'est pas raciste!"; published November 20, 2013 and extracted December 2016 at: http://www.lemonde.fr/idees/article/2013/11/20/non-charlie-hebdo-n-est-pas-raciste_3516646_3232.html. Translation from the French done through Google translate and checked for accuracy.

Charlie Hebdo (2016): "How Did We End Up Here?", published March 30 and extracted December 2016 at: https://charliehebdo.fr/en/edito/how-did-we-end-up-here/.

Chatterjee, Partha (1997): "Development Planning and the Indian State," in Partha Chatterjee, ed., *State and Politics in India*, Oxford University Press, Delhi, pp. 271-297.

Chaturvedi, Swati (2016): *I Am a Troll*, Juggernaut Books, Delhi.

Chhattisgarh (2005): Chhattisgarh Vishesh Suraksha Adhiniyam, (Number 14 of 2006), Raipur, March 21, 2006; extracted December 2016 at: https://cpjc.files.wordpress.com/2007/07/cspsa_english.pdf.

Chishti, Seema (2006): Series of six articles, October 23 to 29, 2006, headline "Sachar Committee", *Indian Express* (New Delhi edition).

Churumuri (2012): "Times of India Readers Affluent, Not Middle Class: Mind It", posted February 2, 2012 and extracted December 2016 at: http://wearethebest.wordpress.com/2012/02/02/toi-readers-affluent-not-middle-class-mind-it/.

Cockburn, Patrick (2014): *The Rise of the Islamic State*, LeftWord, Delhi.

Cohen, G.A. (1983): "The Structure of Proletarian Unfreedom", *Philosophy and Public Affairs*, 12:1, Winter, pp. 3-33.

—— (2011): "Freedom and Money", in *On the Currency of Egalitarian Justice, and Other Essays in Political Philosophy*, Princeton.

Common Cause (2013): In the Supreme Court of India, Civil Writ Petition NO: 880 of 2013; In the matter of: Common Cause (Petitioner) versus Union of India, through its Secretary, Ministry of Information and Broadcasting (Respondent); extracted December 2016 at: http://www.commoncause.in/publication_details.php?id=84.

Content Sutra (2009a): "Indian Express' Shekhar Gupta: 'This Is A Crisis To Which There Seems To Be No End Yet'". The website has since gone out of commission though its successor site continues to host this item though in a highly abbreviated form; accessed December 2016 at: http://paidcontent.org/2009/03/20/419-indian-express-shekhar-gupta-this-is-a-crisis-to-which-there-seems-to-b/.

—— (2009b): "Interview: Indian Express' Shekhar Gupta: 'We'll Survive a Nuclear War, This is Just a Tsunami", published April 6, 2009. The successor website has a summary of the interview, accessed in December 2013 at: http://paidcontent.org/2009/04/06/419-interview-indian-express-shekhar-gupta-well-survive-a-nuclear-war-this/.

—— (2009c): "Interview: The Hindu's N. Ram on Media Regulation, Slowdown and New Media", published February 22, 2009, and accessed in summary form on December 2013 from the successor website at: http://paidcontent.org/2009/02/23/419-interview-the-hindus-n-ram-on-media-regulation-partnerships-and-new-me/.

Coyle, Joseph S. (1998): "Now, The Editor as Marketer", Columbia Journalism Review, July/August, 37-41.

CPJ (2016a): "Press freedom crisis in India's Chhattisgarh state deepens as two journalists flee Bastar", Committee to Protect Journalists, February 29, 2016; extracted December 2016 at: https://www.cpj.org/2016/02/press-freedom-crisis-in-indias-chhattisgarh-deepen.php.

CPJ (2016b): "Indian authorities shut down media outlets in Jammu and Kashmir", Committee to Protect Journalists, July 28, 2016; extracted December 2016 at: https://cpj.org/2016/07/indian-authorities-shut-down-media-outlets-in-jamm.php.

Crispin Miller, Mark (2007): "Introduction" to Vance Packard (1953).

Cruise O'Brien, Conor (1970): *Camus*, Fontana Modern Masters, London.

Crumley, Bruce (2007): "Racism Unfiltered in France", *Time*, January 6, 2007; extracted December 2016 at: http://content.time.com/time/world/article/0,8599,1574817,00.html.

—— (2011): "Firebombed French Paper is No Free Speech Martyr", posted November 2, 2011 and extracted December 2016 at: http://world.time.com/2011/11/02/firebombed-french-paper-a-victim-of-islamistsor-its-own-obnoxious-islamophobia/.

Curran, James and Jean Seaton (1985): Power Without Responsibility, The Press and Broadcasting in Britain, Methuen, London, 1985.

Cyran, Olivier (2014): " 'Charlie Hebdo' not racist? If you say so", published online December 5, 2014 and extracted December 2016 at: http://posthypnotic.randomstatic.net/charliehebdo/Charlie_Hebdo_article%2011.htm.

Daily News and Analysis (2006): "Kill this Broadcast Bill before it kills your rights", Mumbai edition, July 1.

Das Gupta, Jyotirindra and John J. Gumperz (1968): "Language, Communication and Control in North India", in Joshua A. Fishman, Charles A. Ferguson and Jyotirindra Das Gupta (editors), *Language Problems of Developing Nations*, John Wiley, New York.

Dasgupta, Swapan (1991): *The Times of India*, September 30, 1991.

Desai, Santosh (2014): "The New Power of the Media", *The Times of India*, Delhi edition, February 24, p. 4.

Deshpande, G.P. (2002): Introduction to *Jyotiba Phule, Selected Writings*, Left-Word Books, Delhi.

Deuze, Mark (2005): "What is journalism? Professional identity and ideology of journalists reconsidered", *Journalism*, Vol. 6(4), pp. 442–464.

Dhavan, Rajeev (1987): *Only the Good News: On the Law of the Press in India*, South Asia Books, Delhi.

—— (2010): *Publish and be Damned: Censorship and Intolerance in India*, Tulika Books, Delhi.

Dhawale, Sudhir (2014a): "Q&A: Indian journalist Sudhir Dhawale discusses his release from prison"; extracted December 2016 at: https://cpj.org/blog/2014/06/qa-indian-journalist-sudhir-dhawale-discusses-his.php.

—— (2014b): "The country needs an anti-fascist force, says activist acquitted after 40 months in jail"; extracted December 2016 at: http://scroll.in/article/665186/The-country-needs-an-anti-fascist-force,-says-activist-acquitted-after-40-months-in-jail.

Divan, Anil (2011): "Lok Pal Bill and the Prime Minister", *The Hindu*, (Delhi edition), June 30, 2011, p. 12.

Dutta (2009): "Nokia SEZ: Public Price of Success", *Economic and Political Weekly*, October 3.

Economic Times, The (2013): "Deccan Chronicle Suffers ₹ 1,040 cr Loss in 18 Months", January 23, p. 7.

—— (2013): "Strategically, Publicis Omnicom Group does not make any sense at all", Delhi edition, *Brand Equity Supplement*, September 25, pp. 1-2.

—— (2014a): "If You Think TV Isn't an Idiot Box, Read This", February 7, p. 1.

—— (2014b): "Modi in Poll Position, But Needs More Partners on the Ground", January 27, p. 2.

Editors' Guild of India (2002): *Rights and Wrongs*, reproduced in John Dayal (editor), *Gujarat 2002, Untold and Retold Stories of the Hindutva Lab*, Media House, Delhi, pp. 705-72.

Exchange4Media (2001): "Price War in Hyderabad: ToI in for the Long Haul"; extracted January 2007 at: http://www.exchange4media.com/e4m/mediaresearch/research_detail.asp?section_id=2&news_id=3577.

Fanon, Frantz (1952): *Black Skin White Masks*, Pluto Press, London, 1984.

Fast Company (2010): "Google Grabs State Department Star Jared Cohen for 'Think-Do' Tank", published October 18, 2010 and extracted December 2016 at: https://www.fastcompany.com/1695515/google-grabs-state-dept-star-jared-cohen-foreign-policy-think-do-tank.

FCC (2015): "Open Internet", 26 February 26, extracted December 2016 at: https://www.fcc.gov/general/open-internet.

FICCI (2007): *The Indian Entertainment and Media Industry, A Growth Story Unfolds*, FICCI and PriceWaterhouse Coopers, Federation of Indian Chambers of Commerce and Industry March.

—— (2012): *Digital Dawn: The Metamorphosis Begins*, FICCI-KPMG Indian Media and Entertainment Industry Report, Federation of Indian Chambers of Commerce and Industry, Delhi.

—— (2013): *The Power of a Billion, Realizing the Indian Dream*, FICCI-KPMG Indian Media and Entertainment Industry Report 2013, March.

Financial Times (2011): "US urges Twitter to delay service break" posted on 17 June 2009 under the headline and archived by Wikileaks at https://archive.today/ndbmj (extracted December 2016).

Fiske, John (1989): *Reading the Popular*, Routledge, London.

Flanagan, Jake (2015): "Stop comparing Pamela Geller to the murdered staffers of Charlie Hebdo", *Quartz*, published May 4 and extracted December 2016 at: http://qz.com/397726/stop-comparing-pamela-geller-to-the-murdered-staffers-of-charlie-hebdo/.

Flood, Alison (2015): "Charlie Hebdo row leads to Facebook fallout between Salman Rushdie and Francine Prose", *The Guardian*, published April 20, and extracted December 2016 at: http://www.theguardian.com/books/2015/apr/30/charlie-hebdo-pen-award-salman-rushdie-twitter-scrap.

Frontline (1994): "The Trouble with TADA: Misuse, bias and worse", *Frontline*, Chennai, September 23, pp. 4-9.

—— (1995): "End of a black law; and the continuing concerns", *Frontline*, Chennai, June 16.

—— (1996): "Uplinking rights, The outlook for private Indian broadcasters", November 1, pp. 93-4.

—— (1997): "A TV debate, questions of broadcast policy", February 21, pp. 114-5.

—— (1997): "I never interfered with the due process of law", May 30, pp. 25-7.

—— (1999): "Recording media trends", Vol. 16, Issue 20, October 8, pp. 105-6.

—— (2002): "No to FDI in print", Vol. 19, Issue 8, April 26, p. 132.

—— (2002d): "The rise of print", Vol. 19, Issue 14, July 19, pp. 81-2.

—— (2002a): "A Perilous Policy Shift", Vol. 19, Issue 14, July 19, pp. 19-21.

—— (2002b): "Criticism and Concern", Vol. 19, Issue 14, July 19, p. 22.

Galanter, Marc (1984): *Competing Equalities: Law and the Backward Classes in India*, University of California Press, Los Angeles.

Garton Ash, Timothy (2016): *Free Speech: Ten Principles for a Connected World*, Amazon Kindle edition (citations refer to location).

Ghosh, Anindita (2006): *Power in Print, Popular Publishing and the Politics of Language and Culture in a Colonial Society*, Oxford University Press, Delhi.

Gibson, Owen (2006): "Most leading journalists went to private school", *The Guardian*, June 15, 2006; extracted 15 November 2015 at: http://www.theguardian.com/media/2006/jun/15/pressandpublishing.publicschools.

Giddens, Anthony (1990): *The Consequences of Modernity*, Wiley, London.

Giddens, Anthony and Lesley Sklar: *The Globalisation Debate*, (A three part lecture); The London School of Economics and Political Science, extracted in December 2013 at: http://fathom.lse.ac.uk/Seminars/10701014/.

Gilani, Iftikhar (2005): *My Days in Prison*, Penguin, Delhi.

Goldbert, Jeffrey (2015): "Europe is Under Siege", *The Atlantic* Global, posted January 7, 2015; extracted December 2016 at:: http://www.theatlantic.com/international/archive/2015/01/europe-is-under-siege/384305/.

Goldman (2001): Goldman Environmental Prize, Citation for Steve Wilson and Jane Akre; extracted December 2016 at: http://www.goldmanprize.org/recipient/jane-akre-steve-wilson/.

Governance Now (2013): "Murdochs in the Making", Vol. 4, Issue 6, April 16-30, pp. 16-19.

Government of India (1977): *White Paper on Misuse of the Mass Media During the Internal Emergency*, August, Manager of Publications, Delhi.

Gramsci, Antonio (1935): "State and Civil Society" in *Selections from the Prison Notebooks*, edited by Quentin Hoare and Geoffrey Smith, Longmans, Hyderabad, 1996.

Greenhouse, Emily (2012): "The Charlie Hebdo Affair: Laughing at Blasphemy", *The New Yorker*, September 28, 2012; extracted on May 15, 2015 at: http://www.newyorker.com/news/news-desk/the-charlie-hebdo-affair-laughing-at-blasphemy.

Greenwald, Glen (2015): "204 PEN Writers (Thus Far) Have Objected to the Charlie Hebdo Award – Not Just 6", April 30; extracted December 2016 at: https://firstlook.org/theintercept/2015/04/30/145-pen-writers-thus-far-objected-charlie-hedbo-award-6/.

Guardian, The (2013): "Omnicom and Publicis merger creates communications giant", July 28; accessed December 2016 at: http://www.theguardian.com/business/2013/jul/28/omnicom-publicis-merger-france-united-states.

—— (2016): "Facebook accused of censoring conservatives, report says", May 9 2016; extracted December 2016 at: https://www.theguardian.com/technology/2016/may/09/facebook-newsfeed-censor-conservative-news.

Guha Thakurta, Paranjoy (2012): "India needs cross media restrictions", *The Hoot*, posted 10 June; extracted December 2016 at: http://www.thehoot.org/media-watch/media-business/india-needs-cross-media-restrictions-6005.

Guha Thakurta, Paranjoy and Alice Seabright (2011): " 'Murdochisation' of the Indian Media", *Frontline*, July 30 to August 12, 2011; extracted December 2016 at: http://www.frontline.in/navigation/?type=static&page=archive.

Guha, Keshav (2016): "If you care about press freedom, perhaps it's time to boycott Arnab Goswami?", *Scroll*, February 17; extracted December 2016 at: http://scroll.in/article/803733/if-you-care-about-press-freedom-perhaps-its-time-to-boycott-arnab-goswami.

Gujarat High Court (2012): In the High Court of Gujarat at Ahmedabad, *Bharat Desai, Editor, Times of India v State of Gujarat*, judgment dated April 18, 2012, by Harsha V. Devani, Justice.

Gupta, Apar (2015): "What about Section 69A", *The Indian Express*, March 27, 2015, p. 10; extracted December 2016 at: http://indianexpress.com/article/opinion/columns/but-what-about-section-69a/.

Habermas, Juergen (1962): *The Structural Transformation of the Public Sphere*, English translation 1989 by Thomas Burger, Polity Press, Cambridge, 1992.

—— (1983): *Justification and Application: remarks on discourse ethics*, Polity Press, Cambridge.

—— (1995): "Reconciliation Through the Public Use of Reason: Remarks on John Rawls's Political Liberalism", *The Journal of Philosophy*, XCII: 3, March 1995, pp. 109-31.

Halevy, Elie (1928): *The Growth of Philosophical Radicalism*, Beacon Press, New York, 1955.

Halpern, Sue (2011): "Mind Control and the Internet", *The New York Review of Books*, June 23; extracted December 2016 at: http://www.nybooks.com/articles/2011/06/23/mind-control-and-internet/.

Harding, Jeremy (2015): "Looking for 'Charlie Hebdo'", *London Review of Books*, LRB Blog, published January 15; extracted December 2016 at: http://www.lrb.co.uk/blog/2015/01/15/jeremy-harding/looking-for-charlie-hebdo/.

Harriss, John (2003): *Depoliticising Development: The World Bank and Social Capital*, LeftWord Books, Delhi.

Hasan, Mehdi (2015): "Why Islam Doesn't Need a Reformation", *The Guardian*, May 17, 2015; extracted December 2016 at: http://www.theguardian.com/commentisfree/2015/may/17/islam-reformation-extremism-muslim-martin-luther-europe.

Hegel, G.W.F. (1820): T*he Philosophy of Right*, Batoche Books, Ontario, Canada, 2001.

Hickey, Neil (1998): "Money Lust: How Pressure for Profit is Perverting Journalism", Columbia Journalism Review, July/August, pp. 28-36.

Himanshu (2011): "Recent Trends in Poverty and Inequality: Some Preliminary Results", *Economic and Political Weekly*, February 10, pp. 497-508.

Hindu, The (2013): "Most channels benefit from flawed TAM system, stall alternative", August 1; accessed December 2013 at: http://www.thehindu.com/news/national/most-channels-benefit-from-flawed-tam-system-stall-alternative/article3708673.ece.

—— (2013b): "Big broadcasters walk out of TAM, call rating system 'absurd'", June 9, p. 13; accessed December 2016 at: http://www.thehindu.com/news/national/big-broadcasters-walk-out-of-tam-call-rating-system-absurd/article4795716.ece.

—— (1991): See "4 Newspapers Censured for Exaggerating Ayodhya Events", September 26; extracted August 31, 2011 at: http://www.cscsarchive.org:8081/MediaArchive/clippings.nsf/%28docid%29/EA69AB6C89E86BD7E5256B9800319413?OpenDocument.

—— (2006): "Decision on advertisement component in TV channels withdrawn", August 20.

—— (2008a): "Brain behind Ahmedabad blasts nabbed", August 17, p. 1.

—— (2008b): "Terror Mail Threatens to Stop 'India's heartbeat'", September 14, p. 1.

—— (2008c): "From seminary student to SIMI jihadist", August 17, p. 8.

—— (2008d): "SIMI network in many States exposed", August 17, p. 8.

—— (2008e): "2 Terrorists Shot Dead in Delhi", September 20, 2008, p. 1.

—— (2008f): "Killed Indian Mujahideen men provided terror backbone", September 20, p. 1.

—— (2010): "Green Hunt: The Anatomy of an Operation", February 6, p. 1; extracted December 2016 at: http://www.thehindu.com/opinion/op-ed/green-hunt-the-anatomy-of-an-operation/article101706.ece.

—— (2012a): "Activists vandalise scholar's office", May 12.

—— (2012b): "Furore over cartoon atrocious", May 12.

—— (2012c): "Humour is by no means exempt from prejudice", June 8.

—— (2013a): "Crimes death can't wish away", editorial, September 14.

—— (2013b): "Divided industry, 'propriety' of process slow FDI in media proposal", July 12; accessed on December 2016 at: http://www.thehindu.com/news/national/divided-industry-propriety-of-process-slow-fdi-in-media-proposal/article4905861.ece.

—— (2014a): "BJP ropes in professionals for campaign", and "Where the money coming from, asks AAP", February 21, p. 12.

—— (2014b): "Pollsters ready to manipulate surveys for a price: TV report", February 26, p. 15.

Hindu Business Line, The (2000): "Newspaper Price War in Hyderabad", September 24; extracted December 2016 at: http://www.thehindubusinessline.com/2000/09/24/stories/14244498.htm.

—— (2005): "HT Media: Invest at cut-off", July 31; extracted December 2016 at: http://www.thehindubusinessline.com/bline/iw/2005/07/31/stories/2005073100751100.htm.

—— (2006). "Pay Channels @ Rs 5 per month", September 1, p. 1.

Hindustan Times, The (2006): "Media Muzzled I: Is the Broadcast Bill Media Friendly?", Delhi edition, July 26, p. 11.

—— (2011): "Wage Board Outdated: Experts", June 15.

—— (2013): "PM speaks up for free speech on social media at police meet", November 23.

—— (2013): "Varun Gandhi fixed hate speech case: report", May 16; extracted December 2016 at: http://www.hindustantimes.com/delhi/varun-gandhi-fixed-hate-speech-case-report/story-qmKoaba6P6MGRART8nSXXO.html.

—— (2014): "Nielsen on massive hunt for Cong's best poll bets", February 23, p. 1.

—— (2015): "Not Only Internet.Org, Even Airtel Zero has Zero Customers", December 24; extracted December 2016 at: http://www.hindustantimes.com/business/not-only-internet-org-even-airtel-zero-has-no-customers/story-fCGTGbSmicorvY0G2HRodJ.html

Hobbes, Thomas R. (1651): *Leviathan*, Penguin Books, London, 1975.

Hobsbawm, E.J. (1962), *The Age of Revolution*, Penguin Books, London, 2010.

Hoot, The (2007a): "Most profitable Indian media companies"; extracted January 2007 at: http://www.thehoot.org/story.asp?storyid=Web210214166108hoot12302002684&pn=1.

—— (2007b): "India's most profitable media companies"; extracted January 2007 at : http://www.thehoot.org/story.asp?storyid=Web202159222135Hoot43904%20PM1512&pn=1.

—— (2013): "*The Hindu* returns to the family fold", October 23; extracted December 2014 at: http://thehoot.org/web/The-Hindu-returns-to-the-family-fold/7102-1-1-4-true.html.

—— (2015): "*TOI* takes credit", December 27; extracted December 2016 at: http://www.thehoot.org/media-watch-briefs/toi-takes-credit-9087.

—— (2015b): "Assam Rifles Infected with Foot in Mouth Disease!", November 19; extracted December 2016.

Horkheimer, Max (1946), *Eclipse of Reason*, Bloomsbury, London, 2004, http://www.researchersworld.com/vol5/issue3/Paper_08.pdf.

Supreme Court of India (1950): *Romesh Thapar v The State Of Madras*, decided May 26, Equivalent citations: 1950 AIR 124, 1950 SCR 594; extracted December 2016 at: https://indiankanoon.org/doc/456839/.

Huffington Post (2015): "Why The Juvenile In The Nirbhaya Case Deserves A Second Chance", December 19, 2015; extracted December 2016 at: http://www.huffingtonpost.in/2015/12/18/why-the-juvenile-in-the-nirbhaya-case-deserves-a-second-chance/.

Human Rights Watch (2014): *All According to Plan: The Rab'a Massacre and Mass Killings of Protesters in Egypt*, August 12, 2014; extracted with the press release issued on the occasion, December 2016 at: http://www.hrw.org/news/2014/08/12/egypt-rab-killings-likely-crimes-against-humanity.

Hyde, Rosel H. (1987) "FCC Action Repealing the Fairness Doctrine: A Revolution in Broadcast Regulation", *Syracuse Legal Review*, 1987-88, pp. 1175-95.

IFJ-SAMSN (2010): The International Federation of Journalists for the South Asian Media Solidarity Network, *Battle for Democracy, Press Freedom in South Asia 2009-10*, Delhi.

—— (2011): The International Federation of Journalists for the South Asian Media Solidarity Network, *Free Speech in Peril; Press Freedom in South Asia 2010-11*, Delhi.

—— (2012): The International Federation of Journalists for the South Asian Media Solidarity Network, *New Frontiers, New Struggles: Press Freedom in South Asia 2011-12*, Delhi.

—— (2013): The International Federation of Journalists for the South Asian Media Solidarity Network, *Building Resistance, Organising for Change: Press Freedom in South Asia 2012-13*, Delhi.

India Today (2014): "Maximum Campaign: Modi unleashes a blitzkrieg never seen before in Indian electoral history", Cover Story, May 19.

Indian Express, The (2008): "At Mira Road house of techie, family says he left in 2001", August 19, p. 1.

—— (2013): "INS okays 49 per cent FDI in print media", August 1; accessed December 2016 at: http://www.indianexpress.com/news/ins-okays-49-per-cent-fdi-in-print-media/1149467/.

—— (2000): report datelined Mumbai, May 23, and headlined "VNU takeover unlikely to change shape of ORG-MARG's board" the following day; accessed December 2016 at: http://expressindia.indianexpress.com/fe/daily/20000524/fex24049.html.

—— (2013): "A crime less ordinary", Editorial, September 14, 2013; extracted December 2016 at: http://www.indianexpress.com/news/a-crime-less-ordinary/1168940/.

Indian Television (2012): "NY court orders NDTV to file revised lawsuit; WPP, Nielsen dismissal motions to be heard on 14 Dec", September 10; accessed December 2016 at: http://www.indiantelevision.com/mam/headlines/y2k12/sep/sepmam49.php.

—— (2013a): "Times Now Ups Ad Rates Amid Slowdown", March 19; extracted December 2016 at: http://www.indiantelevision.com/mam/headlines/y2k13/mar/marmam89.php.

—— (2013a): "WPP welcomes lower court dismissal of NDTV law suit", March 12; accessed December 2016 at: http://www.indiantelevision.com/mam/headlines/y2k13/mar/marmam56.php.

—— (2013b). "NY court dismisses NDTV law firm's defamation suit against WPP's Martin Sorrell", May 30; accessed December 2016 at: http://www.indiantelevision.com/mam/headlines/y2k13/may/maymam110.php.

—— (2013b): "M&E industry lacks reliable data: Uday Shankar", March 12; accessed December 2016 at: http://www.indiantelevision.com/headlines/y2k13/mar/mar96.php.

—— (2013c): "DAS Phase II commences as analogue TV switched off", April 1; accessed December 2016 at: http://www.indiantelevision.com/headlines/y2k13/apr/apr1.php.

Israel, Milton (1994): *Communications and power: Propaganda and the press in the Indian nationalist struggle, 1920-1947*, Cambridge University Press, Delhi.

Jacklin, Phil, Jeremy Weir Alderson and Joseph Mathews, (1982): "Access to the media: a new fairness doctrine", in Daniel L. Brenner, and William L. Rivers (editors), Free but Regulated: conflicting traditions in media law: collected essays with commentary, pp. 248-71.

Jaffe, Louis L. (1972): "The Editorial Responsibility of the Broadcaster: Reflections on Fairness and Access", *Harvard Law Review*, 85:4, pp. 768-92.

Jagmohan (1991): *My Frozen Turbulence in Kashmir*, Rupa, Delhi.

Jalal, Ayesha (1985): *The Sole Spokesman: Jinnah, the Muslim League and the Demand for Pakistan*, Cambridge University Press, Cambridge.

Janmohamad, Zahir (2014): "India is still no country for free speech", Al Jazeera America, March 17; extracted December 2016 at: http://america.aljazeera.com/articles/2014/3/17/india-is-still-nocountryforfreespeech.html.

Jeffrey, Robin (2000): *India's Newspaper Revolution*, Oxford University Press, Delhi.

—— (2003): *India's Newspaper Revolution, Capitalism, Politics and the Indian-language Press*, Oxford University Press, Delhi.

—— (2010): *Media and Modernity, Communications, Women, and the State in India*, Permanent Black, Delhi.

Johnson, Paul Michael (2015): "Don Quixote, Charlie hebdo, and the 'Politics of Laughter'", Dissident Voice, April 29; extracted January 2016 at: dissidentvoice.org/2015/04don-quixote-charlie-hebdo-and-the-politics-of-laughter/

Kachka, Boris (2015): "At Gala, PEN Doubles Down and Defends Itself", published May 6, 2015; extracted May 15 at: http://www.vulture.com/2015/05/gala-pen-doubles-down-and-defends-itself.html.

Kamleshwar (1991): Interview with Rashme Sehgal, "All my time was spent purging reports", *The Independent*, February 2, 1991; extracted August 31, 2011 at: www.cscsarchive.org:8081/MediaArchive/essays.nsf/%28docid%29/44AF27D5BB28A1016525693F00387CED.

Kant, Immanuel (1788): "Critique of Practical Reason", in Allen W. Wood (editor), *Basic Writings of Kant*, Modern Library, New York, 2001.

—— (1793): "Concerning the Common Saying: This May be True in Theory But Does Not Apply to Practice", in Allen W. Wood (editor) *Basic Writings of Kant*, Modern Library, New York, 2001.

Kaviraj, Sudipto (2001): "In Search of Civil Society", in Kaviraj and Khilnani (editors).

Kaviraj, Sudipto and Sunil Khilnani (editors) (2001): *Civil Society, History and Possibilities*, Cambridge University Press, Delhi.

Keer, Dhananjay (1964): *Jotirao Phule: Father of Our Social Revolution*, Popular Prakashan, Bombay.

Khanvilkar, Sharanya (2011): "Media barons wake up together, sing same song", June 15; extracted December 2016 at: https://wearethebest.wordpress.com/2011/06/15/media-barons-wake-up-together-sing-same-song/.

Kiely, Ray (2005): *The Clash of Globalisations: Neoliberalism, the Third Way and Anti-Globalisation*, Brill, Lieden.

Klein, Naomi (2001): *No Logo*, Flamingo, London.

Kohli, Vanita (2003): *The Indian Media Business*, Response (Sage), Delhi.

Kramer, Adam, Jamie Guillory and Jeffrey Hancock (2014) "Experimental evidence of massive-scale emotional contagion through social networks", *Proceedings of the National Academy of Sciences*, 111:24, June 17, pp. 8788-90.

Krishnan, Kavita (2015): "Zehn ki Loot – The Plunder of Reason in a Times Now TV Studio", *The Scroll*, March 2; extracted December 2016 at: http://scroll.in/article/710458/zehn-ki-loot-the-plunder-of-reason-by-arnab-goswami.

Krishnan, Simantini (2016): "The Problem With Arnab Goswami's Elitist and Techno-Managerial Viewers", *The Wire*, August 2; extracted December 2016 at: http://thewire.in/55692/the-matter-with-arnab-goswamis-viewers/.

Kumar, Anup (2011): *The Making of a Small State, Populist Social Mobilisation and the Hindi Press in the Uttarakhand Movement*, Orient Blackswan, Delhi.

Kumar, Ravish (2015): "Absent Dalit: The Indian Newsroom", *Seminar*.

Lewis, Anthony (2007): *Freedom for the Thought that we Hate: A Biography of the First Amendment*, Basic Books, New York.

Liberman, Robert C. (2001): "A Tale of Two Countries: The Politics of Color Blindness in France and the United States", *French Politics, Culture and Society*, Vol. 19, No: 3, pp. 32-59.

Locke, John (1648): *The Second Treatise on Government*; extracted April 2016 at: http://www.earlymoderntexts.com/assets/pdfs/locke1689a.pdf.

Macpherson, C.B. (1971): "Revisionist Liberalism", in *Democratic Theory, Essays in Retrieval*, Oxford.

—— (1973): *Democratic Theory: Essays in Retrieval*, Clarendon, Oxford.

Mahalingam, Sudha (1998a): "Rights and Wrongs", *Frontline*, March 6, pp. 99-100; extracted December 2016 at: http://www.frontline.in/navigation/?type=static&page=archive.

—— (1998b): "Citizen Jain", *Frontline*, July 3; extracted December 2016 at: http://www.frontline.in/navigation/?type=static&page=archive.

—— (1998c): "A Newspaper Scandal", Frontline, June 19; extracted December 2016 at: http://www.frontline.in/navigation/?type=static&page=archive.

—— (1998d): "The Press Council vs the INS", *Frontline*, December 4; extracted December 2016 at: http://www.frontline.in/navigation/?type=static&page=archive.

Mallet, Victor (2014): "IT-savvy army takes Modi's campaign to new levels", *Financial Times*, May 14.

Mamdani, Mahmood (2004): *Good Muslim, Bad Muslim: Islam, the USA, and the Global War Against Terror*, Permanent Black, Delhi.

Marx, Karl (1842): "Debates on Freedom of the Press", from Marx and Engels, *Collected Works, Volume I*, Progress, Moscow, 1975.

——— (1844a): "On the Jewish Question", in *Marx: Early Writings*, Penguin Books, London, 1977.

——— (1844b): "Critique of Hegel's Doctrine of the State", in *Marx: Early Writings*, Penguin Books, London, 1977.

McLuhan, Marshall (1964): *Understanding Media*, Routledge, London, 2012.

Meghalaya High Court (2015): Uma Nath Singh, CJ, T. Nandakumar Singh and S.R. Sen, JJ, Writ Petition (Civil) Number 127/2015; judgment delivered May 27, 2015, Shillong; extracted December 2016 at: http://megpolice.gov.in/notification/HC's_Meghalaya_order_WP(C)_127-2015.pdf.

Mehrotra, Rajiv (2006): "Social Justice on the Airwaves", *The Hindustan Times*, July 28, p. 11.

Mehta, Nalin (2008): *India on Television*, Harper Collins India, Delhi.

Mill, John Stuart (1859): "On Liberty", in Six Great Humanistic Essays of John Stuart Mill, Washington Square Press, 1969.

Milne, Seamus (2015): "Now the truth emerges: how the US fueled the rise of Isis in Syria and Iraq", *The Guardian*, June 3; extracted December 2016 at: http://www.theguardian.com/commentisfree/2015/jun/03/us-isis-syria-iraq.

Ministry of Home Affairs (1965): Government of India, Annual Report, 1964-65.

Ministry of Information and Broadcasting (1975): Government of India, *Report of the Fact Finding Committee on Newspaper Economics*, New Delhi.

Ministry of Information and Broadcasting (2005a): Policy guidelines for second round of FM radio broadcast licences; posted at following URL, since expired: http://mib.nic.in/informationb/POLICY/frames.htm.

Ministry of Information and Broadcasting (2005b): http://mib.nic.in/fm/fmmainpg.htm.

Ministry of Information and Broadcasting (2006): Guidelines for Community Radio Services, posted December 2006; extracted from the following address which has since expired: http://mib.nic.in/informationb/CODES/CRBGUIDELINES041206.doc.

Mint (2008): "Delayed Gratification", December 24, p. 11.

——— (2008a): "News channels say they have policies for 'anchor investors'", February 18, p. 4.

——— (2008b): "For right candidates, sky's the limit in broadcasting industry", February 4, p. 8.

—— (2008c): "DNA scripts expansion, acquisition plans", March 3, p. 8.

—— (2008d): "Bennett, Coleman to launch public relations agency", Feb 11, p. 1.

—— (2009a): "Current IRS agency makes pitch for National Readership Survey", January 23.

—— (2009b): "New audience measurement initiative face stumbling blocks", April 14, p. 8.

—— (2009c): "MRUC fails to enlist Australian partner for readership survey", May 22, p. 9.

—— (2009d): "Paid content used to cut poll spending", December 2, p. 1.

—— (2013a): "Maheshwar Peri's long way around", November 5, pp. 10-1; extracted December 2016 at: http://www.livemint.com/Specials/13TE2UEtexMf-1GDeEt5rCP/Maheshwer-Peris-long-way-around.html.

—— (2013b): "TV channels to follow 12-minute ad limit from 1 October", May 28, p. 1.

—— (2013c): "Mixed Response from media firms to 49% FDI proposal", June 26, p. 1.

—— (2013d): "TRAI proposes 49% FDI in TV news channels, private FM radio", July 31, p. 9.

—— (2013e): "Publicis Omnicom combine may take time to overtake WPP in India", July 20, p. 8.

—— (2013f): "IMRB to expand coverage for more data on consumer economy", August 1, pp. 1-5.

—— (2013g): "Advertisers, agencies rally behind TAM in fight with broadcasters", June 11, p. 7.

—— (2013h): "TAM agrees to give monthly, absolute numbers to some channels", July 12, p. 1.

—— (2013i):. "Siddharth Varadarajan quits The Hindu; family rift resurfaces", October 21, 2013; extracted in December 2016 at: http://www.livemint.com/Consumer/7Igh9ncxU6SfsvAg9sukZL/Siddharth-Varadarajan-resigns-from-The-Hindu.html.

—— (2013j): "Slowdown takes a toll on media houses", September 6, p. 19.

—— (2013k): "BCCL buys 49% stake in Daiki brands", May 14, p. 1.

—— (2014): "Inside the Network18 takeover", June 23; extracted December 2016 at: http://www.livemint.com/Companies/rqT2Oi8fwv4XVjJcHzlcVN/Inside-the-Network18-takeover.html?utm_source=copy.

—— (2014b): "Poll bonanza projected for print media", February 11, p. 1.

Mitchell, Greg (2008): *So Wrong for so Long: How the Press, the Pundits – and the President – Failed on Iraq*, Union Square, New York.

Mody, Nawaz B. (1987): "The Press in India, The Shah Bano Case and its Aftermath", Asian Survey, Vol. 27, No. 8 (Aug), pp. 935-953.

Mohammadi, Annabelle Sreberny and Ali Mohammadi (1994): *Small Media, Big Revolution: Communication, Culture and the Iranian Revolution,* University of Minnesota Press, Minneapolis.

Moore, Molly (2008): "In France, Prisons Filled with Muslims", *The Washington Post,* April 29; extracted December 2016 at: http://www.washingtonpost.com/wp-dyn/content/article/2008/04/28/AR2008042802560.html.

Morozov, Evgeny (2011): T*he Net Delusion, How Not to Liberate the World,* Penguin, London.

Muralidharan, Sukumar (2005): "The Challenge to the Media", *Seminar,* Number 551, July, pp. 41-45.

—— (2008): "Mumbai, militarism and the media", *Economic and Political Weekly,* December 6.

—— (2009): "Amplifying Chaos, Sowing Discord", *Agenda: Infochange News and Features,* 14, February, pp. 4-10; extracted December 2016 at: http://infochangeindia.org/downloads/agenda_14.pdf.

—— (2011a): "Hazare and his Children", *Economic and Political Weekly,* April 16.

—— (2011b): "Media as Echo Chamber: Cluttering the Public Discourse on Corruption", *Economic and Political Weekly,* September 10.

—— (2012): "Turmoil in Syria, Prelude to Wider Battles in the Arab World", *Economic and Political Weekly,* Vol. XLVII No. 8, February 25, pp. 15-19.

—— (2013): "Express Delivery of Death: a Home Minister Murders the Constitution", *Economic and Political Weekly,* March 2, pp. 13-15.

Narayanan, K. (2006): "Causes, concerns and custom", *The Hindu,* November 27; extracted October 4, 2011 at: http://www.hindu.com/2006/11/27/stories/2006112704781100.htm.

Naregal, Veena (1999): "Colonial Bilingualism and Hierarchies of Language and Power: Making of a Vernacular Sphere in Western India", *Economic and Political Weekly,* December 4.

—— (2001): *Language Politics, Elites, and the Public Sphere: Western India Under Colonialism,* Permanent Black, Delhi.

Natarajan, J. (1955): *History of Indian Journalism,* Publications Division, Government of India, Delhi.

National Academy of the Sciences (2014): "Editorial Expression of Concern and Correction", *Proceedings of the National Academy of the Sciences,* 111:29, July 22.

NDTV (2014): "Facebook COO Sheryl Sandberg's Status Update: Met PM Narendra Modi", datelined July 3, 2014; extracted December 2016 at: http://www.ndtv.com/article/india/facebook-coo-sheryl-sandberg-s-status-update-met-pm-narendra-modi-552382.

New York Supreme Court (2012): New Delhi Television Ltd (Plaintiff) versus Nielsen Holdings NV, Valcon Acquisition BV, The Nielsen Company BV, VNU Intermediate Holding BV, and others; Index Number: 652589/2012; Received July 26, 2012.

New York Times, The (1987): "FCC votes down Fairness Doctrine in a 4-0 Decision", 5 August 1987, extracted December 2016 at: http://www.nytimes.com/1987/08/05/arts/fcc-votes-down-fairness-doctrine-in-a-4-0-decision.html

—— (2012): "Google Has No Plans to Rethink Video Status", 14 September 2012, extracted December 2016 at: http://www.nytimes.com/2012/09/15/world/middleeast/google-wont-rethink-anti-islam-videos-status.html?_r=0.

—— (2013): "France Fights Racism by Outlawing 'Race'", May 17, 2013; extracted December 2016 at: http://rendezvous.blogs.nytimes.com/2013/05/17/france-fights-racism-by-outlawing-race/?_r=0.

—— (2016): "Facebook's Troubling One-way Mirror", May 23, 2016; extracted December 2016 at: http://www.nytimes.com/2016/05/23/business/facebooks-troubling-one-way-mirror.html?_r=0.

—— (2016): a collection of commentators' reactions to the election result, published online and extracted November 9, 2016.

News Laundry (2017a): "The Telegraph Lay-offs: Is It The End Of The Era Of Field Reporting?", February 7; extracted at: https://www.newslaundry.com/2017/02/07/the-telegraph-lay-offs-is-it-the-end-of-the-era-of-field-reporting.

—— (2017b): "Will we ever know how many journalists at HT and Mint lost their jobs?", February 14; extracted at: https://www.newslaundry.com/2017/02/14/will-we-ever-know-how-many-journalists-at-ht-and-mint-lost-their-jobs

Niles, Robert (2005): "Indian media blog shuts down after legal threats from Times of India", March 15, *Online Journalism Review*; extracted December 2016 at: http://www.ojr.org/050315glaser/.

Ninan, Sevanti (1998): "History of Indian Broadcasting Reform", in Monroe E. Price and Stefaan G. Verhulst (editors), *Broadcasting Reform in India, Media Law from a Global Perspective*, Oxford University Press, Delhi.

—— (2000): "History of Broadcast Reform in India", in Monroe Price and Stefaan Verhulst (editors), *Broadcast Reform in India*, Oxford University Press, Delhi, pp. 1-20.

—— (2006): "The New Moguls", *The Hindu*, Sunday magazine, October 8.

—— (2007): *Headlines from the Heartland, Reinventing the Hindi Public Sphere*, Sage, Delhi.

—— (2013): "Broadcasters versus TAM", *Mint*, June 13, p. 8.

Noorani, A.G. (2003): Editor, *The Babri Masjid Question, 1528 – 2003, 'A Matter of National Honour'*, Volumes 1 and 2, Tulika Books, Delhi.

—— (2014): Editor, *Destruction of the Babri Masjid, A National Dishonour*, Tulika Books, Delhi.

Nossel, Suzanne (2004): "Smart Power", *Foreign Affairs*, Vol. 83, No. 2, March-April, pp. 131-42.

O'Brien, Conor Cruise (1970): Camus, Modern Masters, Fontana.

Oakley, Corey (2015): "Charlie Hebdo, the hypocrisy of pencils and the limits of the free speech crusade", 12 January 12; extracted May 15, 2015 at: http://www.stopwar.org.uk/news/charlie-hebdo-the-hypocrisy-of-pencils-and-the-limits-of-the-free-speech-crusade.

Open Society Foundations (2012): *Mapping Digital Media: India*, (Lead Reporters: Vibodh Parthasarathi and Alam Srinivas), December; accessed December 2016 at: http://www.opensocietyfoundations.org/reports/mapping-digital-media-india.

Outlook (1997): "Kesri is an old Friend of the Family", July 16; extracted December 2014 at: http://www.outlookindia.com/printarticle.aspx?203860. Available December 2016 with subscription, at: http://www.outlookindia.com/magazine/story/quotkesri-is-an-old-friend-of-the-familyquot/203860.

—— (2013): "Editor Siddharth Varadarajan's Memorandum to Staff on Election Coverage", Outlook India blog, October 23; extracted December 2014 at: http://www.outlookindia.com/blogs/default.aspx?ddm=10&pid=3064.

Oxford (2016): "Bots and Automation over Twitter during the U.S. Election", Oxford Internet Institute, November 17; extracted December 2016 at: http://politicalbots.org/?p=787.

Packard, Vance (1953): The Hidden Persuaders, IgBooks, Amazon Kindle Edition, 2007.

Packer, George (2015): "The blame for the Charlie Hebdo murders", *The New Yorker*, January 7; extracted December 2016 at: http://www.newyorker.com/news/news-desk/blame-for-charlie-hebdo-murders.

Panagariya, Arvind (2012): "Cracking the Kerala Myth", *The Times of India* (Delhi edition), January 2; extracted December 2016 at: http://timesofindia.indiatimes.com/home/opinion/edit-page/Cracking-the-kerala-myth/articleshow/11329131.cms?referral=PM.

Parashar, Arpit and Govind Krishnan V. (2017): "The media implosion", Fountain Ink, 6:4; February, pp. 38-52.

Pariser, Eli (2011): *The Filter Bubble, What the Internet is Hiding From You*, Viking London, (Kindle Edition).

Parliament of India (1948): Constituent Assembly Debates, Volume VII, Part II, December 2, 1948; extracted December 2016 at: http://parliamentofindia.nic.in/ls/debates/vol7p18b.htm.

—— (1951): The Constitution (First Amendment) Bill, 1951, introduced May 10, 1951; extracted from: http://indiacode.nic.in/coiweb/amend/amend1.htm.

—— (1955): Lok Sabha Debates, Volume 1, Part II, Ninth Session, Lok Sabha Secretariat, New Delhi.

—— (1963): *Constitution (Sixteenth Amendment) Act, 1963*; extracted December 2016 at: http://indiacode.nic.in/coiweb/amend/amend16.htm.

—— (1967): The Unlawful Activities Prevention Act; extracted December 2016 at: http://lawmin.nic.in/ld/P-ACT/1967/A1967-37.pdf.

—— (2002): *Prevention of Terrorism Act*, Act 15 of 2002; extracted December 2016 at: http://www.satp.org/satporgtp/countries/india/document/actandordinances/POTA.htm#1.

—— (2003): Standing Committee on Information Technology, 13th Lok Sabha, 63rd Report, Lok Sabha Secretariat, December 2003.

—— (2013): Standing Committee of Parliament (Fifteenth Lok Sabha), Ministry of Information Technology, 47th Report, Presented to the Lok Sabha, May 6.

Parliamentary Research Service (2011): The Unlawful Activities Prevention (Amendment), Bill, 2011; extracted, December 2016 from: http://www.prsindia.org/billtrack/the-unlawful-activities-prevention-amendment-bill-2011-2159/.

Pavarala, Vinod (2003): "Breaking Free, Battle over the Airwaves", *Economic and Political Weekly*, May 31.

PC World (2014): "Under fire on net neutrality plans, FCC seeks early feedback", April 25; extracted December 2016 at: http://www.pcworld.com/article/2148700/under-fire-over-net-neutrality-plans-fcc-seeks-early-feedback.html

PEN (2015a): Suzanne Nossel (profile); extracted December 2016 at: https://www.pen.org/suzanne-nossel.

—— (2015b): "A Literary Quest", May 15; extracted December 2016 at: http://www.pen.org/event/2015/01/23/literary-quest.

—— (2015c): "World Voices Festival of International Literature"; extracted May 15, 2015 at: http://worldvoices.pen.org/2015-world-voices-sponsors.

Press Commission (1954): *Report of the Press Commission, Part I*, Manager of Publications, Government of India.

—— (1954:1): Report of the Press Commission, Volume I, Delhi.

—— (1989): *Report of the Second Press Commission, Volume 1*, Controller of Publications, Government of India.

Press Council of India (2010): *"Paid News": How corruption in the Indian media undermines democracy*, New Delhi, posted October and extracted December 2016 at: http://presscouncil.nic.in/OldWebsite/Sub-CommitteeReport.pdf.

Press Trust of India (2004): "Trai as broadcast regulator to help convergence: Shourie".

—— (2008): report datelined Delhi, December 16, and published on the website of *The Economic Times* the same day under the headline, "House panel calls for regulation of TRP system"; accessed December 2016 at: http://articles.economictimes.indiatimes.com/2008-12-16/news/28398881_1_trp-system-television-rating-point-indian-broadcasting-foundation.

—— (2012): Report datelined Delhi, June 21, 2012, published the following day in *Mint* under the headline,"Broadcasters unhappy, MSOs welcome digitisation deadline delay"; accessed December 2016 at: http://www.livemint.com/Companies/Z7a1LC6SmoiGas8EfAiPnL/Broadcasters-unhappy-MSOs-welcome-digitisation-deadline-del.html

—— (2013a): News report datelined New Delhi, July 18, 2013, published the following day in *Business Standard* under the headline: "NBA moves TDSAT on cap on ad on TV"; accessed December 2016 at: http://www.business-standard.com/article/pti-stories/nba-moves-tdsat-on-cap-on-ad-on-tv-113071801033_1.html.

—— (2013b): datelined Delhi July 21, 2013, published on the Times of India website the same day under headline "Home ministry opposes any hike of FDI cap in media"; accessed December 2014 at: http://aticles.timesofindia.indiatimes.com/2013-07-21/india/40707977_1_home-ministry-current-affairs-tv-channels-fdi-cap.

—— (2013c): datelined Delhi, July 16, 2013, published in *Business Standard* the following day under the headline: "Government liberalises FDI limits in 12 sectors, including telecom"; accessed December 2016 at: http://www.business-standard.com/article/pti-stories/govt-liberalises-fdi-limits-in-12-sectors-including-telecom-113071601169_1.html.

Price, Monroe E. and Stefaan G. Verhulst (1998): (editors), *Broadcasting Reform in India, Media Law from a Global Perspective*, Oxford University Press, Delhi.

Pulham, Sheila (2005): "Inflammatory Language", *The Guardian online*, November 8; extracted May 15, 2015 at: http://www.theguardian.com/news/blog/2005/nov/08/inflammatoryla.

Punwani, Jyoti (2006): "Khairlanji and the English Press", The Hoot, November 1; extracted July 2016 at: http://www.thehoot.org/media-watch/media-practice/khairlanji-and-the-english-press-2414.

—— (2008): "Creating Tauqeer", *The Hoot*, October 24; extracted July 2016 at: http://www.thehoot.org/media-watch/media-practice/creating-tauqeer-3380.

Rai, Alok (2001): *Hindi Nationalism*, Orient Longman, Hyderabad.

Raja, M. (2004): "Dirty laundry at the Times of India", *Asia Times Online*, May 18; extracted December 2016 at: http://www.atimes.com/atimes/South_Asia/FE18Df05.html.

Ram, N. (1994): "Foreign Media Entry into the Press: Issues and Implications", *Economic and Political Weekly*, Vol. 29, No. 43, October 22, pp. 2787-90.

Raman, Anuradha (2014): "Clogging the Ink: The Modi wave is quietly battering free expression", *Outlook*, February 3; extracted December 2014 at: http://www.outlookindia.com/printarticle.aspx?289263.

Ramanujan, S.R. (2006): "Why is Tamil media so biased?", May 14; at www.thehoot.org.

Rao, Aaron (2014): "Television in Singapore: A Brief Introduction to its Television Industry", *Journal of Arts, Science and Commerce*, Vol. V, Issue 3, July.

Rao, Parimala V. (2010): *Foundations of Tilak's Nationalism: Discrimination, Education and Hindutva*, Orient BlackSwan, Hyderabad.

Rao, Shakuntala (2014): "Covering Rape in Shame Culture: Studying Journalism Ethics in India's New Television News Media", *Journal of Mass Media Ethics*, Vol. 29, pp. 153-67.

Rawls, John (1971), *A Theory of Justice*, Harvard.

—— (1995): "Reply to Habermas", *The Journal of Philosophy*, XCII: 3, March, pp. 132-80.

Rediff (1998): "If my father is a rapist, I cannot, should not, defend him only because he is my father", February 28; extracted December 2016 at: http://www.rediff.com/news/1998/feb/28george.htm.

—— (2008): "TAM domination threatened as govt. eyes a Map tie-up", December 18; accessed December 2013 at: http://www.rediff.com/money/report/prasar-bharati-for-amap-tie-up/20081218.htm.

Remnick, David (1994): *Lenin's Tomb, The Last Days of the Soviet Empire*, Random House, New York.

Reuters (2011): Reported dateline Delhi, October 13, published in *Mint*, Delhi edition the following day under headline "Cabinet approves cable digitisation"; accessed December 2016 at: http://www.livemint.com/Politics/Hc5cKJTQQmYo3xVSYdyKbM/Cabinet-approves-cable-digitisation.html.

Reuters (2014): Report datelined July 2, published on NDTV website under headline "PM Narendra Modi Draws Twitter, Facebook Deeper into Government"; extracted December 2016 at: http://www.ndtv.com/article/india/pm-narendra-modi-draws-twitter-facebook-deeper-into-government-551868.

Rhazoui, Zineb al-l (2013): "If Charlie Hebdo is racist, then so am I", published December 22, 2013 in French at: http://www.cercledesvolontaires.fr/2013/12/22/si-charlie-hebdo-est-raciste-alors-je-le-suis-reponse-de-zineb-el-rhazoui-a-olivier-cyran/; translated into English and published on January 15, 2015 at: http://thecharnelhouse.org/2015/01/15/if-charlie-hebdo-is-racist-then-so-am-i-zineb-el-rhazoui-responds-to-olivier-cyran/; extracted December 2016.

Roberts, Alasdair (2013): *The End of Protest: How Free-Market Capitalism Learned to Control Dissent*, Cornell University Press, Ithaca (Kindle Edition).

Rodrigues, Malika (2014): "Admen in the Mad World of Elections", The Economic Times, April 24, p. 3.

Rosen, Jeffrey (2008): "Google's Gatekeepers", *The New York Times*, November 20; extracted December 2016 at: http://www.nytimes.com/2008/11/30/magazine/30google-t.html?pagewanted=all&_r=0.

Ross, Carne (2011): *The Leaderless Revolution: How ordinary people will take power and change politics in the 21st century*, Simon and Schuster, London.

Rousseau, Jean-Jacques: "The Social Contract", in G.D.H. Cole (editor and translator), *The Social Contract and Discourses,* Dent, London, 1973.

Roy, Arundhati (2013): (Editor) *The Hanging of Afzal Guru*, Penguin Books, Delhi.

Roychowdhury, Paulomi (2013): "'The Delhi Gang Rape': The Making of International Causes", *Feminist Studies,* Vol. 39, No. 1.

Sacco, Joe (2015): "On Satire: A Response to the Charlie Hebdo attacks", *The Guardian*, January 9; extracted December 2016 at: http://www.theguardian.com/world/ng-interactive/2015/jan/09/joe-sacco-on-satire-a-response-to-the-attacks.

Said, Edward (1985): *Orientalism, Western Conceptions of the Orient*, Penguin, London.

—— (1991): *Covering Islam,* Revised Edition, Vintage, London.

Sainath, P. (2009): "The medium, message and the money", *The Hindu*, October 26, p. 12.

—— (2012): "Reaping Gold Through Cotton, and Newsprint", *The Hindu*, May 10, Delhi edition, p. 13; extracted December 2016 at: http://www.thehindu.com/opinion/columns/sainath/reaping-gold-through-cotton-and-newsprint/article3401466.ece.

—— (2014): "Is the 'Era of Ashoka' a New Era for News", *The Hindu,* January 5, p. 1; extracted December 2016 at: http://www.thehindu.com/opinion/columns/sainath/is-the-era-of-ashok-a-new-era-for-news/article56964.ece.

Samrat (2017): "'Malicious and Unjust': Powerful Media Houses vs Journalists", *Economic and Political Weekly*, January 28, pp. 13-16.

Sancton, Julian (2015): "Why Charlie Hebdo's Stupid and Vicious Pencils will Prevail", *Vanity Fair,* January 2015; extracted December 2016 at: http://www.vanityfair.com/news/2015/01/charlie-hebdo-attack-cartoons.

Sans Serif (2008): "Business journalism or the journalism of business?", entry dated February 17 in the media critique blog *Sans Serif*; accessed December 2016 at: http://wearethebest.wordpress.com/2008/02/17/business-journalism-or-the-business-of-journalism/.

Saraf, Pushp (1990): "Job Reservation in Railways and accidents", *Indian Express*, New Delhi edition, September 19, p. 9.

Sayare, Scott (2015a): "The *Charlie Hebdo* I knew", *The Atlantic Global*, January 11; extracted December 2016 at: http://www.theatlantic.com/international/archive/2015/01/charlie-hebdo-secularism-religion-islam/384413/.

—— (2015b): "What *Je Suis Charlie* has Become", *The Atlantic Global*, January 30; extracted December 2016 at: http://www.theatlantic.com/international/

archive/2015/01/je-suis-charlie-france-patriotism/384990/?utm_source=SFTwitter.

Schmidt, Eric and Jared Cohen (2010): "The Digital Disruption: Connectivity and the Diffusion of Power", *Foreign Affairs*, 89:6, November-December, pp. 75-85.

—— (2013): *The New Digital Age*, John Murray, London.

Schmidt, Rick (2010): "Diplomacy 2.0", *Stanford Alumni*, May/June; extracted December 2016 at: https://alumni.stanford.edu/get/page/magazine/article/?article_id=29494 and https://archive.today/Kidpc.

SCOTUS (1980): Supreme Court of the United States, 447 U.S. 557, *Central Hudson Gas & Electric Corp. v. Public Service Commission of New York*, Argued: March 17, 1980 – Decided: June 20, 1980.

SCOTUS (2010): Supreme Court of the United States, *Citizens United v. Federal Election Commission*, Argued March 24, 2009—Reargued September 9, 2009 – Decided January 21, 2010.

Scroll (2015): "Three years after Delhi gang rape, Indian women still under threat, note feminist groups", December 16; extracted December 2016 at: http://scroll.in/article/776082/three-years-after-delhi-gang-rape-indian-women-still-under-threat-note-feminist-groups.

Sen, Amartya (2009): *The Idea of Justice*, Penguin, London.

Seymour, Richard (2015): *Charlie Hebdo*, January 7; extracted May 15, 2015 at: http://www.leninology.co.uk/2015/01/charlie-hebdo.html.

Shils, Edward (1972): *The Constitution of Society*, University of Chicago Press, Chicago.

Shourie, Arun (1991): *The Economic Times*, September 29.

Sinclair, John (2012): *Advertising, the Media and Globalisation: A World in Motion*, Routledge, London.

Singh, Jaswant (2009): Jinnah: India-Partition-Independence, Rupa, Delhi.

Smith, Craig S. (2004): "Islam in Jail: Europe's Neglect Breeds Angry Radicals", *The New York Times*, December 8; extracted December 2016 at: http://www.nytimes.com/2004/12/08/international/europe/08prisons.html?pagewanted=1

Solomon, Andrew and Suzanne Nossel (2015): "Why We're Honouring Charlie Hebdo", *The New York Times*, May 1; extracted December 2016 at: http://www.nytimes.com/2015/05/02/opinion/why-were-honoring-charlie-hebdo.html?_r=0.

South Asia Terrorism Portal (2013): The Terrorist and Disruptive Activities (Prevention) Act, 1987; extracted December 2016 at: http://www.satp.org/satporgtp/countries/india/document/actandordinances/Tada.htm#3.

State Department (2010): Hillary Clinton, U.S. Secretary of State, "Remarks on Internet Freedom", January 21, posted on the website of the U.S. Department of State; extracted December 2016 at: http://www.state.gov/secretary/20092013clinton/rm/2010/01/135519.htm.

—— (2011): "The U.S. and the United Nations Human Rights Council: Principled Engagement", published May 24; extracted December 2016 at: http://www.state.gov/p/io/rm/2011/166802.htm.

Subramanian, Samanth (2012): "Supreme Being: How Samir Jain created the modern Indian newspaper industry", The *Caravan*, December 2012; extracted

July 15, 2015 at: http://www.caravanmagazine.in/reportage/supreme-being#sthash.6LAqeMrb.dpuf.

Supreme Court of India (1950a): *Romesh Thapar vs The State Of Madras*, May 26, 1950; Equivalent citations: 1950 AIR 124, 1950 SCR 594. Extracted December 2016.

—— (1950b): *Brij Bhushan vs State of Delhi*, Equivalent citations: 1950 AIR 129, 1950 SCR 605; extracted December 2016 at: https://indiankanoon.org/doc/43023/.

—— (1957): V*irendra vs The State Of Punjab*, September 6, 1957: Equivalent citations: 1957 AIR 896, 1958 SCR 308; extracted December 2016 at: https://indiankanoon.org/doc/1475436/.

—— (1958): *Express Newspapers Pvt Ltd and Another v Union of India and Others*, decided January 8, 1958.

—— (1959): *Hamdard Dawakhana (Wakf) Lal Kuan, Delhi and Another v Union Of India And Others*; December 18; Equivalent citations: 1960 AIR 554, 1960 SCR (2) 671.

—— (1961): *Sakal Papers (P) Ltd., And Others vs The Union Of India*; Equivalent citations: 1962 AIR 305, 1962 SCR (3) 842); page numbers cited as in latter source.

—— (1962): *Kedar Nath Singh v Union of India*; Equivalent citations: 1962 AIR 955, 1962 SCR Supl. (2) 769; extracted December 2016 at: https://indiankanoon.org/doc/111867/.

—— (1972): *Bennett Coleman and Company Ltd versus the Union of India*, 1973 SCR (2) 759. Judgment is available as of December 2016 at: http://judis.nic.in/supremecourt/qrydisp.asp?tfnm=6674.

—— (1992): *Manubhai Shah v Life Insurance Corporation of India*, 1992 SCR (3), pp 595-626.

—— (1994): Kartar Singh versus State of Punjab: equivalent citations: 1994 SCC (3) 569, JT 1994 (2) 423; extracted December 2016 from: https://indiankanoon.org/doc/1813801/.

—— (1995): *The Secretary, Ministry Of Information and Broadcasting v Cricket Association Of Bengal* on February 9, 1995; Equivalent citations: 1995 AIR 1236, 1995 SCC (2) 161.

—— (2003): People's Union For Civil Liberties versus Union of India, Writ Petition (Civil) 389 of 2002; extracted December 2016 at: https://indiankanoon.org/doc/110957682/.

—— (2011): Civil Original Jurisdiction, Writ Petition (Civil) No 246 of 2011, *Ananda Bazaar Patrika and Another* versus *Union of India and* Others; Judgment written by P. Sathasivam, CJI, Ranjan Gogoi and Shiva Kirti Sing, JJ, concurring.

—— (2014): *Ananda Bazar Patrika Pvt. Ltd. and Another v Union of India and Others*, Writ Petition (Civil) No: 246 of 2011; decided February 7, 2014.

—— (2015): *Shreya Singhal versus Union of India*, Writ Petition (Criminal) No. 167 of 2012, judgment delivered March 24, 2015.

Swami, Praveen (2008): "Safdar Nagori and SIMI's jihad", *The Hindu*, March 28, p. 1.

Taibbi, Matt (2012): "Arizona Debate: Conservative Chickens Come Home to Roost", *Rolling Stone*, February 23; extracted in December 2016 from: http://www.rollingstone.com/politics/blogs/taibblog/arizona-debate-conservative-chickens-come-home-to-roost-20120223.

Tehranian, Majid (1995): Review in *International Journal of Middle East Studies*, 27: 4 (November), pp. 523- 525.

Telecom Regulatory Authority of India (2012a): *Consultation Paper on "Issues Related to Advertisements on TV Channels"*, March 16, Delhi.

—— (2012b): Notification dated May 14, 2012, Delhi.

—— (2013): Consultation Paper on Cross-Media Ownership, posted March 2013 and extracted May 2014 at: http://www.trai.gov.in/Content/Consultation-CommentPreviewALL/2564_675_ConsultationCommentPreviewALL.aspx.

—— (2014): *Recommendations on Issues Relating to Media Ownership*, August 12, 2014, Delhi; available for download at the website of the authority: www.trai.gov.in. The full report could be extracted as of December 2014 by typing in "media ownership" into the search box.

Television Post (2014): "The Ad Cap Ghost", April 16; extracted December 2016 at: http://www.televisionpost.com/research/the-ad-cap-ghost/?code=20140419863195395.

—— (2017): "Ad expenditure could take Rs 3000-cr hit, says Ashish Bhasin", February 10; extracted at: http://www.televisionpost.com/special-reports/ad-expenditure-could-take-rs-3000-cr-hit-says-ashish-bhasin/.

—— (2015): "Unlawful to Report Militant Statements", November 10; extracted December 2016 at: http://www.thehoot.org/free-speech/media-freedom/unlawful-to-report-militant-statements-9015.

Times News Network (2012): "Why TOI readers aren't middle class", posted February 1, at http://timesofindia.indiatimes.com/Why-TOI-readers-arent-middle-class/articleshow/11716104.cms.

Times of India, The (2002): "Language Papers Say it in Black and White", April 5.

—— (2003): "DT: A constant celebration of life", December 24, p. 2.

—— (2003a): "Medianet: Innovative content, integrated offering", March 4; extracted December 2016 at: http://timesofindia.indiatimes.com/india/Medianet-Innovative-content-integrated-offering/articleshow/39286961.cms?-from=mdr.

—— (2006): "New Broadcast Bill just a rehash of existing provisions?", Delhi and Mumbai editions, July 3.

—— (2011): "Opportunism Beckons", Editorial, November 30.

—— (2013): "Nirbhaya case juvenile wasn't the most brutal?", October 4 page 1 (Delhi edition).

—— (2014a): "Blow for newspaper industry as SC upholds wage board's advice", 8 Feb.

—— (2014b): "Newspaper Industry Faces Existential Crises", 3 March, p 22.

—— (2017): "Indian newspaper industry: Red ink splashed across the bottom line", 19 January, p 20.

Todd, Emmanuel (2016): *Who is Charlie?* Translation by Andrew Brown, Amazon Kindle Edition.

Townshend, Jules (2016): Review of Phillip Hansen *Reconsidering C B Macpherson: From Possessive Individualism to Democratic Theory and Beyond*, in Marxism and Philosophy, 16 April 2016, extracted on 1 June 2016 at: marxandphilosophy.org.uk/reviewofbooks/reviews/2016/2294.

TRAI (2015): Telecom Regulatory Authority of India, *Consultation Paper on Differential Pricing for Data Services*, New Delhi, 9 December.

—— (2016): Prohibition of Discriminatory Tariffs for Data Services, Regulation 2 of 2016; issued 8 February.

Trudeau, Garry (2015): "The Abuse of Satire", *The Atlantic Global*, published 11 April 2015 and extracted December 2016 at: http://www.theatlantic.com/international/archive/2015/04/the-abuse-of-satire/390312/.

Tucker, Richard P. (1972): *Ranade and the Roots of Indian Nationalism*, University of Chicago Press, Chicago and London, 1972.

U.S. Court of Appeal (2015): United States Court of Appeal for the Ninth Circuit, California, No 12-57302, D.C. No. 2:12-cv-08315-MWF-VBK; filed 18 May 2015.

—— (2014): *Cindy Lee Garcia v Google Inc. and Youtube, LLC, and Nakoula Basseley Nakoula*, United States Court of Appeal for the Ninth Circuit, California, No. 12-57302, D.C. No. 2:12-cv-08315-MWF-VBK, filed 26 February 2014.

—— (2016): United Court of Appeal for the District of Columbia Circuit, Case No: 15-1063, *United States Telecom Association, et al (Petitioners) vs Federal Communications Commission and United States of America (Respondents)*; decided June 14, 2016.

Underwood, Doug (1998): "Assembly-Line Journalism", Columbia Journalism Review, July/August, pp 42-44.

UNDP (2004): "Cultural Liberty in Today's Diverse World", *Human Development Report*, New York.

Varadarajan, Siddharth (2002): *Gujarat: The Making of a Tragedy*, Penguin Books, India.

—— (2006): "Caste matters in the Indian media", *The Hindu*, June 3, 2006, p 9.

—— (2009): "A stench that is all too familiar", *The Hindu*, March 24, p 10. Extracted December 2016 from: http://www.thehindu.com/todays-paper/tp-opinion/A-stench-that-is-all-too-familiar/article16647491.ece.

—— (2016): "Times Now First Denies Airing Doctored Video, Then Concedes it Did" *The Wire*, 20 February; extracted December 2016 at: http://thewire.in/22148/times-nows-first-denies-airing-doctored-video-then-concedes-it-did/.

—— (2014a): "The Cult of Cronyism", Seminar, April, pp 60-3.

—— (2014b): "Time to curb unfettered electoral expenditure by political parties that impacts poll outcomes", *The Economic Times*, 30 April; extracted December 2016 at: http://economictimes.indiatimes.com/articleshow/34391051.cms?utm_source=contentofinterest&utm_medium=text&utm_campaign=cppst.

Verma J.S. (2001): "Fighting Terrorism under the Rule of Law", Bodh Raj Sawhny memorial oration, December 4, 2001.

Verma, J.S., et al (2013): *Report of the Committee on Amendments to Criminal Law*, January 23, Delhi.

Vijayabaskar, M (2010): "Saving Agricultural Labour from Agriculture: SEZs and Silence in Tamil Nadu", *Economic and Political Weekly*, February 6, 2010.

Volokh, Eugene and Donald Falk (2012): "First Amendment Protection for Search Engine Search Results", Google, Palo Alto, April 12, 2012.

Waldron, Jeremy (2012): *The Harm in Hate Speech*, Harvard.

Wall Street Journal, The (2014): "Sorrell Takes Pleasure From Publicis-Omnicom Deal Collapse", 9 May, extracted in December 2016 at: http://blogs.wsj.com/corporate-intelligence/2014/05/09/sorrell-takes-pleasure-from-publicis-omnicom-deal-collapse/.

Weisskopf, Thomas (2011): "Why Worry About Inequality in the Booming Indian Economy?", *Economic and Political Weekly*, November 19, 2011, pp 41-51.

Woolf, Christopher (2015): "Where did the Paris attackers get their guns?", 15 January 2015, Public Radio International, Extracted December 2016 at: http://www.pri.org/stories/2015-01-15/where-did-paris-attackers-get-their-guns.

ww1.mid-day.com/news/city/2004/may/83022.htm. The link has since turned inoperative.

Zamindar, Vazira Fazila-Yacoobali (2007): *The Long Partition and the Making of Modern South Asia: Refugees, Boundaries, Histories*, Penguin/Viking, Delhi, 2007.

Index

Index of Subjects

Index of Names